HRM

THOMSON NELSON SERIES IN HUMAN RESOURCES MANAGEMENT

Managing Performance Through Training and Development

FOURTH EDITION

THOMSON NELSON SERIES IN HUMAN RESOURCES MANAGEMENT

Managing Performance Through Training and Development

FOURTH EDITION

ALAN M. SAKS
CENTRE FOR INDUSTRIAL RELATIONS AND HUMAN RESOURCES
UNIVERSITY OF TORONTO

ROBERT R. HACCOUN
UNIVERSITÉ DE MONTRÉAL

SERIES EDITOR:
MONICA BELCOURT
YORK UNIVERSITY

THOMSON

NELSON

Australia   Canada   Mexico   Singapore   Spain   United Kingdom   United States

THOMSON

NELSON

Managing Performance Through Training and Development
Fourth Edition

Alan M. Saks and Robert R. Haccoun

Associate Vice President, Editorial Director:
Evelyn Veitch

Publisher:
Veronica Visentin

Acquisitions Editor:
Shannon White

Senior Marketing Manager:
Charmaine Sherlock

Developmental Editor:
Tracy Yan

Permissions Coordinator:
Sheila Hall

Senior Content Production Manager:
Julie van Veen

Production Service:
Interactive Composition Corporation

Copy Editor:
Joyce Grant

Proofreader:
Susan Fitzgerald

Indexer:
Patti Schiendelman

Production Coordinator:
Ferial Suleman

Senior Manufacturing Coordinator:
Joanne McNeil

Design Director:
Ken Phipps

Interior Design Modifications:
Katherine Strain

Cover Design:
Angela Cluer

Compositor:
Interactive Composition Corporation

Printer:
Thomson West

Library and Archives Canada Cataloguing in Publication

Saks, Alan M. (Alan Michael), 1960–
    Managing performance through training and development / Alan M. Saks, Robert R. Haccoun; series editor, Monica Belcourt.—4th ed.

(Nelson series in human resources management)

Includes bibliographical references and index.

ISBN 978-0-17-625244-1
ISBN 0-17-625244-4

1. Employees—Training of—Textbooks. I. Haccoun, Robert R. II. Belcourt, Monica. Managing performance through training & development. III. Title. IV. Series.

HF5549.5.T7S23 2006   658.3′124
C2006-903678-0

To Kelly, Justin, and Brooke, my best friends

Alan Saks

To my late parents, Emma Gammara and Charles Shalom Haccoun

Robert Haccoun

Brief Contents

Detailed Contents

Chapter 3: Learning and Motivation   59

Chapter 15: Training Trends and Best Practices   443

About the Series

More than ever, HRM professionals need the knowledge and skills to design HRM practices that not only meet legal requirements but also are effective in supporting organizational strategy. Increasingly, these professionals turn to published research and best practices for assistance in the development of effective HR policies and practices. The books in the *Thomson Nelson Series in Human Resources Management* are the best source in Canada for reliable, valid, and current knowledge about practices in HRM.

The texts in this series include
- *Managing Performance Through Training and Development*
- *Management of Occupational Health and Safety*
- *Recruitment and Selection in Canada*
- *Strategic Compensation in Canada*
- *Strategic Human Resources Planning*
- *An Introduction to the Canadian Labour Market*
- *Research, Measurement, and Evaluation of Human Resources*

The *Thomson Nelson Series in Human Resources Management* represents a significant development in the field of HRM for many reasons. Each book in the series (except for *Strategic Compensation in Canada*) is the first Canadian text in its area of specialization. HR professionals in Canada must work with Canadian laws, statistics, policies, and values. This series serves their needs. It also represents the first time that students and practitioners have had access to a complete set of HRM books, standardized in presentation, that enables them to access information quickly across many HRM disciplines. The books are essential sources of information that meet the requirements for the Knowledge exam for the academic portion of the HR certification process. This one-stop resource will prove useful to anyone looking for solutions for the effective management of people.

The publication of this series signals that the field of human resources management has advanced to the stage where theory and applied research guide practice. The books in the series present the best and most current research in the functional areas of HRM. Research is supplemented with examples of the best practices used by Canadian companies that are leaders in HRM. Each text begins with a general model of the discipline, then describes the implementation of effective strategies. Thus the books serve as an introduction to the functional area for the new student of HR and as a validation source for the more experienced HRM practitioner. Cases, exercises, and references provide opportunities for further discussion and analysis.

As you read and consult the books in this series, I hope you share my excitement in being involved in the development of a profession that has such a significant impact on the workforce and in our professional lives.

Monica Belcourt
SERIES EDITOR
May 2006

About the Authors

Alan M. Saks

Alan M. Saks, Ph.D., is a Professor of Organizational Behaviour and Human Resource Management at the University of Toronto, where he holds a joint appointment in the Department of Management—UTSC, the Centre for Industrial Relations and Human Resources, and the Joseph L. Rotman School of Management. Prior to joining the University of Toronto, Professor Saks was a member of the Department of Management in the Faculty of Commerce and Administration at Concordia University and in the School of Administrative Studies at York University.

Professor Saks earned his BA in Psychology from the University of Western Ontario, an MASc in Industrial-Organizational Psychology from the University of Waterloo, and a PhD in Organizational Behaviour and Human Resources from the University of Toronto. He conducts research on a number of areas in human resources and organizational behaviour including recruitment, job search, training, and the socialization of new employees. His research has been published in refereed journals such as the *Journal of Applied Psychology*, *Personnel Psychology*, *Academy of Management Journal*, *Journal of Organizational Behavior*, *Journal of Vocational Behavior*, *Human Resource Management*, and *Human Resource Development Quarterly* as well as in professional journals such as the *HR Professional Magazine*, *The Training Report*, *The Learning Journal*, *Canadian HR Reporter*, and the *HRM Research Quarterly*. In addition to this text, he is also the author of *Research, Measurement, and Evaluation of Human Resources*, and a co-author of *Organizational Behaviour: Understanding and Managing Life at Work*.

Professor Saks is currently on the editorial boards of the *Academy of Management Journal*, *Personnel Psychology*, and *Journal of Vocational Behavior*.

Robert R. Haccoun

Educated at McGill University (BA 1969) and the Ohio State University (MA 1970, PhD 1973), Robert R. Haccoun is currently Professor of Psychology at the Université de Montréal. Prior to returning to academia in 1978, Professor Haccoun was a research scientist for Bell Canada in Montreal. He is a founding member and past president of the Industrial-Organizational Psychology section of the Canadian Psychological Association.

He has delivered papers at scientific conferences and published scholarly articles in French and in English in a number of areas including training, absenteeism, gender issues, and research methodology. He has published in many journals including *Personnel Psychology*, the *Journal of Applied Psychology*, *Canadian Psychologist*, *Revue Gestion*, and *Canadian Journal of Administrative Studies*. His research book, *Comprendre l'organisation: Approches de recherches*, co-authored in 1982, has been translated into Spanish. He is also the senior author of a statistics book to be published in French in the fall of

2006. In addition to serving as a reviewer for many scientific journals and research funding agencies, he is Associate Editor of *Applied Psychology: An International Review*.

Active in the transfer of knowledge from academia to applied settings, he has lectured to practitioner audiences and written many professional articles. He has also provided consulting services to a number of leading organizations in Canada, the US, and Europe.

Preface

In order to adapt, compete, and survive in today's frequently changing and uncertain world, organizations must have the capacity for continuous learning and improvement. Continuous learning and improvement, however, depends in large part on the effectiveness of an organization's training and development programs and systems—the focus of this textbook.

Since the last edition of this text was published, the field of training and development has continued to flourish in terms of both the science and the practice of training. The increasing use of technology, the emphasis on blended approaches to training delivery, team task analysis, just-in-time learning, rapid e-leaning, new approaches to training evaluation, and improving the transfer of training are just a few examples of the exciting things that have been happening in the training and development field. The fourth edition of *Managing Performance Through Training and Development* reflects these changes.

For the fourth edition, once again Alan Saks and Robert Haccoun have joined forces. The two authors have been involved in training resarch for over 10 years and have collaborated on numerous research projects on the transfer of training. With the fourth edition, we have continued to develop and improve this textbook in many ways.

First, the fourth edition includes a new chapter on Training Implementation and Delivery. The reviewers of the text felt that there was too much material covered in Chapter 5 on training design and delivery. Therefore, we split this chapter into two, with Chapter 5 focusing exclusively on Training Design and the new Chapter 9 (which comes after the three chapters on training methods) focusing on the implementation and delivery of training. This change not only provides a greater focus of the issues in each chapter, but it also allows us to include some new topics and to expand on existing ones. For example, Chapter 5 now includes a new section on requests for proposals and on integrating errors into learning and training. Chapter 9 provides new material on classroom seating arrangements, creating a climate for learning, and an expanded description of Gagné's nine events of instruction.

Second, Chapter 15 on Training Trends and Best Practices has been substantially revised and now includes coverage of outsourcing and the American Society of Training and Development's new competency model. In addition, almost every chapter in the text contains new material and content. Here are some examples to look for:

Chapter 1: High-performance work systems.
Chapter 2: Differences between formal and informal learning.
Chapter 5: Requests for proposals and integrating errors into learning and training.
Chapter 6: Aptitude-treatment interaction.
Chapter 7: Cross training.
Chapter 8: Customization and personalization of training.
Chapter 9: Classroom seating arrangements and creating a climate for learning.
Chapter 10: The transfer system.

Chapter 13: Ethics training.
Chapter 14: Corporate Universities.
Chapter 15: Outsourcing training and development.

In addition to new content, we have also added two new and exciting pedagogical features that appear at the end of every chapter. The Great Training Debate presents a debatable issue that can be used early in a class to get students discussing a topic or later in a class so students can apply the chapter material to an important training issue. For example, The Great Training Debate in Chapter 15 asks students to debate whether organizations should outsource all of their training and development.

We have also added a case incident to each chapter. This was based on the comments of some reviewers, who felt that some of the cases were too long. Therefore, to satisfy those adopters who like longer cases as well as those who prefer shorter ones, we have retained the cases and added case incidents, which present short descriptions of a training problem followed by several questions. Like The Great Training Debate, they can be used to begin a discussion at the start of a class or later in a class when students can begin to apply the chapter material.

We also made a small change to the exercises at the end of each chapter by breaking them down into two types: In-Class exercises are those that students can do during class time without any pre-class preparation, while In-the-Field exercises require students to gather information in the field by talking to HR and training professionals. These exercises can also be used as projects and assignments. We have also added new discussion questions, Using-the-Internet exercises, and In-Class and In-the-Field exercises, as well as four new cases. The Using-the-Internet exercises require students to visit a website and gather information to answer a question(s) or prepare a brief report on what they have found. In combination, the text now offers a wide variety of pedagogical material at the end of every chapter. Our intent is to provide instructors and students with a wide selection of pedagogical material to choose from, to best suit their learning needs and preferences.

Like the previous edition of the text, every chapter begins with a chapter-opening vignette. Each vignette tells the story of an actual training program in an organization that is of relevance to the material covered in the chapter. The vignette sets the stage for each chapter. Many of the vignettes feature Canadian organizations, and the fourth edition of the text includes seven new ones. Also retained in this edition are The Trainer's Notebook and the Training Today features. The Trainer's Notebook presents practical, hands-on information for trainers and practitioners (e.g., Facilitating Informal Learning in Organizations, Chapter 2) and the Training Today feature describes the latest in training research and practice (e.g., Rotational Assignments at Deloitte & Touche, Chapter 7). Also retained from the previous edition are Weblinks for students who want to learn more about an organization or association mentioned in the text. A Weblink icon appears in the margin of the text and the Web addresses can be found at the end of each chapter. This edition also includes RPC icons, which refer to "Required Professional Capabilities." RPCs represent the learning objectives in the area of Organizational Learning,

Development and Training for the national Certified Human Resources Professional (CHRP) designation. Their appearance in the text alerts students to RPC-relevant content, and the actual RPC content is listed at the end of each chapter.

We have also retained the other features that appeared in the third edition. These include: learning objectives at the beginning of every chapter; key terms, which appear in the text in bold and in the margins and which are also listed at the end of each chapter; and chapter-ending summaries which review the main content of each chapter.

For instructors, this edition is also accompanied by an Instructor's Manual, and PowerPoint slides can be downloaded directly from www.hrm.nelson.com.

We hope that students and instructors find these additions as exciting as we do and that they help to facilitate and maximize learning.

Structure of the Book

The text begins with an overview of the training and development process. In addition to presenting training and development within the larger context of the organization and the human resources management system, Chapter 1 also describes the instructional systems design (ISD) model of the training and development process which sets the stage for much of the subsequent chapters in the text.

Chapters 2 and 3 focus on learning, which is first and foremost what training is all about. We feel that it is important that students first understand learning at both the organizational and individual levels before they begin to learn about the role of training and development in the learning process. Therefore, Chapter 2 describes organizational learning, the learning organization, types of knowledge and intellectual capital, informal learning, and knowledge management practices. The chapter concludes with a multilevel systems model of organizational learning which shows how learning at the organization, group, and individual levels are interrelated, as well as a model that shows how training is related to individual and organizational learning.

Chapter 3 focuses on how individuals learn and their motivation to learn. The major theories of learning, adult learning theory, and theories of motivation are presented along with their implications for training and development. The chapter concludes with a model of training effectiveness, which shows the different variables that influence learning and retention, and how learning and retention are related to individual behaviour and performance and organizational effectiveness. The training effectiveness model is further developed in Chapters 5 and 10.

The training and development process begins with needs analysis, the focus of Chapter 4. Chapter 4 describes the needs-analysis process with particular emphasis on the three levels of needs analysis (organizational, task, and person) and how to determine solutions to performance problems. The chapter also describes the methods and sources of needs anlaysis and some of the obstacles to conducting a needs analysis.

Chapter 5 describes how to design training and development programs. The chapter begins with an overview of the importance of training objectives and how to write good training objectives. The chapter then proceeds to cover the main steps involved in the design of training programs, including whether to purchase or design a training program; requests for proposals; the training content; training methods; active practice and conditions of practice; and integrating errors into learning and training.

One of the most important steps in the design of a training program is choosing training methods. Given the vast array of training methods and instructional techniques available, Chapters 6, 7, and 8 are devoted to this topic. Chapter 6 describes the most frequently used off-the-job training methods including: lectures, discussions, audio-visual methods, case studies, case incidents, behavioural modelling, role plays, games, simulations, and action learning. Each training method is defined and described, along with tips for trainers. The chapter concludes with a discussion of the factors to consider when choosing training methods and the importance of a blended approach.

In Chapter 7, we turn to on-the-job training methods including job instruction training, performance aids, job rotation, apprenticeship programs, coaching, and mentoring. Like Chapter 6, we define and describe each method and provide tips for trainers. The chapter concludes with a discussion of the advantages and disadvantages of off-the-job and on-the-job training methods.

Chapter 8 is devoted to technology-based training methods. The chapter begins with a definition and a list of the different types of technology-based training. Particular emphasis is given to self-directed learning, computer-based training and e-learning, asynchronous and synchronous training, distance learning, electronic performance support systems, and video conferencing. The chapter also describes the advantages, disadvantages, effectiveness, and design of technology-based training methods, and concludes with a discussion of the future of technology-based training.

New to this edition is Chapter 9, on training implementation and delivery. The chapter begins with a description of a lesson plan and then the remainder of the chapter focuses on the main components of a lesson plan including the characteristics and selection of good trainers, the selection of trainees, training materials and equipment, the training site, and scheduling training programs. The chapter also describes how to deliver a training program including how to create a climate for learning, Gagné's nine events of instruction, and various training delivery problems and solutions.

One of the biggest problems facing trainers is how to ensure trainees apply what they learn in training on the job. This is known as the transfer of training and it is the focus of Chapter 10. The chapter begins with a review of the transfer problem and barriers to transfer, followed by a description of Baldwin and Ford's (1988) model of the transfer process. The chapter then describes the different practices that can be undertaken by managers, trainers, and trainees for improving the transfer of training before, during, and after training. The chapter concludes with a description of the transfer system.

Once a training program has been designed and delivered, it needs to be evaluated. Chapters 11 and 12 are devoted to training evaluation. In Chapter 11, we first describe the purpose and difficulties of training evaluation, and then discuss several training evaluation models. The chapter also describes how to measure key variables for training evaluation and the different types of training evaluation designs.

The topic of training evaluation continues in Chapter 12 where the focus shifts to the costs and benefits of training programs. Chapter 12 describes how to calculate the costs and benefits of training programs, as well as the calculation of the net benefit and return on investment. The importance of the credibility of estimates is also discussed as well as the use of utility analysis for determining the financial benefits of training programs. The chapter concludes with a discussion of the activities that support the costing function.

In Chapters 13 and 14 we turn to a consideration of the types of training programs that are provided by organizations. Chapter 13 describes some of the most common forms of training that employees receive including new employee orientation training, basic-skills training, technical skills training, information technology training, health and safety training, quality training, team training, sales training, customer service training, sexual harassment training, ethics training, diversity training, and cross-cultural training. Descriptions of each type of training program are provided as well as statistics on their use by organizations in Canada and in the United States.

Chapter 14 is devoted entirely to management development. This reflects both its importance to organizations and the large investments made by organizations in the development of their managers. The chapter begins with a definition of management development and management, and then describes the core functions, roles, and skills of management. Models of management development are also described as well as the content of management development programs. The final section of the chapter provides an overview of management development programs including management education programs, management training programs, and on-the-job management development (job rotation and coaching). This chapter has been substantially revised and now draws upon and refers back to other chapters in the text to highlight how many of the concepts and techniques are of relevance to the training and development of managers.

Finally, Chapter 15 concludes the text with a discussion of training trends and best practices. This chapter has been substantially revised and now focuses on several major trends in the training field including the changing role of trainers, outsourcing, the aging workforce, and just-in-time learning. The chapter also discusses ethical issues of importance to trainers and training and development. The chapter, and text, conclude with a review and summary of training design features to facilitate learning and transfer and the main reasons why training programs fail, as well as the best practices to make them highly effective.

Throughout the text we have tried to maintain a balance between theory and research on the one hand, and practice and application on the other. We have also tried to provide examples of the concepts and principles presented in the text by showcasing organizations, many of them Canadian, that have successfully designed and delivered effective training programs. Overall, we have tried to provide a thorough and comprehensive text on training and development that reflects both the science and practice of the field as well as our excitement and genuine love of the topic. We hope that the combination of text material as well as the pedagogical features will motivate students to learn about the science and practice of training and development.

Acknowledgments

Writing a textbook requires the support and assistance of many people who either directly or indirectly make important contributions to the process and outcome. We wish to thank all of those who have played important roles in our lives and in writing this text.

First, we thank the reviewers who provided us with insightful and constructive feedback that led to many changes and improvements: Gordon Barnard of Durham College, Susan Fitzrandolph of Ryerson University, Jamie Gruman of University of Guelph, and Stefan Groschl of University of Guelph. Each one contributed to this text by lending us their expertise and by taking the time to share their teaching experiences. Their comments and feedback have helped us improve this text, including the creation of a separate chapter on training implementation and design as well as the addition of case incidents.

Second, we would like to express our appreciation to our many colleagues who have helped us formulate our ideas, provided us with their own ideas and insights, or who were always available to lend a sympathetic ear.

Third, we wish to express our gratitude to the team at Nelson that helped us develop and produce this text. First, we wish to thank two people who worked with us on the third editon and at the beginning of this edition: Acquisitions Editor, Anthony Rezek, who was always very supportive of our ideas and aspirations for this text; and Developmental Editor, Karina Hope, who cared a great deal about this text and had the difficult task of pulling it all together and keeping us on track. We are grateful for the opportunity we had to work with Anthony and Karina over the years and we will miss them.

We also wish to express our gratitude and appreciation to our present team at Nelson: Publisher, Veronica Visentin; Developmental Editor, Tracy Yan; and Senior Content Production Manager, Julie van Veen. We are grateful for their support and all of their hard work. We feel very lucky to be working with a team of professionals who care so much about what they do and about their authors.

Finally, we also wish to thank our families, who have had to endure the burden of living with tired and overworked authors who sometimes don't have time to play or sleep! Alan Saks is grateful to Kelly, Justin, and Brooke for making it all worthwhile. Robert Haccoun thanks his daughter Jennifer and her husband, Bram Abramson, who have provided him with, as the Yiddish expression goes, much in the way of 'nachas.'

Alan M. Saks
University of Toronto

Robert R. Haccoun
Université de Montréal

Chapter 1

The Training and Development Process

Chapter Learning Objectives

After reading this chapter, you should be able to:

- understand the meaning of the terms performance management, training, and development
- describe the organizational, employee, and societal benefits of training and development
- discuss the state of training and development in Canada
- understand and explain the role of the environmental and organizational context of training and development and high-performance work systems (HPWS)
- understand the meaning of strategic human resources management (SHRM) and strategic training and development
- discuss the instructional systems design (ISD) model of training and development

MOLSON COORS BREWING COMPANY

In 2005, Molson Inc. and Adolph Coors Company announced they had completed a merger of equals, to become Molson Coors Brewing Company. Molson Coors Brewing Company's operating scale and balance sheet make it a major player in the brewing industry—the fifth-largest brewer in the world. The company has 11 breweries and more than 10 000 employees worldwide. For the 3000 employees of Molson Inc., the merger meant attending Coors's well-established ethics training program.

Although there has been a great deal of emphasis on ethical business practices in the aftermath of Enron, WorldCom, and Tyco, Adolph Coors Company has been training employees to understand ethical issues and to effectively cope with them for more than a decade. In fact, the company has one of the most comprehensive ethics programs in North America. The program includes interactive on-line courses, ethics leadership training, a decision map, a detailed set of policies, and an ethics help line that complements and supports a user-friendly and accessible code of conduct.

The objective of the program is to teach employees how to think, clarify, and analyze situations as part of a strategy of "prevention" rather than "investigation." In 2002, the company invested $250,000 in an interactive, Web-based ethics training module that guides employees through real-world scenarios to help ensure that they understand key principles of ethics. Using an "ethics expedition" theme, employees must ascend from a base camp to the top of a mountain by completing activities in each of four camps. As employees ascend, the topics evolve from rules to values, from black-and-white issues to shades of grey. The program helps employees understand ethical decision-making in the context of the company's values and business objectives.

All new hires must complete the on-line course within 90 days, as a condition of employment, and existing employees must take a refresher course every couple of years. All employees, from senior executives to those loading trucks, must take the Web-based ethics training module. In addition, a manager-training program focuses on the need to look for warning signs of employees being pressured or otherwise subjected to influences that could lead to unethical activity.

In order to ensure that the training translates into ethical behaviour on the job, employees are evaluated on how well they model the behaviour outlined in the company's ethical code of conduct. And although it is difficult to measure results in terms of numbers or dollars, the company's manager of ethics and audit services believes that the program has paid handsome dividends. When employees understand ethical issues and concerns, they are able to face situations more proactively. Ethics also plays an important role in the company's financial success.

In 2005, Molson Coors was awarded the Optimas Award for Ethical Practice from *Workforce Management* magazine for "implementing a customized program that has directly affected the way employees perceive their work and do their jobs."[1]

Molson Coors Brewing Company is a good example of the role and importance of training and development in organizations. The company's ethics training program ensures that employee behaviour is consistent with the company's ethical code of conduct and that company practices are consistent with the company's values and culture. It is also an excellent example of how to design and implement an effective training and development program.

It is not hard to understand how investments in human capital and training can improve an organization's success and competitiveness. But have you ever considered how the training of employees can impact your life? Consider the emergency landing of an Air Transat Airbus on an island in the Atlantic Ocean on August 24, 2001. With both engines dead and the lives of 293 passengers and 13 crew members on Flight 236 at stake, the pilots successfully made an emergency landing after gliding for 19 minutes without power.

The loss of power was due to a fuel leak in the right engine that caused it to shut down. A chafing fuel line on the right engine, which had recently been replaced, leaked during the flight. Although there was a leak in the right engine causing a loss of fuel, the left engine should have been sufficient to keep the plane in the air. However, fuel from the undamaged left engine tanks was pumped to the leaking right side, where it was dumped overboard. This led to a loss of fuel in the left engine, which then caused it to lose power as well. The Airbus would have been able to fly safely with just the left engine operating had its fuel not been pumped to the leaking right side.

According to Airbus, the maker of the twin-engine A330, Air Transat improperly reconnected the main fuel line to the aircraft's right-side engine when it was changed four days before the near-disaster. The fuel line to the right-side engine chafed against a hydraulic pipe that eventually cracked and created the fuel leak. Air-safety investigators also blamed faulty mechanical work by Air Transat mechanics as the cause of the fuel leak that led to the near-catastrophic emergency landing.

Disaster was averted only by a skilled emergency landing by the pilots, who were hailed as heroes for safely landing the plane. However, one of the pilots, Captain Robert Piché, denied being a hero, stating that landing a plane with no engines is "what you train for."

Transport Canada fined Air Transat $250,000 and ordered the airline to provide pilots and flight crews with special training on fuel management and emergency landings. Senior Transport Canada officials and Air Transat top management agreed that the airline's pilots would take special training sessions. Air Transat also provided Transport Canada with a corrective-action plan to improve the performance of maintenance that included human-factors training for all technical personnel.[2]

In 2004, the official report into the incident concluded that the emergency landing could have been avoided if the pilots had followed established fuel-leak procedures. Accident investigators determined that a fuel leak was turned into a near-disaster because the pilots failed to determine the problem and then tried to correct it from memory rather than by following a computer checklist which would have warned them of the possibility of a fuel leak. The pilots believed the problem was a fuel imbalance so they pumped tonnes of fuel overboard. According to the report, the crew did not correctly evaluate the situation before taking action. At the time, there was no adequate training for the pilots in dealing with a catastrophic fuel leak, because it was considered a remote possibility.[3]

Although we cannot say that inadequate training was the cause of this near-disaster, we do know that training was required in order to prevent a similar incident from happening again. We also know that experience and training had a lot to do with the pilot's ability to safely land the plane. Air Transat has since reviewed its training programs and enhanced its maintenance and flight operations procedures. Its pilots are now required to attend a new training program on the procedures for overseas flights, which includes a review of fuel management. In 2005, Air Transat agreed to a settlement of $7.65 million to a group of passengers who were aboard Flight 236 and had filed a class-action lawsuit against the airline.[4]

This is just one of many examples illustrating how the training of employees affects our lives in ways that we are unaware of and seldom if ever think about. Did you know, for example, that aircraft flying over Canada have nearly collided or come too close to each other at least four times since 1997? Reports indicate that, besides failing to go through the proper checklists before ending their shifts, air traffic controllers are not adequately trained.[5]

And do you remember the worst subway accident in Canadian history on August 11, 1995, in which three people were killed and about 140 others injured in Toronto when two trains collided? The subway operator, who was only on his second shift, admitted he wasn't ready to operate the train. Although he had successfully completed the 12-day subway training course, he had wanted more instruction behind the controls and was not sure he was ready to operate the train. At an inquest into the accident, he said, "I really didn't understand a lot of this stuff, I really didn't understand the mechanics of the train." Since then, the Toronto Transit Commission (TTC) has made many changes, including the way it trains its drivers. For example, the 12-day driver training program has been extended to six weeks and operators are now required to take three days of additional training every two years. Emergency training is also required for the recertification of all subway employees every two years. These changes, along with others, have made the TTC one of the safest transit systems in North America.[6]

Finally, the importance and adequacy of training have recently become an issue for the country's RCMP officers following the killing of four young officers in Alberta in March 2005. A recent report by Canada's auditor general found that inadequate and incomplete training of the country's RCMP officers threatens to compromise public safety. Only 6.2 percent of the national police force's officers completed all of their mandatory training requirements in 2004, a dramatic drop from 57 percent in 2003. Furthermore, newly graduated RCMP cadets do not always spend the required first two months on the job paired with a senior officer or receive the six months of coaching they are supposed to receive once they begin active duty. The report concluded that, "Gaps in training, qualification, and certification may affect the health and safety of peace officers and the public."[7]

As we've seen, employees who are poorly trained can make mistakes and cause accidents that threaten the public's safety and well-being as well as the employee's own safety. And while these examples are among the most extreme, it is important to recognize that poorly trained employees produce defective products and provide poor service. Thus, training is of vital concern not just to employees and their organizations, but for all of us who purchase goods and services every day of our lives.

For organizations, success and competitiveness are highly dependent on employees' continuous learning and education. In fact, continuous learning and education have become key to the success of individuals and organizations. Whether an organization is adopting new technology, improving quality, or simply trying to remain competitive, training and development is a critical and necessary part of the process. A report by The Conference Board of Canada on learning and development in Canadian organizations noted that continuous learning and the transfer of knowledge are key factors in fostering creativity and promoting organizational excellence.[8] Not surprisingly, training and education is one of the distinguishing characteristics of the best companies to work for in Canada.[9]

Therefore, it should not surprise you that organizations today invest millions of dollars each year on training and development. This book will teach you about the exciting world of training and development and how to design, deliver, and evaluate training programs. In this chapter, we introduce you to the topic of training and development and describe the training and development process. We begin with a discussion of performance management, since training and development is first and foremost all about managing performance in organizations.

Performance Management

As the title of the text indicates, training and development is all about managing performance. **Performance management** is the process of establishing performance expectations with employees, designing interventions and programs to improve that performance, and monitoring the success of interventions and programs. This process signals to employees what is really important in the organization, ensures accountability for behaviour and results, and helps to improve performance.[10] Performance management is not a single event, such as a performance appraisal or a training program; rather it is a comprehensive process that involves various activities and programs designed to improve performance. The code of conduct and ethics programs

Performance management

The process of establishing performance expectations with employees, designing interventions and programs to improve performance, and monitoring the success of interventions and programs

Chapter 1: The Training and Development Process

at Molson Coors Brewing Company are good examples of performance management. The code and programs are part of a comprehensive process that indicates the company's expectations for employees in terms of how they should think and act in various situations. The training programs teach employees how to respond to ethical dilemmas, and the performance evaluation process monitors how well employees adhere to the expectations outlined in the company's code of conduct and training programs. As a result, employees know how to recognize ethical issues and effectively cope with and respond to them.

Training and Development

Training is one of the most important ways that performance can be improved. Training refers to the acquisition of knowledge, skills, and abilities to improve performance in one's current job. Training usually consists of a short-term focus on acquiring skills to perform one's job. You have probably experienced this type of training, such as when your company sends you to a workshop to learn a software package like Excel or to learn how to serve customers. The goal is to help you learn to do your current job better.

Development refers to the acquisition of knowledge, skills, and abilities required to perform future job responsibilities and for the long-term achievement of individual career goals and organizational objectives. The goal is to prepare individuals for promotions and future jobs as well as additional job responsibilities. This process might consist of extensive programs such as leadership development, and might include seminars and workshops, job rotation, coaching, and other assignments. The goal is usually to prepare employees for managerial careers. You can read more about management development in Chapter 14.

Training and development is part of a larger human resources system that plays a role in the performance management process. The creation of an organizational environment conducive to optimum performance is a fundamental first step in the process of a performance management system. All systems are concerned with the goal of improving organizational effectiveness through the improvement of human resources. Key to the achievement of this goal is training and development, which has benefits for organizations, employees, and society at large.

The Benefits of Training and Development

Organizations that invest in the training and development of their employees reap many benefits. But so do employees and the society in which they live. In this section, we describe some of the benefits of training and development.

Organizational Benefits

Organizations that invest in training and development benefit in many ways that ultimately help an organization obtain a sustained competitive advantage. Training and development can facilitate the strategy of an organization, increase effectiveness, and improve employee recruitment and retention.

Training
The acquisition of knowledge, skills, and abilities to improve performance in one's current job

Development
The acquisition of knowledge, skills, and abilities required to perform future job responsibilities

1. Organizational Strategy

The goal of all organizations is to survive and prosper. Training and development can help organizations achieve these goals. Organizations can be successful by training employees so they have the knowledge and skills necessary to help organizations achieve their goals and objectives. By linking training to an organization's strategy, training becomes a strategic activity that operates in concert with other programs and activities to achieve an organization's strategic business objectives.

For example, at Space Systems/Loral, a company in the United States that designs and manufactures satellites and satellite systems, training is aligned with the company's strategic goals. The learning and development group meets with the company's executives on a regular basis to plan training and development programs to support the company's strategic goals.[11]

In the service sector, Alimentation Couche-Tard Inc., Canada's second-largest convenience-store operator, uses training as a strategic tool to grow its stores under company labels such as Provi-Soir, Winks, and Red Rooster. Couche-Tard invests twice as much as the national average in training its employees in customer service, management, and merchandising.[12] Training was also a key factor for Quebecor World Inc. in achieving its customer-service strategy and becoming more competitive (see Training Today 1).

2. Increase Organizational Effectiveness

There is a calculable benefit to training employees. Trained employees can do more and better work, make fewer errors, require less supervision, have more positive attitudes, and have lower rates of attrition.[13] These improvements all have a positive effect on an organization's effectiveness.

For example, a survey conducted by American Management Association found that companies that expanded their training programs showed gains in productivity and larger operating profits.[14] In another study, a 10 percent increase in training produced a 3 percent increase in productivity over two years.[15] Companies that invest more heavily in training are more successful and more profitable. These companies spend up to 6 percent of payroll on training, but they achieve 57 percent higher sales per employee, 37 percent higher gross profits per employee, and a 20 percent higher ratio in market-to-book values.

The link between training and an organization's effectiveness is strongly supported by research. Study after study has found that companies that invest more in training have higher revenues, profits, and productivity growth than firms that invest less in training.[16] A review of research on training and organizational effectiveness concluded that training improves organizational productivity, quality, and customer service.[17]

3. Employee Recruitment and Retention

Training can be used by organizations to increase their attractiveness to prospective employees and to retain their current employees. For many organizations today, training is the number one attraction and retention tool.

Strategy and Training at Quebecor World Inc.

Quebecor World Inc. is one of the world's largest commercial printers. Based in Montreal, it has 130 printing facilities located in 17 countries and employs 31 000 people. In 1998, the company embarked on the largest training initiative the organization had ever attempted. After extensive research and a year-long assessment, the company identified some strategic and pressing business realities. The printing industry had undergone some dramatic changes in a short period of time. Gaining a competitive advantage was no longer measured in months and weeks, but in hours and minutes and the company was no longer able to compete on price and quality alone.

As a result of the assessment process, the company determined that customer service was the most important issue on which to focus, and the key to gaining a competitive advantage and differentiating itself from its competitors. This led to the development of the company's Allstar Customer Service training program. The goal of the program was to educate the firm's North American customer service and account representatives in world-class customer service skills. The program's objectives included improving their understanding of customers' needs, improving account management skills, and creating a high-performance, team-based, customer-oriented culture.

The nine-day program consists of three intensive three-day sessions with no more than 25 participants per session. During one of the sessions, employees participate in a team-building cooking exercise in which customer service representatives must design, prepare, and serve a banquet meal within two hours, without any instruction. The exercise forces employees to work together to come up with focused solutions in a short time.

The program also includes role-play situations between "plant employees" and "customers." A low-ropes exercise requires trainees to climb over a 15-foot wall. Trainees must also make presentations to senior managers about what they have learned and how they will apply it at work. Upon completion of the program, trainees evaluate the program and receive a certificate for completing it.

The training program helped Quebecor World Inc. gain a competitive advantage by achieving world-class customer-service skills that have increased customer satisfaction, decreased turnaround time, lowered the cost of errors, and improved internal and external communications. It has received superb feedback within the company and national recognition in the United States. In 2001, *Workforce Management* magazine awarded the company its Optimas Award in the Competitive Advantage category and in 2006, Wal-Mart named Quebecor "Customer Service Supplier of the Year."

Sources: Laabs, J. K. (2001, March). Serving up a new level of customer service at Quebecor. *Workforce Management* magazine, 40–41; Quebecor World Inc. (December 19, 2000). Quebecor World Inc. Human Resources Function Wins. From: www. quebecorworldinc.com; Lake Forest Graduate School of Management. "Lake Forest GSM Corporate Education Client Wins Workforce Magazine Optimas Award." From: www.ifgsm.edu.

An organization that fails to provide training opportunities to its employees will be at a disadvantage in attracting new employees and retaining current ones. In one study, 99 percent of the respondents said that there are job areas in which training would be useful to them, and in which training decreases their willingness to move to another company.[18]

Many organizations offer extensive training and development opportunities to retain employees. For example, at Delta Hotels and Resorts, employees are guaranteed ongoing training. If an employee does not receive proper training, he or she can claim an extra week's salary. About 30 employees a year receive an extra week's salary. Not surprisingly, Delta has an employee retention rate of 89 percent, which is considered one of the best in the hospitality industry. In addition, hotel-school graduates are attracted to Delta because of the training they will receive.[19]

Employee Benefits

Training and development also has benefits to employees. The benefits to employees can be categorized as those that are internal or intrinsic to an individual, such as knowledge and attitudes, and those that are more external to an individual and are extrinsic benefits.

1. Intrinsic Benefits

Employees who are trained benefit by acquiring greater knowledge and skills that enable them to perform their jobs better. In addition to improving their knowledge and skills, trained employees also develop higher confidence or self-efficacy (see Chapter 3 for a discussion of self-efficacy) in their ability to perform their job. They describe feelings of increased usefulness and belonging in the organization, and they seek out opportunities to fully exploit their new skills and abilities.[20] Trained employees also have more positive attitudes toward their job and organization.[21]

2. Extrinsic Benefits

In addition to the intrinsic benefits that reside within employees, there are also extrinsic benefits associated with training. Extrinsic benefits include things such as higher earnings as a result of increased knowledge and skills, improved marketability, greater security of employment, and enhanced opportunities for advancement and promotion. A number of studies have found that company-sponsored training programs increase workers' wages by 4 to 11 percent.[22]

Clearly, employees who have greater knowledge and skills as a result of training will have more and better work-related opportunities, and those who work for organizations that provide extensive training are at an advantage compared to those who work for organizations that do not provide very much training.

Societal Benefits

Training and development also has benefits for society that extend beyond the workplace. The training and development that organizations provide their employees also helps to create an educated and skilled population that benefits the economy and our standard of living.

1. Educated Population

The knowledge and skills that employees receive through workplace training help to create an educated and skilled workforce. For example, some organizations offer literacy and numeracy training for employees who did not obtain them through regular educational channels but who require them to perform their jobs. This training also enables employees to function more effectively in their daily lives and therefore has a number of societal benefits.

Employees who have participated in organization-sponsored training programs report using their new skills to better manage their personal lives. They are more likely to be able to read instructions for assembling products and to be able to calculate bills and expenses. They are also more likely to be able to find employment if they are laid off or their employer closes a plant.

2. Standard of Living

The key to a country's standard of living, incomes, and overall prosperity are its productivity and productivity growth. Canada currently lags behind the United States in its productivity performance. There are a number of ways to improve productivity, and one of them is by improving the education and skills of the workforce.[23] An improvement in Canada's productivity will have a positive effect on the economy and our standard of living.

The federal government spends billions of dollars annually on education and training because it sees a strong link between an educated workforce and a high-wage economy. Higher corporate training investments also leads to the creation of jobs.[24]

Given the benefits of training and development, you might be wondering about the benefits that Canadian workers receive from training and development. Obviously, this depends on the extent to which Canadian organizations invest in training and development, the topic of the next section.

Training and Development in Canada

In order to reap the benefits of training and development, organizations must invest in it. Canadian organizations, however, have tended not to be leaders when it comes to investing in training and development. In fact, Canadian employees receive, on average, only 28 hours of training a year. The most training is received by professional and technical employees (34 hours) while trades (19 hours) and non-technical employees (20 hours) receive the least. Employees in primary industries (34 hours) and government (32 hours) receive the most training, while those in food services (19 hours) receive the least. Employees in medium-sized organizations receive more training (31.5 hours) than those in small (21 hours) or large (25 hours) organizations.[25]

According to The Conference Board of Canada, Canadian organizations under-invest in training and development.[26] For example, the total average investment in training and development across all industries in Canada was reported to be $4.9 million in 2004.[27] In the United States, organizations spend approximately $51 billion a year on formal training programs.[28] Canadian organizations also lag when it comes to the amount spent on training per employee, which has remained relatively static over the past decade. In 2004, the total average direct investment in training per employee was $914 compared to $824 in 2003, $838 in 2002, $859 in 2000, $798 in 2001, $776 in 1998, and $842 in 1996. By comparison, organizational spending on training and development per employee in the United States increased from $1,072 (Cdn) in 1999 to $1,115 in 2000, and $1,135 in 2001 and 2003. In addition, the average investment in training as a percentage of payroll in Canada has remained constant at around 1.75 percent compared to 2.34 percent in the U.S.[29]

These findings suggest that the gap between Canadian and U.S. organizations in training investments appears to be increasing, and that a plateau in Canadian training investment might have been reached, as the amounts invested by the country's organizations have remained relatively stable over the past decade. In other words, Canadian organizations may not be willing to invest much more in training and development. In fact, most organizations (62 percent) expect their training investments to remain the same in the next year.[30]

Canadian organizations also spend less on training and development than organizations in other areas of the world including Europe, Asia, and the Pacific Rim. A report by The Conference Board of Canada concluded that this under-investment in training and development might lead to a gap in essential knowledge and skills, and if Canadian organizations are going to be able to compete effectively, they must increase their investments in training and development.[31]

Given the many benefits of training, it is surprising that Canadian organizations invest less than those in other developed countries. It may be that training is not considered a high priority in Canadian organizations. In fact, Canada currently ranks 20th out of 60 countries in its ranking of employee training as a high organizational priority, behind countries such as Finland (ranked number 1), Denmark, and Japan but just ahead of the United States which ranked 23.[32]

All this is not to say that there are no Canadian organizations that do invest heavily in training and development. In fact, The Conference Board of Canada found that one in five organizations invests more than 3 percent of their payroll in training.[33] Scotiabank, for example, invests $47 million a year in training and education. Employees can receive tuition assistance, language training, and on-line programs for upgrading their skills. In addition, managers receive training on leadership skills and coaching techniques.[34] BMO Bank of Montreal invests an average of $1,800 a year in training per employee, which is more than double the national average, and provides a minimum of seven days of training a year.[35] At Labatt Breweries of Canada, employees from all areas attend beer school to learn how beer is made and to gain a greater knowledge of, and appreciation for, the company's products.[36] And as indicated in the chapter-opening vignette, Molson Coors Brewing Company is a leader when it comes to ethics training.

In order to get more companies to invest in training, the government of Quebec enacted legislation in 1995 that requires companies with payrolls of more than $1 million to spend 1 percent of their payroll on government-sanctioned training, or pay that amount into a provincial fund. The pool of money acquired from companies that do not invest the 1 percent of payroll on

Quebec's Payroll Training Legislation

Companies in Quebec with payrolls over $1 million are required by law to spend 1 percent of their payroll on training, or pay a training tax. They must also carefully document their training activities and complete government forms every February. Some have complained that the process is too complicated and choose to pay the tax rather than complete the forms even if they are providing some training. The main aspects of the legislation are as follows:

1. Every February, companies must file paperwork in which they indicate how they spent 1 percent of their total payroll on training.

2. If they have not spent at least 1 percent of their total payroll on training, they must pay the difference to the government, and that money is then used to fund training programs in companies that have invested at least 1 percent in training.

3. Companies must use accredited training bodies, instructors, and services that follow a code of ethics. All types of training are eligible.

4. General information about the participation of employees in training exercises must be provided.

5. Companies that meet the 1 percent training investment can apply for provincial training grants.

Source: Harding, K. (2003, June 4). A taxing way to train staff. *The Globe and Mail*, C1, C6. Reprinted with permission from *The Globe and Mail*.

---

training is used to provide training grants to companies that do invest at least 1 percent. This is the only payroll training tax in North America, and is believed to be having a positive influence on employee training in Quebec. In fact, research conducted by the authors of this text found that Quebec firms that are subject to the law do invest considerably more in training than firms that are exempted from the law, and firms in Quebec spend more on training than firms in Ontario, where there is no training tax legislation. Furthermore, the average firm in Quebec spends considerably more than the minimum 1 percent required by law.

Although Quebec is the only jurisdiction in North America to have a training tax, countries such as France, Denmark, Singapore, and Brazil have legislated levies to promote training. France introduced a training tax in 1971 and the rate of training has doubled to 1.5 percent of payroll.[37] To find out how the legislation works in Quebec, see The Trainer's Notebook 1, "Quebec's Payroll Training Legislation."

Information about training and development in Canada is summarized in Table 1.1. This information will enable you to compare your organization and training experience against others. This information also highlights some differences in training across job categories and industries. For example, a quick glance shows that those with advanced skills and positions receive the most training. Canadian organizations in the technology/communications and financial services sectors are among the top investors in training and development. Organizations in the health and education sector as well as wholesale/retail invest the least in training per employee.

TABLE 1.1

Training and Development in Canada

- Total average annual training investment in 2004 in all industries in Canada: $4,943,464
- Total average training investment per employee in 2004: $914
- Total average training investment per employee 1996–2004: $846
- Percentage of payroll spent on training: 1.75
- Sectors with the highest training investment per employee: not-for-profit, financial services, government, and technology/communication
- Sectors with the lowest training investment per employee: personal services (e.g., accommodation, food), wholesale/retail, and health/education
- Average number of training hours received annually per employee: 28
- Average number of training hours received annually by employee category: non-technical, 20; professional/technical, 34; trades, 19
- Industries with highest average number of training hours per employee: primary industries, 34; government, 32; high-tech, 29
- Industry with lowest average number of training hours per employee: food services, 19
- Anticipated changes in total training investment: increase, 33 percent; remain the same, 62 percent; decrease, 5 percent

Source: Parker, R. O., & Cooney, J. (2005). Learning & Development Outlook 2005. *The Conference Board of Canada*. Ottawa. Reprinted by permission of The Conference Board of Canada.

The Context of Training and Development

Although we have been discussing training and development as an independent activity, the reality is that training and development are embedded within a larger environmental and organizational context as well as a human resource system. As shown in Figure 1.1, training and development are part of a high-performance work system (HPWS). **High-performance work systems** consist of an interrelated system of HR practices and policies that typically includes rigorous recruitment and selection procedures, performance-contingent incentive compensation, performance management, a commitment to employee involvement, and extensive training and development programs. An increasing number of studies have found that organizations with high-performance work systems have superior productivity and financial performance.[38]

High-performance work systems are influenced by environmental and organizational factors. Environmental factors such as legislation, the economic climate, competition, demographics, and social values have an impact on organizations. For example, if a competitor introduces a lower priced product, the organization will have to decide whether to match the competitor's actions or compete in other ways, such as providing superior service. This strategic decision will in turn affect costs, the ability to pay employees, or the necessity to train and reward employees for effective performance. Events and concerns inside and outside an organization can lead to the need for new knowledge, skills, abilities, and training programs.

High-performance work system (HPWS)

An interrelated system of HR practices and policies that typically includes rigorous recruitment and selection procedures, performance-contingent incentive compensation, performance management, a commitment to employee involvement, and extensive training and development programs

FIGURE 1.1

High-Performance Work System

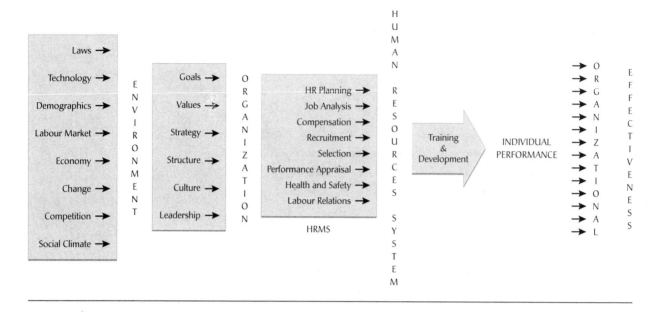

Sometimes sudden and unexpected changes in the environment can lead to changes in organizations and human resources policies and practices. For example, consider how the terrorist attacks in the United States on September 11, 2001, affected airport and flight security training. The Transportation Security Administration in the United States developed new guidelines for the training of baggage screeners and flight crews and made airport security fully federalized.

The training of baggage screeners now includes technical training on metal detectors, X-ray scanners, bag searching, and how to deal with difficult passengers and manage stress. Training was increased to 40 hours of classroom training and 60 hours of on-the-job training. Pilots and flight attendants receive training on how to assess and react to dangerous situations.[39] Other changes in training following the terrorist attacks included a shift to distance technologies and e-learning and an increase in training programs on diversity, security, stress management, and change management.[40] The Training Today 2 feature describes how terrorism has resulted in counterterrorism training programs in Canada.

Below, we discuss how changes in specific environmental and organizational factors can impact training and development.

The Environmental Context of Training and Development

Some of the key environmental factors that drive human resources and training and development are global competition, technology, the labour market, and change.

The Post 9/11 Environment and Counterterrorism Training

After the terrorist attacks in the United States on September 11, 2001, cities such as Toronto responded with improved equipment and co-ordination among police, fire, and medical staff and training at a new counterterrorism centre at Canadian Forces Base (CFB) Suffield.

On a base once known as a secretive centre for biological and chemical warfare research, located on a section of windswept and barren prairie the size of Prince Edward Island in southeast Alberta, municipal emergency response teams are practising for bioterrorist attacks as part of a counterterrorism training program.

CFB Suffield is the only place within NATO where troops can train outside with live chemical agents, one reason it recently attracted a Toronto emergency response team and a group of U.S. Marines that then went on duty in Afghanistan.

Toronto dispatched a group of police, firefighters, and paramedics to Suffield, where they handled the liquid form of sarin and mustard gas in a series of simulated terrorist attacks designed to replicate a chemical assault on a major Canadian city. Ottawa-Carleton and Calgary have also performed this type of exercise.

Wearing sealed protective suits and respirators under the searing sun, the Toronto units practised detecting and decontaminating the blistering agent, and treating mass casualties after a mock terrorist attack.

In another exercise, they handled liquid sarin at a simulated terrorist lab after a mock leak. The nerve agent was made famous when terrorists used it in a gas form during a 1995 attack on the Tokyo subway system.

In addition to a mock terrorist lab, the base has a plane, bus, and post office as well as a mock subway station to replicate possible terrorist targets for training purposes. Several federal government reports have cautioned in recent years that cities were ill-prepared to respond to a commercial chemical accident, while almost none were prepared for a chemical or biological attack.

This is a good example of how changes in the environment can have a direct effect on the training of employees. Prior to September 11, 2001, the type of training taking place at CFB Suffield would not have been considered for Canadian cities. However, the terrorist attacks of September 11 have created a strong need for this type of training.

Source: Stevenson, M. (2002, September 2). Base helps civilians prepare for chemical attacks. *The Globe and Mail*, A6. Reprinted with permission from *The Globe and Mail*.

Global Competition

Increasing global competition has forced organizations to improve their productivity and the quality of their goods and services. Improvements in the production process and quality initiatives almost always require employees to learn new skills. Furthermore, when Canadian organizations send workers on assignments in foreign countries, they need to provide them with cross-cultural training so they will be able to adapt and function in a different culture. Thus, global competition can require numerous changes to human resource practices and the need for training and development.

Technology

Technology has had a profound effect on the way organizations operate and compete. New technologies can provide organizations with improvements in productivity and a competitive advantage. However, such improvements depend on the training that employees receive. Technology will only lead to productivity gains when employees receive the necessary training to exploit the technology.[41] Thus, the adoption of new technologies will have a direct impact on the training needs of employees who will be required to use the technology.

The Labour Market

Changes in the labour market can have a major effect on training and development. For example, consider the impending shortage of skilled labour in Canada. It has been estimated that a critical shortage of skilled workers in Canada could reach one million by the year 2020. To deal with this looming crisis, the country will have to change its approach to education and training.[42] If organizations cannot hire people with the necessary knowledge and skills, they will have to provide more training if they are to compete and survive. Changes in the labour market and the supply of labour will require changes in the amount and type of training.

Change

The technological revolution, increasing globalization, and competition have resulted in a highly uncertain and constantly changing environment. In order to survive and remain competitive, organizations must adapt and change. As a result, managing change has become a normal part of organizational life, and training and development is almost always a key part of the process. This often involves training programs on the change process as well as training that is part of the change program. For example, if an organization implements a change program that involves a team-based work system, then employees will require team training (see Chapter 13 for a description of team training).

The Organizational Context of Training and Development

As indicated in Figure 1.1, training and development are influenced not only by external factors but also by internal events within the organization. Among the most important internal factors are strategy, structure, and culture.

Strategy

Strategic human resources management (SHRM)

The alignment of human resources practices with an organization's business strategy

Strategy is one of the most important factors influencing training and development. As indicated earlier, training and development can help an organization achieve its strategic objectives and gain a competitive advantage when it is aligned with an organization's strategy. The alignment of human resources practices with an organization's business strategy is known as **strategic human resources management** (**SHRM**). Organizations that have greater alignment between their HR practices and their strategies tend to have superior performance.[43]

Training is strategic when it is aligned with business strategy and therefore enables an organization to achieve its strategic goals and objectives. Whether an organization has a strategy for quality, innovation, or customer service, training as well as other human resources practices must be designed to reinforce and support the strategy.

FIGURE 1.2

A Strategic Model of Training and Development

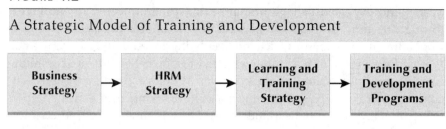

For example, if an organization decides to improve customer service or product quality, then employees will require training in order to learn how to provide better service or improve product quality. If an organization's strategy is to grow as rapidly as possible, then employees need to be trained in the management of mergers, acquisitions, joint ventures, and international ventures. All these growth components necessitate the building of new skills, and training is required to do this. For example, Quebecor World Inc. (see Training Today 1) determined that customer service was a key strategy and this led to the Allstar training program, which was a critical factor in implementing its strategy.

Thus, strategy is often a key factor driving the need for and type of training and development in organizations. By linking training to business strategy, training becomes strategic rather than an isolated and independent activity and as a result, it is more likely to be effective. In fact, there is some evidence that training can lower an organization's market value when it is not strategically focused.[44]

Figure 1.2 depicts the role that strategy plays in the training and development process. The model shows how an organization's business strategy will have implications for its HRM strategy. The HRM strategy will then influence the organization's strategy for learning and training which will determine the type of training and development activities and programs required.

Structure

The structure of an organization also affects training and development activities. Organizations are increasingly becoming flatter, with fewer levels of management. Employees are expected to perform tasks that were once considered managerial tasks and so they must be trained in traditional managerial activities such as problem solving, decision making, team work, and so on. Many organizations have experienced dramatic structural changes such as downsizing and reengineering in an effort to survive. These changes to an organization's structure often lead to changes in employees' tasks and responsibilities and necessitate the need for training.

Culture

The **culture** of an organization refers to the shared beliefs, values, and assumptions that exist in an organization. An organization's culture is important because it determines the norms that exist in an organization and

Organizational culture

The shared beliefs, values, and assumptions that exist in an organization

the expected behaviours. The culture of an organization, along with the norms and expected behaviours, are often communicated to employees through training programs. For example, the ethical practices of Molson Coors Brewing Company, which are deeply ingrained in the company's culture and are visible in the employees' day-to-day behaviour, are communicated to employees through the company's ethics training programs. The company's training programs reflect a culture of integrity and the importance of acting in an honest and trustworthy manner based on business ethics and moral conviction. Thus, its training programs are consistent with the company's core values and are a catalyst for achieving its business goals. In Chapter 4 you will learn about a learning culture and its effect on learning and training.

Human Resources Management System

The human resources management system and other human resources functions also influence training and development in organizations. In fact, in addition to being linked to business strategy, human resources practices should also be aligned and linked to each other. Thus, strategic human resources management involves two kinds of links. First, human resources practices should be linked to business strategy as discussed earlier. Second, human resources practices should be linked to each other so they work together to achieve an organization's strategy. In this regard, what is most important is not individual HRM practices and policies but rather, the entire system of HRM practices.

The objective of human resources management is to attract, motivate, develop, and retain employees whose performance is necessary for the organization to achieve its strategic objectives. The human resources management system accomplishes this through the provision of policies, guidelines, and practices such as HR planning, recruitment and selection, orientation, training and development, performance appraisal, compensation and benefits, health and safety, and employment equity. In combination, these practices form an integrated and tightly linked HRM system or what we described earlier as a high-performance work system.

Each function should be aligned with the others so they work in concert towards the organization's strategic objectives. For example, if an organization's strategy is to provide excellent customer service, then the organization will need to hire employees who have the skills required to interact with customers; they will need to train employees on how to provide excellent customer service; they will need to evaluate employees' customer service behaviour and performance; and they will need to reward employees for providing excellent customer service.

In summary, external factors influence an organization's strategy, structure, and the way human resources are managed, and these factors in turn influence the design and delivery of training and development programs. Training and development should be tightly aligned with an organization's business strategy and the human resources management system. In other words, there should be a good fit between strategy and training and development, and between training and development and other HRM practices. In this way, training and development is strategic and an important part of a high-performance work system that can improve individual performance and ultimately organizational effectiveness. Thus, the model in Figure 1.1 not only explains the context of training and development, but it also helps us to understand the link between training and development and organizational effectiveness.

The Instructional Systems Design (ISD) Model of Training and Development

In this section, we describe an approach to training and development that sets the stage for the remainder of the text. In particular, we describe a systems approach to training and development that is known as the instructional systems design (ISD) model. The **instructional systems design model** of training and development depicts training as a rational and scientific process that consists of three major steps: training needs analysis, training design and delivery, and training evaluation. The process consists of an analysis of current performance and ends with improved performance.[45]

The process begins with a performance gap or an *itch*. An *itch* is something in the organization that is not quite right or is of concern to someone. Perhaps customer complaints are too high, quality is low, market share is being lost, or employees are frustrated by management or technology. Or perhaps there is a performance problem that is making it difficult for employees or departments to achieve goals or meet standards. If some part of the organization itches, or is not satisfied with the performance of individual employees or departments, then the problem needs to be analyzed.

A critical first step in the instructional systems design model is a needs analysis to determine the nature of the problem and if training is the best solution. A needs analysis is performed to determine the difference or gap between the way things are and the way things should be.

Needs analysis consists of three levels known as an organizational analysis, a task analysis, and a person analysis. Each level of needs analysis is conducted to gather important information about problems and the need for training. An organizational analysis gathers information on where training is needed in an organization; a task analysis indicates what training is required; and a person analysis identifies who in the organization needs to be trained.

Based on the data collected from managers, employees, customers, and/or corporate documents, strategies for closing the gap are considered. Before training is determined to be the best solution to the problem, alternatives must be assessed. The solution to the performance gap might be feedback, incentives, or other human resource interventions. If training is determined to be the best solution, then objectives—or measurable goals—are written to improve the situation and reduce the gap. The needs analysis, the consideration of alternative strategies, and the setting of objectives force trainers to focus on performance improvement, not the delivery of a training program. Training is only one solution—and not necessarily the best one—to performance problems.

Instructional systems design model

A rational and scientific model of the training and development process that consists of a needs analysis, training design and delivery, and training evaluation

If training is the solution to a performance problem, a number of factors must be considered in the design and delivery of a training program. The needs analysis information and training objectives are used to determine the content of a training program. Then the best training methods for achieving the objectives and for learning the training content must be identified. Other design factors, which are described in Chapter 5, must also be considered in the design and delivery of a training program in order to maximize trainees' learning.

After a training program has been designed and delivered, the next stage is training evaluation. The needs analysis and training objectives provide important information regarding what should be evaluated in order to determine if a training program has been effective. Some of the critical evaluation questions include: Did the training program achieve its objectives? What did employees learn? Did employees' job performance improve? Is the organization more effective? Was it worth the cost?

The purpose of all training and development efforts is ultimately to improve employee performance and organizational effectiveness. Thus, it is important to know if employee job performance has changed and if the organization has improved following a training program. In this stage, the trainer has to decide what to measure as part of the evaluation of a training program as well as how to design an evaluation study. On the basis of a training evaluation, decisions can be made about what aspects of a training program should be retained, modified, or discarded.

Figure 1.3 presents a simplified version of the instructional systems design model of training and development. As we have described, each stage leads into the subsequent stage with needs analysis being the first critical step that sets the stage for the design-and-delivery and evaluation stages. Also notice that there are feedback loops from evaluation to needs analysis and training design and delivery. This indicates that the process is a closed-loop system in which evaluation feeds back into needs analysis

FIGURE 1.3

The Instructional Systems Design Model of Training and Development

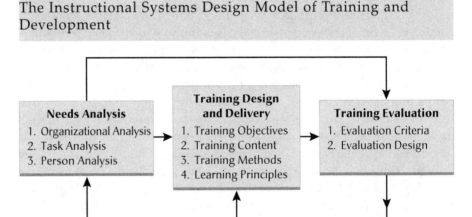

and training design and delivery. In this way, it is possible to know if performance gaps identified in the needs analysis stage have been closed, and if changes are required in the design and delivery of a training program in order to make the training program more effective. Thus, training programs are continuously modified and improved on the basis of training evaluation.

Although the ISD model is considered to be the best approach for managing the training and development process, in reality many organizations do not follow all of the steps of the ISD model. In other words, many organizations do not conduct a needs analysis, they implement training programs that are not well designed, and they do not evaluate their training programs. There has also been some criticism waged against the ISD model in recent years among professionals in the training industry who have seriously challenged its usefulness. However, if used correctly it remains the best approach for managing the training and development process.[46] Training programs often fail because they have ignored an important step in the process such as conducting a thorough needs analysis.

We will have more to say about each of the stages of the training and development process as they are covered in the remainder of the text. For now, you should understand the ISD model and the sequence of activities that are involved in the training and development process. To learn more about how to apply the ISD model, see The Trainer's Notebook 2.

The Trainer's Notebook 2

The Application of the ISD Model

The instructional systems design model begins when somebody identifies a performance gap in the organization. According to the ISD model, the recognition of a performance gap should lead to the following sequence of activities:

1. Conduct an organizational analysis to investigate the performance gap and determine if training is a possible solution (when the cause of the problem is a lack of knowledge or skills).

2. If training is a possible solution, conduct a task analysis in order to determine how the job or jobs in question should be performed and the things that a skilled employee must know and be able to do.

3. Conduct a person analysis to determine how employees currently perform the job compared to how they should perform and how best to train them (e.g., training methods).

4. Design a training program using those methods and approaches that will be most effective to train employees who require training. Include specialists in various media and methods to assist in developing training material.

5. Develop and fine-tune the program. Pilot test it and revise as needed.

6. Deliver the program to its intended audience.

7. Monitor and evaluate the program and its results on an ongoing basis. The program is considered a success if the original performance gap is closed or reduced and if correcting the problem costs less than the cost of not correcting it.

Sources: Gordon, J., & Zemke, R. (2000, April). The attack on ISD. *Training*, 42–53; Zemke, R., & Rossett, A. (2002, February). A hard look at ISD. *Training*, 26–34.

Summary

This chapter has introduced you to the training and development process and emphasized the important role that training and development plays in the effectiveness and competitiveness of organizations. We also stressed the importance of viewing training and development as an investment in human capital, an investment that Canadian organizations must increase. The organizational, individual, and societal benefits of training were described as well as the status of training and development in Canada. We also described training and development as part of a high-performance work system that is embedded within the environmental and organizational context. In particular, we noted that in order for training to be most effective, it should be strategic. That is, it should be tied to an organization's business strategy and aligned with other HRM practices. Finally, we described the instructional systems design model of training and development that sets the stage for the remainder of the text.

Key Terms

development (page 6)

high-performance work system (HPWS) (page 13)

instructional systems design model (page 19)

organizational culture (page 17)

performance management (page 5)

strategic human resources management (SHRM) (page 16)

training (page 6)

Weblinks

Delta Hotels and Resorts: www.deltahotels.com (page 8)

Labatt Breweries of Canada.: www.labatt.com (page 11)

Scotiabank: www.scotiabank.com (page 11)

Quebecor World Inc.: www.quebecorworld.com (page 7)

Discussion Questions

1. According to The Conference Board of Canada, the investments made by Canadian organizations in training and development have remained relatively constant over the last decade and appear to have reached a plateau in terms of the amount organizations are willing to invest in training and development. Comment on the implications of this for organizations, employees, and the Canadian economy. Should governments get involved and enact laws that require organizations to invest a certain percentage of their payroll in training and development as they have in Quebec?

2. Studies comparing the competitive performance of Canadian corporations indicate that among the countries in the G8 (Canada, United States, Japan, Germany, France, Italy, Russia, and the United Kingdom), Canada

ranks very low. Do you think that training and development in Canada has anything to do with this and if so, what should Canada and Canadian businesses do?

3. Discuss some of the reasons why organizations often fail to fully implement the instructional systems design model of training and development. Why do you think the ISD model has come under attack in recent years and been seriously challenged and criticized?

4. Refer to the Training Today 1 feature on Quebecor World Inc. and discuss the extent to which the instructional systems design model was used for the development of the company's Allstar customer service training program. In other words, describe the training program in terms of each stage of the ISD model.

The Great Training Debate

1. Debate the following: Training and development is the single most important factor for the competitiveness and success of an organization.

2. Debate the following: All provinces should enact training tax legislation similar to the law in Quebec.

Using the Internet

1. There are a number of training associations that provide useful information about training and development. To learn more about some of these associations, visit the following websites:

   www.cstd.ca (Canadian Society for Training and Development)
   www.astd.org (American Society for Training & Development)

   Write a brief report in which you describe the association and indicate what information can be obtained from the site about training and development.

2. Go to **www.cstd.ca/resources/tca.html** (Canadian Society for Training and Development) to find out about the Training Competency Architecture (TCA). What is the TCA and what are the five competency categories defined by the TCA?

3. To learn more about the benefits of training for Canadian organizations, go to Industry Canada at **http://strategis.ic.gc.ca/epic/internet/ incts-scf.nsf/en/h_sl00003e.html**

   Answer the following questions:

   1. Why is training important?
   2. How is the workforce changing?
   3. What are companies doing to train employees?

4. To learn about training and skills development in Canada, go to Industry Canada at **http://strategis.ic.gc.ca/epic/internet/incts-scf.nsf/ en/sl00022e.html**

Why is skills development important in Canada and what are the implications for organizations? What should organizations be doing and what are the implications for training and development? What are some initiatives to assist employee skill development?

Exercises

In-Class

1. Review the training and development facts in Table 1.1. Benchmark your experiences in a current or previous organization against the statistics in the table. Based on the statistics in the table, you might consider things such as: How does your organization compare to the Canadian averages in areas such as the amount of training hours employees receive a year and the amount spent per employee on training? Does your organization fare better or worse than the average Canadian organization? What do the results tell you about your organization? What are the implications of your findings for your learning and job performance and for your organization?

2. Consider how training and development is influenced by, and in turn can influence, other HRM functions. In particular, give an example of how training and development can influence and is influenced by activities within each of the following HRM areas: Recruitment and Selection; HR Planning; Performance Appraisals; Compensation; and Health and Safety.

3. Using the ISD model of training and development, dissect the class your instructor has delivered to you today. In other words, what did your instructor have to do in terms of a needs analysis? How did he or she design and deliver the class? And how should the class be evaluated?

4. Assume that you are a director of training and development in a small organization. In order to reduce expenses, the company president has decided to cut the training budget in half and reduce the amount of training provided to employees. The president has asked to meet with you to discuss these plans. Your job is to prepare a short presentation to try to persuade the president to change his or her mind. What will you say and what can you do to convince the president of the importance and need for more, not less, training?

5. Recall the last time you attended an organization-sponsored training program. Describe the objectives and content of the training program and whether or not you think the program was strategic. In other words, was it an example of strategic training? Be specific in terms of why you think it was or was not a good example of strategic training. What would have made it more strategic?

6. Recall the last time you attended an organization-sponsored training program. Describe the objectives and content of the training program and whether or not you think the instructional systems design model was

used to develop the program. Be specific in terms of each stage of the model and the extent to which it was used in the development of the program. How effective was the training program in terms of your learning and in achieving the program's objectives? Based on your analysis, what could have been done to more fully make use of the ISD model and what effect might this have had on the effectiveness of the program?

In-the-Field

1. Contact the human resource department of your own or another organization in order to discuss the organization's training programs. In particular, try to learn about the extent to which the HR staff use the ISD model of training and development. Find out about each stage of the model and the extent to which it is adhered to in the development of training programs. What aspects of the model are adequately carried out and which ones are not? If some of the stages are not adequately conducted, find out why this is the case and why the HR department does or does not rigorously adhere to the ISD model. Based on the responses, what advice would you give the HR department?

Case Incident

Canadian American Transportation Systems

The Canadian American Transportation Systems began running a new high-speed ferry between Toronto and New York State in 2004. The marine industry is highly regulated and most of the workers have no experience so a great deal of training was needed to meet the rigorous standards set by the U.S. Coast Guard and Transport Canada. There are two mandatory levels of training. One is called SOLAS (safety of life at sea) which involves a very basic familiarization of the vessel, basic life saving procedures, and medical emergencies. There is also a more advanced program of survival training called STCW (seafarers' training certification and watch keeping). Employees were taken to Olympic-sized pools where they had to jump in the water, get people safety rafts, and learn how to use all of the stuff in cold water conditions. Good customer service is also important so employees need to understand the customer experience.

Questions

1. To what extent has the instructional system design (ISD) model of training and development been used? Discuss how the ISD model is relevant for the training of the new staff and how it can be applied.
2. Discuss the benefits of the training described in the case for the organization, employees, and the public.

Source: Garcia, C. (2004, May 17). CloseUp: Training and Development. *Canadian HR Reporter,* 17 (10), 7–10.

Case

Flotation Ltd.

"Great course, Sam!" said the trainees as they walked out the door and headed for the parking lot. Just like the others. Sam Harris, a veteran trainer with Flotation Ltd., a manufacturer of life jackets and other flotation devices, smiled as he gathered his notes together.

He had just finished two hours of wisecracking and slightly off-colour storytelling as he worked his way through the third session of a human relations course for supervisors. "Keep 'em happy" was Sam's motto. Give the troops what they want, keep your enrolments up, and no one will complain.

Sam was good at it, too! For 20 years, he had earned an easy living, working the politics, producing good numbers (of trainees) for the top brass to brag about ("We give each employee up to 26 hours of training every year!"), and generally promoting his small training group as a beehive of activity.

Everybody knew Sam and everybody liked him. His courses were such fun. He had no trouble convincing managers to send their people. He put out a little catalogue with his course list every year in January. He hadn't had a cancellation in more than 10 years. Some managers said that training was the best reward they had. Now, only three years from retirement, Sam intended to coast comfortably into pension-land. All his favourite courses had long been prepared; all he had to do was to make adjustments here and there and create some trendy titles.

But times were changing. The company president was thinking differently. "I need somebody to take a close look at our training function," he said. Sitting in the president's office, Jenny Stoppard, the newly hired vice president of human resources, wondered what he meant. Flotation Ltd. had a reputation as a company with a well-trained workforce.

"We need to increase our productivity per person by 50 percent over the next three years," the president continued. "And you are going to spearhead that effort. Yes, we spend a lot on training. Yes, we cycle people through a lot of courses. But I'm not satisfied with the bottom line. I know that while Dad was president he swore by old Sam—said he was the greatest. I don't know anymore. Maybe a whole new approach is needed. Anyway, I want you to take a close look at Sam's operation."

Later in the day, the president called Sam into his office. "Sam, I want you to meet Jenny Stoppard. I've just hired her as vice president of human resources. She's your new boss. I think the next three years are going to be very exciting around here, and Jenny is going to be a key player in the drive to increase our competitiveness. I want you to do everything in your power to cooperate with her."

Questions

1. Comment on Sam's approach to training. Would you want him working for your company? Why, or why not?

2. To what extent has Sam made use of the instructional systems design (ISD) model of training and development? If he were to more fully use the ISD model, what would he have to do? Comment on each of the steps of the ISD model.
3. How does Sam currently evaluate his training programs? Compare Sam's measures of training effectiveness to the president's objectives. If Sam were to evaluate his training programs based on the president's objectives, what would he have to do?
4. The president has asked Jenny to "take a close look at Sam's operation." What should she do and what should she report back to the president?

References

1. Greengard, S. (2005, March). Golden values. *Workforce Management*. 84 (3), p. 52–53. www.molson.com/newsroom/release. Molson and Coors Complete Merger to Form Molson Coors Brewing Company, February 9, 2005. Retrieved July 14, 2005. www.accounting.smartpros.com/x47331.xml. Coors Ethics Program Among Best in Nation. March 9, 2005. SmartPros Editorial Staff. Retrieved July 14, 2005.
2. Norris, A. (2001, September 1). Transat work faulted. *The Gazette*, A1. Koring, P. (2001, August 31). Transat faces safety crackdown. *The Globe and Mail*, A1. Koring, P. (2002, August 30). Jet crew's handling of fuel leak questioned. *The Globe and Mail*, A1. Brazao, D. (2001, August 29). We had no second chance, pilot in jet emergency says. *The Toronto Star*, A1. Taylor, A., & Verma, S. (2002, August 31). Air Transat told to improve training on fuel handling. *The Toronto Star*, A1.
3. Koring, P. (2004, October 18). Transat report blames pilots; EXCLUSIVE: Emergency landing in Azores could have been avoided if crew followed fuel-management procedures, report says. *The Globe and Mail*, A1. Cernetig, M. (2004, October 19). Pilot's heroic flying tarnished in report; Mishandled fuel leak, probe finds Transat jet glided to safety in Azores. *The Toronto Star*, A7.
4. Koring, P. (2004, October 18); Cernetig, M. (2004, October 19). Koring, P. (2005, March 2). Air Transat agrees to settle lawsuit. *The Globe and Mail*, A6.
5. Auld, A. (2002, August 6). Air traffic controller neglect cited in near-misses. *The Toronto Star*, A6.
6. Campion-Smith, B. (1996, January 24). Rookie driver sorry for crash. *The Toronto Star*, A1, A22. Hall, J. (2005, August 6). Ten years after. *The Toronto Star*, B1, B4–B5.
7. Tandt, M. D. (2005, November 23). Poor training for RCMP imperils safety, auditor says. *The Globe and Mail*, A1, A7.
8. Parker, R. O., & Cooney, J. (2005). Learning & Development Outlook 2005. *The Conference Board of Canada*. Ottawa.
9. Gordon, A. (2000, February). 35 best companies to work for. *Report on Business Magazine*, 24–33.
10. Gosselin, A., Werner, J., & Hall, N. (1997). Ratee preferences concerning performance management and appraisal. *Human Resource Development Quarterly, 8* (4), 315–33.
11. Barbian, J. (2002, March). Training top 100: Space Systems/Loral. *Training, 39* (3), p. 66.
12. Millan, L. (1997, September 26). King of the corner store. *Canadian Business*, pp. 101–104.
13. Bowsher, J. (1990, May). Making the call on the CEO. *Training and Development Journal*, 65–66.
14. Adams, M. (1999). Training employees as partners. *HR Magazine, 44* (2), pp. 64–70.
15. Bernstein, A., & Magnusson, P. (1993, February 22). How much good will training do? *Business Week*, p. 76–77.
16. Betcherman, G., Leckie, N., & McMullen, K. (1997). *Developing skills in the Canadian workplace*. Ottawa: Canadian Policy Research Networks.

17. Tharenou, P. (2000). *Does training improve organizational effectiveness?* Paper presented at the Academy of Management Meetings, Toronto, Canada.

18. Schaaf, D. (1998). What workers really think about training. *Training, 35* (9), 59–66.

19. Roseman, E. (2001, August 29). Delta Hotels knows how to keep workers. *The Toronto Star*, E2.

20. Garavan, T. N., Costine, P., & Heraty, N. (1995). *Training and development in Ireland: Context policy and practice.* Dublin: Oak Tree Press.

21. Schaaf, D. (1998).

22. Bernstein, A., & Magnusson, P. (1993).

23. Crane, D. (2002, October 27). Innovation means productivity gains. *The Toronto Star*, C2.

24. Bernstein, A., & Magnusson, P. (1993).

25. Parker, R. O., & Cooney, J. (2005).

26. Harris-Lalonde, S. (2001). Training and development outlook. *The Conference Board of Canada.* Ottawa.

27. Parker, R. O., & Cooney, J. (2005).

28. Dolezalek, H. (2004, October). Training magazine's 23rd annual comprehensive analysis of employer-sponsored training in the United States. *Training, 41* (10). 20–36.

29. Parker, R. O., & Cooney, J. (2005).

30. Parker, R. O., & Cooney, J. (2005).

31. Parker, R. O., & Cooney, J. (2005).

32. Parker, R. O., & Cooney, J. (2005).

33. Parker, R. O., & Cooney, J. (2005).

34. Galt, V. (2002, June 5). Putting the human back into resources. *The Globe and Mail*, C1.

35. Galt, V. (2001, July 9). Training falls short: Study. *The Globe and Mail*, M1.

36. Galt, V. (2002, November 20). Training on tap. *The Globe and Mail*, C1.

37. Harding, K. (2003, June 4). A taxing way to train staff. *The Globe and Mail*, C1, C6. Haccoun, R. R. & Saks, A. M. (2002). Legislating company investments in training: Does it make a difference? Paper presented at the annual conference of the Society for Industrial and Organizational Psychology, Toronto.

38. Becker, B. E., & Huselid, M. A. (1998). High performance work systems and firm performance: A synthesis of research and managerial implications. *Research in Personnel and Human Resources Management*, 16: 53–101.

39. (2002, April). Airport Training Ready to Take Off. *Training and Development*, pp. 17–18.

40. (2002, February). ASTD survey results: The effect of terrorism on training. *Training and Development*, p. 28.

41. Crane, D. (1998, March 28). Time to take worker training seriously. *The Toronto Star*, B2.

42. McCarthy, S. (2001, February 27). Skilled-worker shortage could reach one million. *The Globe and Mail*, A1.

43. Becker, B. E., & Huselid, M. A. (1998).

44. Gibb-Clark, M. (2000, February 11). Employee training can backfire on firms: Survey. *The Globe and Mail*, B10.

45. Dipboye, R. L. (1997). Organizational barriers to implementing a rational model of training. In M. A. Quinones and A. Ehrenstein (Eds.), *Training for a Rapidly Changing Workplace*, Washington, DC: American Psychological Association.

46. Gordon, J., & Zemke, R. (2000, April). The attack on ISD. *Training, 37* (4), 42–53; Zemke, R., & Rossett, A. (2002, February). A hard look at ISD. *Training, 39* (2), 26–34.

Chapter 2

Organizational Learning

Chapter Learning Objectives

After reading this chapter, you should be able to:

- define organizational learning and describe a learning organization
- explain the five disciplines and the principles of a learning organization
- discuss the four key dimensions that are critical for creating and sustaining a learning organization
- explain what knowledge is and give examples of explicit and tacit knowledge
- describe the meaning and types of intellectual capital
- define knowledge management and discuss four knowledge management practices
- define informal learning and describe what organizations can do to facilitate it
- describe the multilevel systems model of organizational learning
- explain how organizational learning and training and development are related

www.dofasco.ca

DOFASCO

Dofasco is Canada's most successful steel producer and the most profitable steelmaker, per tonne in North America. Dofasco produces high-quality flat rolled and tubular steels and laser welded blanks in facilities in Canada, the United States, and Mexico. Dofasco's many steel products are sold to customers throughout North America and in many industries including the automotive, construction, energy, manufacturing, pipe and tube, appliance, packaging, and steel distribution industries.

Dofasco is known for its highly motivated and skilled workforce and its commitment to product quality and customer service. Dofasco is also a good example of a learning organization. In fact, at Dofasco, it is said, "You are going to learn a living as much as you earn a living." Top management at Dofasco is committed to Dofasco becoming a learning organization and demonstrates their commitment by providing support and resources.

The learning begins as soon as new hires join the organization. New hires attend a four-day orientation program in which they learn about Dofasco's culture, strategy, values, and competencies. This, however, is just the beginning. All employees at Dofasco have a learning and development plan. Employees are empowered to take responsibility for their own learning and managers are encouraged to facilitate employees' learning.

Employees have many opportunities to learn at Dofasco including job skills training at their technical training centre, informal trainers located throughout the plant, and apprenticeship programs conducted in partnership with local community colleges. As well, informal trainers are available to assist employees who are learning on the job.

Dofasco also has a formal mentorship program for new hires and apprentices who are hired right out of college or university. The new hires are assigned a mentor to consult with and ask questions.

Another successful program at Dofasco is the Essential Skills program, which includes training in literacy, numeracy, and basic computer skills. The program has been so successful that it is considered a benchmark for other organizations.

Employees at Dofasco also have the opportunity to continue their formal education. The company reimburses employees for programs completed at high school, college, or university. Lifestyle programs that address employees' needs such as stress management are also available as well as lunch-time programs in yoga, tai chi, and aerobics. Two gymnasiums are also available to employees 24 hours a day.

Because Dofasco is a team-based organization in which various kinds of teams play a central role, team learning is also important. Before the company became a team-based organization, a team of employees from different levels in the organization studied teams in other organizations in order to find out how teams would work best at Dofasco. And to encourage team learning, everyone at Dofasco was required to attend a four-day team-building training program.

The importance of learning at Dofasco also extends to the company's customers. The company has developed learning alliances with their customers through a program called "Solutions in Steel." One example of such a program involved a team of Dofasco employees showing an automobile manufacturer how to build a car with fewer welds and save a significant amount of money.

Learning at Dofasco also extends beyond one's job, to understanding the organization and how one's job fits into the big picture. A tool called the "organizational system framework" is used to help employees understand the whole organization and how the various elements and systems are interrelated and fit together. Learning maps are also used to help employees better understand how the organization makes money.

At Dofasco, learning is seen as an investment in employees and the organization's future. The company spends more than $15 million a year to develop and enhance employee skills. Dofasco has been ranked among the Top 100 Employers and one of the 50 Best Companies to Work for in Canada.[1]

Dofasco is a good example of a "learning organization." Although this book is about training and development, training and development is just one of many ways that employees learn. Furthermore, the extent to which employees learn has a lot to do with the learning systems and infrastructure that exist in an organization. In organizations like Dofasco, learning is considered an important investment and receives a great deal of commitment and support from top management. As a result, employees have access to many opportunities for formal and informal learning.

In this chapter, we describe how organizations learn and how learning occurs at all levels of an organization. Training and development is an important part of the learning system in organizations so you should understand how it fits into the larger picture of organizational learning.

What Is Organizational Learning?

A smart organization knows how to create new knowledge and disseminate it throughout the organization. In other words, it knows how to learn. **Organizational learning** refers to the process of creating, sharing, diffusing,

Organizational learning

The process of creating, sharing, diffusing, and applying knowledge in organizations

and applying knowledge. However, organizational learning is not simply the sum of individual employee learning nor is performance management limited to a training system that enables employees to learn and apply that learning. Organizational learning focuses on the systems used to create and distribute new knowledge on an organization-wide basis of which training and development is one component. Simply put, organizational learning is a dynamic process of creating and sharing knowledge.

The traditional perspective of learning has always been strongly associated with training and development. The goals of training have been viewed from a traditional perspective that focuses on developing and improving employees' knowledge, skills, and abilities (KSAs). This is, of course, key for organizational learning because an organization can't learn unless individual employees learn. As noted by Peter Senge, the originator of the concept of the learning organization, "Organizations learn only through individuals who learn. Individual learning does not guarantee organizational learning. But without it, no organizational learning occurs" (p. 139).[2]

The training of employees usually focuses on current needs or deficiencies and is most effective when the future is relatively stable and predictable. However, in today's highly turbulent environment, organizations have realized the need to do more than just train employees for the current state of affairs. In a learning organization, employees learn through a variety of methods and processes, and they also learn how to continuously learn.

To survive and develop, organizations must learn to manage by managing learning—the capacity to learn and change, consciously, continually, and quickly. A company's knowledge, including that contained in its employees' minds, has always been a source of competitive advantage. The ability to learn faster than the competition is a source of sustainable competitive advantage.

For many organizations, creating learning systems and processes requires that they transform themselves into learning organizations. As you will learn in the next section, becoming a learning organization does not represent the latest management fad. It represents a strategic shift and orientation in how organizations learn that can make an organization more competitive and effective.

The Learning Organization

In 1990, Peter Senge published a book called *The Fifth Discipline: The Art and Practice of the Learning Organization*, which set in motion a whole new approach to organizations that focuses on learning and in particular, the "learning organization."

A **learning organization** is an organization that creates, acquires, organizes, shares, and retains information and knowledge, and uses new information and knowledge to change and modify its behaviour in order to achieve its objectives and improve its effectiveness. Learning organizations have established systems and structures to acquire, code, store, and distribute important information and knowledge so that it is available to those who need it when they need it.

Learning organization

An organization that creates, acquires, organizes, shares, and retains information and knowledge, and uses new information and knowledge to change and modify its behaviour in order to achieve its objectives and improve its effectiveness

As a result, a learning organization is able to transform itself by acquiring and disseminating new knowledge and skills throughout the organization. Thus, it has an enhanced capacity to learn, adapt, and change its culture.[3]

Embedded in this concept is the ability to make sense of and respond to the surrounding environment. Organizational values, policies, systems, and structures support and accelerate learning for all employees. This learning results in continual improvements in work systems, products, services, teamwork, and management practices—a more successful organization. Organizational learning is learning that actually results in improvements.

In his groundbreaking book, Senge identified five "disciplines" that he regarded as guiding principles to becoming a learning organization. The five disciplines are:[4]

1. *Personal mastery.* Individuals have to be open to others and willing to learn on a continual basis. People with personal mastery are always in a learning mode. This is fundamental for a learning organization because organizations only learn if the individuals in them learn. If individuals do not learn, then organizational learning will not be possible.

2. *Building a shared vision.* This involves the development of a picture and vision of the future to which everyone can agree and be committed.

3. *Mental models.* Mental models refer to the images and assumptions that people have about themselves and the world. People need to be able to examine their mental models and be aware of how they influence their behaviour. Because such models can thwart or inhibit learning, people must understand them and hold them up to scrutiny.

4. *Team learning.* Learning takes place in teams through dialogue, discussion, and "thinking together." People need to be able to learn and act together.

5. *Systems thinking.* This discipline integrates the others and has to do with viewing the organization as a whole and being able to see and understand how its parts are interrelated.

Principles of a Learning Organization

Learning organizations have a number of important principles. First, in a learning organization everybody is considered to be a learner. Employees recognize the need for learning and are actively involved in both formal and informal learning programs.

Second, in a learning organization, employees do not learn just by attending formal training programs. They also learn through informal means such as listening and observing others. People learn from each other in a learning organization.

Third, learning is part of a change process and in fact enables change. When people are open to learning, they are able to recognize the need for change and learning is an important part of any change program. Thus, learning and change are closely related.

Fourth, continuous learning is considered to be a hallmark of learning organizations. Formal and informal learning are considered to be a regular part of every employee's job.

Fifth, learning organizations recognize that learning is an investment in the future of employees and the organization rather than an expense. Just as expenditures on plants and equipment are viewed as long-term capital investments, expenditures on learning are viewed as long-term investments in human capital.[5] Returning to the chapter-opening vignette, you will notice that all of these principles are characteristic of Dofasco.

While some people might find the notion of a learning organization somewhat of a fad, there is some evidence that learning organizations are highly effective. Research conducted by The Conference Board of Canada found that learning organizations are almost 50 percent more likely to have higher overall levels of profitability than organizations not rated as learning organizations.[6] High-learning organizations were also found to outperform other organizations in terms of employee retention, employee satisfaction, production of quality products and services, and overall organizational performance.[7] Research has also found a positive relationship between learning organization practices and a firm's financial performance.[8] To find out more about the linkages between learning organization practices and firm performance, see Training Today, "Organizational Learning and Firm Performance."

In the next section, we consider learning organizations in Canada.

Learning Organizations in Canada

As described in the chapter-opening vignette, Dofasco is a good example of a Canadian company that can be described as a learning organization. But to what extent are other organizations in Canada learning organizations? The Conference Board of Canada recently examined this as part of a survey on learning and development in Canadian organizations. They asked Canadian organizations to rate the extent to which they see themselves as learning organizations. What do you think they found? Are most Canadian organizations learning organizations?

As it turns out, not very many organizations in Canada see themselves as learning organizations. In fact, the average respondent rated their organization as "somewhat" of a learning organization (49 percent), only 21 percent rated themselves to a large extent as a learning organization, and 2 percent rated themselves as fully a learning organization. Close to 30 percent of the respondents categorized themselves as little or not at all when it comes to being a learning organization. Furthermore, only 34 percent of respondents indicated that learning is a top priority in their organization and a majority (63 percent) said that it is only "somewhat" of a priority.[9]

The Conference Board also identified the following key dimensions or pillars of a learning organization: 1. Vision, 2. Culture, 3. Learning dynamics or systems, and 4. Knowledge management and infrastructure. Table 2.1 provides a description of each dimension.

Organizational Learning and Firm Performance

Although it is widely believed that organizations that have systems and processes consistent with a learning organization will be better performers, few studies have actually tested the relationship between organizational learning and firm performance. An exception is a study by Andrea Ellinger, Alexander Ellinger, Baiyin Yang, and Shelly Howton.

Managers from 208 U.S. manufacturing firms completed a survey that measured their perceptions of their organization along the following six learning organization dimensions:

1. Create continuous learning opportunities.
2. Promote inquiry and dialogue.
3. Encourage collaboration and team learning.
4. Empower people toward a collective vision.
5. Connect the organization to its environment.
6. Use leaders who model and support learning at the individual, team, and organizational levels.

The managers also completed two perceptual outcome measures in which they indicated their organization's current performance compared to the previous year in terms of financial performance and knowledge performance. In addition, objective accounting and return on investment ratios were also used to measure each firm's financial performance including ROE (the return on share-holder investment), ROA (the return available to shareholders from the investment of all the firm's capital), Tobin's q (the value added by management above the value of the firm's assets), and MVA (the difference between the money invested in the firm and the present value of the cash flows expected to be generated by this capital).

The results indicated that there was a significant relationship between the six dimensions of the learning organization and the two perceptual outcomes (financial performance and knowledge performance). The six dimensions of a learning organization were also significantly related to the four objective measures of financial performance.

These results suggest that there is a positive association between a learning organization and an organization's financial performance. Thus, creating a learning organization has important implications for an organization's profitability and financial success. These findings provide a strong business case for the development of learning organizations.

Source: Ellinger, A. D., Ellinger, A. E., Baiyin, Y., & Howton, S. W. (2002). The relationship between the learning organization concept and firms' financial performance: An empirical assessment. *Human Resource Development Quarterly, 13*, 5–21.

According to the Conference Board of Canada, Canadian organizations need to improve on a number of the key dimensions. For example, it was recommended that senior management be more explicit in terms of the type of knowledge that is important in their organization, and that they serve as learning role models to the rest of the organization (vision). Canadian organizations can also improve by creating a more positive learning culture and by encouraging and rewarding experimentation, risk taking, and challenging the status quo. As well, innovation, knowledge sharing, and productivity improvements should be a more frequent part of organizational life. In the area of learning, Canadian organizations can also improve by providing employees with more opportunities for formal and informal learning, and by supporting and developing managers in their roles as coaches, mentors, and facilitators of learning (learning dynamics and systems). Providing employees with opportunities to improve their learning skills is also needed. They

TABLE 2.1

Key Dimensions of Learning Organizations

The Conference Board of Canada has identified the following four dimensions or pillars as critical in creating and sustaining a learning organization.

1. *Vision.* A clear vision of the organization's strategy and goals in which learning is a critical part and key to organizational success.

2. *Culture.* A learning organization has a culture that supports learning. Knowledge, information sharing, and continuous learning are considered to be a regular part of organizational life and the responsibility of everybody in the organization.

3. *Learning dynamics and systems.* Employees are challenged to think and act according to a systems approach by considering patterns of interdependencies when problem solving.

4. *Knowledge management and infrastructure.* Learning organizations have established systems and structures to acquire, code, store, and distribute important information and knowledge so that it is available to those who need it and when they need it.

Source: Parker, R. O., & Cooney, J. (2005). Learning and development outlook 2005. *The Conference Board of Canada*, Ottawa. Reprinted by permission of The Conference Board of Canada.

should be encouraged to participate in learning activities such as communities of practice, mentoring programs, job rotations, and cross training. Finally, Canadian organizations have to develop knowledge management systems and practices so that important information and knowledge that is essential to organizational success can be stored and made available to those who need it whenever it is needed.[10]

Developing a learning organization is a time-consuming and resource-intensive change process. Thus, it represents a significant transformation for most organizations. Given that the very idea of a learning organization is a relatively recent phenomenon, it should not be surprising that only a small percentage of Canadian organizations are fully learning organizations. What is most important is that organizations understand the value and importance of becoming a learning organization, and that by focusing on the four critical dimensions they can make changes that ultimately lead to the development of a learning organization.

Becoming a learning organization involves understanding the importance of knowledge and knowing how to manage it. In the following sections, we focus on knowledge management and intellectual capital.

The Meaning and Types of Knowledge

Knowledge has become a critical resource for organizations in the information economy and is the main resource used to perform work in organizations. Employees require new knowledge in order to improve the products and services that their organizations provide, and organizations require knowledge in order to change and remain competitive in today's increasingly competitive and turbulent environment.[11]

Employee knowledge is a synthesis of information: all the facts, theories, and mental representations employees know about the world and, in the context of work, about their jobs and organization. **Knowledge** is the sum of what is known: a body of truths, information, and principles. Knowledge can be found in the minds of employees or transferred and stored in systems in the organization.

Knowledge is more than information, which we have in abundance, represented by dusty books filling shelves and facts floating across the Internet. Knowledge, on the other hand, is information that has been edited, put into context, and analyzed in a way that makes it meaningful, and therefore valuable to an organization.[12]

Knowledge can be grouped in two ways: explicit knowledge and tacit knowledge.

Explicit knowledge refers to those things that you can buy or trade, such as patents or copyrights and other forms of intellectual property. The formula for making Coca-Cola and the brand name Coke are examples of intellectual properties that are extremely valuable. These tangible assets can normally be codified or formalized. Explicit knowledge can be written into procedures or coded into databases and is transferred fairly accurately. However, less than 20 percent of corporate knowledge is explicit.[13]

The other 80 percent of corporate knowledge is implicit and is difficult to quantify or even describe accurately.[14] Implicit or **tacit knowledge** refers to the knowledge learned from experience and insight, and has been defined as intuition, know-how, little tricks, and judgment. Seasoned executives with tacit knowledge of a situation make million-dollar decisions.

Tacit knowledge is used by employees but is almost impossible to transfer. To grasp the concept of explicit knowledge and tacit knowledge, imagine describing the physical characteristics of your best friend; now try to describe the methods your friend would use to influence a supervisor. The former involves explicit knowledge while the latter involves your tacit knowledge of your friend.

A well-known example of tacit knowledge is that of the decision-making behaviour of dealers in financial markets. That behaviour appears to be instinctual, but it is based on their past experience, what they read and hear, and the climate of the market. Extracting this knowledge from these dealers and then training others in this winning behaviour is extremely difficult.[15] The transfer of tacit knowledge requires personal contact. The personal contact must be extensive and built on trust and can include partnerships, apprenticeships, and mentoring.

The Meaning and Types of Intellectual Capital

Intellectual capital is more than knowledge; intellectual capital is more like intelligence. Intelligence is the ability to create knowledge and includes the ability to learn, to reason, to imagine, to find new insights, to generate alternatives, and to make wise decisions.[16] By increasing the general level of intelligence of employees, organizations hope to create new knowledge that will result in new products, services, and processes.

Knowledge

The sum of what is known; a body of truths, information, and principles

Explicit knowledge

Those things that you can buy or trade, such as patents or copyrights and other forms of intellectual property

Tacit knowledge

Knowledge that is learned from experience and insight, and has been defined as intuition, know-how, little tricks, and judgment

Intellectual capital

An organization's knowledge, experience, relationships, process discoveries, innovations, market presence, and community influence

Human capital

The knowledge, skills, and abilities of employees

Renewal capital

Intellectual property, which consists of patents, licences, copyrights, and marketable innovations including products, services, and technologies

Structural capital

Formal systems and informal relationships that allow employees to communicate, solve problems, and make decisions

Intellectual capital refers to an organization's knowledge, experience, relationships, process discoveries, innovations, market presence, and community influence. Intellectual capital is the source of innovation and wealth production—it is knowledge of value.[17] Intellectual capital has to be formalized, captured, and leveraged to produce a more highly valued asset.[18]

Intellectual capital is not like other assets; it grows with use. When an employee learns and uses that learning, he/she usually learns even more, and is motivated to learn again. He/she can share the learning and not deplete it or use it up, like other assets. Sharing results in the acquisition of even more knowledge, as you probably learned when you worked on projects with other people.

Many organizations today realize the value of intellectual capital and are willing to purchase it. For example, Nortel paid $450 million for a company that had never produced a single product; they bought brainpower (e.g., 150 telecommunication specialists in high-speed networking equipment at Cambridge Systems Corporation, in Kanata, Ontario). They paid $3 million per brain.[19]

Microsoft is a good example of a company in which investors are putting a price tag on intellectual capital, because the total market value of the company exceeds its book value. Investors must believe in the future earnings potential, based not just on goodwill, but on the intellectual potential of the company.

Intellectual capital is often divided into four types: human capital, renewal capital, structural capital, and relationship capital.

Human Capital

Human capital is the knowledge, skills, and abilities of employees. Included in this type of capital are some basic components of intelligence, such as the ability to learn, to reason, to analyze. Interpersonal skills, such as the ability to communicate with others and work in teams to generate better work methods, would also be part of an organization's human capital.

Renewal Capital

Renewal capital refers to what we have labelled intellectual property, which consists of patents, licences, copyrights, and marketable innovations including products, services, and technologies.

Structural Capital

Organizations are not amoebas; they need a skeleton or structure to function. Although the organizational chart captures some of the concept of **structural capital**, what we really mean are the formal systems and informal relationships that allow employees to communicate, solve problems, and make decisions. Structural capital is the set of structures, routines, and information systems that stay behind when employees go home. Sometimes these structures are represented by policies and procedures. For example, a company might require you to obtain the approval of the vice president of marketing before launching an innovative but costly advertising campaign. Another part of structural capital can be stored in databases and knowledge documents.

For example, a consultant at IBM developed a high-quality analysis of the forest industry, which predicted nearly perfectly the rise and fall of timber prices. A consultant in the same firm, but located in Japan, had access to this document to prepare an impressive bid for a contract for a Thai forestry company.[20]

Relationship Capital

Organizations, like individual employees, do not exist as islands. **Relationship capital** refers to an organization's relationship with suppliers, customers, and even competitors that influence how they do business. These relationships, particularly if they are based on trust and integrity, can be a source of competitive advantage.

Customer capital is a subset of relationship capital. **Customer capital** is the value of an organization's relationships with its customers. For example, many small businesses enjoy high degrees of customer capital. Neighbours will shop at the local milk store even though the milk is more expensive because they know the owner and his/her family. In larger organizations, customer capital refers to all the efforts that a company makes to keep customers returning to buy their products or services.

The four types of intellectual capital work in a cycle to increase intellectual capital. As more investments are made in human capital, the employees are more capable and committed to increasing renewal and structural capital, leading to more productive relationship capital, resulting in better financial performance. The money can then be recycled to increase intellectual capital.

In this chapter, we focus on human capital: the sum and synergy of employee knowledge. Organizations want to develop their intellectual capital, and one way to do it is to create an environment in which learning is valued and actively managed. The term "learning organization" refers to the programs and culture required to increase an organization's capacity to learn and to create intellectual capital. Creating and leveraging that knowledge has become a goal of many organizations. Training and performance specialists must understand that the creation and transfer of knowledge are strategic imperatives. Learning organizations have to actively manage this knowledge.

In the next section, we discuss the different ways to acquire, interpret, disseminate, and store knowledge.

Knowledge Management Practices

Knowledge management involves the creation, collection, storage, distribution, and application of compiled "know-what" and "know-how."[21] The value of knowledge occurs when it is available to those who need it, when they need it, and when it is put into action. Many companies today have realized the importance of knowledge management.

Relationship capital

An organization's relationships with suppliers, customers, and competitors that influence how they do business

Customer capital

The value of an organization's relationships with its customers

Knowledge management

The creation, collection, storage, distribution, and application of compiled "know-what" and "know-how"

Skandia, the Swedish insurance company, reports that by managing knowledge, they were able to reduce start-up time for launching a new facility from seven years (the industry average) to three years.[22] Other companies followed Skandia's lead and expressed the value of knowledge management through anecdotes and stories.

For example, at one automotive supplier, 30 percent of the design engineers' time was wasted solving problems that had already been solved in the company.[23] Companies know that knowledge isn't being shared when work is duplicated, or expertise is available but hidden in the company and opportunities are lost, or needless staffing takes place. Platinum Technology saw a $6-million return on an investment of $750,000 in a Web system that allows its sales staff to find product data.[24]

Knowledge at The Dow Chemical Company is managed like a hard asset. Dow tries to assess the hidden value of patents and licences that have not been used. Dow manages its portfolio of more than 30 000 patents by assigning them to individual managers who are then responsible for converting them into profitable businesses.[25] The Canadian Imperial Bank of Commerce (CIBC) tracks the number of new ideas generated, new products created, and percentage of income from new revenue streams.

Recall from our earlier discussion of a learning organization that knowledge management/infrastructure is one of the four critical dimensions of a learning organization. Knowledge management/infrastructure refers to systems and structures that integrate people, processes, and technology so that important knowledge is coded, stored, and made available to members of an organization when they need it. Thus, in a learning organization, knowledge must be shared and distributed so that the organization can benefit from the cumulative knowledge of all employees.[26]

According to research conducted by The Conference Board of Canada, only 31 percent of the respondents indicated that systems and structures exist within their organization to ensure that important knowledge is coded, stored, and made available to those who need it.[27] As noted earlier, Canadian organizations need to develop knowledge management systems and practices to ensure that important information is coded, stored, and made available for use throughout the organization. This is an important element of becoming a learning organization and for improving organizational learning.

In the remainder of this section, we will focus on four processes through which organizations manage knowledge—acquisition, interpretation, dissemination, and retention.[28] The ability to create and use knowledge is what characterizes a learning organization, and the practices in which organizations engage to actively manage knowledge are a critical part of knowledge management.

Knowledge Acquisition

Companies acquire or create new knowledge in many ways. Some focus on well-respected creative processes such as brainstorming. Others may benchmark competitors or the best companies in the world. Others engage in simulations or scenario planning to stimulate new ideas. Most scan the environment looking for new ideas or changing conditions and provide formal training to their employees.

Environmental Scanning

One of the most important ways for organizations to acquire information and knowledge is by scanning the environment. This involves tapping into both internal and external sources of information and establishing internal and external connections.

External sources of information include other organizations, customers, industry watchers, and the marketplace. These sources of information can provide an organization with information on how to improve their practices, services, and products. Internal sources of information include individuals, teams, and departments throughout an organization that might have information and knowledge that would be useful for others in the organization.

Learning organizations establish external connections through partnerships that involve the exchange of information. Internal connections might include the formation of cross-functional teams that meet to discuss changes in the industry and marketplace. Individual members form external connections through participation in professional associations, supplier forums, and through contacts with customers and others in the industry. The cross-functional team is therefore able to keep abreast of industry trends, tactics, and techniques. The key is for the organization to establish both internal and external connections and relationships in order to acquire and share information and knowledge.[29]

Formal Learning

One of the most traditional ways to increase the acquisition of new knowledge in an organization is through formal learning. Formal learning is essentially synonymous with training and development and the focus of this book. It is planned and designed by the organization and usually has explicit goals and objectives. Training and development is an integral and key part of the knowledge-acquisition process in most organizations.

Xerox, one of the first companies to transform itself into a learning organization, trains all of its employees in a six-step problem-solving process that must be used at all meetings and that is used for virtually all decisions. Royal Bank has established a worldwide network of self-development programs, easily accessed from home or work, and promotes a philosophy of lifelong learning. Royal Bank's learning centre manager believes that access to learning is the first step in creating a learning organization.[30] Companies such as Motorola and Delta Hotels and Resorts guarantee their employees a certain number of hours of training a year.[31]

Informal Learning

In addition to formal training and development, employees also learn through informal means. **Informal learning** refers to learning that occurs naturally as part of work and is not planned or designed by the organization.

Informal learning
Learning that occurs naturally as part of work and is not planned or designed by the organization

Informal learning is spontaneous, immediate, and task-specific. By comparison, formal learning has an expressed goal set by the organization and a defined process that is structured and sponsored by the organization.[32] Table 2.2 presents some of the differences between formal and informal learning.

It has been reported that as much as 70 percent of what employees learn and know about their jobs is learned through informal processes rather than through more formal programs. This means that only 30 percent of what employees learn is actually acquired through formal training and development programs sponsored by their organization.[33]

This is really not all that surprising. Employees have always learned without being formally trained. Many employees learn how to handle client problems by trial and error or from co-workers. For example, an employee might show co-workers a way to save time by combining two steps in handling customer complaints. Sometimes learning occurs when an employee returns from a formal training session and teaches others what he or she has learned. In fact, when a research team studied informal training at Motorola, they discovered that every hour of formal training yielded four hours of informal training. Thus, there is a very strong connection between informal learning and formal training and there is some evidence that informal learning has a significant positive relationship to performance.[34]

TABLE 2.2

Differences between Formal and Informal Learning

Factor	Formal Learning	Informal Learning
Control	The control of learning rests primarily in the hands of the organization	The control of learning rests primarily in the hands of the learner
Relevance	Variable relevance to participants because it is not tailored to the individual	Highly relevant and need-specific to the individual
Timing	There is usually a delay in that what is learned is not immediately used on the job	What is learned tends to be used immediately on the job
Structure	Highly structured and scheduled	Usually unstructured and occurs spontaneously
Outcomes	Tends to have specific outcomes	May not have specific outcomes

Source: Day, N. (1998, June). Informal learning gets results. *Workforce Management, 77* (6), 31–35; Parker, R. O., & Cooney, J. (2005). Learning and development outlook 2005. *The Conference Board of Canada*, Ottawa. Reprinted by permission of The Conference Board of Canada.

Organizations are beginning to discover the importance and benefits of informal learning. For example, at Boeing Commercial Airplanes, researchers found that teams, personal documentation, supervisor-employee relationships, and shift changes provided rich examples of informal learning. At Motorola, assembly-line shift workers and their supervisors update the next shift on any problems that had occurred as well as the probable causes and possible solutions during shift changes that overlap by half an hour or more. McDonald's has also begun to focus on informal learning, given the large number of new employees who are hired and need to be trained every year. They are looking for ways to foster episodes of informal learning between crew members. Given the increasing pace of work and the constant changes in technology, organizations are finding that informal learning is more important than ever as there often is not enough time for formal training.[35] To learn more about how to facilitate informal learning, see The Trainer's Notebook 1.

Knowledge Interpretation

Learning occurs when individual employees form their views of the organization and its environment. These views are often called mental models. Peter Senge describes **mental models** as "deeply ingrained assumptions, generalizations, or images that influence how we understand the world and how we take action" (p. 8).[36]

Mental models

Deeply ingrained assumptions, generalizations, or images that influence how we understand the world and how we take action

---

The Trainer's Notebook 1

Facilitating Informal Learning in Organizations

Here are some strategies for facilitating informal learning in organizations:

1. Encourage employees to actively foster informal learning opportunities on their own.
2. Form casual discussion groups among employees with similar projects and tasks.
3. Create meeting areas and spaces where employees can congregate and communicate with each other (e.g., water cooler, cafeteria).
4. Remove physical barriers (e.g., office walls) that prevent employees from interacting and communicating.
5. Create overlaps between shifts so shift workers on different shifts or from different departments can get to know each other and discuss work-related issues.
6. Create small teams with a specialized focus on a product or problem.
7. Allow groups to break from their routines for team discussions.
8. Provide work teams with some autonomy to modify work processes when they have found a better way of doing things.
9. Eliminate barriers to communication and give employees the authority to take training on themselves.
10. Condense office spaces and make room for an open gathering area for coffee breaks and socializing.
11. Match new hires with seasoned employees so they can learn from casual interaction and explicit teaching and mentoring.

Sources: Day, N. (1998, June). Informal learning gets results. *Workforce Management, 77* (6), 31–35; Dobbs, K. (2000, January). Simple moments of learning. *Training, 37* (1), 52–58; Stamps, D. (1998, January). Learning ecologies. *Training, 35* (1), 32–38.

For example, if we have a mental model of managers as manipulators, then we will see all their actions as politically motivated and act accordingly. New knowledge will not be accepted because we cannot recognize and change our mental models. As one researcher noted, the acceptance of new knowledge can be likened to an organ transplant—the possibility of rejection is highly probable.[37] Even when employees are aware of best practices in other companies or units, it might take more than two years for the information to be understood in a way that can be acted upon.

An effective way to develop shared mental models is to establish teams. The most valuable and innovative work-related learning occurs in work teams, solving real problems.[38] At Chevron Corporation, based in San Francisco, best-practice teams save the company millions of dollars annually by improving processes.[39] These groups, learning by doing, are sometimes given a formal name of "communities of practice." **Communities of practice** are networks of people who work together and regularly share information and knowledge.

Communities of practice
Networks of people who work together and regularly share information and knowledge

Knowledge cannot be valued unless there is a shared understanding of its importance. Learning is social, and as teams work together, they not only learn, but they develop a common way of thinking about things and a common identity emerges. These common perspectives are termed mental maps and are vitally important to the interpretation of the work environment and any lessons it contains. New learning is difficult to accept and apply without this shared perspective.

The creation and sharing of knowledge often occurs when people are given the opportunity to talk with each other, and over time, develop a relationship. As we noted earlier, these long-term relationships, such as those that occur with apprentices or protégés, are excellent vehicles for the transfer of knowledge. North Americans generally do not appreciate the importance of the social and emotional context of learning. We see learning as information transfer. Yet, even the youngest student will tell you that he or she learns more from a teacher he or she likes.

The higher your position in an organization, the more likely you are to learn about events in face-to-face conversations. Chief executives spend about 95 percent of their time in conversations and discussions. Workers at the entry level spend less time, but still need to interface to solve problems. For example, employees working on the assembly line at Motorola had no chance to even talk with co-workers—they discussed work problems and solutions as the shifts changed.[40] Perhaps a good way to start creating a learning organization is to build on what is already working at the grassroots level.

Organizations can help employees interpret knowledge by creating networks in which individual learners and teams can share information and insight. For example, at one of the world's top luxury hotels, employees who refine a unique practice for improving reliable and superior customer service are given the opportunity to be an internal consultant by sharing the information with other hotels in the chain. This includes a site visit to ensure that the innovation has been duplicated. If successful, employees are rewarded with assistance in their next career move in the organization.[41]

Knowledge Dissemination

Moving products, services, and money through and between organizations is a standard process for most organizations. Moving ideas requires a different set of skills and even different norms.

Companies must design systems or ways of sharing knowledge so that others can improve their work practices. You might say that information has always been shared between employees, and knowledge management is just a new way of describing communication. Although employees have always passed on new ideas by talking with each other, the difference is that these informal systems can be replaced by formal mechanisms grounded in technology.

Information and communication technologies (ICTs) allow for increased codification of knowledge; that is, its transformation into information that can easily be transmitted. Today, most organizations have electronic bulletin boards, libraries, virtual conference rooms, or connected knowledge bases. Through technology, employees can exchange proposals, presentations, spreadsheets, specifications, and so on.

For example, the CEO of Memphis-based Buckman Laboratories International Inc., a manufacturer of industrial chemicals, noticed informal sharing when he toured the plants and labs in 20 countries. He and his executive team accumulated case histories of best practices developed in one country, and passed on this information in the next country. Obviously, some dilution of information occurred at each stop, because the executive team did not actually do the work.

This experience led Buckman Laboratories to ask "How can we transfer our company's best practices in a better way?" They actually set up a knowledge transfer department, with more than 40 employees in information management and training. As early as 1988, Buckman Laboratories, the winner of the Optimas award for competitive advantage, had established a series of private forums in which employees could share their insights 24 hours a day. Buckman Laboratories credits these on-line forums with an increase of $300 million in revenues, because they reduced the amount of time it takes for new ideas to reach the marketplace.[42]

There is a growth in benchmarking best practices. Normally, benchmarking implies that organizations study the best in the field and then attempt to replicate the best practices in their own companies. But as seen with the Buckman Laboratories example, benchmarking can also occur within organizations. For example, the branch in Regina may have the lowest rate of returns and it would benefit other branches to understand why.

An intranet is a critical component for managing knowledge. An employee who posts a question or seeks advice can receive that information in hours, not weeks. Just as we use the little help wizards in our software, we could use a company expert or subject-matter specialist who would pop up on the monitor while we are working on a new project—an instant coach!

Knowledge Retention

As noted earlier, knowledge resides in the minds of employees or in systems created to store that knowledge. To capitalize on these sources of knowledge, organizations must build tools to quickly compile, store, and retrieve this knowledge, a kind of intellectual inventory. These are called knowledge repositories. Knowledge repositories should not be seen as sacred libraries in which great books are stored and never read. The system has to be designed to encourage its use, to facilitate interaction. One reason for the growth of interest in this area is that the cost of managing it has been significantly lowered through technology.

There are ways to capture and store knowledge in information systems for later use. Some of these are highly structured databases. Digitalized knowledge can be more easily and cheaply processed, indexed, searched, converted, and transmitted.

Some knowledge repositories are more informal lists of lessons learned, white papers, presentations, and so on. Others are more actively stored in discussion groups. Most have links to the originators of the documents or at least to those who tend to access the repositories, thus signalling who is actively interested in that area. These collaborative filters monitor databases and intranet sites, and can tell you which sites others with interests similar to yours have found useful.

Another useful idea is that of on-line mentors. Hughes Space & Communications Company shares knowledge and best practices using just-in-time mentoring. Hughes has an index of mentors who can be called for advice on various aspects of any project. For example, a mentor with experience preparing a business case for a project might be asked to coach an employee who is facing a similar task.[43]

Not all knowledge repositories are based on computer technology. Some knowledge is tacit and not easily codified. Some more traditional means of storing knowledge might include transcripts or audiocassettes from strategic planning sessions, consultants' reports in text or multimedia formats, video-taped presentations, market-trend analyses, and any number of information-rich resources.

IBM, whose core competence is knowledge, maintains dozens of knowledge repositories that consist of project proposals, work papers, presentations, and reports. IBM says that these repositories have reduced project time by as much as two thirds.[44]

Oral histories are another way to capture knowledge, particularly when organizations suffer the memory loss associated with departures and downsizing. For example, in the United Kingdom, Rothschild PLC used an exit interview to capture the vast amount of knowledge that its departing head of public relations held. A professional with HR and PR experience interviewed the executive, for an entire afternoon, and the conversation was recorded. Information that would not normally be transmitted to the successor was uncovered, edited, and indexed.[45] Other companies record oral histories from retiring managers.

TABLE 2.3

Knowledge Management Practices

PRACTICE	PERCENTAGE USING
Creating an intranet	47
Repositories	33
Decision-support tools	33
Groupware to support collaboration	33
Networks of knowledge workers	24
Mapping sources of internal expertise	18
Establishing new knowledge roles	15

Source: Executive perspectives of knowledge in the organization. Ernst & Young Center for Business Intelligence [as cited in] Bassi, L., Cheney, S., & Lewis, E. (1998). Trends in workplace learning: Supply and demand in interesting times. *T+D* (November). Copyright 1998, adapted from *Training and Development* magazine, American Society for Training and Development. Reprinted with permission. All rights reserved.

At Kraft General Foods, the brand manager of Cracker Barrel Cheese was facing declining sales. She consulted the archives where the interview transcripts with the manager who had launched the brand were recorded. Based on these insights into the original goals for the cheese, the current brand manager was able to re-invigorate the brand.

You have just read descriptions of the various practices used by some companies to manage the acquisition, interpretation, dissemination, and retention of knowledge. A survey of knowledge management practices found that the most frequently used method was the intranet. See Table 2.3 for a list of other common methods used.

Few organizations engage in the management of knowledge in a systematic way using all the practices outlined in Table 2.3. Those that do practise knowledge management typically formalize the job by appointing a senior executive who is responsible for this important work. This formalization signals the importance of knowledge management to the success of the organization. To learn more about how an organization can improve the management of knowledge, see The Trainer's Notebook 2, "Improving Knowledge Management."

A Multilevel Systems Approach to Organizational Learning

Although the emphasis of this chapter has been on organizational learning and the learning organization, it is important to understand that learning in organizations requires a multilevel and integrated systems approach. This means that we have to acknowledge and understand the linkages between the organization, groups, and individuals.

Improving Knowledge Management

Here are some of the best knowledge management practices used by organizations today.

1. Create expectations that everyone is responsible for collecting and transferring knowledge.
2. Systematically capture relevant knowledge external to the organization, putting an end to the not-invented-here syndrome.
3. Organize learning events within the organization to capture and share knowledge.
4. Develop creative and generative ways of thinking and learning, keeping in mind, as Einstein put it, "imagination is more important than information."
5. Encourage and reward innovations and inventions.
6. Train staff in storage and retrieval of knowledge.
7. Encourage team mixing, cross-functional teams, and job rotation to maximize knowledge transfer across boundaries.
8. Develop a knowledge base around the values and learning needs of the organization.
9. Create readily accessible mechanisms for collecting and storing information.
10. Develop programs to transfer greater amounts of classroom learning to the job.

Source: Sigler, J. (1999). Best practices and guiding principles: A training guide to successful development of a learning organization. *Futurics, 23* (1&2), 67–73.

Figure 2.1 presents a multilevel systems approach to organizational learning. The model shows that there are three levels of learning in organizations: the organizational level, the group level, and the individual level. Each level is connected to the levels above and below it. The organizational level consists of the organization's leadership, culture, vision, strategy, and structure. Leadership is extremely important because top management needs to articulate a vision for learning and must support it and devote resources and time to the development of a learning organization. The organization must also develop and implement strategies for knowledge management and learning.

Organizational systems are necessary for the organization to acquire information and to distribute it throughout the organization. Thus, an organization must create processes, practices, policies, and structures that enable the acquisition, exchange, and distribution of information and knowledge throughout the organization. As well, the organization's culture for learning will influence the extent to which teams and individuals seek out new information and learning opportunities, and transfer new knowledge and skills on the job. There must be a culture that supports and encourages continuous learning.

Important factors at the group level include group climate, culture, norms, group dynamics, and processes, as well as the nature of the group task in terms of its complexity and task interdependence. Learning at the group level will be influenced by these factors. For example, the extent to which informal learning occurs will be influenced by the group's culture and norms for learning, and the extent to which it is rewarded will be influenced by the group's climate. The nature of the group's tasks will also influence learning.

FIGURE 2.1

A Multilevel Systems Model of Organizational Learning

An environment for learning
and the acquisition and exchange
of knowledge and information.

The opportunity for groups to
interact, communicate, and
share information.

Individuals must have formal
and informal opportunities for
learning. Learning and the
transfer of knowledge and
information must be rewarded.

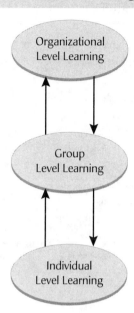

Groups that perform more complex tasks are more likely to realize the benefits of training and learning. When the tasks that group members perform are interdependent, there will be a greater need for the group to interact and share information. Thus, these group level factors will influence the extent to which learning occurs at the group level.

At the individual level, employees must also have both formal and informal opportunities to learn. This means that the organization needs to provide structured and formal training and development programs in order for employees to acquire new knowledge and skills, as well as opportunities to share and exchange information. In addition, employees must also be rewarded for learning and applying what they learn on the job.

In addition to recognizing the importance of each level for learning in organizations, the model also shows how each level is connected to the next level above and/or below it. For example, the systems and processes that exist at the organizational level will influence the extent to which learning occurs at the group level, and group level factors will influence learning at the individual level. In addition, individual learning will influence group learning, and group learning will influence organizational learning.[46]

In summary, the multilevel systems approach to organizational learning demonstrates the importance of each level of the organization for learning. In order for organizations to learn, systems and processes must be in place at each level. After all, organizations cannot learn if individuals and groups do not learn, and individuals and groups cannot learn if organizational level factors do not provide them with opportunities to learn and exchange knowledge and information.

Facilitating Learning in Organizations

Here are 10 strategies for creating a learning system in organizations and facilitating learning in organizations:

1. Develop action learning programs throughout the organization by utilizing learning activities and by creating action learning teams with a facilitator.
2. Increase individuals' abilities to learn how to learn by teaching them how to ask questions that provide new information, how to break up complex ideas and large tasks into smaller parts, how to measure learning, and how to direct learning to meet specific goals.
3. Develop the discipline of dialogue in the organization.
4. Develop career-pathing plans for employability.
5. Establish a budget for self-development programs.
6. Build team learning skills.
7. Encourage and practise systems thinking.
8. Use scanning (of the environment to be prepared for future changes) and scenario planning (strategic and contingency planning) for anticipatory learning.
9. Encourage and expand diversity, multicultural, and global mindsets and learning by opening minds to the ideas of others.
10. Change the mental model to be consistent with learning through a paradigm shift.

Source: Sigler, J. (1999). Best practices and guiding principles: A training guide to successful development of a learning organization. *Futurics, 23* (1&2), 67–73.

In order to better understand what organizations can do at all levels to facilitate learning and create a learning organization, see The Trainer's Notebook 3, "Facilitating Learning in Organizations."

Organizational Learning and Training

In this chapter, we have focused on learning in organizations, the learning organization, and knowledge management. Thus, the emphasis has been on the organizational level, although the focus of this text is on training and development at the individual and group level.

At this point, you might be asking yourself, "What is the connection between organizational learning and training?" Based on the previous section, you know that training and development is an important element of learning in organizations and a learning organization and that a key element of organizational learning is individual learning. In fact, research conducted by The Conference Board of Canada found a positive relationship between a learning organization and an organization's expenditures on formal training programs. In other words, learning organizations invest more in training and development compared to organizations that are not learning organizations (see Table 2.4 for more information about training in learning organizations). Furthermore, learning organizations have higher performance ratings in terms of their overall profitability, productivity, performance, and ability to retain essential employees.[47]

These findings indicate that there is a very close connection between training and development and organizational learning. Learning organizations exceed other organizations in terms of both training practices and

TABLE 2.4

Training and Development in Learning Organizations

Research conducted by The Conference Board of Canada found that high-learning organizations invest more in training and development in the following ways:

1. Average total training expenditure per employee.

2. Average percentage of payroll spent on training.

3. Average total hours per employee.

4. Average percentage of training delivered by technology.

Source: Parker, O., & Cooney, J. (2005). Learning and development outlook 2005. *The Conference Board of Canada.* Ottawa. Reprinted by permission of The Conference Board of Canada.

FIGURE 2.2

Training and Development and Organizational Learning

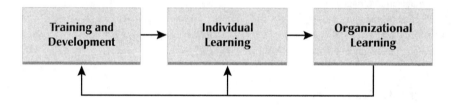

expenditures. Furthermore, learning organizations not only provide more formal training and development, they are also more profitable than other organizations.

In summary, it should now be clear to you how important formal training and development programs are for organizational learning. While we have focused on learning at the organizational level, the fact of the matter is that organizational learning only occurs if individuals learn, and one of the major ways that individuals learn is through training and development.

In the next chapter, we shift our focus to individual learning. For now, we leave you with a model (Figure 2.2) that links training and development to individual learning and organizational learning. The model shows how the design and delivery of training and development programs influence individual learning, and how individual learning leads to organizational learning. The feedback loops show that organizational learning also influences training and development as well as individual learning.

Summary

In this chapter, we described the meaning and importance of learning in organizations, a learning organization, and knowledge management. The five disciplines and the principles of a learning organization were described as well as four dimensions that are critical for creating and sustaining a learning organization. We also discussed the meaning and types of knowledge management and intellectual capital. The methods organizations use to acquire, interpret, disseminate, and retain knowledge were also described. Informal learning was described and distinguished from formal learning, and strategies for facilitating informal learning were presented. The chapter concluded with a multilevel systems model of organizational learning that shows how organizational learning is connected to group and individual learning. The connection between training and development, individual learning, and organizational learning was also discussed. In the next chapter, we focus on learning at the individual level.

Key Terms

communities of practice (page 44)
customer capital (page 39)
explicit knowledge (page 37)
human capital (page 38)
informal learning (page 41)
intellectual capital (page 38)
knowledge (page 37)
knowledge management (page 39)

learning organization (page 32)
mental models (page 43)
organizational learning (page 31)
relationship capital (page 39)
renewal capital (page 38)
structural capital (page 38)
tacit knowledge (page 37)

Weblinks

CIBC: www.cibc.com (page 40)

Dow Chemical: www.dow.com (page 40)

IBM: www.ibm.com/ca (page 39)

Kraft General Foods: www.kraftfoods.com (page 47)

Microsoft: www.microsoft.com (page 38)

Nortel: www.nortel.com (page 38)

Royal Bank: www.royalbank.com (page 41)

Discussion Questions

1. Discuss the role of teams and leaders in a learning organization. How do teams and leaders contribute to a learning organization and what are some of the tasks and activities that they should perform?
2. Discuss the importance and relevance of technology for a learning organization and knowledge management. How important is technology and how should it be used in a learning organization and for knowledge management?
3. Discuss the role of the training function and the role of the trainer in a learning organization. How will these roles change in a learning

organization? What knowledge and skills will a trainer in a learning organization require?

4. Discuss the multilevel systems model of organizational learning. How are the three levels related and what should organizations do for learning to occur at each level?

5. Why do you think there are not more learning organizations in Canada? What do Canadian organizations have to do to become learning organizations?

6. What is the difference between formal and informal learning and what can organizations do to facilitate informal learning? What are the advantages and disadvantages of formal and informal learning?

The Great Training Debate

1. Debate the following: Informal learning is more important that formal learning (e.g., training programs) and organizations should focus more on informal learning and less on formal training programs.

Using the Internet

1. Review the chapter-opening vignette on Dofasco and also visit their website at **www.dofasco.ca**. What are some of the things that make Dofasco a learning organization? Discuss Dofasco in terms of Peter Senge's five disciplines, the principles of a learning organization, and the four key dimensions that are critical for creating and sustaining a learning organization. What can organizations learn from Dofasco if they want to become a learning organization?

2. To learn more about organizational learning and the learning organization, go to: **www.brint.com/papers/orglrng.htm** and find answers to the following questions:

   1. What is organizational learning?
   2. What is a learning organization?
   3. What is the difference between organizational learning and a learning organization?
   4. What is adaptive learning versus generative learning?
   5. What's the manager's role in the learning organization?
   6. What's the relationship between strategy and organizational learning?
   7. What is the role of information systems in the learning organization?
   8. Does IT impose any constraints on organizational learning?

3. To find out more about learning organizations in Canada, go to Industry Canada at **http://strategis.ic.gc.ca/epic/internet/incts-scf.nsf/en/sl00019e.html**

Answer the following questions:

1. What is a leading-edge learning organization?
2. What are the performance characteristics of a leading-edge learning organization?
4. To learn about two companies that are considered to be learning organizations, go to: **http://strategis.ic.gc.ca/epic/internet/incts-scf.nsf/en/sl00053e.html#Vancouver**. What makes these two companies learning organizations and what role does training play in making them learning organizations?

Exercises

In-Class

1. Using the information in this chapter, develop a checklist to determine if the organization in which you work (or have worked) is a learning organization. How many of the four critical elements and principles of a learning organization are characteristic of your organization? What does your organization have to do to become a learning organization?
2. Reflect on a previous or current job in terms of what you have learned and how it was learned. Make a list of the three or five most important things you learned on your job. Once you have made your learning list, indicate how each item on your list was learned. Was it through formal or informal means? Be specific in terms of the formal or informal activity that contributed to your learning. What does your list tell you about learning in organizations? What should you do if you want to improve your learning?
3. Imagine that you are a director of training in an organization and the company president wants to meet with you to discuss becoming a learning organization. What will you tell him or her about learning organizations and what the organization must do to become a learning organization? Prepare a short presentation in which you present your main ideas and suggestions for becoming a learning organization. When complete, pair up with another member of the class and take turns presenting and evaluating each other's presentation. If time permits, presentations to the class can also be made.
4. Imagine that you are a director of training and development in an organization and the company president wants to meet with you to discuss how the organization can improve its management of knowledge. What will you tell him or her about knowledge management and what the organization must do to improve its management of knowledge? Prepare a short presentation in which you present your main ideas and suggestions for knowledge management. When complete, pair up with another member of the class and take turns presenting and evaluating each other's presentation. If time permits, presentations to the class can also be made.

5. As a student, you spend a great deal of your time learning. But how exactly do you learn? Make a list of the formal and informal ways that you learn. Do you learn more from formal or informal methods? If you want to improve your learning, what are some of the things you might do? Be specific in terms of both formal and informal ways to improve your learning.

In-the-Field

1. Contact the human resources department of an organization and ask them if you can talk about their attempts to become a learning organization. Ask them if they are a learning organization and what they have done in order to become a learning organization. How do they rate on the four key dimensions of a learning organization (see Table 2.1)? Do you think they are a learning organization? What do they still need to do to become a learning organization?

2. Contact the human resources department of an organization and ask them if you can talk about how they manage knowledge and information in the organization. Ask them about their knowledge management practices and what they do to acquire, interpret, disseminate, and retain knowledge. Use Table 2.3 to find out what knowledge management practices they have in place. How can the organization improve its management of knowledge?

3. Conduct an interview with several people you know who are currently employed. Interview them about how they learn in their organization. Ask questions about how and what they have learned through formal and informal learning opportunities. Based on their responses, answer the following questions:

   a. Did they learn more or less from formal or informal learning?
   b. Did they have more or less formal or informal opportunities for learning?
   c. Which type of learning was most effective for them: formal or informal learning?
   d. What did they learn from formal and informal learning? Did they learn similar or different things from each?
   e. What kinds of practices were used in their organization for formal and informal learning?

Case Incident

NASA's Knowledge Management Crisis

In the 1990s, NASA's lunar program lost critical knowledge as a result of downsizing when Saturn 5 engineers were encouraged to take early retirement. Commenting on the early retirements, one NASA manager said, "If we want to go to the moon again, we'll be starting from scratch . . . all of that knowledge has disappeared. It would take at least as long and cost at least as much to go back." Now NASA wants to ensure that the expertise of other senior engineers isn't lost when they retire.

Questions

1. What kind of knowledge and intellectual capital is NASA losing and what effect does this have on the organization?
2. What should NASA do to prevent the loss of knowledge when senior engineers retire?

Source: Foord Kirk, J. (2005, December 3). The cost of disappearing knowledge. *The Toronto Star*, D10; Weinstein, M. (2005, December). NASA training program blasts off. *Training, 42* (12), 8–9.

Case

Frozen Rock-Solid

At General Motors of Canada Ltd., Nick Vanderstoop is in charge of implementing a system that he created to prevent the "erosion of knowledge." He loves to scare the daylights out of GM executives and managers by telling them a true story about the company.

The story goes something like this: Several years ago a worker at the head office of General Motors of Canada Ltd. in Oshawa retired. Among the many tasks that were performed by him, one was particularly important. Every fall he would spend about an hour sending messages to inform others that certain freezable chemicals like upholstery cleaners must be shipped in heated trucks during the winter.

A few months after he retired, the parts distribution centre in Woodstock, Ontario, began to receive calls from angry customers across Canada who were upset because the chemicals that they were receiving were frozen rock-solid. The reason: nobody in the company knew enough about the retiree's job to make sure that the chemicals were properly transported during the winter.

A minor oversight? Not quite. It cost the company $1.5 million. Other incidents at GM have also been reported. For example, 400 perfectly good carburetors were accidentally destroyed at a cost of $300,000 because the worker who kept them off the scrap list retired. It has also been reported that a $250,000 car prototype was crushed into scrap metal because the employee who was responsible for it was transferred. Incidents like these are known to occur at other companies.

Source: Livesey, B. (1997, November). Glitch doctor. *Report on Business Magazine*, pp. 96–102. Reprinted with permission of Bruce Livesey.

Questions

1. Why do you think this is an important story to tell company executives and managers? What is the main point of the story?
2. What kind of knowledge is most relevant for understanding the incidents mentioned in the case? What does the case tell us about the role of knowledge in organizations?

3. Organization mishaps like those reported in the case appear to be common occurrences. A traditional organization might blame or attribute the causes of them to a number of different sources. What reasons might be given for such mishaps?
4. What could GM and other companies do to solve the problems reported in the case? What knowledge management practices would you recommend and why?
5. What would a learning organization do to identify and solve the types of incidents described in the case?

References

1. Geary, S. (2002). What does it take to implement the learning organization? *The Canadian Learning Journal, 6* (2), 27–30. www.dofasco.ca Dofasco Inc.; Iron Age New Steel; Dofasco: A Company Overview.
2. Senge, P. M. (1990). *The fifth discipline: The art and practice of the learning organization.* New York: Doubleday.
3. Bennet, J. K., & O'Brien, M. J. (1994, June). The building blocks of the learning organization. *Training, 31* (6), 41–49.
4. Senge, P. M. (1990).
5. Sigler, J. (1999). Best practices and guiding principles: A training guide to successful development of a learning organization. *Futurics, 23* (1&2), 67–73.
6. Harris-Lalonde, S. (2001). Training and development outlook. *The Conference Board of Canada.* Ottawa.
7. Parker, R. O., & Cooney, J. (2005). Learning & Development Outlook 2005. *The Conference Board of Canada.* Ottawa.
8. Ellinger, A. D., Ellinger, A. E., Baiyin, Y., & Howton, S. W. (2002). The relationship between the learning organization concept and firms' financial performance: An empirical assessment. *Human Resource Development Quarterly, 13,* 5–21.
9. Parker, R. O., & Cooney, J. (2005).
10. Harris-Lalonde, S. (2001); Cooney, J., & Cowan, A. (2003). Training and development outlook 2003. *The Conference Board of Canada.* Ottawa.
11. Sigler, J. (1999).
12. Tapscott, D. (1998). Make knowledge an asset for the whole company. *Computerworld, 32* (51), p. 32.
13. Stamps, D. (1999, March). Is knowledge management a fad? *Training, 36* (3), 36–42.
14. Stamps, D. (1999, March).
15. Baets, W. R. J. (1998). *Organizational learning and knowledge technologies in a dynamic environment.* Boston: Kluwer Academic Publishers.
16. Miller, W. (1999, January). Building the ultimate resource. *Management Review,* 42–45.
17. Miller, W. (1999, January).
18. Stewart, T. (1994, October 3). Intellectual capital. *Fortune,* pp. 68–74.
19. Pezim, S. (1999, January 11). Fishing in the knowledge pond. *Canadian HR Reporter,* pp. 15–16.
20. Tapscott, D. (1998).
21. Miller, W. (1999, January).
22. Bassi, L., Cheney, S., & Lewis, E. (1998, November). Trends in workplace learning: Supply and demand in interesting times. *Training and Development,* 51–77.
23. Kransdorff, A. (1997, September). Fight organizational memory loss. *Workforce Management,* 34–39.

24. Stahl, S. (1999, April 5). Knowledge yields impressive returns. *Information Week*, p. 115.
25. Neely Martinez, M. (1998, February). The collective power. *HRM Magazine*, pp. 88–94.
26. Sigler, J. (1999).
27. Cooney, J., & Cowan, A. (2003).
28. Garvin, D. A. (1998). The processes of organization and management. *Sloan Management Review, 39* (4), 33–50.
29. Jeppesen, J. C. (2002). Creating and maintaining the learning organization. In K. Kraiger's (Ed.), *Creating, implementing, and managing effective training and development: State-of-the-art lessons for practice*, (pp. 302–30). San Francisco. CA: Jossey-Bass.
30. Trainor, N. L. (1998, April 20). Learning creates value for organizations. *Canadian HR Reporter*, p. 9.
31. Stamps, D. (1998, January). Learning ecologies. *Training, 35* (1), pp. 32–38; Roseman, E. (2001, August 29). Delta Hotels knows how to keep workers. *The Toronto Star*, E2.
32. Stamps, D. (1998).
33. Day, N. (1998, June). Informal learning gets results. *Workforce Management, 77* (6), 31–35; Dobbs, K. (2000, January). Simple moments of learning. *Training, 37* (1), 52–58.
34. Day, N. (1998, June).
35. Stamps, D. (1998); Dobbs, K. (2000, January).
36. Senge, P. M. (1990).
37. Stamps, D. (1999).
38. Stamps, D. (1997). Communities of practice: Learning is social, training is irrelevant? *Training, 3* (2), 34–42.
39. Neely Martinez, M. (1998, February).
40. Stamps, D. (1998).
41. Jeppesen, J. C. (2002).
42. Sunoo, B. P. (1999). How HR supports knowledge sharing. *Workforce Management, 78* (3), 30–34.
43. Stuller, J. (1998). Chief of corporate smarts. *Training, 35* (4), 28–37.
44. Tapscott, D. (1998).
45. Kransdorff, A. (1997, September).
46. Kozlowski, S. W. J., & Salas, E. (1997). A multilevel organizational systems approach for the implementation and transfer of training. In J. K. Ford, S. W. J. Kozlowski, K. Kraiger, E. Salas, and M. S. Teachout (Eds.), *Improving training effectiveness in work organizations*. Mahwah, N. J.: Lawrence Erlbaum Associates.
47. Parker, R. O., & Cooney, J. (2005).

Chapter 3

Learning and Motivation

Chapter Learning Objectives

After reading this chapter, you should be able to:

- define learning and describe Gagné's five learning outcomes
- describe the three stages of learning and Kolb's learning styles
- describe conditioning theory and social learning theory and their implications for training and development
- describe adult learning theory and its implications for training and development
- define motivation and describe need and process theories of motivation and their implications for training and development
- define training motivation and discuss its predictors and consequences
- define all of the variables in the model of training effectiveness and describe how the variables in the model are related

www.fairmont.ca

FAIRMONT HOTELS AND RESORTS

At the Toronto-based hotel chain, Fairmont Hotels & Resorts, new employees have a lot to learn. Prior to their first day on the job, new employees receive an invitation to the hotel. They are asked to arrive at the front door, where a valet waits to park their car. They are then greeted by senior hotel management and taken to an elegant dining room for coffee, breakfast, and an informal discussion about the hotel. Once treated to a meal or given vouchers for an overnight stay at the hotel, they view a short video message from the members of the corporate executive team welcoming them and letting them know where to go for further assistance.

The second day of orientation includes more presentations, and role-playing activities that simulate encounters with guests. Trainers don't just tell new employees how customers should be treated, they show them. Trainers model customer service by treating new employees as special guests.

Each hotel has its own creative way of showing the property to new employees. Some hotels have scavenger hunts, creating a fun competition among teams of new hires. Others have developed celebrity tours, showing new employees where, for example, John Lennon and Yoko Ono had their love-in at the Queen Elizabeth hotel in Montreal.

At the Fairmont Banff Springs, employees are taken on a tour of rooms believed to be haunted by ghosts. These stories not only share the history and culture of the luxury hotels, but they also prepare new employees for success.

A third day of orientation takes place once employees have been on the job 60 to 90 days. During this time, employees are paired with a mentor of their choosing as a way to receive extra help and build relationships with co-workers. Supervisors also guide new employees through a personal development interview, identifying goals and providing informal feedback.

The Fairmont orientation program attempts to strike the same passion in its employees as the hotel hopes to create for its guests. By experiencing the hotel as guests and hearing the stories along with corporate strategy, employees are better able to take ownership of their jobs and where they work.[1]

Training is first and foremost about learning and at Fairmont Hotels & Resorts, new employees are trained so that they learn about the company, the art of customer service, the building of relationships, and how to perform their new jobs and roles.

In Chapter 2, we discussed organizational learning and the learning organization. However, in order for organizations to learn and to become learning organizations, the people in them must learn. In this chapter, we focus on how people learn and their motivation to learn. First, we define what we mean by learning and describe learning outcomes. We then discuss the stages of learning followed by a review of learning and motivation theories. We conclude the chapter with a model that links training to learning, behaviour, and organizational effectiveness.

What Is Learning?

Although training is the focus of this book, it is important to keep in mind that what we are really trying to accomplish through the process of training and development is learning. In other words, training is simply the means for accomplishing the goal, which is learning.

Learning is the process of acquiring knowledge and skills. It is a process in which an individual's behaviour is changed through experience.[2] For our purposes, that experience is training and development. Learning occurs "when one experiences a new way of acting, thinking, or feeling, finds the new pattern gratifying or useful, and incorporates it into the repertoire of behaviours" (p. 833).[3] When a behaviour has been learned, it can be thought of as a skill.

Learning
The process of acquiring knowledge and skills, and a change in individual behaviour as a result of some experience

Learning Outcomes

Learning can be described in terms of domains or outcomes of learning. Robert Gagné developed the best known classification of learning outcomes. According to Gagné, learning outcomes can be classified according to five general categories:[4]

1. *Verbal information* refers to facts, knowledge, principles, and information or what is known as declarative knowledge.
2. *Intellectual skills* involve the learning of concepts, rules, and procedures and are sometimes referred to as procedural knowledge.
3. *Cognitive strategies* refer to the application of information and techniques, and understanding how and when to use the information.
4. *Motor skills* involve the coordination and execution of physical movements that involve the use of muscles; for instance, learning to swim.
5. *Attitudes* refer to preferences and internal states associated with one's beliefs and feelings. Attitudes are learned and can be changed. However, they are considered to be the most difficult domain to influence through training.[5]

A training program can focus on one or more of these learning outcomes. The important thing to realize is that different training methods might be more or less effective depending on the learning outcome a training program was designed to influence. According to Gagné, different instructional events and conditions of learning are required for each of the learning outcomes. However, regardless of the learning outcome, learning generally occurs over a period of time and progresses through a series of stages as described in the next section.

Stages of Learning

Learning and the acquisition of new knowledge and skills occur over a period of time. A theory developed by John Anderson, which he calls the Adaptive Character of Thought theory or ACT theory, describes the learning process as it unfolds over three stages.[6]

According to ACT theory, learning takes place in three stages that are known as declarative knowledge, knowledge compilation, and procedural knowledge or proceduralization.

The first stage of learning involves learning knowledge, facts, and information or what is known as **declarative knowledge**. For example, think of what it was like when you learned how to drive a car. At first, you acquired a great deal of information such as what to do when you get into the car, how to start the car and put it in gear, how to change gears if it is a standard shift and so on. These pieces of information or units are called chunks.

During this first stage of learning one must devote all of one's attention and cognitive resources to the task of learning. In other words, it is not likely that you could make a phone call, listen to the radio, or carry on a conversation during this period of learning to drive a car. This is because all of your attention and cognitive resources are required to learn the task of driving. Furthermore, your driving performance at this stage is slow and prone to errors.

During the declarative stage of learning, performance is resource-dependent because all of one's attention and cognitive resources are required to learn the task. Any diversion of attention is likely to affect your learning and lower your performance. Just think of what it is like when you are in class and somebody starts talking to you. Your learning is seriously affected because you need all of your attention and cognitive resources for the task of learning. Listening or talking to somebody during class will require your attention and your learning will suffer.

The second stage of learning is called **knowledge compilation**. Knowledge compilation involves integrating tasks into sequences to simplify and streamline the task. The learner acquires the ability to translate the declarative knowledge acquired in the first stage into action. During this stage, performance becomes faster and more accurate. For example, when learning how to drive a car, you are able to get into the car and begin to drive without having to carefully think about every single thing you must do. In other words, what was once many single tasks or units and chunks during the declarative stage (e.g., put your seatbelt on, lock the car, adjust the seat, adjust the mirror, start the car, etc.), is now one smooth sequence of tasks. You get into the car and do all of the tasks as part of an integrated sequence.

Although the attention requirements during the knowledge compilation stage are lower than the declarative stage, performance is still somewhat fragmented and piecemeal. So when you are learning to drive a car, this might

Declarative knowledge

Learning knowledge, facts, and information

Knowledge compilation

Integrating tasks into sequences to simplify and streamline the task

mean popping the clutch from time to time and occasionally rolling backwards when on an incline, stalling the car, and so on.

The final stage of learning is called **procedural knowledge** or proceduralization. During this stage, the learner has mastered the task and performance is automatic and habitual. In other words, the task can now be performed without much thought. The transition from knowledge acquisition to application is complete. This is what most of us experience when we drive. We simply get into a car and drive without giving much thought to what we are doing. The task of driving becomes habitual and automatic.

Because tasks at this stage can be performed with relatively little attention, it is possible to divert one's attention and cognitive resources to other tasks such as conversing with passengers or talking on the phone. Performance at this stage is fast and accurate and the task can be performed with little impairment even when attention is devoted to another task. At this stage, performance is said to be resource-insensitive because changes in attention will not have much of an impact on performance.

ACT theory has some important implications for learning and training. First, it recognizes the fact that learning is a stage-like process that involves three important stages. Second, it indicates that different types of learning take place at different stages. And third, motivational interventions might be more or less effective depending on the stage of learning. As you will learn later in the chapter, goal setting is a motivational theory with implications for training and development. However, research has shown that goal setting can be harmful to learning during the early stages of learning when all of one's attention and cognitive resources must be devoted to learning the task. During the early stages of learning, cognitive ability is more important than motivational strategies.

However, when goals are set during the later stages of learning (e.g., procedural knowledge), they have a positive effect on learning and performance and cognitive ability is less important than it was during the declarative stage of learning. Thus, the effects of both cognitive ability and motivational interventions such as goal setting on learning and performance depend on the stage of learning.[7]

Learning Styles

An important aspect of learning is the way in which people learn. David Kolb focused on the different ways that people prefer to learn. According to Kolb, individuals differ in terms of how they prefer to learn or what are known as learning styles. A **learning style** is the way in which an individual gathers information and processes and acts on it during the learning process.[8]

An individual's learning style is a function of the way an individual gathers and processes information or what is known as a learning mode. According to Kolb, there are four learning modes: 1. Concrete experience (CE), 2. Abstract conceptualization (AC), 3. Reflective observation (RO), and 4. Active experimentation (AE).

Procedural knowledge

The learner has mastered the task and performance is automatic and habitual

Learning style

The way in which an individual gathers information and processes and evaluates it during the learning process

People who prefer to learn through direct experience and involvement as opposed to thinking are CE types. Those who prefer to learn by thinking about issues, ideas, and concepts are AC types. If you prefer to learn by observing and reflecting on information and different points of view you are an RO type. Finally, people who prefer to learn by acting on information and actually doing something to see its practical value are AE types.[9]

An individual's learning style is a function of two of the modes of learning. For example, a convergent learning style combines abstract conceptualization and active experimentation (thinking and doing). People with this learning style focus on problem solving and the practical application of ideas and theories. A divergent learning style combines concrete experience and reflective observation (feeling and watching). People with this orientation view concrete situations from different points of view and generate alternative courses of action. An assimilation style combines abstract conceptualization and reflective observation (thinking and watching). These people like to process and integrate information and ideas into logical forms and theoretical models. Finally, an accommodative learning style combines concrete experience and active experimentation (feeling and doing). People with this learning style prefer hands-on experience and like to learn by being involved in new and challenging experiences.[10]

Kolb's theory has several implications for learning. First, it recognizes that people differ in how they prefer to learn. This means that a person's comfort and success in training will depend on how well the training approach matches their learning style. Thus, trainers need to be aware of these differences and design training programs to appeal to people's different learning styles.

Second, although people might prefer a particular learning style, ideally people can learn best by using all four styles. In fact, Kolb notes the importance of a learning cycle in which people use each of the four modes of learning in a sequence. The learning cycle begins with concrete experience (learning by experience), followed by reflective observation (learning by reflecting), then abstract conceptualization (learning by thinking), and finally active experimentation (learning by doing). This kind of learning cycle has been shown to improve learning and retention as well as the development of behavioural skills. Learning is most effective when all four steps in the learning cycle are part of the learning experience.[11] Thus, training programs should be designed with each learning mode as part of a sequence of learning experiences.

Kolb's learning cycle and learning styles have important implications for how to design training programs. For example, at Capital One Financial Corp., after employees are taught a new set of skills they are given work projects to implement the skills and then they must report on the experience. The approach closely mirrors Kolb's learning cycle.[12] To find out how another company has applied Kolb's learning styles and matches trainees' learning style to training, see Training Today, "Learning Styles and Training at AmeriCredit."

Learning Styles and Training at AmeriCredit

AmeriCredit is an auto finance company in Fort Worth, Texas. The company has a unique approach to training that has its basis in David Kolb's learning cycle model and learning styles. The company has developed an instrument called the I-Opt Learning Style Rollout to measure employees' learning styles.

The company's vision is to measure the preferred learning styles of all the company's 4,800 employees from the CEO to janitors and then log it into a database where course content will be tailored to the individual, the facilitator, and the design of the course.

Before a training program begins, the company runs an I-Opt group profile on all trainees and gives them a motivation questionnaire. Data analysis then yields data on an employee's likelihood of success in learning from the course based on course design, their motivation to attend, and the style of the facilitator.

Course facilitators receive a report prior to a training session that allows them to adjust course delivery, content, and design based on the learning styles of the trainees. Facilitators can then make any necessary changes to the content of a program. They must be fluid in each of the different learning styles so that they can shift their methods to match the styles of the trainees.

In addition, employees are given cards that indicate their personal learning style. Before and after a training session, they can give the cards to the instructor for an instant "style" check, allowing the instructor to fine-tune his or her delivery on the fly.

Source: Barbian, J. (2002, March). Training top 100: AmeriCredit. *Training, 39* (3), 46–47. Reprinted by permission of *Training* magazine.

Learning Theories

Researchers have studied learning and have developed a body of knowledge and theories about the learning process. Theories are very important because they help us understand how something works or why it happens. Theories represent an attempt to organize knowledge so that we can use it in a variety of situations.

Intuitively, most trainers use some guidelines derived from learning theories. For example, the value of rewarding good performance and providing positive feedback is well known, as is the importance of confidence for learning and performing a task. In this section, we describe two theories of learning that have important implications for the design and effectiveness of training and development programs: conditioning theory and social learning theory.

Conditioning Theory

The famous psychologist B. F. Skinner defined learning as a relatively permanent change in behaviour in response to a particular stimulus or set of stimuli.[13] Skinner and the behaviourist school of psychology believe that learning is a result of reward and punishment contingencies that follow a response to a stimulus.

FIGURE 3.1

The Conditioning Process

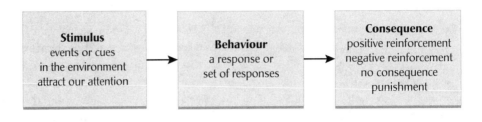

The basic idea is that a stimulus or cue is followed by a response, which is then reinforced. This in turn strengthens the likelihood that the response will occur again and that learning will result.

For example, behaviourists argue that similar principles are at work when an adult submits an innovative proposal and is praised, and when a pigeon pecks a red dot and is given a pellet of food. When a response is reinforced through food, money, attention, or anything pleasurable, then the response is more likely to be repeated. If there is no reinforcement, then over time the response will cease. If the response is punished, then it will not be repeated. The conditioning process is illustrated in Figure 3.1.

Negative reinforcement is the removal of a stimulus after an act. To illustrate this concept, think of an alarm clock ringing. When you turn it off, the noise stops (the stimulus is removed). Similarly, think of your course instructor chewing out the class for not participating and threatening to start picking students at random to answer questions. When students participate, the instructor stops chewing them out and threatening to choose students at random. Thus, the response of increased class participation results in the removal of a negative stimulus.

It is important to realize that this is not the same as punishment, in which one receives a negative consequence for doing something undesirable. In the example above, a desirable behaviour is being learned and increased (e.g., class participation) by a negative reinforcer that is removed when the desirable behaviour occurs.

Managers and trainers use conditioning theory principles when they attempt to influence employee behaviour. For example, at Capital One, a financial services company in the United States, new hires attend monthly reinforcement sessions in which they discuss what they did on the job that directly relates to the skills being developed. Once the skills are mastered they are taught new skills and the reinforcement cycle continues.[14] Linking desired behaviour to pleasurable consequences is based on three connected concepts: *shaping, chaining,* and *generalization*.

Shaping refers to the reinforcement of each step in the process until it is mastered, and then withdrawing the reinforcer until the next step is mastered. Shaping is extremely important for learning complex behaviour. Behaviour modeling is a training method (see Chapter 6) that makes extensive use of this

Shaping

The reinforcement of each step in a process until it is mastered concept by rewarding trainees for the acquisition of separate skills performed sequentially.

Chaining is the second important concept and involves the reinforcement of entire sequences of a task. During shaping, an individual learns each separate step of a task and is reinforced for each successive step. The goal, however, is to learn to combine each step and perform the entire response. This combination is what chaining involves, and it is accomplished by reinforcing entire sequences of the task and eventually reinforcing only the complete task after each of the steps have been learned.

The third important concept is **generalization**, which means that the conditioned response occurs in circumstances different from those during learning.[15] Thus, while a trainee might have learned a task through shaping and chaining, he or she might not be able to perform the task in a different situation or outside of the classroom. To achieve generalization, the trainer must provide trainees with opportunities to perform the task in a variety of situations. For example, the trainer can change a role-play script from negotiating with one's supervisor on the deadline of a project to negotiating the starting salary with a new employer. As a result, the trainee learns to generalize the skill from a simple, controlled environment to a different, more difficult one. This is a goal of training—that learning acquired during training will be generalized to, and used in, different situations and contexts.

IMPLICATIONS FOR TRAINING   When applied to training, conditioning theory suggests that trainees should be encouraged and reinforced throughout the training process. In other words, they should be reinforced for attending training, learning the training material, and applying it on the job. Based on conditioning theory, training should be more effective to the extent that trainees are reinforced for learning and the successful performance of training tasks.

Social Learning Theory

According to social learning theory, people learn by observing the behaviour of others, making choices about different courses of action to pursue, and by managing their own behaviour in the process of learning.[16] Thus, learning does not just occur as a result of reward and punishment contingencies. Learning also occurs through cognitive processes such as imitation and modelling. We observe the actions of others and make note of the reinforcing or punishing outcomes of their behaviour. We then imitate observed behaviour and expect certain consequences to follow.

For example, as part of the new-employee orientation and training program at Fairmont Hotels & Resorts, trainers show new employees how to treat customers by modelling customer service behaviour and treating new employees as guests. In addition, employees participate in role-playing activities that simulate encounters with guests. This is a good example of the process of learning through observation and imitation. Considerable research has shown that people observe and reproduce the actions and attitudes of others.[17]

Social learning theory involves three key components: observation, self-efficacy, and self-management.

Chaining
The reinforcement of entire sequences of a task

Generalization
The conditioned response occurs in circumstances different from those during learning

Observation

Learning by observing the actions of others and their consequences

As already indicated, people learn by **observation**. They observe the actions of others and the consequences of those actions. If the person being observed (the role model) is credible and knowledgeable, their behaviour is more likely to be imitated. The imitation will occur particularly if the role model is reinforced for the behaviour. New recruits watch the intense work hours of the senior staff. They then work the same long hours, in the expectation that they, too, will be rewarded with promotions.

There are four key elements that are critical for observational learning to take place: attention, retention, reproduction, and reinforcement. Learners must first attend to the behaviour (i.e., be aware of the skills that are observable). Second, they must remember what they observed and encode it in their own repertoire so that they can recall the skills. Third, they must then try out the skill (i.e., try to reproduce it) through practice and rehearsal. Fourth, if the reproduction results in positive outcomes (i.e., it is reinforced), then the learner is likely to continue to reproduce the behaviour and retain the new skills.

Many training programs use social learning theory concepts to model desired behaviour that is then followed by opportunities for practice and reinforcement. At Fairmont Hotels & Resorts, trainers show new hires how customers should be treated. They model customer service by treating new employees as special guests. Some organizations assign new recruits to mentors or senior co-workers so that they can learn by observing them. At Fairmont Hotels & Resorts, new employees are paired with a mentor of their choosing. The financial services firm Edward Jones has a mentoring program in which new investment representatives are paired with more established ones. New employees shadow their mentor for three weeks to learn about the company and how things are done.[18]

While observation may provide the observer with information necessary to imitate the modelled behaviour, we know that people do not always attempt to do the things that they observe other people doing. For example, a novice skier might watch his friends skillfully make their way down a steep hill but refuse to follow suit. This is because he or she might not have the confidence or the belief that he or she will be able to do it. Such beliefs are known as self-efficacy.

Self-efficacy

Judgments that people have about their ability to successfully perform a specific task

Self-efficacy refers to judgments that people have about their ability to successfully perform a specific task. Self-efficacy is a cognitive belief that is task-specific, as in the example of the skier's confidence that he or she can ski down a steep hill. The novice skier might have low self-efficacy to ski down the hill but very high self-efficacy that he or she can get an "A" in a training course!

Self-efficacy is influenced by four sources of information. In order of importance they are: task performance outcomes, observation, verbal persuasion and social influence, and one's physiological or emotional state.[19] The self-efficacy of the skier can be strengthened not only by observing his or her friends' behaviour, but also by their encouragement that he or she can make it down the hill, his or her feelings of comfort and relaxation rather than fear and anxiety, and most important, his or her own successful attempts at skiing down the hill.

Self-efficacy has been shown to have a strong effect on people's attitudes, emotions, and behaviour in many areas of human behaviour. Self-efficacy influences the activities people choose to perform, the amount of effort and persistence they devote to a task, affective and stress reactions, and performance outcomes.[20]

Self-efficacy is also a key factor in training. Research has shown that the effectiveness of many training programs is partly due to the strengthening of trainees' self-efficacy to perform the training task. In other words, training increases trainees' self-efficacy to perform a task, and self-efficacy is related to improved task performance.[21]

The third component of social learning theory is self-management. **Self-management** involves managing one's own behaviour through a series of internal processes.

Conditioning theory takes the position that an individual's behaviour is regulated by external factors such as rewards and punishments. However, self-management suggests that people can control and manage their own behaviour through a series of internal processes that enables them to structure and motivate their behaviour. These internal processes involve observing one's own behaviour as well as the behaviour of others, setting performance goals, practising new and desired behaviours, keeping track of one's progress, and rewarding oneself for goal achievement.[22]

Self-management has been found to be related to cognitive, affective, and behavioural outcomes and to be an important method of training. For example, one study found that self-management training increased the job attendance of employees with above average absenteeism. The results indicated that, compared to a group that did not receive the training, employees who received self-management training had higher self-efficacy for attending work and increased job attendance. In a follow-up study, the authors found that these benefits continued up to nine months after training.[23] Several other studies have also demonstrated that self-management training leads to improvements in skill acquisition, maintenance, and performance.[24]

IMPLICATIONS FOR TRAINING   Social learning theory has important implications for the design of training programs. In particular, trainee learning can be improved by providing trainees with models who demonstrate how to perform a training task; by strengthening trainee self-efficacy for successfully learning and performing the task; and by teaching trainees to regulate and manage their own behaviour and performance.

Adult Learning Theory

RPC 3.1

Consider the learning environment most people have experienced throughout their lives. As students, we are told what, when, and how to learn. Learning is supposed to pay off in some unknown way in the distant future. The question is whether this is an appropriate way to educate and train adults given that adults differ from children in a number of important ways.

Self-management

Managing one's own behaviour through a series of internal processes

TABLE 3.1

Teaching Children versus Adults		
FACTOR	CHILDREN	ADULTS
Personality	Dependent	Independent
Motivation	Extrinsic	Intrinsic
Roles	Student	Employee
	Child	Parent, volunteer, spouse, citizen
Openness to change	Keen	Ingrained habits and attitudes
Barriers to change	Few	Negative self–concept
		Limited opportunities
		Time
		Inappropriate teaching methods
Experience	Limited	Vast
Orientation to learning	Subject–centred	Problem–centred

First, unlike children, adults have acquired a great deal of knowledge and work-related experiences that they bring with them to a training program. Adults also like to know why they are learning something, the practical implications of what they are learning, and its relevance to their problems and needs. Adults are also problem-centred in their approach to learning and prefer to be self-directed. They like to learn independently and they are motivated to learn by both extrinsic and intrinsic factors. Other contrasts between the learning needs of children and adults are highlighted in Table 3.1.

These differences have led to the development of an adult learning theory known as andragogy. **Andragogy** is a term coined by adult learning theorist Malcolm Knowles and refers to an adult-oriented approach to learning that takes into account the differences between adult and child learners. Andragogy involves making the learning experience of adults self-directed and problem-centred, and takes into account the learner's existing knowledge and experience. By contrast, the term **pedagogy** refers to the more traditional approach of learning used to educate children and youth.[25]

IMPLICATIONS FOR TRAINING   Adult learning theory has important implications for trainers at every stage of the training process including needs analysis, training design and delivery, and evaluation. The design and instruction of training programs and learning should be the joint responsibility of the trainer and trainees. See The Trainer's Notebook, "Implications of Adult Learning Theory for Training" to learn more about the practical implications of adult learning theory for training and development.

Andragogy

An adult-oriented approach to learning that takes into account the differences between adult and child learners

Pedagogy

The traditional approach to learning used to educate children and youth

Implications of Adult Learning Theory for Training

- Adults need to know why they are learning.
- Adults should have some input into the planning and instruction of training programs.
- Adults should be involved in the needs analysis and have input into things such as training content and methods.
- The designers of training programs should consider the needs and interests of trainees.
- The training content should be meaningful and relevant to trainees' work-related needs and problems.

- Trainers should be aware of trainees' experiences and use them as examples.
- Adults can learn independently, and may prefer to do so.
- Adults are motivated by both intrinsic and extrinsic rewards.
- Adults should be given safe practice opportunities.

Theories of Motivation

Learning and the success of a training program are also a function of people's motivation. Motivation is an important predictor of performance and, as you will learn shortly, it is also a key factor for learning and training. First, it is important to understand what motivation is, the major theories of motivation, and the implications of motivational theories for training and development.

Motivation refers to the degree of persistent effort that one directs toward a goal. Motivation has to do with effort or how hard one works; persistence or the extent to which one keeps at a task; and direction, or the extent to which one applies effort and persistence towards a meaningful goal. In organizations, this usually means that one directs one's effort and persistence towards organization goals or in a manner that benefits the organization, such as high productivity or excellent customer service.

There are two forms of motivation: extrinsic and intrinsic motivation. **Extrinsic motivation** is associated with factors in the external environment such as pay, fringe benefits, and company policies. These are motivators that are applied by somebody in the work environment such as a supervisor. **Intrinsic motivation** is the result of a direct relationship between a worker and the task. Unlike extrinsic motivation, it is self-applied and includes feelings of achievement, accomplishment, challenge, and competence that are the result of performing a task or one's job.

Theories of motivation can be described as need theories or process theories. Need theories have to do with the things that motivate people and the conditions in which they will be motivated to satisfy them.

Process theories of motivation address the process of motivation and how motivation occurs. In the remainder of this section, we will describe need theories of motivation as well as two process theories of motivation (expectancy theory and goal setting theory).

Motivation

The degree of persistent effort that one directs toward a goal

Extrinsic motivation

Motivation that stems from factors in the external environment such as pay, fringe benefits, and company policies

Intrinsic motivation

Motivation that stems from a direct relationship between a worker and the task

Need Theories

Need theories of motivation are concerned with the needs people have and the conditions in which they will be motivated to satisfy them. Needs refer to physiological and psychological desires. In organizations, individuals can satisfy their needs by obtaining incentives such as money to satisfy physiological needs, or by challenging work that allows them to fulfill higher level psychological needs. Therefore, needs are motivational to the extent that people are motivated to obtain things that will satisfy their needs.

Maslow's Need Hierarchy

The best known theory of motivation is Abraham Maslow's need hierarchy. According to Maslow, humans have five sets of needs that are arranged in a hierarchy with the most basic needs at the bottom of the hierarchy and higher order needs at the upper levels of the hierarchy. The five needs from lowest to highest are physiological, safety, belongingness, esteem, and self-actualization needs.[26]

Physiological needs are needs that people must satisfy to survive and include things such as food, water, and shelter. Physiological needs can usually be satisfied with pay. Safety needs refer to needs for security, stability, and freedom from anxiety. Safe working conditions and job security can satisfy safety needs. Belongingness needs have to do with the need for social interaction, companionship, and friendship. The opportunity to interact with others at work and friendly and supportive co-workers and supervision can satisfy belongingness needs. Esteem needs have to do with feelings of competence and appreciation and recognition by others. The opportunity to learn new things and challenging work can satisfy esteem needs.

The highest need in Maslow's hierarchy is self-actualization. Self-actualization involves developing one's true potential as an individual and experiencing personal fulfillment. This can be fulfilled by work experiences that involve opportunities for creativity, growth, and self-development.

According to Maslow, people are motivated to satisfy their lowest level unsatisfied need. If one's physiological need is unsatisfied, then one will be motivated to satisfy it. The basic premise is that the lowest level unsatisfied need has the greatest motivating potential, which means that motivation depends on one's position in the need hierarchy. Once a need has been satisfied it will no longer be motivational and the next highest need in the hierarchy will become motivational. The one exception to this is the self-actualization need, which becomes stronger.[27]

Alderfer's ERG Theory

Another need theory of motivation was developed by Clayton Alderfer. Alderfer's ERG theory consists of three needs. Existence needs are similar to Maslow's physiological and safety needs. Relatedness needs are similar to Maslow's belongingness need. And growth needs are similar to Maslow's esteem and self-actualization needs.[28]

Alderfer's ERG theory differs from Maslow's need theory in a number of ways. To begin with, ERG theory is not a rigid hierarchy of needs in which one must move up the hierarchy in a lock-step fashion. Although both theories argue that once a lower level need is satisfied the desire for higher level needs will increase, ERG theory does not state that a lower level need must be gratified before a higher level need becomes motivational. Thus, one can be motivated to fulfill relatedness or growth needs even if they have not fulfilled their existence needs. Maslow, however, would argue that a lower need must first be satisfied before a higher level need will become motivational.

Another difference is that ERG theory states that if individuals are unable to satisfy a higher level need, the desire to satisfy a lower level need will increase. Maslow of course would say that this is not possible because once a need has been satisfied it is no longer motivational.

IMPLICATIONS FOR TRAINING   Regardless of their differences, both Maslow's and Alderfer's need theories have important implications for training and development. They highlight the fact that employees' needs must be considered in the design of a training program. For example, if trainees' needs are not being fulfilled on the job then their behaviour and performance are not likely to change as a result of a training program unless the training program leads to need fulfillment. Improving employees' knowledge and skill through training and development will be most effective when employees are motivated on the job.

Another implication of need theories for training and development has to do with employees' motivation to attend a training program, to learn the training material, and to apply it on the job. Employees are not likely to be motivated to attend training or to learn and apply the training material if doing so does not fulfill their needs. Therefore, trainers and managers should be aware of trainees' needs and ensure that training programs are designed in part to fulfill them.

Expectancy Theory

Expectancy theory is a process theory of motivation. According to expectancy theory, the energy or force that a person directs toward an activity is a direct result of a number of factors. These factors are known as expectancy, instrumentality, and valence:[29]

1. Expectancy refers to an individual's subjective probability that they can achieve a particular level of performance on a task. For example, what is the probability that you can get an "A" in this course? What is the probability that you can get a "C" in this course? These outcomes are referred to as first-level outcomes since they are a direct result of one's effort or motivational force.
2. Instrumentality refers to the subjective likelihood that attainment of a first-level outcome such as an "A" or "C" in this course will lead to attractive consequences that are known as second-level outcomes.

The consequences can be either intrinsic or extrinsic outcomes. For example, what is the probability that an "A" in this course will result in a job offer or a sense of accomplishment? What is the probability that a "C" will result in a job offer or a sense of accomplishment?

3. Valence refers to the attractiveness of the first- and second-level outcomes. The attractiveness of a second-level outcome such as a job offer or a sense of accomplishment is simply one's subjective ratings. For example, on a scale of 1 to 10 with 10 being the most attractive, how attractive would you rate receiving a job offer? The valence or attractiveness of a first level outcome (an "A" or "C" grade in this course) is a result of the instrumentalities multiplied by the valence of each second-level outcome ($I \times V$). For example, the attractiveness of receiving an "A" in this course would be a function of:

$$(I \times V \text{ of receiving a job offer}) + (I \times V \text{ of experiencing a sense of accomplishment})$$

This calculation will determine the valence or attractiveness of the first-level outcome (receiving an "A" in this course). The same calculation would also be done to determine the valence of receiving a grade of "C" in the course.

To determine one's motivation or effort, the expectancy or probability of receiving an "A" or "C" grade must be multiplied by the valence of the first-level outcomes. This would result in a force or motivational value for pursuing an "A" and a "C" grade. In other words, it will indicate what grade you are most motivated to attain. If you feel that you can put in the effort and time required to obtain an "A" (i.e., your expectancy), and you believe that obtaining an "A" will result in a high probability of getting a job offer and experiencing a sense of accomplishment (instrumentality), then chances are you will be motivated to get an "A" in the course.

The expectancy theory linkages can be written as the following equation:

$$\text{Effort} = \text{Expectancy} \times (\text{Instrumentality} \times \text{Valence})$$

In effect, what all this means is that people's effort or motivation is a function of their beliefs that they can achieve a particular level of performance (first-level outcome), and that this will lead to consequences that are attractive to them (the valence of the first-level outcome). The attractiveness of a first-level outcome is simply the probability that it will lead to attractive consequences (e.g., the probability that getting an "A" in the course will result in a job offer and a sense of fulfillment). Thus, you are likely to be motivated to obtain an "A" in this course if you believe that there is a high probability that you can get an "A" and if you believe that getting an "A" will lead to consequences that are attractive to you.

IMPLICATIONS FOR TRAINING   There are a number of implications of expectancy theory for training and development. First, trainees must believe that there is a high probability that they will be able to learn the training material and fulfill the training objective(s) (high expectancy). Second, learning the training material and fulfilling the training objectives must result in consequences (high instrumentality) that are attractive to trainees (high valence of second-level outcomes). Simply put, you are more likely to learn something if you believe that you can in fact learn it and that you will be rewarded with something that is attractive to you once it has been learned.

The major implication of expectancy theory for training revolves around trainees' motivation to attend a training program, to learn, and to apply what is learned on the job. Along these lines, trainees must believe that there is a high probability that they will be able to learn and apply the training material, and that doing so will result in attractive consequences for them.

Goal-Setting Theory

Another process theory of motivation, with implications for training and development, is goal-setting theory. Goal-setting theory is based on the idea that people's intentions are a good predictor of their behaviour.

According to the theory, goals are motivational because they direct people's efforts and energies and lead to the development of strategies to help them reach their goals. For goals to be motivational, however, they must have a number of characteristics.

First, goals must be *specific* in terms of their level and time frame. General goals that lack specificity tend not to be motivational. Second, goals must be *challenging* to be motivational. Goals should not be so easy that they require little effort to achieve, and they should not be so difficult that they are impossible to reach. Third, goals must be accompanied by *feedback* so that it is possible to know how well one is doing and how close one is to goal accomplishment. Finally, for goals to be motivational, people must accept them and be *committed* to them.[30]

Research on goal-setting theory has provided strong support for the motivational effects of goals. Studies across a wide variety of settings have consistently shown that challenging and specific goals that are accompanied with performance feedback result in higher levels of individual and group performance.[31]

IMPLICATIONS FOR TRAINING   Goal-setting theory has a number of implications for training. For example, prior to a training program trainees should have specific and challenging goals for learning, and they should be provided with feedback during and after the training program so that they know if they have accomplished their goals. Setting specific and challenging goals should improve trainees' motivation to learn as well as their performance on the training task. However, recall from earlier in the chapter that setting goals for performance during the declarative stage of learning can actually be detrimental for learning. Therefore, special attention needs to be given to the stage at which goals are set. It is also important to distinguish between a learning goal and a performance goal, a topic that we now turn to.

Goal Orientation

Another important characteristic of goals is the type of goal or what is known as goal orientation. There are two general types of goal orientations—a mastery or learning goal and a performance goal orientation.

Mastery goals are process-oriented and focus on the learning process. They enhance understanding of the task and the use of task strategies. **Performance goals** are outcome-oriented goals that focus attention on the achievement of specific performance outcomes.

Goal orientation is important because it can influence task performance as well as cognitive, affective, and motivational processes. There is evidence that the type of goal set (i.e., mastery versus performance) affects skill acquisition and self-efficacy. Mastery goals appear to lead to faster skill acquisition and task self-efficacy.[32]

There is also evidence that individuals differ with respect to their goal orientation or goal preference. In other words, goal orientation has been found to be a stable individual difference such that some individuals have a preference for mastery goals while others have a preference for performance goals. Individuals with a mastery goal orientation are most concerned about developing competence by acquiring new skills and mastering new situations. Individuals with a performance goal orientation are more concerned about demonstrating their competence by seeking favourable judgments and avoiding negative judgments.

Research has found that a mastery goal orientation is especially important for performance and leads to higher performance compared to a performance goal orientation. One study on the salespeople of a medical supplies distributor found that a mastery goal orientation was positively related to sales performance but a performance goal orientation was not. A mastery goal orientation has also been found to be positively related to effort, self-efficacy, and goal-setting level. Thus, mastery goals appear to be important for motivation and learning outcomes.[33]

IMPLICATIONS FOR TRAINING Research on goal orientation suggests that trainers should consider the goal orientation of trainees and the type of goals that are set for training. Mastery goals that focus on skill development appear to be particularly important for learning, especially for individuals who have a performance goal orientation and need to be assigned learning goals for training. Although individuals tend to differ in their preference for a mastery or performance goal, it is possible to influence goal orientation. Therefore, trainers should emphasize the importance and need to focus on mastery goals during training. High mastery goals appear to be especially important for challenging tasks and when new skills must be learned.[34]

Training Motivation

In the previous section, we described a number of theories of motivation and their implications for training and development. In this section, we focus more specifically on the role of motivation in training. In particular, we

---

Mastery goals

Process-oriented goals that focus on the learning process

Performance goals

Outcome-oriented goals that focus attention on the achievement of specific performance outcomes

Managing Performance Through Training and Development

introduce the concept of *training motivation* and describe both the predictors and consequences of trainees' motivation to learn.

Training motivation (or what is also known as motivation to learn) refers to the direction, intensity, and persistence of learning-directed behaviour in training contexts. Research has found that training motivation predicts learning and training outcomes and is influenced by individual and situational factors.[35]

Among the individual factors that predict training motivation, personality variables as well as factors associated with one's job and career are important. Personality variables that predict training motivation include locus of control, achievement motivation, anxiety, and conscientiousness.

Locus of control refers to people's beliefs about whether their behaviour is controlled mainly by internal or external forces. Persons with an internal locus of control believe that the opportunity to control their own behaviour resides within themselves. Persons with an external locus of control believe that external forces determine their behaviour. Thus, internals perceive stronger links between the effort they put into something and the outcome or performance level they achieve. Persons with an internal locus of control tend to have higher levels of training motivation.

In addition, persons who are high in achievement motivation or the desire to perform challenging tasks and are high on conscientiousness also tend to have high training motivation. Persons with higher anxiety, however, tend to have lower training motivation. Self-efficacy is also positively related to training motivation.

Several job and career variables are also related to training motivation. For example, employees with higher job involvement or the degree to which an individual identifies psychologically with work and the importance of work to their self-image have higher training motivation. Organizational commitment and career planning and exploration are also associated with higher training motivation. Organizational factors such as supervisor support, peer support, and a positive climate also predict training motivation.

Training motivation is important because it is related to a number of training outcomes. For example, training motivation is positively related to declarative knowledge and skill acquisition. It is also related to trainees' reactions to training and the likelihood that trainees apply what they learn in training on the job.

IMPLICATIONS FOR TRAINING There are at least two things a trainer can do to ensure that trainees' motivation to learn is high. First, they can assess trainee motivation prior to a training program. In fact, this is what the auto finance company AmeriCredit does. Employees complete a motivation questionnaire that is used to predict their likelihood of success in learning from a training program.[36] Second, trainers and managers can try to increase trainees' motivation to learn by demonstrating the importance and relevance of training for their job performance.

In summary, training motivation is an important factor in the training process. Training is more likely to be effective and result in learning, skill

Training motivation
The direction, intensity, and persistence of learning-directed behaviour in training contexts

Locus of control
People's beliefs about whether their behaviour is controlled mainly by internal or external forces

acquisition, and improved job performance when trainees are motivated to learn.[37] Thus, it is important that trainers understand the importance of training motivation and increase trainees' motivation to learn early in the training process.

A Model of Training Effectiveness

In this final section of the chapter, we present a model of training effectiveness that highlights the linkages between training and learning as well as between learning and individual performance and organizational effectiveness.

Figure 3.2 presents a model of training effectiveness. Recall from Chapter 1 that training involves the acquisition of knowledge, skills, and abilities to improve performance on one's current job, and development refers to the acquisition of knowledge, skills, and abilities required to perform future job responsibilities. Thus, the first important link in the model is a path from training to learning and retention. In other words, training leads to declarative knowledge and the acquisition of skills and abilities and the retention of them over time.

In addition to training, we also know that there are personal factors that influence learning. Among the most important is **cognitive ability**, which is one of the most often examined individual characteristics in training research. Cognitive or mental ability is similar to intelligence. It reflects an individual's basic information processing capacities and cognitive resources. It generally refers to the knowledge and skills an individual possesses and may include

Cognitive ability

An individual's basic information processing capacities and cognitive resources

FIGURE 3.2

Model of Training Effectiveness

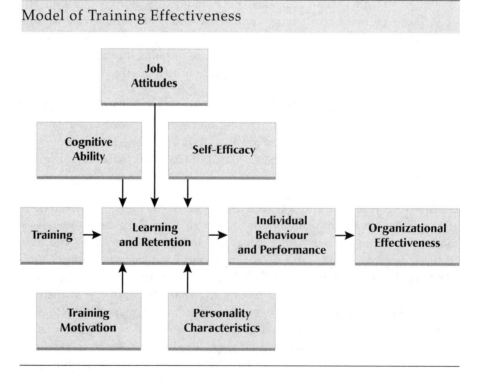

cognitive skills and psychomotor skills. Examples of cognitive skills include basic numeracy and literacy, the intelligence to learn complex rules and procedures, and so on. Cognitive ability (verbal comprehension, quantitative ability, and reasoning ability) is related to the ability to learn and to succeed on the job.

Recall the earlier discussion of ACT theory in which it was noted that cognitive ability is particularly important during the early stages of learning. In fact, research has consistently shown that general cognitive ability is a strong predictor of learning, training success, and job performance. It is an especially good predictor of job performance on complex jobs. In training research, cognitive ability has been found to predict declarative knowledge, skill acquisition, and the application of trained skills on the job.[38]

In addition to cognitive ability, training motivation is also a strong predictor of learning and training outcomes. Like cognitive ability, training motivation predicts declarative knowledge, skill acquisition, and the application of trained skills on the job. Self-efficacy and personality characteristics also have an effect on learning. Trainees with higher self-efficacy are more likely to learn during training. In addition, trainees with an internal locus of control and a high need for achievement also learn more during training.

An additional factor that can influence learning is trainees' attitudes. Three attitudinal variables that are important for learning are job involvement, job satisfaction, and organizational commitment. Employees with higher job involvement, job satisfaction, and organizational commitment are more likely to learn and apply what they learn on the job.[39]

The model also shows a path from learning to individual behaviour and performance. This is called transfer of training and refers to the application of learning on the job. Employees must first learn and retain training content in order to change their behaviour and improve their job performance.

The final path in the model is between individual behaviour and performance and organizational effectiveness. This path indicates that employees' behaviour and job performance have an effect on organizational effectiveness. In other words, more effective employee behaviours and higher job performance will result in a more effective organization.

In summary, the model of training effectiveness shows how training and personal factors influence learning and retention. We will further develop the model in Chapter 5 when we discuss training design and again in Chapter 10 when we discuss the transfer of training.

Summary

We began this chapter by stating that a major goal of all training and development is learning. We also described five learning outcomes that can result from training and development programs. The learning process was described in terms of three stages (declarative, knowledge compilation, and procedural knowledge) and Kolb's learning styles were also discussed. Two major theories of learning (conditioning theory and social learning theory) as well as adult learning theory were described along with their implications for training and development. This chapter also described need theories and process theories of motivation and their implications for training. Training motivation was also discussed, with particular emphasis on its predictors and consequences. The chapter concluded with a model of training effectiveness that shows the links between training, personal factors, and attitudes with learning and retention, individual behaviour and performance, and organizational effectiveness.

Key Terms

andragogy (page 70)
chaining (page 67)
cognitive ability (page 78)
declarative knowledge (page 62)
extrinsic motivation (page 71)
generalization (page 67)
intrinsic motivation (page 71)
knowledge compilation (page 62)
learning (page 61)
learning style (page 63)
locus of control (page 77)

mastery goals (page 76)
motivation (page 71)
observation (page 68)
pedagogy (page 70)
performance goals (page 76)
procedural knowledge (page 63)
self-efficacy (page 68)
self-management (page 69)
shaping (page 66)
training motivation (page 77)

Weblinks

Capital One: www.capitalone.com (page 64)

Edward Jones: www.edwardjones.com (page 68)

RPC Icons

RPC 3.1 Ensures the application of appropriate development methods and techniques based upon generally accepted principles of adult learning.

Discussion Questions

1. Given the importance of motivation for learning and other training outcomes, what should trainers do to ensure that trainees are motivated to learn? Discuss the pros and cons of different approaches.
2. What are the differences between pedagogy and andragogy and what are the implications of adult learning theory for the design of training programs?
3. Discuss Kolb's four learning styles and the implications of them for the design of training programs. How should training programs be designed if people differ in their learning styles?
4. What are the sources of information that influence self-efficacy? How can trainers improve trainees' self-efficacy?

5. What are the three stages of learning according to ACT theory? Give an example of how a training program might be designed according to ACT theory.
6. If an instructor of one of your courses wanted to maximize student learning, what should he/she do according to conditioning theory, social learning theory, and adult learning theory? If he/she wanted to motivate students to attend class and learn, what should he/she do according to need theories, expectancy theory, and goal-setting theory?

The Great Training Debate

1. Debate the following: Given that cognitive ability is a strong predictor of learning, only trainees with high cognitive ability should be allowed to attend training programs, since those with low cognitive ability are not likely to learn and benefit from costly training programs.

Using the Internet

1. Learn about your learning and motivation styles, by visiting the Learnativity website at **www.learnativity.com**. To find out your preferred learning style, click on "Assessments" under "Good Reading" on the home page and then click on "Learning Styles Assessment" and complete the assessment. To find out about your motivation style, click on "Motivation Styles Assessment" and complete the assessment. Write a brief report in which you indicate your primary and auxiliary learning style, and your primary and auxiliary motivation style. What do your results say about your learning and motivation preferences, and what are the implications of this for your learning? What can you do with this information to improve your learning?

Exercises

In-Class

1. If you had a friend who was about to attend a training program on how to use computers and she had very low self-efficacy about her ability to learn and use a computer, what would you do to increase her self-efficacy? Describe some of the things you might do prior to the training program to increase your friend's self-efficacy to learn to use a computer.
2. Consider Kolb's four learning modes and how they might apply to your course on training and development or another course you are taking. How might you structure the course so that students' learning occurs in the following sequence of experiences: concrete experience, reflective observation, abstract conceptualization, and active experimentation? Be specific in terms of what the instructor will have students do at each stage of the learning cycle.

3. Using the material on goal-setting theory, set a goal for your training and development course. That is, set a specific and challenging goal that you will be committed to. In addition, determine how and when you will be able to obtain feedback. Be sure to also set a mastery goal and a performance goal. Once you have set your goals, meet with another member of the class and review and evaluate each other's goals for the course.

4. Consider a course you are currently taking and examine it in terms of adult learning theory. To what extent does your course incorporate the principles of adult learning theory? What aspects of the course incorporate adult learning theory and what aspects do not? If you were to redesign the course to make it more consistent with adult learning theory, what are some of the things you would change and do?

5. Training motivation is an important predictor of training outcomes so it is important that trainers ensure that trainees' motivation to learn is high. You might have noticed how your own motivation to learn influences your performance in a course or training program. Using each of the theories of motivation (Maslow, Alderfer, expectancy, and goal setting), describe what a course instructor or trainer might do to increase students' or trainees' motivation to learn. Be specific in describing the techniques that follow from each theory.

6. Review the model of training effectiveness in Figure 3.2. Assess your potential learning and retention of a course you are currently taking by evaluating yourself as best you can on each of the predictors in the model (i.e., cognitive ability, attitudes, self-efficacy, personality characteristics, and training motivation). Based on your assessment, how successful will your learning and retention of the course material be? What predictors can you try to change in order to enhance your learning and retention of the course material?

7. Review the material on self-management in the chapter and then design a self-management training program to help you learn and improve a skill or behaviour that you want to improve (i.e., making presentations, time management, exercising, quitting smoking, etc.). Once you have chosen a skill or behaviour, prepare a self-management program. Be specific in terms of what exactly you are going to do at each step in the process (i.e., how and when you will observe and keep track of your behaviour and observe the behaviour of others; set specific performance goals; when you will practise and rehearse the desired behaviours; how you will keep track of your progress; and how you will reward yourself for goal achievement). Once you have prepared your program, meet with another member of the class to review and evaluate each other's self-management program.

In-the-Field

1. Contact the human resource department of your own or another organization in order to discuss the organization's training programs. In particular, try to find out the extent to which aspects of conditioning theory, social learning theory, and adult learning theory are used to improve trainees' learning, and the extent to which aspects of need theories,

expectancy theory, and goal-setting theory are used to motivate trainees to attend training programs and learn from them. What aspects of these theories are being used for training and what can the HR department do to improve trainee learning and motivation?

Case Incident

Management at IKEA

IKEA is a Sweden-based home furnishings chain with stores in Canada and the United States. A single store can have 40 managers, making the task of training enough new managers quickly and well a challenge. So to get managers trained for new store openings, IKEA has established certain stores as centres of excellence. These centres of excellence become learning sites for one or more management competencies that managers must master.

Manager trainees have a carefully developed, objectives-based curriculum and access to a 17-module online learning program that covers the basics of each of nine management competencies. Once a trainee has mastered the learning material as well as a series of practicum assignments, he or she is eligible to be certified as successful by the competence centre store manager. Trainees can be at a competence centre for two to six weeks depending on the competency to be mastered and number of competencies to be mastered at each centre. Part of the process involves shadowing successful managers. This is followed by two weeks of classroom training at IKEA Business College where managers are introduced to the philosophies and theories behind IKEA store operations. They get exposed to the "big picture," the theory of how the company operates, and what the IKEA vision is all about. Six months after a location opens, managers begin rotating back to Business College for advanced store operations training.

Questions

1. What learning outcomes are the focus of the IKEA manager training program? What do managers learn and how do they learn it?
2. Comment on the stages of learning as well as Kolb's learning styles, modes, and cycle with respect to the manager training program.

Source: Zemke, R. (2004, March). Training Top 100: Editor's Choice: IKEA U.S.A, *Training, 41* (3), 70. V N U Business Publications. This work is protected by copyright and it is being used with the permission of Access Copyright. Any alteration of its content or further copying in any form whatsoever is strictly prohibited.

Case

The Performance Appraisal Training Program

Although the performance appraisal process is an important part of employee evaluation and development, many organizations do not conduct performance appraisals and managers tend to not like doing them. This was the case at a large hospital where nurse supervisors seldom met with nurses to review and discuss their performance. At the same time, the administration was introducing a new model of nursing that required the nurses to perform certain critical behaviours when interacting with and counseling patients and their families. It was therefore imperative that performance appraisals be conducted to ensure that nurses were implementing the new model of nursing.

The administration decided to hire a performance management consultant to provide a one-day workshop on how to conduct performance appraisals for all nurse supervisors. The nurse supervisors would be required to evaluate their nurses' performance every six months and then conduct a performance appraisal interview with each nurse in which the previous six months' performance would be discussed. An action plan would then be developed with specific goals for improvement.

Many of the supervisors seldom conducted performance appraisal interviews and some had never done one. They complained that there was no time to meet with every nurse and that it was a difficult and unpleasant process that was a waste of time. Some were uncomfortable with the process and found it to be very stressful for everybody concerned. They said that it caused a lot of anxiety for them and the nurses.

Nonetheless, the training program was mandatory and all nurse supervisors had to attend. Many of them reluctantly did so complaining that it would be a waste of time and that it would not make any difference in how things were done in the hospital.

The training program began with a lecture about how to conduct performance appraisal interviews. The consultant first explained that the purpose of a performance appraisal interview is to give feedback to employees on how well they are performing their jobs and then plan for future growth and development. He then discussed different types of performance appraisal interviews such as the "tell-and-sell interview," the "tell-and-listen interview," and the "problem-solving interview." This was followed by a list of guidelines on how to conduct effective interviews such as asking the employee to do a self-assessment, focus on behaviour not the person, minimize criticism, focus on problem-solving, and be supportive. The trainees were then instructed on how to set goals and develop an action plan for improvement.

After the lecture, the trainees were asked to conduct role plays in which they take turns playing the part of a supervisor and employee. They were provided with information about a nurse's job performance and had to discuss it in the role play and then develop an action plan. However, some of the trainees left the session, refusing to participate. Others did not take it seriously and made a joke out it. There was a lot of laughing and joking throughout this part of the program.

After the role play there was a group discussion about the role-play experience and this was followed by a review of the key points to remember when conducting performance appraisal interviews.

Although the supervisors were supposed to begin conducting performance appraisal interviews shortly after the training program, very few actually did. Some said they tried to do them but could not find time to interview all of their nurses. Others said that they followed the consultant's guidelines but they did not see any improvement in how they conducted interviews or in how nurses reacted to them. Some said it continued to be a stressful experience that was uncomfortable for them and their nurses and decided to stop doing them.

One year later, performance appraisal interviews were still a rare occurrence at the hospital. Furthermore, many of the nurses were not practising the new nursing model and as a result, nursing care was inconsistent throughout the hospital and often unsatisfactory.

Questions

1. Consider Gagné's learning outcomes for the performance appraisal interview training program. What were some of the expected learning outcomes of the training program and what did trainees learn?
2. Explain the success of the training program using conditioning theory and social learning theory. How do these theories explain why the training program was not more effective? How could the program be improved using some of the concepts from each theory?
3. Discuss the extent to which adult learning principles were incorporated into the training program. What principles were included and which ones were absent? What could the consultant have done differently to make better use of adult learning theory?
4. Evaluate the training program in terms of Kolb's learning styles and learning cycle. What aspects of the program relate to each of the modes of learning? What learning style or styles are most likely to benefit from the program and which ones are not? How could the program be changed to make better use of Kolb's learning cycle?
5. Comment on the supervisors' motivation to learn. What effect might their motivation to learn have had on the success of the training program? Using the different theories of motivation, explain how the hospital administration and the consultant might have increased the supervisors' motivation to learn.

References

1. Schettler, J. (2002, August). Welcome to ACME Inc. *Training, 39* (8), pp. 36–43.
2. Hinrichs, J. R. (1976). Personnel training. In M. D. Dunnette (Ed.), *Handbook of industrial and organizational psychology* (pp. 829–60). Skokie, IL: Rand McNally.
3. Hinrichs, J. R. (1976).
4. Gagné, R. M. (1984). Learning outcomes and their effects: Useful categories of human performance. *American Psychologist 39*, 377–85.
5. Zemke, R. (1999). Toward a science of training. *Training 36* (7), 32–36.
6. Kanfer, R., & Ackerman, P. L. (1989). Motivation and cognitive abilities: An integrative/aptitude-treatment interaction approach to skill acquisition. *Journal of Applied Psychology, 74*, 657–90.
7. Kanfer, R., & Ackerman, P. L. (1989).
8. Kolb, D. A. (1984). *Experiential learning*. Englewood Cliffs, NJ: Prentice-Hall.
9. Kolb, D. A. (1984).
10. Kolb, D. A. (1984).

11. Whetten, D. A., & Cameron, K. S. (2002). *Developing management skills* (5th ed.). Upper Saddle River, NJ: Prentice Hall.

12. Delahoussaye, M. (2001, March). Training top 50: Capital One. *Training, 38* (3), 70–71.

13. Skinner, B. F. (1953). *Science and human behaviour.* New York: McMillan.

14. Delahoussaye, M. (2001, March).

15. Pearce, J. M. (1987). A model of stimulus generalization in Pavlovian conditioning. *Psychological Review, 94*, 61–73.

16. Bandura, A. (1986). *Social foundations of thought and action: A social cognitive theory.* Englewood Cliffs, NJ: Prentice-Hall.

17. Luthans, F., & Davis, T. (1983). Beyond modelling: Managing social learning processes in human resource training and development. In C. Baird, E. Schneier, & D. Laird (Eds.), *The training and development sourcebook.* Amherst, MA: Human Resource Development Press.

18. McLaughlin, K. (2001, March). Training top 50: Edward Jones. *Training, 38* (3), 78–79.

19. Bandura, A. (1997). *Self-efficacy: The exercise of control.* New York: W.H. Freeman & Co.

20. Bandura, A. (1997).

21. Haccoun, R. R., & Saks, A. M. (1998). Training in the twenty-first century: Some lessons from the last one. *Canadian Psychology, 39*, 33–51.

22. Bandura, A. (1986).

23. Frayne, C. A., & Latham, G. P. (1987). Application of social learning theory to employee self-management of attendance. *Journal of Applied Psychology, 72*, 387–92. Latham, G. P., & Frayne, C. A. (1989). Self-management training for increasing job attendance: A follow-up and a replication. *Journal of Applied Psychology, 74*, 411–16.

24. Gist, M. E., Stevens, C. K., & Bavetta, A. G. (1991). Effects of self-efficacy and post-training intervention on the acquisition and maintenance of complex interpersonal skills. *Personnel Psychology, 44*, 837–61.

25. Knowles, M. (1990). *The adult learner.* Gulf Publishing: Houston, TX.

26. Maslow. A. H. (1970). *Motivation and personality* (2nd ed.). New York: Harper & Row.

27. Maslow. A. H. (1970).

28. Alderfer, C. P. (1969). An empirical test of a new theory of human needs. *Organizational Behavior and Human Performance, 4*, 142–75.

29. Vroom. V. H. (1964). *Work and motivation.* New York: Wiley.

30. Locke, E. A., & Latham, G. P. (1990). *A theory of goal setting and task performance.* Englewood Cliffs, NJ: Prentice–Hall.

31. Locke, E. A., & Latham, G. P. (1990).

32. Cannon-Bowers, J. A., Rhodenizer, L., Salas, E., & Bowers, C. A. (1998). A framework for understanding pre-practice conditions and their impact on learning. *Personnel Psychology, 51*, 291–320.

33. VandeWalle, D., Cron, W. L., & Slocum, J. W. Jr. (2001). The role of goal orientation following performance feedback. *Journal of Applied Psychology, 86*, 629–40.

34. VandeWalle, D., Brown, S. P., Cron, W. L., & Slocum, J. W. Jr. (1999). The influence of goal orientation and self-regulation tactics on sales performance: A longitudinal field test. *Journal of Applied Psychology, 84*, 249–259. VandeWalle, D., Cron, W. L., & Slocum, J. W. Jr. (2001).

35. Colquitt, J. A., Lepine, A., & Noe, R. A. (2000). Toward an integrative theory of training motivation: A meta-analytic path analysis of 20 years of research. *Journal of Applied Psychology, 85*, 678–707.

36. Barbian, J. (2002, March). Training top 100: AmeriCredit. *Training, 39* (3), 46–47.

37. Colquitt, J. A., Lepine, A., & Noe, R. A. (2000).

38. Colquitt, J. A., Lepine, A., & Noe, R. A. (2000).

39. Burke, L. A. (2001). Training transfer: Ensuring training gets used on the job. In L. A. Burke (Ed.), *High-impact training solutions: Top issues troubling trainers.* Quorum Books: Westport, CT. Colquitt, J. A., Lepine, A., & Noe, R. A. (2000).

Chapter 4

The Needs-Analysis Process

Chapter Learning Objectives

After reading this chapter, you should be able to:

- define needs analysis and describe the needs-analysis process
- define and explain how to conduct an organizational, task, and person analysis
- define and describe the purpose of a cognitive task analysis and a team task analysis
- describe the process of determining if training is the best solution to performance problems
- describe the different methods and sources for conducting a needs analysis
- describe the obstacles to conducting a needs analysis and how to overcome them

www.att.com

AT&T BUSINESS SERVICES

Several years ago, AT&T Business Services realized the need for a new business strategy in response to changes in the telecommunications industry as well as competitive pressures. The company determined that it needed to become more dominant in a non-traditional market segment. This was deemed to be of enormous importance to the company. In fact, the company's executive team acknowledged that this shift was a critical factor to survival in the industry.

To succeed, the company's account executives would have to generate new leads in a critical new business segment and improve their productivity. However, this would require different types of selling skills and knowledge about specific products and services. The company's Learning Services Group was approached to provide the training required to support the new strategy. However, it was not entirely clear what type of training was required. Line managers speculated that current sales were lacking in the new segment because account executives could not identify sales opportunities.

To be certain of the training required for the account executives, an in-depth needs analysis was conducted and the findings confirmed the need for training that focused on identifying and generating sales opportunities. A training program was then designed that targeted about 2000 account executives and 200 of their sales managers. The program focused on the account executives' lead-generation performance.

After the program was implemented, a comparison between account executives who had attended the program and those who had not attended indicated that participants in the program had 62 percent more leads in products and services over non-participants. The company estimated that the projected revenue from these additional leads was $4.8 million U.S. with a return on investment (ROI) of 168 percent.[1]

This vignette highlights an important aspect of the training and development process. In particular, it shows how a new business strategy has important implications for training and development, and how a needs analysis is required to determine who needs training and what type of training they need. It also shows how training is often necessary to improve productivity and a company's success. As you can tell from this case, needs analysis is a critical first step in the training and development process. In this chapter, you will learn about the needs-analysis process and how to determine if training is the best solution to performance problems.

What Is a Needs Analysis?

Needs analysis (also known as needs assessment) is the cornerstone and foundation of training and development. In fact, it is often referred to as the most important step in the training and development process.[2] **Needs analysis** is a process designed to identify gaps or deficiencies in employee and organizational performance. Needs analysis is concerned with the gaps between actual performance and desired performance. It is a "formal process of identifying needs as gaps between current and desired results, placing those needs in priority order based on the cost to meet each need versus the cost for ignoring it, and selecting the most important needs (problems or opportunities) for reduction or elimination."[3]

Needs analysis helps to identify gaps or deficiencies in individual, group, or organizational performance. The way to identify performance gaps is to solicit information from those who are affected by the performance problem. A needs analyst gathers information from key people in an organization about the organization, jobs, and employees to determine the nature of performance problems. This information identifies the problem, which is simply the difference between the way the work is being done and the most cost-effective way of doing it. In the simplest terms, needs = required results − current results.[4]

The goal of needs analysis is to identify the differences between what is and what is desired or required in terms of results, and to compare the magnitude of gaps against the cost of reducing them or ignoring them. Obviously, performance gaps could be the result of many factors, and the solutions might include training as well as other interventions. A thorough needs analysis can help an organization prioritize its needs and make informed decisions as to what problems need to be resolved. Thus, needs analysis identifies, prioritizes, and selects needs that will have an impact on internal and external stakeholders.[5] Needs analysis helps to identify the causes and solutions to performance problems.

Needs analysis

A process to identify gaps or deficiencies in employee and organizational performance

The Needs-Analysis Process

RPC 4.1

Needs analysis is a process that consists of a series of interrelated steps. Figure 4.1 outlines the needs-analysis process that we will be discussing in this chapter. As described in Chapter 1, the process starts with an *itch* or a problem. If the performance problem is important, stakeholders are consulted and a needs analysis is conducted. There are three levels of needs analysis: an organizational analysis, a task analysis, and a person analysis. The collection of information and the needs-analysis process concludes with a number of important outcomes.

Step One: A Concern

The process of identifying training needs originates slowly and informally with a concern. This concern is sometimes referred to as an *itch* or a *pressure point*, something that causes managers to notice it. This concern might be as subtle as noticing that employees are treating customers in an abrupt manner, or observing that employees are spending a lot of time asking one another for

FIGURE 4.1

The Needs-Analysis Process

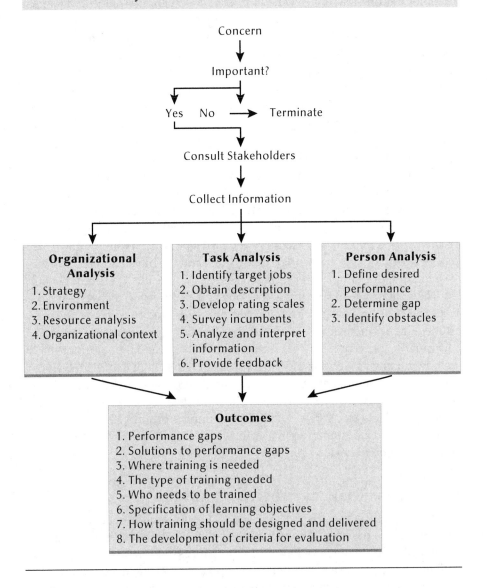

Concern

↓

Important?

Yes   No → Terminate

Consult Stakeholders

↓

Collect Information

Organizational Analysis

1. Strategy
2. Environment
3. Resource analysis
4. Organizational context

Task Analysis

1. Identify target jobs
2. Obtain description
3. Develop rating scales
4. Survey incumbents
5. Analyze and interpret information
6. Provide feedback

Person Analysis

1. Define desired performance
2. Determine gap
3. Identify obstacles

Outcomes

1. Performance gaps
2. Solutions to performance gaps
3. Where training is needed
4. The type of training needed
5. Who needs to be trained
6. Specification of learning objectives
7. How training should be designed and delivered
8. The development of criteria for evaluation

help with a new system. Other concerns might be recognizing a shift in regular activities, such as an increase in defective parts, accidents, or complaints.[6] At Boston Pizza, the top casual dining chain in Canada, a growing skills gap among the company's store managers was noticed. Although managers are familiar with the Boston Pizza concept and have the necessary hard skills, they are lacking in soft skills because most of them have come up through the ranks and have not had any formal management education. In order to remedy the soft-skills concern, the company launched Boston Pizza College, a classroom-based management training program.[7]

Sometimes the pressure comes from the external environment such as when legislation regarding employee relations is changed, or the competition introduces a highly competitive service feature. At IBM, one needs-identification program began with the CEO's comment that about 10 percent of all complaints addressed to him involved client dissatisfaction with IBM's handling of telephone calls.[8]

Step Two: Importance

After a concern has been raised, the next step is to determine if the concern is central to the effectiveness of the organization. The training manager must be aware of the strategic orientation of the organization. The goals, plans, introduction of products and services, changes in technology, practices, and regulations should be clear. Human resource policies must be linked with the strategic directions of the company as discussed in Chapter 1, and the training strategy should support the organization's efforts to achieve its goals.[9] As indicated in the chapter-opening vignette, the need for account executives to improve their sales was a critical factor and necessary to support AT&T Business Services' new focus.

In IBM's case, one strategic goal was customer satisfaction, and further analysis revealed that 70 percent of all customer contact was by telephone. The complaints about telephone calls had to be taken seriously because the concern was central to the effectiveness of the organization.[10]

Another important concern is the cost implications of a problem. Does current performance cost the company in lost productivity or dissatisfied customers? If the performance problem is important, then there must be some way to demonstrate that correcting the problem will result in increased productivity or client satisfaction. A concern is important (i.e., worthy of further exploration and analysis), if it has an impact on outcomes that are important to the organization and its effectiveness.

Step Three: Consult Stakeholders

The next step in the needs-analysis process is to involve the stakeholders who have a vested interest in the process and outcomes. Support from key players in the organization is necessary from the beginning of the needs-analysis process.

At a minimum, top management should understand the rationale for the needs analysis. Training analysts must obtain agreement on why the needs analysis is being done and who will be involved. Managerial expectations must be clarified.[11] Likewise, other stakeholders, such as employees or their collective representatives, should be consulted. At IBM, interviews with employees revealed that they believed they treated customers courteously, and that the managers were antagonistic about learning telephone skills. The attitude was, "just train the secretaries and switchboard operators," even though managers and even financial analysts were receiving calls from customers. The trainers at IBM worked hard to obtain agreement and support from employees on the need for a full analysis. Management sent out a strongly worded message to employees that there was a problem and that together they were going to fix it. Indeed, the manager of U.S. operations made telephone effectiveness one of five key measures of effectiveness. (The others included profit and revenue measures.)[12] At AT&T, the company's executive team believed in the importance of the new business strategy and line managers provided input on possible reasons for the lack of sales.

All stakeholders must buy into the needs-analysis process to ensure that the data collection will result in accurate information and that they have a vested interest in the success of the program. The linking of the training plans to business strategy and the involvement of key stakeholders resulted in dramatic improvements in customer satisfaction at IBM.

Step Four: Data Collection

The next stage in the needs-analysis process is the most extensive and involves the documentation of the concern through the collection of information from three levels of analysis. The three levels of needs analysis are the *organizational*, the *task*, and the *person* or *employee*.

Although overlaps between the three areas of analysis occur, each plays a distinctive role. The analysis of the organization provides information about its strategies and context and answers the question, "Where is training needed in the organization?" The task analysis provides information about the tasks and the relevant knowledge, skills, and abilities needed to perform selected jobs and answers the question, "What knowledge, skills, and abilities are required to perform the job effectively?" And a person analysis provides information about an employee's level of performance and answers the question, "Who needs to be trained?" Returning to the chapter-opening vignette, an in-depth needs analysis at AT&T indicated that account executives required training on the knowledge and skills necessary to generate leads and sales in a new segment of the market.

Needs-Analysis Outcomes

At the beginning of this chapter we referred to needs analysis as the cornerstone of the training and development process and noted that it is one of the most important steps. This is due in large part to the outcomes of needs analysis as shown in Figure 4.1.

Once a needs analysis has been completed, the information has to be examined and interpreted. The focus then shifts to an understanding of the performance problem and the search for the most effective solution.

The needs analysis results in a number of outcomes that set the stage for the rest of the training and development process. Besides clarifying the nature of performance gaps, a needs analysis helps to determine if training and development is a good solution to performance problems or if some other intervention might be more effective. If training and development is part of the solution, needs analysis information is used to determine where training is needed in the organization, what type of training is required, and who in the organization should receive training.

Needs analysis information is also used to write training objectives and to design training programs (e.g., what training content should be included in the training program, what training methods would be most effective, etc.). Finally, the information obtained from a needs analysis is also used in the development of measures for training evaluation.

Most of the outcomes of the needs-analysis process revolve around determining the best solution to performance problems and how to proceed if training is determined to be part of the solution. Later in the chapter we discuss a process for determining if training is the best solution to performance problems. In the following sections, we describe how to conduct an organizational, task, and person needs analysis.

Organizational Analysis

Organizational analysis involves the study of the entire organization: its strategy, environment, resources, and context. An understanding of each of these components will provide information not only for the identification of training needs, but also for the probability of the success of a training program. Key to an organizational analysis is finding out if a training program is congruent with an organization's strategy, and the existence of any constraints as well as support for the delivery and success of a training program. An organizational analysis can help identify potential constraints and problems that can derail a training program so that they can be dealt with prior to the design and delivery of a costly program.

Strategy

Most organizations have a strategy that consists of an organization's mission, goals, and objectives such as a dedication to quality or innovation. These broad statements trickle down to specific goals and objectives for each department or unit, and reflect an organization's plan for growth, adaptation, profitability, and survival.

In the past, an organization's strategy was set and implemented independently of the training function and human resources. During the last decade, however, it became increasingly apparent that human resource functions such as training and development are essential for the accomplishment of an organization's strategy and objectives. As a result, vice presidents and directors of human resources are now often involved in the setting of an organization's strategy and as a result, the human resource function has become more strategic.

In Chapter 1, we defined strategic human resources management (SHRM) as the alignment of human resource practices with an organization's business strategy. Although SHRM refers in general to the human resource system, in actuality it involves aligning specific HRM functions and activities with an organization's business strategy. In this regard, we can describe particular HR functions such as training and development as being strategic. Thus, **strategic training** can be defined as the alignment of an organization's training needs

RPC 4.2

Organizational analysis
The study of the entire organization including its strategy, environment, resources, and context

Strategic training
The alignment of an organization's training needs and programs with the organization's strategy and objectives

and programs with an organization's strategy and objectives. You might recall from Chapter 1 that one of the organizational benefits of training and development is facilitating and supporting an organization's strategy.

An organization's strategy should indicate the type and amount of training required. Training is more likely to be effective and contribute to an organization's success when it is congruent with its business strategy. When training and development programs are designed and implemented in isolation of an organization's strategy, they are not likely to be effective in helping an organization achieve its goals. In fact, as indicated in Chapter 1, there is some evidence that training can actually detract from an organization's bottom line and negatively impact shareholder value if it is not aligned with an organization's strategy. Training that is not linked to an organization's strategy can lower a company's market value by as much as 1.9 percent.[13] Thus, companies need to take a strategic approach to training and development. In the chapter-opening vignette, the training program for account executives was directly linked to the company's strategy to become more dominant in a non-traditional market segment.

Environment

In Chapter 1, we described how training and development is embedded within the external environment and how factors in the environment can impact the organization, human resource practices, and training and development. The environment is dynamic and uncertain. New technologies, competitors, recessions, and trade agreements can profoundly affect not only the need for and content of training, but also employees' receptivity to being trained.

For example, training programs are often a direct result of government regulations (e.g., safety regulations). In the United States, several recent laws require organizations to provide certain kinds of training. For example, a new sexual harassment prevention training law in California requires organizations with 50 or more employees to provide at least two hours of sexual harassment training to all supervisory employees.[14] The Sarbanes-Oxley Act of 2002, which was passed in the United States to protect investors from fraudulent accounting activities by corporations in the wake of high-profile scandals such as Enron and WorldCom, requires organizations to provide compliance training which must be documented. The implications for training are especially being felt by accounting firms where the Act has forced auditors and accountants to do their jobs differently. As a result, some firms have had to double the time their staff spend in training and substantially increase their investment in training.[15]

Besides this regulatory influence, organizations are conscious of the strategies of their competitors. The nature of a training program can be a direct result of an organization's attempt to establish a new market niche. This of course, was an important factor for AT&T. Changes in the telecommunications industry as well as competitive pressures were key determinants of the company's efforts to become more dominant in a nontraditional market segment.

Resource Analysis

An important component of an organizational analysis is determining an organization's ability to design and deliver a training program. Does the organization have the resources (money, time, and expertise) to design and deliver a training program if one is needed?

A **resource analysis** involves identifying the resources available in the organization that might be required to design and implement training and development programs. Training programs are costly and require considerable resources. In addition to the financial costs, the design and implementation of a training program requires considerable time and expertise. Not all organizations have the expertise required to design and deliver training programs. In addition, the human resource staff might not have the time required to design new training programs. Furthermore, training programs also require materials, equipment, and facilities and these too can be expensive.

A resource analysis enables an organization to determine if they have the resources required for a training and development solution or if another less costly solution will be better. Ultimately, one has to answer the question of whether or not the organization has the resources required for training if in fact it is needed. Chapter 12 describes how to determine the costs and benefits of training programs.

Resource analysis
The identification of the resources available in an organization that might be required to design and implement training and development programs

Organizational Context

Organizations consist of more than buildings, equipment, and paper. They are social entities made up of people. The people within the buildings have feelings, attitudes, and values that make up the climate of an organization. The climate of an organization refers to the collective attitudes of its employees toward work, supervision, and company goals, policies, and procedures. One aspect of climate that is particularly important for training is the training transfer climate.

Training transfer climate refers to characteristics in the work environment that can either facilitate or inhibit the application of training on the job. A strong training transfer climate is one in which there exist cues that remind employees to apply training material on the job, positive consequences such as feedback and rewards for applying training on the job, and supervisor and peer support for the use of newly acquired skills and abilities. The training transfer climate has been found to be a strong predictor of training effectiveness and whether or not trainees apply newly trained skills on the job.[16]

Training transfer climate
Characteristics in the work environment that can either facilitate or inhibit the application of training on the job

Another important component of an organization's context is its culture. Recall from Chapter 1 that an organization's culture refers to the shared beliefs and assumptions about how things are done in an organization. Organizations can be differentiated from each other on the basis of their culture. For example, some organizations have innovative cultures while others have risk-taking cultures. One type of culture that is particularly important for training and development is a learning culture.

A **learning culture** refers to a culture in which members of an organization believe that knowledge and skill acquisition are part of their job responsibilities and that learning is an important part of work life in the organization.[17]

Information about an organization's training transfer climate and learning culture is important because it can help to determine if a training program is likely to be effective in an organization as well as whether a pre-training intervention might be required to improve the climate and/or culture prior to the design and delivery of a training program. It might also indicate that an alternative solution to a performance problem would be more effective than a training program. This is an important part of an organizational analysis because training is not likely to be effective in organizations where the climate for training transfer and/or the culture for learning are not strong.

The influence of the training transfer climate and learning culture on training effectiveness demonstrates how important the role of the organizational context is for a training program's success and the need to conduct an organizational analysis. Whether or not employees apply what they learn in training on the job has a lot to do with an organization's transfer climate and learning culture because they can either facilitate or hinder the implementation and success of a training program. In Chapter 10 we discuss the role of climate and culture in the transfer of training in more detail.

Once the strategy, environment, resources, and context of an organization have been assessed, the information gathered can be used to determine if a training program is required to help an organization achieve its goals and objectives and if it will be successful. However, additional information is required about the tasks that employees perform, as well as employees' knowledge, skills, and abilities and current level of job performance and task mastery. This additional information can be obtained by conducting a task analysis and a person analysis.

Task Analysis

Before we discuss task analysis, it is useful to first review the terms used to describe jobs. A job consists of a number of related activities, duties, and tasks. A task is the smallest unit of behaviour studied by the analyst and describes the specific sequence of events necessary to complete a unit of work.

A **task analysis** consists of a description of the activities or work operations performed on a job and the conditions under which these activities are performed. A task analysis reveals the tasks required for a person to perform a job and the knowledge, skills, and abilities that are required to perform the tasks successfully.

There are six steps involved in a task analysis:

1. Identify the target jobs.
2. Obtain a job description.
3. Develop rating scales to rate the importance of each task and the frequency with which it is performed.
4. Survey a sample of job incumbents.
5. Analyze and interpret the information.
6. Provide feedback on the results.

Managing Performance Through Training and Development

1. Identify the Target Jobs

After a problem or performance discrepancy has been identified in an organization, the focus shifts to the job level in order to determine which jobs are contributing to the performance problem and have a performance gap. More than a job title is required here. For example, the title *associate* often describes quite different types of jobs, depending upon the department or level within any organization. These target jobs may be identified by managers. At AT&T, the target job was account executive.

2. Obtain a Job Description

A **job description** lists the specific duties carried out through the completion of several tasks. In large organizations, most positions have a description of the tasks and minimum qualifications required to do the job. If this description has not been updated within the last year, consult with both the manager and several employees in the position (subject-matter experts) to obtain a current listing of tasks and qualifications. The job description should contain a summary of the major duties of the job, a listing of these duties, the knowledge, skills, and abilities required to perform the tasks, and the conditions under which they are performed. All tools and specialized knowledge should be listed.

After preparing a job description, the list of duties should be reviewed with subject-matter experts, managers, job incumbents in interviews, or focus groups. The analyst will then develop a list of tasks to be performed; the knowledge, skills, and abilities needed to perform the tasks; a list of necessary tools, software, or equipment; and an understanding of the conditions under which the tasks are performed. You can see that the result looks very much like a job description with job specifications (a job specification is a statement of the knowledge, skills, and abilities required to perform a job).

Creating job descriptions and making lists of tasks and duties does have its downside. Critics argue that jobs change too rapidly and these lists are quickly out of date. Therefore, some job analysts have begun to develop a list of job competencies. A **competency** is a cluster of related knowledge, skills, and abilities that forms a major part of a job and that enables the job holder to perform effectively.[18] Competencies are behaviours that distinguish effective performers from ineffective performers. Competencies can be knowledge, skills, behaviour, or personality traits. However, most analysts prefer not to use personality traits such as "charisma," and instead prefer to describe the behaviour underlying the trait.

Examples of competencies for managers include setting goals and standards, coaching, making decisions, and organizing. As you can see, competencies are very similar to skills. Skills, however, can be very specific, such as "negotiate a collective agreement," whereas competencies are generic and universal such as "win agreement on goals, standards, expectations, and time frames." The Banff Centre for Management has developed competency profiles for senior leaders so that they can assess needs and then train.[19] An example taken from their profile is listed in Table 4.1.

Job description

A statement of the tasks, duties, and responsibilities of a job

Competency

A cluster of related knowledge, skills, and abilities that enables the job holder to perform effectively

TABLE 4.1

A Competency Profile for Senior Leaders

Core Competency Ability to obtain buy-in of key stakeholders to new directions

Level 1: Communicates new directions so that everyone affected knows the new directions

Level 2: Leads team through discussions and research to identify key new themes and goals that everyone can accept and use

Level 3: Key stakeholders are consulted and have input into direction-setting

Level 4: All stakeholders are engaged in a process to rewrite the new directions in terms that relate specifically to their roles

Source: MacNamara, D. (1998, November 16). Learning contracts, competency profiles the new wave in executive development. *Canadian HR Reporter*, pp. G8–G10. Reprinted by permission of Carswell, a division of Thomson Canada Ltd.

The goal is to develop competencies that are teachable (i.e., we can observe them and describe them). If these competencies are then associated with effective performance, we can use them as a base to increase the effectiveness of employee's on-the-job work behaviour. Competencies can then be used instead of job descriptions.

3. Develop Rating Scales to Rate the Importance of Tasks and the Frequency with Which They Are Performed

Rating scales must be developed in order to rate the importance of each task as well as how often a task is performed. Tasks that are more important for the effective performance of a job as well as those that are frequently performed need to be identified. These ratings are important for determining the content of a training program and for identifying what employees must do in order to perform a job effectively.

4. Survey a Sample of Job Incumbents

Job incumbents as well as supervisors and subject-matter experts who are familiar with the job must then provide task importance and frequency ratings. A questionnaire and a structured interview, as well as observation of employees performing their jobs can be used to rate the importance of tasks and the frequency with which they are performed. An example of a survey is shown in Table 4.2.

5. Analyze and Interpret the Information

Once the tasks have been identified and the importance and frequency ratings have been made, the information must be analyzed and interpreted. This usually involves some elementary statistical analyses to identify those tasks that

TABLE 4.2

Sample Task Analysis Survey

For each of the following areas of skill, knowledge, and ability, please make two ratings. Looking at your own job, assess the importance of the task by circling a number from 1 (not important) to 5 (very important). Then, consider your own level of competence in that task and rate it from 1 (not at all competent) to 5 (extremely competent).

TASK	IMPORTANCE	COMPETENCE
Knowledge: ability to explain technical information to co-workers.	1 2 3 4 5	1 2 3 4 5
Control: ability to develop procedures to monitor and evaluate activities.	1 2 3 4 5	1 2 3 4 5
Planning: ability to schedule time, tasks, and activities efficiently.	1 2 3 4 5	1 2 3 4 5
Coaching: ability to provide verbal feedback to assist in the development of more effective ways of handling situations.	1 2 3 4 5	1 2 3 4 5

are the most important and most frequently performed. Statistical software packages can assist in this task and can be used for more complex analyses. Comparisons between groups may reveal additional important information. Job incumbents may rate their own performance highly, while their managers may feel that employees are not working up to standard. New employees may feel that there are no barriers to optimum performance, while those with several years of service might perceive problems.

One study found that experienced police officers spent less time in traffic activities, and more in non-crime-related tasks than recent recruits, validating the need to collect background information on respondents.[20] Conducting a training course without understanding the participants and the environment may result in less-effective learning and transfer of skills to the workplace.

6. Provide Feedback on the Results

Because employees and managers might not be aware of the need for training, it is important to provide small groups of managers and employees with feedback about the responses to task analysis. This feedback encourages employees to talk about areas of strengths and weaknesses and to propose solutions to problems. By owning the problem and generating the solution, employees may be more willing to change their behaviours and managers will be more likely to support a training program.

The result of a task analysis should be information on the key task requirements for certain job categories and the associated job specifications (knowledge, skills, and abilities). This sets the stage for the design of training programs because it specifies the tasks that employees must be trained to perform as well as the knowledge and skills that they need to learn. At AT&T, a task analysis indicated that account executives required selling knowledge and skills about specific products and services.

A limitation of a task analysis, however, is that it emphasizes observable behaviours rather than mental processes, and it assumes that the tasks are performed by individuals rather than groups. Many jobs today, however, involve mental processes and teamwork. In the following sections, we briefly describe some new approaches to task analysis that focus on mental processes and teamwork.

Cognitive Task Analysis

The traditional approach to a task analysis focuses on behaviours rather than mental processes such as decision-making. However, many jobs today involve complex mental tasks. How then does one conduct a task analysis for jobs that involve mental tasks that are not easy to observe? The answer is a cognitive task analysis.

A **cognitive task analysis** refers to a set of procedures that focuses on understanding the mental processes and requirements for performing a job.[21] It differs from the more conventional task analysis in that the focus is on the mental and cognitive aspects of a job rather than observable behaviours like typing or driving that are the focus of a traditional task analysis.

Cognitive task analysis describes mental and cognitive activities that are not directly observable such as decision-making, problem-solving, pattern recognition, and situational assessment. A traditional task analysis focuses on what gets done while a cognitive task analysis focuses more on the details of how tasks get done.

Although cognitive task analysis is useful for any job that has cognitive elements, it is especially useful in jobs that are complex, dynamic, and have high-stakes outcomes. It can identify important elements of job performance such as decisions, cues, judgments, and perceptions that are important for effective job performance, and are usually not identified by a traditional task analysis. As a result, important cognitive elements can then be incorporated into training and development programs. Although cognitive task analysis has begun to receive a great deal of attention in recent years, it is a relatively new technique that is still being developed.[22]

Team Task Analysis

As indicated earlier, the traditional task analysis is not suited to the analysis of jobs that involve group work. However, many jobs today involve groups. Thus, a task analysis must be able to identify the knowledge and skills required to work in a group. In recent years, there has been an attempt to find ways to conduct a team task analysis.

A **team task analysis** is similar to a task analysis in that the tasks of the job must be identified. However, an assessment of team-based competencies (knowledge, skills, and attitudes) associated with the tasks is also required.

Teamwork competencies include things such as how to communicate, interact, and coordinate tasks effectively with team members. The main

Cognitive task analysis

A set of procedures that focuses on understanding the mental processes and requirements for performing a job

Team task analysis

An analysis of tasks as well as the team-based competencies (knowledge, skills, and attitudes) associated with the tasks.

objective is to identity the key team competencies required for the tasks of the job, which will be used to write training objectives and to design a training program.[23]

There are a number of important differences between a traditional task analysis and a team task analysis. The main difference is that a team task analysis must identify the interdependencies of the job as well as the skills required for task coordination. Another difference is that a team task analysis must also identify the cognitive skills that are required for interacting in a team.

In general, a team task analysis should focus on the knowledge of task-specific goals; knowledge of task procedures, strategies, and timing; knowledge of team members' roles and responsibilities; interpositional knowledge; and knowledge of teamwork. A team task analysis can be conducted through the use of individual and group interviews, a review of existing documents, observation, questionnaires, and by examining past important events.[24]

Like a task analysis, a team task analysis and cognitive task analysis identifies the tasks that an employee must be able to perform and the knowledge, skills, and abilities required. However, they do not indicate how well employees are able to perform the tasks or whether they have the necessary knowledge, skills, and abilities. This information must be obtained from a person analysis, the topic to which we now turn.

Person Analysis

The third level of a needs analysis focuses on the person performing a job. **Person analysis** is the process of studying employee behaviour to determine if performance meets the work standards. A standard is the desired level of performance—ideally the quantifiable output of a specific job.

A person analysis examines how well an employee performs the critical tasks and their knowledge, skills, and abilities. The objective is to provide answers to these kinds of questions: How well does the employee perform the tasks? Who, within the organization, needs training? And what kind of training do they need? A three-step process should help answer these questions:

1. Define the desired performance.
2. Determine the gap between desired and actual performance.
3. Identify the obstacles to effective performance.

1. Define the Desired Performance

The first step is to establish standards for performance. These norms will be important in the needs analysis, during training, and in evaluating the effectiveness of training. The idea is to determine the standard or the acceptable level of task performance. This enables a comparison of each employee's performance level against the standard in order to identify discrepancies and the need for training.

2. Determine the Gap between Desired and Actual Performance

In this step, a comparison is made between the standard level of performance and each employee's performance. Employee performance data can be

Person analysis

The process of studying employee behaviour to determine whether performance meets standards

TABLE 4.3

Barriers to Effective Performance

HUMAN	TECHNICAL	INFORMATION	STRUCTURAL
Lack of knowledge	Poor job design	Ill-defined goals/objectives	Overlapping roles and
Lack of skills	Lack of tools/equipment	Lack of performance	responsibilities
Lack of motivation	Lack of standardized	measurements	Lack of flexibility
Counterproductive	procedures	Raw data, not normative or	Lack of control systems
reward systems	Rapid change in technology	comparative data	Organizational political
Group norms	Ineffective feedback	Resources sub-optimized	climate
		Informal leaders	

Source: Adapted from Chevalier, R. D. (1990). Analyzing performance discrepancies with line managers. *Performance and Instruction, 29* (10). www.ispi.org. Reprinted by permission of International Society for Performance Improvement. Copyright 1990.

obtained from performance appraisals, work samples, observations, self-assessments of competencies, and formal tests. CIBC uses formal tests to determine competencies of financial advisers.[25] Results from the "Financial Advisor Skills and Capabilities Assessment" are used by employees to gain self-awareness and to prepare a developmental plan. More objective sources might be found in records of output, complaints, accidents, rejects, lost time, maintenance hours, and equipment efficiency. The employee's performance can be compared with industry norms or with that of other workers.

3. Identify the Obstacles to Effective Performance

When a gap exists between the standard and an employee's performance, it is necessary to determine the cause or source of the gap. Performance problems can be the result of deficiencies in execution as well as deficiencies in knowledge, skills, or abilities. Sometimes, the gap is the result of the worker not knowing the standard, not receiving adequate feedback about performance relative to the standard, and not being rewarded for meeting the standard. A lack of goals and feedback is often the reason for substandard performance. Table 4.3 lists a variety of potential barriers to effective performance.

Once the obstacles to performance have been identified, the next step in the needs-analysis process is to determine solutions to performance problems and if training is a possible solution to a performance problem. In the next section, we present a framework for determining solutions to performance problems.

RPC 4.3

Determining Solutions to Performance Problems

If you consider all the barriers to performance listed in Table 4.3, only the first two (lack of knowledge and skills) suggest a training solution. Clearly, the solution to performance problems is not always going to be training.

Saying "I've got a training problem" is like going to the doctor and saying you have an aspirin problem.[26] Training, like aspirin, is a solution, not a problem. How then do we determine if training is the best solution to performance problems?

Figure 4.2 presents a flowchart developed by Mager and Pipe to assist in analyzing performance problems and determining solutions to performance problems. Let's review the steps in the flowchart.

First, when there is a performance problem, the manager must first describe the discrepancy and decide if the problem is worth spending either time or money to correct. Is it worth pursuing? For example, a manager might be irritated by employees who wear their hair shoulder-length, but having short hair will make absolutely no difference to productivity or other measures of performance. The exception might be in a manufacturing environment, where long hair would pose a safety hazard (solved easily by wearing a head covering).

If the performance deficiency is deemed important and worth pursuing, then the true analysis begins.

First, we consider some basic solutions or quick fixes. For example, are the work expectations, standards, and goals clear? Does the employee have adequate resources? Is the outcome of the employee's performance visible and known to the employee? If the answer to any of these questions is No, then the solution might involve clarifying expectations, standards, and setting goals; providing necessary resources; and/or providing performance feedback.

If the problem cannot be solved by these quick fixes, the analyst must then attempt to determine the cause of poor performance by asking a number of additional questions about the environment. For example, Is the person punished for desired performance? While this question seems odd, organizational life is full of examples of punishment for good performance. The assistant who works twice as hard as co-workers is punished by being given more work. The manager who stays within his/her budget is punished by having it slashed the following year. In these and other cases, behaviour that should be rewarded is actually being punished. Such penalties and punishments for what is in effect good performance should be eliminated.

Sometimes undesirable performance is rewarded, such as when employees get paid for each unit produced. Under these circumstances you might find that employees are very good at producing lots of defective units. Of course, if they get paid for each unit produced they will continue to produce as many as they can regardless of quality. Thus, it is also important to ensure that undesirable behaviour is not rewarded. High volume should not be rewarded if quality is desired.

The next issue is whether or not rewards are linked to effective performance. Are there positive consequences for performing as desired? Sometimes when an employee does something good, the manager says nothing, on the assumption that the employee is being paid to do the work. Good performance that is not rewarded will eventually disappear. Sometimes, employees

FIGURE 4.2

Mager and Pipe's Performance Analysis Flowchart for Determining Solutions to Performance Problems

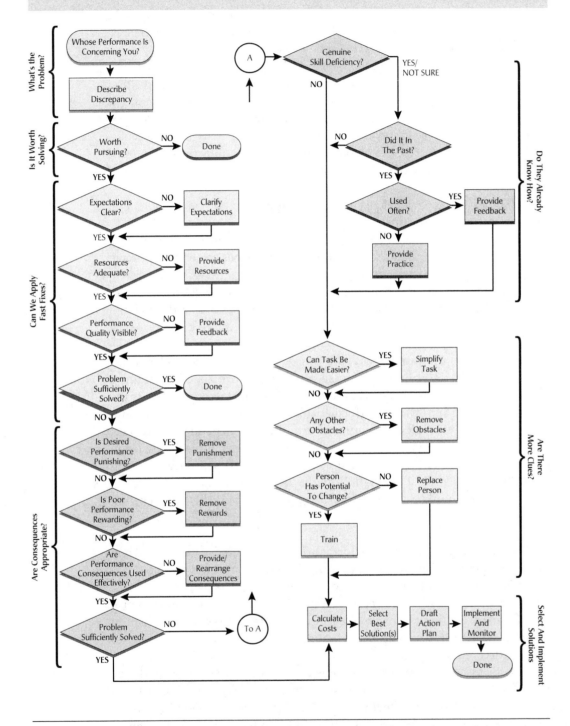

Source: © 1997, The Center for Effective Performance, Inc., Atlanta, Georgia. Adapted from Analyzing Performance Problems, 3rd Edition by Robert F. Mager & Peter Pipe. www.cepworldwide.com, 800-558-4237.

assume that their performance does not matter to anyone. When managers sit in their offices and fume over sloppy work but give no feedback to employees, or arrange no consequences for poor performance, the sloppy work will continue.

Working with the human resource staff, managers need to develop contingency management programs that reward employees for good performance. **Contingency management** is grounded in the belief that every act has a consequence and if the consequence is a reward then the act will be repeated. If there is no consequence or the consequence is something negative or punishing, the action will not be repeated.

Imagine a classroom where the instructor never acknowledges students whose hands are raised to ask questions. Eventually, the students will learn to keep their hands down. Ensuring that no students ask questions can be done even faster by punishing those who ask questions with sarcastic or humiliating replies. Thus, the behaviour of hand raising or asking questions is eliminated, even when the instructor insists that he or she values classroom participation and discussion.

By analyzing rewards and punishments, managers might realize that they are asking for safe procedures but be punishing those who slow down production. Quality might be the all-important word on the sign in the factory, but employees might be praised for quantity. The determination of what constitutes effective performance, and the management of reinforcement for achieving it, is a far more powerful instrument of change than a training program.

If contingency management does not solve the problem, the next step is to consider whether or not there is a genuine skill deficiency. The key to getting at this issue is to ask a critical question: Could the employee perform the task if his or her life depended on it? Could your employees produce six units per hour if their lives depended on it? If the answer is "Yes," then the solution is not to teach them something they already know how to do. Rather, the solution is to provide an environment that allows or encourages them to do it.

Following the right side of Figure 4.2, consider if the employee has ever performed the task and perhaps does not do it often and just needs some practice. Or perhaps the task is done frequently and the employee needs feedback. Thus, if an employee knows how to perform a task, it is important to consider practice and feedback before training.

To restate the critical question asked earlier: Could the employee perform the task if his or her life depended on it? If the answer is "Yes," they could perform the task if their life depended on it, then say "No" to training. If the employee cannot do the task if his or her life depended on it, then consider a number of other changes before training.

Other solutions might be to lower expectations, simplify the task, or perhaps transfer the employee to a job that better fits his or her knowledge and skills. It is also important to remove any other obstacles in the environment. Training will not be a good solution when the environment is the cause of poor performance. Environmental obstacles to effective performance might

Contingency management
Practices based on the belief that every act has a consequence and if the consequence is a reward then the act will be repeated

involve a lack of authority, inadequate tools or technology, conflicting responsibilities, work overload, and so on. Removing these obstacles in the work environment and replacing them with a more supportive environment might be the best solution to a performance problem.

Finally, if there exists a genuine skill deficiency and the person does not have the potential to change, then replacing the person might be the only solution. If, however, the person does have the potential to change, then consider training as a potential solution.

As you can see, training is just one solution for managing performance problems. There are other solutions that might be more effective and less costly than training. Furthermore, even the best-designed training programs are not always effective because the environment does not support the change in behaviour and performance. Thus, one has to consider the cost of each potential solution as well how practical and feasible it will be as well its overall potential to solve the problem.

Training, however, is often the best solution to performance problems under the following conditions:

- the task is performed frequently
- the task is difficult
- correct performance is critical
- the employee does not know how to perform as required (cannot do it)
- performance expectations and goals are clear, and employees receive feedback on their performance
- there are (or will be) positive consequences for correct work behaviour; there are not negative consequences for performing as required
- other solutions (such as coaching) are ineffective or too expensive (e.g. terminating employees and rehiring those with required skills)

If the needs analysis reveals that the tasks are not frequently performed, that they are not critical, and that perfection is not required, then performance-improvement solutions such as job aids and on-the-job training might be more appropriate. Sometimes more radical solutions might even be necessary such as changing employees through firing and hiring, re-designing the job, changing the equipment, or changing the organizational structure.

Even if training is determined to be the best solution, the costs and benefits of training must first be estimated. Trainers must ask questions such as "What is the cost of the training?" and "What are the benefits to training?" (Chapter 12 addresses these questions.) Another consideration is the legal requirement to certify knowledge and skill levels of employees. A further point is the pressure exerted by top management to conduct the training. It is hoped that this pressure is a result of the organization's strategies and objectives.

In summary, the best way to determine if training is an appropriate solution to performance problems is to first conduct a thorough needs analysis, identify performance obstacles, and then consider various solutions to a

The Training Solution Checklist

Trainers are often asked to provide training to correct a performance problem. Training is not always the best solution, and trainers should ask the following questions to determine if training is an appropriate solution:

1. What are the performance (or operating) problems? Don't ask, "What is the training need?"
2. Describe the current performance and desired performance.
3. Can employees perform as desired if they had to? Did they ever perform as expected in the past?
4. If employees have performed as expected in the past, do they need practice, feedback, or specific and challenging goals?
5. If employees perform as you want them to, what are the consequences for them? Are they rewarded for good performance and goal accomplishment?
6. Are there any other reasons why employees might not be performing as desired?
7. If we find a solution to the performance problem, how will we know that the problem has been solved? What behaviours, skills, or results will change?
8. Is training the solution?

performance problem as shown in Figure 4.2. A checklist of the questions to ask to determine if training is the best solution to performance problems is provided in The Trainer's Notebook.

Needs-Analysis Methods

We have been discussing the needs-analysis process and the collection of information about the organization, task, and employees. By this point, you might be wondering where the information for a needs analysis comes from and how it is collected. In this section, we review the methods of needs analysis and the following section discusses the sources of needs analysis information.

There are many methods and techniques for conducting a needs analysis. The methods tend to differ in terms of the quality and type of information obtained, as well as the time and cost of collecting it. This section describes some of the most common methods of needs analysis.

Steadham has developed a useful summary of nine basic needs analysis methods that are described in Table 4.4 along with their advantages and disadvantages. The nine methods are: observation, questionnaires, key consultation, print media, interviews, group discussion, tests, records and reports, and work samples.

There is some research that suggests that some methods of needs analysis are better than others in terms of response rate, quality, usefulness of the data, and cost. One study tested three techniques: closed-ended survey, open-ended survey, and focus groups. A combination of the closed-ended survey and focus-group interviews provided the most practical, useful, and cost-effective information.[27] The best method, however, depends on the time

TABLE 4.4

Advantages and Disadvantages of Nine Basic Needs-Analysis Methods

METHODS	ADVANTAGES	DISADVANTAGES
Observation • Can be as technical as time–motion studies or as functionally or behaviourally specific as observing a new board or staff member interacting during a meeting. • May be as unstructured as walking through an agency's offices on the lookout for evidence of communication barriers. • Can be used normatively to distinguish between effective and ineffective behaviours, organizational structures, and/or process.	• Minimizes interruption of routine work flow or group activity. • Generates in situ data, highly relevant to the situation where response to identified training needs/interests will impact. • (When combined with a feedback step) provides for important comparison checks between inferences of the observer and the respondent.	• Requires a highly skilled observer with both process and content knowledge (unlike an interviewer who needs, for the most part, only process skills). • Carries limitations that derive from being able to collect data only within the work setting (the other side of the first advantage listed in the preceding column). • Holds potential for respondents to perceive the observation activity as "spying."
Questionnaires • May be in the form of surveys or polls of a random or stratified sample of respondents, or an enumeration of an entire "population." • Can use a variety of question formats: open-ended, projective, forced-choice, priority-ranking. • Can take alternative forms such as Q-sorts, or slipsorts, rating scales, either predesigned or self-generated by respondent(s). • May be self-administered (by mail) under controlled or uncontrolled conditions, or may require the presence of an interpreter or assistant.	• Can reach a large number of people in a short time. • Are relatively inexpensive. • Give opportunity of expression without fear of embarrassment. • Yield data easily summarized and reported.	• Make little provision for free expression of unanticipated responses. • Require substantial time (and technical skills, especially in survey model) for development of effective instruments. • Are of limited utility in getting at causes of problems or possible solutions. • Suffer low return rates (mailed), grudging responses, or unintended and/or inappropriate respondents.

Key Consultation
• Secures information from those persons who, by virtue of their formal or informal standing, are in a good position to know what the training needs of a particular group are:
  a. board chairman
  b. related service providers
  c. members of professional associations
  d. individuals from the service population
	• Is relatively simple and inexpensive to conduct.
	• Permits input and interaction of a number of individuals, each with his or her own perspectives of the needs of the area, discipline, group, etc.
	• Establishes and strengthens lines of communication between participants in the process.
		• Carries a built-in bias, since it is based on views of those who tend to see training needs from their own individual or organizational perspective.
		• May result in only a partial picture of training needs due to the typically nonrepresentative nature (in a statistical sense) of a key informant group.

Print Media • Can include professional journals, legislative news/notes, industry "rags," trade magazines, in-house publications.	• Is an excellent source of information for uncovering and clarifying normative needs. • Provides information that is current, if not forward-looking. • Is readily available and is apt to have already been reviewed by the client group.	• Can be a problem when it comes to the data analysis and synthesis into a useable form (use of clipping service or key consultants can make this type of data more useable).

Interviews
- Can be formal or casual, structured or unstructured, or somewhere in between.
- May be used with a sample of a particular group (board, staff, committee) or conducted with everyone concerned.
- Can be done in person, by phone, at the work site, or away from it.

Advantages:
- Are adept at revealing feelings, causes of, and possible solutions to problems that the client is facing (or anticipates); provide maximum opportunity for the client to represent himself spontaneously on his own terms (especially when conducted in an open-ended, nondirective manner).

Disadvantages:
- Are usually time-consuming.
- Can be difficult to analyze and quantify results (especially from unstructured formats).
- Unless the interviewer is skilled, the client(s) can easily be made to feel self-conscious.

Group Discussion
- Resembles face-to-face interview technique, e.g., structured or unstructured, formal or informal, or somewhere in between.
- Can be focused on job (role) analysis, group problem analysis, group goal setting or any number of group tasks or themes, e.g., "leadership training needs of the board."
- Uses one or several of the familiar group facilitating techniques: brainstorming, nominal group process, force-fields, consensus rankings, organizational mirroring, simulation, and sculpting.

Advantages:
- Permits on-the-spot synthesis of different viewpoints.
- Builds support for the particular service response that is ultimately decided on.
- Decreases client's "dependence response" toward the service provided since data analysis is (or can be) a shared function.
- Helps participants to become better problem analysts, better listeners, etc.

Disadvantages:
- Relies for success on a skilful interviewer who can generate data without making client(s) feel self-conscious, suspicious, etc.
- Is time-consuming (therefore initially expensive) both for the consultant and the agency.
- Can produce data that are difficult to synthesize and quantify (more a problem with the less structured techniques).

Tests
- Are a hybridized form of questionnaire.
- Can be very functionally oriented (like observations) to test a board, staff, or committee member's proficiency.
- May be used to sample learned ideas and facts.
- Can be administered with or without the presence of an assistant.

Advantages:
- Can be especially helpful in determining whether the cause of a recognized problem is a deficiency in knowledge or skill, or by elimination, attitude.
- Results are easily quantifiable and comparable.

Disadvantages:
- The availability of a relatively small number of tests that are validated for a specific situation.
- Do not indicate if measured knowledge and skills are actually being used in the on-the-job or "back home group" situation.

Records, Reports
- Can consist of organizational charts, planning documents, policy manuals, audits, and budget reports.
- Employee records (grievance, turnover, accidents, etc.)
- Include minutes of meetings, weekly, monthly program reports, memoranda, agency service records, program evaluation studies.

Advantages:
- Provide excellent clues to trouble spots.
- Provide objective evidence of the results of problems within the agency or group.
- Can be collected with a minimum of effort and interruption of work flow since they already exist at the work site.

Disadvantages:
- Causes of problems or possible solutions often do not show up.
- Carry perspective that generally reflects the past situation rather than the current one (or recent changes).
- Need a skilled data analyst if clear patterns and trends are to emerge from such technical and diffuse raw data.

Work Samples
- Are similar to observation but in written form.
- Can be products generated in the course of the organization's work, e.g., ad layouts, program proposals, market analyses, letters, training designs.
- Written responses to a hypothetical but relevant case study provided by the consultant.

Advantages:
- Carry most of the advantage of records and reports data.
- Are the organization's data (its own output).

Disadvantages:
- Case study method will take time away from actual work of the organization.
- Need specialized content analysts.
- Analyst's assessment of strengths/weaknesses disclosed by samples can be challenged as "too subjective."

Source: From Steadham, S. V. (1980, January). Learning to select a needs assessment strategy. *Training & Development, 30,* 56–61. Copyright January 1980, Adapted from Training and Development magazine, American Society for Training and Development. Reprinted with permission. All rights reserved.

and money available, the experience of the analyst, and the nature of the responses.

Surveys are one of the most often used methods of needs analysis due to their low cost and the ability to collect information from large numbers of respondents. Some software firms have developed surveys that can be customized to include questions from broad-climate issues to specific job standards. There are many firms that have designed needs analysis software, some of which can be tailored to clients' needs. This technology allows HR staff to develop customized surveys quickly, and to analyze results by region, unit, and so on. One HR system contained 200 000 pieces of information on 500 employees. This system tapped every skill of every employee ranging from forklift and fuel-tank exchange procedures to probing abilities.[28]

Needs-Analysis Sources

There are many sources of needs-analysis information. Among the most important and often used are employees and managers as well as subject-matter-experts who are familiar with a job. Some retail stores assess the competence of their sales staff through the use of professional shoppers who rate sales performance against established standards. A bank tests employee knowledge using a computer-based analysis, and then compares the results with supervisory rankings.[29]

In many cases, data on employees' performance and training needs is obtained from employees who rate their own performance and indicate their training needs. This is usually referred to as self-assessment. Self-assessment has its benefits and its limitations. Employees might be more motivated to be trained if they have some input in deciding on their needs. However, expressions of needs include feelings or desires and may have no relation to performance.[30]

Several studies have found weak relationships between employees' self-assessment of performance and managerial assessments.[31] A review of 55 studies failed to find a strong relationship between self-evaluation of ability and other measures of performance.[32] However, a study at IBM demonstrated that employees can be trained in self-assessment by learning to break down a job into its component parts and to analyze skills.[33] This method has the added benefit of the employees' accepting ownership of their development plans.

In summary, there are many methods and sources for conducting a needs analysis. Because of the differences in information provided by the various methods and sources, the best approach is usually one that includes multiple methods and sources. Surveying only job incumbents about their perceptions of their own abilities might not result in the most objective information about performance gaps. Employees may have wish lists for training that do not meet the needs of their units or that do not address their own weaknesses. Managers, too, should be asked for their performance evaluations. Those who have frequent interaction with job incumbents, such as customers and employees in other departments, should also be surveyed. These different perspectives will result in more accurate and complete information. It also enables analysts to distinguish between perceived needs (what training employees feel they need), demand needs (what managers request), and normative needs (training needed to meet industry, unit, or job comparative standards).

Obstacles to Needs Analysis

Now that you know all about the needs-analysis process, you might be surprised to learn that many organizations do not conduct a thorough needs analysis, at least not to the extent that it is described in training and development textbooks.[34] Given the importance of needs analysis in the training process, you might wonder why this is the case.

As it turns out, there are a number of obstacles to conducting a formal needs analysis. Understanding what these obstacles are is important because if you are aware of them then you can also learn how to overcome them.

To begin with, trainers often claim that they are not rewarded for taking the time (and money) to conduct a needs analysis. Managers prefer action over analysis and therefore want to see training resources used to train employees. They may also feel that they can accurately identify training needs and that more analysis is a waste of time and money. Managers may even have their own agendas, such as rewarding employees by sending them to exotic locations for training, and therefore resist any attempt to redefine training needs.

Sometimes time is a constraint. New equipment might be arriving and it is easier to train all employees on all procedures instead of determining who needs training on which aspects of the new equipment. In fact, time is increasingly becoming a concern as a full-blown needs analysis can take months to complete and yet employees need to be trained and back on the job in a matter of weeks or even days.

Ultimately, what everyone is most concerned about is getting people trained as soon as possible. Because needs analysis is costly and time consuming, it is often seen as an unnecessary constraint on resources, staff, and time. The identification of training needs can turn into a comprehensive research study that takes months to complete.

The cost, time, and the rigour necessary for doing a thorough needs analysis means that many organizations will simply not do one. However, conducting some data collection and analysis, rather than having no information, will almost always result in a better training program. It is therefore important for trainers to persuade management of the importance of conducting a needs analysis, and to ensure that it is included in the training budget. Furthermore, trainers need to be creative in finding ways to conduct a needs analysis within the constraints that exist in their organizations. To learn more about how some of the creative techniques that training experts have used to overcome the obstacles to conducting a needs analysis, see Training Today, "Just-in-Time Needs Analysis."

Just-in-Time Needs Analysis

Needs analysis can be a time-consuming process that is hard to sell to managers who want just-in-time solutions to urgent problems. When an organization is introducing new equipment, or an employee has to learn to perform an important task, the last thing that managers want to hear is "Wait, we have to do a needs analysis."

Very few trainers have the time and resources to follow the complete needs-analysis process described in a textbook. However, most trainers would use some means of detecting the underlying cause of a performance problem and training needs. Here are some ways experienced trainers conduct a needs analysis in a timely and less cumbersome manner.

- *Ask a series of questions*. When a manager demands a training course for employees, the trainer should start by asking questions related to the nature of the problem and its impact on the business. (The questions of the needs-analysis decision tree could be used.) Some trainers even agree to conduct a training course, as per the manager's demand, and then renegotiate the assignment as information emerges from interviews with employees before the course. Managers may be receptive to the emerging data,

recognizing the need to design solutions that solve the problem.
- *Use existing information*. Surveys, interviews, and observations are expensive data-collection methods. But most organizations keep customer complaint letters, grievance files, exit interviews, and sales data, which can be re-assessed for needs-assessment purposes.
- *Speed up data collection*. Use the intranet to survey employees. Start discussion groups around issues, concerns, and problems.
- *Link assessment and delivery*. Rather than conduct a lengthy needs analysis and then design a training program, some trainers attempt to join the two together, in small steps. For example, if there are star performers, bring them together in a forum with poorer performers to discuss effective techniques. The poorer performers not only are able to compare performance, but they learn how to improve at the same time.

Source: Adapted from Zemke, R. (1998). How to do a needs assessment when you think you don't have time. *Training*, *35* (3), 38–44. Training: the Human Side of Business by Zemke, R. ©1998–2006 VNU Business Media, Inc. Used with permission from *Training*.

Summary

This chapter has described the needs-analysis process. Three levels of needs analysis were discussed: organizational, task, and person analysis as well as a cognitive task analysis and a team task analysis. We also described the process of how to determine solutions to performance problems and if training and development is the best solution to performance problems. Data collection methods and sources of information were also described as well as the obstacles to needs analysis. It should now be clear to you that a needs analysis is critical for determining the nature of performance problems and whether or not training and development is the best solution to a performance problem. The importance of a needs analysis, however, does not end here. As you will see in the next chapter, a needs analysis is also necessary for writing training objectives and deciding on the content of a training program.

Key Terms

cognitive task analysis (page 100)
competency (page 97)
contingency management (page 105)
job description (page 97)
learning culture (page 96)
needs analysis (page 89)
organizational analysis (page 93)

person analysis (page 101)
resource analysis (page 95)
strategic training (page 93)
task analysis (page 96)
team task analysis (page 100)
training transfer climate (page 95)

Weblinks

The Banff Centre: www.banffcentre.ca/departments/leadership/ (page 97)

Boston Pizza: www.bostonpizza.com (page 90)

CIBC: www.cibc.com (page 102)

IBM: www.ibm.com/ca (page 91)

RPC Icons

RPC 4.1 Establishes priority of responses to needs-assessment results.
RPC 4.2 Conducts training needs assessments by identifying individual and corporate learning requirements.
RPC 4.3 Recommends the most appropriate way to meet identified learning needs (e.g., courses, secondments, and on-the-job activities).

Discussion Questions

1. Organizations often have data on file that can be used for the purposes of a needs analysis. Discuss the kinds of information that might already exist in an organization and how it might be useful for the purposes of an organizational, task, and/or person analysis.
2. If needs-analysis information has not been used as the basis for the design and delivery of a training program, what are some of the reasons why organizations decide to design and deliver training programs? Are these good reasons for investing in training and development programs?
3. Discuss the reasons why organizations do not always conduct a needs analysis and what a trainer might do to overcome needs-analysis obstacles. What are the implications of designing and implementing a training program without conducting a needs analysis?
4. Discuss the advantages and disadvantages of the different sources of needs-analysis information.

5. Discuss the process involved in determining solutions to performance problems. When is training likely to be a good solution? When is training not likely to be a good solution?
6. What is the difference between a training transfer climate and a learning culture? Why should an organization obtain information about the transfer climate and learning culture before designing and implementing a training program?
7. What is the difference between a task analysis, cognitive task analysis, and team task analysis? Discuss when and how each type of analysis should be conducted.

The Great Training Debate

1. Debate the following: Needs analysis is a waste of time. What is most important is getting people trained as soon as possible rather than wasting precious time to find out who needs training.

Using the Internet

1. To learn more about the different methods of needs analysis and how to decide on a method for conducting a needs analysis, go to **http://mime1.marc.gatech.edu/mm_tools/analysis.html**. Explain what the Needs Assessment Matrix is and how it works as well as the Needs Assessment Decision Aid. How can these instruments be used as part of the needs-analysis process and do you think they are useful? What are the advantages and disadvantages of using the following methods for needs analysis: questionnaires, interviews, and focus groups.
2. To find out how some companies are conducting training needs analysis, go to Industry Canada at **http://strategis.ic.gc.ca/epic/internet/incts-scf.nsf/en/sl00032e.html**. Click on the link for Case Studies and briefly summarize the approaches that each organization is using for needs analysis and the kind of diagnostic tools they are using.

Exercises

In-Class

1. Think of a problem you had or were aware of at an organization that you have worked for. Describe the problem and then using Magar and Pipe's flow diagram for determining solutions to performance problems (Figure 4.2), determine the best solution. Also consider each of the solutions in the figure and explain why it would or would not be a good solution to the problem. Finally, if you know what the organization did about the problem, describe what they did and if it was an effective solution.

2. Consider your job and performance as a student and conduct each of the following types of needs analysis: a) a task analysis, b) cognitive task analysis, c) team task analysis, and d) person analysis. Based on your results, indicate the critical tasks of a student as well as how well you perform each task, and on which tasks you need to improve your performance. What do you need to do to become a better student?

3. Find a partner in the class and take turns conducting a task analysis interview. Before beginning your interview, prepare a task analysis interview guide with questions that will help you identify tasks; rate their importance and frequency; and determine the task specifications (knowledge, skills, and abilities). The interviewee can refer to a current or previous job when answering the interviewer's questions. Also consider the relevance of a cognitive task analysis and a team task analysis.

4. Table 4.4 describes nine different methods of needs analysis. Review each of the methods and then explain what methods you think would be most appropriate for each of the following kinds of needs analysis: a) organizational analysis, b) task analysis, c) cognitive task analysis, d) team task analysis, and e) person analysis. Be sure to explain your reasoning as to why a particular method would be best for each type of needs analysis.

5. Recall a training program that you have attended as part of a current or previous job. To what extent do you think the program was based on an organizational, task, and person analysis? Try to relate specific aspects of the training program to each level of needs analysis. What performance problem was the program designed to address, and how effective was the program as a solution to the performance problem?

6. Imagine that you are a trainer in an organization that prides itself on providing employees with frequent opportunities for training. The president of the company has asked you to design and deliver a training program on team skills so that employees will be able to work in groups. He or she wants you to start training employees as soon as possible and does not want you to spend time and money conducting a needs analysis. He or she wants you to develop an action plan for the design and delivery of the program and present it in a week. How will you handle the needs analysis issue and what will you recommend? Prepare your presentation and present it to the class.

In-the-Field

1. To find out the extent to which organizations conduct needs analyses, contact the human resources staff of an organization and request an interview about needs analysis. In particular, find out if the organization conducts an organizational, task, and person analysis; the kinds of information they gather when they conduct each level of needs analysis; what methods and sources they use to gather the information; and what they do with the information and how it is used as part of the training and development process. If they do not conduct needs analyses, find out why, and how they determine training needs. Students should come to class prepared to present the results of their interviews.

Case Incident

Beer School

As part of Labatt's training and development strategy, all non-unionized employees attend beer school to learn about the art of brewing and serving. In fact, the company plans to send 4000 of its employees through the program, either at the employee pub at the company's head office in Toronto or at satellite locations across the country. Labatt employees who have completed beer school can talk knowledgeably about the fine points of beer with clients, friends, and family.

Questions

1. What information from a needs analysis (organizational, task, and person) might have suggested the need for employees to attend beer school?
2. Beer school is part of the company's training and development strategy. Do you think it is an example of strategic training?

Source: Humber, T. (2003, November 17). Serving up training. *Canadian HR Reporter, 16* (20), G1, G4. Reprinted with permission—Torstar Syndication Services.

Case

U-Haul and the Highway Traffic Act

In Ontario, the Highway Traffic Act has in place tough sanctions and fines that apply to commercial vehicles. However, there is an exemption in the Act that some refer to as a loophole, which indicates that trucks rented for short-term personal use are not commercial vehicles and are therefore exempt from some of the sanctions and tough penalties. The exemption includes do-it-yourself movers who are the target market for U-Haul. In fact, U-Haul is the market leader among do-it-yourself truck rental companies.

If police feel that the general maintenance on a commercial truck is poor, they can issue a $20,000 fine against the trucking company. However, a company falling under the exemption such as a U-Haul truck is immune from fines and also from having its safety violations recorded against the company's provincial Commercial Vehicle Operating Record (CVOR).

In July 2005, the *Toronto Star* conducted an investigation of the safety of U-Haul vehicles. One of their conclusions was that if you rent a U-Haul, you have a 50-50 chance of getting a truck that will not pass a road safety check. The *Star* based its investigation on three sources: Ontario Provincial Police data that show police failed 109 of 220 U-Haul vehicles during road-side safety checks between 2002 and 2004. An independent test conducted by the Ontario Safety League of four U-Haul vehicles rented at random, in which all four failed a standard North American provincial and state commercial vehicle safety inspection that every truck must pass yearly to continue operating. And U-Haul's driving record, accessed through the Ontario Ministry of Transportation, which showed that 17 of 35 U-Haul vehicles failed safety inspections over a two-year period.

Some of the violations found by the Ontario Safety League included holes on the floor on the driver's side, axle sealant leaking onto brake pads, one flat tire, one bulging tire, one tire with a nail in it, power-steering fluid leaks, coolant leaks, oil leaks, a loose king pin on the front axle. In all the trucks there were problems with the lights and signals.

Upon hearing of the Ontario Safety League investigation, U-Haul pulled the four vehicles in question out of service and hired independent mechanics to look at them. U-Haul agreed that three of the four trucks had "unacceptable" flaws and should not have been rented. The vice president of U-Haul Ontario said the company was dealing with the four locations that rented the four vehicles and stated that "employees and dealers are responsible for seeing that our equipment is in safe operating condition, scheduling repairs throughout the life of the vehicle."

U-Haul says it runs preventative maintenance inspections at 8000 kilometres, 24 000 kilometres, and 48 000 kilometres that "meet or exceed the federal specifications." Prior to the rental of a vehicle, the employee or dealer is required to check for fuel leaks, engine-oil leaks and levels, power steering leaks and levels, transmission-oil levels, broken seals, anti-freeze levels, tires for treads and air pressure, and to make sure all lights and signals are working and that the windshield is clean. And after every rental, an employee is required to ask the renter if there are any problems that need to be fixed "before the next customer rents this truck" including braking problems, engine overheating, and electrical problems.

U-Haul operates 1800 vehicles in Ontario. According to U-Haul's provincial operating record for the past two years, 35 trucks have had safety inspections and 17 failed. If not for the exemption, every OPP citation against U-Haul would be on record. During one weekend safety blitz, U-Haul vehicles failed six of eight inspections and were pulled off the road until they are repaired.

At the time, Harinder Takhar, Ontario's Minister of Transportation, said he will investigate closing the loophole in the Highway Traffic Act. "If we are having some evidence that there are safety concerns out there . . . I will get a full report. I'm asking the Ministry, what kind of problems did we find and if those problems are serious. I want to make sure the consumers are protected and safety is maintained on our highways." Police and the Ontario Safety League are calling for the loophole to be closed.

Following the *Toronto Star* investigation, the Ontario transportation ministry launched a province-wide investigation of the truck rental industry including surprise spot checks of U-Haul vehicles and other major truck rental companies and determined that U-Haul had the poorest safety record. This resulted in high-level meetings among MTO, OPP, and U-Haul executives. U-Haul subsequently promised that it would clean up its act and begin removing older vehicles from service, and more thoroughly check vehicles before they are rented. In December of the same year, however, a 43-year-old Peterborough man died after being thrown from a U-Haul truck when it flipped over.

Sources: McGran, K. (2005, July 4). Traffic act loophole puts drivers at risk. *Toronto Star*, A1; McGran, K. (2005, July 5). ABCs of do-it-yourself rentals. *Toronto Star*, A10; McGran, K. (2005, July 5). U-Haul rentals to get spot checks. *Toronto Star*, A1; McGran, K. (2005, July 5). U-Haul trails after trucks. *Toronto Star*, A10; McGran, K. (2005, July 6). Province to probe truck rental industry. *Toronto Star*, A1; McGran, K. (2005, December 5). Driver faults U-Haul in death. *Toronto Star*, A4. Reprinted with permission—Torstar Syndication Services.

Questions

1. Assume that you have been hired by U-Haul to conduct a needs analysis. Explain what you might want to find out from an organizational, task, and person analysis. How can each level of needs analysis shed light on the safety problem and whether or not training might be needed to solve it?

2. If you were to conduct a needs analysis at U-Haul, what methods and sources would you use? Be specific when indicating why you would or would not use a particular method and source.

3. Using the Mager and Pipe Flowchart in Figure 4.2, try to determine some possible solutions to the safety problem at U-Haul. Do you think that training is part of the solution? If so, who should be trained and what kind of training should they receive? What other solutions might be called for?

4. What effect if any do you think the government's surprise spot checks will have on U-Haul, its employees, and its training? If the Ontario Government closes the loophole in the Highway Traffic Act, what effect do you think this will have on U-Haul? Will it have an effect on training? Explain your answer.

References

1. Galvin, T. (2003, March). The 2003 training top 100. *Training, 40* (3), 18–36.
2. Salas, E., & Cannon-Bowers, J. A. (2001). The science of training: A decade of progress. *Annual Review of Psychology, 52*, 471–99.
3. Leigh, D., Watkins, R., Platt, W. A., & Kaufman, R. (2000). Alternate models of needs assessment: Selecting the right one for your organization. *Human Resource Development Quarterly, 11*, 87–93.
4. Kaufman, R. (1991). *Strategic planning plus: An organizational guide.* Glenview, IL: Scott Foreman Professional Books.
5. Leigh, D., Watkins, R., Platt, W. A., & Kaufman, R. (2000).
6. Mills, G. R., Pace, W., & Peterson, B. (1989). *Analysis in human resource training and organization development.* Reading, MA: Addison-Wesley.
7. Hall, B. (2003, February). The top training priorities for 2003. *Training, 40* (2), 38–42.
8. Estabrooke, M., & Foy, N. F. (1992). Answering the call of tailored training. *Training, 29* (10), 84–88.
9. Carr, C. (1992, June). The three Rs of training. *Training, 29* (6), 60–61.

10. Estabrooke, M., & Foy, N. F. (1992).

11. Goldstein, I. L. (1993). *Training in organizations* (3rd ed.). Pacific Grove, CA: Brooks/Cole.

12. Estabrooke, M., & Foy, N. F. (1992).

13. Gibb-Clark, M. (2000, February 11). Employee training can backfire on firms: Survey. *The Globe and Mail*, B10.

14. Heller, M. (2005, March). State's measure could undercut damage awards. *Workforce Management, 84* (3), 21–22.

15. Johnson, G. (2004, October). The perfect storm. *Training, 41* (10), 38–49.

16. Rouiller, J. Z., & Goldstein, I. L. (1993). The relationship between organizational transfer climate and positive transfer of training. *Human Resource Development Quarterly, 4*, 377–90.

17. Tracey, J. B, Tannenbaum, S. I, Kavanagh, M. J (1995). Applying trained skills on the job: The importance of the work environment. *Journal of Applied Psychology, 80*, 239–52.

18. Parry, S. B. (1998). Just what is a competency? *Training, 35* (6), 58–64.

19. MacNamara, D. (1998, November 16). Learning contracts, competency profiles the new wave in executive development. *Canadian HR Reporter*, pp. G8–G10.

20. Landey, F. J., & Vasey, J. (1991). Job analysis: The composition of SME samples. *Personnel Psychology, 44*. 27–50.

21. Salas, E., & Cannon-Bowers, J. A. (2001).

22. DuBois, D. A. (2002). Leveraging hidden expertise: Why, when, and how to use cognitive task analysis. In K. Kraiger's (Ed.), *Creating, implementing, and managing effective training and development: State-of-the-art lessons for practice*, (pp. 80–114). San Francisco. CA: Jossey-Bass.

23. Salas, E., Burke, C. S., & Cannon-Bowers, J. A. (2002). What we know about designing and delivering team training: Tips and guidelines. In K. Kraiger's (Ed.), *Creating, implementing, and managing effective training and development: State-of-the-art lessons for practice*, (pp. 234–59). San Francisco. CA: Jossey-Bass.

24. Salas, E., Burke, C. S., & Cannon-Bowers, J. A. (2002).

25. Trainor, N. L. (1998, November 16). Using measurement to predict performance. *Canadian HR Reporter*, pp. 7–8.

26. Mager, R. F., & Pipe, P. (1970). *Analyzing performance problems or you really oughta wanna*. Belmont, CA: Lear Siegler, Inc./Fearon.

27. Preskill, H. (1991). A comparison of data collection methods for assessing training needs. *Human Resource Development Quarterly, 2* (2), 143–156.

28. Rockburn, J. (1991, October 15). Streamlining human resources. *The Globe and Mail*, B15.

29. Tritsch, C. (1991, May). Assessing your training. *Human Resource Executive*.

30. Latham, G. P. (1988). Human resource training and development. *Annual Review of Psychology, 39*, 545–582.

31. McEnery, J., & McEnery, J. M. (1987). Self-rating in management training needs assessment: A neglected opportunity. *Journal of Occupational Psychology, 60*, 49–60. Staley, C. C., & Shockley-Zalaback, P. (1986). Communication proficiency and future training needs of the female professional: Self-assessment versus supervisors' evaluations. *Human Relations, 39*, 891–902.

32. Mabe, P. A., & West, S. G. (1982). Validity of self-evaluation of ability: A review and a meta-analysis. *Journal of Applied Psychology, 67*, 280–96.

33. Bardsely, C. A. (1987, April). Improving employee awareness of opportunity at IBM. *Personnel, 64* (4), 58–63.

34. Saari, L. M., Johnson, T. R., McLaughlin, S. D., & Zimmerle, D. M. (1988). A survey of management training and education practices in U.S. companies. *Personnel Psychology, 41* (4), 731–44.

Chapter 5

Training Design

Chapter Learning Objectives

After reading this chapter, you should be able to:

- define and write training objectives and describe the five elements and three components of them
- discuss the factors to consider when deciding to purchase or design a training program
- discuss the purpose of a request for proposal (RFP) and how to create an effective one
- describe the ways to determine the content of a training program
- describe on-the-job and off-the-job training methods
- define practice and active practice and the conditions of practice before and during training
- explain what error training involves and how it can be incorporated into the design of a training program

www4.bmo.com

BMO FINANCIAL GROUP

For the BMO Financial Group, employee training and development is a top priority. Over the past 10 years, BMO has invested more than $500 million in employee training and development. As a result, more than 8000 employees annually receive training at the company's Institute for Learning. Built in 1994 at a cost of $50 million, the Institute for Learning is a 13-acre complex with 14 high-tech classrooms, 150 bedrooms to accommodate out-of-town students, and a presentation hall that seats 400, as well as dining facilities and a gymnasium.

The Institute for Learning offers more than 700 courses to more than 34 000 employees who receive about six and a half days of training a year. Because BMO courses are custom-made, they are able to connect learning to the organization's strategies and by sending employees to the institute for training, they help to reinforce BMO's corporate culture and engender a sense of community among co-workers.

BMO offers a wide variety of courses but its primary programs include a four-year MBA program in financial services operated in conjunction with Dalhousie School of Management and the Institute for Canadian Bankers. Managerial leadership training is designed to prepare new managers by enhancing their strategic capabilities. Risk management training, offered in partnership with York University's Schulich School of Business, is available for seasoned risk managers. Project management programs are aimed at instilling change-management expertise.

The company recently designed a Corporate Audit Professional Upgrading of Skills program to improve the internal audit division's value to the company. Auditors complete an on-line, role-specific competency assessment that is used to create a customized learning plan. The program has resulted in a 100-percent increase in the audit division's service score, which is provided by clients based on the quality of auditors' work. And a series of selling training sessions to personal banker sales teams resulted in a 35 percent increase in personal deposits and sales points.

Whatever the program, training and development programs at BMO deal with real-world issues the company faces. Trainees are often asked to draft solutions and strategies for existing BMO concerns rather than tackle hypothetical scenarios. And because almost 30 percent of BMO's annual revenue comes from the United States, the company goes to great lengths to incorporate U.S.-specific rules and legislative matters into its training programs. In order to ensure the quality and relevance of its programs, the company conducts employee surveys to gather feedback from employees.

Not surprisingly, *Training* magazine ranked BMO Financial Group 14th in its highly respected Top 100 ranking of the best companies for training and development in 2006.[1]

BMO Financial Group is a good example of a company that invests a great deal of resources in the design of training and development programs. In order to stay competitive and ensure that employees have the knowledge and skills they need to perform their jobs, companies regularly need to design new training programs. In the case of BMO Financial Group, it recently designed the Corporate Audit Professional Upgrading of Skills program, which was recognized by *Training* magazine as an outstanding initiative.[2]

The design of training and development programs involves many important decisions such as whether to purchase a training program from a vendor or design it in-house; deciding on the content of a program and the training methods to use; and how to design a program so that trainees have opportunities for practice that maximize their learning and retention.

In the previous chapter, we described the process of identifying training needs and determining solutions to performance problems. When it has been determined that training is part of the solution to performance problems, the needs-analysis information must then be translated into training objectives and a training program. This involves the following activities which are described in this chapter:

1. Write training objectives.
2. Decide to purchase or design a training program.
3. Create an effective request for proposal (RFP) to purchase training services and programs.
4. Determine the training content.
5. Decide on the training methods.
6. Incorporate active practice into the training program.
7. Integrate errors into learning and training.

Training Objectives

A **training objective** is a statement of what trainees are expected to be able to do after a training program. Training objectives answer the question, "What should trainees be able to do at the end of a training program?" Put another way, an objective is the expected outcome of training. The objectives also describe the knowledge and skills to be acquired.

The emphasis of training is usually learning, on-the-job behaviour, and job performance. Learning involves the process of acquiring new knowledge, skills, and attitudes, while performance involves the use of these new skills, knowledge, and attitudes on the job. Training objectives usually refer to the acquisition of knowledge and/or skills as well as behaviour on the job.

Training objective

A statement of what trainees are expected to be able to do after a training program

TABLE 5.1

Purposes of Training Objectives

Training objectives serve a number of important purposes for trainers, trainees, and managers.

TRAINERS

1. Trainees can be assessed prior to instruction to determine if they have mastered any of the objectives. Depending on the results, trainees can either omit certain sections of a training program or undertake additional training to master the prerequisites.
2. The selection of training content and methods is simplified by objectives. The choice of content and methods will be guided by the need to achieve certain objectives.
3. Learning objectives enable evaluators to develop measures for evaluation and to determine how to calculate the benefits and outcomes of a program.

TRAINEES

4. Objectives inform trainees of the goals of a training program and what they will be expected to learn and do at the end of a training program.
5. Objectives allow trainees to focus their energies on achieving specific goals, rather than waste energy on irrelevant tasks or on trying to figure out what is required of them.
6. Objectives communicate to employees that training is important and that they will be accountable for what they learn in training.

MANAGERS

7. Objectives communicate to supervisors, professional groups, and others what the trainee is expected to have learned by the end of a training program and what the trainee should be able to do.
8. Management and supervisors know exactly what is expected of trainees and can reinforce and support newly trained knowledge and skills on the job.

Training objectives are an important link between the needs-analysis stage and the other stages of the training and development process. In addition to stating what employees will learn and be able to do following a training program, training objectives serve a number of purposes for trainees, trainers, and managers which are described in Table 5.1.

ⓇⓅⒸ 5.1   Writing Training Objectives

The writing of training objectives is a skill that can be learned. Skill in writing training objectives does not mean that trainers can make lists of behaviour verbs such as "recognize" and "evaluate." The real skill is the ability to rework needs-analysis information into performance outcomes. A training objective should contain five key elements of the desired outcome as follows:

1. *Who is to perform the desired behaviour?* Employees and managers are the easiest to identify. In a training situation more accurate descriptors might be "all first-level supervisors," "anyone conducting selection interviews," or "all employees with more than one month of experience." The trainer is not the "who," although it is tempting for some trainees to write, for example, that the trainer will present five hours of information on communication. The goal of the instructor is to maximize the efficiency with which all trainees achieve the specified objectives, not just present the information.[3]

2. *What is the actual behaviour to be employed to demonstrate mastery of the training content or objective?* Actions described by words like "type," "run," and "calculate" can be measured easily. Other mental activities such as comprehension and analysis can also be described in measurable ways.

3. *Where and, 4., When is the behaviour to be demonstrated and evaluated (i.e., under what conditions)?* These could include "during a 60-minute typing test," "on a ski hill with icy conditions," "when presented with a diagram," or "when asked to design a training session." The tools, equipment, information, and other source materials for training should be specified. Included in this list may be things the trainee may not use, such as calculators.

5. *What is the standard by which the behaviour will be judged?* Is the trainee expected to type 60 words per minute with fewer than three errors? Can the trainee list five out of six purposes for training objectives?

An example of a training objective that includes the five elements is as follows:

> *The sales representative* (who) *will be able to make 10 calls a day to new customers in the territory assigned* (what, where, when), *and will be able to generate three (30 percent) sales worth at least $500 from these calls* (how, or the criterion).

Finally, when the five elements are included in a training objective, then the final written objective should contain three key components:

1. **Performance:** What the trainee will be able to do after the training. In other words, what work behaviour the trainee will be able to display.

2. **Condition:** The tools, time, and situation under which the trainee is expected to perform the behaviour. In other words, where and when the behaviour will occur.

3. **Criterion:** The level of acceptable performance or the standard or criteria against which performance will be judged.

The first attempt at writing training objectives will be difficult. However, after some experience, a generalization of these planning skills will occur. Representative workers should be involved in the development of the training objectives. A team consisting of the trainer, trainees, and their supervisors would be ideal.[4] At some point, the objectives should be reviewed with, and approved by, the management and the supervisors of the trainees. Nadler cites a case in which a sales training program, based on a needs analysis of sales representatives, was rejected by senior management because management were secretly planning fundamental organizational changes.[5]

At this stage, the training objectives should closely resemble the task analysis. For example, one task of the job of a receptionist could be: *The receptionist* (who) *sorts 100 pieces of incoming mail by categories of complaints, requests for information, and invoices* (what) *within 60 minutes, with less than one percent processing errors* (how). This could easily become a training objective. A training objective that reads like an actual job behaviour is more likely to be approved, learned, and used on the job.

In summary, a training objective contains an observable action with a measurable criterion outlining the conditions of performance. Once training objectives have been developed, the next step is to design a training program. However, at this point the question that arises is whether a training program will be designed in-house by the organization or by an external consultant. Thus, one must first decide whether or not a training program will be purchased all or in part or designed in-house by the organization.

The Purchase-or-Design Decision

Once it has been determined that a training program is an appropriate course of action to manage a performance problem, and training objectives have been developed, the organization faces a make-or-buy decision. Many private training companies and consultants in Canada offer an extensive array of courses on general topics such as computer training and customer service (see the Using the Internet exercise at the end of this chapter).

In many cases, it is more economical for an organization to purchase these materials, packaged in a professional format, than to develop the materials themselves, which in many cases will be used only once or twice.

For example, most organizations do not design training courses in basic skills; they form alliances with educational institutions, community colleges, or private organizations that specialize in developing and delivering basic skills training programs.[6] Recall in the chapter-opening vignette that BMO forms alliances with several universities that provide them with specialized training programs in areas such as the MBA program, in financial services, and in risk management training. Organizations are particularly likely to purchase training programs that do not require organization-specific content and are of a more generic nature. For example, organizations prefer to use outside consultants for sexual harassment training.[7]

The advantages of packaged programs are high quality, immediate delivery, ancillary services (tests, videos), the potential to customize the package to the organization, benefits from others' implementation experience, extensive testing, and often less expense than internally developed programs.[8]

Training programs developed internally by an organization also have some advantages including security and confidentiality, use of the organization's language, incorporation of the organization's values, use of internal content expertise, understanding of the specific target audience and organization, and the pride and credibility of having a customized program.[9]

Because many of BMO's programs are custom-made they are able to connect learning to the organization's strategy and the training reinforces the company's corporate culture.

Purchase Decision Considerations

Given the pros and cons of purchasing and designing a training program, what factors should be considered in making a decision? Obviously, one of the most important factors to consider is the cost of each alternative. A cost-benefit analysis would be necessary to determine the best option. Some types of training programs will be much more costly to design than to purchase. However, there are other factors that should also be considered in addition to cost.

For example, does the human resource department have the time and expertise to design a training program? Designing a training program from scratch requires expertise in many areas such as training methods and principles, and theories of learning. If the human resource department does not have this expertise in-house then it will need to purchase all or part of a training program. As well, developing a training program is a time-consuming endeavour. Unless a human resource department has a training function and training staff or is otherwise well staffed, it may not have the time to design training programs.

Time is also a factor in terms of how soon the organization wants to begin training. Given the amount of time required to design a new training program, if there is a need or desire to begin training as soon as possible then the organization will need to purchase a training program. In effect, the sooner the organization wants to begin training, the less likely there will be sufficient time to design a new training program.

Another important consideration is the number of employees who will need to be trained and the extent to which future employees will also require training. If a relatively small number of employees require training, then it is probably not worthwhile to design an entire training program. However, if a large number of employees need to receive training now and in the future, then designing a new training program from scratch makes more sense. In other words, to the extent that the training program will be used for many employees in both the short- and long-term, a decision to design the program is more favourable.

Although we have been referring to the purchase of an entire training program, it is important to realize that purchasing can involve buying particular training materials such as a video package or buying an entire training program that is specially designed for the organization. As well, a consultant could be hired to design and deliver a training program or it can be delivered by people within the organization once it has been designed by a consultant.

Organizations can also purchase off-the-shelf training programs that are already designed and which contain all the materials required to deliver a training program.

 **5.2**

Request for proposal (RFP)

A document that outlines to potential vendors and consultants an organization's training and project needs

Request for Proposal (RFP)

When an organization decides to purchase a training program, it needs to begin the process of finding a vendor or consultant who will be able to design and/or deliver the program. The process of identifying and hiring a vendor or consultant begins with a **request for proposal (RFP)** which is a document that outlines to potential vendors and consultants the organization's training and project needs. Vendors and consultants can then review the RFP and determine if they are able to provide the products and services required by the organization and if they should prepare a proposal and bid on the job. The organization must then evaluate the proposals it receives and choose a vendor that can provide the best solution and is also a good match for the organization.

A request for proposal should provide detailed information about the organization's training needs and the nature of the project and will often include the following sections:[10]

- Pre-qualification checklist.
- Detailed description of the opportunity.
- Description of the company and its culture.
- Scope of the project.
- Detailed statement of work.
- Detailed instructions on how to respond to the RFP.
- Schedule for the entire RFP and selection process with milestones.
- Basis of the award.
- Definition of the level of service required.
- Request for additional information.
- Confidentiality agreements.

Creating an RFP is an important step in searching for a vendor because it requires the organization to describe its most critical training needs and the nature of the training solution required. This will help to ensure that the organization purchases what it really needs and also communicates the training needs and required project to stakeholders and potential vendors. Failure to prepare a detailed RFP can result in an organization purchasing a program that it really does not need and at a much higher cost than necessary. There are many stories of companies that failed to create a good RFP and then purchased programs and systems that went well beyond what they really needed.[11] To learn more about how to create an effective RFP, see the Trainer's Notebook 1.

One of the most important things that an organization needs to determine is the extent to which a vendor's products and services match the needs of the organization. To learn about how one company found a vendor for its needs, see the Training Today feature "Training for Consistency at Wendy's International."

How to Create an Effective Request for Proposal (RFP)

Creating an effective RFP is a difficult and time-consuming task. However, a good RFP will ensure that an organization gets the training program and systems it needs from the right vendor at an appropriate cost. Here are eight things to consider when creating an RFP.

- *Have a clear vision of your overall learning strategy:* There must be a master strategy that is based on the primary needs of the various departments involved.
- *Create proper scope for the project:* Set a budget and align the most critical needs with project requirements.
- *Develop a vendor pre-qualification checklist:* Write a pre-qualification checklist before writing the RFP so that vendors can quickly decide if they can provide the required products and services. The checklist should have between 10 and 20 items and indicate the qualifications for the most critical needs.
- *Create a vendor scorecard:* Create a scorecard to grade vendors before writing the RFP to ensure that you request the necessary information in the RFP. The evaluators should rate each item on the scorecard on a scale of zero to five.
- *Use a template:* Use a template to create the RFP if one exists in the organization. Even one used for non-training purchases can be helpful in creating an RFP.
- *Don't overstate the positive or understate the negative:* Be candid about the project so vendors can adequately determine their suitability for it.
- *Design a request-for-information questionnaire:* The questionnaire should be designed to obtain additional information about a vendor's products, services, experience, and background. Most of the questions should be directly related to the needs of the project and the vendor's ability to provide a solution that meets the organization's needs.
- *Allow sufficient time for responses:* Provide at least two to three weeks for most standard projects so that vendors can carefully analyze the requirements and prepare a detailed response.

Source: Based on Chapman, B. (2004, January). How to create the ideal RFP. *Training, 41* (1), 40–43.

Training Content

Once a decision has been made to design a training program, decisions must be made about the training content. This is a crucial stage, as one wants to be sure that the training content matches the training needs and objectives. The importance of this has been noted by Campbell who states, "By far the highest-priority question for designers, users, and investigators of training is, 'What is to be learned?' That is, what (specifically) should a training program try to accomplish, and what should the training content be?" (p. 188).[12]

To understand the importance of this issue, consider an organization that sells dental equipment and supplies. Although the company regularly offers new products, they do not sell very well. The reason appears to be because the sales force concentrates on repeat sales of more common supplies and materials. There are a number of reasons why this might be the case. For example, the sales force might not be sufficiently informed about the new products or they might not have the skills required to sell them. Other reasons could be a lack of motivation or an attitude problem. The point is that the content of a training program can be directed toward any one or more of these areas.

Training for Consistency at Wendy's International

W W W Wendy's International is one of the largest restaurant chains in the world, with a global workforce of more than 227 000 employees and an annual turnover rate that ranges from 180 to 200 percent. This adds up to about half a million employees, at thousands of franchises around the world, who need to be trained every year.

In order to achieve its goals for growth and to expand brand equity, the company realized that it needed to develop a training strategy. According to Wendy's vice president of solutions delivery, "Training and development is a very key part of providing our customers with a consistent experience in every restaurant regardless of store location." Thus, providing customers with a consistent experience means that Wendy's employees must have access to consistent training.

Unfortunately, the company had no way to ensure that training was consistent throughout the organization and relied on a paper-based tracking system to manage employee training. It also lacked the capability to provide some of its training on-line which would reduce the cost of training a constantly changing workforce.

Wendy's began to search for a system that would improve the consistency of the company's training programs across its brands and locations, provide just-in-time training, and shorten the waiting time for getting employees trained. They also wanted a solution that would integrate classroom and computer-based training. A search began for a vendor that could provide these products and services and also scale the program to the size of the organization so that one solution could be used throughout the company.

Wendy's found a solution with Plateau Systems, a provider of Web-based software for developing and managing organizational skills and talent. Plateau's global deployment system allows Wendy's to consolidate, schedule, track, deliver, and manage training more efficiently. The system also supports blended learning, classroom training, computer-based training, and just-in-time training. Web-based, CD-ROM, instructor-led, and on-the-job training are now available on one system in various languages.

In addition, Wendy's can now assess employee competencies and skills and track the level of training and certification in each restaurant. And by integrating the system with its human resource information system, they are now able to design learning development plans for employees based on their job positions and requirements. The system alerts employees when training is required or when an organizational procedure has changed, and it also manages all food safety certification and re-certification requirements for employees. Wendy's is also able to track and manage the costs of training in each franchise.

The new system has not only ensured consistency in training by automating and consolidating all corporate training onto a single platform, but it has also resulted in significant improvements in store profitability. The impact of training on store performance has been substantial. And consistency in training means that customers will have the same Wendy's experience wherever they are in the world.

Source: Based on (2006, February). Wendy's: Consistently excellent through training. *T+D, 60* (2), 68–69. Copyright © February 2006, *T+D*. Reprinted with permission of American Society for Training & Development.

Obviously, designing a training program to inform the sales force about the new products will not be very effective if what they are lacking are sales skills. Getting the content right is one of the most important stages in training design.

A trainer will have a good idea of the nature of the training content from the needs analysis and the training objectives. This is another reason why it is so important to conduct a thorough needs analysis prior to designing a training program. As well, employees' current levels of knowledge and skills can be compared to the organization's desired levels as indicated by the performance goals or objectives. The gap between the two represents the organization's training needs and determines the precise content of the training course.

According to Donald Kirkpatrick, trainers should ask themselves, "What topics should be presented to meet the needs and accomplish the objectives?" (p. 11).[13] The answers to this question should help in identifying the content to include in a training program. In some cases, the required training is legislated, such as the Workplace Hazardous Materials Information System (WHMIS), which requires that workers in certain occupations across Canada receive training on the potential hazards of chemicals in the workplace and emergency procedures for the clean-up and disposal of a spill (see Chapter 13). In such cases, the content of training is specified in the legislation as well as in the requirements for employee certification.

In other cases, however, it might not be clear exactly what content should be included in a training program or how to translate training objectives into training content and the sequence in which the content should be learned.[14]

(R)(P)(C) 5.3

Being more precise about training content can occur in a number of ways. One of the most common and effective ways to identify training content is to consult with subject-matter experts who are knowledgeable in a particular area and know the topic well enough that they can specify the training content.[15] For example, to determine the content of a training program on sales techniques, one can consult with experienced salespersons, consultants, or managers. At BMO, the behavioral characteristics of top performers are integrated into training programs. For example, they surveyed the highest-ranking commercial account managers in order to identify their best work habits and key drivers of success. Their responses were then incorporated into a guide that was given to all employees within the account management sales force.[16] Thus, on the basis of the subject-matter experts' judgments, experiences, and behaviours, one can identify the training content required to achieve training objectives.

Training Methods

Once the training content has been determined, the next step is to decide what training methods will be used.[17] The topic of training methods is extensive and as a result, the next three chapters are devoted to it. For now we will present a brief introduction to this important part of training design.

Training methods can be arranged into a number of different categories such as active versus passive methods or one-way versus two-way communication. For our purposes, we will distinguish training methods in terms of where they take place since this is a fairly tangible distinction. That is, some training methods occur on the job, such as coaching and performance aids, while others take place off the job and usually in a classroom, such as lectures or games and simulations.

(R)(P)(C) 5.4

A variety of off-the-job and on-the-job training methods are described in Chapters 6 and 7. These methods differ in terms of their effectiveness for teaching different types of training content and for various learning outcomes. The fact is that there are many training methods from which to choose. The choice will be constrained by time, money, or tradition.

Research shows that learning and retention are best achieved through the use of training methods that promote productive responses from trainees.[18]

Productive responses are those in which the trainee actively uses the training content rather than passively watches, listens, or imitates the trainer. In addition, it is also believed that training methods that encourage active participation during training also enhance learning.[19] Recall in the chapter-opening vignette that BMO requires trainees to draft solutions and strategies for existing concerns facing the company. Thus, trainees are required to solve real-world problems the company faces. In the next section, we discuss the importance of active practice in the design of a training program.

Ultimately, the objectives of a training program and the training content should help to determine the most appropriate training methods. The best approach, however, is usually a **blended** approach that consists of a combination of classroom training, on-the-job training, and self-paced instruction using computer technology such as CD-ROMs or the Internet.

Active Practice

An important consideration in the design of a training program is how to facilitate and maximize trainees' learning and retention of the training content. One of the most important ways that people learn and acquire new skills is through practice.[20] It is therefore important to incorporate practice into the design of a training program. But what exactly is practice?

Practice refers to physical or mental rehearsal of a task, skill, or knowledge in order to achieve some level of proficiency in performing the task or skill or demonstrating the knowledge.[21] There is a certain degree of truth to the adage "practice makes perfect." A student who practices answering exam questions learns more than someone who just reads the text book. A manager will probably learn more about interviewing by actually conducting a mock interview than by listening to a lecture on interviewing. In general, both adults and children learn through active practice.

In the context of training, we often refer to **active practice**, which means that trainees are provided with opportunities to practice the task or use the knowledge being learned during training. Therefore, training programs should include opportunities for active practice. The effectiveness of active practice, however, depends on a number of conditions that occur before and during a training program. In the following sections, we describe different practice conditions that take place before (prepractice) and during a training program that influence the effectiveness of practice and can maximize trainee learning and retention.

Prepractice Conditions

A number of conditions that occur prior to practice can improve learning and retention. These are strategies or interventions that can be implemented prior to a training program to prepare trainees for practice and include: 1. Attentional advice, 2. Metacognitive strategies, 3. Advance organizers, 4. Goal-orientation, 5. Preparatory information, and 6. Prepractice briefs.[22]

Attentional advice involves providing trainees with information about the task process and general task strategies that can help them learn and perform

---

Blended training

The use of a combination of approaches to training such as classroom training, on-the-job training, and computer technology training such as CD-ROMs or the Internet.

Practice

Physical or mental rehearsal of a task, skill, or knowledge in order to achieve some level of proficiency in performing the task or skill or demonstrating the knowledge

Active practice

Providing trainees with opportunities to practice performing a training task or using knowledge during training

Attentional advice

Providing trainees with information about the task process and general task strategies that can help them learn and perform a task

a task. This helps to focus trainees' attention on task strategies that can aid them in learning and performing a task and to generalize what is learned in practice to other situations in which the general strategies can be applied.

Trainees can also benefit more from practice if they know how to regulate their learning through a process known as metacognition. **Metacognition** refers to a self-regulatory process that helps people guide their learning and performance (recall the discussion of self-management in Chapter 3). In this way, people can assess and adjust their progress and strategies while learning to perform a task. Metacognition consists of two primary functions: monitoring and control. Monitoring involves identifying the task, checking and evaluating one's progress, and predicting the outcomes of that progress. Control involves decisions about where to allocate one's resources, the specific steps to complete a task, the speed and intensity to work on a task, and the prioritization of activities.[23]

Metacognition involves the use of various metacognitive activities or strategies. **Metacognitive strategies** (e.g., thinking out loud, self-diagnosing weaknesses, posing questions to yourself during practice, answering the question, "Why am I doing this?") refer to ways in which trainees can be instructed to self-regulate their learning of a task. Metacognitive strategies can be taught to trainees prior to training so they can self-regulate and guide their own learning and performance during practice sessions. The use of metacognitive strategies during training has been found to be positively related to declarative knowledge, self-efficacy, and training performance.[24] To find out if you use metacognitive strategies when learning, see Table 5.2.

Advance organizers refer to activities that provide trainees with a structure or framework to help them assimilate and integrate information acquired during training. In other words, they help trainees structure and organize information. Examples of advance organizers include outlines, text, diagrams, and graphic organizers. Advance organizers have been found to be particularly useful for learning highly complex and factual material and for low-ability trainees.

Goal orientation refers to the type of goal that is set during training. You might recall the discussion from Chapter 3 that there are two types of goal orientations: a mastery goal orientation and a performance goal orientation. Mastery goals focus trainees' attention on the learning process while performance goals focus attention on the achievement of specific performance outcomes. Because mastery goals focus trainees' attention on the process of learning and skill acquisition, they tend to be more effective. In fact, mastery goals have been found to be related to more metacognitive activity and to result in faster skill acquisition. Thus, mastery goals appear to be most effective for practice because they focus trainees' attention on learning the task rather than on their performance during training. Research has found a mastery goal orientation to be positively related to a number of training outcomes including knowledge, self-efficacy, and performance.[25]

Preparatory information involves providing trainees with information about what they can expect to occur during practice sessions (e.g., events and consequences) so that they can develop strategies to overcome performance obstacles. As a result, trainees who are provided with preparatory information prior to practice are better prepared to learn and perform a task. They know

---

Metacognition

A self-regulatory process that helps people guide their learning and performance

Metacognitive strategies

Refers to ways in which trainees can be instructed to self-regulate their learning of a task

Advance organizers

Activities that provide trainees with a structure or framework to help them assimilate and integrate information acquired during practice

Goal orientation

The type of goal that is set during training (mastery goal or performance goal)

Preparatory information

Providing trainees with information about what they can expect to occur during practice sessions so that they can develop strategies to overcome performance obstacles

TABLE 5.2

Rate Your Metacognitive Activity

Metacognitive activity involves the use of strategies to monitor and control one's learning. More broadly, it has been described as "thinking about your thinking." In a study by Arron Schmidt and J. Kevin Ford, trainees who scored higher on this scale of metacognitive activity acquired more declarative knowledge, had higher levels of self-efficacy, and demonstrated superior training performance. To find out the extent to which you engage in metacognitive activities when learning, answer the following questions the next time you attend a training program or after your next class!

Answer each question using the following scale:

1 = Almost never

2 = Not very often

3 = Sometimes

4 = Often

5 = Almost always

1. During this class or training program, I made up questions to help focus on my learning.
2. During this class or training program, I asked myself questions to make sure I understood the things I had been trying to learn.
3. During this class or training program, I tried to change the way I learned in order to fit the demands of the situation or topic.
4. During this class or training program, I tried to think through each topic and decide what I am supposed to learn from it, rather than just jumping in without thinking.
5. During this class or training program, I tried to determine which things I didn't understand well and adjusted my learning strategies accordingly.
6. During this class or training program, I set goals for myself in order to direct my activities.
7. If I got confused during this class or training program, I made sure I sorted it out as soon as I could before moving on.
8. During this class or training program, I thought about how well my tactics for learning were working.
9. During this class or training program, I thought carefully about how well I had learned material I had previously studied.
10. During this class or training program, I thought about what skills needed the most practice.
11. During this class or training program, I tried to monitor closely the areas where I needed the most improvement.
12. During this class or training program, I thought about what things I needed to do to learn.
13. During this class or training program, I carefully selected what to focus on to improve on weaknesses I identified.
14. During this class or training program, I noticed where I made mistakes and focused on improving those areas.
15. When I practiced a new skill in this class or training program, I monitored how well I was learning its requirements.

Source: Schmidt, A. M., & Ford, J. K. (2003). Learning within a learner control training environment: The interactive effects of goal orientation and metacognitive instruction on learning outcomes. *Personnel Psychology, 56,* 405–429; Blackwell Publishing, 2003.

Prepractice briefs

Sessions in which team members establish their roles and responsibilities and performance expectations prior to a team practice session

what to expect and how to overcome performance obstacles. Preparatory information is particularly useful for learning to perform stressful tasks where the ability to cope and overcome obstacles is critical for task performance.

A final example of a prepractice condition is specific to team training. **Prepractice briefs** involve sessions in which team members establish their roles and responsibilities and performance expectations prior to a team practice session. Prepractice briefs can improve team practice sessions especially for tasks that are fast-paced and stressful.

Conditions of Practice during Training

In addition to prepractice conditions, there are also a number of practice conditions that occur during training. They include: 1. Massed or distributed practice, 2. Whole or part learning, 3. Overlearning, 4. Task sequencing, and 5. Feedback and knowledge of results.

Massed versus distributed practice has to do with how the segments of a training program are divided. Massed practice, or cramming, is practice with virtually no rest periods, such as when the training is conducted in one single session instead of being divided into several sessions with breaks or rest periods between them. Distributed or spaced practice conditions include rest intervals during the practice session.

Students might argue that they can succeed on an exam for which they have crammed, but research shows that memory loss after cramming is greater than if a student had studied over several weeks. Furthermore, organizations would prefer that trainees retain material over many months, rather than just knowing it for the course, test, or simulation.

Research has shown that material that was learned under distributed practice is retained longer.[26] Furthermore, a recent review of research on practice conditions found that distributed practice sessions resulted in higher performance than massed practice conditions.[27] Thus, practice is more effective when practice periods are spread over time, rather than massed together. Trainers teaching a new skill, such as negotiation, could increase learning by spacing the training and practices over a week of two-hour sessions, rather than cramming it into an eight-hour day. Distributed practice is most effective for trainees with little or no experience, when the rest periods are shorter early on but longer later in training, and for learning motor skills.[28]

Whole versus part learning has to do with whether all of the training material is learned and practiced at one time or one part at a time.[29] For example, piano students often learn complex pieces one hand at a time. Research has found that the best strategy depends on the trainee and the nature of the task. Whole learning is more effective when the trainee has high intelligence, practice is distributed, the task organization of the training material is high, and task complexity is low. Generally speaking, when the task itself is composed of relatively clear and different parts or sub-tasks, it is best for trainees to learn and practice each part at a time and then perform all parts in one whole sequence. However, if the task itself is relatively simple and consists of a number of closely interrelated tasks, then a strategy of whole learning makes more sense.[30]

Overlearning is another condition of practice that refers to learning something until the behaviour becomes automatic. In other words, trainees are provided with continued opportunities for practice even after they have mastered the task.[31] It is an effective way to train people for emergency responses or for complex skills in which there is little time to think in a job situation. It is also important for skills that employees might not need to use

Massed versus distributed practice
Refers to how the segments of a training program are divided and whether the training is conducted in a single session (massed) or is divided into several sessions with breaks or rest periods between them (distributed)

Whole versus part learning
Refers to whether the training material is learned and practiced at one time or one part at a time

Overlearning
Continued practice even after trainees have mastered a task so that the behaviour becomes automatic

very often on the job. Overlearning will help to ensure that performance of the task will be habitual or automatic. Automaticity refers to the performance of a skill to the point at which little attention from the brain is required to respond correctly.[32] Typing is the most common example of automaticity.

Overlearning is an effective method for both cognitive and physical tasks. The greater the degree of overlearning, the longer the resulting retention of the training material.[33]

Task sequencing

Dividing training material into an organized and logical sequence of sub-tasks

Task sequencing has to do with the manner in which the learning tasks are organized and arranged. The basic idea is that learning can be improved by dividing the training material into an organized sequence of sub-tasks. The idea behind task sequencing was first proposed by Robert Gagné, who argued that practice is not enough for learning to occur.[34] What is most important is that the distinct sub-tasks be identified and arranged in a logical sequence. In this manner, a trainee will learn each successive sub-task before the total task is performed. The trainee learns to perform each step or task in the proper order or sequence. According to Gagné, what is most important in the design of training is the identification of the component tasks or sub-tasks and the arrangement of them into a meaningful and suitable sequence.[35]

Feedback or knowledge of results

Providing trainees with information and knowledge about their performance on a training task

Feedback or knowledge of results involves providing trainees with information and knowledge about their performance on a training task. Research indicates that feedback is critical for learning for at least three reasons.[36] First, it allows trainees to correct mistakes and improve their performance. Second, positive feedback can help build confidence and strengthen trainees' self-efficacy. Third, positive feedback can be reinforcing and stimulate continued efforts and learning.

During training, feedback can be provided to guide trainees as they attempt new behaviours. This feedback should be designed to correct performance. When incorrect responses are given, the feedback should include the correct response. Negative feedback ("You failed to acknowledge the client's problem.") will not be perceived as punishing if the source is knowledgeable, friendly, trustworthy, and powerful enough to affect outcomes like promotions.[37] However, to be most effective, feedback should be accurate, specific, credible, timely, and positive.[38]

In a study of the effect of feedback on the performance of hourly workers, Miller concluded that the relevance, specificity, timing, and accuracy of the feedback are the critical factors in mastery of learning.[39] Trainees receiving this type of feedback are more likely to adjust their responses toward the correct behaviour, more likely to be motivated to change, and more likely to set goals for improving or maintaining performance.[40] Training methods such as computer-assisted instruction and structured behaviour modelling have feedback as an integral and embedded component. See The Trainer's Notebook 2 on the key elements for providing effective feedback.

In summary, training programs can be designed to facilitate and maximize trainees' learning and retention by providing trainees with opportunities for active practice. In addition, a number of conditions of practice before and during training can be used to improve the benefits of active practice for learning and retention. Table 5.3 summarizes the conditions of practice before and during training.

How to Give Feedback

Feedback can be very effective for learning and changing behaviour if the feedback is perceived as being constructive, not critical. Here are some tips on how to do give feedback.

- *Timing:* Try to provide the feedback immediately after the behaviour or performance is observed.
- *Be specific:* Feedback works best when it is specific. Don't say, "You moved the arm wrong," but, "You have the arm tilted at 30 degrees."
- *Guide:* After discussing what was poorly done, provide guidance on the correct performance. ("You had the arm tilted at a 30-degree angle; you will find it easier or quicker to tilt it 90 degrees.")
- *Reward correct performance:* "Good, you have the right 90-degree angle," not just "good."

TABLE 5.3

The Conditions of Practice

Active practice is an important component of training and can facilitate trainee learning and retention. The following conditions of practice can be used before and during training in order to maximize the benefits of practice.

PREPRACTICE CONDITIONS

1. *Attentional advice:* Providing trainees with information about the task process and general task strategies that can help them learn and perform a task.
2. *Metacognitive strategies:* Refers to ways in which trainees can be instructed to self-regulate their learning of a task.
3. *Advance organizers:* Activities that provide trainees with a structure or framework to help them assimilate and integrate information acquired during practice.
4. *Goal orientation:* The type of goal that is set during training (mastery or performance).
5. *Preparatory information:* Providing trainees with information about what they can expect to occur during practice sessions.
6. *Prepractice briefs:* Sessions in which team members establish their roles and responsibilities and establish performance expectations prior to a team practice session.

CONDITIONS DURING TRAINING

1. *Massed or distributed practice:* Refers to how the segments of a training program are divided and whether the training is conducted in a single session or is divided into several sessions with breaks or rest periods between them.
2. *Whole or part learning:* Refers to whether the training material is learned and practised at one time or one part at a time.
3. *Overlearning:* Continued practice even after trainees have mastered a task so that the behaviour becomes automatic.
4. *Task sequencing:* Refers to dividing training material into an organized and logical sequence of sub-tasks.
5. *Feedback and knowledge of results:* Providing trainees with information and knowledge about their performance on a training task.

Integrating Errors into Learning and Training

In the previous section, we described various conditions of practice that can be integrated into the design of training programs to maximize trainee learning and retention. But what about designing training programs so that trainees make errors while they are learning? At first, this might seem like a ridiculous idea. After all, we usually try to avoid making errors since they can be frustrating and lead to anger and despair. But think again. Isn't it the case that errors and mistakes do happen quite frequently during the learning process? If so, then why not design training programs so that trainees make errors and learn from them?

First, it is helpful to understand why errors might be important for learning. According to Michael Frese and his colleagues who have studied errors in training, errors are a source of negative feedback which can have a positive and informative function in training. In fact, they argue that negative feedback is a necessary prerequisite for learning. Thus, rather than being avoided, errors should be incorporated into the training process. They refer to it as "error training."[41] As a form of negative feedback, we can consider error training or the integration of errors into training as another example of a practice condition during training.

But what exactly is error training? **Error training** involves explicitly allowing trainees to make errors while learning to perform a task. Thus, it increases trainee exposure to errors. This can be done by providing trainees with only basic information or minimal instructions about how to perform a task they are learning. As a result, trainees need to try out different approaches when practicing a task, which means that they will make a number of errors in the process. When the training is **error-avoidant**, the trainees are given detailed instructions on how to do a task so they are less likely to make errors and if they do make an error then the trainer intervenes and corrects it for them.[42]

There are a number of reasons why error training can improve learning and performance. First, errors force people to develop thoughtful strategies and deeper processing of information that leads to better memory and the development of a mental model. In addition, errors can lead to greater practice because people tend to practice those things that they have not yet mastered. Errors also force people to learn "error-recovery strategies" which means they are better able to respond to and correct errors which can lead to improved performance. Errors also lead to greater exploration because people often want to find out why an error occurred. Thus, errors are likely to result in greater learning and therefore better performance on the learned task.[43]

However, because error training can be frustrating to trainees, it should be accompanied with **error-management instructions** that emphasize the positive function of errors. They explain to trainees that errors are a necessary and natural part of learning and that they should make errors and learn from them. Thus, in order for error training to be effective, it is important that trainees are protected from any negative emotional effects that can result from making errors. Error-management instructions reduce the negative effects of errors and enable people to be open to learning from error feedback. In terms of the earlier discussion of prepractice conditions, error-management instructions can be considered an example of an attentional device and a metacognitive strategy.[44]

Error training

Training that explicitly allows trainees to make errors while learning to perform a task

Error-avoidant training

Training that explicitly avoids or minimizes trainee errors while they are learning to perform a task

Error-management instructions

Statements that emphasize the positive function of errors

Michael Frese and his colleagues have conducted a number of studies on error training. Their results indicate that error training results in higher performance than training that reduces the chances to make errors or error-avoidant training. Furthermore, error training with error-management instructions results in better performance than error training without error-management instructions and error-avoidant training. Thus, it is the combination of error training and error-management instructions that results in higher performance. In other words, error-management instructions are essential for the effectiveness of error training because they reduce the frustration and stress associated with making errors.[45]

Model of Training Effectiveness—Training Design

Before concluding this chapter, let's return to the model of training effectiveness that was presented in Chapter 3. Recall that the model showed that, in addition to training, trainees' cognitive ability, training motivation, self-efficacy, personality, and attitudes have a direct effect on trainee learning and retention; learning and retention have a direct effect on individual behaviour and performance; and individual behaviour and performance have a direct effect on organizational effectiveness.

Based on what you have learned in this chapter, we can add training design factors to the model. Recall that active practice and practice conditions before training (prepractice) and during training influence learning and retention. Figure 5.1 shows a revised model of training effectiveness in which training, trainee characteristics, and training design influence learning and retention.

FIGURE 5.1

Model of Training Effectiveness

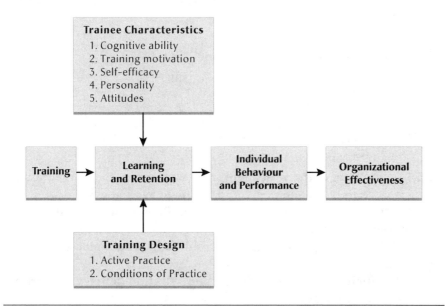

Summary

This chapter described the main activities involved in the design of a training program. First, we described the elements, components, and writing of training objectives. Next we discussed the decision to purchase or design a training program including the advantages and disadvantages of each and the factors to consider when making a decision. The importance of a request for proposal (RFP) was also discussed as well as how to create an effective one. We then described the components involved in designing a training program including training content, methods, active practice, and the conditions of practice. The effects of error training and error-management instructions were also discussed. One of the most important factors discussed in this chapter was deciding on the use of training methods. As you will see in the next three chapters, there are many possible off- and on-the-job methods of training as well as many forms of technology-based training.

Key Terms

active practice (page 132)

advance organizers (page 133)

attentional advice (page 132)

blended training (page 132)

error training (page 138)

error-avoidant training (page 138)

error-management instructions (page 138)

feedback or knowledge of results (page 136)

goal orientation (page 133)

massed versus distributed practice (page 135)

metacognition (page 133)

metacognitive strategies (page 133)

overlearning (page 135)

practice (page 132)

preparatory information (page 133)

prepractice briefs (page 134)

request for proposal (RFP) (page 128)

task sequencing (page 136)

training objective (page 123)

whole versus part learning (page 135)

Weblinks

Wendy's International: www.wendys.com (page 128)

Plateau Systems: www.plateau.com (page 130)

RPC Icons

RPC 5.1 Recommends the most appropriate way to meet identified learning needs (e.g., courses, secondments, and on-the-job activities).

RPC 5.2 Develops requests for proposals (RFP) and reviews submissions by third parties.

RPC 5.3 Ensures legislated training obligations are met within the organization.

RPC 5.4 Participates in course design and selection/delivery of learning materials via various media.

Discussion Questions

1. Discuss the purpose of training objectives for trainees, trainers, and managers.
2. What factors should an organization consider when deciding to purchase or design a training program?
3. What are the advantages and disadvantages of purchasing a training program and designing a training program in-house?
4. Why is it important to include active practice in a training program? Give an example of how active practice was used in a training program you have attended.
5. Discuss the conditions of practice before and during training and how they can improve learning and retention.
6. Explain the difference between error training and error-avoidant training and how you would design an error training program.
7. Explain what a request for proposal (RFP) is and why an organization should carefully write one before purchasing a training program.
8. What are the main sections of a request for proposal (RFP) and what are the steps involved in creating an effective one?

The Great Training Debate

1. Debate the following: Practice makes perfect and enough practice will always lead to learning and retention.
2. Debate the following: Errors are frustrating and upsetting to trainees and should therefore be minimized in training.

Using the Internet

1. To find out about the kinds of training programs that can be purchased, go to **www.trainingreport.ca** and click on Directory and then Directory of Training Consultants and Suppliers (or go directly to **www.trainingreport.ca/dir2000/direct.cfm**).

   First, review the category listings and try to find an area that you are familiar with, perhaps something relevant to a current or previous job or an area that interests you. Second, go to the listings within your chosen category and find out about the kinds of training programs that can be purchased. Describe the content of the programs, the methods, and any other design characteristics that are indicated. Prepare a short report about the category and the kind of training programs available for purchase.

   You can also find out about training suppliers by visiting Industry Canada at **http://strategis.ic.gc.ca/epic/internet/incts-scf.nsf/en/sl00125e.html**.

   What can you find out about training suppliers on this site? What are the different types of training providers and what kind of training do they offer? Does your college or university provide training and if so, what kind of training?

2. Go to Industry Canada at **http://strategis.ic.gc.ca/epic/internet/ incts-scf.nsf/en/sl00032e.html.** Click on the link for the Checklist for Developing a Training Program. Review the questions in each section of the checklist and comment on how the answers to the questions can improve the design of a training program. Write a report in which you briefly describe the types of questions asked in each section of the checklist and how they can help in the design of a training program. Can you think of any other sections or questions that should be added to the checklist?

3. To find out more about how to choose a training supplier in Canada, go to Industry Canada at **http://strategis.ic.gc.ca/epic/internet/incts-scf.nsf/en/h_sl00011e.html**. When choosing a training supplier, what questions should be asked and what issues should you consider?

Exercises

In-Class

1. Think of the best and worst training experience you have ever had. For each one, indicate the purpose of the training, the objectives, content, and methods. Then, using the material presented in this chapter, make a list of all the reasons why you feel that it was the best or worst training experience you have ever had. Based on your lists, what are some of the things that make a training program effective?

2. If you have a driver's licence then you probably remember what it was like to learn how to drive. Chances are you stepped into a car with a friend or family member who told you what to do. And if you have ever taught someone how to drive, you probably did the same thing. Did you remember to tell them everything they needed to know? What did you tell them to do first? Could you have done a better job teaching them to drive? Probably. Refer to the section of this chapter on task sequencing. Recall that task sequencing involves dividing a task into its component parts or sub-tasks, and then ordering them into a meaningful or logical sequence. Now try to design a driver training program based on task sequencing. In other words, make a list of all of the sub-tasks involved in driving a car and then organize them into a logical sequence for the purpose of teaching somebody how to drive.

3. Have you ever wondered what your instructor does to prepare for a class? To find out, choose one of your classes and try to describe each of the following:

   • the objectives of the class
   • the content of the class
   • the training methods used
   • opportunities for active practice
   • conditions of practice

Based on your description, how effective was the class? How can it be improved?

4. Recall a training program that you attended in a previous or current job. Describe the objectives and content of the program and any opportunities for active practice. What did you practice and how helpful was it for your learning and retention? Describe the extent to which any of the conditions of practice were used either before or during the training program and how they affected your learning and retention. What changes would you recommend to improve learning and retention?

5. Identify a skill that you would like to acquire. Some examples might be to use a particular software package or perhaps to improve your written or oral presentation skills. Now develop training objectives for a training program on the skill that you have chosen, using the five elements and three components of training objectives described in the chapter. Exchange your objectives with another student and assess each other's objectives in terms of the criteria outlined in the chapter for writing training objectives.

6. Read the following training objectives and identify what is wrong with them. Then rewrite them so that they conform to the elements and components of training objectives described in the chapter.

   - The trainer will spend 30 minutes discussing time-management tips.
   - The trainees will be able to manage their time more effectively.
   - The purpose of the seminar is to teach time-management techniques.
   - After attending the course, employees will be able to make lists and put letters beside the items on the list, enabling them to manage time more effectively.

7. Recall a training program that you attended in a previous or current job. Describe the objectives and content of the program and the extent to which errors were part of the program. Did you make any errors while learning and what effect did it have on your learning and the training experience? If you were to redesign this training program, how would you change it so that it included error training?

In-the-Field

1. Contact the human resources department of an organization and request a meeting with somebody in the department whom you can interview about the organization's training programs. Develop a series of questions so that you can learn about each of the following design issues in terms of a particular training program that the organization has implemented:

   - Was the training program designed by the organization or purchased? What were the reasons for designing or purchasing the program?
   - If the training program was purchased, was a request for proposal (RFP) used and what was included in it?
   - What is the content of the training program and how was it developed?
   - What training methods were used and why?

- Was active practice designed into the training program and what kind of practice opportunities did trainees have?
- To what extent were the conditions of practice listed in Table 5.3 incorporated into the training program?

Based on the information you have acquired, conduct an evaluation with respect to how effectively you think the training program was designed and list some recommendations for improvement.

Case Incident

Play to Win at Dofasco

Hamilton-based steel manufacturer Dofasco has a training program that it calls "play to win." Nearly every new hire participates in the program as an initiation to the company which takes place at a resort. Employees go to the resort in groups of between 50 and 70 and there are about four trips a year to the resort. Over 7000 employees have taken part in the program since it was launched in 1993. The intent is to get a better understanding of the organization and the things it is trying to accomplish. The program focuses on issues facing the company, what the company does, and who the company's customers are. The program is placed within the context that nobody can do it alone and that they need to look out for each other. Employees also take part in a variety of unique exercises such a rope course and climbing up a pole. In addition, new hires get a chance to sit down with senior management and participate in a question-and-answer session. The context is that when you are back at the company you can help out. The program teaches respect and concern for others, that strength is our people, and what those things mean.

Questions

1. What are the training objectives of Dofasco's play-to-win training program and what purpose do they serve for employees and managers?
2. Discuss the training content and methods used in the training program. What is the nature of the content and what type of methods are used and why?

Source: Humber, T. (2003, November 17). Serving up training. *Canadian HR Reporter, 16* (20), G1, G4.

Case

Training the Sales Force

Sales at a large telecommunications company were down for the third quarter. Management reviewed several strategies to improve sales and concluded that one solution would be to improve training for the large, dispersed sales force.

For the sake of expediency, the training department began using a needs analysis it had conducted several years before as a basis to develop enhanced training. Their plan was first to update the original needs analysis, and then to develop new training strategies on the basis of what they found. They also began investigating new training technologies as a possible means to reducing training delivery costs. However, management was so intent on doing something quickly that the training department was ultimately pressured into purchasing a generic, off-the-shelf training package from a local vendor.

One of the features of the package that appealed to management was that the course could be delivered over the Web, saving the time and expense of having the sales force travel to the main office to receive the training. Hence, even though the package was costly to purchase, the company believed that it was a bargain compared to the expense of developing a new package in-house and delivering it in person to the sales force.

Six months after the training had been delivered, sales were still declining. Management turned to the training department for answers. Because no measures of training performance had been collected, the training department had little information upon which to base its diagnosis. For lack of a better idea, members of the training department began questioning the sales force to see if they could determine why the training was not working.

Among other things, the sales people reported that the training was slow and boring, and that it did not teach them any new sales techniques. They also complained that, without an instructor, it was impossible to get clarification on things they did not understand. Moreover, they reported that they believed that sales were off not because they needed training in basic sales techniques, but because so many new products were being introduced they could not keep up. In fact, several of the sales people requested meetings with design engineers just so they could get updated product information.

The training department took these findings back to management and requested that they be allowed to design a new training package, beginning with an updated needs analysis to determine the real training deficiencies.

Source: Excerpt taken from Salas, E., & Cannon-Bowers, J. A. (2000). Design training systematically. In E. A. Locke (Ed.), *Handbook of principles of organizational behavior*. Oxford, UK. Blackwell Publishers Ltd. Case questions prepared by Alan Saks.

Questions

1. Comment on the company's decision to purchase a generic, off-the-shelf training package by a local vendor. What were the advantages and disadvantages of this and do you think that it was a good idea for the company to purchase the training rather than to have it designed in-house? Explain your answer.

2. Explain how the use of a request for proposal (RFP) might have changed the company's decision to purchase the training program. Do you think that the company would have purchased the same training program from the same vendor if they had created a detailed RFP? Explain your answer.

3. What effect did the use of the original needs analysis have on the content of the training program and the decision to have it delivered over

Chapter 5: Training Design

the Web? Do you think that a new needs analysis should have been conducted and what effect might it have had on the design of the training program?

4. Comment on the use of the Web as the main method of training. What are the advantages and disadvantages of this method of training? What other methods might have been more effective?

5. Discuss the role that practice played in the training program and on its effectiveness? What does the case say about the role of active practice in training?

6. If you were to design the training program, describe what you would do in terms of training objectives, training content, training methods, active practice and the conditions of practice. How would your training program be different from the one described in the case and would it be more effective?

References

1. Waxer, C. (2005, October 24). Bank of Montreal opens its checkbook in the name of employee development. *Workforce Management, 84* (11), 46–48; Anonymous (2006, March). Top 100 ranking. *Training, 43* (3), 42; Lee, C., Dolezalek, H., & Johnson, G. (2005, March). Training top 100: Top 10. 30.

2. Lee, C., Dolezalek, H., & Johnson, G. (2005, March). *Training, 42* (3), 26–47.

3. Kibler, R. J., Barker, L. L. & Miles, D. T. (1970). *Behavioral objectives and instruction.* Boston: Allyn and Bacon, Inc.

4. Laird, D. (1985). *Approaches to training and development* (2nd ed.). Reading, MA: Addison-Wesley.

5. Nadler, L. (1990). *Designing training programs: The critical events model.* Reading, MA: Addison-Wesley.

6. Hays, S. (1999, April). Basic skills training 101. *Workforce Management, 78* (4), 76–78.

7. Ganzel, R. (1998, October). What sexual harassment training really prevents. *Training, 35* (10), 86–94.

8. Nadler, L., & Nadler, Z. (1990). *The handbook of human resource development* (2nd ed.). New York: John Wiley and Sons.

9. Nadler, L., & Nadler, Z. (1990).

10. Chapman, B. (2004, January). How to create the ideal RFP. *Training, 41* (1), 40–43.

11. Chapman, B. (2004, January).

12. Campbell, J. P. (1988). Training design for performance improvement. In Campbell, J. P. & Campbell, R. J. (Eds.), *Productivity in organizations: Frontiers of industrial and organizational psychology* (pp. 177–216). San Francisco, CA: Jossey-Bass.

13. Kirkpatrick, D. L. (1994). *Evaluating training programs: The four levels.* San Francisco, CA: Berrett-Koehler Publishers.

14. Campbell, J. P. (1988).

15. Campbell, J. P. (1988).

16. Waxer, C. (2005, October 24).

17. Campbell, J. P. (1988).

18. Campbell, J. P. (1988).

19. Thoms, P., & Klein, H. J. (1994). Participation and evaluative outcomes in management training. *Human Resource Development Quarterly, 5,* 27–39.

20. Hinrichs, J. R. (1976). Personnel training. In Dunnette, M. D. (Ed.), *Handbook of industrial and organizational psychology* (pp. 829–60). Skokie, IL: Rand McNally.

21. Cannon-Bowers, J. A., Rhodenizer, L., Salas, E., & Bowers, C. A., (1998). A framework for understanding pre-practice conditions and their impact on learning. *Personnel Psychology, 51*, 291–320.

22. Cannon-Bowers, J. A., Rhodenizer, L., Salas, E., & Bowers, C. A., (1998).

23. Schmidt, A. M., & Ford, J. K. (2003). Learning within a learner control training environment: The interactive effects of goal orientation and metacognitive instruction on learning outcomes. *Personnel Psychology, 56*, 405–429.

24. Schmidt, A. M., & Ford, J. K. (2003).

25. Schmidt, A. M., & Ford, J. K. (2003).

26. Baldwin, T. T., & Ford, J. K. (1988). Transfer of training: A review and directions for future research. *Personnel Psychology, 41*, 63–105.

27. Donovan, J. J., & Radosevich, D. J. (1999). A meta-analytic review of the distribution of practice effect: Now you see it, now you don't. *Journal of Applied Psychology, 84*, 795–805.

28. Bass, B. M., & Vaughn, J. A. (1969). *Training in industry: The management of learning.* Belmont, CA: Wadsworth; Donovan, J. J., & Radosevich, D. J. (1999).

29. Baldwin, T. T., & Ford, J. K. (1988).

30. Baldwin, T. T., & Ford, J. K. (1988).

31. Baldwin, T. T., & Ford, J. K. (1988).

32. Yelon, S., & Z. Berge. (1992, September). Practice-centred training. *Performance and instruction*, 8–12.

33. Driskell, J. E., Willis, R. P., & Copper, C. (1992). Effects of overlearning on retention. *Journal of Applied Psychology, 77*, 615–22.

34. Gagné, R. M. (1962). Military training and principles of learning. *American Psychologist, 17*, 83–91.

35. Gagné, R. M. (1962).

36. Baldwin, T. T., & Ford, J. K. (1988).

37. Ilgen, D. R., Fisher, C. D., & Taylor, M. S. (1979). Consequences of individual feedback on behaviour in organizations. *Journal of Applied Psychology, 64*, 349–71.

38. Campbell, J. P. (1988).

39. Miller, L. (1965). *The use of knowledge of results in improving the performance of hourly operators.* General Electric Company, Behavioral Research Service: Detroit.

40. Locke, E. A., & Latham, G. P. (1990). *A theory of goal setting and task performance.* Englewood Cliffs, NJ: Prentice-Hall.

41. Heimbeck, D., Frese, M., Sonnentag, S., & Keith, N. (2003). Integrating errors into the training process: The function of error management instructions and the role of goal orientation. *Personnel Psychology, 56*, 333–361.

42. Heimbeck, D., Frese, M., Sonnentag, S., & Keith, N. (2003).

43. Heimbeck, D., Frese, M., Sonnentag, S., & Keith, N. (2003).

44. Heimbeck, D., Frese, M., Sonnentag, S., & Keith, N. (2003).

45. Heimbeck, D., Frese, M., Sonnentag, S., & Keith, N. (2003).

Chapter 6

Off-the-Job Training Methods

After reading this chapter, you should be able to:

- describe the following training methods: lecture, discussion, audio-visual, case study, case incidents, behavioural modelling, role plays, games, simulations, and action learning
- list the advantages and disadvantages of each training method
- describe how and when to effectively use each training method
- define physical and psychological fidelity
- describe the factors to consider when choosing a training method
- define aptitude-treatment interaction and discuss its implications for training
- discuss a blended delivery approach to training

www.telus.com

TELUS

TELUS Corporation is one of Canada's leading telecommunications companies and employs close to 30000 people. TELUS provides a full range of communications products and services and has been recognized as one of the most respected companies in Canada.

Several years ago, the company decided that it needed to adopt a fundamental change in its selling strategy in order to increase shareholder value and sustainable growth in the highly competitive telecommunications sector. A shift in focus from a tactical, "product-based" sales approach to a more strategic "solutions-based" sales approach was needed. This shift would require the sales force to learn selling strategies and skills that focus on engaging "C-level" customers (CEO/COO-level clients) in meaningful, reciprocal dialogue.

In order to achieve this goal, the sales force and sales managers had to acquire the skills and confidence necessary to interact with C-level customers. Objectives for the change strategy included an assessment of the strengths and weaknesses of the sales force interacting with C-level customers; a safe environment in which to learn and practice C-level selling skills; an opportunity for the sales force to experience what will realistically be expected of them as they move forward; and the identification of high-priority skill gaps that would become the basis for a targeted development plan.

A major part of the solution involved simulations in which the entire sales force participated in a three-day, complex and realistic simulated selling environment. The objective was to show the sales force what the new selling environment looked like, allow it to experience it first-hand, provide a basis to build a longer-term, change-management and performance improvement program, and to enable the sales force to apply new behaviours and skills in an authentic and realistic business environment.

A full-scale actual replication of the new environment was established, which included a fictitious client corporation with actual office locations, audited financials, a corporate website, press releases, and an executive assistant. The company was staffed with real-life executives who role-played specific C-level positions in the fictitious company.

The simulation was set up as a competition in which four sales teams in each session competed against each other to win the account. The teams actually made sales calls to executives and had to uncover business needs. The team that demonstrated that it understood the client's needs and presented the most appropriate solution in the most professional manner won the business.

Assessments were conducted throughout the simulation by sales managers/directors and trained observers, and feedback from the executives on each participant's performance was also obtained. In addition, the sales force performed self-assessments and peer-assessments. The assessments were then used to provide on-the-job support as well as performance goals and plans for sales staff. The assessment information was also used to develop future training and coaching programs. In addition, classroom workshops provided guided, consultative sessions focused on self-exploration in which facilitators provided perspectives on change and new approaches to client relationship-building and selling skills.

The results for TELUS have been a marked increase in sales calls at the C-level and new sales opportunities and business. It also led to the identification of high-priority development needs and new programs to address them.[1]

Source: Reprinted with permission of *The Training Report*, Crownhill Publishing Inc.

In this chapter, we introduce you to training methods that take place away from the job site and are usually referred to as off-the-job training. This chapter discusses the most common off-the-job training methods. The TELUS selling simulation is good example of how trainees can acquire new knowledge and skills off-the-job by participating in a simulation that involves a competitive game, role playing, and classroom instruction.

The chapter presents training methods in order of degree of trainee involvement, from passive to active. We start with lectures, because there is relatively little trainee input, and end with action learning where trainees manage the learning process. Table 6.1 lists the 10 off-the-job training methods described in this chapter.

 **6.1**

Many of the instructional methods presented in this chapter take place in a classroom setting although some methods such as games and simulations also take place outside a classroom, like the selling environment and fictitious client corporation that was part of the TELUS simulation. In both Canada and the United States, classroom delivery is the primary method of providing training. In Canada, 76 percent of all training is delivered via the classroom while in the United States 70 percent of formal training occurs in the classroom with live instructors.[2]

Lecture Method

There are few people who have not experienced a lecture. A **lecture** transmits information orally with little trainee involvement. The trainer organizes the content to be learned and then presents it to trainees. Thus, it involves a unidirectional flow of information from the instructor to the trainee.

There are a number of advantages of a lecture. Large amounts of information can be transferred to large groups of trainees in a relatively short period of time, at a minimal expense. Key points can be emphasized and repeated. Trainers can be assured that trainees are all hearing the same message, which

Lecture

A training method in which the trainer organizes the content to be learned and presents it orally with little trainee involvement

TABLE 6.1

Off-the-Job Training Methods

1. Lecture. A training method in which the trainer organizes the content to be learned and presents it orally with little trainee involvement.

2. Discussion. Two-way communication between the trainer and trainees as well as among trainees.

3. Audio-visual methods. Various forms of media that are used to illustrate key points or demonstrate certain actions or behaviours.

4. Case study. A training method in which trainees discuss, analyze, and solve problems based on a real situation.

5. Case incident. A training method in which one problem or issue is presented for analysis.

6. Behaviour modelling. A training method in which trainees observe a model performing a task and then attempt to imitate the observed behaviour.

7. Role play. A training method in which trainees practice newly learned skills in a safe environment.

8. Games. Activities characterized by structured competition that allow employees to learn specific skills.

9. Simulations. Operating models of physical or social events designed to represent reality.

10. Action learning. A training method in which trainees accept the challenge of studying and solving real-world problems and accept responsibility for the solution.

is useful when the message is extremely important, such as instructions or changes in procedures. A lecture is also useful as a method to explain to trainees what is to follow in the rest of a training session. For example, a lecture could be used to highlight the key learning points of a video or role play. Many employees are comfortable with the lecture method because they are familiar with it and it requires little participation.

However, a lecture, as some of us have experienced, does have its drawbacks as a training method. While useful for the acquisition of declarative knowledge and immediate recall, it is not as effective for the development of skills or for changing attitudes. The lecture does not accommodate any differences in trainee ability, and all trainees are forced to absorb information at the same rate. Trainees are also forced to be passive learners with little opportunity to connect the content to their own work environment, or to receive feedback on their understanding of the material. To overcome these disadvantages, trainers often build in time for discussion, questions and answers, and other opportunities for trainee involvement.

Tips for Trainers

Trainers can use the lecture method effectively by following a number of guidelines. For example, "Where do I begin?" is a question asked by most first-time trainers. The answer is: "First you have to know what you want to do (the objective) and how much information you need to impart." Training objectives were described in Chapter 5, but on a pragmatic level the trainer should be able to write a concise statement describing what the trainees will be able to do or accomplish by attending a lecture.

Either through previously gained knowledge or the ability to research a topic, the trainer will gather and arrange information in a logical manner. Logic could dictate a progression from the general to the specific or from the specific to the general, depending upon the subject matter. This information can be transcribed onto cards or sheets of paper. An effective technique is to rule off a wide (5 cm to 8 cm) margin down the right-hand side of each page. Then detailed information can be placed in the body of the page, while headings are written in the margins.

It has been suggested that no more than six major points should be illustrated during each half hour of a lecture.[3] It takes practice to get the timing of a lecture right. Only through experience can one judge the amount of material needed for any given amount of time. It is helpful to break the lecture into 10- to 15-minute segments with a short stretch of time in between and to summarize the material at both the beginning and the end, stopping occasionally to allow trainees to catch up and to write their own summaries. Finally, time should be scheduled for questions and answers.

A trainer who drones on for an entire hour is rarely effective. Depending on audience needs and motivation level, the delivery should be punctuated with a variety of supplementary material or exercises. Stories, case incidents, graphics, humour, trainee presentations, videos, and question-and-answer sessions are some of the techniques a trainer can use to maintain interest and, perhaps even more important, to instill in the trainee the love of, or at the least, respect for the subject matter. Trainers not only represent themselves but also function as ambassadors for their institution or firm and their discipline. A poor lecture not only shows the trainer in a bad light but also can lead to negative trainee attitudes toward the training.

Discussion Method

The **discussion method** is one of the primary ways to increase trainee involvement in the learning process by allowing two-way communication between the trainer and trainees as well as among trainees. It has been known for some time that group discussion serves at least five purposes:

Discussion method

Allows two-way communication between the trainer and trainees as well as among trainees

1. It helps trainees recognize what they do not know but should know.
2. It is an opportunity for trainees to get answers to questions.
3. It allows trainees to get advice on matters that are of concern to them.
4. It allows trainees to share ideas and derive a common wisdom.
5. It is a way for trainees to learn about one another as people.[4]

Group discussions facilitate the exchange of ideas and are good ways to develop critical thinking skills. Social and interpersonal skills are also enhanced. However, group discussions are not effective with large numbers of participants because many remain silent or unable to participate. Some group members will dominate while the contributions of others will not be useful. Still others may become dogmatic in their positions on issues. Group discussions take a lot of training time and must be carefully facilitated to manage the outcomes.

Tips for Trainers

The discussion method is most effective when the trainer can convince group members that a collective approach has some advantage over individual approaches to a problem.[5] Thus, the trainer should create a participative culture at the beginning of a training program. The trainer's task, then, is to get trainees to buy into the process as an activity that is both interesting and useful.

The major difficulty with the discussion method is that comments tend to be addressed to the trainer. When faced with this situation, the best technique is to reflect the questions or comments back to the trainees. Not surprisingly, positive reinforcement is critical. Reluctant participants are drawn out, while the trainer utilizes the energy of more assertive individuals. When the group strays off topic, the trainer gently refocuses the discussion, supporting the participation while changing the substance.[6]

The key to successful discussions is to ensure that one trainee does not dominate the discussion. The trainer does not have to be obvious (e.g., putting all the dominant personalities together). More subtle techniques can be used. For example, trainees can be given roles that change with each discussion—scribe, presenter, and discussion leader. If groups are kept small—four to six seems to work best—then most trainees have something to do, increasing participation and decreasing chances for some individuals to dominate the process. It is harder to be aggressive when taking notes or trying to summarize the thoughts of others.

Trainers dealing with groups of mixed educational backgrounds must also be aware of reading speed and literacy problems. Often group discussions require trainees to read a passage, case incident, or problem. Reluctance or hostility to do so might point to illiteracy. Be gentle, work the informal group process by finding a place in a hallway for someone to quietly read the material, or if this process is too obvious, summarize the main points before you assign the work. People who don't read well often have excellent memories; with care, they'll get by.[7]

Of note, too, is that groups should be assigned a well-defined, easily understood task, one that is doable within the allotted time frame. Trainees should be given every opportunity to look good in front of their peers, especially if they have to report back to the group. Since many training facilities are less than ideal, seating arrangements will vary. Any configuration that puts trainees in close proximity to one another will do, but a circle arrangement with no obvious leader's position or place is probably best. Size of the group is also important. More than 10 would be hard to handle if everyone is to participate.

Audio-Visual Methods

Audio-visual methods refer to various forms of media that trainers can use to illustrate key points or demonstrate certain actions or behaviours. Videos and slides are often used by trainers to supplement lectures and discussions. A video is often used to illustrate a way to behave in a certain situation or to demonstrate effective and ineffective behaviours. Many managers have learned correct interviewing techniques through videos. Slides highlight the important parts of a lecture or discussion allowing trainees to remember key points.

One advantage of audio-visual methods is the ability to control the pace of the training. A slide or a video clip can be used to clarify a concept. Trainees receive consistent information from these methods no matter where or how often the training is given. Most important, a video can show a situation that is difficult for a trainer to describe, such as a hostile customer or a dangerous malfunction in equipment. Video allows a trainer to show complex and dynamic situations in a realistic manner. Not surprisingly, videos remain one of the most popular methods of training.

Audio-visual methods
Various forms of media that are used to illustrate key points or demonstrate certain actions or behaviours

Tips for Trainers

Before a video is shown, the trainer should discuss the learning objectives, the key points, and instruct trainees to pay particular attention to certain key parts. Trainees should understand how the video fits into the rest of the training program and should be given sufficient guidance so that they know what to look for and focus on. Slides should not overwhelm trainees with information and they should be easy to read and follow. Too much information or print that is too small and difficult to read can undermine their usefulness.

Case Study Method

A **case study** is a training method in which trainees discuss, analyze, and solve problems usually based on a real situation. The primary use of the case study method is to encourage open discussion and analysis of problems and events. Trainees apply business-management concepts to relevant real-life situations.

Case study

A training method in which trainees discuss, analyze, and solve problems based on a real situation

The case study method teaches trainees to think for themselves and develop problem-solving skills while the trainer functions as a catalyst for learning. Case studies develop analytical ability, sharpen problem-solving skills, encourage creativity, and improve the organization of thoughts and ideas.[8]

The objectives of a case study are 1. to introduce realism into trainees' learning; 2. to deal with a variety of problems, goals, facts, conditions, and conflicts that often occur in the real world; 3. to teach trainees how to make decisions; and 4. to teach trainees to be creative and think independently.[9] Therefore, most cases present situations in which the problems are correctable.

The case study method is often used in business schools to teach students how to analyze and solve realistic organizational problems. In fact, more than 70 percent of business schools use the case study method. Several studies have found that using cases improves communication skills, problem-solving, and enables students to better understand management situations.[10]

For the case method to be effective, however, certain requirements must be met. For example, the qualifications of both the trainees and the trainer affect the ability to analyze cases and to draw conclusions. As well, space and time dimensions are important. Trainees need time to analyze cases properly. Finally, case studies and discussions work best in an open and informal atmosphere.[11]

Cases may be written in various styles, presenting either single problems or a number of complex, interdependent situations. They may be concerned with corporate strategy, organizational change, management, or any problem relating to a company's financial situation, marketing, human resources, or a combination of these activities. Some case reports describe the organization's difficulties in vague terms, while others may state the major problems explicitly.

In addition to the various styles of case writing, methods of presentation also differ. Cases do not always have to be in written form. Sometimes it is more effective to present cases using audio-visual techniques. This approach has advantages for both the trainees and the trainers in that trainers do not have to do as much research and writing, and trainees are able to identify better with the characters.[12] A second alternative to a written case presentation is the live case method. Businesses may contact schools to report certain problems. Students then analyze the situation and report back to the company. This approach has been called operational consulting.[13]

Tips for Trainers

Certain requirements should be met when writing a case study. The case should be a product of a real organizational situation. A fictitious case could be regarded with boredom and distrust as the setting might seem too unrealistic.[14] Ideally, cases should be written by more than one person. Collaboration on the presentation of facts ensures a more realistic situation and helps to reduce biases. Although it is difficult, the case writer must not make assumptions and only facts should be included. The author of a case, then, must relate core issues to the reader, not personal bias.

Case studies often concentrate on the corporate strategy of a company within an industry setting. The complexity of business situations makes decisions and analyses challenging. In addition, despite their length, most cases do not contain complete information on the organization or all the relevant inputs. This incompleteness is part of the benefit of using the case method, as trainees must learn to deal with incomplete data.[15]

Because a case study is a description of a typical management situation, it is often difficult to know what to include and what to omit. Most cases give an overall description of the company and the industry situation although the length of a case report varies. A typical case, however, will be up to 20 type-written pages. The key issues and the relevant details should be included to give the reader enough information to make a qualified decision.

Cases vary depending on the intended purpose of the writer and according to the issue being examined. Some case studies disclose what management decisions were made when attempting to solve an organization's problems while others require one to develop solutions and recommend courses of action.

A teaching note provides communication between the case writer and those who teach the case. In its strictest sense, a teaching note would include information on approaches to teaching a specific case. Some teaching notes, however, are more detailed, containing samples of analyses and computations. In addition, teaching notes may state the objectives of the case and contain additional company information not available to trainees.[16]

As most of these cases are excessively long and extremely complex, they have not generally found favour with trainers in business, particularly those training front-line supervisors. There is an offshoot of this technique, however, called the case incident method that can be used to great advantage with a wide variety of trainees at many levels.

Case Incident Method

Unlike the typical case study, a **case incident** is usually no more than one page in length and is designed to illustrate or to probe one specific problem, concept, or issue. Most management textbooks include a case incident at the end of each chapter. The case incident has become one of the most accessible ways of injecting an experiential or real-world component into a lecture.

Case incidents are useful when the trainer wants to focus on one topic or concept. Because they are short, trainees can read them during a training session and valuable time will not be taken up by differences in trainees' reading speeds. When larger, more traditional cases are used, advance preparation is necessary to read and review the case material. The brevity of a case incident reduces the need for preparation and reading skills so all trainees can participate without a lot of advance reading and preparation.

Another advantage of a case incident is that trainees are able to use their own experiences. If the material is written well, the problem presented in each incident will encourage the application of current knowledge, leading to increased confidence, and trainee input and participation.

The main disadvantage of case incidents is that some trainees are bothered by the lack of background material. Indeed, at times it is necessary for trainees to make assumptions and trainers may be asked by some trainees to sketch in the background. They can be especially problematic for trainees who have limited knowledge and work experience. A lack of work or life experiences tends to elicit shallow answers based on speculation and ill-informed opinion.

Case incidents have been used successfully in higher education and organizations. Supervisors seem to like the hands-on aspects of solving a specific management problem. Similarly, students have found the case incident method to be a welcome relief from the traditional lecture method. Case incidents have been found to be valuable in class sizes of up to 70.

Case incident

A training method in which one problem or issue is presented for analysis

Tips for Trainers

Case incidents can be used in several ways. Trainees can be divided into groups with one member assigned the task of making notes while another can be designated the group spokesperson. The groups discuss the case incident and answer questions. The trainer then has each group spokesperson present their answers. This process can then lead into a general group discussion.

Another approach is to have the trainees read the case incident and then discuss it as one group. This method is especially useful when an example is needed to illustrate a specific point. The technique here would be to stop the training, ask the trainees to read the incident, and then lead the group in a short discussion. As soon as the point has been made, the trainer should continue quickly, so as not to lose the trainees' interest. Alternatively, a case incident can be used to illustrate a point at the start of a training program or used as an exercise at the end of a training program.

Behaviour Modelling

People learn by observing the behaviour of others and so it should not surprise you that observation is a popular and effective method of training. **Behaviour modelling** is a training method in which trainees observe a model performing a task and then attempt to imitate the observed behaviour.

Behaviour modelling is based on social learning theory and observation learning that was described in Chapter 3. It is an extremely effective method for learning skills and behaviours and it is one of the most widely used and researched training methods.[17] Behaviour modelling has been used to teach interpersonal skills such as supervision, negotiation, communication, and sales as well as motor skills.

Behaviour modelling is based on four general principles of learning: 1. Observation (modelling), 2. Rehearsal (practice), 3. Reinforcement (reward), and 4. Transfer.[18] The process is fairly straightforward. Trainees observe a model performing a specific task such as handling a customer complaint or operating a machine and then practice performing the task. The performance of a task can be observed on video or it can be performed live.

The training task should be broken down into key learning points or behaviours to be learned as a series of critical steps that can be modelled independently. After viewing the model, the participants practice the behaviour, one step at a time. When one step is mastered and reinforced, the trainer moves to the next critical skill. Specific feedback must follow the performance of each step. This step-by-step process results in the development of skills and self-efficacy needed to use them. The final step involves specific actions to maximize the transfer of learning on-the-job.[19]

A recent review of research on behaviour modelilng training found that it has a particularly strong effect on learning but also has a positive effect on skills development and job behaviour. The effect on skills development was greatest when learning points were used and presented as rules to be followed and when training time was longest. Transfer of learning on-the-job

Behaviour modelling

A training method in which trainees observe a model performing a task and then attempt to imitate the observed behaviour was greatest when models displaying both positive and negative behaviours were used, when trainees were instructed to set goals, when trainees' superiors were trained, and when rewards and sanctions were provided for using or failing to use newly learned skills on the job.[20]

Tips for Trainers

The model used in behavioural modelling training should be someone with whom the trainee can identify and who is perceived as credible. Under these conditions, the trainee is more likely to want to imitate the model's behaviour. In addition, trainers have to carefully plan behaviour modelling training and ensure that trainees are provided with opportunities to practice the observed behaviour, receive feedback on their performance of the task, and are motivated to use the new behaviour on the job. Trainees will resist behaviour modelling if the behaviours are incongruent with common work practices.

To be effective, trainees must have sufficient trust in the trainer to experiment (i.e., to try new behaviour in front of a group). Sometimes, a traditional and ineffective scenario is demonstrated first to increase motivation to try the new positive behaviour. John Cleese of Monty Python fame used this technique very effectively in his humorous video series on interviewing.

Transfer of the new skill and behaviours to the workplace is always the weak link in the process. Old patterns are comfortable and familiar, especially when there is some resistance in the work environment to new ways of doing things. However, by overlearning the skill as discussed in Chapter 5, its use can become automatic. In addition, the reinforcement of newly acquired skills on the job ensures their repetition and continued application. When these reinforcers are in place, behaviour modelling can have long-lasting and positive outcomes.[21]

Role Play

A **role play** is a method of training in which employees are given the opportunity to practise new behaviours in a safe environment. The emphasis is on doing and experiencing. This training method is most useful for acquiring interpersonal and human relations skills and for changing attitudes. You might recall that the TELUS selling simulation involved a fictitious company in which executives role played employees and the objective of the training was for the sales force and sales managers to learn to interact with "C-level" customers.

A role play consists of three phases: 1. Development, 2. Enactment, and 3. Debriefing. First, a role play must be carefully designed to achieve its objectives. Development involves the design of a role play that usually consists of a scenario in which there are two actors. For example, if sales clerks are learning how to interact with customers, a role play might involve a customer returning an item and asking for a refund. The scenario provides information on the time, place, roles, encounter, and instructions on what each role player should do.

Role play

A training method in which trainees practise newly learned skills in a safe environment

During the enactment phase, trainees are provided with the role play information and scenarios and are assigned roles. Usually there are two role players and sometimes a third trainee who is an observer. Trainees are given some time to become familiar with the scenario and their roles, and then act out the role play. Usually the trainees will rotate so that each one spends some time in each role.

By playing a role, trainees can develop empathy for others and learn what it feels like to be in a particular role. For example, when a customer service representative is given instructions to play the part of a disgruntled customer with a major problem, he or she can experience the frustrations of responses like, "That's not my department," and, "Just fill in that form over there, no, not that one."

After the enactment phase is the debriefing phase, which is considered to be the most important stage of a role play, and should last two to three times longer than the enactment phase. In this phase, participants discuss their experiences and the outcomes of their role play. Correct behaviours are reinforced and connections with key learning points and trainees' jobs are made. This is done by establishing the facts (what happened, what was experienced), analyzing the causes and effects of behaviours, and planning for skill or attitude changes on the job.

Role playing can take on various forms and does not always have to involve just two actors. Role plays can also involve groups of trainees acting out various roles in what is known as multiple role playing. They can also vary in terms of how much detail the actors are provided in terms of a script or structure. In some role plays the actors are provided a great deal of detail about what they are supposed to do and feel, while less structured role plays might just indicate the actor's roles without any detail about them. A role play can also involve one trainee playing him or herself (e.g., manager) while the other trainee acts out a role (e.g., employee who is being coached). Another variation on the use of role plays is to have a single role play performed that is observed by the rest of the trainees. In other cases, it might be preferable to have all of the trainees participate in role plays. The type of role play chosen will depend on the training content and objectives.

Tips for Trainers

While role playing allows trainees to practise and learn new skills, trainees sometimes resist it. As a result, the role of the trainer is crucial. Trust has to be established and an open and participative climate is necessary. Trainees should be warmed up by involving them in minor role situations. The trainer can reinforce risk-taking and use mistakes as learning opportunities. Trainers could ask people to show all the incorrect ways to handle an angry customer. When a critical mistake is made, the trainer can start again or rewind the case. In one role play, a police officer was testing methods of talking to a potential suicide victim on a bridge. The officer made the fatal mistake of saying, "Go ahead, I dare you," and the role play partner jumped. The trainer immediately stated, "Well, that approach didn't work, would you like to try another?" He rewound the case and demonstrated the true value of role playing—the opportunity to practice behaviours in a safe environment.

One of the limitations of a role play is that unlike behaviour modelling, trainees are not shown exactly what to do and how to behave prior to participating in a role play. As a result, some trainees might not be successful in a role play and might even display incorrect behaviours. Furthermore, much of what happens during a role play is left in the hands of the role players. This means that it is extremely important for the trainer to draw out the incorrect and correct behaviours during the debriefing phase. Otherwise, trainees might not learn the appropriate behaviours following a role play. Recall that an important part of the TELUS training program was assessments that were conducted by sales managers/directors and trained observers as well as feedback from the executives on each participant's performance. The trainees also did self-assessments and peer assessments.

Games

Games involve activities characterized by structured competition that allow trainees to learn specific skills. Recall that the TELUS selling simulation was also a game in that four sales teams had to compete against each other to win the account. Games tend to have rules, principles, and a system for scoring. For example, an employment law game called *Winning through Prevention* teaches human resource managers about lawful termination, discrimination, and workplace safety. Players who answer correctly get promoted and those who answer incorrectly are faced with a lawsuit.[22] In the TELUS selling competition, the team that demonstrated the best solution in the most professional manner won the account.

Business games often require teams of players to compete against each other to gain a strategic advantage, market share, or to maximize profits. They can involve all areas of management practice and often require the players to gather and analyze information, and to make business management decisions. As a result, business games tend to focus on the development of problem-solving, interpersonal skills, and decision-making skills.

Some business games are relatively simple and focus on a particular functional area such as marketing, human resources, or finance. Other games are much more complex and try to model an entire organization such as in the TELUS training program. Participants might have to operate a company and make all kinds of decisions and solve business problems. They would then receive feedback and have the opportunity to practice particular skills.

Games incorporate many sound principles of learning such as learning from experience, active practice, and direct application to real problems. They are used to enhance the learning process by injecting fun and competition, generating energy, and providing opportunities for people to work together.

A disadvantage of the use of games is the possibility of learning the wrong things, a weak relation to training objectives, and an emphasis on winning.[23] In addition, trainees sometimes get so caught up in the game that they

Games

Activities characterized by structured competition that allow trainees to learn specific skills

lose sight of the importance of learning. Although trainees seem to enjoy games and respond enthusiastically to them, there is not very much evidence on how effective games are for improving skills and on-the-job performance.

To find out more about the kinds of games being used for training, see Training Today 1, "The Games Trainees Play."

Tips for Trainers

The design of a game begins with a critical question: "What is the key task to be learned?" At the beginning of the exercise, the trainer should state the learning objective so that trainees don't just focus on winning the game but understand what they will learn. In addition, the roles of the players must be clearly defined.

Games should be as realistic as possible and be a meaningful representation of the kind of work that participants do. If they are not realistic, participants might not take them seriously. This will obviously undermine learning and the application of new skills on the job. To be most effective, games

Training Today 1

The Games Trainees Play

A number of companies today specialize in corporate training programs that are anything but traditional. Games such as "human slingshot" and "Sumo wrestling" and one in which trainees fly in a two-seater plane and engage in an aerial dogfight with lasers are fun, unusual, and not for the faint of heart. They stretch trainees' limits but can offer valuable insights.

Some of the most intense courses in Canada are offered by a company called Survival in the Bush, Inc. Located in rural eastern Ontario, they offer programs from Thunder Bay to Labrador.

Interested companies must first determine the goals they want to achieve and how gung-ho they are about bushwhacking. The training can take place on the grounds of the company or at one of many secluded outdoor locales. The courses run all year round, which means that trainees might have to trudge through ice and snow.

Companies that decide to rough it in the bush can expect to find themselves building shelters and fires, foraging for edible items such as non-poisonous wild plants, learning how to navigate in the woods and preparing wild game for meals. Trainees develop leadership skills, an appreciation for team work, and learn how to make decisions under very stressful situations.

In the United States, a company called Total Rebound regularly hosts programs in Toronto, Vancouver, Montreal, and Calgary in which they provide over-the-top interactive games that are designed to be fun and educational.

Among the games are "human slingshot," which involves bungee cords, "soft bouncy racing lanes," and "Sumo Wrestling" in which participants wear giant, flesh-coloured, vinyl, foam-filled suits. In a game called "Hornet Adventure," trainees are taken to a United States' aircraft carrier called the Hornet where they are shown how to build and launch rockets at a target floating 3000 feet off in San Francisco Bay. The company also custom designs games according to a company's needs.

These games are designed to teach trainees how to communicate and collaborate, to break down barriers between people, and to help team members recognize qualities and skills that they did not know they or others in their group had. One of the most important aspects of such cutting-edge training programs is that they allow trainees to develop individual skills and leadership abilities.

Source: Excerpt from Hendley, N. (2002, October). Games without frontiers: Extreme corporate training. *The Training Report*, pp. 1–2. Reprinted by permission of *The Training Report*, Crownhill Publishing Inc.

should be well planned and prepared, linked to training objectives, and include a debriefing session so that trainees understand the purpose of the game and the critical skills and behaviours to be learned.[24] As well, because there are many kinds of games available, trainers need to be familiar with them and to carefully choose one that best meets an organization's needs and objectives.

Simulations

Simulations are a form of training that involves the use of operating models of physical or social events that are designed to represent reality. They attempt to recreate situations by simplifying them to a manageable size and structure. They are models or active representations of work situations that are designed to increase trainee motivation, involvement, and learning. They are also used when training in the real world might involve danger or extreme costs. This of course, is what the TELUS selling simulation involves. A realistic selling simulation was designed along with a fictitious company and a realistic selling environment.

Simulations are a popular method of training that are widely used in business, education, and the military. For example, simulations are typically used in medicine, maintenance, law enforcement, and emergency management settings. The military and the commercial aviation industry are purported to be the biggest users of simulation-based training.[25]

Some simulations, known as equipment simulators, use equipment that mimics the equipment and machinery in the workplace. **Equipment simulators** are mechanical devices that are similar to those that employees use on the job. They are designed to simulate the kinds of procedures, movements, and/or decisions required in the work environment.

A good example of an equipment simulator is a flight simulator that is used to train pilots to fly. Flight simulators mimic flights exactly but pose no risk to humans or equipment. Equipment simulators are also used to train astronauts, air traffic controllers, and maintenance workers.

Simulations can also be designed to simulate social situations and interactions. Royal Bank Financial Group of Canada trained 58 000 employees in coaching skills using a five-hour CD-ROM simulation.[26] The TELUS simulation is a good example of how social situations and interactions can be designed into a simulation.

Simulations can also be used to develop managerial and interpersonal skills. For example, organizational simulations require participants to solve problems, make decisions, and interact with various stakeholders. Trainees can learn how organizations operate and acquire important managerial and business skills.

Simulations are commonly used to train employees involved in emergency response work such as firefighters and police officers. You might recall the Training Today feature in Chapter 1 on counterterrorism training that described how police, firefighters, and paramedics are being trained to handle biological weapons in a series of simulated terrorist attacks designed to replicate a chemical assault on a major Canadian city. Trainees practised

Simulations
Operating models of physical or social events designed to represent reality

Equipment simulators
Mechanical devices that are similar to those that employees use on the job

detecting and decontaminating chemical agents and treating mass casualties after a mock terrorist attack. In another exercise, they handled liquid sarin at a simulated terrorist lab after a mock leak.[27]

These kinds of simulations are becoming more common since the terrorist attacks of 9/11 in the United States. For example, in May 2003 a week-long staged disaster was conducted to test Canadian and U.S. preparedness for a terrorist attack. Simulated attacks in Seattle were designed to test the local, state, and federal government response to a possible terrorist attack. The simulation involved 8500 people from 100 local, state, and federal agencies in the United States as well as the Canadian government at a cost of US$16 million.[28] For an example of a recent simulation in Toronto that involved riot police clashing with fake protestors, see the Training Today 2 feature, "Training for Canada Calm."

A major disadvantage of equipment simulators and simulations is that they are usually very expensive to develop and in the case of emergency response simulations, very expensive to stage. On the positive side, simulations are an excellent method for adding some realism into a training program. They are especially useful in situations where it would be too costly or dangerous to train employees on the actual equipment used on the job.

Tips for Trainers

In order to be most effective, simulations should have physical and psychological fidelity. **Physical fidelity** has to do with the similarity of the physical aspects of a simulation (e.g., equipment, tasks, and surroundings) to the actual job. Simulators should be designed to physically replicate and resemble the work environment. That is, the simulation should have the appearance of the actual work site. For example, a flight simulator should look like the cockpit of an actual airplane with respect to the various controls, lights, and instruments.

Psychological fidelity has to do with the similarity of the psychological conditions of the simulation to the actual work environment. Simulations should be designed so that the experience is as similar as possible to what trainees experience on the job. In other words, the simulation should include on-the-job psychological conditions such as time pressures, problems, conflicts, and so on.

Simulations allow a great deal of flexibility as complicating factors or unexpected events can be built into the program. For example, in a pilot-training simulation, a blizzard can be introduced. However, trainers should ensure that simulations have both physical and psychological fidelity.

To learn more about how to make experiential training methods such as role plays, games, and simulations more effective, see The Trainer's Notebook, "Getting the Most out of Experiential Training Methods."

Action Learning

In Chapter 5, active practice was described as an important component of a training program for trainee learning and retention. A good example of a training method that provides active practice is action learning.

Physical fidelity

The similarity of the physical aspects of a simulation (e.g., equipment, tasks, and surroundings) to the actual job

Psychological fidelity

The similarity of the psychological conditions of the simulation to the actual work environment

Training for Canada Calm

In December 2005, a series of truck bombs in Toronto knocked out the city's power, destroyed a terminal at Pearson airport, an office tower on Bay Street, and much of the St. Michael's Hospital. Fortunately, this was just an imaginary scenario that was part of a training exercise for riot police to practise their emergency response strategy.

On a vacant lot in Toronto, a rock-throwing mob stormed a medical station behind coils of barbed wire set up by Canadian soldiers. The mob, who were actually reservists with the domestic response unit, chanted "Give us the drugs," and confronted dozens of camouflage-wearing soldiers stationed by makeshift medical and warning stations. After an initial face-off with some pushing and shoving, the order was given to back away.

The Toronto police wearing riot gear were then called in to manage the crowd.

The simulation included army reservists as well as Toronto police, firefighters, and paramedics and signals the military's transition into something it calls "Canada Calm," the ability not only to perform duties overseas on international operations, but to look internally and focus on the defence of Canada and to aid local civilian authorities in a time of crisis. The objective of the program was to look for areas that can be improved as well as coordinate with other agencies, and to be prepared in case such a scenario ever transpires.

Excerpt from Powell, B. (2005, December 5). Troops rehearse for disaster. *Toronto Star*, B1. Reprinted with permission—Torstar Syndication Services.

Action learning provides trainees with opportunities to test theories in the real world. Reginald Revans, the originator of action learning principles, emphasizes that the learner develops skills through responsible involvement in some real, complex, and stressful problem.[29] The action learning method compels trainees to identify problems; develop possible solutions; test these solutions in a real-world, real-time situation; and evaluate the consequences. The aim is to solve a business problem.

The goals of action learning are to involve and to challenge the trainee and move employees from passive observation to identification with the people and the vision of the organization. This method moves trainees from information receivers to problem solvers. Action learning incorporates more of the adult learning principles than any other method of training.

The majority of the time spent in action learning is dedicated to the diagnosis of problems in the field. The problems and the inherent value systems supporting the problems are assessed and challenged. This work is always done in groups and learning by-products include group and interpersonal skills, risk-taking, responsibility, and accountability.[30]

Professions use action learning to train and socialize their students. For example, students in social work are often sent to work with the homeless or welfare recipients. These students are encouraged to apply their theoretical knowledge in the field. Industry is using the precepts of action learning when employees take responsibility for quality-improvement projects.

Action learning

A training method in which trainees accept the challenge of studying and solving real-world problems and accept responsibility for the solution

Getting the Most out of Experiential Training Methods

Experiential training methods such as role playing, games, and simulations encourage trainee participation. Learning theory teaches us that by increasing trainee participation and active involvement, learning and retention will be enhanced. But not always.

Many training methods put trainees on the spot— literally in the spotlight, forced to act in situations in which they feel very uncomfortable. One executive was encouraged to describe a time at work when he had faced a difficult situation in order to illustrate how corrective counselling worked. The person playing the role of counsellor criticized him extensively, with no intervention from the trainer. The outcome can be worse than losing face and not learning. Trainees may not want to return to any training program or they may actively sabotage subsequent sessions.

Here are some tips for trainers to make effective use of experiential training methods:

- Don't use games and role plays just to play and have fun. There must be a purpose, a learning outcome that you should share with the trainees.
- Try the exercise you have designed or chosen. If you are uncomfortable doing it, don't use it.

- Don't think that unlearning previous habits means going through extremely difficult events, like boot camp. People don't learn to swim by being thrown into the deep end of the swimming pool.
- Not everyone has to participate in a participative workshop. Some people can play different roles (such as observing or note taking) rather than the high profile "let us show them how they are doing it wrong" simulations.
- Warm-up exercises and limiting the size of the group might also create a supportive environment in which to risk behaviour by role playing or asking questions.
- If an individual does lose face, trainers can make favourable comments by focusing on the correct actions, inviting observers to empathize with the person facing the difficulties of the task in the exercise, and asking the others to appreciate the risks taken by those who did play the game.

Source: Becker, R. (1998). Taking the misery out of experiential training. *Training, 35* (2), 79–88. Training: The Human Side of Business by Becker, R.

Action learning requires a commitment of energy and time from participants and their managers. Solving real organizational problems can be stressful for trainees. The difficulties of working in teams on real problems can lead to conflict and increased anxiety and stress.

Although action learning is more popular in Europe than in North America, a number of Canadian companies have recently developed action learning programs. For example, TD Bank Financial Group has a new leadership development program in which action learning plays an integral part. The bank's senior managers attend a three-day course to learn about the competencies that comprise a new leadership profile. Then they must use the learning to solve an action learning opportunity that they identified before attending the courses. TELUS also has an action learning program for its director-level managers. The company partnered with several universities to deliver courses in several key areas. After taking the courses, participants are expected to use the learning to solve work-related problems and they are held accountable for applying the learning and making changes.[31]

Tips for Trainers

Action learning projects must be challenging and deal with real organizational concerns. Trainees should buy into the importance of the project and the organizational problem and receive some release time to work on the project. In addition, some training in group skills to enable collaboration might also be necessary. The group working on the project should be small (four to seven members) enough to develop trust but contain a diverse set of skills to enable creative solutions. The learning process should be monitored and the trainees held accountable for their proposed solutions.

What Training Method Is Best?

Ⓡ Ⓟ Ⓒ 6.2

In this chapter, we have described some of the most common off-the-job training methods. In Chapter 7, you will learn about on-the-job training methods, and in Chapter 8 you will find out about technology-based training methods. With so many training methods available, it is natural to ask, "What training method is best?" and "How does a trainer choose a training method?" There is of course no easy or straightforward answer to this question. However, we will try to provide some guidelines for choosing training methods.

In terms of the effectiveness of the various methods, one survey conducted by one of the authors of this text that was completed by 150 experienced professional trainers (members of the Canadian Society of Training and Development) revealed a hierarchy of effectiveness. As a general principle, the more highly involved the trainee in the learning process and the more the training situation resembles the job, the more likely it is that transfer to the job will occur. These methods include on-the-job and one-on-one training, simulations, role plays, behaviour modelling, self-study, case studies, and multimedia. A combination of these methods results in even greater transfer. Other methods, such as lectures, discussions, video conferencing, and lunch and learn programs, were not as effective for transfer to the job, perhaps because these techniques allow (and indeed require) that trainees be passive absorbers of information.[32]

Two large surveys of training directors found that nine different training methods were effective in achieving different types of training goals.[33] For example, the case study method was rated as most effective for problem-solving skills and computer-based instruction was rated best for knowledge retention. The role-play method was evaluated as the best for changing attitudes and developing interpersonal skills. However, these are only individual perceptions and do not provide information on actual trainee achievements.

It is important to realize that ultimately the effectiveness of a training method depends on its achievement of training objectives. Thus, the choice of what training method to use for a particular training program should start with the program's objectives. For example, if the objective is declarative knowledge, you might choose the lecture method. However, if the objective is the acquisition of interpersonal skills, then you might want to use the role-play method. In general, the lecture method will be most effective when you want to impart large amounts of information quickly and at low cost to large groups of trainees. To teach skills such as interviewing or negotiations, the most effective methods are behaviour modelling and role playing.

In addition to a training program's objectives, other factors that need to be considered when choosing a training method include cost and resource availability, on-the-job application, trainer skill and preferences, and trainee characteristics.

COST AND RESOURCE AVAILABILITY   A training method might be extremely effective for achieving a program's objectives, but it might be too costly to develop and implement. For example, a simulation might be appropriate for a training objective but very expensive. Thus, trainers must also consider the cost of and resources available for developing and implementing various training methods.

ON-THE-JOB APPLICATION   Another important factor to consider is whether or not trainees will be expected to apply what they learn in training on the job. Trainers will choose some methods over others if trainees are expected to apply the newly acquired skills on the job. For example, a lecture is probably not a good choice if the objective is for trainees to apply new knowledge and skills on the job. If trainees are expected to apply new knowledge and skills on the job then a role play or behavioural modelling would be more effective.

TRAINER SKILL AND PREFERENCES   A trainer might be more skilled at using some methods than others and might also have a personal preference for using some methods. For example, if a trainer is not experienced or comfortable conducting role plays or simulations then these methods might not be considered. Some trainers might have preferences for some methods and are most effective using them. Thus, the choice of a training method will also depend on the skills and preferences of trainers.

TRAINEE CHARACTERISTICS   Another important factor to consider is the characteristics of trainees. Trainees are likely to vary in terms of what training methods will motivate them and maximize their learning. For example, not all trainees are going to be motivated enough for action learning and some will not have the literacy skills necessary to understand a lengthy case study. Perhaps even more important is a trainees' ability to benefit from a particular method of instruction. There is some evidence that training methods have differential effects on trainees as a result of differences in aptitudes (e.g., abilities, skills, knowledge). This is known as an aptitude-treatment interaction.

Aptitude-treatment interaction

When a training method has differential effects on trainees with different aptitudes

An **aptitude-treatment interaction** occurs when a training method is more effective for some trainees than others. In other words, the training method has differential effects on trainees with different aptitudes. An aptitude is broadly defined as any characteristic of trainees that affects their ability to learn from the training method. For example, there is some evidence that high-ability students benefit more from programs with less structure and greater complexity while low-ability students benefit more from explicit and structured programs.[34]

Thus, it is important that the training methods chosen are appropriate given trainees' aptitudes.

Table 6.2 summarizes 10 on- and off-the-job training methods against three criteria (objectives, costs, and on-the-job transfer).

Blended Training

Finally, although we have been discussing training methods one by one, in reality trainers mix and combine them (e.g., case studies with lecturing). In fact, you might recall that in Chapter 5 we described blended training as an approach that combines traditional classroom training, on-the-job training, and on-line learning. Blended training programs that make use of various training methods are becoming the norm rather than the use of any one particular method.

A blended delivery approach has a number of benefits. It allows participants to learn in ways that work for them, allows multiple learning outcomes to be achieved, and increases the possibility that the training will be applied on the job. Trainers must therefore be skilled in a variety of approaches to learning. According to a recent survey in the United States, 15 to 30 percent of responding organizations reported that they use both traditional training methods and e-learning.[35]

In conclusion, when it comes to training methods, each method has its place. There are many factors to consider when deciding on training methods. The choice depends on the following five factors: 1. The training objectives,

TABLE 6.2

Choosing a Training Method

Method is Effective for the . . .

Method	Training objectives[1]			Costs[2]		Use on the job[3]
	Knowledge	Skills	Attitudes	Dev$	Admin$	Transfer
Lecture	yes	no	no	low	low	low
Video	yes	no	yes	high	low	med
Discussion	no	no	yes	low	low	low
Behaviour modelling	no	yes	no	high	high	high
Role play	no	yes	yes	med	med	high
Case study	yes	med	yes	med	low	med
Case incident	med	med	med	med	med	med
Games	no	med	no	med	med	low
Simulations	yes	yes	no	high	high	high
Tech-based training	yes	yes	no	high	low	high

[1] Determine the training objective and match the training methods to that objective
[2] Consider the costs of the method (development and administration) and its potential benefits
[3] Determine suitability for transfer to the job

2. The cost and resources available, 3. On-the-job application, 4. The trainer's skill and preferences, and 5. Trainee characteristics. Ultimately, mixing, adapting, and blending methods is likely to be the best approach for maximizing trainee learning and a training program's effectiveness.

Summary

This chapter focused on off-the-job training methods and described 10 of the most frequently used methods. The advantages and disadvantages of each method were described as well as suggestions for their use. The chapter concluded with a discussion of how to choose training methods and identified five factors to consider. The importance of combining methods and using a blended delivery approach was also discussed.

Key Terms

action learning (page 165)

aptitude-treatment interaction (page 168)

audio-visual methods (page 155)

behaviour modelling (page 158)

case incident (page 157)

case study (page 155)

discussion method (page 153)

equipment simulators (page 163)

games (page 161)

lecture (page 151)

physical fidelity (page 164)

psychological fidelity (page 164)

role play (page 159)

simulations (page 163)

Weblinks

Royal Bank Financial Group of Canada: www.royalbank.com (page 163)

RPC Icons

RPC 6.1 Using a variety of methods facilitates the delivery of development programs to groups and individual learners.
RPC 6.2 Recommends the most appropriate way to meet identified learning needs (e.g., courses, secondments, and on-the-job activities).

Discussion Questions

1. What is the difference between role plays and behavioural modelling and what are the advantages and disadvantages of each method?
2. With the rising concerns about airport security in Canada and the United States, there has been an urgent need to change the way that security personnel are hired and trained. In the United States, the

U.S. Department of Transportation was given one year to recruit, screen, hire, and train more than 28 000 airport passenger and baggage screeners for every airport in the United States. In terms of training, what training methods do you think should be used? Review the training methods listed in Table 6.1, and discuss the advantages and disadvantages of using each method to train the airport passenger-and-baggage screeners. What methods do you think will be most effective and why?

3. What are the advantages and disadvantages of each of the training methods listed in Table 6.1, and when would it be best to use each method? What method do you prefer when you are being trained and why?

4. What are main factors that a trainer should consider when choosing a training method?

5. What is the difference between physical and psychological fidelity and how would you design a training program to have both?

The Great Training Debate

1. Debate the following: Lectures are not a very effective method of training and should not be used as often as they have in the past.

Using the Internet

1. To find out about the kinds of games and simulations that are used in training, visit the following websites:

www.survivalinthebushinc.com
www.totalrebound.com

Indicate the kinds of games and simulations that each company offers for corporate training. What are the objectives of these games and what do employees actually do? What knowledge and skills do employees learn from these games and how effective do you think they are? Using the factors described in the chapter for choosing a training method, evaluate the use and effectiveness of these games for training.

2. To learn more about training and development at TELUS, go to **http://about.telus.com/community/social_responsibility/en/ workplace/developingteam.html**.

What training methods are used at TELUS and what kind of training is provided? How many formal courses were completed last year?

How much is spent on learning at TELUS and what percentage of salaries and wages is invested in learning? How much is spent per employee?

Exercises

In-Class

1. Prepare a five-minute lecture on a topic of your choice following the information on lectures outlined in the text. Find a partner in your class and review each other's lecture. If time permits, give your lecture to the class or a small group and discuss its effectiveness. What would make your lecture more effective?

2. Choose a training program you have taken that you really liked and one that you did not like. For each one, indicate the training methods that were used (see Table 6.1) and how they were used. What effect did the methods have on your satisfaction of the program and your learning? What methods might have improved your satisfaction and learning?

3. Think of a work situation you have either experienced or observed that would lend itself to a role play (e.g., a customer complaining to an employee). Design a role play in which you describe a situation and the role of two role players. Be clear about the purpose of the role play in terms of its objectives and what the role players are expected to learn from it. Be sure to include instructions to participants about the situation and the relationship between the characters. The instructor can now either have you describe your role play to the class and/or have class members enact it. If role plays are enacted, be sure to also include a debriefing session afterwards.

4. Describe the major tasks involved in performing a previous or current job and how employees are trained. Then review each of the training methods in Table 6.1 and describe how they might be used to train employees for the job. What training methods do you think would be most effective? Which ones would you recommend and why?

5. For this exercise, your task is to design a short game that can be played in class to learn a skill such as communication, team skills, leadership, negotiations, etc. In groups of two or three, choose a skill to focus on, and then design a game to learn the skill. Your game must be designed so that other members of the class can play it during class time. Write a brief description of your game indicating the objectives, the players, the rules, and what team members have to do to get points or win. The instructor can now either have you describe your game to the class and/or have class members actually play it. After playing the game, be sure to discuss how effective it was for learning the skill and the players' reaction to it.

6. You have been asked to develop a course to teach senior executives how to use e-mail. Which training method would you use and why (see Table 6.1)?

7. Consider the potential of action learning as an instructional method for your course on training and development. Do you think that action learning would be an effective method? Design an action learning project for your training and development course. Be specific in terms of the objectives, the skills to be developed, and the problems to be worked on and solved.

In-the-Field

1. Contact the human resources department of an organization to learn about the training methods they use to train employees. In particular, you should inquire about:

   - What training methods they use, what they use them for, and why they use them? (Refer to Table 6.1).
   - Do they use a blended approach to training. Why or why not?
   - Do they use certain training methods for particular training programs?
   - Do they prefer to use certain training methods more than others?
   - What training methods do they believe to be the most effective for training employees in their organization?
   - What factors do they consider when choosing training methods?

Case Incident

In-Flight Crew Training at JetBlue

JetBlue Airways was launched in 2000. In 2005, the company had just over 20 000 applicants for in-flight crew (flight attendants) positions with only 600 selected for training. After a rigorous recruitment and selection process, new hires must attend in-flight crew training and learn how to serve customers miles in the air and how to respond to emergencies. JetBlue also requires that trainees learn how to open cabin doors and shout the appropriate commands and evacuate the aircraft in 90 seconds.

Questions

1. How should JetBlue train new flight attendants? What are the advantages and disadvantages of each method of off-the-job training?
2. Which training methods do you think are most effective for training new flight attendants and why?

Source: Weinstein, M. (2006, April). JetBlue: Training in the air. *Training, 43* (4), 26–27.

Case

Making Customers Happy

Intense competition among retailers today has made customer service a top priority. At stores such as the Gap and Wal-Mart, employees welcome customers into the store with cheery greetings. Sales staff now have to do much more than simply operate the cash register. They need to have good communication and interpersonal skills in order to provide customers with excellent service. They need to be courteous, polite, and helpful.

Providing good customer service requires training programs that teach employees how to interact with customers. Many retail companies provide customer service training programs that teach employees how to be friendly, courteous, and helpful. Consider a large retail clothing store that decided it too needed to improve customer service. To be competitive, the store wanted employees to be more active and involved with customers. A training program was designed so that in addition to learning how to use the company's sales register system, which had always been the focus of the training program, the employees would learn how to greet customers, offer assistance, help them find what they are looking for, solve customer complaints and problems, and provide courteous, helpful, and friendly service.

The training program began with a lecture in which the trainer described the importance of customer service and the objectives of the training program. Trainees were also instructed on how to provide good service and how they should behave when they are interacting with customers.

Following the lecture, a video tape was shown that consisted of different scenarios in which employees were shown interacting with customers. In one scenario, a customer could not find what he was looking for and asked the employee for assistance. The employee was not friendly and told the customer to try looking down another aisle. In another incident, a customer complained to an employee about something she had purchased that was less expensive at another store. She demanded a price reduction or her money back. The customer began raising her voice and the employee yelled at the customer and told her to leave the store. Similar incidents of poor customer service were also shown in the video.

After the video, the trainer asked trainees what was wrong with each scenario and how the employee should have behaved to provide better customer service. At the end of the discussion, the trainer provided a brief lecture outlining the key points shown in the video. This was followed by another video that showed scenarios of employees providing good customer service. A brief discussion and lecture followed in which the trainees were asked to describe what the employee did to provide good service. The trainer then concluded the session by highlighting the key customer service behaviours.

Trainees then had to take a test on their knowledge of customer service. The test consisted of multiple choice questions that asked trainees to choose the most appropriate behaviour in different situations with customers. Most of the trainees did very well on the test and upon completing the training program, they all received a customer service qualification certificate.

Back on the job, however, some employees had difficulty dealing with customers. For example, in one incident a customer demanded his money back for a pair of pants that had shrunk after cleaning. He started blaming the employee for the store's poor quality and called the employee an idiot. The employee didn't know what to do and just walked away. In another incident, a customer came into the store to pick up a shirt that he had asked an employee to hold for him. The item had been sold and it was the last one in the store. The employee apologized saying that it was sold to somebody else by accident. However, the customer insisted that the employee call the customer who bought the shirt and have them return it. The employee said she could not do that and told the customer how sorry she was. The customer refused to leave the store unless the employee called the customer who bought the shirt. The employee threatened to call security if the customer did not leave the store. He finally left but not before causing a big scene in the store in front of many other customers.

Questions

1. How effective was the training program? What are its strengths and weaknesses?
2. Describe the training methods used in the customer service training program. Do you think these were appropriate methods to use and were they used appropriately?
3. What other training methods could have been used to make the training program more effective? Review the methods in Table 6.1 and indicate how effective each one would be using the criteria in the chapter to select training methods.
4. If you were to redesign the customer service training program, what training methods would you use and why?
5. What does this case say about training methods and the effectiveness of a training program?

References

1. Connal, D., & Baskin, C. (2002, November). Transforming a sales organization through simulation-based learning: a TELUS Communications case study. *Training Report*, 4–5; http://www.telus.com.
2. Parker, R. O., & Cooney, J. (2005). Learning & development outlook 2005. *The Conference Board of Canada*. Ottawa; Dolezalek, H. (2005, December). 2005 industry report. *Training, 42* (12), 14–28.
3. Renner, P. (1988). *The quick instructional planner*. Vancouver: Training Associates Ltd.
4. Zander, A. (1982). *Making groups effective*. San Francisco: Jossey-Bass Publishers.
5. Gabris, G. 1989. Educating elected officials in strategic goal setting. *Public Productivity and Management Review, 13* (2), 161–75.
6. Conlin, J. (1989). Conflict at meetings: Come out fighting. *Successful Meetings, 38* (6), 30–36; Renner, P. (1988); Wein, G. (1990). Experts as trainers. *Training and Development Journal, 44* (7), 29–30.
7. Keller, S., & Chuvala, J. (1992). Training: Tricks of the trade. *Security Management, 36* (7).
8. Pearce, J. A., Robinson, R. B., Jr., & Zahra Shaker, A. (1989). *An industry approach to cases in strategic management*. Boston: Irwin Publishing.
9. Yin, R. K. (1985). *Case study research: Design and methods*. Beverly Hills: Sage Publications.
10. Wright, P. (1992). The CEO and the business school: Is there potential for increased cooperation? *Association of Management Proceedings: Education, 10* (1), 41–45.
11. Craig, R. L. (1987). *Training and development handbook: A guide to human resource development* (pp. 414–29). New York: McGraw-Hill Inc.
12. Craig, R. L. (1987).
13. Schnelle, K. (1967). *Case analysis and business problem solving*. New York: McGraw-Hill.

14. Craig, R. L. (1987).

15. Kenny, B., Lea, E., & Luffman, G. (1992). *Cases in business policy* (2nd ed.). Oxford: Blackwell Publishers.

16. Leenders, M. R., & Erskine, J. A. (1973). *Case research: The case writing process*. London: University of Western Ontario Press.

17. Taylor, P. J., Russ-Eft, D. F., & Chan, D. W. L. (2005). A meta-analytic review of behavior modeling training. *Journal of Applied Psychology, 90,* 692–709.

18. Robinson, J. C. (1982). *Developing managers through behaviour modelling*. Austin: Texas.

19. Georges, J. C. (1988). Why soft-skills training doesn't take. *Training, 25* (4), 44–45.

20. Taylor, P. J., Russ-Eft, D. F., & Chan, D. W. L. (2005).

21. Buller, M., & McEvoy, G. (1990). Exploring the long-term effects of behaviour modelling training. *Journal of Organizational Change Management, 3* (1).

22. Atkins, E. (1999, March) Winning through prevention. *Workplace News,* p. 9.

23. Greenlaw, B., Herron, M., & Ramdon, L. (1962). *Business simulation in industrial and university education*. Englewood Cliffs, NJ: Prentice-Hall.

24. Tannenbaum, S. I., & Yukl, G. (1992). Training and development in work organizations. *Annual Review of Psychology, 43,* 399–441.

25. Salas, E., & Cannon-Bowers, J. A. (2001). The science of training: A decade of progress. *Annual Review of Psychology, 52,* 471–99.

26. Salopek, J. (1998). Workstation meets Playstation. *Training and Development, 52* (8), 26–35.

27. Stevenson, M. (2002, September 2). Base helps civilians prepare for chemical attacks. *The Globe and Mail,* A6.

28. Patrick, K. (2003, May 13). Staged disaster a test for assault readiness. *The Globe and Mail,* A13.

29. Revans, R. W. (1982). *The origins and growth of action learning*. Gock, Sweden: Bratt–Institute for Neues Lernen.

30. Revans, R. W. (1984). Action learning: Are we getting there? *Management Decision Journal, 22* (1), 45–52.

31. Vu, U. (2005, April 25). Action learning popular in Europe, not yet caught on in Canada. *Canadian HR Reporter, 18* (8), 1, 17.

32. Belcourt, M., & Saks, A. M. (1998, February). Training methods and the transfer of training. *Canadian Learning Journal,* 3.

33. Newstrom, J. W. (1980). Evaluating the effectiveness of training methods. *Personnel Administrator, 25* (1), 55–60; Carrol, S. J., Paine, F. T., & Ivancevich, J. J. (1972). The relative effectiveness of training methods—expert opinion and research. *Personnel Psychology, 25,* 495–510.

34. Tannenbaum, S. I., & Yukl, G. (1992). Training and development in work organizations. *Annual Review of Psychology, 43,* 399–441.

35. Dolezalek, H. (2005, December). 2005 industry report. *Training, 42* (12), 14–28.

Chapter 7

On-the-Job Training Methods

www.ssloral.com

SPACE SYSTEMS/LORAL

In 1990, Space Systems/Loral acquired Ford Aerospace and its 30-year tradition of satellite innovation. Since then, the Palo Alto, California-based company has been designing, manufacturing, and integrating satellites and satellite systems that provide the foundation for the burgeoning wireless age. For prospective employees of the aerospace industry, Space Systems/Loral's history of playing among the stars continues to lure the next generation of scientific intelligentsia.

With breakthrough technology continually reshaping its industry, Space Systems/Loral's workforce is constantly evolving. Scientific experts act as coaches and mentors so that each fresh generation of engineers and physicists is guided through the application of the complicated technology involved in satellite design and development.

The process begins with the Space Systems/Loral College Hire and Leadership Development Program, which targets about 12 U.S. colleges and universities to attract and recruit the specialized talent it needs. Graduates are welcomed at New Hire Orientation and immediately begin the industry assimilation program or "Satellite 101" class.

Within their first month, they are matched with a mentor and participate in a workshop to learn how to make the most of the mentoring opportunity. During the early weeks of the new hires' careers at Space Systems/Loral, management creates individualized learning tracks made up of three six-month rotational assignments. To broaden their skill sets even further, the new recruits are also offered a concurrent program of leadership development courses.

To train its nearly 2700 employees, the company employs seven senior trainers who make up the company's professional training team. The team is responsible for delivering more than 145 courses to employees each year. To complement the training staff, the company maintains a cadre of 40 or so "adjunct" trainers, recruited and trained to support the professional training team. This ensures that employees have high-quality training opportunities on a just-in-time basis.

According to the manager of learning and development, people are drawn to the company because of the nature of the work as well as the extensive technical training, leadership development, team training, mentoring, and the integration with the more experienced workforce.[1]

Source: Barbian, J. (2002, March). Training Top 100: Space Systems/Loral, *Training*, V N U Business Publications. This work is protected by copyright and it is being used with the permission of Access Copyright. Any alteration of its content or further copying in any form whatsoever is strictly prohibited.

TABLE 7.1

On-the-Job Training Methods

1. Job instruction training—A formalized, structured, and systematic approach to on-the-job training.
2. Performance aid—A device that helps an employee perform his or her job.
3. Job rotation—A training method in which trainees are exposed to many functions and areas within an organization.
4. Apprenticeship programs—Training that combines on-the-job training with classroom instruction.
5. Coaching—A training method in which a seasoned employee works closely with another employee to develop insight, motivate, build skills, and to provide support through feedback and reinforcement.
6. Mentoring—A method in which a senior member of an organization takes a personal interest in the career of a junior employee.

Training at Space Systems/Loral is a good example of an organization that uses a number of on-the-job training methods to train and develop employees. In this chapter, we will focus on some of the most common methods of on-the-job training such as coaching, mentoring, and job rotation that are all part of the Space Systems/Loral training program.

Table 7.1 lists the six types of on-the-job training methods described in this chapter. We begin with the most basic form of on-the-job training—when one person trains another person on how to do something—and conclude with some of the more expensive and time-consuming methods.

On-the-Job Training (OJT) Methods

The most common method of training is **on-the-job training** in which a trainee receives instruction and training at his/her workstation from a supervisor or an experienced co-worker. According to The Conference Board of Canada, over 90 percent of Canadian organizations report using on-the-job training.[2] Most of us can probably remember a time when someone was assigned the job of training us to perform a task such as operating a cash register or learning how to make a request for supplies. Although on-the-job training has been practised since at least the Middle Ages, the United States army formalized the concept during World War II.

There are a number of approaches for on-the-job training. Table 7.2 provides a description of the many ways in which on-the-job training can be accomplished such as training a group of employees on the spot, observing performance and providing feedback, and so on.

On-the-job training is an important part of training at McDonald's Canada. As one of Canada's largest employers of youth, the company needs

 **7.1**

On-the-job training
A training method in which a trainee receives instruction and training at his or her workstation from a supervisor or an experienced co-worker

TABLE 7.2

Approaches to On-the-Job Training

On-the-spot lecture	Gather trainees into groups and tell them how to do the job.
Viewed performance/ Feedback	Watch the person at work and give constructive feedback, such as when the sales manager makes a call with a new salesperson.
Following Nellie	The supervisor trains a senior employee, who in turn trains new employees (showing the ropes).
Job-aid approach	A job aid (step-by-step instructions or video) is followed while the trainer monitors performance.
The training step Sequence	The trainer systematically introduces the task. Following a planned sequence. On-the-spot lecture, gather trainees into groups, and tell them how to do the job.

to train thousands of new crew members every year. Although the company once used videos and classroom training, it now uses a buddy system combined with hands-on training and visual aids. A more experienced employee or "buddy" works with a new member individually on the job. In addition, laminated visual aids are used to show the steps in a task at each station and as a form of visual reinforcement. New crew members can refer to it during training and on the job. The combination of hands-on training and visual reinforcement is believed to result in higher levels of trainee self-efficacy and performance.[3]

OJT is especially useful for small businesses where most new employment is being created. Small businesses rarely offer courses and workshops for employees. Thus, OJT is ideal for them because of the limited investment needed to conduct the training. In fact, a recent survey found that 43 percent of small- and medium-sized enterprises use informal training methods such as on-the-job training, tutoring, and mentoring, while just 2 percent use only formal training such as the classroom, seminars, and workshops. Forty-three percent said that they use both informal (on-the-job) and formal training methods.[4]

Although on-the-job training is the most common approach to training, it has also been described as the most misused.[5] This is due to a number of problems that limit its effectiveness. One of the biggest problems is that on-the-job training is often not well planned or structured.

A related problem is that most people assigned the task of training others on the job have not received training on how to be a trainer. As a result, managers and employees do not have the knowledge and skills required to be effective trainers and are not familiar with important learning principles such as practice, feedback, and reinforcement.

Another problem is that inept employees will transfer undesirable work habits and attitudes to new employees. Furthermore, the traditional ways of doing things will be passed on to new employees, which means that existing problems as well as poor attitudes and behaviours will persist.

Other problems occur when those doing the training are worried that newly trained employees will one day take over their jobs. Further, some trainers might abuse their position by making the trainee do all the dirty work and the trainee might not learn important skills. In addition, OJT can be time consuming and some employees feel penalized when they can't earn as much money or meet their goals because of the time they have had to spend training others. It is for all these reasons that OJT is not always effective and has been referred to as the most used and misused training method.[6]

The main problem with the traditional unstructured approach to on-the-job training is that it results in training that is inconsistent, inefficient, and ineffective. However, when the process is carefully planned and structured, it can be a highly effective method of training that is also consistent and efficient.[7]

In fact, in one of the few studies to test the effectiveness of on-the-job training, structure was shown to be very important. In the study, a group of newly hired workers received training on how to operate a manufacturing process. One group received traditional on-the-job training in which one worker was trained by the supervisor, and then each person trained another one (similar to the Following Nellie approach described in Table 7.2). A second group was trained by a supervisor who used a structured approach to on-the-job training.

The results showed that the structured approach was considerably more effective. Trainees who received structured on-the-job training reached a predetermined level of skill and productivity in one-quarter of the time it took to train the other group. They also produced 76 percent fewer rejects, and their troubleshooting ability increased by 130 percent. This study highlights the importance of building structure into on-the-job training and how it can have a positive effect on the performance of trainees and the organization.[8]

In the next section, we describe a method for carefully planning and structuring on-the-job training that is known as job instruction training.

Job Instruction Training

While the traditional unstructured approach to on-the-job training is ineffective, more structured approaches can be highly effective. The best known structured approach to on-the-job training is job instruction training. **Job instruction training** is a formalized, structured, and systematic approach to on-the-job training.

Job instruction training consists of four steps: 1. Preparation, 2. Instruction, 3. Performance, and 4. Follow up. During the preparation phase, the trainer breaks down the job into small tasks, prepares all the equipment and supplies necessary to do the task, and allocates a time frame in which to learn each task. The instruction phase involves telling, showing, explaining, and demonstrating the task to the trainee. During the performance stage, the trainee performs the task under guidance from the instructor who provides feedback and reinforcement. Each task is learned in a similar way until the whole job can be

Job instruction training
A formalized, structured, and systematic approach to on-the-job training

completed without error. In the follow-up stage, the trainer monitors the trainee's performance and provides feedback. Each of these steps is described in more detail below.

Preparation

The key activity during the preparation phase is to develop a communications strategy that fits the trainee and to find out what the trainee already knows. The instructor needs to understand the background, capabilities, and attitudes of his or her trainees as well as the nature of the tasks to be performed before choosing a technique or combination of techniques. If the training is too easy or difficult for a trainee, the instructor can make adjustments to suit his or her needs. Note that trial and error has *not* been included here. Very few circumstances justify throwing an employee into a new position without proper training. Learning from one's mistakes is not only inefficient, but can be humiliating, dangerous, or lead to poor customer relations.

The second part of the preparation phase concerns the trainee. There are three stages: putting the trainee at ease, guaranteeing the learning, and building interest and showing personal advantage.[9]

1. The trainer must remember that the trainee might be apprehensive. It is unwise to begin too abruptly. Some small talk might be appropriate to relax the trainee and to set the tone for the training sessions. Most individuals learn more readily when relaxed. A short conversation concerning any matter of interest—the weather, sports, a work-related item—should be effective. Obviously, the topic chosen must be suitable for the situation.

2. When the conversation does turn to the training session, the trainer needs to guarantee to the employee that learning is possible. Again, use a simple statement, "Don't worry about this machine, Sally; in about three hours you'll be operating it almost as well as everyone else. I've trained at least 10 people in this procedure." The trainee now knows that it is possible to learn (i.e., learning will take place) and that the instructor has the ability to teach the process, adding to her confidence and self-efficacy.

3. Although the instructor might be interested, the trainee might be apprehensive or might not understand the effect that training will have on the quality of his or her work-life. Developing trainee enthusiasm sometimes is difficult, but pointing out some personal gain helps to create interest. The idea that the training activity will lead to something positive creates the opportunity to design rewards: more self-esteem, easier work, higher-level work, less routine, more control over work, greater opportunity or security. Once the appropriate reward is found (provided it can be obtained), most employees will respond positively.

Some people will resist as training is change and individuals accept change at different rates. The trainee preparation phase will identify those who are not responding. As the trainer is responsible for meeting measurable objectives, it is important to evaluate the likelihood of cooperation among trainees so that individual remedial action can be taken. One way to defuse resistance is to train employees in order of their perceived enthusiasm. When the resisters see others reaping the rewards of training, they usually agree to be trained, albeit grudgingly.

Instruction

If the trainee is to perform a task or an operation, he or she should be positioned slightly behind or beside the instructor so that the job is viewed from a realistic angle. The trainer can then proceed as follows:

1. Show the trainee how to perform the job.
    - Be sure to break the job into manageable tasks and present only as much as can be absorbed at one time. Remember, too, that individuals learn at different speeds, so while some trainees might be able to learn six or seven sequences at once, while others can absorb only four or five.
    - Repeat Step 1 as necessary and be patient.
    - Don't forget to tell why as well as how.
    - Point out possible difficulties as well as safety procedures.
    - Encourage questions.
2. Repeat and explain key points in more detail.
    - Safety is especially important.
    - Take the time to show how the job fits into any larger systems.
    - Show why the job is important.
    - Show why key points are more important than others.
    - Repeat Step 2 as necessary and be patient.
    - Encourage questions.
3. Allow the trainee to see the whole job again.
    - Ask questions to determine the level of comprehension.
    - Repeat Step 3 as necessary and be patient.
    - Encourage questions.

Performance

Following the instruction phase, the trainee should be given an opportunity to perform the task. This can be done in the following manner:

1. Ask the trainee to perform less difficult parts of the job.
    - Try to ensure initial success.
    - Don't tell how. If possible, ask questions, but try to keep trainee's frustration level low.
    - Ask the trainee to explain the steps.
2. Allow the trainee to perform the entire job.
    - Gently suggest improvements where necessary.
    - Provide feedback on performance.
    - Reinforce correct behaviour.

Effective On-the-Job Instructors

OJT instructors should be selected and trained and even certified before they begin instructing others in job tasks. The experience they must obtain and skills that they must learn include:

- At least one year's experience working in the job task area, including possessing hands-on experience performing all tasks that will be taught
- Ability to conduct task analysis, write measurable and observable performance objectives, and prepare effective training aids

- Skills in coaching techniques
- Ability to evaluate performance, give feedback, and reinforcement
- Organizational and time management skills
- Flexibility in adapting to trainees with different levels of skills experience, and abilities.

Source: Adapted from Walter, D. (1998, March/April) Training and certifying on-the-job trainers. *Technical Training*, pp. 32–34.

Follow-up

Once the performance stage is complete, the trainee will be left on his/her own to perform the task. This does, not, however mean that the training is over. It is important that the trainer keep track of the trainee's performance and provide support and feedback. The trainer should leave the trainee to work alone, indicate when and where to find help if necessary, supervise closely and check performance periodically, and then gradually taper off instruction as the employee gains confidence and skill.

Tips for Trainers

Sloman studied three British National Training Award winners that paid particular attention to the OJT delivery. From their programs he developed a set of rules governing good on-the-job training.[10]

First, job instruction training should not be managed differently from other types of training. Second, it should be integrated with other training methods. Third, ownership must be maintained even when consultants are used. And fourth, trainers must be chosen with care and trained properly. In addition to being experts in the skill area, they must want to be trainers and have good communication skills. Patience and respect for differences in the ability to learn are also important as the trainer sets the initial mood or climate of the learning experience.[11] (See The Trainer's Notebook 1 on the characteristics of effective on-the-job instructors.)

Once suitable individuals are found they should be trained (train-the-trainer) and then recognized and rewarded for training others. It is of little use to give training responsibilities to an already busy employee without restructuring his or her job to include a training element. Nor is increased pay always the most sought after reward (although it doesn't hurt). Recognition, the chance to add variety to the work day, respect from new employees, training certificates, and the prospect of either promotion or cross training all help to make the experience worthwhile for the individual.

While the steps of job instruction training might seem elaborate, they must be applied with the complexity and possible safety hazards of the job in mind. Very simple tasks might require only one demonstration. As well, employees bring different skills and backgrounds to the workplace. Competent preparation will eliminate overtraining and the resultant boredom and inattention.

Performance Aids

A **performance aid** is any device that helps an employee perform his/her job. Performance aids can be signs or prompts ("Have you turned off the computer?"); trouble-shooting aids ("If the red light goes on, the machine needs oil"); instructions in sequence ("To empty the machine, follow the next five steps"); a special tool or gauge (a long stick to measure how much gas is in an inaccessible tank); flash cards to help counsel clients; pictures (of a perfectly set table, for example); or posters and checklists.[12]

Performance aid

A device that helps an employee perform his/her job

For example, employees learning about hazardous-waste management could be provided with a checklist that summarizes the major steps for handling radioactive material. This checklist, if prepared as a colourful poster, will increase the chances of employee application. As indicated earlier, McDonald's uses laminated visual aids to remind trainees of the steps in a task and as a form of visual reinforcement that trainees refer to during training and once they are on the job.

The reasoning behind the use of performance aids is that requiring the memorization of sequences and tasks sometimes takes too much training time, especially if the task is not repeated daily. They are also useful when performance is difficult, is executed infrequently, can be done slowly, and when the consequences of poor performance are serious.[13] As well, new employees can be on the job more quickly if armed with a series of temporary performance aids. Finally, routine (and not-so-routine) trouble-shooting and repair responses can be performed much more quickly and with less frustration.

Employees who are placed in positions where they must react very quickly might not be able to rely on memory. A panel operator in a nuclear power plant, for example, may have 15 seconds (or less) to perform a series of safety sequences. In the less hectic world of insurance sales, one manager found that a potentially sound sales trainee constantly neglected to complete the entire sales sequence and paperwork. Both these employees, despite their vastly different work environments, were helped by performance aids.

In the first instance, an indexed manual containing various operating sequences was developed and placed on a wheeled trolley within easy reach of all the operators' positions. The sales problem was solved by creating a checklist containing all the steps or tasks to be completed each time the salesperson visited a prospective client. The employee completed and checked off each step and the sheet was signed and dated. The manager then reviewed each call with the trainee. In this case, the checklist was discarded after about three weeks as the sales trainee was performing to the standards set by management.[14]

Tips for Trainers

When designing visual performance aids that help employees remember key information, all the skills of the graphic artist's craft should be utilized. Ease in reading, space between letters, colour, boldness, symbols, and graphic language ("Pull Here!") are all used to communicate more effectively.[15] Audio aids also must clearly communicate intent. A taped warning ("Connect your safety harness!") may be useless, but a buzzer alarm is hard to ignore.

When designing a training program, it is important to consider how performance aids might save time and money. With ingenuity, the trainee's work-life not only can be made easier, but significant improvements in performance, downtime, and safety records can result. Performance aids work even better with the use of technology. Performance aids that use technology are called electronic performance-support systems and they are described in Chapter 8.

Job Rotation

Job rotation

A training method in which trainees are exposed to different jobs, functions, and areas within an organization

Job rotation is a training method in which trainees are exposed to different jobs, functions, and areas within an organization. Job rotation is often used as part of an ongoing career-development program, especially for employees who are destined to management positions. The objective is for an employee to learn a variety of skills from both doing a variety of tasks and by observing the performance of others. Typically the individual will be supervised by a supervisor who is responsible for the individual's training. Through this process a trainee can acquire a number of skills required to perform different tasks and also learn about the organization.

Job rotation broadens an individual's knowledge and skills by providing him/her with multiple perspectives and areas of expertise. This is precisely why Space Systems/Loral creates individual learning tracks for new hires that consist of three six-month rotational assignments. The purpose is to broaden new hires' skill sets.

Cross training

Training employees to perform each other's jobs

Job rotation is also an effective means of cross training employees. **Cross training** involves training employees to perform each other's jobs so that anyone can step in and perform any member's job if necessary. Cross training is particularly popular with cross-functional teams. By rotating team members to the various positions on a team, each team member learns the skills required to perform all of the team's tasks and jobs. Cross training not only provides greater flexibility for organizations, but it also enables employees to learn and use more skills.

Job rotation can also be used as a leadership development strategy to strengthen employees' leadership capabilities.[16] Indeed, the practice of line managers temporarily taking staff jobs has met with some success.[17] A variety of cross-job and project-based experiences can be devised to create a pool of leadership talent capable of responding to emergencies and to rapidly changing business environments while making the constant incremental changes necessary for corporate survival.[18]

Some organizations benefit from job rotation more than others. In highly technical environments, for example, it may be difficult for some employees to be productive in areas for which they are untrained. Short-term assignments and planned observations may prove more useful so that non-technical managers gain familiarity with technical processes without actually managing the unit or division.[19]

Job rotation is an effective method of training employees who need to learn a variety of skills. By providing employees with a series of on-the-job experiences in which they work on a variety of tasks, jobs, and assignments, they will acquire the skills required to perform their current job as well as future job responsibilities.

Research on job rotation has generally been supportive. It not only results in an improvement in knowledge and skills but it also has a number of career benefits such as higher job satisfaction, more opportunities for career advancement, and a higher salary.[20]

To find about how one company successfully uses job rotation, see the Training Today feature, "Rotational Assignments at Deloitte & Touche."

Training Today

Rotational Assignments at Deloitte & Touche

Deloitte & Touche has four programs for rotational assignments that include both domestic and international assignments. The management development program places high-performing managers in technically challenging assignments in which they spend two years at a national office or a domestic practice office working for a partner with national responsibilities. The assignments are intended to help managers build skills and develop a more complete understanding of the firm's mission, strategies, and resources. It also helps the firm staff key positions with top talent.

Another example of rotational assignments is the learning development program for audit professionals. Employees have the opportunity to facilitate live training seminars and mentor both facilitators and seminar participants. They choose from 17 learning tracks and commit to facilitating for four or five weeks, during which they serve as the on-site representative of a regulatory body and gather feedback for the development of future seminars. The assignment helps employees improve facilitation and public speaking skills and to develop technical proficiencies and self-confidence.

The global development program is geared for top performers from different service areas in the company who want to work on large and prestigious client engagements. Participants are transferred around the globe each year as they complete the program. The program not only provides employees with career-broadening experiences but it also enhances the firm's ability to serve multinational clients.

The global just-in-time program provides opportunities for managers in South Africa, Sweden, India, and Mexico to transfer to and work in other countries on assignments that last between three and five months.

Job rotation at Deloitte & Touche has been so effective that it has been featured as a best practice in *Training* magazine where the company was ranked sixth among the top 100 companies for training and development in 2005.

Source: Excerpt from (2005, March). Training Top 100: Best Practices. *Training, 42* (3), p. 69. V N U Business Publications. This work is protected by copyright and it is being used with the permission of Access Copyright. Any alteration of its content or further copying in any form whatsoever is strictly prohibited.

Tips for Trainers

A disadvantage of job rotation is that if an employee does not spend enough time in a department or working on an assignment, he or she might not have sufficient time to get up to speed and complete an assignment. Thus, a trainee might acquire only a superficial understanding of a job or department and this might result in some frustration. Therefore, it is important that job rotation be carefully planned and structured so that trainees receive sufficient exposure and experience on each assignment to make it a worthwhile learning experience. In addition, the assignments should be tailored to each individual's training needs as is the case at Space Systems/Loral where management creates individualized learning tracks for each new hire's rotational assignments.

It is also important that job rotation be part of a larger training program and integrated with other training methods. That is, job rotation should be only one component of a training program and learning process and supplemented with classroom instruction and coaching or mentoring. For example, at Space Systems/Loral new hires receive classroom instruction, coaching, and mentoring in addition to job rotation. Thus, the rotational assignments are just one component of the training of new hires. Coaching and mentoring are important because trainees need some guidance and supervision throughout the job rotation process.

Apprenticeship Programs

Apprenticeship programs

Training for skilled trades that combines on-the-job training and classroom instruction

Apprenticeship programs are for skilled trades that combine on-the-job training and classroom instruction. The on-the-job component is used to teach the requisite skills of a particular trade or occupation and also enables apprentices to "earn while they learn." Classroom instruction which usually takes place in community colleges comprises a relatively minor portion of the program (usually about 10 percent or 180 hours), teaches related theory and design concepts.

For example, the four-year plumber program includes only three eight-week in-school sessions. In the classroom, plumber apprentices learn such things as the physical properties of piping and other plumbing materials, industry codes, safety rules and operating procedures, trade tools and equipment, soldering techniques, and the characteristics of various fittings and piping systems. On the job, the trainees become familiar with relevant codes, regulations, and specifications, and learn to install, service, and test systems and equipment.

In Canada, the apprenticeship system covers more than 65 regulated occupations in four occupational sectors: construction (e.g., stone mason, electrician, carpenter, plumber), motive power (motor-vehicle mechanic, machinist), industrial (industrial mechanic, millwright), and service (baker, cook, hairstylist). In some of these regulated occupations, apprentices must be trained and supervised by at least one qualified tradesperson and also pass a provincial government examination to earn a certificate of qualification. Apprentices who pass an interprovincial examination with a minimum grade of 70 percent are awarded a red seal, indicating their qualifications are acceptable across Canada.

Apprenticeship training differs from other training methods in that it is regulated through a partnership between government, labour, and industry. In Canada, the federal government pays for in-school training and income support. Provincial governments administer the programs and pay for classroom facilities and instructors. Employers absorb the costs of workplace training and apprentices initiate the process by finding employers willing to sponsor them.

Unlike corporate-sponsored training programs that address the specific needs of an organization, apprenticeships are focused on the collective training needs of specific occupations within broad industrial categories.[21] Consequently, the skills learned through apprenticeship training are transferable within an occupation, across a province, and across Canada.

In the construction industry, carpenters, electricians, plumbers, and masons are trained to meet standards recognized throughout the trade. This flexibility provides advantages to the worker and the industry when regional fluctuations occur in the supply and demand of skilled labour. However, the system is highly dependent on employers, for they must accept the responsibility for establishing and maintaining adequate standards of job performance. However, a recent survey found that only 18 percent of Canadian employers take on and train apprentices. This is a serious problem given the growing shortage of workers in the skill trades and the fact that apprenticeship training is the primary point of entry for careers in skilled trades.[22]

Furthermore, despite the recent infusion of government funding, much of Canada's apprenticeship system remains antiquated. Outmoded legislation, outdated curricula, poor pay for teachers, archaic entry and completion regulations, and low-prestige entry modes still combine to discourage many young people from considering careers in the skilled trades. Program expansion and enhancement would be key elements in creating apprenticeships that meet the needs of current and future industries, while developing attractive and challenging career alternatives for a greater segment of our labour force.

Tips for Trainers

In determining acceptable qualifications and performance standards for the future, industry and government must address the special needs of new labour groups like women and minorities, eliminating standards or test criteria that might unjustly limit opportunities. For example, criteria pertaining to physical strength might be relaxed or eliminated by making simple changes in job design. Employers that intend to utilize apprenticeships also will need to become more sensitive to the special needs of working mothers and to the various religious or cultural backgrounds of employees. As well, more flexible work schedules may be required to better accommodate those with family or other commitments.

Given the skills shortage crises faced by many industrial sectors, it is likely that increased emphasis will be placed on apprenticeship programs, as this method is one of the most effective and practical ways of teaching skills occupations. It has been predicted that the shortage of skilled workers in Canada could reach one million by the year 2020 unless there is a change in the country's approach to education and training. Over the years, the federal government has organized a series of round table meetings with government, business, and labour to find ways to address the skills shortage problem including apprenticeship programs.[23]

Coaching

Coaching is a training method in which a seasoned employee, usually a manager, works closely with an employee to develop insight, motivate, build skills, and to provide support through feedback and reinforcement. The coach also guides the employee in learning by helping to find experts and resources for learning and development.

Coaching has become very popular in many organizations today. Coaching programs have been effective in enhancing skills and improving performance in a wide range of areas including interpersonal skills, communication skills, leadership skills, cognitive skills, and self-management skills. It is especially effective for helping people apply what they have learned in the classroom on the job.[24]

Research has found coaching to be highly effective for both individuals and organizations. In general, the results of a number of studies indicate that individuals who participated in coaching showed dramatic improvements in specific skills and overall performance. Coaching has also been found to improve working relationships and job attitudes, and to increase the rate of advancement and salary increases.

Benefits to organizations have been found in productivity, quality, customer service, reduced customer complaints, retention, cost reductions, and bottom-line productivity. Thus, coaching is not only popular but it is also effective.[25]

The coaching process involves the planned use of opportunities in the work environment to improve or to enhance employee strengths and potential. Weaknesses are considered only if they prevent the employee from functioning, or if they are below the manager's tolerance level.[26]

The key elements in the coaching process are "planned," "opportunities in the work environment," and "strengths." First, the process revolves around an agreed-upon plan or set of objectives developed mutually by employee and coach. Development does not occur haphazardly or by chance. The process proceeds in a logical agreed-upon fashion. Second, the work environment is the training laboratory (sometimes expanded to include the community). Transfers, special assignments, vacation replacements, and conference speaking engagements are all potential coaching opportunities. The necessary formal infrastructure, perhaps attached to the firm's appraisal or evaluation system, must be in place for the system to work.[27]

The coaching process begins with a dialogue between coach and employee, during which a set of objectives is defined. Then, coaching opportunities are identified by a mutual examination of the environment. A long-term plan is struck, along with an evaluation or measurement procedure. As well, the process is fitted into the employee's career-development goals and made part of the organization's long-term strategies.

The employee performs the agreed-upon task and then reports to the coach both informally and formally during the annual or semi-annual evaluation. They discuss the results of the current program and then plan the next round of activity.[28] With practice, this approach develops into a continual transfer of skills and an ongoing process.[29]

Several devices can be used as coaching tools. For example, a special-project assignment that will enhance a specific skill is a useful approach, as there is no need to reorganize other work or to hire additional staff. Conversely, job rotation often requires extensive preparation for employees to exchange entire jobs on a long-term basis.

Another useful coaching technique is to design a method or schedule of representation, either at meetings or as committee members. Depending upon the skill or knowledge to be developed, the benefits can be significant, as this long-term exposure to more senior colleagues benefits the employee, while freeing the coach for other tasks. In large retail organizations, for example, a management trainee may be rotated through several departments before choosing one in which to specialize.

Where assignments outside the regular work area are impractical, job redesign or restructuring might be considered. Here, some portion of the job is changed so that new skills must be used. The restructuring of one job may, of course, affect the work of others. Job redesign should be part of an overall work strategy that embraces an entire work unit.

There may be situations in which even job restructuring is impossible. The coach might then have no choice but to suggest job enlargement—the employee taking on more work. Although often not a popular alternative, it may be necessary that an employee perform certain new tasks to grow professionally. A larger job may be the only answer. This approach will work best with individuals who have been on the job for some time and have mastered the tasks. A less-experienced person might panic when faced with more work.

As the last three coaching activities to be mentioned here—conference attendance, professional memberships, and teaching/publishing—take place outside the firm, the coach must be concerned with control over the process. Conferences, in particular, can be treated as social events rather than as serious opportunities to learn. Although there may be spin-off benefits (e.g., exposure to leading experts or networking), conferences must be chosen where attendance will meet a clearly defined purpose.

Similarly, professional societies can be used for a number of purposes— networking, publicity, leadership development, training, updating, and group-participation enhancement. Again, these functions need to serve a planned purpose. If, for example, an employee's job provides little opportunity to manage others, the coach might suggest a term as chairperson of the annual conference committee. Likewise, an employee who shows promise as a speaker might be coaxed into volunteering as master of ceremonies for a fundraiser, thus gaining more experience in public speaking.

Undoubtedly, many more ideas for coaching could be found. For example, some senior executives hire professional coaches to improve their skills. The key is to constantly remind oneself that coaching is the *planned* acquisition of skills and knowledge through the use of existing, or carefully

A Well-Designed Coaching Process

A well-designed coaching process should address the following issues:

1. **Contracting**: The process should begin by identifying the key stakeholders (the coach, the person being coached, the person's boss or designated sponsor, and human resource contact). The coach should discuss expectations, roles, and responsibilities with each of them. Specific learning goals and clear expectations for how and when performance will improve should also be discussed.
2. **Coaching Sessions**: There are three parts to the coaching session: 1. The Opening—Expectations should be clarified and a working agenda should be established. The two parties should get to know each other, build trust, and establish rapport. 2. Practice—This is the heart of the coaching process. The coach facilitates learning through hands on practice of real-world situations, instructions, modelling, feedback, and discussion. 3. Action Planning—This involves coming up with a specific plan to put new behaviours into action by specifying things such as what to do, when to do it, how to do it, how to evaluate the outcome, how they will get feedback from others, and how they will modify or build on what they did.
3. **On-the-Job Activities between Sessions**: Participants need to be encouraged to practice and apply what they have learned on a daily basis.
4. **Evaluation of Progress**: Progress should be discussed periodically with each of the stakeholders and participants should be encouraged to regularly seek feedback, encouragement, and support from their organizational sponsors.

Source: Based on Peterson, D. B. (2002). Management Development: Coaching and Mentoring Programs. In *Creating, Implementing, and Managing Effective Training and Development: State-of-the-Art Lessons for Practice* by Kraiger © 2002 and Jossey-Bass. Reprinted with permission of John Wiley & Sons, Inc.

modified, opportunities in the work or professional environments. This focus will prevent both the squandering of developmental opportunities on those who won't benefit and the loss of many potential training activities.

Tips for Trainers

To make coaching work, the employee and the coach must trust each other. Otherwise the employee will see development as extra work. Indeed, perhaps the most important aspect of the coaching process is ongoing dialogue and feedback. It is only under these conditions that employees participate willingly in a two-way process that often requires extra effort and risk taking.[30]

Therefore, it is important that the coach build trust and understanding so that employees will want to work with him/her. It is also important that a coach is able to relate to the person he/she is coaching. And to be most effective, coaching should be used as part of a broader process of learning rather than a standalone program.[31]

Finally, like any training program, the effectiveness of coaching should be evaluated. Coaching programs are expensive and time-consuming so it is important to determine if they are accomplishing what they are supposed to.

To learn more about how to design an effective coaching program, see The Trainer's Notebook 2, "A Well-Designed Coaching Process."

Mentoring

A key part of Space Systems/Loral's training of new hires is a mentoring program that matches each new hire with a mentor within their first month in the organization. Further, new hires participate in a workshop to learn how to make the most of their mentoring experience. But what is mentoring and what is its purpose?

Mentoring is a method in which a senior member of an organization takes a personal interest in the career of a junior employee. A mentor is an experienced individual, usually a senior manager, who provides coaching and counselling to a junior employee.

Mentors play two major roles: career support and psychosocial support. **Career support** activities include coaching, sponsorship, exposure, visibility, protection, and the provision of challenging assignments. **Psychosocial support** includes being a friend who listens and counsels, who accepts and provides feedback, and who offers a role model for success.[32]

The mentor-protégé relationship used to be an informal one with a senior person recognizing the talent of a junior employee and wishing to help. However, organizations now recognize mentoring as a valuable employee development tool and have moved to formalize the relationships by implementing formal mentoring programs.

Like coaching, mentoring is also popular in organizations today and is also an expensive investment.[33] However, mentoring has a more narrow focus than coaching in that its focus is on the career development of junior employees.

According to David Peterson, mentoring can serve a number of purposes for organizations. It can help to accelerate the career progress of underrepresented groups; transmit the culture and values to newer managers; and pass on the accumulated wisdom of seasoned leaders.[34] Mentoring involves exposure to senior management activities that are valuable and beneficial for one's growth and development.

Research has found that mentoring is highly effective for those who are mentored and their organizations. Both professional and academic research consistently has indicated that mentored individuals have greater career prospects and higher incomes than those who have not been mentored. A recent review of mentoring research found that compared to non-mentored individuals, mentored individuals had more promotions, higher compensation, as well as greater career commitment and higher career and job satisfaction. Furthermore, career mentoring was more strongly related to objective career success such as compensation and promotion while psychosocial mentoring was more strongly related to satisfaction with the mentor.[35]

Tips for Trainers

Mentoring can be an effective method of learning that benefits both the mentor and the person being mentored. However, to be effective it is important that the roles and expectations of the mentor and protégés are clear and well understood. It is also important that they agree on how often they will meet, what types of topics they will discuss, and what career activities will be part of the protégé's development.

Mentoring

A method in which a senior member of an organization takes a personal interest in the career of a junior employee

Career support

Mentoring activities that include coaching, sponsorship, exposure, visibility, protection, and the provision of challenging assignments

Psychosocial support

Mentoring activities that include being a friend who listens and counsels, who accepts and provides feedback, and a role model for success

Both the mentor and protégé should have some guidelines on how the process will work. Researchers have highlighted several areas of concern to managers wishing to implement formal mentoring programs:[36]

- *Choice of mentors.* Mentors must be motivated to participate in the program and to make sufficient time available to their protégé. They also need to be knowledgeable about how the organization really works. Participation should be voluntary. Inevitably, some assigned relationships will not work out. A procedure needs to be in place to allow either party to cancel the arrangement without too much loss of face, and employees should feel free to end the relationship without fear of retaliation.

- *Matching mentors and protégé(s).* Matching is an important process that needs to be handled with care. Should males be matched with males; females with females? There may not be enough senior women to mentor all the junior women. Hostility from men when women network with one another make some women reluctant to take on the mentoring role.[37] Those mentors close to retirement perform better in both the vocational and psychosocial functions.[38] It is important that the relationship remain confidential and for the protégé to know that it will be confidential. The right mentor must be chosen. The protégé is unlikely to feel comfortable, for example, if the mentor is his or her boss.

- *Training.* Mentors and protégés both need training. This process should entail more than giving mentors a book to read about mentoring. It should, for example, involve the opportunity to share experiences about mentoring. The training of protégés, usually as part of the induction process, is partly concerned with demonstrating the organization's commitment to mentoring, but also involves setting appropriate expectations for the mentoring relationship. Mentors could be chosen for this training, based on their previous track record in developing employees.

- *Structuring the mentoring relationship.* Some programs set out time limits on the relationship and specify minimum levels of contact. Goals, projects, activities, and resources are spelled out. The program is evaluated and those areas in which either mentors or protégés report dissatisfaction are redesigned. While commitment must be made at all levels, it is at the individual level that the process can most easily break down. Signals sent by derailed mentoring schemes include delay between assignment and first meeting with protégé, poor meeting locations (e.g., the cafeteria), and infrequent contacts.

Finally, to be effective, mentoring programs must receive continued support from management. And because most mentors are volunteers, there should be some benefits and incentives to those who participate as mentors in mentoring programs. The workshop at Space Systems/Loral is a good example of how to make the most out of mentoring by preparing mentors and protégés. To learn more about how to design a formal mentoring program, see The Trainer's Notebook 3, "Developing a Formal Mentoring Program."

Developing a Formal Mentoring Program

A well-designed formal mentoring program should consider the following issues:

1. **Business objectives**: Determine the business objectives of establishing a mentoring program in order to tie it back to business success.
2. **Selection criteria**: Determine key criteria for the recruitment and selection of mentors and mentees (job descriptions, expectations, capabilities).
3. **Mentee assessment**: Mentees should be assessed on their appetite for risk, handling mistakes, and their mindset.
4. **Training**: Determine the type of training participants should receive.
5. **Matching process**: Make sure there is an effective process for optimum matching between participants.

6. **Criteria for success**: Determine what the success factors will be. How will you be able to measure success?
7. **Rewards**: Decide what the rewards of being involved in the mentoring program should be.
8. **Timeline**: Establish a concrete timeline for the mentoring relationship. Most mentoring relationships average one or two years.
9. **Feedback**: Build a feedback loop for continuous improvements to ensure a viable and dynamic mentoring program.

Source: Based on Butyn, S. (2003, July 27). Mentoring your way to improved retention. *Canadian HR Reporter, 16* (2), 13 & 15. Reprinted by permission of Carswell, a division of Thomson Canada Ltd.

Off-the-Job versus On-the-Job Training Methods  7.2

You have now learned a great deal about on- and off-the-job training methods. In Chapter 6, we discussed some of the factors to consider when choosing a training method. A related issue is whether to use on- or off-the-job training methods. In the final section of this chapter, we will review some of the advantages and disadvantages of on- and off-the-job training methods.

Off-the-Job Training Methods

ADVANTAGES   Off-the-job training methods have a number of advantages. First, a trainer can use a wide variety of training methods when training is done off the job. For example, a trainer can use a lecture method with discussion along with audio-visual methods such as a video and slides, a case study or case incident, as well as games and simulations. Thus, a trainer has many possibilities when training is provided off-the-job and will therefore be better able to tailor a training program to the needs and preferences of trainees. The trainer is also able to choose a combination of methods that will be most effective given the objectives and content of a training program and the characteristics of the trainees.

Another advantage of off-the-job training is that the trainer is able to control the training environment. In other words, the trainer can choose a training site that is comfortable, free of distractions, and conducive to learning. A trainer does not have as much control over the learning environment when training is conducted on the job.

A third advantage is that a large number of trainees can be trained at one time. This is particularly the case when the lecture method is used. Thus, off-the-job training is generally more efficient given that so many more trainees can be trained at one time.

DISADVANTAGES There are of course a number of disadvantages of off-the-job training methods. First, off-the-job training can be much more costly than on-the-job training. This is due to the costs associated with the use of training facilities, travel, accommodation, food, and so on. However, as you will see in the next chapter, such costs can be almost completely eliminated with the use of technology.

A second disadvantage of off-the-job training is that because the training takes place in an environment that is different from the environment in which trainees will be required to apply what they learn in training, trainees might have some difficulty making the transition from the training environment to the work environment. For example, while a trainee might be able to perform a training task in a role play during training, he or she might have some difficulty performing the task on the job. Thus, the application of training material on-the-job or what is known as the transfer of training (see Chapter 10) can be more difficult with off-the-job training.

On-the-Job Training Methods

ADVANTAGES There are also a number of advantages and disadvantages of on-the-job training. A major advantage of on-the-job training is that the cost is much lower given that the need for training facilities, travel, accommodation, and so on is eliminated. Thus, on-the-job training tends to be much less costly than off-the-job training.

A second advantage is the greater likelihood of the application of training material on the job. That is, because training takes place in trainees' actual work area, the application is much more direct and in some cases immediate. Thus, there is less difficulty in the transfer of training since the training site and work site are the same.

DISADVANTAGES There are a number of disadvantages of on-the-job training. First, the work environment is full of distractions that can interfere with learning and interrupt training. Noise might make it difficult for trainees to hear and understand the trainer, and at times the trainer might be interrupted and called to solve a problem or work on something else.

Second, when trainees are being trained on an actual machine or equipment in the work place, there is always the potential for damage to expensive equipment. This could also shut down production for a period of time adding to the cost of damaged equipment that needs to be repaired or replaced.

A third problem is the disruption of service or slow down in production that occurs during training. You have probably had the experience of being served by an employee who is being trained. The result is usually slower service and the potential for errors. Thus, on-the-job training can result in a reduction in productivity, quality, and service.

Finally, when there are safety issues associated with the use of equipment or dangerous chemicals, on-the-job training can compromise safety. A trainee learning on-the-job can make a mistake and harm him or herself, other employees, or customers. Therefore, extra precaution and care need to be taken whenever on-the-job training involves working with equipment or dangerous chemicals.

Combining On- and Off-the-Job Methods

As you can see, there are advantages and disadvantages associated with on- and off-the-job training methods. Being aware of and understanding them can be helpful when choosing a training method. For example, when there is a need to train a large number of employees, off-the-job training would be more practical. When the cost of training is an issue, on-the-job training might be more feasible. Thus, issues of practicality and feasibility are important considerations when choosing a training method.

Finally, it should be apparent to you that the choice of a training method is not really about whether it is on- or off-the-job. In fact, effective training programs often combine on- and off-the-job training methods. Recall that Space Systems/Loral combines both on- and off-the-job training methods to orient and train new hires.

Ultimately, what is most important is mixing and combining methods to best suit a particular training need and objective. In fact, a recent government study found that a combination of on-the-job and off-the-job training methods is the best approach for getting employees up to speed. The report found that on average Canadian organizations provide off-the-job or classroom training to 63 percent of their workforce, and on-the-job training to 66 percent of the workforce. However, it also found that larger organizations are more likely to use only off-the-job training while smaller organizations can't afford off-the-job training and therefore tend to rely on on-the-job training.[39]

Thus, once again the best approach appears to be a blended approach that combines different methods of training. This is not only the case with respect to on- and off-the-job training methods, but also for technology-based training methods, which are discussed in Chapter 8.

Summary

This chapter has described some of the most common methods of on-the-job training and serves as a complement to the off-the-job training methods described in Chapter 6. It was noted that on-the-job training is the most common method of training as well as the most misused. However, when on-the-job training is carefully planned and structured, it can have a positive effect on employee learning and performance. Although each of the methods of training described in this chapter takes place on the job, they differ in terms of what they are best suited for and when they should be used. Therefore, it is important to match each method with the objectives of a training program and the needs of trainees. Finally, we noted that there are advantages and disadvantages of on- and off-the-job training methods, and that effective training programs mix and combine both kinds of training methods along with technology-based methods, which are described in the next chapter.

Key Terms

apprenticeship programs (page 188)

career support (page 193)

coaching (page 190)

cross training (page 186)

job instruction training (page 181)

job rotation (page 186)

mentoring (page 193)

on-the-job training (page 179)

performance aid (page 185)

psychosocial support (page 193)

Weblinks

McDonald's Canada: www.mcdonalds.ca (page 179)

RPC Icons

RPC 7.1 Using a variety of methods facilitates the delivery of development programs to groups and individual learners.

RPC 7.2 Recommends the most appropriate way to meet identified learning needs (e.g., courses, secondments, and on-the-job activities).

Discussion Questions

1. Describe the similarities and differences between coaching and mentoring. When would you use coaching and when would you use mentoring?
2. What are the main issues to consider when developing a mentoring program?
3. How should an organization decide if it should use on-the-job training? What are the advantages and disadvantages?
4. Why do you think on-the-job training is the most common method of training? Why is it also called the most misused method of training? What can organizations do to avoid the problems of on-the-job training?
5. Describe the objectives of apprenticeship programs and how they are used in Canada. Why do you think the apprenticeship program in Canada has not been more successful, and what can be done to improve it? What are the consequences of not improving it?
6. Describe the four steps of job instruction training and what you would do in each step if you were training someone on the job.
7. Discuss the advantages and disadvantages of on-the-job and off-the-job training methods.

The Great Training Debate

1. Debate the following: On-the-job training can result in employees who are poorly trained and should therefore be avoided whenever possible.

Using the Internet

1. Do you have what it takes to be a good mentor? To find out, go to **www.mentors.ca** and click on "All about Mentoring" and then click on "Take" to take the mentor test. After you have found out your score, see if you can find a mentor. Click on "Profile" and then "Tips to find a Mentor." What are some of the ways you can find a mentor on your own?
2. To find out about job rotation and cross training, go to **www.jobquality.ca/indicator_e/des001.stm**.

   1. To what extent do organizations of different sizes use job rotation?
   2. To what extent is job rotation and cross training used in different provinces?
   3. Comment on the use of job rotation and cross training across industries.
   4. What are the benefits of job rotation and cross training?

3. To find out about implementing a job rotation system, go to **www. danmacleod.com/Articles/job%20rotation.htm**. Answer the following questions:

   1. What are the roadblocks in setting up a job rotation system?
   2. What are the limitations of job rotation?
   3. What are the steps involved in implementing a job rotation system?

Exercises

In-Class

1. Recall the most recent job you had and how you were trained. Were you trained on the job? If you were trained on the job, describe the experience. What exactly did the trainer do and how did it impact your learning? Was your on-the-job training experience effective? Why or why not? What could have been done differently to make it more effective? If you have not been trained on the job, describe how on-the-job training might be used to train employees doing your job.
2. As a student, you have probably experienced some problems studying, writing assignments, or perhaps writing exams. If you were to act as a

tutor to train another student with some of these problems, what method of training would you use and why? Consider each of the on-the-job training methods in Table 7.1 and indicate how you would use them and how effective they would be for training a student to become a "better" student.

3. Assume that you have just been hired as a trainer in an organization that hires many recent college and university graduates every year. The company does not have a formal mentoring program and your job is to try to get one started. Prepare a proposal to convince management of the importance and need for a formal mentoring program. You should also describe how the program will work and what will be required to get it started. You can then either have another member of the class review your proposal and provide feedback or you can present your proposal to the class.

4. Using the job instruction training method, design a training program to perform a task you are familiar with. It could be a task you have had to perform in a current or previous job, or it could be something that is not work-related such as how to fix a flat tire, how to drive a car, how to ride a bike, etc. Design your training program following the steps outlined in the chapter. Then have another member of the class review your training program and provide feedback. Alternatively, you can provide a demonstration in front of the class and have the class critique your training program and provide feedback.

5. Very often, experienced employees are called upon to train a new employee on the job. In most cases, the employee has not received any training on how to train others. Chances are that some day you will be asked to train a new employee or perhaps you have already had to. To prepare yourself for this task, consider how well prepared and qualified you are. Review the material in The Trainer's Notebook 1, "Effective On-the-Job Instructors." Using this information, assess your qualifications to train somebody on the job. What are your strengths and weaknesses? Prepare an action plan to develop areas that need improvement. If you have already had to train somebody on the job, how effective were you and what do you need to work on to improve?

In-the-Field

1. Ask your friends if they would accept a paid training experience that consisted of the following benefits:
   - they would be given structured classroom training and on-the-job assignments
   - they would be coached and supervised throughout the learning experience
   - they would be paid to learn
   - they would be certified at the end of learning the job
   - they would be guaranteed employment at high wages

   If they answer "Yes!" then tell them about becoming an apprentice electrician or carpenter. What is their reaction? Do students resist the certification programs in the traditional vocations and embrace certification in human resources or technology? Why? What can be done to increase the likelihood that students will choose a skilled trade and enter an apprenticeship program?

2. Contact the human resource department of an organization to find out about their use of on-the-job training. In particular, you should inquire about:

- Do they use on-the-job training, and if so what do they use it for (what employees, what kinds of job), why do they use it, and how effective is it?
- How formal and systematic is their on-the-job training? Is it carefully planned, do trainers receive training and instruction, are the trainers carefully selected, are they rewarded for their efforts, and are they evaluated?
- Do they follow the steps of the job instruction training method? How well is each of the steps performed?
- Based on what you have learned in this chapter, is the organization doing a good job in providing on-the-job training? What are they doing right and wrong?
- What advice would you give the organization to improve their on-the-job training?

Case Incident

Davco Machine Ltd.

Davco Machine Ltd. is located in Grande Prairie in northern Alberta where it designs and builds equipment for the forestry, construction, oil and gas industries. The company has 66 employees most of whom are machinists, welders, mechanics, or millwrights. Davco formed a partnership with technical schools in Edmonton and was able to generate interest among students to apprentice at the company. However, the facility didn't have enough journeymen to meet the requirement of one journeyman tradesperson for every apprentice. So company representatives traveled to Germany to take part in a job fair hosted by the provincial government. When a worker in Germany is unemployed the government requires him/her to go back to school. As a result, Germany has a low unemployment rate and a highly educated labour pool. Once in Germany, Davco had no problem recruiting four journeymen machinists.

Questions

1. What does this case tell us about apprenticeship training in Canada and its future as a method of on-the-job training?
2. What should companies like Davco and governments do to increase the number of apprentices and journeymen in Canada?

Franceschini, T. (2005, December). CloseUp: CEOs talk workforce development. *Canadian HR Reporter, 18* (21), 7–10.

Case

TPK Appliances

When TPK, a manufacturer of small appliances—electric kettles, toasters, and irons—automated its warehouse, the warehouse crew was reduced from 14 to 4. Every one of the displaced stockmen was assigned to another department, as TPK had a history of providing stable employment.

Jacob Peters, a stockman with more than 15 years of service, was transferred to the toaster assembly line to be retrained as a small-parts assembler. When he arrived to begin his new job, the foreman said, "This may be only temporary, Jacob. I have a full staff right now, so I have nothing for you to do, but come on, I'll find you a locker." As there really was no job for him, Jacob did nothing for the first week but odd jobs such as filling bins. At the beginning of week two, Jacob was informed that a vacancy would be occurring the next day, so he reported for work eager to learn his new job.

The operation was depressingly simple. All Jacob had to do was pick up two pieces of metal, one in each hand, place them into a jig so that they were held together in a cross position, and press a button. The riveting machine then put a rivet through both pieces and an air jet automatically ejected the joined pieces into a bin.

"This job is so simple a monkey could do it," the foreman told Jacob. "Let me show you how it's done," and he quickly demonstrated the three steps involved. "Now you do it," the foreman said. Of course, Jacob did it right the first time. After watching him rivet two or three, the foreman left Jacob to his work.

About three hours later, the riveter started to put the rivets in a little crooked, but Jacob kept on working. Finally, a fellow worker stopped by and said, "You're new here, aren't you?" Jacob nodded. "Listen, I'll give you a word of advice. If the foreman sees you letting the rivets go in crooked like that, he'll give you hell. So hide these in the scrap over there." The co-worker then showed Jacob how to adjust the machine.

Jacob's next problem began when the air ejection system started jamming. Four times he managed to clear it, but on the fifth try, he slipped and his elbow hit the rivet button. The machine put a rivet through the fleshy part of his hand, just below the thumb.

It was in the first-aid station that the foreman finally had the opportunity to see Jacob once again.

Questions

1. Comment on the strengths and weaknesses of Jacob's on-the-job training.
2. What does this case tell you about the traditional approach to on-the-job training?
3. If you were the trainer, how would you have trained Jacob?
4. If the job instruction training method was used, how would Jacob's training have been conducted? Explain how each step would proceed.

5. Describe any other methods of on- or off-the-job training that might be used to train Jacob. What do you think would be the most effective, practical, and feasible methods?

References

1. Excerpt from Barbian, J. (March 2002). Training top 100: Space Systems/Loral. *Training*, 66.
2. Parker, R. O., & Cooney, J. (2005). Learning & development outlook 2005. *The Conference Board of Canada.* Ottawa.
3. (1999, May/June). McDonald's stresses hands-on training. *The Training Report*, p. 10.
4. Dulipovici, A. (2003, May). Skilled in training: Results of CFIB surveys on training.
5. Sisson, G. R. (2001). *Hands-on training.* Berrett-Koehler Publishers, Inc. San Francisco: CA.
6. Sisson, G. R. (2001).
7. Sisson, G. R. (2001).
8. Sisson, G. R. (2001).
9. Broadwell, M. (1969). *The supervisor and on-the-job training.* Reading, MA: Addison-Wesley.
10. Sloman, M. (1989). On-the-job training: A costly poor relation. *Personnel Management 21* (2), 38–42.
11. Renner, P. F. (1989). *The instructor's survival kit.* Vancouver: Training Associates Ltd; Tench, A. (1992). Following Joe around: Should this be our approach to on-the-job training? *Plant Engineering, 46* (17), 88–92.
12. Meyers, D. (1991). Restaurant service: Making memorable presentations. *Cornell Hotel and Restaurant Administration Quarterly, 32* (1), 69–73; Ukens, C. (1993). Cards help pharmacists counsel patients in a flash. *Drug Topics, 137* (1), 24–27.
13. Ruyle, K. (1991, February/March). Developing intelligent job aids. *Technical and Skills Training,* 9–14.
14. Arajis, B. (1991). Getting your sales staff in shape. *Graphic Arts Monthly, 63* (5), 125–127.
15. Arajis, B. (1991); Cowen, W. (1992). Visual control boards are a key management tool. *Office Systems, 9* (10), 70–72; King, W. (1994). Training by design. *Training and Development, 48* (1), 52–54.
16. Orr, J. (2006, January 30). Job rotations give future leaders the depth they need. *Canadian HR Reporter, 19* (2), 17, 20.
17. Zemke, R. (1998). In search of self-directed learners. *Training, 35* (5), 61–68.
18. McCall, M. (1992). Executive development as a business strategy. *Journal of Business Strategy, 13* (1), 25–31; Miller, F. (1993). Management development. *Training and Development, 11* (8), 16.
19. Rothwell, W. (1992). Issues and practices in management job notation programs as perceived by HRD professionals. *Performance Improvement Quarterly, 5* (1), 49–69.
20. Campion, M. A., Cheraskin, L., & Stevens, M. J. (1994). Career-related antecedents and outcomes of job rotation. *Academy of Management Journal, 37,* 1518–542.
21. Moskal, B. (1991). Apprenticeship: Old cure for new labor shortage? *Industry Week, 240* (9), 30–35.
22. Galt, V. (2006, March 22). Few employers taking on apprentices: New survey. *The Globe and Mail,* C2.
23. McCarthy, S. (2001, February 27). Skilled-worker shortage could reach one million. *The Globe and Mail,* A1.
24. Peterson, D. B. (2002). Management development: Coaching and mentoring programs. In K. Kraiger (Ed.), *Creating, implementing, and managing effective training and development: State-of-the-art lessons for practice,* (pp. 160-91). San Francisco. CA: Jossey-Bass.
25. Peterson, D. B. (2002).

26. Lovin, B., & Casstevens, E. (1971). *Coaching, learning, and action*. New York: American Management Association; Frankel, L., & Otazo, K. (1992). Employee coaching: The way to gain commitment. *Employment Relations Today, 19* (3), 311–20.

27. Blakesley, S. (1992). Your agency . . . leave it better than you found it. *Managers Magazine, 67* (4), pp. 20–22.

28. Kroeger, L. (1991). Your team can't win the game without solid coaching. *Corporate Controller, 3* (5), 62–64.

29. Azar, B. (1993). Striking a balance. *Sales and Marketing Management, 145* (2), 34–35; Whittaker, B. (1993). Shaping the competitive organization. *CMA Magazine, 67* (3), p. 5.

30. Kruse, A. (1993). Getting top value for your payroll dollar. *Low Practice Management, 19* (3), 52–57.

31. Peterson, D. B. (2002).

32. Noe, R. A. (1999). *Employee training and development*. Boston: Irwin McGraw-Hill.

33. Peterson, D. B. (2002).

34. Peterson, D. B. (2002).

35. Allen, T. D., Eby, L. T., Poteet, M. L., Lentz, E., & Lima, L. (2004). Career benefits associated with mentoring for protégés: A meta-analysis. *Journal of Applied Psychology, 89*, 127–36.

36. Jackson, C. (1993). Mentoring: Choices for individuals and organizations. *The International Journal of Career Management, 5* (1), 10–16; Noe, R. A. (1999).

37. Gallege, L. (1993). Do women make poor mentors? *Across the Board, 30* (6), 23–26.

38. Mullen, E. J. (1998). Vocational and psychosocial mentoring functions: Identifying mentors who serve both. *Human Resource Development Quarterly, 9* (4), 319–31.

39. Harding, K. (2003, May 9). Combined training works best, study says. *The Globe and Mail*, C1.

Chapter 8

Technology-Based Training Methods

Chapter Learning Objectives

After reading this chapter you should be able to:

- define, compare, and contrast technology-based training and traditional training methods
- define the different methods of technology-based training
- compare and contrast instructor-led and self-directed learning
- define and give examples of asynchronous and synchronous training
- define and discuss computer-based training, e-learning, distance learning, electronic performance support systems, and video conferencing
- discuss the advantages and disadvantages of technology-based training
- discuss the effectiveness of technology-based training programs
- describe how to design technology-based training programs and how to maximize trainee engagement and learning

www.hbc.com

HUDSON'S BAY COMPANY

If you walk into a restaurant in any of the Hudson's Bay Company stores, you might come across the best cinnamon buns the restaurant has ever made. That's because HBC has an e-learning program that includes courses on everything from health and safety, merchandise loss prevention, employee development for managers, and even cinnamon bun making.

Computer-based training is not new at HBC. Canada's oldest retailer decided to meld computers and training back in 1991 when they offered mainframe computer-based courses to their employees. That mainframe system carried the company's training load—a total of 146 courses and 60 000 course-units being taken every year on average until 1997. By then many people had PCs in their homes. The system dropped off in popularity and the company stopped developing courses for it. The company needed something new and current because it planned to do more training than ever.

With 70 000 employees in roughly 550 locations, e-learning made sense. It would allow the company to cut down on its travel and class-room training expenses, and could even help administer quick training modules to the 10 000 employees hired over the Christmas holiday season.

The company turned to the Bell e-Learning Centre, which works with companies to create a complete training environment for employees including self-serve and live on-line courses. The vision is to have hundreds of compelling on-line courses for employees, available any time, anywhere.

The new system can handle all of the extras that typically make courses attractive to employees, including video and sound capabilities, synchronous learning and the ability to track their performance and forward it to their supervisors for consideration in promotions.

The cost of developing on-line courses is roughly $10,000—because of all the added bells and whistles—compared to the $3,000 to $5,000 HBC used to spend to develop material for its mainframe system. And the system itself came with a significant price tag. But once all of the course development is completed, getting an employee to take an on-line course probably costs about $10, compared to the $200 a company can easily spend, per person, on travel expenses and classroom costs.

The new system also includes what HBC terms "product knowledge" courses, meaning an employee hired to staff the jewellery counter will be able to sit down and take a one-hour course on the

Like many companies today, the Hudson's Bay Company has begun to invest in technology-based training. Besides being able to offer a wide assortment of training programs, computer-based training can be provided to large numbers of employees at any time with many benefits to employees and the organization.

In Chapters 6 and 7, we described traditional methods of off- and on-the-job training. In this chapter, we describe technology-based training methods. We begin by defining technology-based training and then describe some of the different types of technology-based training methods.

What Is Technology-Based Training?

RPC 8.1

Organizations are increasingly using technology-based training to deliver training.[2] In the United States, 15 to 30 percent of organizations now use both technology-based training and traditional methods.[3] In Canada, the use of technology represents 13 percent of all training time and this is expected to almost double to 23 percent by 2007.[4] However, it has been reported that 77 percent of Canadian employers now provide some form of technology-based training. Thus, technology-based training has arrived and is on the rise.[5]

The importance of technology-based training became especially apparent following the September 11, 2001, terrorist attacks in the United States. Many organizations found themselves with no choice but to turn to technology-based training. This was seen immediately following the attacks as thousands of workers required instant training. Various forms of technology-based training proved to be an essential means of getting thousands of people trained in a short period of time.[6]

In addition, because of the cancellation of many training programs following the terrorist attacks, due in large part to people's reluctance to fly, many organizations turned to technology-based methods that allowed employees to take training without having to travel. For example, Pfizer, the large pharmaceutical company, cancelled many international training programs following the attacks. To replace the cancelled classroom training programs, it accelerated the use of its Interactive Distance Learning program, which involves a virtual studio at its learning centre where training courses are digitally broadcast via satellite and broadband to the homes of more than 1000 managers and sales representatives.[7]

In their Annual Industry Report of formal training in the United States, *Training* magazine defines **technology-based training** as any training that involves using technology to deliver it, such as Web-based training, computerized self-study (including CD-ROMs, DVDs, and diskettes), satellite or broadcast TV, and video-, audio- or teleconferencing. Any technology that delivers education or training, or supports the delivery of these subjects,

Technology-based training
Training that involves using technology to deliver courses

TABLE 8.1

Types of Technology-Based Training

Internet: A loose confederation of computer networks around the world that is connected through several primary networks

Intranet: A general term describing any network contained within an organization. It refers primarily to networks that use Internet technology

Extranet: A collaborative network that uses Internet technology to link organizations with their suppliers, customers, or other organizations that share common goals or information

CD-ROM: A format and system for recording, storing, and retrieving electronic information on a compact disc that is read using an optical drive

Electronic performance support system (EPSS): An integrated computer application that uses any combination of expert systems, hypertext, embedded animation, and/or hypermedia to help a user perform a task in real time quickly and with a minimum of support by other people

Electronic simulation: A device or system that replicates or imitates a real device or system

Multimedia: A computer application that uses any combination of text, graphics, audio, animation, and/or full-motion video

Teleconference: The instantaneous exchange of audio, video or text between two or more individuals or groups at two or more locations

Television (cable, satellite): The transmission of television signals via cable or satellite technology

Source: Cooney, J. & Cowan, A. (2003). Training and development outlook 2003. Reprinted by permission of The Conference Board of Canada. Ottawa.

would be included in the definition.[8] Thus, although it might appear as if this kind of training is something new and different, in reality it is really about the use of technology to facilitate learning and training.[9]

Traditional training

Training that does not involve using technology to deliver courses

By contrast, **traditional training** is defined as any training that does not involve using technology to deliver it, such as classroom training with a live instructor (regardless of the instructor's or learners' use of technology during the class); non-computerized self-study, such as textbooks or workbooks; non-computerized games; seminars; lectures; or outdoor programs.[10]

While most people understand that computers are being used for training, one of the most confusing things about technology-based training is the many different terms and labels that are used to refer to the various forms of technology-based training. Although there are technical distinctions between some of the methods, the distinctions are generally not apparent to trainees and often have to do with where the programs and data are located and the ease with which they can be updated.[11]

Nonetheless, it is important to be aware of the terms used to describe the different types of technology-based training. Table 8.1 provides a list and definitions of the different types of technology-based training.

Managing Performance Through Training and Development

TABLE 8.2

Percentage of Courses Using Technology-Based Training Methods to Deliver Training in Canada in the Year 2002

METHODS	PERCENT
Internet	12.4
Intranet	18.3
CD-ROM	8.3
Electronic Performance Support System (EPSS)	10.9
Simulators	13.0
Multimedia	24.1
Teleconference	7.2
TV (cable, satellite)	9.2

Source: Cooney, J. & Cowan, A. (2003). Training and development outlook 2003. Reprinted by permission of The Conference Board of Canada. Ottawa.

By all measures, the use of technology-based training methods has been steadily increasing and some organizations have a separate training budget for technology-based training. The use of training technologies in Canada has also increased dramatically over the last decade and some companies have made major advances.[12] For example, at Cisco Systems Canada Co., 80 percent of sales staff training is now done on-line compared to just a few years ago when 90 percent was done in the classroom. Employees access the company's website to find out about new Cisco networking products and how to install products. Because the courses are up and running much faster than traditional classroom programs, employees can learn about new products in one week compared to three months.[13]

In terms of the use of technology-based training methods in Canada, The Conference Board of Canada found that in the year 2002, 19.6 percent of organizations reported using television signals (cable, satellite); 58.9 percent used CD-ROMs; 51.3 percent used internal Internet technology (intranet, extranet); 50.6 percent used external Internet technology (Internet, World Wide Web); 13.9 percent used simulators; 36.7 used multimedia; and 43.7 used teleconferencing.[14] Table 8.2 shows the percentage of courses using technology-based methods to deliver training in Canadian organizations.

As for the type of training, a recent survey of organizations in Canada and the United States found that technology-based training is being used primarily for the training of information technology (IT) skills (e.g., programming skills) and mostly in the technology/telecommunications field. A growing number of organizations are also using technology-based training for business and soft skills such as management, leadership, communication, customer service, quality management, and human resources skills.[15]

One of the ways that technology-based methods differ is in terms of whether the training is instructor-led or self-directed, the focus of the next section.

Instructor-Led and Self-Directed Learning

Technology-based training can take many forms. Like more traditional approaches to training, some forms of technology-based training involve an instructor or facilitator who might lead, facilitate, or teach on-line. Technology-based training that is instructor-led is known as **instructor-led training** or **ILT**. Some examples of ILT are on-line discussions and video conferencing.

In some cases, the instructor is highly involved in the training and leads the process. In other cases, a course or program involves self-study and the instructor is available for answering questions and providing assistance.[16]

However, one of the main advantages of technology-based training is that it does not always have to be instructor-led but rather, can be self-paced and controlled by the trainee. This is known as self-directed learning.

Self-directed learning (SDL) is a process that occurs when individuals or groups seek out the necessary resources to engage in learning that enhances their careers and personal growth. Employees assess their own needs, use a variety of organizational resources to meet those needs, and are helped with evaluating the effectiveness of meeting their needs. SDL can be as simple as a booklet that describes a new procedure or a multimedia program that teaches project management skills.

Self-directed learning has become increasingly popular because traditional methods of training lack the flexibility to respond quickly to dramatic and constant organizational change and trainees' needs. Technology-based self-directed learning allows trainees to access training materials and programs when they want to, at their own pace, and sometimes in the sequence they prefer. This usually involves computer-based or Web-based training materials.

Motorola Inc. implemented an SDL approach to its training program. Forty percent of their employees undertook self-study courses. The research showed that the average cost for the SDL was $7.76 per hour, compared to $13.34 hourly for classroom instruction. The results demonstrated that SDL was as effective as, or better than, the traditional training approach. At Motorola U, about 30 percent of employee training now involves self-directed learning. The major benefit for Motorola has been the time savings. With technology-based self-directed learning, employees can complete a course in five hours rather than eight hours in a traditional classroom. This also means that the company can triple the amount of training that employees receive since they require a minimum of 40 hours a year per employee.[17]

See Table 8.3 for some of the benefits and the limitations of self-directed learning.

Computer-Based Training and E-Learning

Over the last decade, the use of a computer to deliver training has been referred to as computer-based training and e-learning. Although these terms are often used synonymously, there are differences. **Computer-based training**

Instructor-led training (ILT)

Training methods that involve an instructor or facilitator who might lead, facilitate, or teach on-line

Self-directed learning (SDL)

A process in which individuals or groups identify the resources necessary to learn and then manage the learning experience

Computer-based training

Training that is delivered via the computer for the purpose of teaching job-relevant knowledge and skills

TABLE 8.3

The Benefits and Limitations of Self-Directed Learning

BENEFITS

- Trainees can learn at their own pace and determine their desired level of expertise
- Trainees build on their knowledge bases and training time may be reduced; trainees learn what is relevant to their needs
- Trainees become independent and acquire skills enabling them to learn more efficiently and effectively, reducing dependence on formal training
- People can learn according to their own styles of learning

LIMITATIONS

- Trainees may learn the wrong things or may not learn all there is to know; one suggestion to remedy this problem is to negotiate a learning contract with specific learning objectives and performance measures
- Trainees may waste time accessing resources and finding helpful material; the trainer could become a facilitator, directing employees toward useful resources
- SDL takes time—the employee has to learn active knowledge-seeking skills, has to acquire knowledge-gathering skills, must learn to tolerate inefficiencies and mistakes; the trainer, too, must learn to give up a power base and move from expert to helper

---

refers to training that is delivered via the computer for the purpose of teaching job-relevant skills. It can include text, graphics, and/or animation and be delivered via CD-ROMs, intranets, or the Internet.[18] Among the various forms of computer-based training, Web-delivered and CD-ROM formats have received the most attention.

A related and increasingly popular term for technology-based training is e-learning. **E-learning** refers to the use of computer network technology such as the intranet or Internet to deliver information or instruction to individuals.[19] Thus, e-learning is a specific type of computer-based learning and is limited to the use of computer network technology. It would not include the use of CD-ROMs. In this chapter, we will use the broader term, computer-based training, which includes e-learning.

It has been estimated that Canadian companies spent $1.7 billion on computer-based training in the year 2000.[20] Although computer-based training represents a small proportion of the total spending on training, more and more organizations are moving in this direction. To find out about some Canadian companies that have won awards for their computer-based training programs, see Training Today 1, "Computer-Based Training Excellence."

E-learning

The use of computer network technology such as the intranet or Internet to deliver information or instruction to individuals

Computer-Based Training Excellence

Once a year, the Canadian Society for Training and Development recognizes outstanding training programs with the Canadian Awards for Training Excellence. Winners are chosen based on a program's originality and instructional design as well as the program's business value.

In 2005, Mental Health Works, an initiative of the Canadian Mental Health Association (Ontario) was one of four winners for a CD-ROM called, "Working it Out: A Manager's Guide to Mental Health and Accommodation in the Workplace." The CD-ROM, which is based on Mental Health Works' full-day workshop, trains employers to manage mental health problems in the workplace. It has three modules that help managers identify the signs and symptoms of mental health issues, informs them of their rights and responsibilities towards employees, and shows how to develop accommodation plans and other solutions to help employees with mental health problems such as depression and anxiety.

Interactive exercises and scenarios demonstrating approaches to mental illness at work help employers understand how to help employees remain productive by identifying issues, understanding the duty to accommodate, and managing the accommodation process. The program tests participants' knowledge and suggests which material to review if the participant does poorly. The entire program takes about three hours to complete and can be done with audio or only text, a flexible function that accommodates individual learning preferences.

Another award winning program was the "Fire Safety" program developed by Hydro One Networks. Safety training is a top priority for Hydro One. It developed an e-learning program to complement its existing classroom training to ensure that its employees have as much knowledge as possible to aid in preventing fires and to improve their ability to follow procedures and ensure their safety and the safety of others. The program's use of audio, graphics, and animation makes it interesting and easy to use. It is also easy for the company to track who has completed the training and report that information to the government as part of its health and safety requirements.

Source: Based on Shannon Klie (2005, November 7). Trainers prove their worth: Awards recognize T&D programs with good business sense. *The Canadian HR Reporter*, 1–2; 2005 Awards: Canadian Awards for Training Excellence 2005. Mental Health Works "Working It Out: A Manager's Guide to Mental Health and Accommodation in the Workplace" and Hydro One Networks Inc. and Provinent Corporation, Now Vitesse Learning "Fire Safety." www.cstd.ca/awards/current/2005_awards.html.

Asynchronous and Synchronous Training

An important characteristic of technology-based training has to do with when it is available. In this regard, computer-based training can be asynchronous or synchronous.

Asynchronous training

Training that is pre-recorded and available to employees at any time and from any location

Synchronous training

Training that is live and requires trainees to be at their computer at a specific time

When training is **asynchronous**, it is pre-recorded and available to employees at any time and from any location. When training is **synchronous,** it is live and in real-time so trainees must be at their computer at a specific time. Currently, asynchronous learning is much more common than synchronous learning.

Asynchronous and synchronous training programs vary in their level of sophistication. For example, at the most basic level, an asynchronous program might simply involve the posting of text, information or instructions on a website. More sophisticated programs can include graphics, animation, audio and video thereby providing a multimedia program. This combined with simulations, interactive exercises, tests, and feedback can result in a much more engaging and active learning experience. While the use of multimedia involves greater involvement on the part of the trainee, it is much more expensive to design and develop.

A basic synchronous program might simply involve "chat" sessions in which trainees log on at the same time and participate in a discussion of some topic. More sophisticated programs might have trainees from various locations log into the training at a set time and receive instruction from a trainer who facilitates a discussion, shows slides, and answers trainees' questions and provides feedback.[21]

In the following sections, we present two common forms of asynchronous training, distance learning and electronic performance support systems. We then discuss a popular form of synchronous learning called video conferencing.

Distance Learning

Computer-based training is increasingly being used for distance learning. **Distance learning** and distance education are general terms that refer to learning methods in which information is communicated from a central source to individuals or groups at locations separate from the source, usually through the use of technology. The most common methods of distance learning include correspondence courses, which can include audio- and videocassettes or CD-ROMs, supplemented by workbooks and even supervised off-site exams.

Distance learning is considered valuable for students or employees who live in remote areas, when there is an insufficient number of students enrolled in a course to justify hiring an instructor, for trainees who are less mobile than others because of parenting or work responsibilities, and for trainees who have disabilities.

A major advantage for students is the ability to control the pace and place of learning. However, motivation seems to be a big problem in learning. Students report feeling isolated and missing the collegial nature of classroom learning.[22] Another problem is the high cost of course development, particularly when advanced technology is used. However, the advantage of nearly universal access overrides concerns about motivation and cost.

An increasing number of universities are now providing Internet courses. Students log on to a website where they can access course materials. There is, however, a great deal of variation in terms of how these courses are designed and what they deliver. Some simply provide text information such as the instructor's notes and slides. Others show videotaped lectures and some include audio-recorded lectures that are accompanied by slides.

Some universities now provide degree programs taken entirely over the Internet. For example, Athabasca University in Alberta now offers an on-line MBA program. The number of students taking distance education courses at the university has doubled in three years and the university now has 25 percent of the Canadian e-learning MBA market.

Distance learning

Learning methods in which information is communicated from a central source to individuals or groups at locations separate from the source, usually through the use of technology

Given the increasing enrollment in Canadian colleges and universities expected over the next decade, Internet courses and degree programs are likely to become even more popular.[23]

Electronic Performance Support Systems

Electronic performance-support system (EPSS)

A computer-based system that provides information, advice, and learning experiences on the job to improve performance

An **electronic performance support system (EPSS)** is a computer-based system that provides on-the-job access to integrated information, advice, and learning experiences.[24] They are computer programs that help solve work-related problems. These systems provide several types of support including assisting, warning, advising, teaching, and evaluating. Thus, in some ways they are a modern version of a performance aid.

The goal of an EPSS is to provide whatever is necessary to aid performance and learning at the time it is needed. When the accounting firm KPMG needed to train all its employees on a new tax planning service, it chose EPSS over classroom training. The EPSS saved in delivery time (consultants did not need to spend three weeks in classrooms) and reduced costs in updates.[25]

Alberta Pacific Forest Industries at its Sarnia plant extols the advantages of EPSS for safety, maintenance, and laboratory training: learning occurs when workers need it most, on-site; it allows for continual upgrading; it allows for individual differences in the pace of learning; and it allows links to suppliers' training and tracks learning accomplishments.[26]

EPSS offers even more advantages than computer-based training programs. With EPSS, information is accessed only when it is needed. Only the information that is needed is given; there is no information overload. It is unrealistic to expect that enough information can be crammed into everyone's memory during training and then banked for access later. EPSS is particularly useful for training in high-turnover jobs, like hotel staff and tasks that are difficult, performed infrequently, and must be performed perfectly.[27]

As increasing numbers of employees use personal computers, EPSS will become more common for training employees such as cashiers, bank tellers, insurance agents, and so on. If you want to experience using an EPSS, then just ask for help the next time you are preparing a Microsoft PowerPoint presentation or even trying to figure out how do a task when writing a letter in Microsoft Word.

Video Conferencing

Video conferencing

Linking an expert to employees via two-way television and satellite technology

Video conferencing consists of linking a subject-matter expert to employees by means of two-way television. This can involve the transmission of television signals via cable or through satellite technology. Whatever the actual means of transmission, the basic idea is that people at two or more locations are able to see, hear, and speak with one another thus permitting simultaneous meetings in different locations.

Video conferencing is used to bring in an expert from another location, to hold meetings with staff working in various locations, and to communicate corporate information that needs to be rapidly disseminated.

Political conditions and incidents like the Gulf War and the September 11, 2001, terrorist attacks in the United States (which made some executives wary of travel terrorism) as well as decreases in the costs of technology, have made video conferencing more acceptable and affordable than ever. In addition, employees in remote locations and those with limited flexibility (e.g., with child-care arrangements) stand to benefit from this technology, which allows them to be trained at their own workplace.

Companies like Stentor claim that training by live TV reduces the travel and labour costs of training, gets consistent or uniform training quickly to a large number of people, brings the subject-matter expert to all trainers, enhances company revenues by implementing training faster (down from three months to two weeks), and distributes complex information over shorter periods of time. The consulting firm Booz Allen Hamilton invested $250,000 in an e-learning centre designed to emulate a television studio that can provide synchronous online instruction and video- and teleconferencing for its 13,500 worldwide employees.[28]

The disadvantage of video conferencing is that less personal attention is given to trainees. However, this problem can be remedied by having a facilitator on-site or by allowing for interactive questioning while training takes place. For a good example of this, see Training Today 2, "Satellite Television at Scotiabank."

Training Today 2

Satellite Television at Scotiabank

Scotiabank has begun to use interactive training sessions that are broadcast to employees across the country by satellite television.

Using satellite television technology, the bank is able to train employees in branches across Canada. For example, they trained 2000 employees at 25 locations across the country on RRSPs. Trainees had to first use the Internet to review course materials on-line prior to attending the training. To keep employees engaged, they completed quizzes and participated in opinion polls throughout the session by pushing buttons on their phone sets. During breaks, there were group discussions and case study analyses that were led by previously trained managers at each meeting site. During the broadcast, trainees asked questions by telephone.

For Scotiabank and its employees, this method of training has many advantages. With some 28 000 employees spread all over the country, the bank is able to train thousands of employees at one time without having to bring them together in one location or to send trainers all over the country. It also ensures that a consistent message is sent to all employees and everyone hits the ground running at the same time. In fact, employees return to their branches the day after training and begin to apply their new product knowledge.

An added benefit to employees is the opportunity to learn about what their fellow employees around the country are doing and to share ideas and best practices. This also helps to create a sense of cohesion, which is difficult in such a large and geographically diverse organization.

Source: Galt, V. (2003, January 22). Bank tunes in to TV training. *The Globe and Mail*, C1, C5. Reprinted with permission from *The Globe and Mail.*

Technology-Based Training: Advantages and Disadvantages

Now that you are familiar with technology-based training, you might be wondering how it compares to traditional methods of training. Like on- and off-the-job training methods, there are advantages and disadvantages of technology-based training for trainees and organizations.

Advantages

TRAINEES A major advantage of technology-based training for trainees is greater flexibility. For example, trainees do not have to coordinate and arrange their schedule and workload to accommodate training schedules. Trainees do not have to take courses when they are offered or wait until a group of trainees are ready to take a course. They can learn when they want to or "just in time." Trainees also do not have to leave work to attend training, and can even learn while they are at home or away from work.

Another advantage for trainees is greater control over their learning or what is known as learner control. In other words, trainees can enter and leave training as they choose and can also progress at their own pace. Self-pacing means that trainees can work on training tasks as quickly or as slowly as they want. In some cases, trainees even have control over various instructional elements of a program such as the sequence of instructional material, the content of instruction, and the amount of instruction during training.[29]

There is also some evidence that trainees are not as shy on-line as they might be in a more formal classroom training program. Trainees who are having problems are less likely to feel embarrassed about their pace or success of learning, and they don't have to admit that they don't know something. As a result, they are more likely to feel comfortable on-line than in a classroom and this can improve their satisfaction with the training as well as their self-efficacy and learning.[30]

Perhaps most beneficial for trainees is the convenience of being able to learn whenever they want to or need to, and to do so from any location where they have access to a computer. This, of course, is the ultimate example of "just-in-time" training. Employees do not have to sign up and wait for a course to be available; it is available whenever they need it. And during training, employees can pause and continue at a later time without missing a beat. Furthermore, because of the ability to learn at work or at home, employees do not have to spend time traveling to distant training locations. Geographic flexibility is a major advantage.

ORGANIZATIONS From the organization's perspective, there are a number of advantages of technology-based training. One advantage is that they can ensure that all trainees receive the same training. The main reason that the Hudson's Bay Company uses computer-based training is that it can standardize training for all of its employees.[31] Thus, organizations can deliver standardized and consistent training to large numbers of employees across the organization and even worldwide. This is especially important for training programs in which all employees need to be trained across many locations. Leaving the training to each location could result in differences in terms of content, delivery, and effectiveness.

Another advantage is that large numbers of employees can be trained within a short period of time as was the case following the terrorist attacks in the United States. With technology-based training, there is no limit to the number of employees who can be trained, as one is not constrained by the number of instructors available or the need for classroom space.

Technology-based training also makes it possible to track employees' performance on learning exercises and tests. This kind of tracking is especially important for training programs that are mandatory and completion, certification, or attaining a certain level of performance is legally mandated such as for health and safety training. The technology can generate tests that can provide legal documentation for proof of competency levels. When an accident or safety incident results in a lawsuit, the employer can prove that a training program was completed and that a desired level of competence was achieved. These training statistics could reduce corporate liability. Technology also allows trainees to track their own progress and test themselves.

Perhaps the greatest advantage from the organization's perspective is the cost savings. Computer-based training can result in increased efficiencies and a reduction in the cost of training.[32] Although the costs of development can be very high, in the long-term the cost of training is lower due to the elimination of the costs associated with travel, training facilities, hotel rooms, meals, trainers, and employee time off from work while traveling and attending training. In addition, the high overhead costs of traditional training make technology-based training especially advantageous to companies with national or international employees.

The savings reported by some companies are quite significant. For example, Dow Chemical estimates that the implementation of a Web-based training system saved the company $30 million in one year. They saved $20 million as a result of a reduction in the time employees spend in training, and $10 million due to a reduction in administrative time, classroom facilities, trainers, and the cost of printed material.[33]

Disadvantages

TRAINEES There are of course some disadvantages of technology-based training. For trainees, there is less interaction with other trainees and interpersonal contact. Furthermore, individuals have learning preferences and styles and if a trainee prefers to receive training in a classroom with a trainer and other trainees, then the use of technology would disadvantage that employee.

Trainers who are not computer literate might also resist and fear the change to technology. A low-threat opportunity to allow trainers to test the multimedia approach is to place the learning stations in the classroom.[34] Most industry analysts perceive these two barriers as temporary problems. Technology-based training will become a standard way of supplying information, particularly for the current generation that is comfortable with computers and technology.

ORGANIZATIONS For organizations, a disadvantage is that some employees will be uncomfortable with computers and might resist training. This is particularly likely for older workers who are more likely to be inexperienced using computers. There is also the potential for problems to arise if employees do not have computers that can run the programs.

The major disadvantage for organizations is the cost of development, especially for sophisticated multimedia programs. Estimates are that it takes 200 to 300 hours of design and development time to produce one hour of instruction.[35] Full-motion colour-and-sound courseware would likely cost $200,000 for 30 hours of instruction. This requires a considerable upfront investment in information technology and staff. At Motorola, where about 30 percent of employee training is computer-based, it was estimated that $20 million to $27 million will be spent in one year on e-learning.[36]

Although the cost to design and develop technology-based training is considerably higher than traditional classroom training, once a program has been developed there is the potential for considerable cost savings given the elimination of a number of variable costs such as travel, lodging, meals, materials, and in many cases an instructor's salary. Thus, technology-based training has the potential to be less costly than classroom training once the program has been developed. This is most likely to be the case when there are large numbers of employees to be trained, they are geographically dispersed, and the training will be frequently repeated.[37]

How Effective Is Technology-Based Training?

While technology-based training provides many advantages for trainees and organizations, ultimately what really matters is how effective it is for learning. Unfortunately, few studies have actually studied the effectiveness of technology-based training, especially compared to more traditional methods of classroom training. Nonetheless, there is some research that does bear directly on this issue although most of it has been conducted in educational settings rather than organizational settings.[38]

Some of the earliest reports on the effectiveness of technology-based training were very optimistic and often touted the huge gains such as increased task mastery, higher motivation and retention, improvements in job performance, and reductions in learning time compared to traditional classroom training. Unfortunately, such claims do not have their basis in empirical research. In fact, at this time, the most we can say is that technology-based training can be effective for trainee learning, especially for training that emphasizes cognitive learning and for less complex material. On the other hand, it might not be as effective for learning complex material, soft skills, psychomotor skills, or team skills.[39]

Although there is some research that indicates technology-based training is on average more effective than traditional classroom training, given the limited amount of research and the fact that some studies found no differences between technology-based training and classroom training, one must be cautious about concluding that technology-based training is more effective. In fact, it is not really possible to say if technology-based training is more, less, or equally effective for learning than traditional classroom-based training because the results have been so varied across studies.[40] Furthermore, the effectiveness of technology-based training is likely to depend on a number of factors such as the design of the program, the content of the program, the trainees, and the type of technology.[41]

Some research has also studied the time it takes to complete training. There is some evidence that technology-based training can result in a reduction in the time to completion. However, this appears to be most likely only when trainees have some prior experience using technology. In some cases, such as when trainees do not have IT experience or when trainees experience technology problems and interruptions, the time to completion might actually be greater for technology-based training compared to classroom training.[42]

A final issue regarding the effectiveness of technology-based training is trainees' motivation to take technology-based training programs, if they complete them, and their attitudes towards technology-based training. There is some research that indicates that employees are not likely to take or complete courses that are optional or have little impact on the trainee. That is, unless a course is required or when there is a strong reason for employees to complete a course, they are not likely to do so. Employees have been found to be more likely to complete an e-learning training program when there is an incentive for doing so, some form of accountability, or when the program content is job-relevant and useful.

Finally, unless trainees experience technical problems, they tend to respond positively to technology-based training programs. A number of studies have reported that after taking a technology-based training program, trainees report satisfaction with their learning experience, more positive attitudes towards technology-based training, and a willingness to try it again.[43]

In summary, while the research does not indicate that technology-based training is superior to more traditional methods of training, there is sufficient evidence to indicate that technology-based training can be effective for trainee learning and for improving work behaviour. Furthermore, technology-based training can reduce the time it takes to complete training although this is by no means guaranteed. To learn how to make technology-based training more effective, see the Trainer's Notebook 1, "Strategies for Making Technology-Based Training Effective."

The Design of Technology-Based Training

RPC 8.2

The advent of technology for the use of learning and training has created somewhat of a craze and many organizations have been quick to jump on the e-learning bandwagon. Unfortunately, because technology is the focus, many of the important design principles described in Chapter 5 are forgotten or ignored.

It is important to keep in mind that the technology simply provides a new means or medium for providing and delivering training and learning experiences. Whether or not a training program is effective depends more on how it is designed rather than the sophistication of the technology that is used to deliver it. Therefore, in this section, we will review some of the important issues and concerns with regard to the design of technology-based training programs.

The Trainer's Notebook 1

Strategies for Making Technology-Based Training Effective

At the 2002 On-line Learning Conference, Susan Boyd, who is an expert on e-learning, offered the following 10 suggestions for making e-learning effective.

1. **Develop a job-focused curriculum**. Determine the needs of trainees before developing or purchasing a program and identify any gaps between skill levels, business goals, and customer requirements. Design courses with specific needs in mind and include objectives, tasks, prerequisite skills, and assessment tools.

2. **Make learning interactive**. Engage trainees with photos, animations, and videos and use graphics and thought-provoking questions, analogies, and surveys. Build in feedback mechanisms through discussion boards, instructor e-mail, and feedback on assessments.

3. **Offer support materials**. Ensure clear instructions for registration and course access and use a getting-started guide as well as quick-reference guides.

4. **Prepare learners**. Demonstrate the technology everywhere you can and during classroom training programs. Market the benefits of on-line learning such as trainee control and flexibility and include testimonials from actual users.

5. **Prepare managers**. Present the technology to managers and highlight the benefits such as the cost savings realized from reduced travel and time away from work. Emphasize that computer-based training is a priority and identify the financial impact of interruptions and non-completes.

6. **Support learners**. Send e-mail confirmations and reminders and identify trainees' equipment and technical needs. Designate a person they can call for technical support during training and assign a mentor to participants who are new to on-line learning. Provide trainees with a checklist of things to do.

7. **Monitor and report results**. Keep track of attendance and completion rates and follow up with participants who drop out to identify barriers and improve completion rates.

8. **Evaluate**. Include an on-line pop-up evaluation at the end of the course to assess trainee reactions as well as a post-training test one to two weeks after completion to assess learning. Three to four weeks after completion survey participants on their application of learning on-the-job and six to eight weeks after ask managers if the training has made an impact on business objectives and if the course was valuable. Ask for specific suggestions for course improvements.

9. **Enhance the course**. Summarize feedback and evaluation data and prioritize course changes. Inform trainees and managers of the changes and pilot them as needed.

10. **Identify future training needs**. Meet with trainees to identify other on-line courses that would help them do their jobs and discuss business needs with managers. Prioritize training needs with business objectives and customer concerns.

Source: This text is republished with the express written consent of IOMA ©2006; any further use requires the publisher's permission. Please contact IOMA directly at: content@ioma.com or by phone, 212-576-8744; www.ioma.com.

As described in Chapter 5, to maximize learning and retention, training programs should incorporate adult learning principles, active practice, and the conditions of practice. These principles and conditions should also be incorporated into technology-based training programs. Trainees need to have opportunities for active practice even if they are sitting at a computer terminal.

Fortunately, there are many ways to actively engage and involve trainees using computer technology. This is because interactive features can be designed into computer-based training programs such as providing trainees with choices that link them to various parts or segments of a program and to related sites for additional information. Some programs enable trainees to choose the sequence in which they want to complete training modules as well as exercises and activities they want to complete. This not only actively engages trainees, but it also gives them control over their learning in terms of how they structure their learning experience.

Making computer-based training programs more experiential and interactive can also help to engage trainees and improve learning. This can be done through the use of games, simulations, and role plays as well as by using stories, customizing and personalizing the training, and providing feedback.

GAMES Games can be effective for engaging trainees with realistic and entertaining experiences. Learning games such as crossword puzzle games have been used in the presentation and practice of training material. Games can improve trainee learning and performance by increasing the appeal of e-learning, encourage trainees to practice, and facilitate the discovery of patterns and relationships in the training material.[44] Some games involve multimedia simulations that are designed to entertain and motivate trainees to learn. For example, in a leadership training program called Executive Challenge, teams of executives are given a virtual company with information and scenarios tailored to different positions in the company. Using computers, team players work on tasks presented as stories with colourful images and are tested on leadership skills, teamwork, and the ability to make their virtual companies successful.[45]

COMPUTER SIMULATIONS Computer simulations provide trainees with hands-on-training for a particular task. They are designed to replicate on-the-job experiences by providing trainees opportunities to practice and master knowledge and skills in an interactive environment. Mr. Lube uses an on-line simulation for new technicians to learn how to perform an oil change. The simulation takes trainees through all the checks and assessments and times them on the tasks. The simulation provides new technicians with a safe learning environment to learn and master their job before they actually work on an actual vehicle. As a result, on-the-job training time and errors are reduced. The program also ensures that the same process will be used by all technicians across the country. Other organizations are using computer simulations for soft skills training for various skills such as leadership, sales, customer service, and financial services.[46]

ROLE PLAYS Role plays can also be used in the design of computer-based training programs. For example, Rogers Wireless Communications Inc. has an interactive customer-service training program for sales representatives that includes on-line role playing. Trainees interact with animated characters that present different customer service challenges and learn different approaches for interacting with them. An animated coach provides guidance and feedback. Rogers noticed improvements in service and employee satisfaction not long after the program was implemented. The role-playing makes the program engaging and the lessons which are based on real-life scenarios are having an effect on employees' performance.[47]

STORIES Stories and narratives have also been used in e-learning in order to engage trainees. Abstract concepts as well as dry material can be livened up with stories that involve dialogue and characters. The characters can be created to be similar to the trainees and learning can occur as the characters solve problems in the story. Sprint and Volvo have used stories to train employees on how to deliver the company's brand image when interacting with customers. Trainees also practice communicating the brand image in simulated customer interactions.[48]

CUSTOMIZATION   Trainees can also be engaged through the customization of the training. **Customization** involves tailoring instructional elements to meet trainee preferences and needs. This can increase trainee satisfaction with the training and improve learning. Hewlett-Packard is an example of one company that has been very successful at customization. The company has found that preferences for e-learning and other training media differ around the world. For example, they found that employees in Asia prefer instructor-presented or blended learning while in the United States and Europe employees prefer self-paced and instructor-presented learning approaches. Differences in e-learning preferences indicate that one type of e-learning program is not likely to meet the needs and preferences of all employees.[49]

PERSONALIZATION   Personalizing the training experience can also improve trainee engagement. **Personalization** refers to structuring the program so that trainees feel that they are engaged in a conversation with the program. This can be achieved by using conversational rather than formal language in the on-screen text and audio recording.[50]

FEEDBACK   Regardless of the nature of the training experience, it is important that feedback be provided to trainees as described in Chapter 5. Fortunately, this is something that can be done very effectively using computer-based training because tests and exercises can be incorporated into a program that provides trainees with immediate feedback on test performance. The feedback can range from a simple prompt indicating that the answer is right or wrong to the execution of another program segment in which trainees are routed through a complex maze of reviews and reinforcements based on their responses and answers.

Feedback can also be incorporated into simulations and role plays. For example, in a role play in which trainees must choose from a number of options how they would respond to different customers, immediate feedback can be provided following each response chosen by a trainee. In addition, a coach can be designed into the program to provide trainees with feedback about the correctness of their choices, what they did wrong, and hints on how to proceed and improve. Trainees can then take the program again until their performance improves.

Finally, it is important to realize that in order for trainees to benefit from technology and in particular, computer-based training, they must have the motivation and ability to use the technology and computers. Trainees must have computer literacy and self-efficacy. This means that some individuals will be more willing and able to learn through technology-based training while others will be better suited for more traditional methods of training. It

Customization

Tailoring instructional elements to meet trainee preferences and needs

Personalization

Structuring the program so that trainees feel that they are engaged in a conversation with the program also means that some trainees will require computer training to improve their computer literacy and computer self-efficacy prior to taking a computer-based training program.

Clearly, there are many things to consider when designing technology-based training programs. See The Trainer's Notebook 2 for some additional design principles.

The Future of Technology-Based Training

The field of training technology is changing rapidly and the use of computers to deliver training has increased dramatically over the last several years. It has been predicted that organizations will reduce classroom training by nearly 20 percent and replace it with computer-based training. The increase in storage capacity of personal computers, the growth of expert and authoring systems, and the development of generic courses support this change.[51]

Thus, there is little doubt that the use of computers and technology for training has taken off and is here to stay. The advantages and benefits far outweigh the disadvantages. At this point, the main issues have to do with how to best design technology-based training programs, how best to blend them with more traditional methods, and how to make them more effective for trainee learning, retention, and transfer to the job.

While many have predicted the demise of more traditional classroom methods of training, the reality is that they will continue to be used and combined with technology-based methods. In fact, most training in organizations today remains in the classroom with live instructors both in Canada and in the

---

The Trainer's Notebook 2

Design Principles for Technology-Based Training

The following principles cover many different aspects of e-learning design and are well grounded in both theory and research.

1. **The multimedia principle**. Graphics and text should be used in e-learning rather than simply text alone. Trainees will engage in a deeper and more active processing of the learning material.

2. **The contiguity principle**. When text is used to explain a graphic or vice versa, the text and graphics should be placed near each other on the screen. This permits trainees to focus on the instructional material rather than on trying to match a miscellaneous set of pictures to text.

3. **The modality principle**. Audio technology should be used to present information instead of on-screen text.

Trainees are likely to become overwhelmed with visual information when only presented with text, graphics, illustrations, and figures during learning.

4. **The personalization principle**. Text for e-learning programs should be written in first and second person and trainees should have access to on-screen virtual coaches that provide guidance and direction. This will help trainees to see the computer as a conversational partner rather than as an information delivery agent.

Source: DeRouin, R. E., Fritzsche, B. A., & Salas, E. (2005). E-Learning in organizations. *Journal of Management, 31*, 920–40. Based on Clark, R. C., & Mayer, R. E. (2003). *E-learning and the science of instruction: Proven guidelines for consumers and designers of multimedia learning*. San Francisco: Jossey-Bass.

United States. Furthermore, many organizations realize the value of a blended approach to training that combines traditional classroom methods with technology-based methods. A blended approach is likely to be most effective especially for delivering certain types of training and for appealing to trainees with different learning styles and preferences.

The real question is not whether one should use a traditional method of training versus technology-based training, but rather, what combination of the two will be most effective. In general, computer-based training programs are most effective for providing trainees with knowledge and information at a pace dictated by the trainee, while traditional methods of training are best suited for more interactive learning experiences.[52]

For trainers, the important issues revolve around when to use technology-based training and when is it most likely to be effective. This means that trainers need to consider training objectives, the content of training, design factors, and trainee characteristics. For some types of skills such as soft skills, psychomotor skills, and team skills, more traditional forms of training will still be necessary and perhaps more effective than technology-based training. Thus, not surprisingly, most experts agree that technology-based training will never completely replace traditional classroom or face-to-face training methods.[53]

Finally, given the high cost involved in the design and development of technology-based training, the costs and benefits will be a major factor in whether or not an organization chooses to use technology or more traditional methods of training. The costs are most likely to lead to benefits when there are many trainees, numerous locations where training is required, considerable distance to the training site, and when the training is frequently repeated.[54]

Summary

This chapter described technology-based training methods and serves as a complement to the on- and off-the-job training methods described in Chapters 6 and 7. The different types of technology-based training methods were described including computer-based training, e-learning, distance learning, electronic performance-support systems, and video conferencing. We also described how technology-based training can differ in terms of whether it is instructor-led or self-directed, and whether it is asynchronous or synchronous. The advantages, disadvantages, and effectiveness of technology-based training were also discussed as well as how to design technology-based training programs. The chapter concluded with a discussion of the future of technology-based training.

Key Terms

asynchronous training (page 212)

computer-based training (page 210)

customization (page 222)

distance learning (page 213)

e-learning (page 211)

electronic performance-support system (EPSS) (page 214)

instructor-led training (ILT) (page 210)

personalization (page 222)

self-directed learning (SDL) (page 210)

synchronous training (page 212)   traditional training (page 208)
technology-based training (page 207) video conferencing (page 214)

Weblinks

Athabasca University: www.athabascau.ca (page 213)

Cisco Systems Canada Co.: www.cisco.com (page 209)

Dow Chemical: www.dow.com (page 217)

Motorola Inc.: www.motorola.com (page 210)

Scotiabank: www.scotiabank.com (page 215)

RPC Icons

RPC 8.1 Using a variety of methods facilitates the delivery of development programs to groups and individual learners.
RPC 8.2 Participates in course design and selection/delivery of learning materials via various media.

Discussion Questions

1. In both Canada and the United States, the actual use of training technologies has fallen below projections and, in fact, the adoption of training technologies has been relatively slow. What are some of the reasons for this and what are the potential barriers to the adoption of training technologies?
2. Compare and contrast technology-based training methods to traditional methods of training. Why would an organization choose to use some forms of technology-based training rather than traditional methods? Are there some types of industries, organizations, or jobs in which technology-based training or traditional training would be more appropriate and effective?
3. What are the advantages and disadvantages of technology-based training for trainees, trainers, and organizations?
4. If you had the choice, would you choose to take a distance education course that involved on-line learning or a traditional classroom course? Which would you prefer and why? Do you think your study habits, course satisfaction, learning, and grades would differ in an on-line course versus a traditional classroom course? Explain your reasoning.
5. Discuss how e-learning programs can be designed to engage trainees and improve motivation and learning.
6. Discuss how games, simulations, and role plays can be used in computer-based training programs.

The Great Training Debate

1. Debate the following: Given the many benefits of technology-based training, organizations should consider converting all of their traditional training programs to technology-based programs and make formal classroom training a thing of the past.

Using the Internet

1. To learn more about e-learning in Canada, read the report by The Conference Board of Canada, "E-Learning in Canada: Findings From 2003 E-Survey" at **www.conferenceboard.ca/education/reports/pdfs/ TopLine_report.pdf**.

   Review the report and then summarize the main findings and concerns facing Canadian organizations. Some of the things to consider include:

   1. What are the challenges to implementing e-learning?
   2. What are the benefits of e-learning?
   3. How should e-learning programs be evaluated?
   4. What is the future use of e-learning by Canadian organizations?

2. To find out about technology-based training in Canada, visit Industry Canada at **http://strategis.ic.gc.ca/epic/internet/incts-scf.nsf/ en/h_sl00009e.html**.

   Read the following sections and summarize the main findings:

   1. What is the impact of learning technologies?
   2. Does e-learning help companies save money and improve productivity?
   3. How can you find out which learning technology is right for you?
   4. How can you assess the quality of e-learning products and services?
   5. Read the case studies and briefly summarize how each organization has used technology-based learning and the benefits and outcomes that resulted from it.

3. To learn about when an organization should use technology-based training, go to **www.coastal.com/PressReleases/online_technology.html**. Read the article, "When Should Your Organization Use Technology-Based Training?" and summarize the main things to consider when deciding to use technology-based training. Then review the Multimedia Training Questionnaire and the CD-ROM versus WBT Training Questionnaire and consider how useful they are for making a decision about the use of technology-based training.

Exercises

In-Class

1. Describe the most recent traditional training program you have attended in terms of its objectives, content, methods, and conditions of practice. Now think about how the program might be converted into a computer-based training program. Describe what the program would be like and how you would design it. Do you think it would be more or less effective than the traditional training program?

2. Choose a class from a course you are currently taking, and describe it in terms of the following design factors from Chapter 5:

   - What are the objectives?
   - What is the content?
   - What training methods are used?
   - What practice conditions are used?

   Now consider how the class might be designed and delivered as a computer-based course. Review your answers to each of the above design factors, and then convert them into a computer-based program. In other words, what would be the objectives, content, methods, and practice conditions?

   How effective do you think the class will be as a computer-based course? Compare and contrast it to the classroom version. What are the advantages and disadvantages for students, instructors, and the university or college? Which one would you prefer and why?

3. One of the concerns about technology-based training is the tendency to focus too much on the technology and not enough on learning and the conditions of practice. Refer back to Chapter 5 and the conditions of practice in Table 5.3. Describe how each of the conditions of practice might be designed into a computer-based training program.

4. After learning about technology-based training, you realize that your organization can benefit by converting some of its traditional classroom training programs to technology-based methods. Describe how you would proceed if you were to convert a particular training program (e.g., customer service, sales, negotiations, etc.) to a technology-based program. What would you have to do in order to convert the program and how would you proceed?

5. You have just been hired by an organization to help them convert some of their training programs to technology-based programs. However, the company does not have a tradition of using technology in the workplace and there is likely to be a great deal of resistance from managers and employees. You have to meet with employees and managers to help them understand why technology-based training will be better for them and the organization than classroom training. Prepare a brief presentation of what you will tell the employees and managers and then present it to a partner or the class.

In-the-Field

1. Contact the human resource department of an organization and ask them if you can conduct a brief interview with the training staff about their use of technology-based training methods. Some of the things you might consider include:

   a. Do they use technology for training, and if so, what forms of technology-based training are they using and what are they using them for?
   b. Why did they decide to use technology for training?
   c. How effective has the use of technology been for training? How have they evaluated its effectiveness and what has the impact been on employees and the organization?
   d. Do they plan to use technology-based training in the future, and if so, in what way, for what purposes, and for what reasons?

2. Contact the human resource department of an organization to find out if they have e-learning training programs. Once you have found an organization that has developed an e-learning program, find out how they designed the program and how it works. Some of the things to consider include:

   a. What are the training objectives?
   b. What is the training content?
   c. Who are the trainees?
   d. How has the program been designed and does it include interactive elements?
   e. Does the program incorporate learning principles and if so, how have they been incorporated into the program?
   f. How effective has the program been and how does it compare to traditional forms of training?

Case Incident

SKU at Nike

One of the biggest problems facing retailers is turnover where retention is very low in certain retail businesses and turnover is 100 percent. This makes training a real challenge. At Nike, for example, every few months an employee leaves and another starts and so does the training process. As a result, training new staff in a classroom setting is not cost-effective. So Nike decided to design an on-line training program that the company could offer to employees in its own stores as well as at other retailers that sell its products. The program would have to convey a lot of information quickly but also be easy to digest.

The solution was a program called Sports Knowledge Underground or SKU. The layout for the program resembles a subway map with different stations representing different training themes. For example, Apparel Union station branches off into the apparel technologies line, the running products line and the Nike Pro products line. The Cleated Footwear Station offers paths to football, whereas the Central Station offers broad lines like customer skills. Each segment is three to seven minutes long and gives the employee the basic knowledge they need about various products.

Questions

1. How effective do you think Nike's SKU e-learning program will be for employee learning? Do you think it will reduce turnover?
2. How should the SKU program be designed to be most effective for learning and retention? Should other retailers design similar e-learning programs?

Source: Marquez, J. (2005, August). Faced with high turnover, retailers boot up e-learning for quick training. *Workforce Management, 84* (8), 74–75.

Case

E-learning at Flotation Ltd.

Jenny Stoppard was excited about her new position as vice president of human resources at Flotation Ltd., a manufacturer of life jackets and other flotation devices. However, she knew she had her work cut out for her.

The president of the company had clearly stated that one of her first tasks was to take a close look at the training function. Although Flotation Ltd. had a reputation as a company with a well-trained workforce, the president now wanted to see some hard evidence to back up the company's training investment. The president wanted to increase productivity per person by 50 percent over the next three years, and Jenny was expected to spearhead the effort.

Sam was the company's veteran trainer who was liked by everybody in the organization. For 20 years he had been training employees at Flotation Ltd. He was only three years away from retirement and was not likely to respond favourably to Jenny and her new mandate.

The president introduced Jenny to Sam as his new boss and the key player in the drive to increase the company's competitiveness. He also asked Sam to do everything in his power to cooperate with her.

Jenny not only had to revamp the training function, but she also had to deal with Sam who was pretty much set in his ways. How was she going to achieve the president's goals and at the same time get Sam on board?

After thinking about her situation for several days, Jenny came across an article on e-learning and how it has saved some companies millions of dollars a year in training costs. Suddenly, she had an idea.

"Why not convert some of Sam's courses to e-learning programs on the company's website?" she thought to herself. "This would certainly be a whole new approach and I could save the company money and get Sam involved since he would be responsible for preparing his course material for the program. Surely Sam would be excited to know that his training courses would continue even after he has retired."

Both the president and Sam were very excited about the potential of e-learning at Flotation Ltd. Jenny was given the go ahead to begin designing the first course. Jenny and Sam decided that the first course would be Sam's sales training program, which was one of his best. It would also be useful for the company's sales staff who would be able to take the program while they were on the road selling.

The first thing that Jenny did was to arrange for Sam to be videotaped delivering the course. Then she had Sam prepare some text material and additional information about some of the key learning points. With the help of the IT people, the video and text were placed on the company's website. The program was designed so that when an employee logged onto the site they could watch the video of Sam and at certain points during the video they could click on an icon for more information. The video would then stop and the additional information would appear on the screen. After reading the material they could then return to the video.

When the program was set up and ready to go, the sales staff received a memo telling them about the company's first e-learning program and how to access it on the company's website. The memo was titled "Learn how to improve your sales skills on the road" and "Attend Sam's best training program any time and anywhere." Everybody was very excited about this new approach to training, and Sam was thrilled to know that he was the main attraction.

However, although the program was launched with much fanfare, the results were less than glowing. In fact, after the first six months very few of the sales staff had taken the course. Many said that they did not have time to take it. And of those who did, less than half actually completed it.

When asked about it, some of the sales staff said that it was not very interesting. Some said they would rather attend a live version of the course in the classroom and others said they didn't see what the advantage was of taking an e-learning course. Some thought it was just a big waste of the company's time and money.

The president asked to see Jenny to find out how things were going and if they were on track for achieving the company's productivity goals. Jenny did not know what she would tell him. Sam tried to console her by telling her that it had only been six months and the sales staff just needed a little more time to get used to learning on-line. Jenny wasn't so sure. She began to wonder if the e-learning strategy was a big mistake.

Questions

1. Do you think that e-learning was a good idea for Flotation Ltd.? Could e-learning help the company realize the president's productivity goals?
2. Comment on the e-learning program that Jenny and Sam designed. What are the indicators that suggest that it has not been a success? Is it

possible that there are other indicators that might suggest that it is more effective than it appears?

3. Comment on how the program was designed and the use of learning principles and the conditions of practice. Do you think the program could be redesigned to make it more effective, and if so how would you proceed?

4. If you were Jenny, what would you tell the president and what would you do about e-learning at Flotation Ltd.? Should Jenny give up on e-learning or wait another six months before making a decision?

References

1. (2002, December). Canada's oldest store embraces e-learning. *The Training Report*, p. 4. Reprinted by permission of *The Training Report*.

2. Tomlinson, A. (2002, March 25). T & D spending up in U.S. as Canada lags behind. *Canadian HR Reporter*, p. 1.

3. Dolezalek, H. (2005, December). 2005 industry report. *Training, 42* (12), 14–28.

4. Parker, R. O., & Cooney, J. (2005). Learning & development outlook 2005. *The Conference Board of Canada*. Ottawa.

5. Galt, V. (2004, June 12). Employers jumping on e-learning bandwagon. *The Globe and Mail*, B10.; Eure, R. (2001, March 21). Companies embrace e-training. *The Globe and Mail*, B16; (2001, June 18). Businesses find a new class of e-learning. *The Globe and Mail*, R12.

6. Caudron, S. (2002, February). Training in the post-terrorism era. *Training and Development*, 24–30.

7. Galvin, T. (2002, October). 2002 industry report. *Training, 39* (10), 24–73.

8. Dolezalek, H. (2005, December).

9. Welsh, L. T., Wanberg, C. R., Brown, K. G., & Simmering, M. J. (2003). E-Learning: Emerging uses, empirical results and future directions. *International Journal of Training and Development, 7*, 245–58.

10. Dolezalek, H. (2005, December).

11. Brown, K. G., & Ford, J. K. (2002). Using computer technology in training: Building an infrastructure for active learning. In K. Kraiger (Ed.), *Creating, implementing, and managing effective training and development: State-of-the-art lessons for practice*, (pp. 160–91). San Francisco. CA: Jossey-Bass.

12. Harris-Lalonde, S. (2001). Training and development outlook. *The Conference Board of Canada*. Ottawa.

13. Ray, R. (2001, May 25). Employers, employees embrace e-learning. *The Globe and Mail*, E2.

14. Cooney, J. & Cowan, A. (2003). Training and development outlook 2003. *The Conference Board of Canada*. Ottawa.

15. DeRouin, R. E., Fritzsche, B. A., & Salas, E. (2005). E-Learning in Organizations. *Journal of Management, 31*, 920–40.

16. Welsh, L. T., Wanberg, C. R., Brown, K. G., & Simmering, M. J. (2003).

17. Eure, R. (2001, March 21).

18. Brown, K. G., & Ford, J. K. (2002).

19. Welsh, L. T., Wanberg, C. R., Brown, K. G., & Simmering, M. J. (2003).

20. McLaren, C. (2002, May 31). E-training cooks up customer service tips. *The Globe and Mail*, T4.

21. Welsh, L. T., Wanberg, C. R., Brown, K. G., & Simmering, M. J. (2003).

22. Robinson, J. C. (1982). *Developing managers through behaviour modelling*. San Diego, CA: Learning Concepts.

23. Johnston, A. D. (2002, November 18). The university crunch. *Maclean's, 115* (46), 20–28.
24. Raybould, B. (1990, November–December). Solving human performance problems with computers—A case study: Building an electronic performance support system. *Performance and Instruction,* 4–14.
25. Smith, K. (1996, April). EPSS helps accounting firm reduce training time, improve productivity during transition to new service emphasis. *Lakewood Report on Technology for Learning,* p. 8.
26. Kulig, P. (1998, March 23). When training meets performance support. *Canadian HR Reporter, 11* (6), 17–18.
27. Gebber, B. (1991). Help! The rise of performance support systems. *Training, 28* (12), 23–29; Ruyle, K. (1991, February/March). Developing intelligent job aids. *Technical and Skills Training,* 9–14.
28. Johnson, G., Johnson, H., & Dolezalek, H., Galvin, T., & Zemke, R. (2004, March). Training top 100: Top five profile and ranking. *Training, 41* (3), 42–51.
29. DeRouin, R. E., Fritzsche, B. A., & Salas, E. (2005).
30. Galt, V. (2004, June 12).
31. Allan, K. (1993, June). Computer courses ensure uniform training. *Personnel Journal,* 65–71.
32. Brown, K. G., & Ford, J. K. (2002).
33. Welsh, L. T., Wanberg, C. R., Brown, K. G., & Simmering, M. J. (2003).
34. O'Keefe, B. (1991, September/October). Adopting multimedia on a global scale. *Instruction Delivery Systems,* 6–11.
35. Miles, K. W., & Griffith, E. R. (1993, April/May). Developing an hour of CBT: The quick and dirty method. *CBT Directions,* 28–33.
36. Eure, R. (2001, March 21).
37. Welsh, L. T., Wanberg, C. R., Brown, K. G., & Simmering, M. J. (2003).
38. DeRouin, R. E., Fritzsche, B. A., & Salas, E. (2005).
39. Welsh, L. T., Wanberg, C. R., Brown, K. G., & Simmering, M. J. (2003).
40. DeRouin, R. E., Fritzsche, B. A., & Salas, E. (2005).
41. Welsh, L. T., Wanberg, C. R., Brown, K. G., & Simmering, M. J. (2003).
42. Welsh, L. T., Wanberg, C. R., Brown, K. G., & Simmering, M. J. (2003).
43. Welsh, L. T., Wanberg, C. R., Brown, K. G., & Simmering, M. J. (2003).
44. DeRouin, R. E., Fritzsche, B. A., & Salas, E. (2005).
45. Anonymous. (2005, December 12). Simulation games score with trainees. *Workforce Management, 84* (15), 70.
46. Bowness, A. (2004, September 27). Hands-on learning through computer simulations. *Canadian HR Reporter, 17* (16), 15.
47. Galt, V. (2004, June 12).
48. DeRouin, R. E., Fritzsche, B. A., & Salas, E. (2005).
49. DeRouin, R. E., Fritzsche, B. A., & Salas, E. (2005).
50. DeRouin, R. E., Fritzsche, B. A., & Salas, E. (2005).
51. Brown, K. G., & Ford, J. K. (2002).
52. Welsh, L. T., Wanberg, C. R., Brown, K. G., & Simmering, M. J. (2003).
53. Eure, R. (2001, March 21).
54. Welsh, L. T., Wanberg, C. R., Brown, K. G., & Simmering, M. J. (2003).

Chapter 9

Training Implementation and Delivery

www.starbucks.com

STARBUCKS

Starbucks takes coffee very seriously. In fact, they have a boot camp for store development partners called Store Development Boot Camp. Since 1997, store development partners have been attending the training program, which is a required one-week course on the process and participants involved in developing a new Starbucks store.

Each session takes place at the company's headquarters in Seattle and is attended by 15 to 20 participants, most of whom are store development partners along with some others from operation areas. They listen to subject-matter experts make presentations from various departments on how IT systems support development, how the real estate team selects store sites, how construction budgets are created, how to make purchasing decisions about materials, equipment, and furniture, and how designers lay out a new store. Participants also learn how the store development finance team contributes, and how store development fits in with recycling and other corporate social responsibility issues.

In addition to presentations, the program also involves games and learning activities to help participants review what they have learned such as coffee tasting, a tour of downtown Seattle stores, and a social evening at the end of the program with presenters and other operations partners.

It has been estimated that between 750 and 1100 participants have gone through the program, which usually takes place quarterly but due to demand may eventually become a monthly event. The program has also changed over the years and has been adjusted and modified to reflect new aspects of the business.

Store development partners usually attend boot camp between three and six months after their start date, although this might be changed to about 90 days after starting based on participants' feedback that it is harder for them to get away the longer they are in the position.[1]

Source: Dolezalek, H. (2004, July). Boot camp brew-ha-ha, *Training*, V N U Business Publications. This work is protected by copyright and it is being used with the permission of Access Copyright. Any alteration of its content or further copying in any form whatsoever is strictly prohibited.

In the previous four chapters, we described how to design training programs and the use of different methods of training. However, as you can tell from the Starbucks Boot Camp training program, there are other important training issues such as deciding on the trainer and trainees, scheduling the training program, and the location of the training. In this chapter, we focus on issues that have to do with implementing and delivering training programs. These issues follow from the design issues covered in Chapter 5 and include the following:

1. The lesson plan.
2. The trainer.
3. The trainees.
4. Training materials and equipment.
5. The training site.
6. Scheduling the training program.
7. Training administration.
8. Delivery of the training program.

The Lesson Plan

Once a training program has been designed, the trainer needs to prepare a lesson plan. The **lesson plan** is the blueprint that outlines the training program in terms of the sequence of activities and events that will take place. As such, it is a guide for the trainer that provides a step-by-step breakdown for conducting the training program. A lesson plan is important for a number of reasons.

Lesson plan
The blueprint that outlines the training program in terms of the sequence of activities and events that will take place

First, a competently prepared lesson plan will make the task of competing for funding easier. Second, a good plan will enable training activity to be directed toward real training problems, not symptoms of problems. Third, the planning document will ensure that the problems under consideration can be solved by training and not some other intervention or method. Fourth, good planning enhances credibility with line managers. All of these factors combined will help the training department implement and deliver sound training programs.

A good lesson plan should be prepared in advance of a training program and be detailed enough that any trainer could use it to guide him or her through the training program. Most of what will be required to deliver a training program will be indicated in the lesson plan. Some of the things that should be listed on the first page or cover of a lesson plan are the training objectives, the trainees, instructor, time allocation, location, classroom requirements and seating, training materials and equipment, and trainee supplies and handouts.[2]

The development of a lesson plan is a critical phase in the design of a training program. It allows for the approval and the smooth operation of training activities. It also enables expenditures to be budgeted for and monitored. The development of a lesson plan sets the stage for the implementation of the training program and it is a signal to other members of the organization that training is to be conducted in a professional manner.

Table 9.1 presents the cover page of the lesson plan for a training program on structured employment interviews. Table 9.2 presents the detailed lesson plan for the same training program. In the following pages we will describe in more detail the main elements included in a lesson plan.

TABLE 9.1

Lesson Plan Cover Page

Organization: Vandalais Department Stores
Department: Human Resources
Program Title: Structured Employment Interviews
Instructor(s):   Interview Training Consultant
Time Allocation: 1 day
Trainees: All employees in the Human Resource Department
Where: Vandalais Learning Centre

Training Objectives

Employees will be able to conduct a structured behaviour description interview and correctly perform the seven key behaviours.

Classroom Requirements

Seating for 50 people that allows for high involvement.

Training Materials and Equipment

VCR and TV monitor; videotape: "How to Conduct a Structured Employment Interview"; Computer and projector with screen; flipchart; paper; and markers.

Trainee Supplies

Pen and paper.

Trainee Handouts

1. Course objectives and outline.
2. Article on structured employment interviews.
3. Article on behaviour description interviews.
4. List of the seven key behaviours for conducting a structured employment interview.
5. Copy of the behaviour description interview for the sales associate position with interview questions and scoring guide and instructions.
6. Role-play exercise.

TABLE 9.2

Structured Employment Interview Lesson Plan

OBJECTIVE

Employees will be able to conduct structured behaviour description employment interview and correctly perform the seven key behaviours.

Trainees: Members of the Human Resource Department.
Time: 9 a.m.–5 p.m.

9:00–10:00	Introduction lecture on the problem of poor employee performance and high turnover and the use of structured and unstructured employment interviews for selection.
10:00–10:30	Show video of an unstructured employment interview followed by a discussion.
10:30–10:45	Break
10:45–11:15	Show video of a structured employment interview followed by a discussion.
11:15–12:00	Review the seven key behaviours of conducting a structured employment interview.
12:00–1:00	Lunch
1:00–2:00	Lecture on behaviour description interview questions and review of the interview questions and guide developed for sales associates.
2:00–2:30	Review of the seven key behaviours in conducting a structured employment interview.
2:30–2:45	Break
2:45–3:30	Role-play practice exercise: In groups of three, assign participants the roles of interviewer, interviewee, and observer. Review script for roles and instruct trainees to demonstrate the seven key behaviours of a structured interview using the sales associate behaviour description interview questions. Have observer provide feedback using feedback guidelines contained in the role-play exercise booklet and evaluate the interviewer's performance on the seven key behaviours using the evaluation form provided. Switch roles until each group member plays the role of the interviewer.
3:30–4:30	Regroup for discussion of role-play exercise. Discuss how it felt to be the interviewer and the interviewee, and get the observer's feedback and evaluation.
4:30–4:45	Review the seven key behaviours of the structured employment interview and the importance of using structured interviews and the behaviour description interview for hiring sales associates.
4:45–5:00	Closing. Review objectives and give pep talk about conducting structured employment interviews and using the behaviour description interview. Thank participants and hand out training certificates.

The Trainer

The lesson plan cover sheet in Table 9.2 indicates that the trainer will be a consultant. But how is it decided who will deliver a training program? At first, this might seem like a trivial question. After all, isn't this the job of the human resources department or the training staff? In some cases the answer is yes, but in many training situations the answer to this question depends on a number of important factors.

First, it is important to realize the importance of a good trainer. Regardless of how well a training program is designed, the success of a program rests in large part on the trainer. In other words, no matter how good the training program is, if the trainer is ineffective, the program will suffer.

What then are the qualities of a good trainer? This question should be easy for students to answer if they consider the courses they have enjoyed and those that they found less memorable. One of the first things that comes to mind is probably the extent to which the instructor is knowledgeable about the course material. Such a person is known as a subject-matter expert (SME). A **subject-matter expert** is someone who is familiar with the knowledge, skills, and abilities required to perform a task or job and has what is known as subject-matter expertise. A trainer should be an expert on the topic or content area being taught. Not only will trainees learn more, but also the trainer will be perceived as more credible. Very often those persons who conduct training in an organization do so because they have expertise in a particular area. At Starbuck's Store Development Boot Camp, subject-matter experts from various departments give presentations.

Unfortunately, not all subject-matter experts are good trainers. Students know, perhaps all too well, that no matter how well informed or knowledgeable an instructor, a course can still be inadequate to the extent that the instructor is not very good at delivering the material. In addition to subject-matter expertise, good trainers must also have good verbal and communication skills, interpersonal skills, and organizing and planning skills. In other words, a trainer must be able to deliver the training material and content in a manner that is understandable to trainees. Trainees are more likely to learn and be better able to recall training content when the trainer is well organized and easy to follow.[3]

A third category of trainer characteristics is the ability to make the material interesting rather than dull and boring. Students probably have had instructors who knew the material and were able to deliver it, but all the same, they did not make it very interesting. A good trainer should be enthusiastic and excited about the training material and capable of motivating and arousing the interest of trainees.

One way for trainers to generate interest and increase trainee motivation is by being expressive during the delivery of a training program. Expressive trainers are more physically animated (e.g., posture, gesturing, eye contact) and use linguistic devices such as an enthusiastic voice as opposed to a monotone voice, and vocal fluency rather than speaking with hesitancies (e.g., "ums"). Research has shown that trainees recall a greater amount of the training content when a trainer is more expressive. There is also evidence that a trainer's expressiveness enhances trainees' motivation to learn and their self-efficacy.[4]

Subject-matter expert (SME)

A person who is familiar with the knowledge, skills, and abilities required to perform a task or job

In addition to being expressive, a good trainer is also engaging. In other words, a good trainer is able to draw trainees into the training program and keep them interested, focused, and involved in learning. No doubt, you can think of course instructors you have had who either put you to sleep or kept you on the edge of your seat, perhaps even absorbed in what was being taught. When a trainer is engaging, trainees are more likely to be motivated to learn, attentive, and absorbed in the learning process. To find out how to be an engaging trainer, see the Trainer's Notebook 1, "The Engaging Trainer."

The Trainer's Notebook 1

The Engaging Trainer

Although adults are better than children at paying close attention to a lengthy presentation, even adults tend to drift off after 20 minutes. Thus, many adult learners will tune out during a training program. A good trainer can keep trainees awake and focused by actively engaging them. Engagement ignites the learning process and stimulates trainees. Without it, the trainee in the corner is likely to fall asleep. Here are 10 ways in which a trainer can actively engage trainees.

1. **Determine what's in it for them**. Ask participants what they want to learn from the course and help them form a clear idea of why they are there.
2. **Probe frequently**. During the session, stop frequently and ask participants to paraphrase or explain what has been learned. Ask trainees if they are tuned in and understand what you have been covering.
3. **Encourage application**. Provide trainees with opportunities to apply what is being taught through the use of discussions, case studies, role plays, or simulations that require them to integrate the learning points into an effective solution in a situation that is similar to those they encounter on the job.
4. **Test and give feedback**. A well-designed test can confirm that much has been learned. The results can provide positive feedback and also clarify what has not been learned. The act of taking a test also tends to increase interest in the subject matter as trainees like to know how they did and what the correct answers are.
5. **Start with questions**. Rather than start a program by providing information, ask questions. For example, instead of telling trainees how to make up interview questions, ask them what questions they ask in an interview and why they ask them.
6. **Run counter to expectations**. Show trainees that there are different ways of doing things that are contrary to

their beliefs. You can begin by asking a question and based on trainee responses, demonstrate alternative ways of performing a task or responding to a problem.
7. **Start with what learners know**. Start with what learners know because it makes them feel that they are in familiar territory and in a safe place for encountering new information and learning. Questions can be used to ask about previous material covered in a program. This allows trainees to reconstruct their frame of reference and readies them for new information and learning.
8. **Use visual modes**. Sitting through a course in which all of the information is transmitted verbally can be frustrating especially for visual learners. Provide some form of visual representation of what trainees are hearing even if this is done during the training using wallboards, flipcharts, or blank transparencies.
9. **Provide an advanced organizer**. Help trainees put information into a meaningful context. For example, you can provide a mental outline or visual organizer so trainees can organize information that they will receive during training. This might take the form of a visual handout that lists key learning points, key definitions, or a table that contains the main learning principles.
10. **Use humour**. Bring a sense of humour into the training by recognizing opportunities to laugh over a funny mistake or a humourous coincidence or event. Humour helps relax and stimulate trainees and can also create a bond between the trainer and participants.

Based on Deming, B. (2001, January). Ten steps to being positively engaging. *Training and Development, 55* (1), 18–19. Copyright © January 2001, *T+D*. Reprinted with permission of American Society for Training & Development.

Chapter 9: Training Implementation and Delivery

Training Subject-Matter Experts to Be Trainers

Because of their technical expertise, an increasing number of employees are being drafted into the role of trainer. Organizations, especially smaller ones without training departments, have long relied on their resident experts to teach others to program their voice mail, send faxes, and log on to their computers. But as technology has transformed office equipment into souped-up vehicles on multi-lane electronic autobahns, it's not always possible to navigate just by reading the manual and relying on intuition.

Just because a person has crafted countless Microsoft PowerPoint presentations or designed award-winning Web pages doesn't mean he or she will be able to teach others to do the same. Often, organizations assume that teaching should come naturally to employees who know their stuff and have spent countless hours sitting in classes themselves. "Unfortunately, many companies have said all one needs to be a good technical instructor is subject-matter expertise," says Michael Nolan, president of

Friesen, Kaye and Associates, an Ottawa firm that works with non-trainers or subject-matter experts (SMEs) who find themselves having to teach what they know to others. "It goes much farther than that. They have to have other skills that they haven't developed in the environment in which they've worked." They have to understand, for example, how adults learn, what to do when participants behave like mules, and how not to feel as though they've been caught in a klieg light when someone asks them a question they can't answer.

Nolan predicts SMEs won't replace professional trainers—even in the IT field. But when these experts are called on to share their knowledge, they need support. That's where the training department comes in. "Instructors in the training department can provide a fabulous experience by coaching and mentoring," he says.

Excerpted from Kiser, K. (1999, April). When those who "do," teach. *Training, 36* (4), 42–48. Training: The Human Side of Business by Kiser, K.

Finally, one of the difficulties in choosing a good trainer is that individuals who have subject-matter expertise often do not have the knowledge and skills required to be a good trainer. On the other hand, those who are skilled trainers such as members of a human resource department or training staff often do not have the subject-matter expertise to conduct every training program in their organization.

One solution to this problem has been to teach subject-matter experts how to become effective trainers. These programs are known as train-the-trainer and focus on the skills that are required to be an effective trainer. **Train-the-trainer** refers to training programs that teach subject-matter experts how to design and deliver training programs. As described in the Training Today feature, with the increasing use of technology in the workplace, more subject-matter experts are being asked to become trainers.

Train-the-trainer

Training programs that teach subject-matter experts how to design and deliver training programs

The Trainees

The lesson plan in Table 9.2 indicates that the trainees will be members of the human resources department. This raises another important question. Who should attend a training program? This is an important question because money and time can be wasted if the wrong people attend and, of course, problems are likely to continue if those who really need the training do not attend. As a starting point, one must carefully select trainees based on their abilities, aptitudes, and motivation. If a person analysis has been conducted, then it should provide some indication if employees are deficient in any required knowledge or skills for performing their job.

Additional information can be obtained if employees are assessed or tested to determine current knowledge and skill levels. Performance tests or interviews could be conducted to develop a base line of competencies. These tests can also act as motivators in the sense that they indicate the need for change and can also indicate if some employees already know some of the material. These knowledgeable employees can either bypass a training program or can act as coaches during the training process.

One way to determine if an employee should attend a training program is to have him or her take a trainability test. A **trainability test** is a test that measures an individual's ability to learn and perform training tasks in order to predict whether an individual will successfully complete a training program.[5] This is typically done by having individuals take a mini-course or learn a sample of the training that is representative of the training content of a training program. They then take a test that measures their learning and performance of the tasks.

Trainability tests have been shown to be effective in predicting training success and job performance in many jobs such as carpentry, welding, dentistry, and forklift operating. Although they have most often been used for psychomotor skills, they are just as applicable for other types of skills and knowledge tests. These kinds of training pre-tests can also be used to determine what kind of remedial training an individual might require in order to prepare them for a training program or to tailor a training program to their needs. Thus, managers can maximize trainee learning by assessing employees' readiness to learn and trainability prior to training.[6]

In addition to employee readiness for training, a number of other factors also need consideration. According to Kirkpatrick, the following four decisions need to be made when selecting participants for a training program:[7]

1. Who can benefit from the training?
2. What programs are required by law or by government edict?
3. Should the training be voluntary or compulsory?
4. Should the participants be segregated by level in the organization, or should two or more levels be included in the same class?

Some employees stand to benefit from a training program given the tasks they perform and the extent to which the training will provide them with knowledge and skills that will help them improve their performance. Some training programs are required by law, such as health and safety programs for employees who work with hazardous materials. Other training programs like Starbucks' Store Development Boot Camp are compulsory for all employees in a particular job category or position. According to Kirkpatrick, some programs should be compulsory. If a training program is voluntary then there will be some employees who need the training but will not attend. When the

Trainability test

A test that measures an individual's ability to learn and perform training tasks

training is required for a group of employees, the program should be compulsory as is the case for store development partners at Starbucks.[8]

As for segregating participants by organizational level or including them in the same training session, this really depends on the culture of the organization and the rapport that exists between different levels in the organization. The main issue is whether employees will feel comfortable enough to speak and participate if their supervisors are present. If this is the case then it is often a good idea for different levels to attend a training program together.

Information on who requires training can be incorporated into a training plan. A **training plan** indicates who in an organization needs training (e.g., human resource staff), the type of training needed (e.g., structured employment interviewing), and how the training will be delivered (in a formal classroom).[9]

 9.1

Training Materials and Equipment

All training programs require the use of training materials, supplies, and equipment and should be indicated on the lesson plan cover page. The content of a training program as well as the methods and exercises determine the materials, supplies, and equipment that will be required. Materials refer to expendable items such as note pads, pens, markers, tape, and so on. Equipment refers to things that have a life beyond a single use such as projectors, computers, VCR, and so on. The trainer must identify the materials and equipment that will be required for a training program.[10]

With the determination of the materials and equipment necessary for training, the training budget is more easily determined, the program more accurately costed, and the actual training session more likely to run smoothly. Common supplies include computer equipment, a projector, VCRs and tapes, and workbooks or manuals. Handouts such as course outlines that indicate the course objectives, the material to be covered, and a schedule of training activities, as well as articles and copies of the trainer's slides, are often required and will have to be prepared in advance.

As shown in Table 9.1, the materials and equipment required for the structured employment interview training program include a VCR and TV monitor, a videotape on how to conduct a structured employment interview, a computer and projector with screen, a flipchart, pen, paper, and markers. Handouts for trainees include a course outline, readings, a list of the key learning behaviours, and a role-play exercise.

The Training Site

The training site is the actual facility or room where the training will take place. Off-the-job training can take place at the organization if there are rooms available or at an organization's headquarters such as Starbucks' Store Development Boot Camp, or at a rented facility such as a hotel or conference centre. Some organizations like the Bank of Montreal have their own learning centres that are designed for training and development. However, for organizations that do not have training facilities, space must be found and rented. In this case, an important concern will be the amount of travel time required for trainees to get to the training site and ensuring that trainees have transportation. If trainees have to stay overnight, plans for transportation, accommodation, and meals will have to be made and included in the training budget. As indicated in Table 9.1, the structured employment interview training takes place at the company's learning centre.

Whether the training takes place in an organization's facilities or one that needs to be rented, a number of factors need to be considered to ensure that the training program runs smoothly. First, the training site should be conducive to learning. This means that the training environment should be comfortable in terms of things like space, lighting, and temperature. This might seem like a trivial point, but have you ever attended a class and the room temperature was a bit on the cold side? Or how about one that was too crowded and you had to stand or sit on the floor because there was not enough space? Chances are it caused you some discomfort and interfered with your learning.

Second, the training site should be free of any noise or distractions that might interfere with or disrupt trainee learning. How often have you been in a class where you had to strain to hear the instructor over the chatter coming from outside the classroom? Obviously, noise can interfere with learning. Distractions can also be a problem. This is one reason why it is sometimes preferable to conduct a training program away from the organization. Otherwise, trainees might be tempted to step out of the training session to check for messages or take care of business. This, of course, is not likely if they are far from their desk and the workplace.

Third, the training site should be set up in a manner that is appropriate for the training program. For example, if trainees will be viewing a video, will they be able to see the screen and hear the sound? If trainees will be required to work in groups, will there be sufficient room for them to move around the room and interact with group members? Are break-out rooms necessary for group work? Are the seats arranged in a way that will allow trainees to interact and work with each other, and will the trainer be able to interact with trainees? Are the chairs movable or fixed? These are important considerations that the trainer needs to determine before the training.

The seating arrangement is especially important because it can facilitate or limit trainee involvement and participation, it can energize or inhibit trainees, and it also communicates the trainer's style.[11] Figure 9.1 shows examples of different seating arrangements for low, moderate, and high levels of trainee involvement. The low involvement seating represents a traditional classroom arrangement in which the instructor is in control and stands or sits at the front of the room behind a desk or table. With this seating arrangement, communication is one-way and flows from the instructor to trainees. Communication among the trainees is not possible. This arrangement is most common for the lecture method.

When a moderate amount of involvement is desired, the instructor is still at the front of the room. However, trainees are seated around a table, thereby allowing them to interact and exchange ideas with each other. Although the

FIGURE 9.1

Seating Arrangements

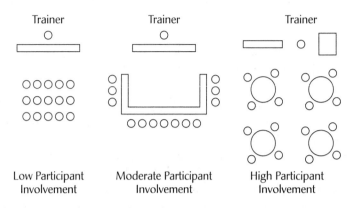

Source: Eitington, J. E. (1989). *The Winning Trainer: Winning Ways to Involve People in Learning.* Houston, TX: Gulf Publishing Company. Reprinted with permission from Elsevier.

instructor remains in control and one-way communication still dominates, participants can also communicate and learn from each other.

Finally, with a high involvement seating arrangement, small groups of trainees are seated together in groups around small tables. As a result, the groups can interact and work together on projects. The instructor's role is more of a resource person or facilitator. This allows for the instructor to present material to the class (the work table and flip chart are at the front of the room), engage the class in discussions, and move around the room and listen in on the groups, provide help and assistance, and spend time with each group while they work on projects and solve problems.[12]

Thus, as you can see, the seating arrangement has important implications for both the role of the trainer and trainees and needs to be arranged in accordance with the training program and the desired level of trainee involvement. The set-up of the training room is an important contributor to trainee motivation and learning. It is vital, then, that trainers inspect and prepare the room in advance to ensure that it will be conducive for learning. The trainer should also arrive early on the day of the training to make sure that the room is properly set up and that the required equipment has arrived and is functioning. Finally, as you will see later in this chapter, the training site and facilities are also important in creating a climate for learning.

Scheduling the Training Program

As shown in Table 9.1, the structured employment interview training program is scheduled as a one-day program. Scheduling a training program must take into consideration a number of important factors. In effect, one has to arrange the training schedule so that it can accommodate all of the participants. For example, when is the best time for employees to attend a training program in terms of the day of the week, the time of day, and the time of year? When will they be available to attend training? This will probably depend on the organization and the nature of its business. Most businesses have periods or seasons when they are especially busy and scheduling a training program during these times is likely to result in some resistance and perhaps low attendance.

It is also important to be sensitive to the needs and desires of employees and their supervisors. Would it be preferable to hold the training during office hours or after hours, such as in the evenings or on the weekend? Employees and their supervisors should be consulted to determine the best time and schedule for them to attend a training program.[13] Recall that the store development partners at Starbucks attend Store Development Boot Camp between three and six months after their start date but this might need to be changed to 90 days because it is harder for them to get away the longer they have been on the job.

A second consideration is the availability of the trainer. Whether the trainers are from the human resource department or elsewhere in the organization, they will likely have many other responsibilities that will restrict their availability. Trainers from within the organization will have to receive release time from their other duties to prepare and deliver the training program. If the trainers are from outside of the organization, then they will also have some restrictions regarding their availability and will have to be contracted for a particular date.

A third consideration in scheduling the training program is the availability of the training site, equipment, materials, and so on. If the training site and facilities are regularly used, one will have to schedule them in advance. In addition, if materials need to be designed or purchased, they will need to be prepared in advance and available in time for the training program.

Finally, when scheduling a training program, one also has to consider whether it would be best to offer it all at once, such as one day versus four two-hour sessions in the case of an eight-hour program, or all in one week versus one day each week for five weeks (or once a month for five months) in the case of a five-day program. As indicated in Chapter 5 when we discussed massed versus distributed practice, this depends in part on the complexity of the training material and the experience level of the trainees. There are also issues of resources and logistics. Sometimes it is just not feasible to conduct a training program over a longer period of time. Whenever possible, however, Kirkpatrick recommends that it is best to spread the training out as an ongoing program, such as a three-hour session once a month.[14] The Store Development Boot Camp program at Starbucks takes place over the course of one week.

Training Administration

ⓡⓟⓒ 9.2

Once the lesson plan has been completed, there are a number of activities that must be undertaken in order to effectively manage and administer a training program. **Training administration** involves the coordination of all of the people and materials involved in a training program. The maintenance of trainee records, training histories, customized learning opportunities, schedules, and course and material inventories is a routine, but necessary, activity. In addition to tracking registrations for programs, it is also useful to

Training administration
The coordination of all the people and materials involved in the training program

track individual career development and learning plans. Software is available that can do all these things.

In terms of particular training programs, employees and their supervisors have to be informed of each program with respect to its purpose and content, as well as where and when it will take place. In addition, employees who are required to attend must be notified and enrolled in the program. Trainers must also be informed of this information, as they will need to know how many trainees will be attending and the scheduling of the program. If trainees are to receive training materials or information prior to attending the program, then this will have to be prepared and sent to them in advance.

In addition, all of the materials and equipment must be ordered and prepared in time for the training program. The training site must be booked and any equipment required must be made available. In some cases, this might involve renting equipment. As well, supplies such as pens and paper must be ordered.

Finally, the training administrator will need to prepare a budget that includes the costs of all of the expenses incurred in the design and delivery of the training program. The calculation of the costs and benefits of training programs is discussed in Chapter 12.

Delivery of the Training Program

Once the lesson plan has been prepared and the administrative activities have been completed, the program is ready to be delivered. For many trainers and especially novices, this is actually the most difficult part of the training process. There are, however, a number of important steps to follow when delivering a training program. In this section, we describe how to create a climate for learning and Gagné's nine events of instruction.

Creating a Climate for Learning

One of the first things that a trainer has to be concerned about is ensuring that the training climate is conducive for learning. In other words, the trainer needs to ensure that trainees feel relaxed, comfortable, and safe in the training environment. Creating a climate that is conducive for learning is a key factor for trainee learning and involves four elements: pre-arrival factors, the greeting of participants, the learning facility/environment, and the trainer's style and behaviour.[15]

Pre-Arrival Factors

Although trainees will be forming perceptions of the learning climate when the training begins, there are some things a trainer can do before the training program. For example, contacting trainees before the training begins can help to set a positive tone. This might just be a welcome message that explains the program and its objectives but it can also include information about the location, when the program starts and ends, meals, clothes to wear, what to bring, and so on. Other pre-arrival factors might include pre-work readings or assignments, a pre-session get-together (to hand out materials or perhaps for a cocktail party or dinner), or an attempt to find out about trainees' needs, ideas, and input for the program.

The Greeting of Participants

While the tone of the climate can be set before participants arrive for training, even more important will be the perceptions they form once they arrive at the training site. Trainees might be anxious about the training and some will be skeptical about its value and the fact that they are spending time away from work. Therefore, upon arrival the trainer should meet and greet participants and make them feel welcome. A nice touch is to also have a welcome message posted on the board or a flipchart in the room. Some trainers like to have trainees write their name on a name card to get them doing something simple rather than sitting alone and waiting for the program to start. An early morning welcome session with coffee and refreshments can help to facilitate interactions with and among trainees and create a relaxed and comfortable atmosphere.

Learning Facility/Environment

A major factor in trainees' climate perceptions is the training site itself. In this regard, the trainer should ensure that the physical set-up of the training room is attractive, comfortable, bright, relaxing, and clean. Some of the things that the trainer needs to pay attention to include lighting, noise, space, and room temperature as discussed earlier. Making sure that drinks, refreshments, and lunch arrive on time is also important for creating a positive training climate.

Trainer's Style and Behaviour

Trainees' perceptions of the learning climate will be in large part based on how the trainer interacts with them and conducts the training. If the trainees do not know the trainer, then one of the first things trainers should do is provide a brief personal introduction about themselves and their involvement in the training program. The trainer should let trainees know how they can address him or her (e.g., first name is fine) and should address trainees by their first name. The trainer should circulate throughout the room and at times be seated rather than standing at the front of the room throughout the session. It is also a good idea to take advantage of opportunities to get closer to participants. This can be achieved by mingling with them during breaks, joining them at lunch and other meals, and showing understanding towards late arrivals.

Finally, key to creating a positive climate is the style of the trainer. A trainer can create a positive climate by listening with empathy, accepting different ideas, sensitivity to the communication process, supporting people who take risks, providing a fun-type atmosphere, stressing opportunities for discovery, making learning gradual, asking for feedback, and making oneself accessible for questioning.[16]

Creating a positive climate that is conducive for learning is a critical factor in the successful delivery of a training program. Also important is how the trainer actually delivers the training, our next topic.

Gagné's Nine Events of Instruction

Once a climate conducive for learning has been created, the trainer can begin to deliver the training. According to Gagné, a training program should have nine events of instruction. Table 9.3 lists the nine events, along with the learning and design principles (discussed in previous chapters) that are reflected in the events. Following is a brief description of the nine events of instruction.[17]

TABLE 9.3

Gagné's Nine Events of Instruction

Gagné's nine events of instruction reflect important principles of learning and training design discussed in previous chapters of the text.

1. **Gain attention**. Reflects the adult learners' need to know why they are learning something and their motivation to learn.

2. **Describe the objectives**. Reflects adult learners' need to know how the learning relates to their job and goal-setting theory.

3. **Stimulate recall of prior knowledge**. Reflects the adult learner's existing knowledge and experience and how that can be linked to the training material. Providing a framework for learning is similar to an advance organizer.

4. **Present the material to be learned**. Reflects task sequencing as well as incorporating adult learners' job-relevant experiences into the training.

5. **Provide guidance for learning**. Reflects the use of metacognitive strategies, attentional advice, and advance organizers.

6. **Elicit performance practice**. Reflects the importance of active practice and experiential training methods (e.g., role plays, games, simulations).

7. **Provide informative feedback**. Reflects the importance of feedback and knowledge of results during training.

8. **Assess performance**. Reflects the importance of linking training objectives to trainee learning and ensuring that the objectives are being met as well as the stages of learning.

9. **Enhance retention and transfer**. Reflects generalization from conditioning theory and self-management from social learning theory as well as the importance of self-efficacy and motivation to apply training on the job.

Gain Attention

The first thing a trainer needs to do is to draw trainees into the learning process. In other words, get the attention of trainees (recall the earlier discussion of trainee engagement). This can be achieved in a number of ways. For example, the trainer might present a thought-provoking problem. For the structured employment interview training, the trainer might ask trainees, "What should we do to ensure that we hire great employees?" Other questions might help to focus trainees on the problem at hand and the need for training, such as, "How do you conduct a valid employment interview?" Or the trainer might point out that bad hiring is costing the organization thousands of dollars. Having the CEO make an impassioned plea on the importance of the training program can also get the attention of trainees. Getting trainees interested and motivated is an important way to begin a training program. Trainees should know why the training program is important for them and the organization.

Describe the Objectives

In Chapter 5, we discussed the purpose of objectives for trainees, trainers, and managers (see Table 5.1). However, objectives are important for trainees only if they have been informed of them. Therefore, the trainer must communicate to trainees what they will learn in a training program, what to expect, and what they will be able to accomplish at the end of the program. Trainees should understand what they will learn and how they will be able to use it on the job. The trainer might even provide a demonstration of the desired performance, to help trainees form a mental picture of the skill to be performed. This will help trainees begin to focus on what they will need to learn and do after training and think about goals for learning.

Stimulate Recall of Prior Knowledge

Discuss what trainees already know that is relevant to the training material (facts, rules, procedures, or skills). It is important to show trainees that they know some things that are related to what they will learn in training. This enables trainees to think about what they know and can do that is related to what they will learn in the training program. The trainer might also provide a framework to help trainees learn and retain the training material. By providing a solid grounding, trainees will feel more confident about their ability to learn. For example, trainees might begin to think about what they have already learned about hiring and interviewing and how they currently conduct employment interviews.

Present the Material to Be Learned

The organization and presentation of the training material should be done in a logical and consistent manner. As discussed in Chapter 5, this involves teaching the material in a logical sequence or one sub-task at a time (i.e., task sequencing). The trainer can ensure learning and understanding by asking questions at various points or junctures during the training and by asking trainees to provide examples from their own work experience. For the interview training, the trainer might present each of the seven key behaviours in a logical order and ask trainees how they perform the behaviours when conducting employment interviews (e.g., how have you decided what questions to ask job candidates?).

Provide Guidance for Learning

In addition to presenting the training content, the trainer should provide trainees with guidance and direction on how best to learn the material. Provide trainees with relevant examples that demonstrate what they need to learn or do and ask questions to help them generate ideas and solutions. The combination of examples, questions, and discussion should help to guide trainees towards the main learning points.

Elicit Performance Practice

Give trainees an opportunity to practice and apply the training knowledge and skills. Allow sufficient training time so that trainees can actually do something with the information they have received during training. In a training program on the employment interview, trainees would be given time to actually practise conducting an interview. If they have been taught seven key learning points, they would be allowed to practise them in a mock interview during training.

Provide Informative Feedback

Let trainees know if their responses and behaviours in the practice session are correct as well as why they are correct or incorrect. Recall the discussion of feedback and knowledge of results from Chapter 5 where we described the importance of feedback as a condition of practice during training. It is essential that trainees know and understand what they did correct, what they did wrong, and how to correct what they did wrong. Trainees should leave training with an understanding of what they can do well and what they need to improve.

Assess Performance

It is important to test trainees on their learning of the training material and mastery during and after a training program. Ideally, learning should be assessed after each topic is completed. The assessment of learning can be either declarative (recall the discussion in Chapter 3 on the stages of learning), in which case trainees are simply asked to recall information, or it can involve knowledge compilation or procedural knowledge, in which case trainees have to explain how they would do something or actually display the learned behaviour in a role play or behavioural demonstration. The assessment of performance can involve a formal test or it might simply involve an informal question-and-answer session on the material covered in the training program up to a particular topic. The main issue is to ensure that trainees have learned the material before moving on to new topics.

Enhance Retention and Transfer

Trainees need to know how their learning can be used and applied on the job. Therefore, it is important that trainers discuss how the training material can be applied to their job and actual work situations that they encounter. The trainer might actually show trainees how the material they are learning applies to actual situations that they will encounter. Asking trainees to describe situations in which they will be able use the training content in their job can also help to enhance their retention and transfer. More detail about how to facilitate transfer is described in Chapter 10.

Finally, once a training program has ended, the trainer must adequately close the program. Like the rest of the program, the closing should be well planned and include a closing activity that signals the successful completion of the program. Some kind of event or form of recognition is common such as a ceremony in which certificates are awarded to trainees who have completed the program. Recall that the Starbucks Store Development Boot Camp program ended with a social evening with presenters and other operations partners. The lasting impression following the closing should be that the next step is a change in behaviour and performance.[18]

Training Delivery Problems

Although Gagné's nine events of instruction might seem straightforward, there are many potential problems that trainers might experience when delivering a training program. One of the most common problems is the uncooperative and difficult trainee. While most trainees are cooperative, some can make it difficult for a trainer to deliver a training program by talking too much, putting others down, complaining, displaying negative or hostile behaviour, or just being plain irritating.

Table 9.4 lists some of the types of problem participants. Dealing with problem participants requires patience and avoiding arguments and put downs. In most cases, it is best to deal with them in a polite fashion and, if possible, let the group decide how to manage them.[19]

To learn about the various types of delivery problems, Richard Swanson and Sandra Falkman conducted a study in which they asked novice trainers about the problems they have had when delivering a training program. After content-analyzing of the responses, the authors identified the following 12 common training delivery problems:[20]

1. *Fear.* Fear that is due to a lack of confidence and a feeling of anxiousness while delivering the training program.
2. *Credibility.* The perception that they lack credibility in the eyes of the trainees as subject-matter experts.
3. *Personal experiences.* A lack of stories about personal experiences that can be used to relate to the training content.
4. *Difficult learners.* Don't know how to handle problem trainees who may be angry, passive, or dominating.
5. *Participation.* Difficulty getting trainees to participate.
6. *Timing.* Trouble with the timing and pacing of the training material and worries about having too much or too little material.

TABLE 9.4

Types of Problem Participants

Some of the most common types of problem participants in training include the following:

1. **The hesitant one**. Shy, reluctant, and silent most of the time.

2. **The monopolizer**. The "big talker" who will use up all of the available air time if permitted.

3. **The voice of experience**. Has a strong need to be heard and to bring in incidents and anecdotes that are tedious and unnecessary.

4. **The arguer**. Constantly looks for opportunities to disagree, to show up the other participants and the trainer.

5. **The non-listener**. Tends to interrupt, cuts others off, leaps in before others have had their say, and does not listen to others.

6. **The idea zapper**. Puts down other participants' ideas and anything new or different.

7. **The complainer**. A problem magnifier who finds the world unfair and is a specialist in blaming and fault-finding.

8. **The rigid one**. Staunchly takes a position on an issue and will rarely, if at all, move from it.

9. **The hostile one**. Presents highly hostile questions that are designed to embarrass or inflame the trainer.

10. **The angry one**. Will find loopholes in your ideas and present impossible "what-if" scenarios.

11. **The negative one**. Finds the gloomy side of things and will dredge up gripes, past grievances, and cantankerous complaints.

12. **The clown**. Has an abundance of ill-fitting and sometimes irritating and annoying humour.

13. **The show off**. Likes to parade his/her knowledge before everyone.

14. **The tangent-taker**. Has interesting inputs but they do not relate to the topic.

Source: Based on Eitington, J. E. (1989). *The Winning Trainer: Winning Ways to Involve People in Learning*. Houston, TX: Gulf Publishing Company. Reprinted with permission from Elsevier.

7. *Adjusting instruction*. Difficulty adjusting the training material to the needs of trainees or being able to redesign the presentation of material during delivery.

8. *Questions*. Difficulty using questions effectively and responding to difficult questions.

9. *Feedback*. Unable to read trainees and to use feedback and evaluations effectively.

10. *Media, materials, facilities*. Concerns about how to use media and training materials.

11. *Opening, closing techniques.* The need for techniques to use as ice-breakers, introductions, and effective summaries and closings.
12. *Dependence on notes.* Feeling too dependent on notes and having trouble presenting the material without them.

These 12 common delivery problems of novice trainers have three basic themes: 1. Problems pertaining to the trainer, 2. Problems pertaining to how the trainer relates to the trainees, and 3. Problems pertaining to presentation techniques. Fortunately, the authors of this study also asked expert trainers for strategies and solutions for dealing with each of the 12 delivery problems. For example, to deal with the problem of fear, a trainer should be well prepared, use ice-breakers, begin with an activity that relaxes the trainees and gets them talking and involved, and acknowledge one's fear, understanding that it is normal.[21] See The Trainer's Notebook 2 for solutions to the 12 delivery problems.

The Trainer's Notebook 2

Solutions to the Most Common Training Delivery Problems

1. Fear.

A. Be well prepared and have a detailed lesson plan.
B. Use ice-breakers and begin with an activity that relaxes trainees.
C. Acknowledge the fear and use self-talk and relaxation exercises prior to the training.

2. Credibility.

A. Don't apologize. Be honest about your knowledge of the subject.
B. Have the attitude of an expert and be well prepared and organized.
C. Share personal background and talk about your area of expertise and experiences.

3. Personal experiences.

A. Relate personal experiences.
B. Report experiences of others and have trainees share their experiences.
C. Use analogies, refer to movies or famous people who relate to the subject.

4. Difficult learners.

A. Confront the problem learner and talk to them to determine the problem.
B. Circumvent dominating behaviour by using nonverbal behaviour such as breaking eye contact or standing with your back to the person.
C. Use small groups to overcome timid behaviour and structure exercises where a wide range of participation is encouraged.

5. Participation.

A. Ask open-ended questions and provide positive feedback when trainees participate.
B. Plan small-group activities such as dyads, case studies, and role plays to increase participation.
C. Invite participation by structuring activities to allow trainees to share early in the program.

6. Timing.

A. Plan for too much material and prioritize activities so that some can be omitted if necessary.
B. Practise presenting the material many times so that you know where you should be at 15-minute intervals.

(continued)

7. Adjusting instruction.

A. Determine the needs of the group early in the training and structure activities based on them.
B. Request feedback by asking trainees how they feel about the training during breaks or periodically during the training.
C. Redesign the program during breaks and have a contingency plan in place.

8. Questions.

Answering questions

A. Anticipate questions by writing out key questions that trainees might have.
B. Paraphrase and repeat a question so everyone hears the question and understands it.
C. Redirect questions you can't answer back to the trainees and try to find answers during the break.

Asking questions

A. Ask concise and simple questions and provide enough time for trainees to answer.

9. Feedback.

A. Solicit informal feedback during training or breaks on whether the training is meeting their needs and expectations and watch for nonverbal cues.
B. Do summative evaluations at the conclusion of the training to determine if the objectives and needs of trainees have been met.

10. Media, materials, facilities.

Media

A. Know how to operate every piece of equipment you will use.
B. Have back-ups such as extra bulbs, extension cords, markers, tape, and so on, as well as bringing the material in another medium in case one has problems.
C. Enlist assistance from trainees if you have a problem and need help.

Materials

A. Be prepared and have all the material placed at trainees' workplace or ready for distribution.

Facilities

A. Visit facility beforehand to see the layout of the room and where things are located and how to set up.
B. Arrive at least one hour early to set up and handle any problems.

11. Opening, closing techniques.

Openings

A. Develop a file of ideas based on experimentation and observation.
B. Develop and memorize a great opening.
C. Relax trainees by greeting them when they enter, taking time for introductions, and creating a relaxed atmosphere.

Closings

A. Provide a simple and concise summary of the course contents using objectives or the initial model.
B. Thank participants for their time and contribution to the course.

12. Dependence on notes.

A. Notes are necessary.
B. Use cards with an outline or key words as prompts.
C. Use visuals such as notes on the frames of transparencies or your copy of the handouts.
D. Practise and learn the script so you can deliver it from the key words on your note cards.

Source: Swanson, R. A., & Falkman, S. K. (1997). Training delivery problems and solutions: Identification of novice trainer problems and expert trainer solutions. *Human Resource Development Quarterly, 8,* 305–14. © 1997 by Jossey-Bass Inc. Reprinted with permission of John Wiley & Sons, Inc.

Summary

This chapter described the main issues associated with implementing and delivering training programs. We began with a discussion of the lesson plan which should follow from the design of a training program and describe how a training program should be conducted. This was followed by a description of the characteristics of effective trainers as well as how to determine who should attend a training program. We also described the issues related to training equipment and material, the training site, scheduling, and training administration. Finally, we discussed how a training program can be effectively delivered in terms of creating a positive climate for learning and Gagné's nine events of instruction. The chapter concluded with a discussion of common delivery problems and solutions.

Key Terms

lesson plan (page 235)
subject-matter expert (SME) (page 238)
train-the-trainer (page 240)

trainability test (page 241)
training administration (page 245)
training plan (page 242)

Weblinks

Bank of Montreal: www4.bmo.com (page 242)

RPC Icons

RPC 9.1 Participates in course design and selection/delivery of learning materials via various media.
RPC 9.2 Ensures arrangements are made for training schedules, facilities, trainers, participants, and equipment and course materials.

Discussion Questions

1. Discuss Gagné's nine events of instruction and how they relate to various learning and design principles.
2. What are some of the common problems encountered in training delivery and what are some solutions for them?
3. What are the characteristics of a good trainer and what effect do these characteristics have on trainee learning? Do you think that you can learn to be a good trainer or is it something you are born with?
4. How can you decide if an employee should attend a training program?

5. Describe the different types of problem trainees and how a trainer might manage them during training.
6. What factors need to be considered when deciding on a training site?
7. Why is it important for a trainer to be engaging and how can a trainer be more engaging?

The Great Training Debate

1. Debate the following: Great trainers are born, not made.
2. Debate the following: All training programs should be compulsory.

Using the Internet

1. Robert Gagné has made some important contributions to the science of training including the nine events of instruction. To learn more about Robert Gagné, go to **www.psy.pdx.edu/PsiCafe/KeyTheorists/ Gagne.htm**. Click on "The Nine Events of Instruction" and for each one, find out what tactics can be used. Write a brief summary of the tactics for each of the nine events of instruction.
2. To find out what it means to be a Certified Training and Development Professional (CTDP) in Canada, visit the Canadian Society of Training and Development (CSTD) at **www.cstd.ca/certification/index.html**. What does it mean to be a CTDP? What are the objectives and requirements? Describe the CTDP process.

Exercises

In-Class

1. Think about the last time you attended a training program or a course. How effective was the trainer or instructor and what effect did it have on your motivation to learn and learning? What is it about the trainer that had a positive or negative effect on your motivation and learning? What could the trainer or instructor have done differently to improve your motivation and learning?
2. How expressive are you as a trainer? To find out and improve your expressiveness, prepare a short (5–10 minutes) lecture on a topic of interest to you or perhaps something on training from the text. Then give your lecture to the class. The class can then evaluate your verbal and nonverbal expressiveness. Make a list of the things that you can do to improve your expressiveness.

3. Evaluate your instructor's use of Gagné's nine events of instruction. Choose a class and evaluate the instructor on each of the following events:

- Gain attention
- Describe the objectives
- Stimulate recall of prior knowledge
- Present the material to be learned
- Provide guidance for learning
- Elicit performance practice
- Provide informative feedback
- Assess performance
- Enhance retention and transfer

Based on your evaluation, how effective was the instructor's delivery? How can it be improved?

4. Recall a training program that you attended in a previous or current job. Describe the extent to which the trainer used Gagné's nine events of instruction. Provide specific examples of how each of the events was applied. How effective was the training program and what might the trainer have done differently to make it more effective?

5. Consider some of the factors that make a training site conducive for learning. Now consider the room of one of your current courses. Is the room adequate for learning? What aspects, if any, are affecting your ability to learn and what needs to be improved?

6. Think about the last time you attended a training program or one of the courses you are currently taking. Describe the climate for learning and its effect on your motivation, learning, and satisfaction with the program or course. What can the trainer or instructor do to improve the climate?

In-the-Field

1. Contact the human resources department of an organization and request a meeting with somebody in the department whom you can interview about the organization's training programs. Develop a series of questions so that you can learn about each of the following issues in terms of a particular training program that the organization has implemented:

- Was a lesson plan prepared for the program? If not, why? If so, what things were included on it?
- Who is the trainer of the program and how was he or she chosen?
- Who were the trainees and how and why were they chosen to attend the program?
- What training materials and equipment were used?
- Describe the training site and why it was chosen.
- Describe the scheduling of the training program and how it was determined.
- Who administered and coordinated the training program and what did this involve?

- How was the training program delivered (refer to Gagné's nine events of instruction)? What are some problems that have occurred in the delivery of the training program and what strategies are used to deal with them?

Based on the information you have acquired, conduct an evaluation with respect to how effective you think each of the above were performed and list some recommendations for improvement.

Case Incident

Training the Trainer at the Running Room

The Running Room has more than 60 stores and 600 employees across Canada and plans for expansion into the United States. The company does not have an HR department and relies heavily on a train-the-trainer approach to training. The store managers are in effect the human resource managers and training takes place at the store level. Each year, all store managers are brought together to talk about training issues, initiatives, and challenges. The focus is usually floor sales training because customer service on the floor is the essence of the business. Training is dynamic and interactive and does not rely on lectures. Role playing is used to teach such things as how to greet customers, how to do merchandising, how to handle security, and how to sell. The goal is make it fun and enjoyable.

Questions

1. What do you think about the train-the-trainer approach to training used at the Running Room? What are the advantages and disadvantages?
2. As the company grows and expands into the United States, do you think it will have to change its approach to training and development and if so, how should it change and why?

Source: Garcia, C. (2004, May 17). CloseUp: Training and development. *Canadian HR Reporter*, *17* (10), 7–10.

Case

Houghton Refrigeration Company

Houghton Refrigeration Company builds refrigerators for large appliance companies. It employs about 300 people, mostly assembly line workers, and is located in a small rural town in Ohio. The company typically builds, on a contract basis, chest-type freezers and small bar-type refrigerators. On occasion, however, it also builds standard size refrigerators. The president of the company is a former engineer, as are most of the other executives. These individuals are very knowledgeable about engineering, but have received little training in the basic principles of management.

During the summer months, volume at the factory increases significantly, and the company needs to hire about 40 new employees to handle the heavy workload. Most of these new employees are college students who attend a small private college located about 15 minutes from the plant. Some high school students are hired as well.

When a new employee is hired, the company asks him or her to complete an application blank and then to show up at the plant gate ready for work. Employees receive no orientation. The worker is shown to a work station and, after a minimum amount of on-the-job training, the new employee is expected to start performing a job. Most of the jobs are quite simple, hence, the training is typically completed within 10 minutes. The first-line supervisor usually shows the employee how to do a job once, then watches while the employee does the job once, leaves, and comes back about 20 minutes later to see how the employee is progressing. Typical jobs at the plant include screwing 14 screws into the sides of a freezer, placing a piece of insulation into the freezer lid, and handing out supplies from the tool room.

The company has had excellent experience with college students over the years. Much of the success can be attributed to the older workers coming to the aid of the new employees when difficulties arise. Most new employees are able to perform their jobs reasonably well after their on-the-job training is completed. However, when unexpected difficulties arise, they are usually not prepared for them and therefore need assistance from others.

The older workers have been especially helpful to students working in the "press room." However, Joe Gleason, the first-line supervisor there, finds it amusing to belittle the college students whenever they make any mistakes. He relishes showing a student once how to use a press to bend a small piece of metal, then exclaims, "You're a hot-shot college student; now let's see you do it." He then watches impatiently while the student invariably makes a mistake and then jokingly announces for all to hear, "That's wrong! How did you ever get into college anyway? Try it again, dummy."

One summer, the company experienced a rash of injuries to its employees. Although most of the injuries were minor, the company felt it imperative to conduct a series of short training programs on safe material-handling techniques. The company president was at a loss as to who should conduct the training. The Human Resource Director was a 64-year-old former engineer who was about to retire and was a poor speaker. The only other employee in the Human Resource Department was a new 19-year-old secretary who knew nothing about proper handling techniques. Out of desperation, the president finally decided to ask Bill Young, the first-line supervisor of the "lid-line," to conduct the training. Bill had recently attended a training program himself on safety and was active in the Red Cross. Bill reluctantly agreed to conduct the training. It was to be done on a departmental basis with small groups of 10 to 15 employees attending each session.

At the first of these training sessions Bill Young nervously stood up in front of 14 employees, many of whom were college students, and read his presentation in a monotone voice. His entire speech lasted about one minute and consisted of the following text:

Statistics show that an average of 30 persons injure their backs on the job each day in this state. None of us wants to become a "statistic."

The first thing that should be done before lifting an object is to look it over and decide whether you can handle it alone or if help is needed. Get help if there's any doubt as to whether the load is safely within your capacity.

Next, look over the area where you're going to be carrying the object. Make sure it's clear of obstacles. You may have to do a little housekeeping before moving your load. After you have checked out the load and route you're going to travel, the following steps should be taken for your safety in lifting:

1. Get a good footing close to the load.
2. Place your feet 8 to 12 inches apart.
3. Bend your knees to grasp the load.
4. Bend your knees outward, straddling the load.
5. Get a firm grip.
6. Keep the load close to your body.
7. Lift gradually.

Once you've lifted the load, you'll eventually have to set it down—so bend your legs again—and follow the lifting procedures in reverse. Make sure that your fingers clear the pinch points. And, finally, it's a good idea to set one corner down first.

After Bill's speech ended, the employees immediately returned to work. By the end of the day, however, everyone in the plant had heard about the training fiasco, and all, except the president, were laughing about it.

Source: From Applications in Human Resource Management, Cases, Exercises, and Skill Builders, 5th Edition, by Nkomo/Fottler/McAfee © 2005. Reprinted with permission of South-Western, a division of Thomson Learning: www.thomsonrights.com. Fax 800 730-2215.

Questions

1. Comment on the president's choice to conduct the training. Was it a good idea to have Bill Young be the trainer? How else might the president have chosen a trainer?
2. How effective was Bill Young as a trainer? What characteristics of a good trainer did he display and which ones were lacking?
3. Discuss how the company determined who should attend the training. How else might they have decided who should attend the safety training program?
4. Describe the climate for learning. How positive was the climate? What might Bill Young have done to create a more positive climate?
5. Evaluate Bill Young's delivery of the training program in terms of Gagné's nine events of instruction. Which of the events was included in his delivery? Describe some things that he might have done if he had followed Gagné's nine events of instruction in his delivery of the safety training program.

References

1. Dolezalek, H. (2004, July). Boot camp brewhaha. *Training, 41* (7), 17.
2. Donaldson, L., & Scannell, E. E. (1986). *Human resource development: The new trainer's guide* (2nd ed.). Reading, MA: Addison-Wesley.
3. Towler, A. J., & Dipboye, R. L. (2001). Effects of trainer expressiveness, organization, and trainee goal orientation on training outcomes. *Journal of Applied Psychology, 86*, 664–73.
4. Towler, A. J., & Dipboye, R. L. (2001).
5. Tannenbaum, S. I., & Yukl, G. (1992). Training and development in work organizations. *Annual Review of Psychology, 43*, 399–441.
6. Goldstein, I. L., & Ford, J. K. (2002). *Training in organizations*. Belmont, CA: Wadsworth.
7. Kirkpatrick, D. L. (1994). *Evaluating training programs: The four levels*. San Francisco, CA: Berrett-Koehler Publishers.
8. Kirkpatrick, D. L. (1994).
9. Ford, J. K., Major, D. A., Seaton, F. W., & Felber, H. K. (1993). Effects of organizational, training system, and individual characteristics on training director scanning practices. *Human Resource Development Quarterly, 4*, 333–51.
10. Nadler, L., & Nadler, Z. (1994). *Designing training programs*. Houston, TX: Gulf Publishing Company.
11. Eitington, J. E. (1989). *The winning trainer*. Houston, TX: Gulf Publishing Company.
12. Eitington, J. E. (1989).
13. Kirkpatrick, D. L. (1994).
14. Kirkpatrick, D. L. (1994).
15. Eitington, J. E. (1989).
16. Eitington, J. E. (1989).
17. Zemke, R. (1999). Toward a science of training. *Training, 36* (7), 32–36.
18. Nadler, L., & Nadler, Z. (1994).
19. Eitington, J. E. (1989).
20. Swanson, R. A., & Falkman, S. K. (1997). Training delivery problems and solutions: Identification of novice trainer problems and expert trainer solutions. *Human Resource Development Quarterly, 8*, 305–14.
21. Swanson, R. A., & Falkman, S. K. (1997).

Chapter 10

Transfer of Training

Chapter Learning Objectives

After reading this chapter, you should be able to:

- define transfer of training as well as positive, negative, zero, far, near, horizontal, and vertical transfer
- describe the major barriers to transfer of training
- describe Baldwin and Ford's model of the transfer of training process
- describe the activities that managers, trainers, and trainees can do before, during, and after training to improve the transfer of training
- define identical elements, general principles, and stimulus variability and explain how they can improve the transfer of training
- explain what a transfer of training intervention is and describe relapse prevention, self-management, and goal-setting interventions
- define transfer system and describe the transfer system factors

www.healthpartners.com

HEALTH PARTNERS

Health Partners is a non-profit organization that administers Medicard and Medicare coverage for 130 000 patients in Philadelphia. The company spent two and half years and $3 million building and installing a major upgrade to its data-processing system. For the organization, the new system was seen as a godsend—a software tool sophisticated enough to cope with the mountains of data on doctor visits, wheelchair authorizations, and other services of which Health Partners had to make sense. To the company's 360 employees, however, the new system was an unfamiliar program with complicated commands and multiple windows—a monster waiting on their desktops to devour them.

Although the company had spent tens of thousands of dollars on outside training consultants, because of delays in the installation of the system the training was a distant memory in most employees' minds. As a result, a new round of training was needed as well as follow-up support not to mention a motivational campaign to boost slumping corporate morale.

The task was handed over to the company's new Organizational Learning Centre (OLC). Rather than outsource the training, the OLC identified a handful of employees who were the top performers in the initial training course and persuaded them to become part-time instructors and support resources for the rest of the staff. In addition, rather than conducting grueling day-long crash courses, OLC broke the training into a longer series of 45-minute sessions that employees could fit into their work schedules, and offered plenty of chances for employees to retake the training and reinforce their skills. And rather than organize the curriculum by tasks, OLC organized it by department and invited staffers from other departments to attend so they could get a better understanding of how the entire company utilized the system. The OLC also devoted a portion of the training time to talking with employees about the inevitable stress of going through changes in the workplace and the benefits that might be gained from successfully weathering it.

Within weeks managers reported that their employees, who had been stuck pondering screen menus for 10 minutes at a time on day one, were able to click through in a third of the time after taking the courses. The initial wave of complaints from client hospitals and administrators about log-jams just as quickly dropped to virtually nil. And the palpable sense of dread among the workforce had been replaced by an eagerness to sign up for refresher courses.[1]

Source: Reprinted with permission, Workforce Management, 81 (12), November 2002. Copyright Crain Communications Inc.

Health Partners invested a great deal of time and money in a new data-processing system. However, in order for it to be a success, employees had to learn the new system and then actually use it on the job. This is not an easy task. Research has shown that many trainees do not actually apply what they learn in training on the job. In fact, at Health Partners employees dreaded the change to the new system. Nonetheless, the company was successful in getting employees to learn the new system and to use it on the job. This process is known as the transfer of training. This chapter describes the transfer of training process and the many ways of facilitating and improving the transfer of training.

What Is Transfer of Training?

Organizations concerned about their training investment are interested in knowing how much of what is learned in training translates into changes on the job. A training program is just the acquisition phase for knowledge, skills, and/or attitudes. Trainers can often demonstrate that trainees leave training with new knowledge and skills. But if trainees do not apply their newly acquired knowledge and skills on the job, then most of the resources spent on training are wasted.

Organizations are increasingly concerned about the value-added aspect of human resource programs. When it comes to training, they are concerned about the transfer of training. **Transfer of training** refers to the application of the knowledge and skills acquired in a training program on the job and the maintenance of acquired knowledge and skills over time.[2] Thus, there are two conditions of transfer of training. **Generalization** refers to the use or application of learned material to the job. **Maintenance** refers to the use or application of learned material on the job over a period of time. Transfer of training occurs when learned material is generalized to the job context and maintained over a period of time on the job.

The extent to which a training program transfers to the job can be described as zero, positive, or negative transfer. When transfer is positive, trainees effectively apply their new knowledge, skills, and attitudes acquired in training on the job. If transfer is zero, then trainees are not using new knowledge and skills on the job. When transfer is negative, training has had a negative effect and trainees are performing worse as a result of a training program. The purpose of this chapter is to find out why transfer is sometimes zero or negative and what can be done to make it positive.

Transfer of training can also be considered in terms of the type of situations in which trainees can apply what was learned in training on the job. For example, **near transfer** refers to the extent to which trainees can apply what was learned in training to situations that are very similar to those in which they were trained. On the other hand, **far transfer** refers to the extent to which trainees can apply what was learned in training to novel or different situations from those in which they were trained.[3]

A final distinction to note about the transfer of training is the difference between horizontal and vertical transfer. **Horizontal transfer** involves the transfer of knowledge and skills across different settings or contexts at

Transfer of training

The generalization of knowledge and skills learned in training on the job and the maintenance of acquired knowledge and skills over time

Generalization

The use or application of learned material to the job

Maintenance

The use or application of learned material on the job over a period of time

Near transfer

The extent to which trainees can apply what was learned in training to situations that are very similar to those in which they were trained

Far transfer

The extent to which trainees can apply what was learned in training to novel or different situations from those in which they were trained

Horizontal transfer

The transfer of knowledge and skills across different settings or contexts at the same level

the same level. This is in fact the focus of this chapter and is consistent with how we have defined transfer of training. That is, we are concerned about the extent to which trainees transfer what they learn in training from the training setting to the job setting.

Vertical transfer refers to transfer from the individual or trainee level to the organizational level. In other words, it is concerned with the extent to which changes in trainee behaviour or performance transfer to organizational level outcomes. For example, will a change in trainees' customer service result in an improvement in the organization's service and customer satisfaction? Vertical transfer represents the link between employee behaviour and organizational effectiveness.

This is an important distinction to understand because transfer to the job (i.e., horizontal transfer) might not lead to changes in organizational outcomes (i.e., vertical transfer). Furthermore, there are differences in terms of how to improve each type of transfer. The focus of this chapter is on horizontal transfer, which is a necessary condition for vertical transfer.[4]

The Transfer Problem

Transfer of training is a major problem for trainers and organizations. For decades it has been reported that there exists a transfer of training problem in organizations. Although the estimates of transfer have varied over the years, they have for the most part been quite low, with studies reporting that between 60 and 90 percent of what is learned in training is not applied on the job.[5]

In the only Canadian study conducted by one of the authors of the text, it was found that although trainees apply 62 percent of what they learn in training on the job immediately after attending a training program, it declines to 44 percent after six months, and to 34 percent one year after attending training. The respondents, who were experienced training professionals, also indicated that an average of 51 percent of training investments results in a positive change or improvement in employees' performance, and an average of 47 percent results in an improvement in organizational performance.[6]

There are many reasons why training does not transfer. Table 10.1 provides a list of some of the major barriers to the transfer of training. One of the things you will notice about this list is that many of the barriers have to do with factors in the work environment and can be traced to trainees, managers, and the organization. Furthermore, many of the barriers have to do with a lack of support from supervisors and the organization. Supervisor support has to do with the extent to which supervisors reinforce and support the use of learning on the job.[7] As you can see in Table 10.1, the number one barrier to transfer is the immediate manager's lack of support for training. Supervisor support has been found to be one of the most important factors for transfer along with the social support system in an organization.[8]

In the next section, we will describe the transfer of training process, which sets the stage for understanding how to improve and facilitate the transfer of training.

Vertical transfer

Transfer from the individual or trainee level to the organizational level or the extent to which changes in trainee behaviour or performance transfer to organizational level outcomes

TABLE 10.1

Barriers to the Transfer of Training

- Immediate manager does not support the training.
- The culture in the work group does not support the training.
- No opportunity exists to use the skills.
- No time is provided to use the skills.
- Skills could not be applied to the job.
- The systems and processes did not support the skills.
- The resources are not available to use the skills.
- Skills no longer apply because of changed job responsibilities.
- Skills are not appropriate in our work unit.
- Did not see a need to apply what was learned.
- Old habits could not be changed.
- Reward systems don't support new skills.

Source: Phillips, J. J., & Phillips, P. P. (2002). 11 reasons why training and development fail . . . and what you can do about it. *Training, 39* (9), 78–85. © ROI Institute, www.roiinstitute.net. Used with permission.

The Transfer of Training Process

ⓇⓅⒸ 10.1

One way to understand how to improve the transfer of training is to first identify the factors that contribute to positive transfer of training. A good place to start is with a well-known model of the transfer of training process by Tim Baldwin and Kevin Ford.[9]

As shown in Figure 10.1, Baldwin and Ford's model of the transfer of training process can be understood in terms of three main factors: training inputs, training outputs, and the conditions of transfer. The training inputs include trainee characteristics, training design, and the work environment. The training outputs include learning and retention. The conditions of transfer refer to transfer generalization and maintenance.

According to the model, trainee characteristics, training design, and the work environment have a direct effect on learning and retention. Trainee characteristics, the work environment, and learning and retention have a direct effect on transfer generalization and maintenance.

An important implication of the model is that learning and retention are a necessary but not sufficient condition for transfer. This is because trainee characteristics and the work environment also play a critical role in whether or not trainees apply what they learn in training on the job. To better understand the role of the training inputs, we will describe them in more detail.

Training Inputs

Training inputs include trainee characteristics, training design, and the work environment.

FIGURE 10.1

Baldwin and Ford's Model of the Transfer of Training Process

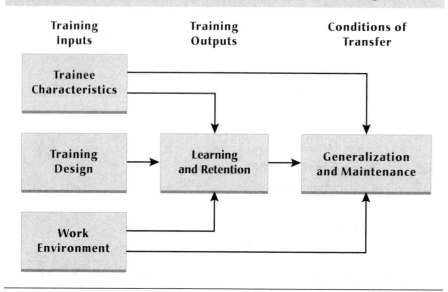

Source: From Baldwin, T. T. and Ford, J. K., "Transfer of Training: A Review and Directions for Future Research." Personnel Psychology 41, 63–105; Blackwell Publishing, 1988.

Trainee Characteristics

As described in Chapter 3, trainee characteristics are an important determinant of trainee learning and retention. Thus, it should not surprise you that trainee characteristics are also important for the transfer of training. In fact, the same trainee characteristics that influence learning are also important for transfer. Trainee differences in these characteristics can help us understand why some trainees are more likely to transfer than others.

In Chapter 3, the importance of cognitive ability, training motivation, self-efficacy, and personality characteristics were discussed in relation to learning and retention. Recall that these factors were included in the training effectiveness model and that they have a direct effect on learning and retention. They also have a direct effect on the conditions of transfer. In other words, trainees with higher cognitive ability, motivation to learn, and self-efficacy are more likely to transfer. In addition, trainees with an internal locus of control and a high need for achievement are also more likely to apply what they learn in training on the job.

Recall from Chapter 3 that another factor that influences learning and transfer is trainee attitudes. Employees with higher job involvement, job satisfaction, and organizational commitment are more likely to learn and transfer.[10]

Training Design

Another important training input is the design of a training program. Sometimes training programs do not result in positive transfer because of the failure to incorporate design factors that enable trainees to understand how to apply what they learn on the job. Recall the discussion in Chapter 5 on active practice and the conditions of practice for learning and retention. Trainee learning is likely to suffer if these conditions are not included in a training program.

There is also a number of learning principles that can be incorporated into the design of a training program to improve the transfer of training. These learning principles include identical elements, stimulus variability, and general principles.

First, trainers should ensure that the training situation reflects the work environment or what is known as identical elements. **Identical elements** involve providing trainees with training experiences and conditions that closely resemble those in the actual work environment. Identical elements theory states that transfer will occur only if identical elements are present in both the old (training course) and new situations.[11] Identical elements are especially important for near transfer and have been shown to increase trainees' retention of motor and verbal behaviours.[12]

But what exactly is identical? We discussed this issue in Chapter 6 with respect to simulations. At that time it was noted that to be most effective, simulations should have physical and psychological fidelity. Physical fidelity involves making the conditions of a training program such as the surroundings, tasks, and equipment similar to the work environment. Psychological fidelity has to do with the extent that trainees attach similar meanings to the training experience and the job context.

A second principle is known as general principles. **General principles** involve teaching trainees the general rules and theoretical principles that underlie the use and application of trained knowledge and skills. In other words, the training program provides trainees with an explanation of the theory and principles behind a skill or task that they are learning how to perform. On-the-job application is more likely when trainees are taught the general rules and theoretical principles that underlie training content.[13]

Finally, **stimulus variability** involves providing trainees with a variety of training stimuli and experiences such as multiple examples of a concept or practice experience in a variety of situations. The idea is that trainees' understanding of training material can be strengthened by providing numerous examples of a concept because they will see how the concept can be applied in a variety of situations. This will enable greater generalization of the new skills and prevents the potential problem that learning will be limited to a narrow range of situations.[14] Thus, stimulus variability is especially important for far transfer.

Stimulus variability can be incorporated into a training program in a number of ways, such as by using different models that vary in terms of their characteristics (e.g., gender or age), modelling different situations (e.g., different types of negotiation scenarios for a training program on negotiation skills), and by using models with different levels of competence in performing the training task (successful and unsuccessful). As well, trainers can increase stimulus variability simply by describing a variety of examples and experiences related to the training content, and by asking trainees to discuss their own work

Identical elements

Providing trainees with training experiences and conditions that closely resemble those in the actual work environment

General principles

Teaching trainees the general rules and theoretical principles that underlie the use and application of particular skills

Stimulus variability

Providing trainees with a variety of training stimuli and experiences, such as multiple examples of a concept, or practice experiences in a variety of situations

experiences in relation to the training material. Using several examples during the course of a training program has been found to be more effective than simply repeating the same example.[15]

The Environment

The third input factor in Baldwin and Ford's model is the work environment. Characteristics of the work environment can influence transfer before training (the pre-training environment) as well as after training (the post-training environment). Let's first consider the pre-training environment.

Management actions prior to training sends signals and messages to employees about the importance of training and the extent to which the organization supports training. These messages can influence employees' training motivation. For example, if management's actions convey messages that training is not important, employees will not be motivated to attend training and less likely to learn. In addition, if employees face constraints in their job such as a lack of time, equipment, and/or resources, they will not be highly motivated to learn given that the work environment would prevent them from using new skills.[16]

Events that occur after a training program in the post-training environment can also influence the transfer of training. Factors in the post-training environment can encourage, discourage, or prevent employees from applying new knowledge and skills on the job. As indicated earlier, one of the most important characteristics of the post-training environment is the amount of support provided by trainees' supervisors. Supervisor support for training is a key factor that affects the transfer process. Trainees who have supervisors who are more supportive of training are more likely to be motivated to attend training, to learn and retain training content, and to transfer what they learn in training on the job. There are a number of important activities that supportive supervisors can do before and after training that are described later in this chapter.[17]

At this point, it would be helpful to recall the discussion from Chapter 4 on the organizational context. At that time, two important aspects of the work environment were described: the training transfer climate and a learning culture. As described in Chapter 4, a **training transfer climate** refers to characteristics in the work environment that can either facilitate or inhibit the application of training on the job. A strong transfer climate is one in which there exist cues that remind employees to apply training material on the job, positive consequences such as feedback and rewards for applying training on the job, and supervisor and peer support for the use of newly acquired skills and abilities. A positive and supportive transfer climate has been shown to result in greater learning, retention, and the transfer of training.[18]

A **learning culture** refers to a culture in which members of an organization believe that knowledge and skill acquisition are part of their job responsibilities and that learning is an important part of work life in the organization. Research has shown that the transfer of training is greater in organizations that have a learning culture.[19] Refer to The Trainer's Notebook 1, "Learning Culture Diagnosis" to find out how to determine if an organization has a learning culture.

Training transfer climate

Characteristics in the work environment that can either facilitate or inhibit the application of training on the job

Learning culture

A culture in which members of an organization believe that knowledge and skill acquisition are part of their job responsibilities and that learning is an important part of work life in the organization

Learning Culture Diagnosis

Here are some ways that you can determine if an organization has a learning culture. Use the following scale to answer each of the statements below:

1 = Strongly disagree
2 = Disagree
3 = Neither agree nor disagree
4 = Agree
5 = Strongly agree.

- Acquiring knowledge and skills is an essential part of the job.
- Assignments are challenging and are designed to help employees develop new skills.
- Co-workers help each other to learn by sharing their job knowledge and helping to understand how jobs are interconnected.
- Employees are rewarded for learning new things.
- Employees are given opportunities on the job to apply what they have learned.

- Employees feel that they work in a place where innovation is encouraged.
- Employees receive excellent on-the-job training.
- Supervisors give employees recognition and credit when they use new knowledge and skills to do their job.
- Supervisors openly express their support of continuous learning.
- Co-workers encourage each other to use new knowledge and skills on the job.

Total your scores for all 10 items. Your total score can range from 10 to 50. Higher scores indicate a stronger learning culture.

Source: Adapted from: Tracey, J. B, Scott, I. T., & Kavanagh, M. J. (1995). Applying training on the job: The importance of the work environment. *Journal of Applied Psychology, 80* (2), 239–52.

In summary, Baldwin and Ford's model of the transfer of training process indicates that transfer generalization and maintenance is a function of trainee characteristics, the work environment, and learning and retention. Learning and retention are a function of trainee characteristics, training design, and the work environment. The model provides a number of practical implications for facilitating and improving the transfer of training that is the focus of the remainder of this chapter.

Facilitating and Improving Transfer of Training

In the previous section, we described how the transfer of training is influenced by factors before a training program (i.e., the pre-training environment), during training (training design), and after training (the post-training environment). In this section, we describe practices and activities before, during, and after training to improve the transfer of training. Further, we will also show that positive transfer of training requires the involvement of three key role players: management, trainers, and trainees and describe the activities that each role player can do at each of the three time periods.

Table 10.2 presents a transfer of training framework that guides this section of the chapter. It shows the activities that can be performed by each of the

TABLE 10.2

Transfer of Training Framework

TRANSFER OF TRAINING ACTIVITIES BEFORE TRAINING

Management

- Decide who should attend training.
- Meet with employees prior to training to discuss training programs (e.g., WIIFM).
- Get employee input and involvement in the training process.
- Provide employees with support for learning and training (e.g., release time to prepare for training).

Trainer

- Ensure application of the ISD model.
- Make sure that trainees and supervisors meet and discuss the training.
- Find out supervisor and trainee needs and expectations.
- Make sure that trainees are prepared for the training.

Trainees

- Find out about training programs prior to attendance.
- Meet with supervisor to discuss the training program and develop an action plan.
- Prepare for the training program.

TRANSFER OF TRAINING ACTIVITIES DURING TRAINING

Management

- Participate in training programs.
- Attend training programs before trainees.
- Reassign employees' work while they are attending training.

Trainer

- Incorporate conditions of practice, adult learning principles, and other learning principles (e.g., identical elements) in the design of training programs.
- Include content and examples that are relevant and meaningful to trainees.
- Provide transfer of training interventions at the end of the content portion of a training program (e.g., relapse prevention, self-management, goal-setting).
- Have trainees prepare and commit to a performance contract for the transfer of trained skills on the job.

Trainees

- Enter a training program with a positive attitude and the motivation to learn.
- Engage yourself in the training program by getting involved and actively participating.
- Develop an action plan for the application of training on the job.

Management

- Ensure that trainees have immediate and frequent opportunities to practice and apply what they learn in training on the job.
- Encourage and reinforce trainees' application of new skills on the job.
- Develop an action plan with trainees for transfer and show support by reducing job pressures and workload, arrange practice sessions, publicize transfer successes, give promotional preference to employees who have received training and transfer, and evaluate employees' use of trained skills on the job.

Trainer

- Conduct follow-up or booster sessions following a training program.
- Stay involved in the training and transfer process by conducting field visits to observe trainees' use of trained skills, provide and solicit feedback, and provide continued support and assistance to trainees.

Trainees

- Begin using new knowledge and skills on the job as soon and as often as possible.
- Meet with supervisor to discuss opportunities for transfer.
- Form a "buddy system" or a network of peers who also attended the training program.
- Consider high-risk situations that might cause a relapse and develop strategies for overcoming them and avoiding a relapse.
- Set goals for transfer and use self-management.

role players before, during, and after training to facilitate and improve the transfer of training.

Transfer of Training Activities before Training

Effective training and the probability of positive transfer should begin before a training program is delivered. There are many pre-training activities that are relatively easy to implement as part of a training program that can facilitate the transfer of training. This is in part due to the fact that the pre-training work environment has a direct effect on trainees' motivation to learn, learning, and transfer. The work environment can send messages to employees about the importance of training and should therefore be carefully constructed and managed. This means that management has an especially important role to play before training.

Management

One of the first things that a manager or supervisor should do prior to training is to carefully decide who should attend training. This involves more than just the identification of employees' needs for training. Recall from our earlier discussion that trainee characteristics are an important determinant of learning and retention as well as transfer. Therefore, it is important that trainees who are selected to attend training programs will learn to perform training tasks and transfer what they learn on the job.

The extent to which a trainee is likely to learn and benefit from a training program is known as readiness to learn and trainability. **Readiness to learn and trainability** refer to the extent to which an individual has the knowledge, skills, and abilities and the motivation to learn the training content. An equation for readiness to learn and trainability combines ability, motivation, as well as perceptions of the work environment as follows:[20]

Readiness to Learn and Trainability = (Ability × Motivation × Perceptions of the Work Environment)

According to this equation, trainees are more likely to learn or are more trainable when they have the ability to learn the training content, when they are motivated to learn, and when they perceive the work environment as supportive of their learning and use of new knowledge and skills on the job. All three of these components are important and they are not additive. In other words, being high on one factor will not make up for a low rating on another factor. For example, a trainee might have the ability to learn and be motivated to learn, but if he/she does not believe that the work environment will support learning, then he/she will score low on readiness to learn and trainability. Therefore, it is important that all three components are high before sending trainees to a training program.

One way to determine if an employee has the ability to learn the training content is have him/her take a trainability test as described in Chapter 9. If employees are lacking the motivation to attend training, there are several ways for a manger to increase motivation to learn. First, they can meet with employees to discuss their training needs and decide on a training plan to meet those needs. Prior to actually attending a training program, managers can discuss the content and the benefits of a training program with their employees and set goals for learning and how they will apply what they learn on the job. They should also discuss the objectives of a training program so that employees know what is expected of them and what they will be accountable for in terms of learning and the use of new knowledge and skills on the job. Trainees who know that they will be required to participate in follow-up activities or an assessment have stronger intentions to transfer what they learn in training.[21]

Employees also need to know why they are attending a training program and the benefits. It is up to management to inform trainees about the importance and relevance of attending a training program and the potential benefits of learning and transfer. Trainees need to know what's in it for them or what is sometimes referred to as "**WIIFM**" (what's in it for me).

These benefits could range from fewer client problems and increased speed in processing orders to more personal incentives such as promotion or increases in pay. As indicated at the beginning of the chapter, a portion of the training time at Health Partners was devoted to talking with employees about the inevitable stress of going through changes in the workplace and the benefits that might be gained from successfully weathering it.

Readiness to learn and trainability

The extent to which an individual has the knowledge, skills and abilities and the motivation to learn the training content

WIIFM

What's in it for me

There is some evidence that trainees will be more motivated and will achieve greater learning when they have some choice in attending a training program than when attendance is mandatory. In one study, managers who could choose whether to attend a performance-appraisal workshop achieved more from attending the workshop than those who were forced to attend. Providing detailed information about the workshop, which was designed to facilitate the managers' attendance decision, rather than just providing the typical positive overview, also resulted in greater achievement.[22]

Some, however, argue that it is better to make attendance mandatory. The idea behind this argument is that by making attendance mandatory, managers communicate the importance of training and ensure that all employees are using the same skills.[23] One study did find that a mandatory course resulted in higher intentions to transfer training to the workplace.[24] However, this appears to be the case when training is highly valued in an organization. When training is not so highly valued, however, providing employees with some choice is beneficial. The main point is that trainee involvement and input in the training process, whether it is discussing training needs, allowing trainees to decide what training programs to attend, and/or providing input regarding training content and methods, can enhance motivation to learn, learning, and transfer.

Finally, managers also need to show their support for training before an employee is sent to a training program. One way of doing this is to have them complete a questionnaire and respond to questions about the need for and potential application of training material. For example, managers who have requested training might be required to answer questions such as: What is the training need? What are the employees doing now and what should they be doing? Why do you feel that training will solve the problem? What would you want employees to be able to do after the training? Having managers complete a contract can also commit them to a training program and ensure their support for it. Such a contract is presented in Table 10.3. Supervisors can

TABLE 10.3

Training Support Contract—Supervisor

I, _____ , agree to

- provide time for the employee to complete pre-course assignments.
- provide release time for attendance, and ensure that the employee's workload is undertaken by others to eliminate interruptions.
- review the course outline with the employee, and discuss situations in which the newly acquired knowledge and skills can be used.
- provide timely opportunities to implement the skills, and reinforce new behaviours upon the return of the trainee.

Signature _____

Title _____

also demonstrate their support for training by providing employees release time to prepare for training and by providing encouragement.[25]

Trainer

There are a number of things that trainers can do before training to facilitate the transfer of training. First, trainers should ensure that the training system is operating according to the instructional systems design (ISD) model presented in Chapter 1. That is, a trainer should ensure that a needs analysis has been conducted, appropriate training objectives have been developed, and that important learning and design principles have been incorporated into the design of the training program.

Second, the trainer should ensure that supervisors and trainees are prepared for the training program. For example, the trainer should ensure that supervisors have taken appropriate actions with respect to the trainability of trainees as discussed in Chapter 9. The trainer should also make sure that supervisors and trainees meet to discuss the objectives, content, and benefits of the training program and that trainees know what is expected of them in terms of learning and changes in their on-the-job behaviour.

Third, the trainer should know what supervisors and trainees expect from the trainer and the training program. Thus, to some extent a trainer might have to tailor a training program to the particular needs and expectations of supervisors and trainees. The trainer should also be aware of the needs of trainees in terms of relevant content, examples, and methods. Thus, the trainer must ensure that the training program is relevant and meaningful for trainees. This way a trainer can adjust a training program to meet trainees' needs and improve the probability of learning and transfer.

Finally, the trainer should ensure that trainees are prepared for the training program and have taken any required prerequisite courses and have the necessary readings, assignments, and/or pre-training exercises. Preparation might also include asking trainees to think about any work-related problems and issues that they are currently dealing with and how the training program might help to solve them. These efforts on the part of the trainer should ensure that trainees show up for a training program ready and motivated to learn.

Trainees

Trainees often show up for training programs with little knowledge of what they are going to learn or what is expected of them. This is obviously not going to lead to a high level of motivation, learning, or transfer. Trainees need to be much more involved in their training and the training process. There are a number of things that trainees can do before training to increase their involvement and the likelihood that they will learn and transfer.

First, trainees should find out why they are being asked to attend a training program, what the training objectives are, and what is expected of them in terms of learning and on-the-job behaviour. Second, trainees should meet with their supervisors to discuss the training program and develop a plan of action for learning and transfer. Trainees should also ask their supervisor about the support they can expect while they are away from work and attending a training program, and the support they will receive when they return to their job.

Finally, trainees should prepare for the training program to ensure that they are ready to learn and that they will benefit from the training. This might involve doing some preparatory reading, pre-training exercises or assignments, or simply thinking about work-related problems they are experiencing that they can bring with them to the training program. These activities will help ensure that trainees are knowledgeable about the training program and its objectives and are prepared and motivated to learn.

Transfer of Training Activities during Training

Although it is the responsibility of the trainer to actually implement and deliver a training program, there are also important activities that trainees and managers can perform during training to improve learning and transfer.

Management

Managers can facilitate the transfer of training during training by showing their support for training. One way of doing this is to actually attend a training program. If managers cannot attend a training program, then they should consider speaking about the importance and relevance of the training at the start of a program or participating as a trainer if possible. At the very least, they should visit the session at some time to show their support.[26]

It also helps if managers have already taken a training program. Managers are more likely to support training if they have been trained or have participated as trainers in a training program. In this way, managers can model the behaviour and observe its occurrence. Senior executives at Vancouver-based Finning Ltd., the world's largest Caterpillar dealer, are the first to attend training and help deliver the training.[27] This cascading effect tells employees that management is serious about learning and the application of new skills on the job. In addition, when managers are required to teach the new skills, they learn them very well. They are also aware that their employees are watching them to see if they practice what they preach.

There are also a number of things that management can do to assist employees while they are away from work and attending a training program. For example, they can reassign some of their workload so that they don't have to worry about falling behind while they are being trained. They can also ensure that trainees will not be interrupted during training. This not only puts trainees at ease while they are being trained, but it also signals to employees that management supports training and considers it a high priority.

Trainer

As described earlier, there are several ways to design training programs to improve and facilitate the transfer of training. In particular, training programs should include active practice and the conditions of practice (e.g., task sequencing, feedback and knowledge of results), adult learning principles (e.g., problem-centred focus, use of work-related experience), as well as principles of learning such as identical elements, general principles, and stimulus variability.

Trainers can also increase trainees' motivation to learn during training. This can be done by explaining the future value of a skill and by using training content and examples that are familiar and meaningful to trainees.[28] Trainees learn and remember meaningful material more easily than material unrelated to their work.[29] Trainers can use information, problems, and anecdotes collected from the needs analysis to provide the link between training material and work situations. New material should be introduced using terms and examples familiar to trainees.

Before a training program ends, trainers should also provide some instruction on the difficulty of transfer and ways to facilitate it. One way of doing this is provide an intervention at the end of the content portion of a training program that is designed specifically for the purpose of improving the transfer of training. These transfer interventions include relapse prevention, self-management, and goal-setting and are discussed in more detail later in the chapter.

Something else trainers can do before trainees leave a training program is to have them prepare a performance contract. A **performance contract** is a statement, mutually drafted by the trainee and the trainer near the end of a training program, that outlines which of the newly acquired skills are beneficial and how they will be applied to the job. A copy can then be given to the trainer, a peer, or the supervisor, who will monitor progress toward these goals. Trainees could then submit progress reports to human resources and their supervisor. A variation on the timing (i.e., signing the contract jointly before a training program) alerts the trainee to the critical elements of the program and commits the supervisor to monitoring progress.[30] Trainees should also receive a follow-up report to training from the training department. They should know what will be expected and that these results will be discussed with their supervisors. To find out how technology can be used to follow-up on trainees, goals and action plans, see the Training Today 1 feature, "Transfer of Training Meets Technology."

Performance contract

An agreement outlining how the newly learned skills will be applied on the job

Trainees

There a number of things trainees can do during training to maximize their learning. First, trainees should begin a training program with a positive attitude and a willingness and motivation to learn. During the actual training program, trainees should actively engage themselves by taking notes, participating in discussions and exercises, asking and answering questions, and interacting with the trainer and the other trainees.

Before leaving a training program, trainees should develop an action plan for the application of training on the job and be prepared to discuss their learning and plan of action with their supervisor and co-workers. These activities should help maximize trainee learning and facilitate the transfer of training.

Transfer of Training Meets Technology

Training leaders and managers quickly lose sight of trainees once a training program has ended. As a result, unless follow-up systems and action plans are in place, transfer of training is not likely to happen. In order to address this need, the leadership consulting firm of Zenger-Folkman developed a Web-based tracking and communications software program called ActionPlan Mapper to help organizations increase the likelihood that participants will follow through on their post-training commitments.

The software is designed to help managers and training professionals monitor and track the post-training implementation goals, activities, and progress of participants. It is also designed to help participants organize, communicate, and remain focused on their post-training goals and follow-up action plans. It provides an on-line format that leads participants through the process of entering their post-training goals and action plan commitments into an on-line database that can be accessed by their manager and trainer. At later intervals chosen by the organization, participants receive e-mail reminders asking them to create brief reports in the database on their accomplishments and plans. The participant's manager, coach, mentor, or trainer can access copies of the goals and reports. The process continues for as long as the organization chooses.

Intercontinental Hotels Group (IHG) is trying ActionPlan Mapper as a six-month pilot in their five-day general manager training program. The program educates general managers on revenue management reports, the guest service tracking system, loss prevention and risk management. According to Tom Ruby, manager of curriculum and certifications, "The software will allow us to do the one thing we've never been able to do before—to add a little coaching beyond the initial face-to-face training. As project managers, we will now be able to go on-line and check on general managers' progress and send them customized feedback via e-mail. If we see action steps that are not working, we will be able to let the participant know."

Source: Based on Anonymous (2005, June). The wired taskmaster: Making learning stick. *Training, 42* (6). V N U Business Publications. This work is protected by copyright and it is being used with the permission of Access Copyright. Any alteration of its content or further copying in any form whatsoever is strictly prohibited.

Transfer of Training Activities after Training

After a training program has ended and trainees return to work, they are often motivated to try to use their new skills on the job. However, only some are able to do so successfully. Some will stop trying after a few attempts because they receive no support or reinforcement for the use of their new knowledge and skills on the job. Others will give up because they encounter barriers and obstacles that make it difficult if not impossible for them to apply their new knowledge and skills on the job. Still others will give up just because the old ways of doing things are easier and faster. Therefore, it is extremely important that managers, trainers, and trainees participate in post-training activities that facilitate the transfer of training.

Management

Transfer of training can be inhibited by the "bubble" syndrome, in which the trainee is expected to use the new skills without support from the environment.[31] Management can burst the bubble by ensuring that the time between training and on-the-job application is minimal, and by providing trainees with support and reinforcement for the use and application of their new knowledge and skills on the job. Follow-up support was an important factor in the successful transfer of Health Partners training program described at the beginning of the chapter.

One of the most important things that managers can do following a training program is ensure that employees have immediate and frequent opportunities to practice and apply what they learned in training on the job. Assignments and opportunities to try new skills should be given as soon as trainees return from a training program. Managers can also help by allowing trainees time to try or experiment using new behaviours without adverse consequences.

Managers must also encourage and reinforce the application of new skills on the job. In fact, one of the major reasons for a lack of transfer is that reinforcement is usually infrequent or nonexistent. Behaviour that is not reinforced is not repeated. If the sales representative dutifully submits the reports as learned in training but no one even notices they are filed, then the representative will waste no further energy doing this task.

A Xerox study showed that only 13 percent of trainees were using their new skills six months after training when management did not coach and support their use.[32] Therefore, managers must reward and reinforce employees for using new skills and behaviours acquired in training on the job. Trainees who use new skills on the job should be provided with praise, recognition, positive feedback, more challenging assignments, additional opportunities for training, and other extrinsic rewards. This not only directly reinforces employees for their transfer behaviour, but it also sends a signal to other employees that training is important and learning and transfer will be rewarded. In effect, it helps to create a positive transfer climate and learning culture.

There are many other things that managers can do to facilitate transfer such as the development of an action plan for transfer, reducing job pressures and workload, arranging for co-workers to be briefed by trainees about a training program, arranging practice sessions, publicizing successes, promotional preference to employees who have received training, and evaluating employees' use of trained skills on the job.[33] Calgary-based Western Gas Marketing, Ltd., a subsidiary of TransCanada PipeLines Ltd., rates their managers on the application of new skills on their performance-appraisal form.[34] At the Bank of Montreal, managers conduct performance assessments to gauge the transfer of learning to the job.[35]

Trainer

Once a training program has ended, it is important for trainers to remain involved in trainees' learning and transfer. Trainers should maintain their involvement in the training and transfer process by conducting field visits to observe trainees' use of trained skills, provide and solicit feedback, and provide continued support and assistance to trainees.[36]

It is also common for trainers to meet with trainees at some point after a training program has ended in what is known as a booster session. **Booster sessions** are extensions of training programs that involve periodic face-to-face contact between the trainer and trainees. They can involve a review of the

Booster sessions

Extensions of training programs that involve periodic face-to-face contact between the trainer and trainees

training material or a kind of refresher course and/or a discussion of any problems trainees have had using their trained skills on the job as well as success stories. The main objective is for the trainer to meet with trainees sometime following a training program to find out if they have been able to transfer the training and to discuss any problems or difficulties they might be having and how to manage them.

Trainees

After attending a training program, one of the first things that trainees should do is begin to use their new knowledge and skills on the job. Failure to use the training material when one returns to work is likely to result in a low likelihood of transfer. To ensure adequate opportunities for skill application and support, trainees should meet with their supervisor and discuss opportunities for transfer. Trainees might also benefit by establishing a "buddy system" or a network of peers who also attended a training program and can provide assistance and support as well as reinforce each other for using their trained skills on the job.[37] This can also help ensure that trainees persist in the application of trained skills on the job and avoid a relapse.

Along these lines, trainees should think about high-risk situations that might make it difficult for them to apply the training material on the job. They should anticipate potential difficulties and develop strategies for overcoming them. It is also helpful for trainees to set goals for practicing their newly acquired skills on the job.

Transfer of Training Interventions

As indicated earlier, one of the things that a trainer can do towards the end of a training program is to discuss the transfer problem with trainees and instruct them on how to transfer their newly acquired knowledge and skills on the job. In the last decade, many studies have found that a number of interventions provided at the end of a training program can be effective for improving the transfer of training. In this section, we briefly discuss three types of transfer of training interventions: relapse prevention, self-management, and goal-setting.

Relapse Prevention

Relapse prevention (RP) interventions teach trainees to anticipate transfer obstacles and high-risk situations in the work environment and to develop coping skills and strategies to overcome them. A relapse occurs when trainees revert back to using the old skills or their pre-training behaviour. Relapse prevention sensitizes trainees to the possibilities of a relapse and "immunizes" them against obstacles in the environment that might cause one.[38] It sensitizes trainees to barriers in the workplace that might inhibit or prevent successful transfer.

Relapse prevention interventions make trainees aware that relapse can occur and that temporary slips are normal. Trainees are asked to identify obstacles and barriers to transfer and high-risk situations in which a relapse is

Relapse prevention

Instructs trainees to anticipate transfer obstacles and high-risk situations in the work environment and to develop coping skills and strategies to overcome them likely to occur. Some high-risk situations that might lead to a relapse are time pressure and deadlines, work overload, lack of necessary tools, equipment, and resources, and the lack of opportunities to apply trained skills on the job.[39] For each barrier or high-risk situation, trainees develop a coping strategy. For example, if workers think they will abandon their new skills when there is too much work, time-management techniques could be discussed and used to prevent a relapse. In this way, trainees are prepared to anticipate and prevent relapses and recover from temporary lapses.

Relapse prevention programs have been found to be effective. Trainees who receive training in relapse prevention have higher levels of course knowledge and use the knowledge on the job more than trainees who do not receive it. Relapse prevention has also been found to improve trainees' ability and desire to transfer. There is also some evidence that relapse prevention interventions are especially effective when the transfer climate is not very supportive of training.[40]

To find out how one company prepares trainees for transfer obstacles, see Training Today 2, "Improving Transfer at Delta Hotels and Resorts."

Self-Management

In Chapter 3 we discussed self-management as one of the components of social learning theory. We also noted that employees can be trained to learn how to manage their behaviour. **Self-management** interventions focus on behavioral change and usually involve teaching trainees to perform a series of steps to manage their transfer behaviour. The steps of self-management include anticipating performance obstacles, planning to overcome obstacles, setting goals to overcome obstacles, monitoring one's progress, and rewarding oneself for goal attainment. A number of studies have found that self-management results in greater skill generalization and higher performance on a transfer task.[41]

See The Trainer's Notebook 2 for a guide to implementing a self-management intervention.

Goal-Setting

In Chapter 3, we described goal-setting theory and its relevance for the design and effectiveness of training programs. Many studies have shown that individuals who set specific, difficult, and challenging goals achieve higher levels of performance.[42]

The importance of goal-setting for training has been the focus of many studies in recent years. From these studies, we know that learning and transfer is more likely when trainees set specific and challenging goals. Therefore, it makes sense to introduce goal-setting into training as a post-training transfer intervention.

Goal-setting interventions teach trainees about the goal-setting process and to set specific goals for the use of trained skills on the job. This usually involves a discussion of why goal-setting is important and a definition of goals; a description of the goal-setting process; characteristics of effective goals (specific and challenging); an explanation for the effectiveness of goals;

Self-management

A post-training transfer intervention that teaches trainees to manage their transfer behaviour

Goal-setting intervention

An intervention that instructs trainees about the goal-setting process and how to set specific goals for the use of trained skills on the job

Improving Transfer at Delta Hotels and Resorts

At Delta Hotel and Resorts where employees are guaranteed ongoing training, the company expanded a one-day training program into a two-day program by adding practice sessions to each module and a final session for identifying roadblocks to on-the-job application. Trainees developed an action plan for those problems they could control and another plan for those they had only indirect control over. They also made a list of problems beyond their control that they presented to management.

In a group of 17 trainees of whom 10 were identified by trainers and managers as skeptics, an action plan was presented to Delta's general manager. A few weeks after the training ended, the trainees not only met their own objectives, but they challenged management to make the changes they suggested.

Examining roadblocks was a key part of the program. When trainees are asked to come up with reasons why they might not use the training, they are also likely to come up with solutions to overcome the roadblocks and use the training.

Source: Gardner, P. (1998, November). Cynics, snorters, doodlers and skeptics—whatcha gonna do? www.trainingreport.ca/articles/story.cfm?StoryID=88. Reprinted by permission of The Training Report, Crownhill Publishing Inc.

A Guide for Implementing Self-Management

A five-step self-management program, which has proven to be effective in increasing the transfer of training, consists of the following:

- *Identify performance obstacles*. Ask trainees to identify situations that make it difficult to apply the material in their work situations.
- *Plan to overcome obstacles*. After a group discussion of the obstacles, give trainees time to develop strategies to deal with the obstacles. As a group, prepare a list of do's and don'ts.
- *Set goals*. Ask trainees to set goals for transfer.
- *Self-monitor progress*. Based on their goals, require trainees to develop means of determining whether they met those goals.
- *Self-administer rewards*. Ask trainees to design a system for rewarding themselves if their goals are achieved.

examples of how goal-setting has been used in organizations; and a discussion of how goal-setting can be effective in one's own organization. Following a discussion of how to set specific and challenging goals, trainees develop their own goal-setting plan that indicates the steps they will take to achieve their goals and the date that each step will be achieved.[43]

Several studies have found that goal-setting interventions are effective. Goal-setting interventions have been shown to improve learning and the extent to which trainees apply their newly learned skills on the job. In addition, one study found that goal-setting was particularly effective for enhancing transfer for trainees who worked in a supportive work environment.[44]

The Transfer System

In this chapter, we have described many factors that contribute to the transfer of training. These factors can occur throughout the training process and have to do with the training program itself as well as trainees, trainers, management, and the organization. One way of thinking about all of these factors is in terms of a transfer system. According to Elwood Holton and colleagues, the **transfer system** refers to all factors in the person, training, and organization that influence transfer of learning to job performance.[45]

There are sixteen factors that make up the transfer system. The sixteen factors represent important predictors of transfer that we have already discussed in the chapter including trainee ability, motivation, and the work environment. Learning as well as the transfer system factors influence transfer performance which in turn influence organizational performance.[46]

Holton and his colleagues have developed a diagnostic instrument called the Learning Transfer System Inventory (LTSI) to assess the transfer system in organizations. The instrument consists of the sixteen factors that have been found to be the most important in transfer research. Some of the factors are used to assess a specific training program while others are general factors that are important for all training programs. Table 10.4 lists the sixteen factors and their definitions.

The LTSI can be used by organizations to diagnose their transfer system. It is usually administered to trainees after a training program in order to identify potential barriers in an organization's transfer system and to determine the type of intervention to overcome barriers and facilitate transfer. Factors with particularly low scores can be identified and the focus of interventions.[47]

One of the benefits of this approach to transfer is that it recognizes the importance of a systematic approach to the transfer of training. Organizations are able to diagnosis their transfer system, identify barriers, and implement programs to eliminate the barriers. This is important because transfer systems differ across organizations, which means that the barriers and the type of intervention to eliminate them will also differ from organization to organization.[48]

TABLE 10.4

Transfer System Factors

The Learning Transfer System Inventory (LTSI) consists of sixteen factors that assess the transfer system in organizations. Eleven factors are for specific training programs (Factors 1 to 11) and the remaining five (Factors 12 to 16) are more general and apply to all training programs.

Specific Factors

1. **Learner readiness**. The extent to which individuals are prepared to enter and participate in training.
2. **Motivation to transfer**. The direction, intensity, and persistence of effort toward utilizing in a work setting skills and knowledge learned.

Managing Performance Through Training and Development

3. **Positive personal outcomes**. The degree to which applying training on the job leads to outcomes that are positive for the individual.

4. **Negative personal outcomes**. The extent to which individuals believe that not applying skills and knowledge learned in training will lead to outcomes that are negative.

5. **Personal capacity for transfer**. The extent to which individuals have the time, energy, and mental space in their work lives to make changes required to transfer learning to the job.

6. **Peer support**. The extent to which peers reinforce and support use of learning on the job.

7. **Supervisor support**. The extent to which supervisors-managers support and reinforce use of training on the job.

8. **Supervisor sanctions**. The extent to which individuals perceive negative responses from supervisors-managers when applying skills learned in training.

9. **Perceived content validity**. The extent to which trainees judge training content to reflect job requirements accurately.

10. **Transfer design**. The degree to which (1) training has been designed and delivered to give trainees the ability to transfer learning to the job, and (2) training instructions match job requirements.

11. **Opportunities to use**. The extent to which trainees are provided with or obtain resources and tasks on the job enabling them to use training on the job.

General Factors

1. **Transfer effort-performance expectations**. The expectation that effort devoted to transferring learning will lead to changes in job performance.

2. **Performance-outcomes expectations**. The expectation that changes in job performance will lead to valued outcomes.

3. **Resistance or openness to change**. The extent to which prevailing group norms are perceived by individuals to resist or discourage the use of skills and knowledge acquired in training.

4. **Performance self-efficacy**. An individual's general belief in the ability to change performance at will.

5. **Performance coaching**. Formal and informal indicators from an organization about an individual's job performance.

Source: Holton, E. F., III, Bates, R. A., & Ruona, W. E. A. (2000). Development of a generalized learning transfer system inventory. *Human Resource Development Quarterly*, *11*, 333–60. © 2000 Jossey-Bass Inc. Reprinted with permission of John Wiley & Sons, Inc.

Model of Training Effectiveness—Transfer of Training

Before concluding this chapter, let's return to the model of training effectiveness that was presented in Chapters 3 and 5. Recall that the model shows that:

1. Trainee characteristics (i.e., cognitive ability, training motivation, personality,

self-efficacy, and attitudes) and training design (i.e., active practice and the conditions of practice) have a direct effect on trainee learning and retention; 2. Learning and retention have a direct effect on individual behaviour and performance; and 3. Individual behaviour and performance has a direct effect on organizational effectiveness. We can now add a number of other factors and links to the model based on the material presented in this chapter as shown in Figure 10.2.

First, we can add the work environment to the model which includes the training transfer climate, a learning culture, and the transfer system. Second, we can add the learning principles (i.e., identical elements, stimulus variability, and general principles) to training design. In terms of the paths, we can add a direct link from trainee characteristics and the work environment to individual behaviour and performance. This follows from Baldwin and Ford's model of the transfer process. We can also add a direct link from training design to individual behaviour and performance given that the learning principles are important for transfer. Thus, the model now shows that individual behaviour and performance (i.e., transfer) is influenced by trainee characteristics, training design, the work environment, and learning and retention.

The final linkage in the model is from transfer behaviour and performance to organizational effectiveness. Recall that this linkage is known as vertical transfer. Vertical transfer refers to the link between individual-level training outcomes and organizational outcomes. While a change and improvement in employees'

Figure 10.2

Model of Training Effectiveness

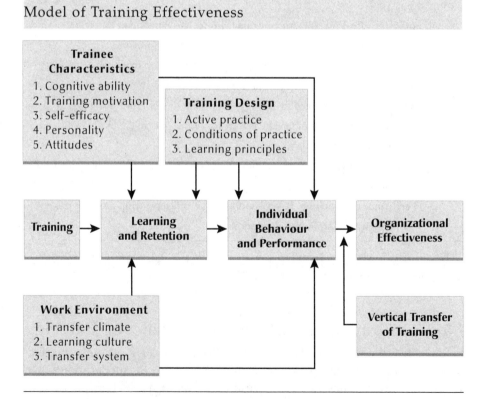

behaviour and performance (i.e., horizontal transfer) is necessary for vertical transfer, it is important to realize that the relationship is not one-to-one. In other words, positive horizontal transfer does not guarantee vertical transfer because many other factors also contribute to organizational effectiveness.

Summary

This chapter has described the different types of transfer of training and the factors that influence it. Baldwin and Ford's model of the transfer of training process was presented as a framework for understanding how to facilitate and improve the transfer of training. In addition, activities for improving the transfer of training at different time periods (before, during, and after training) and the roles of management, trainers, and trainees were also described. The chapter concluded with a discussion of three kinds of transfer of training interventions (relapse prevention, self-management, and goal-setting) and the transfer system which refers to all factors in the person, training, and organization that influence the transfer of training.

It should now be clear to you that transfer of training is something that must be addressed throughout the training process—before, during, and after training. Furthermore, positive transfer of training is the responsibility of management, trainers, and trainees. This means that improving the transfer of training requires a systematic approach that involves activities and practices on the part of all of the key players throughout the training process.

Key Terms

booster sessions (page 280)
far transfer (page 265)
general principles (page 269)
generalization (page 265)
goal-setting intervention (page 282)
horizontal transfer (page 265)
identical elements (page 269)
learning culture (page 270)
maintenance (page 265)
near transfer (page 265)

performance contract (page 278)
readiness to learn and trainability (page 274)
relapse prevention (page 281)
self-management (page 282)
stimulus variability (page 269)
training transfer climate (page 270)
transfer system (page 284)
transfer of training (page 265)
vertical transfer (page 266)
WIIFM (page 274)

Weblinks

Delta Hotels and Resorts: www.deltahotels.com (page 283)

Finning Ltd.: www.finning.com (page 277)

Western Gas Marketing, Ltd.: www.transcanada.com (page 280)

Xerox: www.xerox.com (page 280)

RPC Icons

RPC 10.1 Facilitates coaching and post-training support activities to ensure transfer of learning to the workplace.
RPC 10.2 Participates in course design and selection/delivery of learning materials via various media.

Discussion Questions

1. Refer to Table 10.1, "Barriers to the Transfer of Training." For each of the barriers, indicate who is responsible for the barrier (trainer, trainee, management) and when the barrier is most likely to occur (before, during, and/or after).
2. Refer to Table 10.1, "Barriers to the Transfer of Training." For each of the barriers, describe what can be done in order to remove the barrier and facilitate the transfer of training. Be sure to indicate at what stage in the training process you would do something to remove the barrier (i.e., before, during, and/or after), and who would be involved (i.e., manager, trainer, and/or trainee).
3. Refer to the Health Partners vignette at the beginning of the chapter and describe the activities that helped to facilitate the transfer of training. At what point during the training process were these activities implemented and who was involved?
4. What is the difference between horizontal and vertical transfer and how are they related? What is the difference between near transfer and far transfer and what should a trainer do in order to maximize each of them?
5. Describe the main factors in Baldwin and Ford's model of the transfer of training process and how they are related. What are the practical implications of the model for improving transfer of training?
6. What is the transfer system and what are the specific and general factors associated with it? Review each of the factors in Table 10.4 and discuss who is responsible for each factor (i.e., trainee, trainer, supervisor) and what can be done to increase a trainee's rating of each of them.
7. Discuss how technology can be used to facilitate the transfer of training in organizations.

The Great Training Debate

1. Debate the following: Low rates of transfer of training are inevitable and will always be a problem for trainers and organizations.
2. Debate the following: Trainers should only be responsible for trainee learning and retention because what happens when trainees return to the work environment and the transfer of training is beyond their control.

Using the Internet

1. To find out more about the Learning Transfer System Inventory (LTSI), go to **www.edholton.com/_private/New%20EdHolton/LTSI.htm**. Answer the following questions:

   1. What is the LTSI?
   2. How should it be administered?
   3. Describe the LTSI conceptual model.
   4. How was the LTSI developed?
   5. Describe the learning transfer system change process.

Exercises

In-Class

1. After the final exam, many students claim to forget most of what they learn in their courses. How could you design an educational experience for students so that they would remember and use most of the material learned in the classroom?

2. Think about the most recent training experience you had in a current or previous job. What did you learn and to what extent did you apply what you learned on the job? Did you transfer immediately after training? Six months after training? One year after training? What factors do you think explain why you did or did not transfer what you learned in training on the job? Is there anything that the trainer or your supervisor could have done to increase your chances of transfer? Is there anything you could have done yourself to improve your transfer? (Note: This exercise can also be done by interviewing somebody about their training experiences, e.g., another member of the class, a friend, or family member.)

3. Students acquire a great deal of knowledge and information from their courses but does this learning transfer to their work experiences? Describe any courses you have taken that resulted in transfer from school to work. What factors do you think contributed to your transfer and could they be used in the design of other courses?

4. Describe how you would use the principles of identical elements, general principles, and stimulus variability to improve the learning and transfer of your courses. In other words, what can an instructor do to incorporate these learning principles into his/her classes?

5. Assume the role of a training consultant who has been hired by an organization with a transfer of training problem. Your task is to conduct a diagnosis of the transfer system to find out why there is a transfer problem. Therefore, you need to develop a diagnostic tool to find out what barriers exist. Using the material in this chapter, develop a series of questions that take into account the different time periods of the training

process (i.e., before, during, and after), and the main role players (management, trainer, and trainees). What questions will you ask and who will you interview and/or survey?

6. Review the transfer of training interventions described in the chapter and think about how they might be used to help students learn their course material and apply it on the job. You could consider your course on training and development or perhaps a course on managerial skills. Your task is to design one of the following interventions: relapse prevention, self-management, or goal-setting. You can then either have another member of the class review your intervention and provide feedback or if time permits, present your intervention to the class.

In-the-Field

1. To find out about transfer of training in an organization, contact the human resource department of an organization and ask the following questions:

   - To what extent do trainees apply what they learn in training on the job immediately after training, six months after training, and one year after training?
   - What are the main barriers or obstacles to transfer of training in your organization?
   - What kinds of things do you do to try to improve the transfer of training?
   - Are there things you do before, during, and after training to improve transfer?
   - What are the responsibilities of managers, trainers, and trainees for the transfer of training?
   - What have you found to be most effective for ensuring that trainees apply what they learn in training on the job?

   Based on your interview, how well do you think the organization is managing the transfer of training process? What recommendations do you suggest for the organization in order to improve its transfer system and the transfer of training?

Case Incident

Standard Life Canada

Standard Life Canada has a total customer satisfaction philosophy based on seven core competencies: customer focus, teamwork, action orientation, leadership, business acumen, strategic thinking, and professional development. Several years ago, the company decided it was time to repeat its total customer satisfaction training and brought all of its employees from Canada to Montreal for one day of training on customer service. The focus was on what sorts of things are essential for the customer, what adds value to the customer, and looking at things from the customer's perspective.

Questions

1. What should employees be able to do on-the-job after attending this training program? In other words, what is it that should transfer?
2. What factors might limit the extent to which employees transfer what they learn in this training program on the job? What can be done in order to facilitate their transfer of training?

Source: Garcia, C. (2004, May 17). CloseUp: Training and development. *Canadian HR Reporter, 17* (10), 7–10.

Case

The School Board

For years, parents, students, and teachers had been complaining that nobody listened, that decisions were made without participation, and that good ideas went unacknowledged. A needs analysis that involved a survey of teachers and students confirmed that these problems were widespread.

As a recently appointed trainer with a strong background in teaching, Carlos DaSilva tackled the communications problem as his first assignment. He designed what he considered to be the finest three-day communications program in any school board. He spent months on the design: finding videos, exercises, and games that taught active listening, upward communication, brainstorming, and other areas identified in the survey.

Carlos was excited to deliver his new training program and was sure that the participants would like it. On the first day, Carlos began with a brief introduction on the importance of communication, followed by a lecture on communication channels. Afterwards, he showed a video about manager-employee communication problems and how to improve communication. This was followed by a discussion of the key points in the video and what the trainees might do to improve their communication skills.

On day two of the training program, Carlos began with a lecture on brainstorming. He then had trainees participate in a group brainstorming exercise. Each group had to brainstorm as many ideas as possible for improving communication in the school board. Afterwards, the groups presented their ideas followed by a discussion of the most creative ways to improve communication with teachers, students, and parents.

On the third day of the training program, Carlos began with a lecture on active listening. Trainees then participated in an exercise in which they had to develop a message and then communicate it to the other trainees. At the end of the exercise, each trainee had to recall the message sent by the other trainees. This was then followed by a discussion of how to be a more effective listener and with tips on active listening.

Carlos then ended the training program by having the trainees participate in a communication game. First, he had trainees complete a self-assessment of how they send messages and the channels they use for communication. Then groups of trainees had to develop a message that they would communicate to the other groups. Each group had to determine the best way for their message to reach the other groups as accurately and timely as possible. At the end of the game, each group read out the message they received from the other groups. Carlos then scored each group in terms of the accuracy of the message received by the other groups as well as how long it took for each group to receive the message.

The game was a lot of fun for the participants, who left the training program on a high. Carlos thanked them for attending the training program and encouraged them to try to apply what they learned in training when they return to work. The trainees then applauded Carlos and thanked him for providing such an enjoyable training experience.

Two months after the training program, Carlos was sitting at his desk in the training office, thinking about his meeting scheduled for 2 p.m. with the school board superintendent. He was looking forward to the meeting with the superintendent, knowing that he would be praised for the successful interactive communications program he had designed.

However, the meeting with the superintendent went poorly. Although some participants loved the exercises and games in the communications course, most did not change their behaviour at work. Furthermore, a review of the situation showed that the old problems persisted and communication remained a serious problem at the school board. Carlos did not know what to say or what he would do.

Several days later, Carlos approached several of the participants who attended the training program and asked them how things were going. One participant laughed at him and said, "Well that was a lot of fun, but training is training and work is work. Besides, nothing ever changes around here." Carlos asked her what she meant and she explained to him that supervisors don't get it and continue to call the shots. "The only thing they know about communication is downward," she said. "Maybe they should have attended your training program."

Questions

1. What are some of the reasons why Carlos's training program did not transfer?
2. Discuss some of the barriers to transfer that might be operating at the school board. Who is responsible for these barriers?
3. Describe some of the things that Carlos might have done before, during, and after the training program to improve the transfer of training.
4. Discuss the role of the training transfer climate and the transfer system. How might they have contributed to the transfer problem at the school board?
5. What should Carlos do about the transfer problem?

References

1. Kiger, P. J. (2002, November). Health Partners delivers training that works. *Workforce Management, 81* (12), 60–64.
2. Baldwin, T. T., & Ford, J. K. (1988). Transfer of training: A review and directions for future research. *Personnel Psychology 41*, 63–105.

3. Broad, M. L., & Newstrom, J. W. (1992). *Transfer of training*. Reading, MA: Addison–Wesley.

4. Kozlowski, S. W. J., Brown, K. G., Weissbein, D. A., Cannon-Bowers, J. A., & Salas, E. (2000). A multilevel approach to training effectiveness: Enhancing horizontal and vertical transfer. In K. J. Klein & S. W. J. Kozlowski (Eds.), *Multilevel theory, research, and methods in organizations* (pp. 157–210). San Francisco: Jossey-Bass.

5. Phillips. J. J., & Phillips, P. P. (2002, September). 11 reasons why training and development fails . . . and what you can do about it. *Training, 39* (9), 78–85.

6. Saks, A. M. (2002). So what is a good transfer of training estimate? *The Industrial-Organizational Psychologist*, 29–30.

7. Cromwell, S. E., & Kolb, J. A. (2004). An examination of work-environment support factors affecting transfer of supervisory skills training to the workplace. *Human Resource Development Quarterly, 15*, 449–71.

8. Cromwell, S. E., & Kolb, J. A. (2004); Tracey, J. B, Scott, I. T., & Kavanagh, M. J. (1995). Applying training on the job: The importance of the work environment. *Journal of Applied Psychology 80* (2), 239–52.

9. Baldwin, T. T., & Ford, J. K. (1988).

10. Colquitt, J. A., Lepine, A., & Noe, R. A. (2000). Toward an integrative theory of training motivation: A meta-analytic path analysis of 20 years of research. *Journal of Applied Psychology, 85*, 678–707.

11. Bass, B. M., & Vaughn, J. A. (1969). *Training in industry: The management of learning*. Belmont, CA: Wadsworth.

12. Baldwin, T. T., & Ford, J. K. (1988).

13. Baldwin, T. T., & Ford, J. K. (1988).

14. Baldwin, T. T., & Ford, J. K. (1988).

15. Baldwin, T. T., & Ford, J. K. (1988).

16. Tannenbaum, S. I., & Yukl, G. (1992). Training and development in work organizations. *Annual Review of Psychology, 43*, 399–441.

17. Baldwin, T. T., & Ford, J. K. (1988); Tannenbaum, S. I., & Yukl, G. (1992).

18. Rouiller, J. Z., & Goldstein, I. L. (1993). The relationship between organizational transfer climate and positive transfer of training. *Human Resource Development Quarterly, 4*, 377–90.

19. Tracey, J. B, Scott, I. T., & Kavanagh, M. J. (1995)

20. DeSimone, R. L., Werner, J. M., & Harris, D. M. (2002). *Human resource development*. Orlando, FL: Harcourt.

21. Baldwin, T. T., & Magjuka, R. J. (1991). Organizational training and signals of importance: Linking pretraining perceptions to intentions to transfer. *Human Resource Development Quarterly, 2*, 25–36.

22. Hicks, W. D., & Klimoski, R. J. (1987). Entry into training programs and its effects on training outcomes: A field experiment. *Academy of Management Journal, 30*, 542–52.

23. Broad, M. L., & Newstrom, J. W. (1992).

24. Baldwin, T. T., & Magjuka, R. J. (1991).

25. Tannenbaum, S. I., & Yukl, G. (1992).

26. Burke, L. A. (2001). Training transfer: Ensuring training gets used on the job. In L. A. Burke (Ed.), *High-impact training solutions: Top issues troubling trainers*. Wesport, CT: Quorum Books.

27. Clemmer, J. (1992, September 15). Why most training fails. *The Globe and Mail,* B26.

28. Bass, B. M., & Vaughn, J. A. (1969).

29. McGehee, W., & Thayer, P. W. (1961). *Training in business and industry*. New York: Wiley.

30. Leifer, M. S., & Newstrom, J. W. (1980, August). Solving the transfer of training problems. *Training and Development Journal*, 34–46.

31. Hatcher, T., & Schriver, R. (1991, November-December). Bursting the bubble that blocks training transfer. *Technical and Skills*, 12–15.

32. Zucker, L. (1987). Institutional theories of organization. *Annual Review of Sociology, 13*, 443–64.

33. Broad, M. L., & Newstrom, J. W. (1992).

34. Clemmer, J. (1992, September 15).

35. Waxer, C. (2005, October 24). Bank of Montreal opens its checkbook in the name of employee development. *Workforce Management, 84* (11), 46–48;

36. Burke, L. A. (2001).

37. Baldwin, T. T., & Ford, J. K. (1988); Burke, L. A. (2001).

38. Tziner, A., & Haccoun, R. R. (1991). Personal and situational characteristics influencing the effectiveness of transfer of training improvement strategies. *Journal of Occupational Psychology 64* (2), 167–77.

39. Burke, L. A. (2001).

40. Burke, L. A. (2001).

41. Gist, M., Bavetta, A., & Stevens, C. (1990). Transfer training method: Its influence on skill generalization, skill repetition, and performance level. *Personnel Psychology, 43*, 501–23; Gist, M., Stevens, C., & Bavetta, A. (1991). Effects of self-efficacy and post-training intervention on the acquisition and maintenance of complex interpersonal skills. *Personnel Psychology, 44*, 837–61.

42. Locke, E. A., & Latham, G. P. (1990). *A theory of goal setting and task performance.* Englewood Cliffs, NJ: Prentice-Hall.

43. Richman-Hirsch, W. L. (2001). Posttraining interventions to enhance transfer: The moderating effects of work environments. *Human Resource Development Quarterly, 12*, 105–20; Wexley, K. N., & Nemeroff, W. F. (1975). Effectiveness of positive reinforcement and goal setting as methods of management development. *Journal of Applied Psychology 60*, 446–50.

44. Richman-Hirsch, W. L. (2001).

45. Holton, E. F. III. (2003). What's really wrong: Diagnosis for learning transfer system change. In E. F. Holton III & T. T. Baldwin (Eds.), *Improving learning transfer in organizations.* San Francisco, CA: John Wiley & Sons, Inc.

46. Holton, E. F. III. (2003).

47. Holton, E. F. III. (2003).

48. Holton, E. F. III., Chen, H., & Naquin, S. S. (2003). An examination of learning transfer system characteristics across organizational settings. *Human Resource Development Quarterly, 14*, 459–82.

Training Evaluation

Chapter Learning Objectives

After reading this chapter, you should be able to:

- define training evaluation and the main reasons for conducting evaluations

- discuss the barriers to evaluation and the factors that affect whether or not an evaluation is conducted

- describe the different types of evaluations

- describe the models of training evaluation and the relationship between them

- describe the main variables to measure in a training evaluation and how they are measured

- discuss the different types of designs for training evaluation as well as their requirements, limits, and when they should be used

www.bell.ca

BELL CANADA

Years ago, when Bell Canada installed a new telephone system for its business clients, it also sent out service advisors whose task it was to train the employees to use the new system. These training sessions consisted of "show-and-tell" activities in which the instructors demonstrated the use of the telephone. Simple as the training was, it was expensive, costing millions of dollars annually. With the introduction of electronic equipment, the functionality of the telephone systems—and complexity for the users—increased exponentially.

Initially, the company attempted to use their traditional training approach with purchasers of the electronic systems. However, a training evaluation was conducted and it showed that the training was not effective. At the end of the training, customer knowledge of the operation of the electronic telephones was quite low.

A number of attempts were then made to improve the situation. Different types of training, presented by either Bell Canada or user personnel, were tried and evaluated. None made any significant difference in terms of training effectiveness.

However, these training evaluation studies did detect an important fact. No matter how training was conducted, the users' knowledge of a limited number of functions—those they used a lot—increased after training, indicating that practise seemed to have a significant effect on learning.

This suggested that providing end users with an instructional aid might help them gain greater benefit from the electronic system. To that end, a special instruction booklet was carefully prepared and trainees were provided with a brief instructional session teaching the users how to use the instruction booklet.

The results of the evaluation showed that the use of the instruction booklet resulted in greater user mastery than the formal training course. Thus, the training evaluation was very useful in a) demonstrating that the traditional training method was ineffective, b) that changing the instructors had no effect, but c) that the use of a well-developed instruction booklet had greater effect.

As a result of the evaluation, the traditional training program was discontinued and replaced with the much shorter instruction on the use of the booklet, thereby saving large amounts of money. Thus, the training evaluation paid off because it directly led to modifications to the instructional strategy and showed that a less expensive alternative (the booklet) was superior to the more expensive traditional approach (formal training).

Training programs are designed to have an effect on learning and behaviour. However, as the Bell Canada story demonstrates, this is not always the case. Fortunately, in that case, the organization launched an evaluation program that involved several studies, the results of which served not only to assess the effectiveness of the existing training but also to identify and test different strategies for improving the situation.

In this chapter, you will learn about the evaluation of training and development programs. In particular, you will learn about the training evaluation models, the different types of evaluation, the variables to measure and how to measure them, as well as the different data collection designs for conducting a training evaluation.

What Is Training Evaluation?

Ⓡ Ⓟ Ⓒ 11.1

Training programs may be launched for a number of reasons: they may be used to improve competencies (e.g., learning new software), to modify attitudes (e.g., preparing a manager posted to an international assignment), and/or to modify behaviours (e.g., leadership training). Organizations invest in improving employee competencies, attitudes, and behaviours because such improvements are expected to lead to positive results for organizations (e.g., improved productivity).

Training evaluation is concerned with whether or not these expected outcomes materialize as a result of training. They are designed to assist decision-making about training programs: Should the organization cancel or continue a training program? Should an existing training program be modified? How should it be modified?

Training evaluation is a process designed to assess the value—the worthiness—of training programs to employees and to organizations. Training evaluation assesses this value by analyzing data collected from trainees, supervisors, or others familiar with the trainees and with the job context. Using a variety of techniques, objective and subjective information is gathered before, during, and after training to provide the data required to estimate the value of a training program.

Training evaluation is not a single procedure. Rather, it is a continuum of techniques, methods, and measures that informs management about the value of training programs. At one end of the continuum lie simple procedures that are easy to implement and that can provide some potentially useful information about the value of a training program. Asking participants how much they enjoyed a training program is one example of a simple evaluation procedure.

At the other end of the training evaluation continuum lie more elaborate procedures. These provide managers with more information of a richer quality about the value of a training program. More involved training evaluations might assess how much of the trained skills trainees apply on the job (i.e., transfer of training) and how much performance improvement has resulted from the training effort. More extensive training evaluations might be used to diagnose the training program's success in enhancing key psychological factors, such as trainee motivation and self-efficacy. Some evaluation designs can even estimate the specific contribution of training to any changes

Training evaluation

A process to assess the value—the worthiness—of training programs to employees and to organizations

observed in the organization, sometimes in dollar terms. The more sophisticated the design, the more complete the information, the better the conclusions, and the greater the confidence with which they can be stated.

However, more sophisticated evaluation procedures are more costly and more complex and difficult to implement. Hence, the quality and completeness of the information gathered involves a trade-off with the costs and complexity of the techniques chosen. In some cases, less sophisticated evaluation procedures may be quite suitable, while in other cases the same procedures will not yield useful information.[1] Conversely, very sophisticated procedures required in one situation might be overkill in another. The key is that the specific training evaluation procedures required depend on the specifics of the training situation and on the decisions that need to be made as a result of that evaluation.

Why Conduct Training Evaluations?

The evaluation of training programs and systems is done for many reasons. In the contemporary business environment, understaffing is chronically prevalent. With little time available for training, it is critical that employees and organizations waste little of it on unprofitable training programs. Guided by evaluation results, it is a managerial responsibility to improve training. Training evaluation is therefore of value to:

- Assist managers in identifying the training programs most applicable to employees and to assist management in the determination of who should be trained.
- Determine the cost benefits of a program and to help ascertain which program or training technique is most cost-effective (see Chapter 12).
- Determine if the training program has achieved the expected results or solved the problem for which training was the anticipated solution.
- Diagnose the strengths and weaknesses of a program and pinpoint needed improvements.
- Use the evaluation information to justify and reinforce the value and credibility of the training function to the organization.

Although in practice, training evaluation in most organizations was stagnant for many decades, the last years saw signs that things are beginning to change.[2] Recent industry surveys by the American Society for Training and Development (ASTD)—the major professional association in the field—have begun to formally monitor the evaluation activities of organizations. This signals a growing interest in evaluation as a mechanism for improving training and development.

Barriers to Training Evaluation

Because of the usefulness of training evaluation, many organizations conduct some form of evaluation for most of their training programs. The most recent ASTD[3] survey showed that three quarters of organizations conduct some evaluation of their training programs and that the best companies conduct more of the complex and sophisticated training evaluations. It remains, however, that the overwhelming majority of training evaluations are simple, limited to trainee reactions. A survey of Canadian training evaluation practices found a similar pattern of results.[4] According to The Conference Board of Canada, most organizations (83 percent) evaluate trainee reactions; more than a third (37 percent) evaluate learning; nearly a quarter (23 percent) evaluate behaviour; and only 12 percent evaluate organizational results.[5]

Studies of training professionals[6] showed that many employers do not conduct training evaluations because they are perceived to be too complicated to implement, too time consuming, and/or too expensive. Some training managers do not conduct evaluations because top management does not demand them and because it is difficult to isolate the effects of training among many other variables that might also be having an effect on employees and the organization. Thus, barriers to training evaluation fall into two categories: pragmatic and political.

Pragmatic Barriers to Training Evaluation

Evaluating training programs requires knowledge about research design, measurement, and data analysis. Understandably, some training managers feel insecure about taking on such a task. However, the training evaluation process has been unduly mystified. The principles, techniques, and procedures involved in training evaluation are logical and straightforward, and most can be easily implemented. Moreover, training evaluations require that information (objective and/or perceptual measures) about trainees be gathered from the trainees, their supervisors, and/or co-workers, and in some cases even by subordinates. These measures are sometimes collected before and after training as well as after trainees return to the job. Valuable training and job time needs to be diverted to these data collection tasks, and many managers hesitate or are unable to tax the organizational resources for the purpose of evaluation. However, with the advent of modern information technologies (e.g., Web-based questionnaires and computerized work performance data) the disruptive impact of data collection can now be seriously eased.

Political Barriers to Training Evaluation

Evaluations are conducted when there is pressure from management to do so (see Training Today). In the absence of such pressures, many training managers would rather forego the exercise. One risk associated with training evaluation is that they might demonstrate that part of, or an entire training program, is not effective. Whereas this should be considered a valuable finding (as in the Bell Canada case), some trainers fear that negative evaluation results might reflect poorly on them, the training function, and the training choices they make. Moreover, some trainers do not conduct evaluations themselves because this might be perceived as a conflict of interest (how can the person doing the training also be the one responsible for evaluating its effectiveness?). As a result, many feel that evaluations should be conducted by external professionals, thus siphoning funds from the training budget.

Diverting training money to cover evaluation costs is a choice that, understandably, many training managers find difficult, especially as this might affect the number of training programs and participants that can be accommodated by the training and development function. However, as long as training managers make use of the established methods of evaluation and document them, there is little ground for concern about conflict of interest.

RPC 11.2 ## Types of Training Evaluation

Most training evaluations focus on the impact of a training program on trainees' perceptions and behaviours. Perceptions are assessed through questionnaire measures while behavioural data may require a combination of techniques including self-reports, observation, and performance data. Evaluations may be distinguished from each other with respect to the data gathered and analyzed, and the fundamental purpose for which the evaluation is being conducted.

1. **The data collected:** Evaluations differ with respect to the type of information that is gathered and how that is accomplished.
   a. The most common training evaluations rely *on trainee perceptions at the conclusion of training* (did the participants like it?) while more

---

Training Today

Upper Management's Role in Training Evaluation

A few years ago, there was a rash of serious accidents among employees of a large transportation company. Some of these accidents were the direct or indirect result of operator errors due to the consumption of drugs and alcohol. As a result, the firm declared a zero-tolerance policy concerning the use of such substances. The policy required that no employee may use substances that may impair effective and safe job performance, whether or not these substances are legal. The key element of the policy was that all supervisors were directly and personally responsible for enforcing the policy. Supervisors who failed to enforce the policy would themselves be subject to sanctions that could include dismissal.

The training department was directed to develop and administer a training program to all supervisory and managerial personnel in the company. However, the CEO of the company also insisted that the training program be evaluated to ensure that it was effective. As a result, the training department, which normally only administered "smile sheets" to evaluate their training programs, launched a much more sophisticated training evaluation program that included three measurement times and the collection of information on dozens of variables. Clearly, this effort was launched because the training program had attained high visibility and because top management demanded it. The training evaluation did uncover some problems with the training program and suggested a number of changes. However, none of these changes were ever implemented. This occurred because top management showed no interest in the results of the evaluation study, as these became available several months after the training program was administered.

The moral of the story is that high-level visibility can stimulate evaluation actions. However, maintaining that visibility is important to ensure that the evaluation results will prove of practical use.

sophisticated evaluations go further to analyze the extent of trainee learning and the post-training behaviour of trainees.

b. More recently, there has been a growing emphasis on evaluation studies that also assess the *psychological forces* that operate during training programs and that impact outcome measures such as learning and behaviour change. Research in this area has helped to identify psychological states (affective, cognitive, and skills-based) that are important training outcomes because of the influence they have on learning as well as to improvements in job behaviours.[7]

c. Finally, information about the *work environment* to which the trainee returns can be useful in evaluation.[8] For example, measures of training transfer climate and a learning culture have been developed.[9] Training programs provided by organizations that rank higher in terms of these dimensions tend to be more effective. Specific organizational events and policies—such as on-the-job opportunities to practice new skills or trainee expectations about the type of support they will receive on the job—have been found to influence training success.[10] Other studies showed that (self-reported) transfer of training was higher for trainees who perceived a strong alignment between training and the firm's strategic vision, and training was more effective in firms that tie performance and rewards more tightly.[11]

2. **The purpose of the evaluation:** Evaluations also differ with respect to their purposes. Worthen and Sanders distinguished between *formative evaluation* and *summative evaluation*.[12]

a. **Formative training evaluations** are designed to help evaluators assess the value of the training materials and processes with the key goal of identifying improvements to the instructional experience (the clarity, complexity, and relevance of the training contents, how they are presented, and the training context). Hence, formative evaluation provides data that is of special interest to training designers and instructors.

b. **Summative evaluations** are designed to provide data about a training program's worthiness or effectiveness: Has the training program resulted in pay-offs for the organization? Cost-benefit analyses (see Chapter 12) are usually summative. Economic indices are often an integral and important part of these types of evaluations; consequently, organizational managers show great interest in these results.

A further distinction can be made between *descriptive* and *causal evaluations*. **Descriptive evaluations** provide information describing trainees once they have completed the program. What has the trainee learned in training? Is the trainee more confident about using the skill? Is it used on the job? Most evaluation designs have descriptive components. **Causal evaluations** are used to determine if the training caused the post-training behaviours. Causal evaluations require more sophisticated experimental and statistical procedures.

Formative evaluations

Provide data about various aspects of a training program

Summative evaluations

Provide data about the worthiness or effectiveness of a training program

Descriptive evaluations

Provide information that describes the trainee once he or she has completed a training program

Causal evaluations

Provide information to determine if training *caused* the post-training behaviours

Models of Training Evaluation

Models of training evaluation specify the information (the variables) that needs to be measured in training evaluation and their interrelationships. The dominant training evaluation model is Donald Kirkpatrick's hierarchical model.[13] However, research and practical experience has indicated that Kirkpatrick's model can be improved. COMA and the Decision-Based Evaluation models are two recent efforts in that direction.[14]

Kirkpatrick's Hierarchical Model: The Four Levels of Training Evaluation

Donald Kirkpatrick's hierarchical model is the oldest, best known, and most frequently used training evaluation model. It identifies four levels of training evaluation criteria. According to this model, a training program is "effective" when:

L1. Trainees report positive reactions to a training program (Level 1 = reactions).

L2. Trainees learn the training material (Level 2 = learning).

L3. Trainees apply what they learn in training on the job (Level 3 = behaviours).

L4. Training has a positive effect on organizational outcomes (Level 4 = results).

The model states that the four levels are arranged in a hierarchy, such that each succeeding level provides more important information than the previous level. The model also assumes that all levels are positively related to one another and that each level has a causal effect on the next level. Hence, positive trainee reactions (L1) cause trainees to learn more (L2), which in turn leads to the behavioural display of the new skill at work (L3), which, in turn, impacts on organizational effectiveness (L4)—the ultimate reason for conducting training in organizations. Thus, a complete training evaluation would assess all four levels.

Critique of Kirkpatrick's Model

The contribution of Kirkpatrick's model to training evaluation cannot be underestimated. Organizations evaluate training more frequently now than in the past, largely because of the Kirkpatrick model. Organizations have adopted the model because it makes good sense to managers and trainers alike as it is a clear and simple systematic framework for assessing training. It has greatly demystified training evaluation and provided an impetus for research. As a result, we now know considerably more about the model than was the case when it was introduced, more than 35 years ago. Whereas there is general agreement that the four levels are indeed important outcomes to be assessed, other aspects of the model including its completeness have been questioned.

Research studies, especially those conducted by Elwood Holton (who concludes that Kirkpatrick's is *not* a model!) and by George Alliger and his colleagues have thrown doubt on the validity of the hierarchical aspect of the model.[15] The model would be valid if a positive correlation exists between the four levels. Hence enjoyment (L1) would be correlated with learning (L2) and learning correlated with transfer (L3) and so on. In fact, that is not the case. The correlations between the levels are small or non-existent. Most students can easily explain this result: one may have learned little from an otherwise pleasant course or learned a great deal from a hated one (as exemplified by biochemistry for one of the authors!). As a further example, most people know that smoking is not healthy, yet many still do it—knowledge and behaviours are not synonymous. In short, the hierarchical aspect of the Kirkpatrick model lacks empirical support.

This flaw does not affect the effectiveness of the Kirkpatrick model for conducting summative evaluations, where global pay-off is the main interest. The model remains helpful because no matter the relationships between the levels, there is intrinsic value in assessing whether the training programs leads to learning (L2), results in a pay-off to the organization (L4), or is boring (L1). However, relying on it can prove a handicap in formative evaluations where the goal is to use the results to improve training effectiveness. When "something goes wrong" with a training program (for example low transfer), the model does not indicate the specific nature of the problem or what to do about it. For example, as the relationship between learning and behaviour is small, improving L1 (reactions) or L2 (learning) is unlikely to improve transfer levels. As the model collects no other information (such as trainee motivation, self-efficacy or conditions of the organization) it is unable to provide assistance in the formative evaluation process. For these applications, therefore, the Kirkpatrick model is insufficiently diagnostic.

The model has also been criticized for its lack of precision in the outcomes. For example it fails to specify what is meant by "L2-learning" (Declarative? Procedural? See Chapter 3) or by "L1-reactions." To demonstrate this last point, we used seven different terms to describe L1 in the preceding paragraphs (hated, enjoyment, like, pleasant, boring, detested, interesting). These are all reactions but they do not describe equivalent realities. Similar arguments can be made for the other levels.

But perhaps the most important critique has been that Kirkpatrick requires *all* training evaluations to rely on the same variables and outcome measures. The current view is that the type of evaluation, as well as the measures and procedures, should be selected as a function of the organizational situation and the purposes of the evaluation. One model does not fit all in training evaluation situations. To that end, two improvements to Kirkpatrick's models have been proposed: COMA and DBE.

COMA Model

Haccoun, Jeanrie, and Saks proposed the **COMA** model as a mechanism for enhancing the usefulness of training evaluation questionnaires by identifying and measuring those variables that research has shown to be important for the transfer of training.[16] Instead of relying exclusively on reaction and declarative learning measures, COMA suggests the measurement of variables that

COMA

A training evaluation model that involves the measurement of Cognitive, Organizational, Motivational, and Attitudinal variables

Chapter 11: Training Evaluation

fall into four categories: cognitive, organizational environment, motivational, and attitudinal variables. These can all be measured by questionnaires administered before and immediately after the training session.

- **Cognitive** variables refer to the level of learning that the trainee has gained from a training program. Both declarative and procedural learning might be measured, but the latter is more important because it is more strongly related to transfer than the former.
- **Organizational** environment refers to a cluster of variables that are generated by the work environment and that impact transfer of training. This includes the learning culture, the opportunity to practice, and the degree of support that is provided to trainees once they return to the job.
- **Motivation** refers to the desire to learn and transfer on the job what was presented in training. As indicated in Chapter 10, motivation has been shown to be a powerful and persistent influence on the transfer of training. COMA suggests that motivation to learn (measured at the onset of the program) and motivation to transfer (measured immediately after) both be measured.
- **Attitudes** refer to individuals' feelings and thinking processes. Chief among these beliefs are self-efficacy, perceptions of control, and expectations about self and the environment.

According to the COMA model, training evaluation should assess the degree to which trainees have mastered the skills ("**C**"); accurately perceive that the organizational environment (including peers and supervisors) will support and help them apply the skills ("**O**"); are motivated to learn and to apply the skills on the job ("**M**"); and have developed attitudes and beliefs that allow them to feel capable of applying their newly acquired skills on the job ("**A**").

COMA improves upon the Kirkpatrick model in three ways: it integrates in the reaction questionnaires a greater number of measures (the COMA variables); the measures added *are* causally related to training success (See Chapter 10: Transfer of Training); and it defines these new variables with greater precision. As the COMA model is still relatively new, it is too early to conclude as to its value. Nevertheless, COMA's focus is limited to an analysis of the factors that impact on transfer only. Moreover, COMA does not specify how training evaluations should be conducted. Decision-Based Evaluation, the third evaluation model to be discussed, resolves some of these issues.

Decision-Based Evaluation Model

Decision-Based Evaluation (DBE)

A training evaluation model that specifies the target, focus, and methods of evaluation

Decision-Based Evaluation (DBE) is a model recently developed by Kurt Kraiger. As with the Kirkpatrick and COMA model, Decision-Based Evaluation specifies the variables to be measured. However, it goes further than either of the two preceding models in that DBE identifies the *target* of the evaluation (what do we wish to find out from the evaluation?); its *focus* (what are the variables we will measure?); and it suggests the *methods* that may be appropriate for conducting the evaluation.

The model specifies three potential "targets" for the evaluation: 1. Trainee change, 2. Organizational pay-off, and 3. Program improvement. If trainee change is of consequence, the evaluator is directed to specify the "focus" of the change: Are we interested in assessing the level of trainee changes with respect to learning, behaviours, or to the psychological states (such as motivation and self-efficacy)? Each evaluation study may include one or more foci. Once the focus or foci are selected, the model suggests the appropriate data collection method (e.g., surveys, job sample information, objective data, etc).

Decision-Based Evaluation may well be a marked improvement, for different reasons, over both Kirkpatrick's model and the COMA model. Unlike Kirkpatrick's model, it identifies and ties the specific variables that should be measured in the evaluation (focus) depending on the chosen target. Unlike COMA, DBE is general to any evaluation goals (targets), not just transfer of training. Further, it is the only model that also specifies the types of methods that can be used for an evaluation. And most importantly, DBE is a flexible model. It does not advocate a *one best way* for training evaluation nor does it compel the measurement of a single set of variables (as do Kirkpatrick and COMA) for all evaluations. DBE is the only training evaluation model that clearly specifies that evaluations must always be guided by a key question: What is the target of the evaluation? However, as with COMA, this model is recent and it remains to be tested more fully.

Training Evaluation Variables

RPC 11.4

Training evaluation requires that data be collected on important aspects of training. Some of these variables have been identified in the training evaluation models. Table 11.1 provides a more complete list of the main variables that can be measured in training evaluation and how that is accomplished.

Training evaluation variables are relatively easy to develop. In this section, we will review some of the basic techniques and formats that may be used to develop them. Table 11.2 shows sample questions and formats for measuring each type of variable.

Reactions

Trainee opinions and attitudes about a training program are usually measured immediately following training. Typically, they are survey-type questions in which trainees indicate their answers on a rating scale. Reaction measures are easy to administer, collect, and analyze, and the questions may focus on the trainees' overall reactions to a training program (e.g., Overall, how satisfied were you with the training program?) and/or on specific elements of a program (e.g., To what extent were you satisfied with the instructor?).

In a major study involving thousands of responses to reaction questionnaires, Morgan and Casper identified six dimensions that underlie reaction measures: satisfaction with the instructor, the training process, the materials, the course structure, the assessment process, and the perceived usefulness (utility) of the training.[17]

TABLE 11.1

The Main Variables Measured in Training Evaluation

VARIABLE	DEFINITION	HOW MEASURED
Reactions	Trainee perceptions of the program and/or specific aspects of the course.	Questionnaires, focus groups, interviews.
Learning	Trainee acquisition of the program material. Declarative learning is knowing the information. Procedural knowledge is being able to translate that knowledge into a behavioural sequence.	Multiple choice or True-False tests (declarative); situational and mastery tests (procedural).
Behaviour	On-the-job behaviour display, objective performance measures.	Self-reports, supervisory reports, direct and indirect observations, production records.
Motivation	Trainee desire to learn and/or transfer skills.	Questionnaires.
Self-efficacy	Trainee confidence in learning and/or behaviour display on the job.	Questionnaires.
Perceived and/or anticipated support	The assistance trainees obtain and/or the assistance trainees expect.	Questionnaires.
Organizational perceptions	How trainees perceive the organization's culture and climate for learning and transfer.	Standardized questionnaires.
Organizational results	The impact of training on organizational outcomes.	Organizational records.

Affective reactions

Reaction measures that assess trainees' *likes and dislikes* of a training program

Utility reactions

Reaction measures that assess the perceived *usefulness* of a training program

Reaction measures can be quite different, but two types have received the most attention: affective and utility reaction measures. **Affective reactions** assess trainees' *likes and dislikes* of a training program. **Utility reactions** refer to the perceived *usefulness* of a training program.

Whereas trainers are interested in the likes and dislikes of trainees (affective reactions), research has shown that affective reaction measures bear little relationship to other important training outcomes including learning and

TABLE 11.2

Examples of Questions and Formats Used in Training Evaluations

VARIABLE	EXAMPLE OF QUESTION	EXAMPLE OF ANSWER FORMAT
Reactions	"How much of the course content can be applied in your job?" (utility reaction measure)	1 = None, 2 = Little, 3 = Some, 4 = Much, 5 = All.
	"How satisfied were you with the content of the program?" (affective reaction measure)	1 = Not at all satisfied, 2 = Not satisfied, 3 = Somewhat satisfied; 4 = Satisfied, 5 = Very satisfied
Declarative learning	Declarative: True or False: The earth is square.	Declarative True ____ False ____
	Multiple choice: What statement best describes the earth?	Multiple choice: round, square, triangular, flat.
Procedural learning	Procedural Mastery: You need to write a letter using a computer. From the list below pick the four steps required to do so and list them in the order with which they should be performed.	Procedural Step Required Order Turn computer on Yes 1 Set the margins Yes 4 Select "new document" Yes 3 Open the word processor Yes 2 Test the hard drive No —

(Continued)

TABLE 11.2 *(Continued)*

VARIABLE	EXAMPLE OF QUESTION	EXAMPLE OF ANSWER FORMAT
Behaviour	Self-report: How many "cold calls" have you made in the last week? Observation: By others including the supervisor and the analyst. May also include subordinates or customers.	Open-ended frequency scale (number of times) or rating scale: 1 = Always, 2 = Sometimes, 3 = Rarely, 4 = Never.
Motivation	How important is it to reduce accidents at work?	1 = Very important, 2 = Important, 3 = Neither important nor unimportant, 4 = Somewhat unimportant, 5 = Very unimportant
	The consequences to you of applying the behaviour at work?	Will make my job 1 = much harder, 2 = somewhat harder, 3 = no effect, 4 = somewhat easier, 5 = much easier
	How likely is it that if you do apply the trained behaviours there will be fewer accidents?	1 = Extremely likely, 2 = Somewhat likely, 3 = Neither likely nor unlikely, 4 = Unlikely, 5 = Extremely unlikely
	The product of the three sets of questions produces the motivator scores.	
Self-efficacy	How confident are you that you can explain the new policy to your subordinates?	1 = Not at all confident, 2, 3, 4, to 5 = Very confident.
Perceived and/or anticipated support	I expect that my supervisor will help and support me in my attempts to apply my new skills on the job.	1 = Completely disagree, 2, 3, 4, to 5 = Completely agree.
Organizational perceptions	Supervisors give recognition and credit to those who apply new knowledge and skills to their work.	Standardized questionnaires.
Organizational results	How much has quality improved as a result of the training program?	Number of units rejected per day; number of items returned per month; number of customer complaints per week.

behaviour. On the other hand, *utility* reaction measures demonstrate some relationship to learning and behaviour.[18] Hence, collecting utility reactions is important because they tell us somewhat more about whether or not the trainee will transfer newly acquired skills to the job than do affective reactions.

Irrespective of the type of reaction measure used, they can be collected in a number of ways. The most common method is a questionnaire that is administered at the end of a training program. The questions are listed on one side of the page and a rating scale is placed next to each question (see Table 11.3 for an example). However, reactions can also be measured by open-ended discussions with trainees using focus groups or interviews though such an approach might prove to be more expensive and time consuming and more subject to the biases of the interviewer, especially if the interviewer is also the course designer or leader.

The questions and the answers may be formatted in any number of different ways: 1. In the form of a statement (e.g., "The course materials captured my interest.") for which the trainee indicates his/her degree of agreement (from strongly agree to strongly disagree) or 2. In the form of direct questions (e.g., "How effective was the instructor?") to which the trainee chooses a response from a linear rating scale (from very effective to very ineffective). Most rating scales have between four and seven response choices though more or fewer points can be used.

No matter their relationship to other training outcomes, immediate post-training reaction measures remain somewhat useful because: 1. They are easy to collect and analyze and are easily understood by managers and employees alike; 2. They provide trainers with immediate feedback on their course; 3. Trainees who have had a chance to comment on a program and make suggestions for improvements might be more motivated to transfer their learning than others who leave a program without providing input; and 4. They are so frequently used they are easy and convenient mechanism for measuring, in addition to utility reactions, the variables identified through the COMA or DBE models.

Learning

Although there are many types of learning outcomes that can be measured (Jonassen and Tessmer[19] identify more than 10!), most training evaluations measure "declarative" learning. In rare cases, some evaluators also assess "procedural" learning. The contents of both the declarative and procedural learning measures are selected from the training content.

Declarative learning is by far the most frequently assessed learning measure. It refers to the acquisition of facts and information. **Procedural learning** involves the organization of facts and information into a smooth behavioural sequence. Research has shown that declarative learning has only a minor effect on behaviours. Procedural learning, however, is more strongly related to a number of training outcomes including transfer of training.

Declarative learning is usually assessed with multiple choice or true-false type questions. Students familiar with college or university exams know about these tests of learning. Table 11.4 presents an array of these options. The test

Declarative learning

Refers to the acquisition of facts and information and is by far the most frequently assessed learning measure

Procedural learning

Refers to the organization of facts and information into a smooth behavioural sequence

TABLE 11.3

| Reactions Rating Form |

Course or Session: _____

Instructor: _____

Content:

Please answer the following questions using the scale below:

1. strongly disagree 2. disagree 3. neither disagree nor agree 4. agree 5. strongly agree

_____ The material presented will be useful to me on the job.

_____ The level of information was too advanced for my work.

_____ The level of information presented was too elementary for me.

_____ The information was presented in manageable chunks.

_____ Theories and concepts were linked to work activities.

_____ The course material was up-to-date and reliable.

Instructor:

Please rate the instructor's performance along the following dimensions:

_____ Needs improvement.

_____ Just right, or competent, effective.

_____ Superior or very effective performance.

The instructor:

_____ Described the objectives of the session.

_____ Had a plan for the session.

_____ Followed the plan.

_____ Determined trainees' current knowledge.

_____ Explained new terms.

_____ Used work and applied examples.

_____ Provided opportunities for questions.

_____ Was enthusiastic about the topic.

_____ Presented material clearly.

_____ Effectively summarized the material.

_____ Varied the learning activities.

_____ Showed a personal interest in class progress.

_____ Demonstrated a desire for trainees to learn.

Perceived Impact:

_____ I gained significant new knowledge.

_____ I developed skills in the area.

_____ I was given tools for attacking problems.

_____ My on-the-job performance will improve.

Please indicate what you will do differently on the job as a result of this course.

Overall Rating:

Taking into account all aspects of the course, how would you rate it?

_____ Excellent _____ Very Good _____ Good _____ Fair _____ Poor

Would you take another course from this instructor? _____ Yes _____ No

Would you recommend this course to your colleagues? _____ Yes _____ No

TABLE 11.4

Declarative Learning Test Formats

PART A: OBJECTIVELY SCORED TESTS

True or False

1. A test is valid if a person receives approximately the same result or score at two different testing times. True _____ False _____

Multiple Choice

2. The affective domain of learning refers to

   _____ skills

   _____ attitudes

   _____ knowledge

   _____ all of the above

   _____ 2 and 3

Matching

3. For each of the governments listed on the left, select the appropriate responsibility for training and place its letter next to the term.

   _____ 1. federal   a. displaced workers

   _____ 2. provincial   b. language training

   _____ 3. municipal   c. student summer work

Short Answer

4. Kirkpatrick identified four levels of measurement. These are:

PART B: SUBJECTIVELY SCORED TESTS

Essay

5. Describe the similarities between Kirkpatrick, COMA, and DBE.

Oral

6. The measurement of training has many potential benefits. Identify these benefits. Discuss the reasons why, given these advantages of measurement, most trainers do not evaluate training.

Observation Checklist

7. The customer service representative:

   _____ greeted the customer

   _____ approached the customer

   _____ offered to help

Rating Scale

8. Indicate the degree to which you agree or disagree with the statements below:

   Scale: 1 = strongly disagree 2 = disagree 3 = agree 4 = strongly agree

   During a selection interview, the interviewer:

   used behavioural–based questions   1 2 3 4

   looked for contrary evidence   1 2 3 4

   used probing questions   1 2 3 4

Diaries, Anecdotal Records, Journals

9. In your journal, write about your experiences working with someone from a different culture. Record the date, time, and reason for the interaction. Describe how you felt and what you learned.

items listed in Part A are termed "objectively scored" tests because there is only one correct answer possible. Part B gives some examples of "subjectively scored" test items. Test items that are considered subjective are essay questions, oral interviews, journals, and diaries. Here, several answers might be acceptable, and markers have some latitude in their interpretation of the correctness of the answer, which potentially exposes that judgment to "subjective" biases.

Procedural learning, however, is rarely measured because the development of such measures is much more complex. Desjardins developed a procedural learning measure for a "protecting a crime scene" course given to police officers where the police officers learned the do's and don'ts when called to a crime scene.[20] She interviewed task experts who demonstrated the proper actions and proper sequence of behaviours required and then summarized these steps, added some unnecessary and incorrect steps, and shifted the order of the steps. Trainees had to distinguish between the required and erroneous steps and reposition them into the correct order. Completing this task successfully requires procedural understanding of the training content.

Cheri Ostroff used another approach to develop a measure of procedural learning.[21] Education managers were instructed on how to interact with parents more effectively in tense situations. Different anecdotes drawn from real experience were presented to trainees along with four different ways of handling each situation. The four options were carefully constructed. Trainees who had acquired a basic comprehension of the principles of conflict management would tend to select one option, while those with sophisticated comprehension levels would select another. The intermediate choices reflected comprehension levels between these extremes.

Procedural learning measures can also involve simulations conducted in realistic situations. For example, a pilot could be tested in a virtual-reality airplane. The skills of a drug counselor could be tested using actors as drug addicts. A test could be conducted as a role play (for negotiation skills) or a practice session (for tennis certification). These tests are usually called performance tests or work sample tests.

Learning measures also vary in terms of when they are administered. For example, some researchers have divided learning measures into three subcategories: 1. Immediate post-training knowledge, which measures trainee learning immediately after a training program; 2. Knowledge retention, which measures trainee learning sometime after a training program; and 3. Behaviour or skill demonstration, which measures trainees' ability to perform the training task during the training program.

Learning measures are useful for a number of reasons besides determining if trainees have learned the training material. For example, a testing hurdle anticipated at the end of a course increases trainees' motivation to learn the material.[22] For trainees at General Dynamics this was important because they were not allowed access to the manufacturing resource planning software until they had passed a competency test.

The information that learning tests provide to trainers is invaluable. In cases of accidents and litigation, the employer can prove that the employee was trained to the necessary levels. Furthermore, if trainees consistently score low on some aspect of the course, the trainer is alerted to the fact that this component needs to be revised. More information may be required or exercises might have to be added to ensure that learning does occur. At General Dynamics, trainers became extremely motivated because the trainees had to learn and could not be brushed off by hinting that they could "always learn misunderstood material back on the job." However, the trainer cannot assume that scoring well on tests necessarily means doing well on the job. It is on the job where the real measurement of the pay-off of training begins.

Behaviour

Behaviour refers to the display of the newly learned skills or competencies on the job. This is also what we have referred to in Chapter 10 as "transfer of training" and is arguably the most important of all training effectiveness criteria.[23] The behaviours assessed should be those identified by the training objectives (see Chapter 5). Behaviours can be measured using three approaches:

a. *Self-reports*: The trainee indicates if and/or how often he or she has used the newly trained behaviours on the job.

b. *Observations*: Others observe and record whether and/or how often the trainee has used the newly trained behaviours on the job. Typically it is supervisors who provide these observations, but depending on the opportunity to observe the trained person, trainers, subordinates, or even clients can provide it.

c. *Production indicators*: The trainee's objective output is assessed through productivity records, such as sales or absenteeism.

Self-reports remain the most frequently used measures of behaviours.[24] However, the accuracy of self-report measures can be problematic. How do we know that people are accurately remembering and reporting their own behaviours? It is generally agreed that self-reports tend to be *inaccurate* although they might yet be *valid*. The distinction between accuracy and validity is important. Studies comparing self-reports of absenteeism with company records of absence show that in general, people tend to report fewer absences than were actually taken (low accuracy). However, people who are more absent tend to self-report more absences than those who have fewer absences (validity). Hence, although self-reports are unable to measure transfer in absolute terms, they are able to reveal trends.

Observations by others (mainly supervisors) are sometimes used to measure behaviour. Typically, the observer rates whether or not the person has used the behaviour and/or how often that has occurred. As with self-reports, the issue of accuracy is of significance here. Moreover, the person's opportunity to observe the behaviour is very important. Observational data is more useful when there is strong evidence to suggest that the observer has extensive contact with the trainee thus enabling frequent observations.

For both self-report and observational data, it is important that the measure focus on specific behaviours (how many times in the last month has the trainee used the new machine) as opposed to general ones (has the trainee applied the skill on the job?). Measures of specific behaviours are more likely to be valid and accurate.

Performance indices (sometimes called "objective" measures) are a third type of behaviour data that might be gathered in an evaluation of behaviour. Performance indicators, such as sales performance, can often be obtained directly from company records. They are more frequently used when the evaluator is interested in measuring the impact of training on job performance.

In some cases, performance records can provide highly precise data on specific behaviours. For example, "the number of times that a trainee has accessed a database" can provide highly accurate behaviour data for evaluating a training program designed to train people in the use and application of a database. With the advent of computer technology, it is now increasingly easy to rely on this information to gauge training success. For example, in the Bell Canada opening case computerized records were used to accurately measure, for each trainee, his/her extent of use of each feature of the electronic telephone. However, performance indices are *not always* the best measure as they sometimes contaminate individual performance with other events that impact performance. For example, one "objective" measure of a telephone operator might be the number of calls he or she has taken in an hour. However, that data might not lead to accurate conclusions as the number of calls an operator takes is also affected by the number of calls that are received. Similarly, the performance of a salesperson is influenced by external factors such as sales territory and competition in addition to the salesperson's behaviour.

Xerox uses many methods to ascertain behaviour, including post-course observations of trainees performing their jobs, interviews with their managers, and a review of performance appraisal forms.[25] TD Bank uses a very simple approach. Participants in training programs are asked to describe three or four examples of when they used the new knowledge or skill on the job.[26]

Whatever the approach used, behaviour data collection should take place only after the trainee has become comfortable with the newly acquired skills and has had opportunities to demonstrate them on the job. The time lag for the assessment of behaviour can range from a few weeks to as much as two years, in the case of managerial skills. It is recommended that the measurement of behaviour take place at several points following a training program in order to determine the long-term effects of a training program.

Motivation

Training evaluators consider two types of motivation in the training context: Motivation to learn and the motivation to apply (transfer) the skill on the job. As described in Chapter 3, motivation to learn is a very important factor that influences training success. A number of scales have been designed to measure motivation to learn.[27]

Although there are no definitive and established methods to assess motivation to transfer, one important technique relies on expectancy theory (described in Chapter 3). Three sets of items are used to measure the valence (the attractiveness of transfer outcomes), instrumentalities (the positive or negative consequences of transfer), and expectancies (the probability that transfer will result in successful performance). The principle is that trainees will be motivated to apply the training when they attach importance to the end result of training (valence), that the attainment of that end result leads to positive consequences or avoids negative ones (instrumentalities), and that applying the training is likely to lead to the desired end result (expectancies).

A study by Haccoun and Savard exemplifies the measurement of motivation to transfer. Trainees (supervisors) were trained to apply a new organizational policy designed to reduce employee absenteeism (among other things). Motivation was measured through three sets of questions. 1. Valence: How important is it that absence be reduced in your work group? 2. Instrumentality: If you reduce absence what would be the consequences (positive or negative) for you? And 3. Expectancy: If you did apply the behaviours taught in training, how likely is it that absence levels would drop? Each question was rated on a five-point rating scale. The product of the three sets of answers (Valence X Instrumentality X Expectancy) produces the transfer motivation score.

Self-Efficacy

As described in Chapter 3, self-efficacy refers to the beliefs that trainees hold about their ability to perform the behaviours that were taught in a training program. Self-efficacy assesses a person's *confidence* in engaging in *specific* behaviours or achieving specific goals.

Self-efficacy is measured relative to a specific behavioural target. Measures of self-efficacy vary but most tend to focus on assessing trainees' level of confidence for performing specific tasks and behaviours. In one option people rate the likelihood of obtaining a certain result followed by ratings of the confidence they have in obtaining that result. For example, a measure of self-efficacy for an exam on training evaluation might read as follows: "Are you likely to obtain 50%; 60%; 70%; 80%; 90%; 100% on an exam on training evaluation?" (Yes/No response to each option). Next, the person rates how confident they are about obtaining the grade for each "Yes" response. The question might read: "How confident are you that you can obtain that grade?" (0 = Not confident at all, 10 = Totally confident). Another simple method lists the key behaviours demonstrating transfer and asks trainees to rate each on a confidence scale such as: "How confident are you that you will obtain at least 70% on the training evaluation exam?" The response scales would range from totally confident to not at all confident. Although 10-point rating scales are common, scales employing a smaller number of points are also frequently used.

Perceived and/or Anticipated Support

As indicated in Chapter 10, the support provided to trainees as they return to work is a very important component of transfer and training effectiveness. Two important measures of support are perceived support and anticipated support. **Perceived support** refers to the degree to which the trainee reports receiving support in his or her attempts to transfer the learned skills. **Anticipated support** refers to the degree to which the trainee expects to be supported in his or her attempts to transfer the learned skills.

Perceived support
The degree to which the trainee reports receiving support in his or her attempts to transfer the learned skills

Anticipated support
The degree to which the trainee expects to be supported in his or her attempts to transfer the learned skills

The measurement of perceived and/or anticipated support can be easily constructed for any training program. Specific questions can be designed to include the source of the support (e.g., supervisor, co-workers, or the organization) and the support (perceived or anticipated) in applying the training content in general and/or in transferring specific aspects of the training program.

For example, in a study on the effects of a training program that trained nurses on a model of nursing, questions about anticipated support included: "If I am having difficulty writing a nursing care plan, I know I can obtain (very little—very much) help from my supervisor." An alternative phrasing could be "Based on my previous experiences, I think I can count on (very little—very much) support from my co-workers in applying the training content to my job."

Notice that in the nursing study, the first formulation of the question refers to a specific component of the training program (i.e., nursing care plan) while the latter refers to the training program content in general. These two items also differ in terms of the source of support with the former being one's supervisor and the latter being co-workers. The respondents use a rating scale to fill in the blank spaces (1 = Very little, 5 = Very much). Similar items can be constructed to refer to key parts of a training program and then administered before training to measure anticipated support and then again once trainees have completed training and returned to work to measure perceived support. In their study, Haccoun and Savard measured anticipated support (immediately after training) and both (perceived) actual support and transfer as assessed two years later. They show that the greater the discrepancy between anticipated and actual supports, the lower the transfer. Expecting help from organizational contexts that do not provide it depresses transfer.

Organizational Perceptions

Several researchers have designed scales to measure perceptions of the transfer climate and a learning culture which were discussed in Chapters 4 and 10. Transfer climate can be assessed via a questionnaire developed by Janice Rouiller and Irwin Goldstein. The questionnaire consists of a number of questions that identify eight sets of "cues" that can trigger trainee reactions that encourage or discourage the trainee to transfer the skill. The eight scales include: goal cues, social cues, task and structural cues, positive feedback, negative feedback, punishment, no feedback, and self-control. Trainees are asked questions about training-specific characteristics of the work environment such as, "In your organization, supervisors set goals for trainees to encourage them to apply their training on the job" (1 = Strongly disagree, 5 = Strongly agree).

In addition, J. Bruce Tracey, Scott Tannenbaum, and Michael Kavanagh proposed a scale to measure if an organization has a continuous-learning culture. The questions measure trainees' perceptions, beliefs, expectations, and values with regard to individual, task, and organizational factors that support the acquisition and application of knowledge, skill, and behaviour. The Trainer's Notebook 1 in Chapter 10 presents some of the items from this scale.

Organizational Results

Unlike all of the other variables we have discussed, results focus on the effects of training on the organization rather than on the trainee: How has the organization benefited from the training program? Results criteria are considered to be the "ultimate" criteria for training evaluation and may include such measures as turnover, productivity, quality, profitability, customer satisfaction, accidents, etc. However, some of these may be difficult to measure and, in any case, it is very difficult to clearly attribute changes in these variables specifically to the training program. Testing causality requires experimental designs that are generally difficult to implement in organizations (see "data collection designs in training evaluation" below). In some instances, the objective is to cost the program and determine the net benefit. Chapter 12 is devoted to procedures for doing cost-benefit analysis.

Hard and soft data can be useful in assessing the results of training. **Hard data** is obtained when the information can be measured objectively, while **soft data** usually involves a judgment or observation. Phillips has produced a taxonomy of hard data and soft data that may be measured in training evaluations.[28] Hard data may include quantities (number of items sold or produced), quality (scrap rates and product returns), time (downtime or time to complete assignments), and costs (sales expenses, benchmarks). ACCO Brands Corporation, a manufacturer of school supplies ranging from paper clips to binders, uses hard data (quantity) to track the effect of training on new production hires. After training, new hires were able to produce vinyl binders at a 5 to 10 percent higher rate than tenured operators: a clear pay-off to the organization.

In many cases, however, hard data are difficult to obtain or are simply not relevant to a training program. In these cases, trainers must use soft-data measures that are perceptions. Soft data are results of organizational value that are assessed through perceptions and judgments. Such measures include the perception of work climate, feelings and attitudes, and difficult-to-measure skills like decision-making. Although these measures are not direct indicators of organizational outcomes, they are reasoned to be linked to concrete results. For example, communication skills are not bottom-line measures but they may ultimately have an impact on the organization's bottom line. However, it remains difficult to assign a dollar value to this, or to prove that changes in attitude do make a difference.

In some cases it is difficult or impossible to adequately assess the impact of training directly. An alternative is to calculate **return on expectations**. Those who are involved in training decide exactly what they expect from the training. These expectations form the goals for training, and some time after the course, managers decide if the performance results are in line with their expectations.

For example, an organization that was restructured into product-performance teams was unable to place a dollar value on the cross-functional training employees had received, but managers were able to articulate improvements they noticed after the training. The numbers are not absolute, but managers are not only saying that time is being managed better, but that

Hard data
Results that are assessed objectively

Soft data
Results that are assessed through perceptions and judgments

Return on expectations
The measurement of a training program's ability to meet managerial expectations

95 percent of deadlines are being met. They feel that this anecdotal evidence does have an impact on the bottom line, and that profit improvements are noticeable.

According to the recent ASTD survey, less than 10 percent of organizations in the United States assess results in their training evaluations and, as indicated earlier, only 12 percent of Canadian organizations measure results. This is far from ideal but there are good reasons for this. Not only is it more costly in terms of time (it may take months or years for a training program's effects to manifest themselves on the bottom-line results) and resources, it is very difficult to link training to organizational results. The fact that productivity increases after training may not be automatically attributed to training. Many other things unrelated to training, including other changes in the organization or its environment may have caused the effect and improved productivity.

However, the organization of the evaluation data may be designed in many ways. The more sophisticated training evaluation data collection designs can detect the effect of training in precise ways. Other designs, though useful in some situations, produce more limited conclusions about training's value. Data collection designs are a very important component of training evaluation. They determine the possible conclusions that can be made. Hence, the discussion now turns to a consideration of data collection design in training evaluations.

Data Collection Designs in Training Evaluation

Data collection designs in training evaluation refer to the manner in which the data collection is organized and how the data will be analyzed. All data collection designs compare the trained person to something. They may compare 1. Trained people with untrained ones, 2. The same people before and after training, or 3. Each trained person to an absolute standard. When the comparison does not involve another group of (untrained) people, the designs are labeled **non-experimental**. When that comparison is to another group of people similar to those trained but that do not receive the training, the designs are called **experimental or quasi-experimental**. The main difference between an experimental design and a quasi-experimental design has to do with whether assignment-to-conditions is random or not random.

In experimental designs, the assignment of people to the trained (labeled the "experimental" or "trained" group) and to the untrained group (labeled the "control" group) is done randomly. In quasi-experimental designs, we also compare trained to untrained employees but the assignment to the groups is not done randomly. In that case, instead of speaking about a "control" group we refer to it as a "comparison" group.

Figure 11.1 graphically represents several data collection designs. The uses and limitations of each data collection design are explained below and Table 11.5 summarizes the main difference between the various methodologies. In general, non-experimental designs do not establish if trainee learning and behaviours were *caused* by the training program (with the exception of the IRS strategy, design G below). On the other hand, they are

FIGURE 11.1

Training Evaluation Data Collection Designs

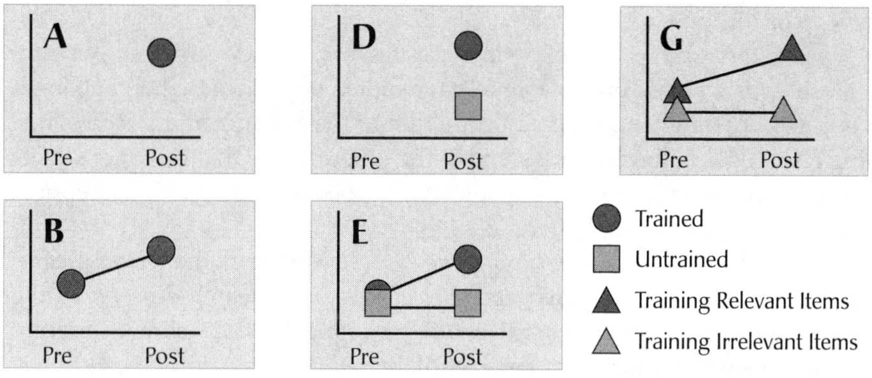

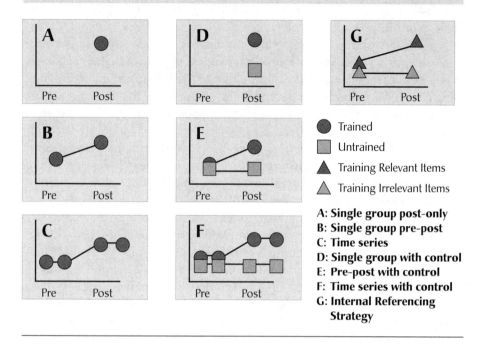

A
Pre
Post
B
Pre
Post
C
Pre
Post
D
Pre
Post
E
Pre
Post
F
Pre
Post
G
Pre
Post
Trained
Untrained
Training Relevant Items
Training Irrelevant Items

A: Single group post-only
B: Single group pre-post
C: Time series
D: Single group with control
E: Pre-post with control
F: Time series with control
G: Internal Referencing Strategy

TABLE 11.5

Uses and Limitations of Non-Experimental, Quasi-Experimental, and Experimental Training Evaluation Designs

Experimental designs estimate the degree to which a training program has *caused* trainee proficiency. They are used to establish if the training program should be eliminated or expanded to other parts of the organization. The downside is that experimental designs are more difficult to use in organizational settings.

Quasi-experimental designs provide indications of cause but the proof is not definitive. However, because they do not require random assignment they are generally more accessible to organizations. Hence, quasi-experimental designs may be appropriate when experimental designs cannot be used and when the training manager is willing to live with some risk.

Non-experimental designs *cannot* provide causal information (except for the Internal Referencing Strategy). Hence, such designs *cannot* be used to infer the quality of the training program. However, they are most practical and can provide useful information when the evaluator has an external standard against which post-training performance can be compared and when demonstrating that training caused that proficiency does not matter.

easy to organize and practical for use in organizations. Quasi-experimental and experimental designs are more complex but they do provide evidence of causality. Compared with quasi-experimental designs, experimental designs provide even stronger evidence of causality, but they are more difficult to use in practice.

One of the reasons that experimental designs provide stronger evidence of causality is because one is able to have more confidence that any changes in trainees' learning and behaviour are due to the training and not to something else. To learn more about some of the other factors that might explain a change in trainees' learning and behaviour, see The Trainer's Notebook, "Understanding Pre-Post Differences."

Training evaluation designs were developed from the principles of experimental scientific research and there are many research designs within each of the three general types. Each of the data collection schemes graphically described in Figure 11.1 is now explained.

Designs A, B, and C are non-experimental designs because the employees who are trained are not compared to untrained employees. Designs D, E, and F are causal models that compare trained and untrained people and, depending on trainee assignment, they may be experimental or quasi-experimental. Finally, design G—the Internal Referencing Strategy—is a hybrid design that permits some of the conclusions made by the causal designs (D, E, F) while collecting data exclusively from trainees.

In general, all training outcome measures may be used irrespective of the training evaluation design chosen: affective, cognitive, or skill-based as well as reactions and behaviours. *Hence, the choice of an evaluation design has less to do with the measures collected but much more to do with the inferences or decisions required about the training program relative to the original aims of the training program.*

Non-experimental, Experimental, and Quasi-Experimental Training Data Collection Designs for Training Evaluation

This section explains each of the seven designs represented in Figure 11.1. Design A is the most simple, while design F is the most complex, with the others falling in between these extremes. More complex designs allow clearer inferences about the effectiveness of the training program. However, these designs are more difficult to implement in practice. Designs A, B, and C are non-experimental because the trained group is not compared to another group. Designs D, E, and F are experimental when subjects are randomly assigned and quasi-experimental when subject assignment to trained and comparison groups is not random.

Non-Experimental Designs

Design A: The Post-Only Design is the simplest and most common training evaluation data collection scheme. Data is gathered once after training and only from those who have completed training. Each trainee is compared to a

Understanding Pre-Post Differences

Suppose we wish to evaluate this chapter's effectiveness in teaching training evaluation. We select a pre-post design in which knowledge is measured with a multiple choice test administered on the first day of class (pre-test) and again on the last day (post-test). The results show that the students greatly improved their test performance: the average score of the students on the post-test is significantly higher than the pre-test scores. Can it be concluded that reading this chapter caused this gain in knowledge? Before jumping to conclusions, you should consider four alternative explanations:

History or Time: Events in the environment that coincide with this course and that have nothing to do with it may, in fact, have caused pre-to-post changes. For example, the class may have done better because many students saw a PBS program on training evaluation that was aired the week before the final exam.

Maturation: People mature and change over time. As the students are taking this course they are also taking other courses. Even if none of the other courses deals explicitly with training evaluation, they may have helped the students develop higher levels of reasoning and critical thinking skills. This growing general competence may translate into better performance on the post-test.

Testing: Taking the pre-test may have made it easier for students to perform better on the post-test. Some students may have remembered some of the questions asked on the pre-test, while others may have gained a better "feel" for the kinds of questions that are asked. Hence, the post-test performance may be due, at least in part, with the mere experience of being pre-tested.

Mortality: Whereas most students who enroll in a course stay until the end, it is almost always the case that some students drop the course. Those who remain in the course and from whom post-test information will be available may be systematically different from those who dropped the course—they may be more interested in the subject matter, more motivated, more able than those who leave, and/or have more time to meet the course demands. These students may very well show large improvements in learning, shifting the average class performance on the post-test upward.

Source: Adapted from Cook, T. D., & Campbell, D. T. (1979). *Quasi-experimentation: Design and analysis issues for field settings.* Skokie, IL: Rand McNally.

pre-determined criterion of success and training is considered "effective" when the trainees meet that standard of proficiency. Three common examples of such programs include the exams in a college course on "organizational training," a course for new drivers, and the basic training program administered to new telephone operators. The basic strength (and popularity) of this design is its simplicity. The two drawbacks of the design are that it cannot indicate if the trainees changed (e.g., trainees may have been proficient before training) or if the achieved outcome is a result of training (their observed proficiency may have been "caused" by some other experience coincidental to training).

Design B: The Single Group Pre-Post Design is a non-experimental design because the comparison is not made to another group. Instead the comparison is made to the trainees themselves prior to training. This is the second most frequently used evaluation design. Training outcome data is gathered from trainees both before as well as after training. Used to assess *changes* in trainees, this design infers training effectiveness when the post-training data shows statistically significant improvement from pre-training. There are a number of drawbacks of this design. When pre-post differences are noted, it is not possible to know if the differences resulted from training because events other than training may have caused the difference. Other drawbacks include history, testing, and maturation effects which are described in The Trainer's Notebook "Understanding Pre-Post Differences."

Design C: The Time-Series Design is, in principle, an extension of the pre-post only data collection technique. Because it requires several measurements, questionnaire data is infrequently used. Instead, the design principally relies on "objective" measures of job performance that can be collected without disturbing the employee. It requires several data collection points before and after training (the pre-post design only requires one pre and one post measure). Training is considered effective when there is a clear, evident and stable difference between pre and post performance. The use of several pre and post measures, essential to this design, yields the decided advantage of this technique over the simple pre-post design. Objective performance measures tend to fluctuate (up or down) due to many circumstances that may have little to do with the employee. Multiplying the measurement moments will tend to cancel out these fluctuations. Further, the time-series design allows the evaluator to test if post-training improvements are persistent and stable over time. However, the quality of the conclusions depends on the number of times data is collected. The more data points the more valid the conclusion. For example, in a time-series design to assess a course on "selling earthquake insurance" the analyst would retrieve for each trainee the number of earthquake policies sold during each of the four quarters prior to training and each of the four quarters after training. Training is considered effective when the number of policies sold jumps after training and remains consistently higher. However, the statistical analyses required to assess the results are more complex than the ones needed with the simpler designs.

Data collection designs D, E, and F compare the trainees to another group of "equivalent" people who have not been trained. These designs can be either experimental or quasi-experimental depending on whether or not the assignment to the comparison group is random.

Design D: The Single-Group Design with Control Group is the simplest quasi-experimental or experimental design. Post-training data is collected from both trainees as well as a group of people who were not trained. Effectiveness is inferred when those trained obtain higher scores on the training outcome than the untrained group. With this design, it is possible to state with considerable confidence that the training program caused the higher outcomes obtained by the trained group. We have greater confidence in this conclusion when the design is experimental (because random assignment ensures that both groups are initially equal). However, the statistical properties of randomness will equate the groups only when the number of people involved is large. This latter restriction is important because many training programs in organizations are administered to a limited number of people. When assignment to groups cannot be randomized (as is typical in organizational settings) the design becomes quasi-experimental and it cannot be categorically stated that the groups were initially equal. In that case the attribution of causality is more risky.

Design E: With **the Pre-Post Design with Control Group**, data is gathered from trainees both before and after training. Simultaneously, data is also gathered from an untrained group. This is a more complete training evaluation design because it allows one to examine the two most important questions about training programs: "Did the trainees change?" and "To what degree was the training program responsible for that change?" Training effectiveness is inferred when pre-post changes are greater for the trained group. The main drawback of this model is practical: rare are the cases where random assignment and multiple measurements can be conducted. The Trainer's Notebook on Corporate Universities presented in Chapter 14 illustrates this design.

Design F: The Time-Series Design with Comparison Group is identical to the time-series design C except that data is simultaneously gathered from a comparison group. This additional group allows for stronger conclusions about changes as well as about the role that the training intervention played in creating that change. Take for example the course on "selling earthquake insurance" described above (see design C). Suppose that shortly after the course is offered, an earthquake does occur. Selling earthquake insurance is likely to become a lot easier and all salespeople, whether or not they had taken the training, would show a marked increase. Had we not had a comparison group, we would have falsely concluded that the training program was responsible for the pre-post changes.

Design G is a hybrid design. As it does not need a comparison group it cannot be considered an experimental design. However, it does generate some of the inferences produced by experimental or quasi-experimental data collection systems.

Design G: The Internal Referencing Strategy is a hybrid design developed by Haccoun and Hamtiaux for use in those frequent cases where a causal inference is required but a control or comparison group is not available.[29] It assesses change from pre- to post-training and estimates if training caused the difference observed without the use of an external comparison group. With this design, it is the outcome measure itself that forms the basis of the comparison. The heart of this technique is the careful construction of the pre-test and the post-test measures. Two types of test items—"relevant" and "irrelevant but germane"—are constructed. Relevant items are those that test the knowledge and behaviours that are covered in a training program. Irrelevant but germane items are those that could have been included in a training program but were not. For example, in testing the effectiveness of this chapter for teaching evaluation designs, one could ask questions about the time-series design. One could also ask questions about the interrupted time-series design. Questions testing your knowledge of time-series design would be "relevant" because the topic is covered in this chapter. Questions testing your knowledge of the interrupted time-series would be "irrelevant" because the chapter does not cover this design but "germane" because the interrupted time-series is a legitimate evaluation design that could have been included.

Comparisons are then made between pre-post differences on the relevant and on the irrelevant but germane items. If the program was effective, the differences on the relevant items should be greater than those pre-post differences noted on the irrelevant but germane ones. This design is a practical and superior alternative to the pre-post design and it can be used for a variety of learning, behaviour, and job performance outcomes.[30]

In summary, trainers have a variety of data collection designs to choose from when evaluating a training program. These designs differ in terms of the time involved, their cost, the level of expertise they require, and the kind of conclusions that one can derive from the evaluation. As stated at the beginning of this chapter, evaluation strategies and data collection designs always involve trade-offs (between the quality and the scope of the information gathered and their costs and practicality). A trainer will have to weigh the importance of each of these factors when deciding on an evaluation design. Ultimately, what is most important is the question that the trainer must answer and the information that management requires.

Summary

This chapter reviewed the main purposes for evaluating training programs as well as the barriers that prevent training evaluation. Models of training evaluation were presented, contrasted, and critiqued. Although Kirkpatrick's evaluation model is the most common and frequently used model, for formative evaluations at least, the more recent COMA and DBE models might be required. We also described the variables required for an evaluation as well as some of the methods and techniques required to measure them. Whereas many of these are measured through questionnaires administered to trainees, their supervisors or others, objective data can also be used. Advantages and disadvantages of each were discussed. The main types of data collection designs were also described along with their advantages and disadvantages. The choice of data collection design, as with most aspects of training, was seen as a trade-off between costs and practicalities and the information needs of management.

Key Terms

affective reactions (page 306)

anticipated support (page 315)

causal evaluations (page 301)

COMA (page 303)

data collection designs in training evaluation (page 318)

Decision-Based Evaluation (DBE) (page 304)

declarative learning (page 309)

descriptive evaluations (page 301)

experimental designs (page 318)

formative evaluations (page 301)

hard data (page 317)

non-experimental designs (page 318)

perceived support (page 315)

procedural learning (page 309)

quasi-experimental designs (page 318)

return on expectations (page 317)

soft data (page 317)

summative evaluations (page 301)

training evaluation (page 297)

training evaluation designs (page 320)

utility reactions (page 306)

Weblinks

ACCO Brands Corporation: www.acco.com (page 317)

American Society for Training and Development (ASTD): www.astd.org (page 298)

Conference Board of Canada: www.conferenceboard.ca (page 299)

General Dynamics: www.generaldynamics.com (page 312)

TD Bank: www.td.com (page 314)

Xerox: www.xerox.com (page 314)

RPC Icons

RPC 11.1 Compiles, analyzes, and documents evaluation data based on feedback.

RPC 11.2 Documents participant feedback to evaluate effectiveness of program delivery.

RPC 11.3 Conducts an evaluation of the program.

RPC 11.4 Ensures participant and organizational feedback is documented and evaluated.

RPC 11.5 Interprets results of development programs in terms of contribution to organizational objectives, and does a post-development follow-up.

Discussion Questions

1. Discuss the similarities and the differences between the evaluation models discussed in the chapter. In your discussion be sure to include the practical implications of preferring one model over another.
2. You have two training programs: a) a course designed to teach the use of a PC and b) a course to improve supervisory feedback to employees. Which evaluation design would you use in each case? What if you wanted to determine if training caused the outcome? Which design would you use?
3. Many organizations do not evaluate their training programs. If you had to convince a manager to evaluate a training program, what would you tell him or her? Why should organizations evaluate their training programs and what should they evaluate?
4. What are the barriers to training evaluation? Discuss the main types of barriers and what a trainer might do to overcome them and evaluate a training program.

5. Discuss the different types of training evaluation and how they can be distinguished from each other.
6. What is the difference between formative and summative evaluation and between descriptive and causal evaluation?
7. Discuss the assumptions of Donald Kirkpatrick's hierarchical model of training evaluation. What are the implications for training evaluation if the assumptions are valid? What are the implications if the assumptions are not valid?
8. Explain each of the following and give an example: Hard data, soft data, and return on expectations. What are the advantages and disadvantages of each type of measure?
9. Explain each of the following and give an example: non-experimental designs, experimental designs, and quasi-experimental designs. What are the advantages and disadvantages of each type of evaluation design?

Using the Internet

1. To find out about the evaluation of executive training, visit the Treasury Board of Canada Secretariat at **www.tbs-sct.gc.ca/eval/pubs/eet-efcs/eet-efcs_e.asp**. Read the article and answer the following questions:

   1. How has the public sector evaluated training in the past?
   2. How have executive development programs been evaluated in the Canadian federal government?
   3. What model of training evaluation is being advocated?
   4. Do you think that this model should be used to evaluate executive training programs?
   5. What other models would you consider to evaluate executive training programs and why?

The Great Training Debate

Conducting evaluation studies using full experimental designs and sophisticated data collection is almost impossible in real organizations. Some managers argue that training evaluation can provide meaningful conclusions only when they are conducted using these techniques. They therefore conclude that in most cases training evaluations are a waste of time and money.

Debate that conclusion: Is it the case that training evaluations should be conducted only when it is possible to use the more sophisticated procedures?

In preparation for this debate you should review the chapter's sections on barriers to training evaluation and models of training evaluation as well as data collection schemes.

Exercises

In-Class

1. Training evaluation principles and variables can also be used to make important individual decisions. Following her graduation Sally, your best friend, felt she lacked "work-life skills." To remedy her perceived problem, she enrolled in a private school that specializes in "enhancing the skills needed for a successful work life." Six months into her program you are meeting Sally, who is briefly visiting home before returning to the school to complete the year-long program. You are graduating at the end of the year and, for the same reasons, are thinking of enrolling in that program after graduation. But you are hesitating as the school fees are very high. You are willing to assume that burden, provided that the program is worthwhile. Assume that Sally is your only source of information about the school's effectiveness. What are the changes in Sally that you will be looking for to help you decide if the school is worthwhile or not? Are there specific questions you would ask Sally? Refer to the models and variables of training evaluations to guide your thinking. Remember that Sally has not yet completed her course.

2. In most universities and colleges, students fill out an end-of-course questionnaire in which they evaluate the course. Describe how these evaluations are typically conducted in your university or college. What variables are measured, how is that done, and what type of data collection design is used? Keeping in mind each model and the variables in Table 11.1, what other variables do you think should be included as part of the evaluation process? Design an evaluation form that you would like to see used to evaluate your university/college's courses. For each variable you include, develop one sample question, and/or a procedure for measuring it.

3. Suppose that your university or college has decided to switch all computers from PC to Mac (or, if your university's current system uses Mac, to PC). Although some staff members already know both systems, the majority will need to learn and master the new system (Mac or PC). The university administration has therefore authorized Human Resources and the IT group to work together to develop and deliver a compulsory training program to all staff members. The top university administration has hired you to conduct an evaluation of the effectiveness of this program as it needs to know if the training program was worthwhile. a) Decide whether your client's request calls for a summative or formative evaluation, and b) depending on that decision, develop the training evaluation plan. Keeping in mind the data collection designs (Figure 11.1) and the models and the variables of training evaluation, describe what will be measured, how, and when that will be done to meet the client's needs.

4. Suppose that in the same circumstances described in problem 3, it is Human Resources and the IT group who are your clients. They are

interested in identifying possible improvements to the course. Would the design you established in 3 be applicable? Would you change anything? If so what would you change and how? What would the plan look like if your clients were simultaneously both the administration and the HR/IT?

5. Consider a situation in which you are the director of training and development in an organization that is going to deliver a very expensive training program. It is very important to find out how effective the training program is, given the expense and the large number of employees who will be trained over the next several years. Your job is to develop a plan for the evaluation. Discuss what you will do in terms of the type of evaluation: What data should be gathered and analyzed? What is the purpose of the evaluation and should it be formative or summative? Should it be a descriptive or causal evaluation? Now consider the different types of evaluation designs in Figure 11.1. What type of evaluation design do you think would be most appropriate? Consider the pros and cons of the various alternatives. Present your training evaluation strategy to the class.

In-the-Field

1. Identify the training manager of a local company, set up an appointment and meet with him or her. During that interview identify

   - The types of training programs that are given in that company and
   - The types of training evaluations (if any) that are conducted.
   - Is the same type of evaluation used across different programs or are different evaluations schemes adopted for different ones?
   - How are the evaluation data used and by whom?
   - Finally, based on all of the information gathered, assess the quality of that company's evaluation efforts: What is it that they can conclude about training effectiveness given the types of evaluations they conduct and what is that they cannot conclude?

2. Identify a member of your family or a friend who is currently working and who has recently taken a training course and interview him or her. The purpose of the interview is for you to estimate the likelihood that the training program was "effective." Establish the interview guide (the questions you will ask) in advance of the interview. Your questions should focus on the dimensions to be measured using both the Kirkpatrick and the COMA models.

Case Incident

The Social Agency

A large governmental social agency, employing thousands of social workers and other specialized workers, trained all of its front-line professionals on a new service-delivery system. Simultaneously, it taught managers how to actively support and encourage their employees to implement the new system: that is, transferring their new skills. A consultant was asked to evaluate the effectiveness of the program directed to the managers and to offer suggestions for improvements.

Questions

1. What information should be collected and from whom should it be collected?
2. Discuss when and how the information should be collected.
3. What should the criteria for "effectiveness" be?

Case

The Alcohol/Drug Abuse Prevention Program (ADAPP)

The North American Transportation Company (NATC) is a very large organization that provides continent-wide facilities for the shipping of goods, from tonnes of wheat and iron ore to individual parcels. Headquartered in Canada, the company uses all forms of heavy equipment to load, transport, and deliver goods and materials for its clients.

In recent years, a number of accidents and near-accidents had occurred. In some cases the accidents caused injuries to people (mainly employees, though some injuries were sustained by bystanders). They also caused substantial material damage to property and/or the environment. In three cases in the last five years, people were killed.

Investigation of these accidents indicated that drug and/or alcohol abuse by company personnel was relatively common and that these may have been contributing factors to the accidents. This analysis also uncovered that absenteeism and job performance problems were also the result of drug/alcohol use by employees.

The CEO of the company asked the Human Resource department to solve the problem. In response, the department formulated a zero-tolerance policy towards workplace alcohol and drug abuse. The policy outlawed alcohol/drug use on the job and made the implementation and enforcement of the policy the direct responsibility of all supervisory personnel in the company. They further developed and implemented a training program to instruct all supervisors of the policy, the means to implement it, and the specific behaviours expected of them. This training program became known as the Alcohol/Drug Abuse Prevention Program (ADAPP).

The day-long training program explained that it was the responsibility of supervisors to be vigilant with respect to drug/alcohol use on the job and to act immediately when there is a problem.

The supervisors were required to do three major things: 1. Explain the policy to their employees as a group; 2. Observe their employees and note if employees show signs of being "under the influence." Were this to be the case, the supervisor was to individually meet the employee and direct him or her to the Employee Aid Program for further investigation and treatment; and 3. Immediately remove from the job any employee assigned to hazardous duties if the supervisor felt that the person was in no condition to do the work safely. Supervisors who failed to implement the procedure would face disciplinary actions including, in some cases, immediate dismissal.

The training program consisted of lectures and video presentations, followed by various role-playing exercises and discussions designed to help them learn the policy, to motivate supervisors into implementing it, and to enhance their confidence in their ability to do so.

Questions

1. Design a training evaluation for the ADAPP. The training evaluation must be both *summative* (has ADAPP led to an increase in the desired supervisory behaviours and has it led to a decrease in employee absence and workplace accidents and injuries?) and *formative* (what aspects of the training program, if any, should be improved?).
2. What model or models of training evaluation would seem appropriate in this case? Explain your answer.
3. What variables should be measured and how should this be done.
   a. Determine the main variables to measure.
   b. Determine the information to be collected to address program improvements.
4. What data collection design or designs would you consider most appropriate for the evaluation? Explain your reasoning.

References

1. Sackett, P. R., & Mullen, E. J. (1993). Beyond formal experimental design: Towards an expanded view of the training evaluation process. *Personnel Psychology, 46*, 613–27.
2. Twitchell, S., Holton, E. F. III, & Trott, J. R. Jr. (2001). Technical training evaluation practices in the United States. *Performance Improvement Quarterly, 13* (3) 84–109.
3. Sugrue, B., & Kim, K-H (2004) ASTD's annual review of trends in workplace learning and performance. The American Society for Training and Development.
4. Blanchard, P. N., Thacker, J. W., & Way, S. A. (2000). Training evaluation: perspectives and evidence from Canada. *International Journal of Training and Development, 4* (4), 295–304.
5. Parker, R. O., & Cooney, J. (2005). Learning & development outlook 2005. *The Conference Board of Canada.* Ottawa.
6. Grider, D. T. (1990). Training evaluation. *Business Magazine 17* (1), 20–24.
7. Kraiger, K., Ford, J. K. and Salas, E. (1993). Application of cognitive, skill based and affective theories of learning outcomes to new methods of training evaluation. *Journal of Applied Psychology, 78* (2) 311–28; Colquitt, J. A., Lepine, J. A., Noe, R. A. (2000). Toward an integrative theory of training motivation: A meta-analytic path analysis of 20 years of research. *Journal of Applied Psychology, 85* (5), 678–707.
8. Pace, R. W., Smith, C. P. & Mills, G. E. (1991). *Human resource development: The field.* Englewood Cliffs, NJ: Prentice-Hall.

9. Roullier, J. Z. & Goldstein, I. L. (1993). The relationship between organizational transfer climate and positive transfer of training. *Human Resource Development Quarterly, 4* (4), 377–90; Tracey, J. B, Tannenbaum, S. I, Kavanagh, M. J. (1995). Applying trained skills on the job: The importance of the work environment. *Journal of Applied Psychology, 80* (2), 239–52.

10. Quinones, M. A. (1995). Pretraining context effects: Training assignment as feedback. *Journal of Applied Psychology, 80,* 226–38; Haccoun, R. R., Savard, P. (2003). Prédire le transfert des apprentissages à long terme role du soutien anticipé et perçu, de la motivation et de l'efficacité personnelle. In G. Delobbe, C. Karnas, & C. Vandenberghe (Eds.) *Evaluation et développement des compétences au travail.* UCLs: Presses Universitaire de Louvain, pp. 507–16.

11. Montesino, M. U. (2002). Strategic alignment of training, transfer-enhancing behaviors and training usage: A posttraining study. *Human Resource Development Quarterly, 13* (1), 89–108; Saks, A. M., Tagger, S., & Haccoun, R. R. (2002). Is training related to firm performance? *The HRM Research Quarterly, 6* (2) .

12. Worthen, B. R., & Sanders, J. R. (1987). *Educational evaluations: Alternative approaches and practical guidelines.* White Plains, NY: Longman.

13. Kirkpatrick, D. L. (1976). Evaluation of training. In R. L. Craig (Ed.) *Training and development handbook: A guide to human resource development* (2nd ed). New York: McGraw-Hill.

14. Kraiger, K. (2002). Decision-based evaluation. In K. Kraiger (Ed.) *Creating, implementing, and managing effective training and development: State-of-the-art lessons for practice,* (pp. 331–75). San Francisco: Jossey-Bass; Haccoun, R. R., Jeanrie, C., & Saks, A. M. (1999). Concepts et pratiques contemporaines en évaluation de la formation: Vers un modèle diagnostic des impacts. In D. Bouthilier (Ed.) *Gérer pour la performance.* Montreal: Presses de HEC.

15. Holton, E. F. III (1996). The flawed four-level evaluation model. *Human Resource Development Quarterly, 7,* 5–21; Alliger, G. M., Tannenbaum, S. L., Bennett, W., Traver, H., & Shortland, A. (1997). A meta-analysis on the relations among training criteria. *Personnel Psychology, 50,* 341–42.

16. Haccoun, R. R., & Saks, A. M. (1998). Training in the 21st century: Some lessons from the last one. Invited Paper, Special Issue: Industrial psychology at the turn of the century. *Canadian Psychology, 39* (1-2), 33–51.

17. Morgan, R. B., & Casper, W. (2000). Examining the factor structure of participant reactions to training: A multidimensional approach. *Human Resource Development Quarterly, 11,* 301–17.

18. Alliger, G. M., Tannenbaum, S. L., Bennett, W., Traver, H., & Shortland, A (1997). Meta analysis of the relationship among training criteria. *Personnel Psychology, 50,* 341–57.

19. Jonassen, D., & Tessmer, M. (1996-97). An outcomes-based taxonomy for instructional systems design, evaluation and research. *Training Research Journal, 2,* 11–46.

20. Desjardins, D. (1995). Impact de la présentation d'un organisateur avancé sur l'apprentissage et le transfert en formation du personnel. Unpublished Master's Thesis, Université de Montréal, Département de Psychologie.

21. Ostroff, C. (1991). Training effectiveness measures and scoring schemes: A comparison. *Personnel Psychology, 44,* 353–74.

22. Smith, J. E., & Merchant, S. (1990). Using competency exams for evaluating training. *Training and Development Journal, 44* (8), 65–71.

23. Flynn, G. (1998). The nuts and bolts of valuing training. *Workforce Management, 17* (11), 80–85; Kozlowski, S. W. J., & Salas, E (1997). A multilevel organizational systems approach for the implementation and transfer of training. In J. K. Ford (Ed.) *Improving training effectiveness in work organizations* (pp. 247–87). Hillsdale, NJ: Erlbaum.

24. Salas, E., & Cannon-Bowers, J. A. (2001). The Science of training: A decade of progress. *Annual Review of Psychology 52,* 471–99.

25. Olian, J. D., & Durham, C. C. (1998). Designing management training and development for competitive advantage: Lessons from the best. *Human Resource Planning, 21* (1), 20–31.

26. Larin, N. (April, 1998). Who understands return on investment better than a bank? *Canadian HR Reporter*, 2–8.
27. Noe, R. A., & Schmitt, N. (1986). The influence of trainee attitudes on training effectiveness: Test of a model. *Personnel Psychology, 39,* 497–523.
28. Phillips, J. (1996). How much is the training worth? *Training & Development*, 20–24.
29. Haccoun, R. R., & Hamtiaux, T. (1994). Optimizing knowledge tests for inferring learning acquisition levels in single group training evaluation designs: The internal referencing strategy. *Personnel Psychology, 47,* 593–604.
30. Frese, M., Beimel, S., & Schoenborn, S. (2003) Action training for charismatic leadership: Two evaluation studies of a commercial training module on inspirational communication of vision. *Personnel Psychology, 56,* 671–97.

Chapter 12

The Costs and Benefits
of Training

Chapter Learning Objectives

After reading this chapter, you should be able to:

- explain why trainers should calculate the costs and benefits of training and development programs
- describe the different approaches for costing training programs
- describe how to calculate the benefits of training programs and the difference between cost-effectiveness and cost-benefit evaluation
- describe how to conduct a net benefit analysis and return on investment
- describe how utility analysis can be used to calculate the financial benefits of training programs
- describe the activities for supporting the costing function

SPRINT CORP.

Sprint's University of Excellence (UE) is a world-class corporate university that provides the company with a systematic approach to workforce development. The UE has helped the company develop some of the most effective performance support tools used in North America. The systematic approach has also meant a shift from what was once an operationally focused training organization that measured success in terms of activity-based measures and unit costs to an organization that is focused on delivering value as seen in the eyes of the company's business units.

One of Sprint's best success stories is the company's Local Telecommunications Division's Consumer Markets Group (CMG), which provides service to residential and home-office customers. Historically, new accounts receivable representatives were given seven weeks of intensive classroom training, and were then expected to perform on the job in difficult situations with slow and non-paying customers.

Working with CMG, the University of Excellence redesigned the curriculum, reduced training by three weeks, and introduced a UE Guide solution for on-the-job performance support. UE Guide is a Web-based help system for Sprint-specific software that is accessed through a shortcut on an employee's desktop. Organized and developed around the tasks required by the software application it supports, the tool also generates context-sensitive information about whatever task the employee is trying to accomplish when the UE Guide icon is activated.

The eight accounts receivable representatives who took part in the pilot program using UE Guides collected more than $800,000 in their first three weeks on the job—time that had previously been spent in the classroom—and produced 72 percent more in average daily revenue per employee than the existing representatives, all of which resulted in a significant positive effect on bottom-line results. In terms of ROI (return on investment), the reduced training time provided a 300 percent net benefit. The increased productivity for the pilot-group representatives resulted in a net annualized benefit of 1616 percent. In addition to these results, the revamping of the training curriculum increased customer satisfaction and revenue.

The University of Excellence also developed a Web-based tutorial for purchasers of an equipment supplier's business telephone system. The tutorial features an image of the supplier's handset model that allows customers to click on different parts of the image to learn the functions of each. It was bundled with the sales package for the system and reduced the number of hours that technicians had to spend helping buyers program their new phones. Based on 2002 sales volume, the tutorial has saved Sprint as much as $300,000.[1]

Source: Galvin, T. (2003, March). Training Top 100: Top five profile and ranking: Sprint, *Training*, V N U Business Publications. This work is protected by copyright and it is being used with the permission of Access Copyright. Any alteration of its content or further copying in any form whatsoever is strictly prohibited.

Organizations have become increasingly concerned about the costs and benefits of their training programs. As you can see from the Sprint example, it is possible to calculate the benefits of training programs in monetary terms and the return on training investments. This information is important for making decisions about whether or not to adopt a training program and as part of the training evaluation process. In fact, some experts consider the calculation of return on investment (ROI) to be Level 5 in Kirkpatrick's evaluation model.[2]

The purpose of this chapter is to describe the different approaches for calculating the costs and benefits of training and development programs and the calculation of return on investment (ROI) and utility analysis.

Training and the Bottom Line

In Chapter 11, we described the process of training evaluation. This often involves measuring trainees' reactions, learning, behaviour, and organization results. The intent is to show some improvement in employees' knowledge, on-the-job behaviour, and organizational outcomes. Typically, one would hope to see an improvement in employees' learning and on-the-job behaviour, and thrilled to see a positive effect on organizational outcomes.

But what about the cost of a training program? What if a training program is very expensive? That is, what if the cost is greater than the benefit? Would improvements in employee behaviour and organizational outcomes still be significant? Would the training program be worth the cost?

Without any information on the cost of training and the monetary value of training benefits, one cannot adequately answer these questions. Clearly, the effectiveness of a training program also depends on its costs and benefits. Management might be pleased to know that a training program has improved customer satisfaction, but managers will be even more interested to know the financial value of an improvement in customer satisfaction.

Costing is a complex and time-consuming process that many training specialists traditionally have avoided. Some managers are skeptical about the theoretical underpinnings of costing, while others suggest, rightly, that in business not everything is quantifiable. Indeed, many managers suggest that some quality and processes—job satisfaction, communication techniques— make people feel good about themselves and the company they work for, and you just cannot put a dollar value on them.

However, there is increasing pressure for human resource and training professionals to demonstrate the financial value of their programs. Organizations increasingly want to know the return on their training investments.[3] Therefore, trainers and human resource professionals must increasingly be able to calculate and demonstrate both the costs and benefits of training and development programs. This not only helps to demonstrate the value of training programs to management and the organization, but it also helps to justify the training function's share of the budget and improve its credibility. Furthermore, other members of the organization are more likely to see training and development as an investment rather than a cost and training budgets are less likely to be slashed during economic downturns. Financial information about the benefits of training programs also places human resource and training professionals on an equal footing with other areas in an organization.

According to The Conference Board of Canada, although most organizations in Canada evaluate Level 1 or reactions to their training programs, only eight percent conduct a Level 5 or investment evaluation.[4] Increasingly, however, more organizations are beginning to conduct financial evaluations of their training programs. For example, at CIBC financial advisers across Canada attended a workshop on how to advise clients on company pension plans. They completed detailed surveys of their knowledge before and after the workshop that was then compared to hard data on new pension-related sales in order to identify the percentage of new business that was due to the workshop.[5]

You might also recall the AT&T example in Chapter 4 in which it was estimated that a training program for account executives and their sales managers resulted in US$4.8 million in revenue and a return on investment of 168 percent.[6] Pharmaceutical giant Pfizer has also begun to pay more attention to the contribution of training to the bottom line and even created a new office for measurement, evaluation, and strategic analysis. The company determined that a program for district managers on how to spot employees at risk of turnover decreased turnover by 2 percent after one year. The initial investment in the program was $150,000 and the resulting drop in turnover saved the company $2.4 million just in its training budget. Pfizer estimated a total return of $3.6 million in cost avoidance and increased productivity.[7]

Perhaps it is no surprise that most of the companies like Sprint and Pfizer that have been ranked in *Training* magazine's top 100 evaluate the effect of training on business results and return on investment.[8]

 12.1

Costing

The process of identifying all the expenditures used in training

Costing Training Programs

Costing is the process used to identify all the expenditures used in training. This is an important procedure in both the design and evaluation of a training program. In Chapter 9, we noted that the trainer must prepare a budget that includes the costs of all of the expenses incurred in the implementation of a training program.

The calculation of the cost of a training program usually involves the assignment of various costs to a number of meaningful cost categories. Over the years, a number of approaches have been developed. One approach categorizes the costs of training according to the stages of the training process. For example, one might calculate the cost of needs analysis, training design, delivery, and evaluation. These costs are usually listed on a costing worksheet. One can then calculate and compare the cost of each stage as well as the total cost of a training program.

An example of this kind of costing worksheet is presented in Table 12.1. Note that in addition to the cost of the needs analysis, program development,

TABLE 12.1

Costing Worksheet

1. Fixed-cost factors
   i. Overhead—AC/heat/light; space; rental/lease; communications; per input hour _____
   ii. Supervisory allocation per input hour _____
   iii. Equipment cost per input hour _____
   iv. Administrative support cost per input hour _____
   v. Training unit fringe benefits cost per input hour _____
2. Total fixed costs per input hour _____
   i. Professional hours ____ @ $____/hour = cost _____
   ii. Support hours ____ @ $____/hour = cost _____
   iii. Transportation expenses _____
   iv. Material _____
   v. Consulting fees _____
   vi. Other costs _____
   Total direct needs-analysis costs _____
3. Program development
   i. Professional hours ____ @ $____/hour = cost _____
   ii. Support hours ____ @ $____/hour = cost _____
   iii. Material _____
   iv. Consulting fees _____
   v. Subject-matter expert/management and staff input
      ____ hours @ ____/hour = cost _____
   vi. Other costs _____
   Total direct program-development costs _____
4. Program delivery
   i. Administration hours _____
      @ $_____/hour = costs _____
   ii. Administrative support hours _____
      @ $_____/hour = costs _____
   iii. Presentation/delivery hours _____
      @ $_____/hour = cost _____
   iv. Technical support hours _____
      @ $_____/hour = cost _____
   v. Trainee materials costs _____
   vi. Transportation/accommodations/meals
      a. staff _____
      b. trainees _____

(Continued)

Chapter 12: The Costs and Benefits of Training

TABLE 12.1 (*Continued*)

vii. Facilities rental   _____

viii. Equipment   _____

Total direct program-delivery costs   _____

5. Evaluation

    i.   @ $_____/hour = cost   _____

    ii.   Support hours   _____

       @ $_____/hour = cost   _____

    iii.   Management input hours   _____

       @ $_____/hour = cost   _____

    iv.   Trainee input hours   _____

       @ $_____/hour = cost   _____

    v.   Transportation costs   _____

    vi.   Material costs   _____

    vii. Consulting fees   _____

Total evaluation cost   _____

6. Revision costs

    i.   Professional hours ___ @ $____/hour = cost   _____

    ii.   Support hours ____ @ $____/hour = cost   _____

    iii.   Management/staff collaboration hours ____ @

      $____/hour = cost   _____

Total evaluation cost   _____

7. Total program cost

    1 + 2 + 3 + 4 + 5 + 6 = Total Cost   _____

delivery, and evaluation, this worksheet also includes a category for fixed costs (e.g., overhead, equipment) as well as the costs of revisions.

Another approach to costing training programs is to categorize the costs according to the nature or kind of cost. A well-known example of this approach uses the following five cost categories: direct costs, indirect costs, development costs, overhead costs, and trainee compensation costs.[9]

Direct costs are costs that are directly linked to a particular training program. This would include the trainers' salary and benefits, equipment rental, course materials, instructional aids, food and refreshments, and the cost of travel to and from the training site. These costs are so directly linked to a particular training program that they would not be incurred if a training program was cancelled.

Indirect costs are costs that are not part of a particular training program per se but they are expenses required to support training activities. Indirect costs include clerical and administrative support, trainer preparation and planning, training materials that have already been sent to trainees, and the cost of marketing training programs. These costs would still be incurred even if a training program were cancelled. In other words, unlike the direct costs, these costs cannot be recovered.

Direct costs

Costs that are directly linked to a particular training program

Indirect costs

Costs that support training activities and are not directly linked to a particular training programs

Developmental costs are costs that are incurred in the development of a training program. This would include the cost of doing a needs analysis, the cost of developing training methods such as videotapes, the design of training materials, and the cost of evaluating a training program.

Overhead costs refer to costs incurred by the training department but not associated with any particular training program. Such costs are required for the general operation of the training function such as the cost of maintaining training facilities (e.g., heat and lighting) and equipment, and the salaries of clerical and administrative support staff. A portion of these costs must be allocated to each training program.

Trainee compensation refers to the cost of the salaries and benefits paid to trainees while they are attending a training program. This might also include the cost of replacing employees while they are in training. The logic behind this cost is simply that employees must be paid while they are not working and this is a cost of the training program.

Table 12.2 presents a costing sheet using this classification of training costs. The example is from a company that produces wood panels. The company has three problems that it wanted solved. First, it wanted to improve the quality of wood panels because they were experiencing a 2-percent rejection rate each day due to poor quality. Second, they wanted to lower the number of preventable accidents, which was higher than the industry average. Third, they wanted to improve the housekeeping of the production area, which was considered poor and a cause of some of the preventable accidents. Visual inspections that used a 20-item checklist indicated an average of 10 problems in housekeeping each week.[10]

The solution was to train supervisors in performance-management and interpersonal skills. Forty-eight supervisors as well as seven shift superintendents and a plant manager attended a three-day behavioural-modelling skill-building training program. The main objectives of the program were to teach the supervisors how to discuss quality problems and poor work habits with employees; to recognize improvements in employee performance; to teach employees on the job; and to recognize employees for above-average performance.

The cost of the training program was calculated for each of the five cost categories. As shown in Table 12.2, the total cost of the training program was $32,564 or $582 per trainee. This was based on total direct costs of $6,507; indirect costs of $1,161; development costs of $6,756; overhead costs of $1,444; and compensation costs of $16,696.

It is important to recognize that the costing sheets presented In Tables 12.1 and 12.2 are only examples. They represent two approaches for categorizing training costs and they might need to be modified to suit an organization's unique circumstances. The idea is to identify the main costs of a training program and not to worry too much about the labels assigned to them. The trainer should be most concerned about how to design a costing approach that has credibility within an organization and that will be accepted by management.

Once the costs of a training program have been calculated, they can be used for at least two purposes. First, they can be used to prepare a budget for a training program and to compare and contrast the costs of different

Developmental costs
Costs that are incurred in the development of a training program

Overhead costs
Costs incurred by the training department but not associated with any particular training program

Trainee compensation
The cost of the salaries and benefits paid to trainees while they are attending a training program

TABLE 12.2

Training Cost Analysis for Wood Panel Plant

Direct costs. The travel and per-diem cost was zero, because training took place adjacent to the plant. Classroom space and audiovisual equipment were rented from a local hotel; refreshments were purchased at the same hotel. Because different supervisors attended the morning and afternoon sessions, lunch was not provided.

Direct Costs	
Outside instructor	0
In-house instructor—12 days × $125 a day	$1,500
Fringe benefits—25 percent of salary	375
Travel and per-diem expenses	0
Materials—$60 × 56 participants	3,360
Classroom space and audiovisual equipment—12 days × $50 a day	600
Refreshments—$4 a day × 3 days × 56 participants	672
Total direct costs	**$6,507**

Indirect costs. Clerical and administrative costs reflect the amount of clerical time spent on making arrangements for the workshop facilities, sending out notices to all participants, and preparing class rosters and other miscellaneous materials.

Indirect Costs	
Training management	0
Clerical and administrative salaries	750
Fringe benefits—25 percent of clerical and administrative salaries	187
Postage, shipping, and telephone	0
Pre- and post-learning materials—$4 × 56 participants	224
Total indirect costs	**$1,161**

Development costs. These costs represent the purchase of the training program from a vendor. Included are instructional aids, an instructor manual, videotapes, and a licensing fee. The instructor-training costs are for a one-week workshop the instructor attended to prepare for facilitating the training. Front-end assessment costs were covered by the corporate training budget.

Development Costs	
Fee to purchase program	3,600
Instructor training	
Registration fee	1,400
Travel and lodging	975
Salary	625
Benefits (25 percent of salary)	156
Total development costs	**$6,756**

Overhead costs. These represent the services that the general organization provides to the training unit. Because figures were not available, we used 10 percent of the direct, indirect, and program-development costs.

Overhead Costs	
General organization support, 10 percent of direct, indirect, top management's time and development costs	....
Total overhead costs	**$1,444**

Compensation for participants. This figure represents the salaries and benefits paid to all participants while they attended the workshop.

Compensation for Participants	
Participants' salaries and benefits (time away from the job)	
Total compensation	**$16,696**
Total training costs	**$32,564**
Cost per participant	**$ 582**

Source: Robinson, D. G., & Robinson, J. (1989). Training for impact. Adapted from *Training & Development*, August, 34–42, American Society for Training & Development.

programs. This is important when making decisions about whether to adopt a particular training program. Second, they can be used along with benefit information to calculate a training program's net benefit and return on investment.

In the next section, we present examples of how to compare the costs of different training programs followed by a discussion of how to determine the benefits of training programs and the return on investment.

Comparing the Costs of Training Programs

While the costing of a training program is necessary for budgeting and reporting purposes, costing training programs is also necessary to determine the relative costs of different training alternatives. Consider the following simplified comparison worksheet:

Program _____	Analyst _____	Date _____
Option	1. _____	2. _____
Performance Value	$ _____	$ _____
Minus Cost	_____	_____
Net Benefit	$ _____	$ _____

To complete the analysis, the program costs (see Table 12.3) are combined with an estimate of the value of the program (performance value) to the organization.

To give you an example of how this type of cost-comparison works and how different organizations might require cost data at various levels of complexity and detail, consider the following situation.[11]

You are part of an organization that designs electronic systems. A recent reorganization has created a project-management division that places all lead engineers on projects in one group rather than being spread across several operations. The purpose of the reorganization was to allow the engineers to have less hands-on technical activity and focus more on theory development, design, and the management of others on projects. A manager from your firm with an outstanding record in project management now heads the management group. The group consists of 10 lead engineers. You have been experiencing an alarming rate of turnover in electronic engineers since this group was established. A needs analysis reveals that the engineer types who make up this management group are very unskilled in communicating directions, delegating, and handling people-crisis issues. Data from the exit interviews reveal that the inability of project managers to manage crises and the inability to transmit clear guidelines and directions have been the primary frustrations. Your needs analysis also confirms that the members of the organization and the management group itself feel that this reorganization was a good decision.

TABLE 12.3

Simplified Comparison Worksheet

| Program _____ | Analyst _____ | Date _____ |
| _____ Option name | 1. _____ | 2. _____ |

Analysis:

Needs assessment_____	_____	_____
Work analysis _____	_____	_____
Proposal to management_____	_____	_____
Other _____	_____	_____
Other _____	_____	_____

Design:

General HRD program design_____	_____	_____
Specific HRD program design _____	_____	_____
Other _____	_____	_____
Other _____	_____	_____

Development:

Draft and prototype _____	_____	_____
Pilot test and revise_____	_____	_____
Production and duplication _____	_____	_____
Other _____	_____	_____
Other _____	_____	_____

Implementation:

Program management _____	_____	_____
Program delivery_____	_____	_____
Participant costs _____	_____	_____
Other _____	_____	_____
Other _____	_____	_____

Evaluation:

Program evaluation and report_____	_____	_____
Performance follow-up_____	_____	_____
Other _____	_____	_____
Other _____	_____	_____
Total training program costs	$ _____	$ _____
	(Option 1)	(Option 2)

The crisis in the organization resulting from the high turnover rate is a financial one. Finding, hiring, and relocating an engineer with the appropriate credentials and experience costs the organization approximately $75,000. In the past nine months, your organization has replaced five engineers. At this rate you anticipate you will replace a total of six engineers before the year is complete. You have been asked to recommend a training program to address the management skills deficiencies in this group. The goal is to reduce the turnover rate to two engineers per year.

Your options are to send each project manager in the group to a management development institute identified by the president of the corporation, arrange for a vendor-delivered training program in-house, or develop a coaching program to help these managers acquire the necessary skills.

Your director has suggested that the last option might take 9 to 12 months to achieve the desired results. The probabilities are low to none that the managers will develop the skills needed on their own on the job. Your organization will not consider salaries or other normal employee maintenance costs as training expenses.

A budget of $7,000 will be provided for materials and $17,000 for consulting fees to support a coaching approach to solving the problem. The following information is provided to help you make your decision:

MANAGEMENT DEVELOPMENT INSTITUTE:

80-hour program delivered off-site over a two-week period—$10,000 per trainee (this includes airfare, lodging, food, and materials).

VENDOR-SUPPLIED PROGRAM:

15 four-hour sessions delivered on site over a six-month period—$15,000 per trainee

MATERIALS BUDGET TO SUPPORT COACHING OPTION: $7,000

Needs Analysis	10%	
Work Analysis	5%	
Design	5%	
Development	15%	
Implementation	50%	
Evaluation	15%	
	100%	allocation

Table 12.4 shows the actual cost analysis worksheet used by the organization.

This example demonstrates a number of important aspects of costing and comparing training program alternatives:

1. It shows how the original costing sheet (Table 12.1) can be modified to meet an organization's needs. The substitution of a "maintenance of behaviour" category for the nebulous term "performance follow-up," for example, makes this cost easier to sell. Also, there was no need to make a "proposal to management." The problem was well understood and immediate.

Table 12.4

Cost Analysis Worksheet

	M.D. Institute	Outside Vendor	Coaching
Analysis:			
Needs Analysis	$	$	$ 10,700
Work Analysis	$	$	$ 4,350
Design:			
Program	$	$	$ 350
Instructional Aids	$	$	$ 0
Development:			
Pilot Testing	$	$	$ 0
Formative Evaluation			
(during the HRD activity)	$	$	$ 0
Instructional Aids	$	$	$ 1,050
Implementation:			
Delivery	$ 100,000	$ 150,000	$ 3,500
Management	$	$	$ 0
Evaluation:			
Summative Evaluation	$	$	$ 3,000
Training Revision	$	$	$ 0
Maintenance of Trainee			
Behaviour	$	$	$ 1,050
(A) Total	$ 100,000	$ 150,000	$ 24,000
(B) Trainees	$ 10	$ 10	$ 10
Cost Per Trainee (A)/(B) =	$ 10,000	$ 15,000	$ 2,400

2. Management was not interested in a cost breakdown for either the institute or the in-house vendor program, hence the single cost entered in the "Delivery" column. In contrast, had this client been a government agency, a detailed breakdown of both bids might have been required.
3. As discussed previously, costs of salaries and benefits, overhead, and cost-productivity measures are not included. In this case, the problem had to be solved. Management was not interested in fine-tuning the costs.
4. Coaching, an on-the-job training method, is by far the cheapest option. Whether coaching will be the method chosen would require a benefit analysis. The important issue, however, is that a formal training program might not be the best investment. All appropriate training and development methods should be considered.

While this type of cost comparison analysis is useful for determining the costs of training programs and hence making sound choices and budgetary allocations, a decision should not be made without an estimate of the benefits likely to be received under each system. In the following sections, we describe how to calculate the benefits of training programs and how to determine the return on training investments.

The Benefits of Training Programs

⊛℗© 12.2

The benefits of a training program can be calculated in monetary or non-monetary terms. When the benefit is calculated in monetary terms, it is referred to as cost-effectiveness evaluation. **Cost-effectiveness evaluation** involves comparing the monetary cost of training to the benefit of training in monetary terms.

Sometimes, however, it is not possible to determine the monetary value of training benefits or to express them in financial terms. Further, in some cases there might be important benefits of a training program that are not monetary benefits. This kind of evaluation is called cost-benefit evaluation.

Cost-benefit evaluation compares the cost of training in monetary terms to the benefits of training in non-monetary terms. Non-monetary benefits are similar to what was described as results or Level-4 evaluation criteria in Chapter 11 and include organization outcomes such as the rate of turnover, absenteeism, customer satisfaction, and so on. It is worth noting that such benefits might have a financial effect on the performance of an organization even though they might not be described in monetary terms.

For example, if a training program is expected to reduce the amount of scrap in the production of a product, then a cost-benefit evaluation would indicate how much the training program cost and the amount or percent reduction in scrap. On the other hand, a cost-effectiveness evaluation would calculate the monetary value of the reduction in scrap.

How benefits are calculated depends on the training situation, management needs, and the data available. Because of these differences, we present several examples of the calculation of cost-benefit and cost-effectiveness evaluation beginning with the example in Table 12.4.

Recall that the coaching option has the lowest cost ($24,000) compared to the other two options ($100,000 for the institute and $150,000 for the outside vendor). However, when the "Net Benefit Value Calculation Worksheet" (Table 12.5) is completed, a different picture emerges.

First, we can calculate the cost-benefit by comparing the cost of each option to the non-monetary benefit of the estimated reduction in turnover. As shown in Table 12.5, the reduction in turnover for the Management Development Institute is estimated to be 4.84; for the outside vendor the estimated reduction is 3.0; and for the coaching option it is 1.0. Thus, the Management Development Institute is estimated to result in the greatest amount of turnover reduction followed by the outside vendor and then coaching. Also note that the Management Development Institute is the most

Cost-effectiveness evaluation

A comparison of the monetary cost of training to the benefit of training in monetary terms

Cost-benefit evaluation

A comparison of the cost of training in monetary terms to the benefits of training in non-monetary terms

TABLE 12.5

Net Benefit Value Calculation Worksheet

	Institute Option 1	Vendor Option 2	Coaching Option 3
A. Data Required for Calculations			
(a) What is the desired performance as a result of worker training?	4 reductions per group	4 reductions per group	4 reductions per group
(b) What unit(s) of measure will be used to describe the performance?			
(c) What is the dollar value that will be assigned to each unit of measure?	$75,000	$75,000	$75,000
(d) What is the estimated training time to reach the goal?	.04 year	.5 year	1.0 year
(e) What is the current level of worker performance?	0 reduction	0 reduction	0 reduction
(f) How many workers will participate in the training?	10	10	10
B. Calculations to Determine Net Performance Value			
(g) What is the estimated performance level during training? Will trainee produce during training? _____ No = 0 _____ Yes = a + e / 2	0	2	2
(h) What is the length of the period being evaluated (at a minimum this will be the longest "d" of all options under consideration)?	1.0 year	1.0 year	1.0 year
(i) What is the estimate of the total number of units (b) that will be achieved during training? [d x g]			
(j) What is the estimate of the total individual performance (or the evaluation period [(h − d) x a] + 1)?	0 4.84 reduction	1 3.0 reduction	2 1.0 reduction
(k) What is the value for the total performance for the evaluation period? [c x j]	$363,000	$225,000	$75,000
(l) What is the net performance value gain? [k + (e x c x h)]	$363,000	$225,000	$ 75,000
(m) Do you want to calculate the total net performance value of all trainees? _____ Yes = l × f __X__ No = net performance value of 1 trainee	$363,000	$225,000	$75,000
Net Benefit	$363,000	$225,000	$75,000
Cost (from Cost-Analysis Worksheet)	$100,000	$150,000	$24,000
Final Net Benefit	*$263,000*	*$75,000*	*$ 51,000*

expensive option followed by the outside vendor and coaching option. In this case, if one were simply interested in the greatest turnover reduction, then the Management Development Institute would be the preferred option.

It is also possible to conduct a cost-effectiveness evaluation using data on the net benefit of each option. But first, we have to determine how to convert the benefit of a training program into monetary terms. Returning to the example in Table 12.4, recall that finding, hiring, and relocating an engineer with the appropriate credentials and experience costs the organization approximately $75,000. Therefore, the monetary benefit of each option is based on the reduction in turnover multiplied by $75,000 as follows: Management Development Institute is $363,000 (4.84 reduction × $75,000); the outside vendor is $225,000 (3.0 reduction × $75,000); and the coaching option is $75,000 (1 reduction × $75,000).

Once we know the cost of a training program as well as the benefit in monetary terms, it is possible to determine the net benefit of the program. The **net benefit** of a training program refers to the estimated value of the performance improvement over the cost of improving performance. Thus, to conduct a net benefit analysis one simply subtracts the cost of a training program from its financial benefit.

The net benefit of each of the three training options is simply the monetary benefit due to the reduction in turnover minus the cost of the program. These values are presented at the bottom of Table 12.5. The Management Development Institute is the most attractive option with a net benefit of $263,000 ($363,000 − $100,000). The net benefit of the vendor-supplied program is $75,000 ($225,000 − $150,000) and for coaching it is $51,000 ($75,000 − $24,000).

Does this mean that the organization should choose the Management Development Institute program? The answer to this question again depends on the criteria used to choose a training program. If one is simply interested in the final net benefit, then clearly the Management Development Institute is the best choice. If one is interested in the least expensive option, than coaching is the best choice.

Another way to determine the financial return of a training program is the calculation of the return on investment or ROI which is described in the next section.

Return on Investment (ROI)

The most popular approach for determining the benefits or value of a training program is the calculation of return on investment. **Return on investment (ROI)** involves comparing the cost of a training program relative to its benefits. The investment refers to the cost of a training program and the return refers to the financial benefits of a training program.

A recent survey of HR trends by *Workforce Management* magazine found that 86 percent of responding organizations formally or informally measure the ROI of training.[12] For example, Cisco Systems calculates the ROI of e-learning by having employees complete a Web-based survey shortly after

Net benefit

The estimated value of the performance improvement over the cost of improving performance

Return on investment (ROI)

A comparison of the cost of a training program relative to its benefits

they have attended a training program. Employees are asked to select a percentage range that indicates the time savings or quality improvement in their performance since taking the course. The results are used to calculate the ROI of e-learning, which has been found to be 900 percent per course. In other words, every dollar the company spends on training results in a gain of $9 in productivity.[13]

The calculation of ROI is relatively simple and can be done using the following equation:

$$\text{Return on Investment} = \frac{\text{Net Program Benefits}}{\text{Cost of the Program}}$$

As an example, if a training program cost $100,000 and the financial benefit or return is $150,000, then the calculation of ROI would simply be $150,000/$100,000. The result is a 1.5 return on investment ratio. When the ROI is above 1 it indicates that the return of a training program is greater than the investment. A higher ratio of results to costs indicates a greater financial benefit to the organization. When the ROI ratio is less than 1 it indicates that the investment or cost is greater than the return. And when the ROI is 1, the return is equal to the investment and the training program breaks even.

A value of 1.5 is obviously a very good return on investment. It indicates that the organization would receive $1.5 for every $1 spent on training (1:1.5). The percentage return can also be calculated by simply multiplying the ratio by 100 so in this case, the return is 150 percent. This can also be described as a 50 percent return on investment (the gain of $50,000 is 50 percent of the $100,000 investment).

If we return to the net benefit and cost values presented in Table 12.5, we can calculate the ROI for each of the options as follows: the Management Development Institute is 3.63 ($363,000/$100,000); the outside vendor is 1.5 ($225,000/$150,000); and the coaching option is 3.12 ($75,000/$24,000). Thus, based on the ROI, the best option is the Management Development Institute. In other words, the organization receives the greatest return for each dollar spent ($3.63) on the Management Development Institute option. This is equivalent to a 363-percent return on investment, which is only slightly better than the return of the coaching option which is 3.12 or 312 percent. However, if one is concerned about obtaining the highest return on one's training investment, the choice would be the Management Development Institute option, which also resulted in the greatest net benefit.

Few managers, however, would make the final decision based on these criteria alone. As previously suggested, there are qualitative concerns that become part of the analysis—reputation of the training institute, past experience, trainee perceptions of the options, the degree to which the training can be customized, and the time factor—all will be considered before a final decision is made. For example, if time is a factor then one might choose the Management Development Institute since it has the lowest estimated training time to reach the goal while the coaching option has the longest estimated time. Thus, the preferred option will depend on the criteria used for selecting a training program.

TABLE 12.6

Calculation of Benefits and ROI for Wood Panel Plant

OPERATIONAL RESULTS AREA	HOW MEASURED	RESULTS BEFORE TRAINING	RESULTS AFTER TRAINING	DIFFERENCES (+ OR −)	EXPRESSED IN $
Quality of panels	percent rejected	2 percent rejected–1440 panels per day	1.5 percent rejected −1080 panels per day	.5 percent 360 panels	$720 per day $172,800 per year
Housekeeping	Visual inspection using 20-item checklist	10 defects (average)	2 defects (average)	8 defects	Not measurable in $
Preventable accidents	Number of accidents	24 per year	16 per year	8 per year	$48,000 per year
	Direct cost of each accident	$144,000 per year	$96,000 per year	$48,000	

Total savings: $220,800

$$\text{ROI} = \frac{\text{Return}}{\text{Investment}} = \frac{\text{Operational Results}}{\text{Training Costs}} = \frac{\$220,800}{\$32,564} = 6.8 \times 100\% = 680\% \quad \text{Net Benefit} = \$220,800 - \$32,564 = \$188,236$$

Source: Copyright August 1989, adapted from *Training & Development* journal, American Society for Training & Development. Reprinted with permission. All rights reserved.

For another example of the calculation of the net benefit and ROI, let's return to the wood panel plant. Recall that a supervisor training program that cost $32,564 was designed to improve the quality of wood panels by lowering the daily rejection rate; to improve the housekeeping of the production area; and to reduce the number of preventable accidents.[14]

Table 12.6 shows how the benefits were measured in each of the three areas and the calculation of the ROI. The results in each area before and one year after training as well as the differences are shown. Before training, the rejection rate of wood panels was 2 percent per day or 1440 panels. After training, this was reduced to 1.5 percent or 1080 panels. The difference of .5 percent per day or 360 wood panels was calculated to be a saving of $720 per day or $172,800 per year. Housekeeping was measured in terms of a visual inspection using a 20-item checklist. Before the training there was an average of 10 defects per week while after training it was reduced to two defects. Thus, the training program resulted in a reduction of eight defects per week (this could not be calculated in monetary terms). The number of preventable accidents before training was 24 per year at a cost of $144,000. After training this was reduced to 16 per year or eight fewer accidents at a cost of $96,000 and a savings of $48,000.

By comparing this information to the cost information in Table 12.2, we can calculate the net benefit and the ROI of the training program. Recall that the total cost of the training program was $32,564. The total net benefit of the

The ROI of Training at Accenture

WWW The consulting firm Accenture invests heavily in training its employees. Entry-level employees receive more than 750 hours of training during their first five years and during the next eight years they receive an additional 550 hours of training. But how much of a return does the company receive for all this training?

In an unprecedented move, the company analyzed the ROI of all training for 261 000 employees over the history of the company. They did this using a technique that begins with a comprehensive analysis of 261 000 employee records. The analysis factors out the effects of inflation, market cycle, experience, and employee level to isolate the training effect on a per-person margin.

This analysis enabled the company to determine that for every dollar invested in training, there was a return of $3.53 in net benefits. In other words, the overall ROI of all training over the history of the company was 353 percent.

On a per-person basis, they found that of the employees who take more training (the top 50 percent versus the bottom 50 percent), the top 50 percent are 70 percent more chargeable, have 20 percent higher bill rates, and stay with the company 14 percent longer.

Not surprisingly, with an ROI of 353 percent the company decided that the per-person funding for training in 2003 will be 50 percent higher than actual spending in 2002 which was already one of the biggest training budgets around.

Source: Galvin, T., Johnson, G., & Barbian, J. (2003, March). The 2003 training top 100. *Training, 40* (3), 18–38; Galvin, T. (2002, March). The 2002 training top 100. *Training, 39* (3), 42–60.

training program in monetary terms can be determined by adding the savings from the reduction in rejected wood panels ($172,800) with the savings from the reduction in preventable accidents ($48,000) and then subtracting the cost of the training program ($32,564). Thus, the final net benefit of the training program is: $220,800 − $32,564 = $188,236.

To calculate the ROI, we simply divide the monetary benefit of the program ($220,800) by the cost of the training program ($32,564): $220,800/$32,564 = 6.78. Therefore, the ROI for one year after training is equal to 6.78 or 678 percent. It is worth noting that while this analysis is an example of cost-effectiveness evaluation, the results for housekeeping (i.e., a reduction of eight defects per week) is an example of cost-benefit evaluation.

While we have shown you how to calculate the ROI for one training program at a time, some organizations might want to know the ROI for all of its training programs. To find out how one company did just that, see the Training Today feature, "The ROI of Training at Accenture."

In summary, this example as well as the previous example provides a good illustration of how the benefits of training programs can be measured in a manner that is consistent with the objectives of a training program (e.g., reduction in preventable accidents), and can then be translated into monetary terms and used to calculate a training program's net benefit and return on investment.

To learn more about how to convert benefits data into monetary values, see The Trainer's Notebook 1, "Converting Measures to Monetary Values."

One of the most difficult aspects of calculating ROI is placing a monetary value on the benefits of training. Jack Phillips, one of the leading experts on the calculation of ROI, suggests the following five steps for converting data to monetary values.

Step 1: Focus on a single unit. Identify a particular unit of improvement in output (e.g., products, sales), quality (e.g., errors, product defects), time (to respond to a customer order or complete a project), or employee behaviour (e.g., one case of employee turnover).

Step 2: Determine a value for each unit. Place a value identified on the single unit identified in step 1. This will be easier for hard measures such as production, quality, and time because most organizations record the value of one unit of production or the cost of a product defect. It will be more difficult to do for softer measures such as the cost of one employee absence.

Step 3: Calculate the change in performance. Determine the change in performance following training after factoring out other potential influences. This change in units of performance should be directly attributable to the training.

Step 4: Obtain an annual amount. The industry standard for an annual performance change is equal to the total change in the performance data during one year.

Step 5: Determine the annual value. The annual value of improvement equals the annual performance change, multiplied by the unit value.

Source: Phillips. J. J. (1996, April). How much is the training worth? *Training & Development*, 20–24. Copyright © April 1996, *T+D*. Reprinted with permission of American Society for Training & Development.

The Credibility of Estimates

We have been discussing the costs and benefits of training programs and how to calculate the return on training investments. However, it is important to realize that this is not an exact science. One must make some assumptions and judgments when estimating the monetary benefits of a training program. As a result, the process only works if managers and clients accept the assumptions that have to be made. The estimation of benefits is an inexact procedure and trainers should be concerned about professional credibility.

Credibility is a major issue in cost-effectiveness evaluation and the data must be accurate and the process believable.[15] Consider the example of a large bank that was experiencing a high rate of turnover. A training program was designed to counter the turnover problem. The cost of employee turnover needed to be estimated to calculate the ROI. But actual cost calculation was difficult because of the many interacting variables—administrative costs, interviewing, testing, relocation, orientation, increase in supervisory time, initial less-than-optimal performance, on-the-job training—all make up the cost of replacing one person. As the bank did not want to devote the considerable resources necessary to developing a precise calculation, turnover was classified as a soft cost and a combination of approaches was used to derive an acceptable figure.

Initially, a literature search was used to determine that another institution in the same industry had calculated a cost of $25,000 per turnover. This figure, derived by an internal-audit unit and verified by a consulting specialist in turnover reduction, was used as a starting point. The application of this statistic to another (even though quite similar) organization, however, was in question. The training staff then met with senior executives "to agree on a turnover cost value to use in gauging the success of the program. Management agreed on an estimate that was half the amount from the study, $12,500. This was considered very conservative because other turnover studies typically yield statistics of greater value. Management felt comfortable with the estimate, however, and it was used on the benefits side of program evaluation. Although not precise, this exercise yielded a figure that was never challenged" (p. 337).[16]

The term "never challenged" is significant. Trainers must perform cost-effectiveness evaluations from a position of strength. In this example, senior managers were brought on-side when they were used as experts. It mattered little that the turnover cost was set at $12,500 rather than $25,000, because the benefit estimation produced from these data was credible and accepted by those with the power to make investment decisions.

Thus, despite the appearance of quantitative rigour, virtually all but the simplest cost-effectiveness evaluations are dependent to a greater or lesser extent on some assumptions and expert opinion.[17] Trainers must ensure that their clients and management agree on the cost factors and the measurement and estimation of benefits. Management and clients must perceive benefit estimates as credible, believable, and acceptable. It is therefore critical that trainers find out what management deems to be most important in terms of the benefits and expected results, and whenever possible, obtain cost estimates (e.g., the cost of turnover) from management.

It also helps to use internal and external experts to assist in making benefit estimates. Because they are experts who are familiar with the situation, they are likely to be seen as credible by management. For example, if one wanted to estimate the cost of employee grievances, a good expert would be a manager of labour relations. Estimates might also be obtained from other sources who are close to the situation such as trainees and their supervisors.[18]

For some guidelines on how to increase the credibility of the estimates of training benefits, see The Trainer's Notebook 2, "Increasing the Credibility of Benefit Estimates."

Utility Analysis

As described in Chapter 11, in a typical training evaluation study the performance of a training group is compared to an untrained or control group that did not receive the training in order to determine how effective the training program was for improving job performance. While the results of this comparison might tell us that there is a significant statistical difference in the job performance between the two groups, it does not tell us the dollar value associated with the training program. Utility analysis, however, can do just that and it is another approach for determining the costs and benefits of training programs.

Utility analysis is a method for forecasting the net financial benefits that result from human resource programs such as training and development. Utility analysis involves procedures in which the effectiveness of a training program can be translated into dollars and cents.[19]

Utility analysis

A method to forecast the net financial benefits that result from human resource programs such as training and development

Increasing the Credibility of Benefit Estimates

Following these guidelines can increase the credibility of your estimates of the benefits of a training program.

1. Take a conservative approach when making estimates and assumptions.
2. Use the most credible and reliable sources for estimates.
3. Explain the approaches and assumptions used in the conversion.
4. When results appear overstated, consider adjusting the numbers to achieve more realistic values.
5. Use hard data whenever possible.

Source: Phillips. J. J. (1996, April). How much is the training worth? *Training & Development*, 20–24. Copyright © April 1996, *T+D*. Reprinted with permission of American Society for Training & Development.

To calculate the utility of a training program, several key factors must be considered. One of the most important factors is the effectiveness of the training program. In other words, what is the difference in job performance between employees who are trained and those who do not receive training? This is sometimes referred to as the effect size. The larger the effect size, the more effective a training program will be and the greater will be its utility.

A second key factor is what is known as the standard deviation of job performance in dollars of untrained employees. This factor has to do with how much of a difference there is in the job performance of untrained employees and the monetary value of this difference. The standard deviation of job performance in dollar terms is an important factor because in jobs in which the contribution of individual employees to the organization is widely different, an effective training program will improve the performance of a greater number of employees and will, therefore, result in larger dollar gains. When individual contributions are relatively similar, an effective training program is less likely to result in large dollar gains. Therefore, it is necessary to know or estimate the value of the standard deviation of job performance of untrained employees to make estimates of utility. There are several approaches for doing this such as asking supervisors to provide an estimate of the dollar value of performance. The larger the standard deviation of job performance of the untrained group the greater the utility of a training program.

A third factor is the number of employees trained. The more employees who are trained the greater the utility. A fourth factor is the expected length of time that the training benefits will last. The longer the effects of training will last, the higher the utility of a training program.

Utility is equal to the multiplication of all of these factors minus the cost of the training program (cost per employee × number of employees trained). The following formula is used to estimate the utility of a training program:[20]

$$\Delta U = (T)(N)(d_t)(SDy) - (N)(C)$$

where

ΔU = utility, or the dollar value of the program

T = the number of years the training has a continued effect on performance

N = the number of people trained

d_t = the true difference in job performance between the average trained and untrained employee in standard deviation units (effect size)

SDy = the standard deviation of job performance in dollars of the untrained group

C = the cost of training each employee

Consider a simple example. To increase the number of toys produced in a toy factory, a training program is implemented and 50 of the plant employees attend. Compared to a group of workers who do not attend the training program, the performance of the 50 trained employees is found to be twice as high (e.g., they produce 100 toys per day compared to 50 produced by untrained workers). We will assume that this equals an effect size of 2. We also assume that the standard deviation of job performance of the untrained employees is $100. The expected length of time that the training will last is estimated to be five years. The cost of the training program is $300 per employee. Using the utility equation above, we can calculate the utility of the training program as follows:

$$\Delta U = 5(50)(2)(\$100) - 50(\$300)$$
$$\Delta U = \$50,000 - \$15,000$$
$$\Delta U = \$35,000$$

Thus, the expected utility of the training program for the 50 employees trained is $35,000. This amount might be even greater if the training program lasts longer than five years or if the untrained employees learn how to improve their performance by working with and observing the trained employees. The ROI can also be calculated by dividing the utility by the total cost of the program: $35,000/15,000 = 2.33.

An interesting extension of the use of the utility formula is conducting a **break-even analysis** or finding the value at which benefits equal costs and utility is equal to zero.[21] This analysis can be done for any of the terms in the utility equation. However, it is most meaningful to conduct a break-even analysis for the effect size or the standard deviation. For example, what is the break-even effect size for the example presented above? This can be calculated by dividing the cost of the training program ($15,000) by the multiplicative function of the other factors; that is, (N)(T)(SDy) or (50)(5)(100). The calculations are as follows:

$$d_t = 15,000/25,000$$
$$d_t = .6$$

Thus, a training program with an effect size of .6 will result in a utility of zero, and an effect size greater than .6 will result in a utility that is greater than zero. Therefore, a training program that is considerably less effective than the one in the example would still be likely to result in a financial gain as long as the effect size is greater than .6.

Break-even analysis

Finding the value at which benefits equal costs and utility is equal to zero

Managing Performance Through Training and Development

Break-even analysis can be very useful because it helps reduce the uncertainty associated with the estimates of the various parameters used to calculate utility. For example, to the extent that the break-even effect size is far below the actual effect size used to calculate utility, the greater the confidence one can have in the results.[22]

Supporting the Costing Function

Costing training programs involves more than simply working with costing sheets and measuring benefits. It also requires the support of a number of activities. In this section, we discuss a number of activities that support the costing function including cost-benefit tracking systems, accounting treatment of training costs, and record keeping.

Cost-Benefit Tracking Systems

One of the most important facets of a costing system is a database that can be used to measure the progress an organization is making toward meeting its objectives. In particular, historical data can be invaluable when costing new proposals or in negotiating for new funding.

The major weakness has been the difficulty in showing a training program's contribution to profits. Without a method of collating and reporting successes in financial terms, the training professional is reduced to a minor supporting role in the corporate enterprise.

Accounting Treatment of Training Costs

Once training costs have been identified, they have to be incorporated into the accounting system so that they can be included in the total cost of production or service rendered. There are three ways to administer training accounts.

1. *Allocation of costs.* Costs can be shared with other departments and may, for example, be allocated according to the number employed in a department and its labour turnover or output. The main advantage of this method is its simplicity. Because of that simplicity, it is the most widely used method. However, this method has disadvantages:

   - It is contrary to the principle that managers should not be held accountable for costs they do not control.
   - It does not relate to actual use of the training facilities or services.
   - It gives no incentive to the training unit or professional to reduce costs and to improve efficiency.

2. *Selling the service.* Under this system, the training unit is required to sell its services at competitive rates to the other departments, the aim being to cover the cost of the training department.[23] For example, at CIBC the training function operates as a business and other divisions

of the organization are billed for the delivery of Web- and classroom-based courses.[24] The main advantages of this method are:

- Control over training costs (training costs have to remain reasonable or the training function will price itself out of the reach of consumer departments)
- A check on the relevance and efficiency of the training offered (training is carefully evaluated by the departmental managers who are required to pay for it)

The main disadvantage of this approach is the fluctuating demand for training services and the consequent planning difficulties.

3. *Policy costs.* Under this system, training costs are regarded as company policy costs and are stated as such in the accounts. Training costs are accumulated and shown as a deduction from the gross profit of the business. This approach is simple but can mean that control over training expenditures is less rigorous than it should be. Use of the method can, however, be justified when training is designed to keep human resources available, irrespective of individual departmental needs, such as in a company-wide, management-development scheme.

Some form of joint responsibility for or division of costs appears to be the best solution. A fixed charge can be made to the departments according to the number of staff undergoing training and the duration and type of training given. This charge should be fixed in advance and be a realistic estimate of the expected cost of training an average employee. The departments utilizing the services know the amount in advance. The training department is treated as a profit centre in its own right; it is expected to show a profit on the fixed charges levied. In the company accounts, the training department's profit or loss is credited or debited, respectively, to the training account in the ledger, to which the total of the charges levied on the departments using the service is also debited. The balance on this training account is then incorporated in the final profit and loss account in the usual way.

Record Keeping

Record keeping is not done for its own sake, but as a communication tool. Evidence needs to be presented that a contribution from training is being made on a day-to-day basis, rather than at a once-a-year review before the next year's training plan is written.[25] In addition, historical and comparative data can be useful in the identification of opportunities. A flow chart can be used to advantage, to discourage "duplicate efforts and unnecessarily complicated procedures," and to prevent bottlenecks.[26]

Summary

As organization investments in training and development increase along with the importance of training for organizational competitiveness and effectiveness, organizations want to know the financial benefits and ROI of their training and development programs. This chapter described the methods and approaches for estimating the costs and benefits of training programs. The differences between cost-effectiveness and cost-benefit analysis were described and examples of the calculation of the costs, benefits, net benefits, and ROI of training programs were provided. This information is not only important for budgeting purposes and for comparing the costs of training programs, but it is also important for training evaluation. Utility analysis was also described as an alternative approach to calculate the financial benefits of training programs. The importance of credibility in estimating the costs and benefits of training programs was also discussed as well as the activities required to support the costing function.

Key Terms

break-even analysis (page 354)
cost-benefit evaluation (page 345)
cost-effectiveness evaluation (page 345)
costing (page 336)
developmental costs (page 339)
direct costs (page 338)

indirect costs (page 338)
net benefit (page 347)
overhead costs (page 339)
return on investment (ROI) (page 347)
trainee compensation (page 339)
utility analysis (page 352)

Weblinks

Accenture: www.accenture.ca (page 350)

Cisco Systems: www.cisco.com (page 347)

RPC Icons

RPC 12.1 Assesses and reports on the costs and benefits of engaging internal and external suppliers of development programs, given the organizational constraints and objectives.
RPC 12.2 Conducts an evaluation of the program.

Discussion Questions

1. Discuss the pros and cons of calculating the ROI of training and development programs. Should trainers always do this as part of a training evaluation?
2. What are some of the things a trainer might do to increase the credibility of his/her monetary estimates of the benefits of a training program?
3. What is the difference between cost-benefit evaluation and cost-effectiveness evaluation? What are some situations in which a trainer might want to calculate one or the other?
4. What is a utility analysis and how is it used to determine the cost and benefits of a training program? What is a break-even analysis and how can it help to understand the value of a training program?

5. What are the three ways to administer training accounts and the advantages and disadvantages of each one?
6. Why should trainers be concerned about calculating the costs and benefits of training programs? What are the advantages and disadvantages of doing so?
7. What are the different ways of categorizing the costs of training programs?
8. Why do you think so few Canadian organizations evaluate the financial benefits of training programs? Do you think that more organizations should do so? What might be required in order to increase the number of organizations that evaluate the financial benefits of training?

The Great Training Debate

1. Debate the following: Calculating the monetary benefits and ROI of training and development is the most important way to evaluate training.
2. Debate the following: The calculation of a training program's ROI is more art than science and should be abandoned.

Using the Internet

1. To find out the latest about ROI and training, visit the website of *Workforce Management*, at **www.workforce.com**. Then click on training and development and do a search for an article on training and ROI. Choose an article that interests you and write a brief review of the article to present to your class.
2. To learn about one approach for calculating the ROI of training, go to **www.workplacebasicskills.com/frame/free_tools/roi/worksheet.htm** and find out about the Training ROI Worksheet. Think about the most recent training course you have taken in a current or previous job, and then calculate the ROI. Alternatively, ask a friend or family member about a recent training program they have attended and calculate the ROI. What is the ROI of the training program? Was the training program worth taking? What parameters would have to change in order to increase the program's ROI? How effective is the ROI Worksheet for calculating the ROI of a training program?
3. To find out how companies in Canada measure the success of training, visit Industry Canada at: **http://strategis.ic.gc.ca/epic/internet/incts-scf.nsf/en/sl00029e.html.**
   Answer the following questions:

   1. How do companies measure training success?
   2. What percentage of companies measure ROI?
   3. What types of training are the most frequently evaluated?

4. To learn about how some Canadian companies are calculating the ROTI (return on training investment) of their training programs, go to **http://strategis.ic.gc.ca/epic/internet/incts-scf.nsf/en/sl00041e.html**. Review the cases of companies that have calculated the return on training investment (ROTI) and write a brief summary with the following information:

   1. How did each company calculate the ROTI?
   2. What was the ROTI for each training program?
   3. What were the training costs and benefits calculated for each training program?
   4. Did the companies do a cost-benefit or cost-effectiveness evaluation?

5. To find out about the Canadian ROI Network, go to: **www.cstd.ca/networking/cop/roi_network.html**.
   Answer the following questions:

   1. What is the Canadian ROI Network?
   2. What tools are available through the Canadian ROI Network?
   3. Click on the ROI resources page and review some of the case studies. Choose one of the cases and briefly summarize how the organization calculated the costs, benefits, and ROI of training.

Exercises

In-Class

1. In order to calculate the benefits of training programs, one has to develop measures that are consistent with a training program and its objectives. As well, some of these measures will need to be converted into monetary terms. For each of the following training programs, identify some of the benefits that can be measured for the purpose of cost-benefit evaluation and cost-effectiveness evaluation:

   a. Sales training
   b. Management development
   c. Customer-relations training
   d. Health and safety training
   e. Quality training
   f. Sexual harassment training

   To learn more about these training programs, refer to Chapters 13 and 14.

2. Consider a situation in which you, a trainer for an organization that manufactures sportswear, must present information on the costs and benefits of a training program to management who is about to decide if

the program will be implemented organization-wide. You have already designed the training program and delivered it to one group of employees and you want to begin offering it to the rest of the organization. How will you present the information to management? Will you present information on the net benefit, ROI, and/or utility analysis? Will you present cost-benefit information or cost-effectiveness information? What are the advantages and disadvantages of presenting information on each of these? Do you think that trainers should present financial information about the benefits of training to management? What are the advantages and disadvantages of doing so?

3. As the housing market began to heat up, the Renswartz Realty Company decided to capitalize by increasing the number of listings and sales on a monthly basis. In order to do this, the company president believed they would have to do two things. First, they would have to better market the company's superior customer service. Second, they would have to train all agents to improve their sales and customer service skills. Choosing an advertising company turned out to be much easier than choosing a training program. Two consulting firms were contacted to provide a proposal to design and implement a training program that would be attended by all 200 of the company's sales agents.

The first consulting firm proposed a five-day program that would consist of lectures on "how to get more listings," "how to improve your service," and "making the sale," and would involve videos and behavioural modelling. According to the consulting firm, research has shown that the sales performance of those who have attended the training is significantly better than those who have not; the effect size of the program is .35. The training is expected to last for two years and will cost $1,500 per employee.

The second consulting firm proposed a similar program with the exception that it would be for only two days and would consist of sessions on "how to improve your sales," and "providing excellent service." Research on the training program has found it to be highly effective, with an effect size of .25. The effects have been found to last for one year at which time follow-up sessions are required. The cost of the training program is $450 per employee.

Based on the current sales performance of all 200 sales agents at Renswartz Realty, the standard deviation of sales is $15,000.

   a. Calculate the utility of the training programs proposed by each of the consulting firms.

   b. Calculate the break-even effect size for both training programs.

   c. What are the advantages and disadvantages of each training program?

   d. Which training program should the company purchase?

   e. What are the advantages and limitations of this approach for calculating the benefits of a training program?

4. Consider the costs and benefits of a university or college course such as the training and development course you are now taking. Using the five cost categories discussed in the chapter, identify the major costs of the course and try to come up with some estimates. Now consider the benefits. What benefits would you include if you were to do a cost-effectiveness and a cost-benefit analysis? How would you determine the ROI and utility of your course? Consider the costs and benefits from the institution's perspective and the student's perspective.

5. Think about the last time you attended a training program. Based on what you know about the program, make a list of the various costs in each of the following cost categories: direct costs, indirect costs, development costs, overhead costs, and compensation for participants. In addition, make a list of the potential benefits of the program. What information would you need in order to determine the monetary value of these benefits? What additional information would you require in order to calculate the utility of the program?

In-the-Field

1. To find out about the evaluation of the costs and benefits of training in an organization, contact the human resource department of an organization and ask the following questions:

   - To what extent do they determine the cost of training programs and how do they do it and who does it? What cost categories are used?
   - To what extent do they determine the benefits of training programs and how do they do it? Who is involved in calculating the monetary value of training?
   - To what extent do they conduct a cost-effectiveness evaluation and a cost-benefit evaluation and who does this?
   - To what extent do they determine the net benefit and return on investment (ROI) of training programs and who is responsible for it?
   - What are some of the reasons why they do or do not evaluate the net benefit and ROI of training?

   Based on your interview, how well do you think the organization is evaluating the costs and benefits of training? What recommendations would you give the organization for improving its evaluation of the costs and benefits of training?

Case Incident

Measuring Results at CIBC

In an effort to measure the benefits of training, CIBC conducted a pilot project with a 100 financial advisers across Canada. The participants took a quiz to diagnose their baseline knowledge of company pension plans, before taking a half-day workshop on how to advise clients on the subject. After the training the participants completed a survey that asks if they actually applied the knowledge and the business impact (e.g., did you build more business or generate more leads?)

Questions

1. Describe how to do a cost-effectiveness evaluation and a cost-benefit evaluation of this training program.
2. What information is required to calculate the net benefit and ROI of the training program? What else has to be done to obtain all of the information required?

Source: Staples, S. (2003, November 9). Cult of accountability. *Canadian Business*, 76 (21), 123–24.

Case

DATAIN

DATAIN is a company started by two students who saw an opportunity to make some money and help pay for their education. With an increasing number of organizations deciding to survey their customers and employees, they saw a need for data input and analyses. With a loan from their parents, they rented space, purchased 20 used computers and set up shop. They hired other students to do data input and analyses and began advertising their services. Within a relatively short period of time they were having trouble keeping up with demand. In fact, business was so good they had to hire more students and purchase more computers.

After about six months, however, they began to notice some problems. The data files were often full of mistakes, and the data analysis was often incomplete and incorrect. As a result, almost 40 percent (20 jobs per month) of all jobs had to be completely redone. This turned out to be a rather costly problem. Each job took approximately 10 hours and cost the company $150 (students were paid $15 per hour).

In order to try to cut down on this unanticipated expense, DATAIN decided to invest in a training program to reduce the mistakes and errors in data input and analyses. They hired a training consultant to conduct a needs assessment, develop and deliver a training program, and conduct the training evaluation.

Based on the figures provided by the consultant, DATAIN thought it would be a good idea to determine if the training program would be a worthwhile investment. The consultant estimated that the needs assessment and training evaluation would each take about 20 hours at a cost of $100 per hour. The fee to purchase the actual training program would be $5,000. The training program itself would be for one day (8 hours) at a cost of $200 per hour to the consultant.

In addition to the consultant fees, DATAIN would also have to give their 25 employees one full day (8 hours) of pay ($15 per hour); lunch that would cost $10 per employee; and coffee and snacks at a cost of $50 for the day. The training would take place at DATAIN so the only cost for classroom space would be a portion of the cost associated with room heating, lighting, and maintenance which was estimated to be $100 for the day. As well, some administrative support work would be required to prepare and plan for the training which would involve about two days (8 hours per day) of work on the part of DATAIN's secretary, who is paid $15 an hour.

According to the training consultant, DATAIN could anticipate a 95-percent drop in mistakes and errors. In other words, instead of 20 jobs a month, only 1 would have to be redone. This sounded like a good investment. However, DATAIN wasn't sure how to calculate the potential financial benefit of the training program and if they should hire the consultant.

Questions

1. Calculate the costs of the training program in terms of the different categories for determining training costs. What is the cost associated with each category as well as the total cost of the training program?
2. Calculate the benefit, net benefit, and return on investment for the proposed training program. Based on your calculations, is the training program a good investment?
3. What other factors besides the benefit, net benefit, and ROI should the company consider in deciding whether or not to purchase the proposed training program?
4. If the company wanted to conduct a utility analysis, what additional information would they need? What would be required in order to obtain this information? In other words, what would they or the consultant have to do in order to obtain the necessary information?

References

1. Excerpt from Galvin, T. (2003, March). 2003 training top 100: Top five profile & ranking. Sprint. *Training, 40* (3), 44–45; Dolezalek, H. (2004, March). Training top 100: Top five profile & ranking. Sprint, *Training, 40* (3), 46–47.
2. Phillips. J. J. (1996, February). ROI: The search for best practices. *Training and Development,* 42–47.
3. Salas, E., & Cannon-Bowers, J. A. (2001). The science of training: A decade of progress. *Annual Review of Psychology, 52,* 471–99.
4. Parker, R. O., & Cooney, J. (2005). Learning & development outlook 2005. *The Conference Board of Canada.* Ottawa.
5. Staples, S. (2003, November 9). Cult of accountability: Does employee training pay off? Accounting techniques and science-inspired metrics evaluate return on investment. *Canadian Business, 76* (21), 123–24.
6. Galvin, T. (2003, March). The 2003 training top 100. *Training, 40* (3), 18–36.
7. Schettler, J. (2003, March). 2003 training top 100: Top five profile & ranking. Pfizer. *Training, 40* (3), 40–41.
8. Galvin, T., Johnson, G., & Barbian, J. (2003, March). The 2003 training top 100. *Training, 40* (3), 18–38.
9. Robinson, D. G., & Robinson, J. (1989, August). Training for impact. *Training & Development Journal, 43* (8), 34–42.

10. Robinson, D. G., & Robinson, J. (1989, August).

11. Prepared by Dr. Gary D. Geroy, Colorado State University at Fort Collins. Reproduced with permission from his client organization.

12. (2002, May). Companies continue to invest in training and evaluate ROI. *Workforce Online*: www.workforce.com

13. Gale, S. F. (2002, August). Measuring the ROI of e-learning. *Workforce Management*, 74–77.

14. Robinson, D. G., & Robinson, J. (1989, August).

15. Bedinham, K. (1998). Proving the effectiveness of training. *Education & Training 40* (4), 166–67; Phillips. J. J. (1996, April). How much is the training worth? *Training & Development*, 20–24.

16. Phillips, J. J. (1991, Autumn). Measuring the return on HRD. *Employment Relations Today, 18* (3), 329–42.

17. Geroy, G. D., & Wright, P. C. (1988). Evaluation research: A pragmatic program-focused research strategy for decision makers. *Performance Improvement Quarterly, 1* (3), 17–26; Wright, P. C. (1990). Validating hospitality curricula within associated-sponsored certification programs: A qualitative methodology and a case study. *Hospitality Research Journal, 14* (1), 117–32.

18. Phillips. J. J. (1996, April).

19. Cascio, W. F. (1991). *Costing human resources: The financial impact of behavior in organizations.* Boston, MA: Kent.

20. Schmidt, F. L., Hunter, J. E., & Pearlman, K. (1982). Assessing the economic impact of personnel programs on workforce productivity. *Personnel Psychology, 35*, 333–47.

21. Cascio, W. F. (1991).

22. Mathieu, J. E., & Leonard, R. L. Jr. (1987). Applying utility concepts to a training program in supervisory skills: A time-based approach. *Academy of Management Journal, 30*, 316–35.

23. Long, R. F. (1990). Protecting the investment in people—Making training pay. *Journal of European Industrial Training, 14* (7), 21–27.

24. Staples, S. (2003, November 9).

25. Brown, M. G. (1992). The Baldrige criteria—Better, tougher, and clearer for 1992. *Journal for Quality and Participation, 15* (2), 70–75.

26. Kaydos, W. (1991). *Measuring, managing, and maximizing performance.* Cambridge, MA: Productivity Press.

Chapter 13

Training Programs

Chapter Learning Objectives

After reading this chapter, you should be able to:

- describe orientation training programs and basic-skills and literacy training
- describe technical skills training and information technology training
- discuss WHMIS legislation and describe the type of information that should be included in health and safety training programs
- describe total quality management and quality training programs
- describe team training and the kinds of skills that team members require to work in teams
- describe sales training and the skills required to be effective in sales
- discuss customer service training and the skills that employees require to interact effectively with customers
- define sexual harassment and describe sexual harassment training
- describe ethics training, diversity training, and cross-cultural training and their use in organizations

www.royalstarfoods.
com

ROYAL STAR FOODS LIMITED

Royal Star Foods Limited is a seafood processing plant in Tignish, Prince Edward Island, and a subsidiary of Tignish Fisheries Cooperative Association Ltd. With a workforce of 350–400, it is the largest single plant processor of lobster in P.E.I. and one of the most modern state-of-the art seafood processing plants in eastern Canada. In addition to processing lobster, Royal Star also processes snow crab, rock crab, dogfish, scallops, mackerel, herring, mussels, and groundfish for international markets in Canada, Europe, Japan, and the United States.

Royal Star Foods' plant is a highly mechanized working environment from weighing product on the dock to using the computerized time clock. Employees' reactions to such "high-tech" gadgets have ranged from complete fear to "show me the button" to "teach me what I need to know." However, new processing equipment with new safety requirements, and the introduction of more sophisticated quality control procedures motivated managers to focus on employees' literacy requirements and the need to raise the literacy levels of employees.

A voluntary project team made up of employees, managers, and a Workplace Education PEI representative was put together to determine a "learning route" for both the company and its employees. An assessment was conducted to find out what learning programs were needed, who was interested in what, and how to go about implementing the learning initiatives.

A company-wide survey of employees indicated that many were interested in taking computer courses. In the winter of 1999, the first workplace literacy program began—a basic computer literacy program that the project team felt would pave the way to a "learning comfort zone" for the company.

Workplace literacy programs at the company are designed to enhance employees' reading and math skills using General Equivalency Degree (GED) materials that have been customized for the workplace. The curriculum has also been customized to the fish processing industry. In 2000, 16 Royal Star Foods employees chose to write the GED examination, and all of them passed. In 2001, of the eight employees who participated in the GED Preparation program, five chose to write the examination and four received their GED certificate. Employees who receive their GEDs get a great deal of recognition at a company-sponsored event where their GED certificates are proudly handed out.

In 2001, employees were so interested in the computer literacy course that the company offered employees four classes that focus on using e-mail, working with spreadsheets, using the Internet, and word-processing techniques. In addition, a communications program focuses on oral and written communications techniques within the structure of the company. Skills in problem-solving, conflict resolution, and teamwork are covered in the program.

Royal Star Foods now has over 17 workplace literacy programs including computer training, General Equivalency Degree (GED) programs, and customized communication programs. The programs have increased the confidence level of employees and the entire company. The result is a more productive and efficient workplace and a skilled workforce that is more willing to express their views and offer suggestions for improving the production process—ultimately helping the company's bottom line.[1]

Source: Watt, D. (2002). "Excellence in Workplace Literacy, Medium Business Winner 2002: Royal Star Foods Ltd." Ottawa: The Conference Board of Canada, 2002.

By now you should be familiar with the training and development process. We have covered all of the major steps in the development of a training program and the instructional systems design (ISD) model of the training and development process: needs analysis, training objectives, design, methods, delivery, transfer of training, and the evaluation and costing of training programs. At this point, you might be asking yourself, "What type of training programs do organizations design and deliver to their employees?"

Organizations offer many different types of training like the workplace literacy programs at Royal Star Foods Limited. The purpose of this chapter is to describe the major types of training programs that are designed and delivered by organizations today.

Types of Training Programs

During the last decade, organizations have made dramatic changes in response to an ever-changing work environment. New work arrangements, combined with new technologies, have led to a demand for skilled employees in both the manufacturing and service sectors. Whether employees are learning to operate a new computer system on the factory floor or how to provide customers with excellent service, some type of training is almost always required. In fact, two-thirds of employee learning in Canadian organizations occurs through formal training programs and 70 percent of formal training courses in the United States are provided in classrooms with live instructors.[2]

Thus, it is not surprising that training and development has experienced dramatic growth in the last decade. It has been estimated that $51.1 billion was spent on formal workplace training in the United States in 2005.[3] According to The Conference Board of Canada, the total average annual training investment by Canadian organizations in 2004 was approximately $4.9 million across all industries. This figure translates into $914 spent per employee and an average of 1.75 percent of payroll invested in training. The not-for-profit, financial services, government, and technology and communication sectors averaged the

Chapter 13: Training Programs

TABLE 13.1

Training Types as a Percentage of Training Expenditures in Canadian Organizations

Professional skills training	14.7
Management/supervisory skills training	12.7
Information technology skills training	9.8
Technical processes and procedures training	9.0
Occupational health and safety/government mandated	7.5
Interpersonal communication training	7.1
New employee orientation training	6.9
Customer relations training	6.8
Executive development	6.7
Product knowledge training	6.3
Quality, competition, and business practices training	4.7
Sales and dealer training	4.6
Basic-skills training	2.2
Other	2.1

Source: Parker, R. O., & Cooney, J. (2005). Learning & development outlook 2005. *The Conference Board of Canada*. Ottawa. Reprinted by permission of The Conference Board of Canada.

most investment in formal training activities in 2004. The personal services, wholesale and retail, and health and education sectors had the lowest average training investment. The highest percentages of total training expenditures in Canadian organizations are for professional and technical and non-technical groups, which accounted for almost half of the total investment.[4]

With so much money and effort being spent on training, you might be wondering what types of training employees are receiving. A recent study asked employees about the training they receive and found that nearly 80 percent of the employees reported that they had received some type of training in the past year.[5] The most common types of training were job-specific and technical skills training followed by the use of new technology. Common types of soft skills training included teamwork, communication, problem-solving, and customer service training. When asked if additional training would be useful to them, 99 percent of the respondents said yes; however, most indicated they wanted more of the same type of training they were already receiving. The exception to this was technology. In terms of training that is not provided by their organization but would be of value, 25 percent indicated computer training or some other type of current technology. If their organization offered it, nearly 75 percent said they would sign up for training on the use of new technology, communication skills to help them work better with other people, job-specific and technical skills, and management training.[6]

To provide you with some idea of the types of training programs provided by organizations, Table 13.1 lists training types as a percentage of training expenditures in Canadian organizations. Table 13.2 indicates the frequency with

Managing Performance Through Training and Development

TABLE 13.2

Percentages of Organizations Providing Common Types of Training in the United States

TYPE OF TRAINING	% PROVIDING*
New hire orientation	66.6
Communication skills	63.0
Team building	62.7
Sexual harassment	62.0
Management skills/development	56.5
Customer service	55.5
Executive development	52.3
Quality/process improvement	49.7
Diversity, cultural awareness	48.2
Basic life, work skills	43.4
Technical skills/knowledge	40.6
Product knowledge	36.6
Safety	35.8
New equipment operation	31.8
Computer systems, applications	28.7
Sales	27.6

*Traditional training methods.

Source: Dolezalek, H. (2005, December). 2005 Industry Report. Training 42 (12), 14–28. V N U Business Publications. This work is protected by copyright and it is being used with the permission of Access Copyright. Any alteration of its content or further copying in any form whatsoever is strictly prohibited.

which the different types of training are offered by organizations in the United States. Notice that in Canada, professional and skills training, management and supervisory skills training, information technology skills training, and technical processes and procedures training account for almost half of the total training investment of Canadian organizations. Furthermore, these four training types dominate across industry sectors. On the other hand, basic-skills training continues to receive the lowest percentage of training investment, with only 2.2 percent.[7] Unfortunately, training programs like those offered by Royal Star Foods Limited are not very common in Canadian organizations.

In the remainder of this chapter, we will review the major types of training programs provided by organizations today.

New Employee Orientation Training

New employee orientation training refers to programs that are designed to introduce new employees to their job, the people they will be working with, and the organization.[8] Formal orientation and training programs have become the main method used by organizations to socialize new employees.[9]

Most organizations provide some type of orientation for new employees. For example, a study of 100 major British organizations found that an overwhelming majority provided new hires with formalized, off-the-job induction training within four weeks of entry. Most of the organizations provided standardized programs that were designed and conducted by in-house human resource practitioners. The content of induction training was general in nature and pertained mostly to health and safety, terms and conditions of employment, organizational history and structure, specific training provisions, and human resource management policies and procedures.[10]

Many companies today realize the value and importance of new employee orientation training. Starbucks, for example, has a comprehensive orientation and training program. New employees receive 24 hours of training in their first 80 hours of employment. CEO Howard Schultz greets new hires via video and they learn about the company's history and obsession with quality and customer service.[11]

This first phase is followed by classes during the next six weeks on topics such as "Brewing the Perfect Cup," "Retail Sales," "Coffee Knowledge," and "Customer Service." Employees are also taught relaxation techniques and guidelines for on-the-job interpersonal relations.[12] According to CEO Howard Schultz, "For people joining the company we try to define what Starbucks stands for, what we're trying to achieve, and why that's relevant to them" (p. 126).[13]

Research has shown that orientation training has a positive effect on the attitudes and adjustment of new hires. According to Daniel Feldman, "the overall training program plays a major role in how individuals make sense of and adjust to their new job settings" (p. 399).[14]

One of the authors of this text examined the training of entry-level accountants in Canadian accounting firms and found that the amount of training received was positively related to their ratings of training helpfulness, and both the amount and helpfulness of training were positively related to job attitudes and negatively related to turnover.[15] Not surprisingly, the turnover rate at Starbucks is around 60 percent, which is considerably less than the average rate of 150 percent in the specialty-coffee industry.[16]

In a recent study on a new employee orientation training program, employees attended a three-hour orientation program that was designed to help them feel more a part of the organization; learn more about the organization's language, traditions, mission, history, and structure; and better understand the organization's basic workplace principles. The program consisted of an introduction and overview; a videotaped welcome from the company president; a game/exercise to familiarize employees with the company's traditions and language; a videotape and discussion about the mission, history, and structure of the organization; and a lecture/discussion of the organization's basic workplace principles.[17]

The results of the study indicated that employees who attended the orientation training program were more socialized in terms of their knowledge and understanding of the organization's goals and values, history, and involvement with people. Furthermore, employees who attended the orientation also had higher organizational commitment as a result of their greater socialization. The authors concluded that orientation training can help employees become more socialized and result in greater organizational commitment.[18]

In summary, the orientation and training of new employees is one of the most common types of training. In order for new hires to learn their jobs and adjust to organizations, they require knowledge and information about their job-related tasks, work roles, group processes, and organizational attributes (e.g., organizational goals, values, history, etc.). Research has shown that newcomers' knowledge in these areas is positively related to their job satisfaction, organizational commitment, and adjustment. Knowledge about one's tasks and role is especially important for successful socialization. Thus, new employee orientation training programs should be designed to provide new hires with information and knowledge about their job, role, work group, and organization. Effective orientation programs can shape corporate culture, increase new employees' speed-to-proficiency, and lower turnover.[19]

For a good example of an orientation training program, see the Training Today feature, "Bauer Beginnings."

Training Today

Bauer Beginnings

Like many companies, Eddie Bauer had an orientation program that provided new associates with far too much information to digest in a short time period and failed to meet its potential. So after months of research and development, including focus groups and a needs analysis, Eddie Bauer University unveiled a new orientation program called "Bauer Beginnings."

New hires attend an initial program that lasts four hours and includes a guided tour through the associate resource guide, two hours of technical training to learn desktop skills, and a campus tour.

The associate resource guide includes a 90-day initial performance plan for the new hire to follow, along with an introduction to the Bauer Beginnings Associate Portal, which provides on-line access to additional information.

New associates also attend four seminars during their first 90 days at work. These seminars cover topics such as corporate history, product, and a brand overview. A performance management seminar provides associates with information regarding performance appraisals and succession planning. Supplemental components cover topics specific to each new hire.

Once the 90-day orientation period is complete, new hires are surveyed for feedback on whether they feel supervisors gave them adequate support during initial orientation. The survey results are sent to all of the corporate officers, directors, and managers to let them know if the team is effectively getting their new associates on board.

The program also contains built-in reminders for new associates to stay in contact and ask questions. Every six weeks, new associates receive targeted e-mails asking them if they have all the information they need, and reminding them of the resources they have in the corporate HR department.

The standardized orientation program ensures that all new associates begin their jobs with the same foundation and information about product and brand direction. It also gives new associates an opportunity to meet people and to understand the history of the company.

Source: Schettler, J. (2002, August). Welcome to ACME Inc. *Training, 39* (8), 36–43. Training: The Human Side of Business by Schettler, J.

Basic-Skills Training

At one time, it was possible to find a job that paid well and that did not require a high-school education. Those days are gone. The ability to read, write, and understand mathematics is now required for an increasing number of jobs. The number of factory workers who have a college education has been steadily rising over the past decade.[20] For young people, this means that a high-school diploma is the minimum amount of education they must have to acquire a good job in today's workplace.

But what about the workers who don't have a high-school education and whose jobs are changing and will require them to read, write, and understand arithmetic? Unfortunately, far too many workers in Canada fall into this category. A recent report by The Conference Board of Canada indicates that 42 percent of all Canadians aged 16 to 65 score at the lowest literacy levels and are only semi-literate. About 4.7 million Canadians score in the upper Level 2 and low Level 3 range and their limited literacy skills pose a significant challenge to their workplace performance and success. It has also been reported that only 58 percent of Canadian adults can read well enough to meet most day-to-day requirements.[21]

Literacy

The ability to understand and employ printed information in daily activities, at home, at work, and in the community—to achieve one's goals, and to develop one's knowledge and potential.

Literacy can be defined as follows:

The ability to understand and employ printed information in daily activities, at home, at work, and in the community—to achieve one's goals, and to develop one's knowledge and potential.[22] Literacy competencies are measured across the following three broad domains:[23]

Prose Literacy: The knowledge and skills needed to understand and use information from texts including editorials, news stories, brochures, and instruction manuals.

Document Literacy: The knowledge and skills required to locate and use information contained in various formats, including job applications, payroll forms, transportation schedules, maps, tables, and charts.

Quantitative Literacy. The knowledge and skills required to apply arithmetic operations, either alone or sequentially, to numbers embedded in printed materials, such as balancing a chequebook, figuring out a tip, completing an order form, or determining the amount of interest on a loan from an advertisement.

Table 13.3 shows the five literacy levels used by the International Adult Literacy Survey (IALS) to describe adult literacy, and the percentage of Canadians at each level. It is estimated that one in four Canadian adults in the labour market has literacy skills at Level 2.[24] This statistic is particularly alarming when you consider that these people will make up the bulk of the labour force for decades to come. A survey by Statistics Canada found that the literacy skills of 20 percent of recent high-school graduates were too low for entry-level jobs. Statistics Canada concluded that the literacy problem in Canada is so serious that it threatens Canada's economic future and global competitiveness.[25]

The implications of low levels of literacy are enormous. For example, "In everyday work life, this deficiency translates into secretaries who can't write letters free of grammatical errors, workers who can't read instructions that govern the operation of new machinery, and bookkeepers who can't manipulate the fractions necessary to compute simple business transactions"

TABLE 13.3

Literacy Levels

The International Adult Literacy Survey (IALS) measures literacy on a five-level scale, where Level 1 is the lowest and Level 5 is the highest. Descriptions of typical competencies and the percentage of Canadians (aged 16 to 65) at each level on the prose scale illustrate the differences between the five levels.

Level 1—16.6 percent of Canadians: At this level, respondents show very poor prose literacy skills. Individuals may, for example, be unable to determine the correct amount of medicine to give a child from information printed on a package.

Level 2—25.6 percent of Canadians: At this level, respondents can deal only with material that is simple, clearly laid out, and in which the tasks involved are not too complex. A Level 2 score denotes a weak level of skill, but more hidden than Level 1. It identifies people who can read, but test poorly. They may have developed coping skills to manage everyday literacy demands, but their low level of proficiency makes it difficult for them to face novel demands, such as learning new job skills.

Level 3—35.1 percent of Canadians: At this level, respondents demonstrate a suitable minimum for coping with the demands of everyday life and work in a complex, advanced society. A Level 3 score approximates the skill level required for successful secondary school completion and college entry. As with the higher levels, it requires the ability to integrate several sources of information and solve more complex problems.

Levels 4 and 5—22.7 percent of Canadians: At these levels, respondents demonstrate a command of higher-order information-processing skills.

Source: Campbell, A. (2005, December). Profiting from Literacy: Creating a Sustainable Workplace Literacy Program. *The Conference Board of Canada*. Ottawa; Campbell, A., & Gagnon, N. (2006, January). Literacy, Life and Employment: An Analysis of Canadian International Adult Literacy Survey (IALS) microdata. *The Conference Board of Canada*. Ottawa.

(p. 71).[26] It is estimated that the lack of basic skills in the workforce costs American organizations $60 billion in lost productivity as a result of mistakes, workplace accidents, and damage to equipment.[27] Low levels of literacy have a negative impact on individuals, businesses, and Canada's overall economy, and threaten Canada's future prosperity.[28]

It is becoming increasingly clear that organizations must provide their workforces with basic-skills training if they are to compete and survive in a global and high-tech workplace. Evidence suggests that without first providing trainees with basic-skills training, other programs and initiatives will not succeed.[29]

Basic-skills training programs are designed to provide employees with critical literacy skills and improve their ability to read things such as change orders, to make numerical calculations, to enter data for tracking, and to use

Basic-skills training

Training programs that are designed to provide employees with critical literacy skills, such as reading and arithmetic, that are required to perform their job

Key Success Factors of Workplace Literacy Programs

Research conducted by The Conference Board of Canada that included a review of the relevant literature, consultations with employers' unions and their learning partners on best practices in workplace literacy design, development, delivery, and evaluation identified the following 12 key success factors. Each success factor is an important design element in the creation and ongoing sustainability of workplace learning programs.

1. Create a learning environment.
2. Recognize literacy needs.
3. Plan before initiating.
4. Find adequate funding and support.
5. Make decision-making inclusive.
6. Design an effective curriculum.
7. Select the right instructor.
8. Use the best delivery mix.
9. Market and sell the program.
10. Engage supervisors.
11. Encourage employee participation.
12. Evaluate programs realistically.

Source: Campbell, A. (2005, December). Profiting from Literacy: Creating a Sustainable Workplace Literacy Program. *The Conference Board of Canada.* Ottawa.

the correct technical vocabulary. There are four primary types of basic-skills or remedial training: reading, basic math or arithmetic, English as a second language, and writing. Reportedly, the most popular way of teaching basic skills to manufacturing employees is on-the-job training. An increasing number of organizations are realizing that it is imperative that employees receive basic-skills training. Motorola Inc., for example, spent $40 million to train 8000 of its employees in basic skills.[30]

Organizations that have implemented basic-skills training have not only experienced improvements in productivity, efficiency, and quality, but some also report a decrease in absenteeism and the number of workers' compensation claims made, and an improvement in cross-cultural communication and morale. Basic-skills training also has advantages for employees. Not only does the training improve their skills, self-esteem, and confidence, but it also improves their chances of remaining employed. The percentages of employees who receive basic-skills training and remain employed or are promoted are higher than those of employees who do not receive training.[31]

Royal Star Foods Limited is an excellent example of an organization that has developed basic-skills and literacy training programs and was recognized for excellence by The Conference Board of Canada in 2002. Unfortunately, Royal Star Foods Limited is the exception rather than the rule. As noted earlier, Canadian organizations spend very little on basic-skills training, an under-investment that The Conference Board of Canada has described as "troubling," particularly in light of their own research, which has found that employees who improve their basic skills are more likely to learn new job-related skills more quickly and accurately, make fewer mistakes, work more efficiently, and be less resistant to change. Literacy is critical to productivity which in turn is essential to Canadian competitiveness and prosperity.[32]

See The Trainer's Notebook 1 for the key success factors of workplace literacy programs.

Technical Skills Training

Technical skills training is training in specific job skills that all employees need to perform their jobs. Among manufacturing firms, specific job skills is the type of training that the largest percentage of firms provided to more than 60 percent of employees. As well, note that in Table 13.2, technical skills and knowledge training was provided by 40.6 percent of organizations.

These figures should not be surprising given the changes in the workplace that have occurred over the past two decades. With increasing global competition, organizations have had to find new ways to stay competitive and to survive, often by adopting new technologies and the redesign of work arrangements and systems. As a result, employees have had to undergo a considerable amount of technical skills upgrading and training. Nowhere is this more apparent than in the manufacturing sector, where low-skilled employees have had to become highly skilled employees to keep their jobs and for their organizations to survive.[33]

During the mid-1980s, companies such as Corning, Motorola, and Xerox began a trend toward high-skills manufacturing. Rote assembly-line workers were replaced with workers who needed to learn new skills to operate new technology and think while they worked. These innovative practices became mainstream in the 1990s as they spread throughout the manufacturing sector. Not only did these organizations realize that investments in training can boost productivity, but that training employees to improve their skills was essential to being competitive. As a result, factory workers in North America are now being trained to improve their technical skills to the level Japanese and German workers have already attained.[34]

As organizations continue to struggle to remain competitive, they are likely to continue to increase their use of new technologies thus making technical skills training a regular and continuous part of the job for manufacturing workers.

Technical skills training
Training in specific job skills that all employees need to perform their jobs

Information Technology Training

Information technology training refers to computers and computer systems training. As shown in Table 13.2, 28.7 percent of organizations indicated that they provide computer systems and applications training. Information systems training has been ranked as one of the top 10 issues of critical importance and is known to be a key factor in the successful implementation of information systems technology.[35] Research has shown that technological failures in the workplace are most often the result of training issues rather than the technology.[36]

Information technology training usually involves either introductory computer training programs in which trainees learn about computer hardware and software, or applications training in which trainees are instructed on specific software applications to be used within the organization.[37] Applications training is required whenever an organization upgrades its computer systems.

With the growing use of computers and computer technology in the workplace, workers increasingly require training in applications. For example, factory workers must now learn to use computer controls to operate new equipment and to read computer-generated information in areas such as inventories, suppliers and customers, costs and prices.[38]

Information technology training
Training programs that focus on the use of computers and computer systems

Computer software training

Training programs that focus on how to use a specific computer software application

One of the most common types of information technology training is computer software training. "**Computer software training** refers to the planned, structured, and formal means of delivering information about how to use a specific computer software application" (p. 271).[39] Computer software training has been shown to increase trainees' ability to use the system and their motivation to use software.

Information technology training is likely to continue to be a critical area of training given the rapid pace of change in computer technology and the increasing use of computers in the workplace. This means that trainers will have to increasingly provide computer-related training to employees.

Health and Safety Training

Workplace health and safety has become an increasing concern in Canadian organizations. The costs of work-related injuries and illnesses are on the rise and present a serious threat to employees and their organizations. Approximately 900 workers die each year in Canada as a result of workplace accidents and more than 350 000 workers suffer an injury serious enough to warrant missing time from work or what is know as a lost-time injury. Workplace injuries are estimated to cost $12 billion a year.[40]

Preventing accidents and injuries and improving workplace health and safety is an important concern of workers, governments, unions, and organizations. Occupational health and safety should begin with preventative and corrective actions that eliminate or reduce accidents and injuries. Safety training is one of the most important ways to deal with accidents before they occur by educating employees in safe work methods and techniques. Employees should also be trained to recognize the chemical and physical hazards in the workplace so that they are prepared and capable of taking corrective action in the event of an accident.

As noted in Table 13.1, occupational health and safety training accounts for 7.5 percent of the average overall expenditures on training and development by Canadian organizations. In the United States, 35.8 percent of the organizations surveyed indicated that they provide safety training. These figures indicate the importance of health and safety training along with the fact that for many organizations it is government mandated.

An effective health and safety training program should include the following:[41]

- The organization's safety rules, practices, and accident and injury reporting procedures
- The duties of the employer, supervisor, and the worker as specified in the Occupational Health and Safety (OHS) legislation
- The importance of strict compliance with warning and emergency signs and signals
- The types and use of emergency equipment (e.g., extinguishers or spill retainers)
- The use, care, and acquisition of personal protective equipment
- The organizational benefits

- The known hazards and safeguards against them
- The importance of reporting other hazards (e.g., defective equipment) and the mechanism for doing so
- The emergency and evacuation procedures for dealing with things such as fires and explosions, spills, toxic exposure, and so on
- The need for good housekeeping
- Courses in first aid, CPR, and defensive driving where applicable

An important component of health and safety training involves the handling of hazardous materials and chemicals. The **Workplace Hazardous Materials Information System (WHMIS)** legislation is designed to ensure that workers across Canada are aware of the potential hazards of chemicals in the workplace and are familiar with emergency procedures for the clean-up and disposal of a spill. An important component of WHMIS legislation is employee training. Training in WHMIS is designed so that employees can identify WHMIS hazard symbols, read WHMIS supplier and workplace labels, and read and apply the information on material safety data sheets (MSDS), which outline the hazardous ingredient(s) in a product and the procedures for the safe handling of that product.[42]

Besides including health and safety education as part of the orientation and training of new employees, organizations should provide it on an ongoing basis, such as through safety meetings during working hours, especially when new procedures or equipment are introduced into the workplace. In addition, all levels of management and supervision should receive training in health and safety. Trained employees are the best deterrent to injuries, material damage, and health problems.[43]

Workplace Hazardous Materials Information System (WHMIS)

Legislation to ensure that workers across Canada are aware of the potential hazards of chemicals in the workplace and are familiar with emergency procedures for the clean-up and disposal of a spill

Quality Training

In the 1980s, North American manufacturing organizations found themselves challenged by the high quality of foreign goods. Given the emphasis on quantity and economies of scale in North America, quality was viewed as simply an inspection of goods at the end of the line.[44]

To remain competitive, however, this approach had to change. In response, organizations in North America began to invest in new programs aimed at building quality into the production process. Today, quality programs can be found in many organizations.[45] The best example of this is total quality management (TQM).

Total quality management is a systematic process of continual improvement of the quality of products and services. In addition to an emphasis on quality and continual improvement, TQM also involves teamwork and a customer focus.[46] Because TQM requires the involvement of all stakeholders in an organization, the concept moves far beyond piecemeal approaches to quality improvement, which often are limited to inspection and quality-control methods carried out by a specialized department. Although this search for quality is not a new concept, TQM can require major organizational changes.[47]

Total quality management (TQM)

A systematic process of continual improvement of the quality of an organization's products and services

TQM places the training function in a pivotal position, as the process often requires significant changes in employees' skills and the way employees work. TQM literature, however, typically contains only superficial information about new approaches to training and development. Fortunately, some training professionals have had to become involved in TQM, and have provided some guidance on how to transform traditional practices into TQM.[48]

For example, employees are empowered by having the decision-making power driven down to those who can do the most for quality improvement. TQM requires that employees at lower levels share managerial responsibility, moving away from conventional command-and-control procedures to a more participative style of management. With empowerment, the roles of employees change and they assume more responsibility. In addition, they are required to work in teams that share decision-making and problem-solving responsibilities.

Most TQM advocates emphasize the importance of training and development.[49] Without proper employee training, the act of empowerment in TQM is meaningless.[50] Training and development is the primary method of reinforcing employee commitment to the consistent delivery of high-quality products and services. Accordingly, leading TQM companies invest heavily in training and development at all levels. In the absence of proper training, many TQM systems that are excellent at identifying and quantifying the cost of performance problems are ultimately unsuccessful because there is no way of changing the behaviours that caused the deficiencies in the first place.[51]

Because quality initiatives such as TQM involve substantial changes to employees' work roles and responsibilities, comprehensive and extensive training is required in a number of areas. Harper and Rifkind have provided the following outline for TQM training:[52]

1. *Overview of the state of the organization.* This overview provides information about the health of the organization and why it is planning to implement TQM.
2. *Statement from the head of the organization.* The best way to communicate the support of top executives for TQM is for a statement by the head of the organization to be delivered in person as part of training.
3. *Overview of TQM.* Employees need to be informed about what TQM involves including the use of teams, continual improvement, customer focus, employee empowerment, and plans for implementation.
4. *Team training.* Employees need to be trained on how teams function, such as the difference between a team and a committee, the rules for team formation, the composition of teams, and team responsibilities.
5. *Training in the use of tools.* TQM involves the use of a number of statistical tools such as Pareto charts, fishbone diagrams, affinity programs, and interrelationship diagrams as part of the problem-solving and decision-making processes. Employees will need to be trained on how to use each of these tools.

Source: "A Training Program for TQM in the Diverse Workplace" by Harper, L. F and Rifkind, L. J © 1994 Jossey-Bass Inc. Reprinted with permission of John Wiley & Sons, Inc.

Although the name of quality programs might differ depending on the approach, a focus on quality will continue to be one of the major initiatives critical to organizational competitiveness and survival. The success of quality initiatives, however, depends on training programs to provide employees with the knowledge and skills required to function in a quality-oriented work system. Quality training is related to quality outcomes, and is considered to be a critical factor in an organization's strategy and ability to achieve a competitive advantage.[53]

Nontechnical Skills Training

Although a great deal of emphasis has been given to technical skills, soft or nontechnical skills have also become an increasingly important set of skills for many jobs. **Nontechnical or soft skills** are skills that are required for working and interacting effectively with other people, such as communication skills, interpersonal skills, conflict management skills, negotiation skills, problem-solving solving, and so on. Many of the changes taking place in organizations, such as the increased use of teams, have resulted in an increasing awareness of the importance of nontechnical skills.

Nontechnical skills have even become important in areas where traditionally they were not deemed as relevant as technical skills. For example, in addition to technical skills upgrading required for many factory workers, new work arrangements often require factory employees to work in teams. As a result, they require nontechnical skills to work effectively with other team members and to make decisions and solve problems as part of a team. In addition to technical skills training, many factory workers now also receive training in areas such as conflict resolution, problem-solving, and customer and supplier relations.[54]

As indicated in Table 13.2, nontechnical skills training programs such as communication skills, interpersonal communication, and customer service are provided by the majority of organizations today. Although there are many types of nontechnical skills training, some of the most common are team training, sales training, customer service training, sexual harassment training, ethics training, cultural diversity training, and cross-cultural training. In the remainder of this chapter, we describe each of these types of training programs.

Team Training

During the last decade, many organizations have implemented team-based work systems. The reasons for this vary but in many cases it is an attempt to improve efficiency, quality, customer satisfaction, innovation, and the speed of production.

Unfortunately, teams often do not work. There are many examples of organizations that have failed to successfully implement teams, with disastrous consequences including a United Airlines plane crash in 1978 in which a breakdown in teamwork was found to be the primary cause of the accident.[55] Team training is an essential and critical requirement for teams to function effectively.

Team training programs are designed to improve the functioning and effectiveness of teams in areas such as communication, coordination, compensatory behaviour, mutual performance monitoring, exchange of feedback, and

Nontechnical skills (soft skills)

Skills that are required for working and interacting effectively with people, such as communication and interpersonal skills

Team training

Training programs that are designed to improve the functioning and effectiveness of teams in areas such as communication and coordination adaptation to varying situational demands.[56] According to Bottom and Baloff, team training is an "attempt to improve a group's process through the use of interventions targeted at specific aspects of the process such as effective communication" (p. 318).[57] Group processes are usually the focus of team training; however, because team members are often expected to perform a variety of the group's tasks, they often must also receive technical training to become multi-skilled.

Thus, team training focuses on two general types of skills: *task-work skills* refer to skills that are required to perform the team's tasks, and *teamwork skills* are skills that team members require in order to interact, communicate, and coordinate tasks effectively with other team members. Both types of skills need to be incorporated into the design of team training programs, and it is recommended that team members first master task-work and technical skills before they are trained on teamwork skills.[58]

Team training is one of the most popular types of human resource development interventions. However, team training programs have not always been effective, primarily because of a lack of a diagnosis of all the relevant factors. For team training to be effective, a comprehensive diagnosis must first be conducted on group input, task, and process variables in order to determine the appropriateness of team training, and to tailor interventions to the needs of the group.[59]

Furthermore, once it has been determined that team training is necessary, a team task analysis as described in Chapter 4 must be conducted. The objective of a team task analysis is to identify the team competencies including the knowledge, skills, and attitudes that are required to perform team tasks effectively and to function as a team member.[60]

In addition to providing team members with both task-work and teamwork skills training, managers and supervisors must also receive training on how to implement teams, and on their role as a team coach and facilitator rather than as a traditional manager. When team training interventions are based on a comprehensiveness diagnosis and team task analysis, there is evidence that they can improve group processes and team effectiveness.[61]

Sales Training

Shorter product cycles, finicky customers, more complex sales channels, and global competition have changed the sales profession and made it much more demanding and challenging.[62] Sales professionals have to do much more than just sell. They need to develop relationships with their customers, understand their needs and problems, and help them develop solutions. This process involves changing from an order-taking mentality, in which an organization competes primarily on price, to more of a business-partnership mentality, in which organizations compete by selling service rather than just commodities.[63]

Sales professionals must develop a different set of skills to be successful in today's competitive sales environment. They need to be more knowledgeable about their products and their business, as well as their customers' businesses. As a result, sales training has become more than simply sending the sales troops off to a motivational pep rally.[64]

Today, sales training programs are being designed to upgrade sales professionals' skills and help them deal with new competitive challenges. At the centre of these new training initiatives is an emphasis on "relationship-based" sales training. Sales professionals are being trained to develop more strategic and complex relationships with clients, and to create relationships across client functions. They are also being trained to become knowledgeable about their customers' business needs, and to develop customized sales strategies. Rather than just selling a commodity, integrated teams of people from sales, support, and service are learning to sell solutions that combine support and service agreements.

Unlike traditional sales training, these new approaches require a high level of management support and commitment since they represent a cultural change in the way an organization conducts its business. However, there is evidence that this new approach can increase sales effectiveness. For example, as described in Chapter 6, Canadian telecommunications company TELUS had the entire sales force participate in a three-day realistic selling simulation that allowed them to experience first-hand a new selling environment. Sales teams had to compete against each other in order to win an account. This required understanding the client's needs and developing solutions. In addition to the simulation, the sales force also took part in classroom-based workshops and a comprehensive assessment process. The workshop focused on new approaches to client relationship building and selling skills and the assessment was used to develop performance goals and plans for the sales staff.[65]

To learn more about how to design effective sales training programs, see The Trainer's Notebook 2, "Successful Sales Training Programs."

Customer Service Training

An organization's front-line employees play a key role in representing the organization to its customers. Good customer service and customer satisfaction are the keys to ensuring that customers return, so it is critical that front-line or customer-contact employees have the skills and abilities necessary to interact and communicate effectively with customers and provide them with excellent service. For many organizations, this requires extensive training in customer service.

Companies with a strong commitment to customer service, such as L.L. Bean, Federal Express, Marriott, and Disney, invest heavily in training their employees. For example, employees at L.L. Bean receive 40 hours of training before they deal with customers, and at British Airways all employees attend two days of training called "Putting People First."[66]

At Delta Hotels and Resorts, employees are trained and empowered to provide customers with excellent service such as settling a disputed mini-bar charge or offering a complimentary room if a guest has a reasonable complaint. As part of its training program, Delta has produced an award-winning training video and promises employees a certain amount of training every year. Delta's employee turnover rate has dropped, morale has improved, and occupancy rates have risen without Delta having to drop prices to be competitive.[67]

Successful Sales Training Programs

A survey of top sales training organizations was conducted to find out why successful companies launched new sales training programs, how they designed and implemented them, and what they were able to achieve as result of their efforts. The following success strategies were identified:

1. **The identification of a real business need that must be addressed before any training is developed.** There was a clear and defining business need that a sales training program had been crafted to address.

2. **Use of a team approach to design and implement new training.** Teams were critical to the success of the sale's programs and usually consisted of IT, sales and product marketing staff, vendors, and outside experts and creative development staff.

3. **Communication is a central component of the development and implementation process.** Communication did not stop with the development team, it also went up to senior managers and executives and out to members of each company's sales force. Each company used existing communication methods, including company newsletters and communications from senior managers, to communicate its message and to build excitement around its training.

4. **Comprehensive blended learning curriculum.** Old classroom training was combined with on-demand e-learning to create a comprehensive blended learning curriculum. This ensured the richness and depth of face-to-face classroom training with the added benefit of being able to deliver more training, more quickly, less expensively, and on-demand to better meet the needs of a busy sales force.

5. **Performance assessment support tools.** Performance assessment support tools and before-and-after learning events helped salespeople and their managers to determine the impact of sales-related training and continue the development cycle long after the training had ended.

Source: Hall, B. (2005, May). Sales Training Makeovers. *Training*, *42* (5), 15–22., V N U Business Publications. This work is protected by copyright and it is being used with the permission of Access Copyright. Any alteration of its content or further copying in any form whatsoever is strictly prohibited.

According to Schneider and Bowen, "The fundamental issue in training, whether it be training of individuals or training of teams, is to ensure that when customer meets employee, the encounter unfolds in ways that yield a sense of seamlessness for the customer" (p. 132).[68] They describe the experience this way:

> By seamlessness, we mean that the service, in all of its dimensions and characteristics, is delivered without a hitch. It is *simultaneously* reliable, responsive, competent, courteous, and so forth, and the facilities and tools necessary for it are all put into play smoothly and without glitches, interruptions, or delay. The same applies to responses to system failures and special requests. Seamless service is something all customers expect (p. 8).[69]

Customer service training can be either informal or formal. Informal training might involve pairing new hires with the organization's best employees in terms of customer service behaviour and philosophy. The kind of formal training required will depend on the type of service business that an organization is in and its service strategy. In other words, the training program must be tailored to an organization's strategy and characteristics as well as its customers.[70]

According to Schneider and Bowen, employees must be motivated and able to meet the following customer expectations for service quality:[71]

1. *Reliability:* Dependability and consistency of performance (e.g., performing the service at the designated time).
2. *Responsiveness:* The willingness and readiness of employees to provide service (e.g., giving prompt service).
3. *Competence:* The required skills and knowledge to perform the service (e.g., research capability of the organization).
4. *Access:* Approachability and ease of contact (e.g., convenient hours and location).
5. *Courtesy:* Politeness, respect, consideration, and friendliness (e.g., clean and neat appearance).
6. *Communication:* Keeping customers informed and listening to them (e.g., assuring customers that a problem will be handled).
7. *Credibility:* Trustworthiness, believability, and honesty (e.g., personal characteristics of employees).
8. *Security:* Freedom from danger, risk, or doubt (e.g., confidentiality).
9. *Understanding or knowing the customer:* Making an effort to understand the customer's needs (e.g., providing individualized attention).
10. *Tangibles:* Physical evidence of the service (e.g., appearance of personnel).

In addition to these quality expectations, employees must be able to deal with service failures, perform beyond customer expectations, and satisfy customer expectations for special requests. Employees must also ensure that customers feel secure, have their self-esteem enhanced, and are treated justly. Finally, service employees must also be able to act as supervisors or co-workers in those situations in which they are involved with customers in co-producing a service.[72]

Service employees must have both the *ability* and *motivation* to perform effectively. Because you cannot always hire people with the required abilities or motivation, you must be able to train them. Many organizations that have reputations for superb customer service are successful because of their commitment to training. Organizations that provide the best service also provide the most training. The key to service quality and competitiveness is customer service training.

Sexual Harassment Training

In recent years, a number of high-profile sexual harassment cases have made the news headlines and brought increased attention to sexual harassment in the workplace. Many well known and respected organizations, including Mitsubishi, Astra, Sears & Roebuck, and Del Laboratories have found themselves embroiled in costly litigation.[73] The failure of these organizations to effectively respond to charges of sexual harassment has cost them millions of dollars in settlements not to mention lower productivity, increased absenteeism, and higher turnover.

Sexual harassment in the U.S. army is reported to cost $250 million a year in lost productivity, absenteeism, and the replacement and transfer of employees.[74] The effects of sexual harassment on employees can include decreased morale and job satisfaction, as well as negative effects on people's psychological and physical well-being.[75] Men who perceive their workplace as hostile toward women and minorities also report lower job satisfaction and trust for their employer.[76]

Sexual harassment is defined as "unwelcome sexual advances, requests for sexual favours, and other verbal or physical conduct of a sexual nature . . . when submission to requests for sexual favours is made explicitly or implicitly a term or condition of employment; submission to or rejection of such requests is used as a basis for employment decisions; or such conduct unreasonably interferes with work performance or creates an intimidating, hostile, or offensive work environment" (p. 401).[77]

There are two kinds of sexual harassment. *Quid pro quo* refers to explicit requests for sexual favours as a condition of employment. A *hostile environment* refers to a work environment in which language or actions or both create an uncomfortable and offensive work environment that interferes with job performance.[78]

With the number of litigation cases and costly settlements on the rise, organizations have become more concerned about sexual harassment. The most effective way for organizations to prevent sexual harassment is to develop sexual harassment policies and procedures for filing complaints and to provide training programs that educate employees about sexual harassment and the organization's policies and procedures.[79]

Training is especially important because the definition of what constitutes sexual harassment is not always clear or understood, and problems have occurred in situations in which employees and managers were unaware of an organization's sexual harassment policy or did not know how to report it and proceed with a complaint. In the United States, sexual harassment training programs have become a popular way to ward off lawsuits.[80]

Organizations that are responsive to complaints of sexual harassment not only have policies and procedures in place, but, among other things, they have comprehensive education and training programs.[81] For example, E.I. Du Pont de Nemours has developed a sexual harassment awareness program called "A Matter of Respect" that includes interactive training programs, peer-level facilitators who are trained to meet with employees who want to talk about sexual harassment, and a 24-hour hotline. As the company has become more international, so has its training on sexual harassment, which is now provided in Japan, China, Mexico, and Puerto Rico.[82]

With increasing incidents of sexual and racial harassment in the workplace, organizations must develop policies to deal with complaints and provide comprehensive education and training programs. Not surprisingly, many organizations are now doing this. As indicated in Table 13.2, 62 percent of organizations reported providing sexual harassment training in the United States.

Sexual harassment
Unwelcome sexual advances, requests for sexual favours, and verbal or physical conduct of a sexual nature that is a condition of employment, interferes with work performance, or creates a hostile work environment

Ethics Training

In the wake of major organizational scandals such as Enron and WorldCom and the increasing lack of trust towards executives and their organizations, ethical guidelines and ethical training have become a top priority for organizations. In the United States, the passage of the Sarbanes-Oxley Act in 2002 which requires publicly traded companies to disclose whether they have adopted a code of ethics for senior officers has also increased the importance of ethics training. As a result, more companies are providing ethics training today than ever before.[83] In fact, there has been a 32-percent increase in the number of organizations offering ethics training since 1994.[84] In Canada, however, although most companies have ethical policies and an ethical code of conduct, less than 30 percent have training programs to support them.[85]

While many companies provide ethics training to comply with legal mandates and to gain liability protection, ethics training is also vital for creating an ethical culture and workplace and for attracting and retaining the right type of employee. Ethics training programs teach employees about the organization's values and ethical policies. This usually involves opportunities for employees to practice applying company values and its code of ethics to hypothetical situations. As a result, employees learn to recognize ethical dilemmas and how to respond to them.[86]

To be most effective, ethical training programs must be mandatory for all employees and include a copy of the organization's code of ethics, a discussion of relevant compliance laws, an ethical decision-making model, resources for help, and role-playing scenarios. Organizations should first set standards for ethical behaviour and determine what the training should accomplish. Key elements of strong ethical programs are responsibility, respect, fairness, honesty, and compassion. Employees should be trained on the laws that apply to their jobs as well as decision-making models with questions they can ask themselves to help them make ethical decisions. Employees should also be taught how to report ethics violations and where they can go for assistance. Practical scenarios should be included in the training so employees can test their ethical knowledge. Ethical topics can include workplace romance, e-mail appropriateness, Internet use, confidentiality, security, and harassment (physical, verbal, and emotional).[87]

Among the companies that have been recognized for their training in ethics is Molson Coors Brewing Company which was featured in Chapter 1. You might recall that the company has one of the most comprehensive ethics programs in North America that includes interactive on-line courses, ethics leadership training, a decision map, a detailed set of policies, and a help line that complements and supports a user-friendly and accessible code of conduct.[88]

Deloitte & Touche also has an extensive ethics training program that includes an on-line course that focuses on rules and regulations for maintaining independence from clients. In addition, the Ethics in Action Learning Program builds critical thinking skills through a blended program that combines a two-hour on-line story-based course with a four-hour live, instructor-led class.[89] United Parcel Service has a multimedia training program that includes several practical exercises. In one exercise called the "glass vault," employees brainstorm their beliefs on core values, principles, and traits of the organization. The training also includes practical ethical dilemma exercises and debriefings and an exercise in which participants design a personal action plan to apply the learning to their own jobs. The training is conducted by senior management to show management's commitment to employees. The company believes that training is essential for making an ethics policy work.[90]

A recent survey found that in organizations of all sizes and industries, 90 percent of employees said that ethics training is useful or somewhat useful to them.[91] Employees are more likely to report misconduct they observe in the workplace when an organization has an ethics program in place that includes a code of conduct and training.[92] Training is the most important factor for an ethics policy to be effective and the most important component of an ethics training program is senior management's continued and public commitment to it.[93]

Diversity Training

There has been a rapid rise in the percentage of ethnic, cultural, linguistic, and religious minorities in Canada, which has resulted in a considerable change in the ethnic and racial origins of employees working in Canadian organizations. Visible minorities now represent approximately 13 percent of the Canadian population and this is expected to increase to 22 percent by the year 2017. In Toronto, where visible minorities are the fastest growing group, they make up 37 percent of the population.[94]

As a result of this diversity and differences in attitudes and values across cultures, it has become increasingly important for organizations to manage diversity in the workplace. The effective management of diversity can have economic and competitive consequences for organizations, and is becoming part of many organizations' business strategy.[95] At IBM, diversity is embedded in the overall strategy, business goals, and policies toward employees, and every new manager is exposed to diversity training as part of the leadership development curriculum.[96]

Diversity training

Training that focuses on differences in values, attitudes, and behaviours of individuals with different backgrounds

Diversity training programs are one of the most common and effective ways for organizations to manage diversity and achieve a competitive advantage. **Diversity training** programs are designed to address the differences in values, attitudes, and behaviours of individuals with different backgrounds. The objectives are to increase awareness and understanding of cultural diversity, and to improve interaction and communication among employees with different backgrounds. Diversity training is reported to be one of the most widely used strategies for managing diversity in the workplace and there has been a dramatic rise in diversity training programs in the last decade.[97]

According to Noe and Ford, "The goal of diversity training programs is to eliminate barriers such as values, stereotypes, and managerial practices which constrain employee contribution to organizational goals and personal development" (p. 357).[98]

Diversity training has three main objectives: 1. Increase awareness about diversity issues, 2. Reduce biases and stereotypes, and 3. Change behaviours to those required to work effectively in a diverse workforce.[99] Some diversity training programs are designed to change people's attitudes by creating an awareness of diversity and an understanding of differences in values and behaviours. The expectation is that, by creating an awareness and understanding of these differences, people will change their behaviour and overcome any stereotypes they might hold. Another approach to diversity training is to change behaviour. This approach emphasizes learning new behaviours that might then lead to changes in attitudes.[100]

A recent study on diversity in the workplace found that diversity experts rated training and education programs as one of the best strategies for managing diversity. According to the experts, training and education was considered to be important for the following reasons:[101]

1. Building awareness and skills
2. Helping employees understand the need for and meaning of valuing diversity
3. Providing education on specific cultural differences and how to respond to those differences
4. Providing the skills required to work on diverse work teams
5. Improving employee understanding of the cultural diversity within the organization
6. Learning about the culture and community that the organization serves
7. Providing skills and activities to assist diverse groups to integrate within the organization, perform their jobs effectively, and increase opportunities for advancement.

In addition, the study noted that diversity training should focus on increasing *awareness* of what diversity is and why it is important; providing *skills* required to work effectively in a diverse workforce; and *application* strategies to facilitate the use of diversity awareness and skills to improve work performance, interactions, and communication. The study also indicated that effective diversity training programs have the following components: commitment and support from top management, inclusion as part of the organizational strategic plan, programs that meet the specific needs of the organization, qualified trainers, association with other diversity initiatives, mandatory attendance, inclusive programs (i.e., include all individuals and groups), and evaluation.[102]

In one of the most comprehensive studies on diversity training, human resource professionals responded to questions about diversity programs in their organizations. The results indicated that the majority of diversity programs last one day or less and use less than 10 percent of the training budget. As well, more than 80 percent reported that they evaluate participants' reactions immediately after training, but less than one third conduct any long-term evaluation. In terms of success, half of the programs were described as having a neutral effect, 18 percent were described as largely or extremely ineffective, and slightly more than 30 percent judged their training to be quite or extremely effective. The adoption and success of diversity training was strongly influenced by top management support as well as other organizational context factors such as organizational size and diversity-supportive policies.[103]

In Canada, many organizations have implemented diversity programs. For example, BC Hydro has an "Aboriginal Cross-Cultural Awareness Program" that focuses on building relationships. BC Hydro's transmission lines cross more than 500 aboriginal reserves so employees need to be aware of aboriginal rights, customs, and laws protecting their lands. Employees learn how diversity can affect their work in a particular community. Aboriginals serve as subject-matter experts for the training program, which includes face-to-face meetings. Training takes place in a traditional setting within a particular community and has included dancing and singing.[104]

In recent years, an increasing number of organizations have begun to treat sexual orientation on par with other dimensions of diversity. Lucent Technologies, a leading global supplier of communications-networking equipment is among a growing number of companies that includes sexual orientation in its diversity training. Whirlpool, a leading home appliance manufacturer, has a training module on diversity that covers sexual orientation and helps employees understand the buying power of gay consumers.[105] Eastman Kodak Co. has a wide range of diversity programs and five education programs that address workplace inclusion of gay, lesbian, bisexual, and transgender employees. Employees at the company first hear about sexual orientation in a series of presentations called the "52 Weeks: Diversity in Action Conversation Series" which is administered worldwide by Kodak's global diversity and community affairs office. The series explains the company's mission, the business case for diversity, and its corporate values of respecting and valuing differences, including sexual orientation.[106]

Organizations are realizing that managing cultural diversity is not only the right thing to do, but that it also makes good business sense.[107] Furthermore, diversity training is one of the most effective strategies for providing employees with the skills required to perform effectively in a diverse workplace. As noted by Wentling and Palma-Rivas, "Organizations need to provide employees with the most important skills for operating in a multicultural environment so that they understand their own as well as others' cultures, values, beliefs, attitudes, behaviours, and strengths and weaknesses. Employers must invest constantly in all employees by providing training and improving competencies if they are to work most effectively in a diverse workplace" (p. 243).[108]

See The Trainer's Notebook 3 to find out more about how to design an effective diversity training program.

Cross-Cultural Training

One of the implications of international business and a global marketplace is that workers, or *expatriates* as they are called, must work in different countries around the globe and interact with people from different cultures. Although

How to Design an Effective Diversity Training Program

Here are some key steps to follow in the design and implementation of an effective diversity training program:

1. **Obtain top-level leadership support**: The support and involvement of a company's CEO and top leadership team is a key factor in predicting the success of diversity programs. Leaders must clearly communicate the importance of diversity as a business value and goal and demonstrate their commitment to diversity initiatives.

2. **Conduct a needs analysis**: Conduct a needs analysis to determine the nature of diversity problems and issues in your organization. A needs analysis allows one to tailor a diversity training program to meet the specific needs of an organization and helps to determine the goals and objectives of a diversity program and the most appropriate training content and methods.

3. **Focus on three levels of learning**: Diversity training programs should be designed around three levels of learning: awareness, skill building, and action planning. *Awareness* involves learning about diversity issues, cultural differences, and bias in the workplace. *Skill building* refers to learning new skills such as new ways of communicating with persons with different backgrounds or managing diversity conflict. *Action planning* involves contributing to a more positive work environment by committing to and applying the knowledge and skills acquired in diversity training on the job.

4. **Embed and integrate diversity in a larger framework**: Diversity issues should be addressed as part of corporate change and development initiatives and as an embedded component of recruitment, development, training, compensation, and promotion. Diversity training should be part of a larger diversity program that is integrated with other business processes and objectives. Diversity initiatives and goals should be long-term and factored into management appraisal, reward, and recognition systems and policies.

5. **Research best practices**: Research companies with successful diversity programs. For example, IBM and AT&T provide outstanding examples of how to design and implement diversity programs that integrate diversity goals into strategic planning and business goals, and take a holistic, systematic approach to embedding diversity themes and priorities into all operational areas at all organizational levels.

6. **Use diversity as a business advantage**: Ensure that your organization fully appreciates the diversity of its employees and the ways in which diversity can be leveraged to marketplace advantage.

7. **Design informational and transformational programs**: Diversity programs need to convey information about specific policies and organization initiatives as well as being transformational in design and content (e.g., why workforce diversity is critical to achieving business goals) in order to create synergy, trust, and greater workplace cooperation and understanding.

8. **Use various methods and media**: Role plays, storytelling, small-group discussions, videos, simulations, vignettes, and exercises should all be incorporated into the design of diversity training programs.

9. **Recognize your role**: As a trainer, take it upon yourself to educate your company's CEO and top leaders about how diversity as a value and business focus can help the organization reach new markets, foster an atmosphere of inclusiveness, and create a world-class workforce. Also make sure that you or the diversity trainer is qualified and capable of discussing sensitive issues about diversity and managing the emotions that often arise during diversity training.

Sources: Koonce, R. (December, 2001). Redefining diversity. *Training & Development*, p. 27 (How to create effective diversity training); Chrobot-Mason, D., & Quinones, M. A. (2002). Training for a diverse workplace. *Creating, implementing, and managing effective training and development: state-of-the-art lessons for practice* by Kraiger, K. © 2002 Jossey-Bass Inc. Reprinted with permission of John Wiley & Sons, Inc.

middle managers are sent on overseas assignments most often, senior managers, sales staff, engineers, IS programmers, scientists, and other professionals are also sent.[109] Canada sends hundreds of technical advisors each year to developing countries as part of its international development assistance programs.[110]

A foreign assignment can last for years and involve contact and interactions with persons who differ from Canadians in terms of culture, values, and language. For an organization to succeed in its international business operations, it requires individuals who can function and work effectively in different cultures.

Unfortunately, both Canadian and American expatriates have typically not performed very well on foreign assignments. During the past two decades, North American expatriates who were assigned to work overseas for their organizations have had a much higher failure rate than European or Japanese expatriates. In other words, they either perform poorly and/or they return home early.[111]

In the United States, it is estimated that 20 percent of U.S. expatriates fail in their global assignment.[112] A study on Canadian technical advisors working in developing countries found that only about 20 percent were highly effective in terms of their ability to transfer skills and knowledge to their counterparts in the host country, 65 percent had little impact, and 15 percent were highly ineffective.[113] The cost of failure is high, costing multinational companies millions of dollars each year. In North America, an estimated $2 to $2.5 billion is wasted when overseas assignments fail.

One of the main reasons for the high failure rate of North American expatriates is the culture shock they and their families experience living in a foreign culture. The study of Canadian technical advisors working in developing countries found that more than 50 percent experienced culture shock, and a major reason for their lack of effectiveness was the inability to interact effectively with their counterparts in the host country.[114] In addition, a major reason for failure is the inability of the expatriate's spouse and family to adjust to the foreign culture.[115] This inability to adjust stems in large part from a lack of cross-cultural training or pre-departure training for the expatriates and their families.

Cross-cultural training

Training that prepares employees for working and living in different cultures and for interactions with persons from different backgrounds

"**Cross-cultural training** is designed to prepare employees for overseas assignments by focusing on developing the skills and attitudes necessary for successful interactions with persons from different backgrounds" (p. 355).[116] Some of the major types of cross-cultural training include:[117]

- Environmental briefings about a country's geography, climate, housing, and schools
- Cultural orientation to familiarize expatriates with cultural institutions and the value systems of the host country
- Cultural assimilators that use programmed learning approaches to expose members of one culture to the concepts, attitudes, role perceptions, and customs of another culture
- Language training
- Sensitivity training to develop attitudinal flexibility, and
- Field experience such as visiting the country where one will be assigned to see what it is like to work and live with people in a different culture.

Despite increasing awareness of the importance of cross-cultural training, only a minority of firms (30 to 45 percent) provide cross-culture training for expatriates and their families—a major contributing factor in expatriate assignment failure.[118] Furthermore, in the few organizations that do provide cross-cultural training, it is usually not very rigorous. In fact, it is often basic and brief, consisting of films and reading books rather than building cross-cultural skills. This is unfortunate because research has shown that cross-cultural training can improve an expatriate's cross-cultural skills, cultural adjustment, and job performance.[119]

A critical factor in the success of cross-cultural training is training rigour. According to Black, Gregersen, and Mendenhall, **training rigour** refers to "the degree of mental involvement and effort that must be expended by the trainer and the trainee in order for the trainee to learn the required concepts" (p. 97).[120]

Training rigour also refers to the length of time spent on training. Generally, cross-cultural training programs that are high on training rigour tend to be more effective. Cross-cultural training programs that are considered to have a high degree of rigour include interactive language training, cross-cultural simulations, and field trips. Programs with a moderate degree of training rigour include role plays, cases, and survival-level language. Cross-cultural training programs that are considered to be the lowest in terms of training rigour include lectures, films, books, and area briefings. More rigorous cross-cultural training programs require trainees to be much more active and involved in practising cross-cultural skills.[121]

The degree of cross-cultural training rigour required by an expatriate for a particular foreign assignment depends on three dimensions: cultural toughness, communication toughness, and job toughness. *Cultural toughness* refers to how difficult it is to adjust to a new culture. Generally speaking, cultural toughness will increase the greater the difference or distance between one's own culture and the foreign culture. For example, cultural toughness will be much higher for a Canadian expatriate in the Middle East than one in the U.S. The Canadian expatriate on assignment in the Middle East will require more rigorous cross-cultural training. An exception to this is the degree of past experience that an expatriate has had living in a foreign culture. For example, a Canadian expatriate with considerable experience living in the Middle East will require less cross-cultural training than one who has never lived there.[122]

Communication toughness is a function of the extent to which the expatriate will have to interact with the locals of the host country. When an expatriate will be required to have frequent interactions with host nationals that will involve face-to-face, two-way, and informal communication, the level of communication toughness will be high, and more rigorous communication training will be required.

Job toughness refers to how difficult the tasks will be for the expatriate compared to what he/she is used to doing. If the expatriate will be working in a new area and the demands of the job will be different and require new responsibilities and challenges, then the degree of job toughness will be greater. As a result, the expatriate will require more rigorous job-specific training.[123]

Training rigour

The degree of mental involvement and effort that must be expended by the trainer and the trainee in order for the trainee to learn the required concepts

An expatriate will have the most difficulty adjusting to foreign assignments that have a high degree of cultural, communication, and job toughness. As the levels of these three dimensions increase, the type of cross-cultural training required will need to be more rigorous. In addition to pre-departure training, it is also important that the expatriates and their families also receive follow-up or in-country cross-cultural training in the host country.[124]

Research on Canadian expatriates has found that interpersonal and intercultural adaptation skills as well as knowledge of the local culture and participation in that culture are important predictors of overseas effectiveness. Furthermore, among Canadian technical advisors, learning the local language was a major factor in overseas effectiveness.[125]

To be successful, expatriates require cross-cultural training that not only informs them of the history and politics of a country, but also teaches them the language, values, and appropriate patterns of behaviour. Cross-cultural training helps employees withstand the culture shock of working abroad and improves their job performance and adjustment.[126]

With the increasing pace of change and the ever-expanding global marketplace, more Canadian workers will be sent on foreign assignments that require them to work and interact with persons in different and diverse cultures. Given that an organization's competitive success in the global marketplace depends to a great extent on its people, it is crucial that expatriates receive rigorous cross-cultural training so that they will perform effectively and adjust to foreign cultures.

See The Trainer's Notebook 4 to find out how to design an effective cross-cultural training program.

The Trainer's Notebook 4

How to Design an Effective Cross-Cultural Training Program

Here are some recommendations for the successful design and implementation of a cross-cultural training program:

1. Cross-cultural training should be considered a mandatory process.
2. The location of training should be established in accordance with the needs of the family as part of the preparation process and corporations need to accept that training can be done at home or in the host country.
3. The depth of training is of utmost importance. If corporations are going to provide cross-cultural training, it needs to be done properly with depth and with care.
4. Families must be incorporated into the training process. Training for expatriates alone is only sufficient if the expatriate is on an individualized assignment.

5. Language training should be incorporated into cross-cultural training wherever possible and should be encouraged as an ongoing aspect of the assignment.
6. Education and expectations of training must be laid out by training companies for international human resource professionals and in turn be easily translated for the preparation of each individual expatriate. This can be through appropriate written information being prepared for the expatriate and reinforced by the service provider reiterating the goals and expectations prior to the training.

Sources: Bross, A., Churchill, A., & Zifkin, J. (2000, June 5). Cross-cultural training: Issues to consider during implementation. *Canadian HR Reporter*, 13 (11), 10, 12. Reprinted by permission of Carswell, a division of Thomson Canada Ltd.

Summary

This chapter has provided an overview of the different types of training programs that are designed and delivered by organizations today. You should now be familiar with new employee orientation training, basic-skills training, technical skills training, information technology training, health and safety training, quality training, team training, sales training, customer service training, sexual harassment training, ethics training, diversity training, and cross-cultural training. These training programs are a result of the many challenges and issues facing organizations in today's rapidly changing and competitive environment. Many of these training programs have become key components of an organization's corporate strategy and are major factors in their efforts to remain competitive.

Key Terms

basic-skills training (page 373)

computer software training (page 376)

cross-cultural training (page 390)

diversity training (page 386)

information technology training (page 375)

literacy (page 372)

nontechnical skills (soft skills) (page 379)

sexual harassment (page 384)

team training (page 379)

technical skills training (page 375)

total quality management (TQM) (page 377)

training rigour (page 391)

Workplace Hazardous Materials Information System (WHMIS) (page 377)

Weblinks

BC Hydro: www.bchydro.com (page 388)

Starbucks: www.starbucks.com (page 370)

TELUS: www.telus.ca (page 381)

WHMIS: www.hc-sc.gc.ca/hecs-sesc/whmis/index.htm (page 377)

Discussion Questions

1. Diversity training programs have been criticized for doing more harm than good. In fact, there is some evidence that they may be ineffective at best and harmful at worst. Why do you think this is the case? Do you think this is true and should organizations abandon diversity training or embrace it?

2. Why do you think Canadian organizations invest so little in basic-skills training (see Table 13.1)? What are the implications of this for employees, organizations, and society? Should Canadian organizations be spending more on basic-skills training? What are the advantages and disadvantages?

3. What would be your reaction if your employer wanted to send you on an overseas assignment? What would be your reaction if the assignment was in: 1. England, 2. France, 3. China, or 4. the Middle East? Would

you accept the assignment and if so, what training would you require? Describe the training you would need in terms of the content and methods.

4. What aspects of a cross-cultural training program affect its degree of training rigour? Discuss the factors that need to be considered in order to determine the degree of cross-cultural training rigour required by an expatriate for a particular foreign assignment. If you were sent on a foreign assignment to France to manage a new restaurant, what degree of cross-cultural training rigour would you require?

5. What is the Workplace Hazardous Materials Information System (WHMIS) and what are its implications for safety training? What should be covered in a health and safety training program?

6. Why is team training important for organizations that want to implement team-based work arrangements? What skills should be the focus of team training programs?

7. Why should an organization provide a new employee orientation training program? If you were going to design a new employee orientation program, what material would you include and how would your program be delivered?

The Great Training Debate

1. Debate the following: Diversity programs result in more harm than good and organizations should abandon them.

2. Debate the following: Basic-skills and literacy training is the responsibility of government, not organizations.

Using the Internet

1. To learn more about workplace literacy and basic skills in Canada, go to **www.conferenceboard.ca/workplaceliteracy** and find out about the challenges that employers face and the solutions. Prepare a brief report in which you summarize the challenges, solutions, and best practices for small, medium, and large businesses.

2. To learn more about the types of safety training programs available, visit the Canadian Centre for Occupational Health and Safety at **www.ccohs.ca/education/**.

What kinds of training programs are available? Choose one of the programs and find out what the program is about, the topics covered, the program objectives, target audience, and delivery options.

3. To find out about WHMIS education and training go to **www.ccohs.ca/oshanswers/legisl/whmis_education.html**. Answer the following questions:

   1. What is WHMIS education and training?
   2. Who should be educated and trained in WHMIS?

3. What is the purpose of WHMIS training?

4. What, in general, is the content of a WHMIS training program?

5. Can people in the same plant receive different training?

6. What are the criteria of a successful program?

4. To find out about different kinds of diversity training, go to **www.sabes.org/resources/brightideas/b2derosa.htm.** Answer the following questions:

1. What are the six different models of diversity training?

2. What are the strengths and limitations of each model?

3. If you had to recommend diversity training to your organization, or one that you have worked in, what model would you recommend and why?

5. To learn more about new employee orientation programs, read the new employee orientation survey report at **www.thetrainingclinic.com/ orientation/orient%20survey.htm.** Answer the following questions:

1. Who conducts orientation?

2. When does orientation start?

3. Where is orientation held?

4. Who attends orientation?

5. What materials are given during orientation?

6. Who is responsible to conduct specific topics?

7. What methods are used?

8. How is orientation evaluated?

9. What would respondents do if they could redesign their orientation program?

Exercises

In-Class

1. The extent to which organizations provide certain types of training programs is often driven by external and internal factors. In other words, social, political, and economic changes in the work environment, as well as internal changes to organizational systems and work arrangements, have a substantial influence on training activities. Choose several of the following training programs as required by your instructor, and discuss the role of external and internal factors and how these factors might influence the need and importance of each type of training:

a. New employee orientation training

b. Basic-skills training

c. Technical skills training

d. Information technology training

e. Health and safety training

f. Quality training

g. Team training

h. Sales training

i. Customer service training

j. Sexual harassment training

k. Ethics training

l. Cultural diversity training

m. Cross-cultural training

2. Assume that you are a training director for a large retail organization. To increase your training budget for next year, you have to make a persuasive argument to convince other members of the organization of your need for an increase in resources. An important part of your argument will involve proving the need for and importance of several training programs. For some of the training programs listed in Exercise 1 above (as indicated by your instructor), describe how you will argue that it is important, the impact it will have on employee attitudes and behaviour, the benefits it will have for employees and the organization, and how it can help the organization gain a competitive advantage.

3. Design a training program for one of the types of training discussed in this chapter. In designing your program, specify each of the following:

a. The training objectives

b. The training content

c. The trainer

d. The trainees who should attend the program

e. The training methods to be used

f. The required training materials and equipment

g. The training site

h. The schedule for the training program

i. The lesson plan

j. The criteria you will use to evaluate the program

4. Describe the orientation training you received in the most recent job that you held. Some of the things to consider are:

a. How long was the orientation training?

b. What content was included?

c. What methods were used?

d. What did you learn from it?

e. Were you satisfied with the program and did it help you perform your job?

f. What did you like about it and what did you not like?

g. How would you change the orientation training you received to make it more effective?

5. Choose one of the types of training programs described in this chapter that you have attended in a current or previous job. Describe the content and methods used and how effective the training was for your learning and on-the-job behaviour. Based on the material in the chapter and your experience, how effective was the program? How would you change it, improve it, and make it more effective?

6. Imagine that your employer has just informed you that you are going on a foreign assignment for three years to a country that you have never been to and know nothing about. Furthermore, the culture is very different from your own. Your employer has informed you that you will be receiving some written information about the country and its culture as well as a videotape to help you prepare for your assignment. Prepare a memo to your employer in which you evaluate the training they are offering you and describe the type of cross-cultural training that you require if you are going to accept the assignment.

7. Students often have to work in groups on course projects without any knowledge of how groups function and what it takes for them to be effective. Students often experience difficulties when working in groups and sometimes they just fall apart and the work never gets completed. Therefore, it might be helpful if students receive team training. Your task is to design a training program for students to prepare them for working in groups. Describe the nature of your training program including the objectives, content, and methods.

In-the-Field

1. To find out more about the training programs discussed in this chapter, contact a training professional or a human resource professional to arrange an interview about the types of training provided in their organization. Choose one or two of the types of training programs described in this chapter and ask them the following questions:

   • Does your organization provide this type of training?
   • What are some of the reasons why you do or do not provide this type of training?
   • What are the objectives of this type of training program?
   • What is the content of this type of training?
   • How is this training program designed (e.g., what methods, techniques, etc.) and who is the trainer?
   • What effect does this type of training have on employees' attitudes and behaviours?
   • What effect does this type of training have on the organization?

Based on your interview, what is your evaluation of the training programs provided by the organization? Do you think they could be improved and if so, what would you recommend and why?

2. Contact several employees who you know, and who work in different organizations, and ask them the following questions about one or two of the types of training programs discussed in the chapter:

- Have you ever received this type of training?
- If yes, what was the reason why you attended the training program?
- What were the objectives of the training program?
- What was the content of the training program?
- How was the training program designed (e.g., methods, techniques, etc.) and who was the trainer?
- What was your reaction to the training program and what did you learn? What effect did the training have on your behaviour and job performance?
- What effect did the training have on the organization?

Based on your interview, do you think the training program was effective? What changes do you recommend to make it more effective?

Case Incident

Saving Theatre Calgary

Theatre Calgary is one of the largest professional theatres in Western Canada, with a 35-year history. However, lagging ticket sales and competing claims on the philanthropy dollar brought Theatre Calgary to near bankruptcy in 1996. A decision was made to overhaul the company's marketing approach that would raise the standard of performance expected from employees, especially those in the areas of sales and customer service. To support the new approach, the company invested in training for aggressive marketing and up-selling. Employees attended seminars on a range of techniques from how to cross-sell to how to analyze demographics for marketing opportunities and how to create a customer profile from the client database. Employees also had to improve their customer contact skills from telephone manner to up-selling to meet-and-greet. They spent time developing scripts and rehearsing how to deal with people and how to deal with people with problems.

Questions

1. How important is training for saving the company from bankruptcy and what kind of training is most important?
2. What do you think about the training programs? What would you recommend for improving them?

Source: Garcia, C. (2004, May 17). CloseUp: Training and development. *Canadian HR Reporter, 17* (10), 7–10.

Managing Performance Through Training and Development

Case

Sensitivity Training

On September 14, 2000, several police officers raided a special event known as the Pussy Palace, a lesbian bathhouse in Toronto in which 355 scantily clad women were gathered. Two undercover female officers entered the bathhouse to check for possible liquor violations. They then called in five male officers, who raided the palace and spent 90 minutes walking around on what was described as a routine liquor licence inspection.

The officers allegedly opened doors, entered private rooms, questioned the women, and lingered in areas where the patrons' nudity was most evident in rooms such as "the sling room" and "the photo room." Complainants alleged that their feelings of violation and intimidation were akin to being strip-searched. Police charged two organizers with six liquor violations and three counts of permitting disorderly conduct. The raid outraged the gay community.

Justice Peter Hryn of the Ontario Court threw out the liquor licence infractions and ruled that the defendants' privacy rights had been seriously violated in a situation that did not require urgent police action. He compared the officers' entry into the club to a strip-search, calling it outrageous, flagrant, deliberate, unjustified, and a violation of the women's Charter rights. During the defamation trial that followed, Justice Janet McFarland of the Ontario Superior Court described the raid as a violation of the Charter of Rights of the women present and declared, "It is no part of a police officer's job to breach the Charter of Rights of any citizen. To do so is misconduct of the most serious kind."

The Toronto Women's Bathhouse Committee launched a human rights complaint, and several of its members also initiated a $1.5-million class-action lawsuit alleging harassment and discrimination. In December 2004, a settlement between the Toronto Police Services Board and seven complainants was announced and approved by the Ontario Human Rights Commission.

The settlement requires all current and future Toronto police officers to attend gay and lesbian sensitivity training. The Toronto Police Service also had to pay $350,000 to the complainants, that went toward charities and to cover legal fees. In addition, the five male officers who raided the bathhouse provided a signed apology to the women who were attending the event stating that they did not intend to breach their rights or privacy. As a result of the settlement, the $1.5-million class-action suit and the complaint to the Ontario Human Rights Commission were dropped.

According to the settlement, everyone on the 7260 member force—from rookie constables to the chief of police—will be required to take training on gay and lesbian sensitivity. The training will pay particular attention to searches involving the gay, lesbian and transgendered communities as well as inspections of gay and lesbian venues, businesses, and bathhouses. The program will be designed in consultation with the Ontario Human Rights Commission and members of the gay community.

Chapter 13: Training Programs

Then-Police Chief Julian Fantino responded to the settlement by stating that the Toronto Police are already bogged down in training programs and scarcely need the added burden of enforced gay and lesbian sensitivity training which he called an unnecessary overreaction. He told a local newspaper that, "it's being forced on us," and "we are conscientious about diversity and sensitivity issues and all those kinds of things. Is it necessary? I think that in many respects this is a duplication of much of the work we already do." He went on to say that the force shouldn't have to "bow to all kinds of pressures," and "we have made extraordinary efforts to reach out and work with all entities in the community." Mayor David Miller called the sensitivity training "a very positive step" and "a very good part" of the settlement.

Sources: Makin, K. (2004, December 17). Toronto police to face gay-sensitivity training. *The Globe & Mail*, A1, A15; Porter, C. (2004, December 18). Fantino attacks deal; Sensitivity training "being forced" on police force, chief says: Agreement ends lawsuit over 2000 raid on lesbian bathhouse. *Toronto Star*, A1; Makin, K., & Gray, J. (2004, December 18) . . . . but calls sensitivity training a burden. *The Globe & Mail*, A17; Reinhart, A. (December 18, 2004). Fantino has proved he can exemplify tolerance . . . *The Globe & Mail*, A17; Brown, D. (2005, January 31). Toronto cops grudgingly accept sensitivity training. *Canadian HR Reporter, 18* (2), 1, 3.

Questions

1. Do you agree that all current and future Toronto police officers should be required to attend gay and lesbian sensitivity training? What do you think the effect of this will be on the police and the gay and lesbian community?

2. If you were to design a training program for the Toronto Police, how would you design it in terms of content and methods? Develop a lesson plan for your training program.

3. Consider the relevance of diversity training for the sensitivity training program. What aspects of diversity training are relevant and might be used in the design of the sensitivity training program? Are there are other types of training programs that are relevant and might be part of the sensitivity training program?

4. Do you think the sensitivity training will be effective? What else might be required in order for it to result in a significant change in police attitudes and behaviour?

5. How would you evaluate the sensitivity training program?

References

1. Excerpt from Watt, D. (2002, September). Excellence in workplace literacy, medium business winner, 2002: Royal Star Foods Limited. *The Conference Board of Canada.* Ottawa.

2. Parker, R. O., & Cooney, J. (2005). Learning & development outlook 2005. *The Conference Board of Canada.* Ottawa; Dolezalek, H. (2005, December). 2005 Industry Report. *Training, 42* (12), 14–28.

3. Dolezalek, H. (2005, December).

4. Parker, R. O., & Cooney, J. (2005).

5. Schaaf, D. (1998). What workers really think about training. *Training 35* (9), 59–66.
6. Schaaf, D. (1998).
7. Parker, R. O., & Cooney, J. (2005).
8. Klein, H. J., & Weaver, N. A. (2000). The effectiveness of an organizational-level orientation training program in the socialization of new hires. *Personnel Psychology, 53,* 47–66.
9. Feldman, D. C. (1989). Socialization, resocialization, and training: Reframing the research agenda. In I.L. Goldstein (Ed.), *Training and development in organizations* (pp. 376–416). San Francisco: Jossey-Bass.
10. Anderson, N. R., Cunningham-Snell, N. A., & Haigh, J. (1996). Induction training as socialization: Current practice and attitudes to evaluation in British organizations. *International Journal of Selection and Assessment 4,* 169–83.
11. Gruner, S. (1998, July). Lasting impressions. *Inc. 20* (10), 126.
12. Reese, J. (1996, December 9). Starbucks: Inside the coffee cult. *Fortune,* pp. 190–200.
13. Gruner, S. (1998, July).
14. Feldman, D. C. (1989).
15. Saks, A. M. (1996). The relationship between the amount and helpfulness of entry training and work outcomes. *Human Relations 49,* 429–51.
16. Gruner, S. (1998, July).
17. Klein & Weaver (2000).
18. Klein & Weaver (2000).
19. Ostroff, C., & Kozlowski, S. W. J. (1992). Organizational socialization as a learning process: The role of information acquisition. *Personnel Psychology 45,* 849–74; Schettler, J. (2002, August). Welcome to ACME Inc. *Training, 39* (8), 36–43.
20. Baker, S., & Armstrong, L. (1996, September 30). The new factory worker, *Business Week,* pp. 59–68.
21. Campbell, A. (2005, December). Profiting from literacy: Creating a sustainable workplace literacy program. *The Conference Board of Canada.* Ottawa; Brown, L., & Girard, D. (2006, May 4). 42 percent of adults semi-literate. *Toronto Star,* R2; Campbell, A., & Gagnon, N. (2006, January). Literacy, life and employment: An analysis of Canadian International Adult Literacy Survey (IALS) microdata. *The Conference Board of Canada.* Ottawa.
22. Campbell, A. (2005).
23. Campbell, A. (2005).
24. Campbell, A. (2005).
25. Calamai, P. (1999, August 28). The literacy gap. *Toronto Star,* J1, J2.
26. Hays, S. (1999). The ABCs of workplace literacy. *Workforce Management 78* (4), 70–74.
27. Hays, S. (1999).
28. Campbell, A. (2005).
29. Kuri, F. (1996, September). Basic-skills training boosts productivity. *HRMagazine 41* (9), 73–79.
30. Hays, S. (1999).
31. Kuri, F. (1996, September).
32. Harris-Lalonde, S. (2001). Training and development outlook. *The Conference Board of Canada,* Ottawa; Campbell, A. (2005).
33. Baker, S., & Armstrong, L. (1996, September 30).
34. Baker, S., & Armstrong, L. (1996, September 30).
35. Harp, C. G., Taylor, S. C., & Satzinger, J. W. (1998). Computer training and individual differences: When method matters. *Human Resource Development Quarterly 9,* 271–83.
36. Martocchio, J. J. (1992). Microcomputer usage as an opportunity: The influence of context in employee training. *Personnel Psychology 45,* 529–52.
37. DeSimone, R. L., & Harris, D. M. (1998). *Human resource development* (2nd ed.). Fort Worth, TX: Dryden Press.
38. Baker, S., & Armstrong, L. (1996, September 30).
39. Harp, C. G., Taylor, S. C., & Satzinger, J. W. (1998).

40. Kelloway, E. K., Francis, L., & Montgomery, J. (2006). *Management of occupational health and safety* (3rd ed.). Toronto: Nelson Canada.
41. Montgomery, J. (1996). *Occupational health and safety*. Toronto: Nelson Canada.
42. Kelloway, E. K., Francis, L., & Montgomery, J. (2006).
43. Montgomery, J. (1996).
44. Kuri, F. (1996, September).
45. Murray, B., & Raffaele, G. C. (1997). Single-site, results-level evaluation of quality awareness training. *Human Resource Development Quarterly 8*, 229–45.
46. Dean, J. W., Jr., & Bowen, D. E. (1994). Management theory and total quality: Improving research and practice through theory development. *Academy of Management Review 19*, 392–418.
47. Armitage, H. M. (1992, January). Quality pays. *CGA Magazine 96* (1), 30–37; Fine, C. H., & Bridge, D. H. (1987). Managing quality improvement. In M. Sepehri (Ed.), *Quest for quality: Managing the total system* (pp. 66–74). Norcross, GA: Institute of Industrial Engineers.
48. Cocheu, T. (1989). Training for quality improvement. *Training and Development Journal 41* (1), 56–62; Rossett, A., & Krumdieck, K. (1992). How trainers score on quality. *Training and Development 46* (1), 11–16.
49. Oakland, J. S. (1989). *Total quality management*. Oxford: Butterworth–Heinemann Ltd; Schonberger, R. J. (1992). Total quality management cuts a broad swath–through manufacturing and beyond. *Organizational Dynamics 20* (4), 16–28; Tenner, A. R., & DeToro, I .J. (1992). *Total quality management, three steps to continuous improvement*. Reading, MA: Addison–Wesley.
50. Gandz, J. (1990). The employee empowerment era. *Business Quarterly 55* (2), 74–79.
51. Kiess–Moser, E. (1990). International perspectives on quality. *Canadian Business Review 17* (3), 31–33; Regalbuto, G. A. (1992). Targeting the bottom line. *Training and Development 46* (4), 29–38.
52. Harper, L. F., & Rifkind, L. J. (1994). A training program for TQM in the diverse workplace. *Human Resource Development Quarterly 5*, 277–79.
53. Murray, B., & Raffaele, G. C. (1997).
54. Baker, S., & Armstrong, L. (1996, September 30).
55. Salas, E., Burke, C. S., & Cannon-Bowers, J. A. (2002). What we know about designing and delivering team training: Tips and guidelines. In K. Kraiger (Ed.), *Creating, implementing, and managing effective training and development: State-of-the-art lessons for practice*, (pp. 234–59). San Francisco. CA: Jossey-Bass.
56. Tannenbaum, S. I., & Yukl, G. (1992). Training and development in work organizations. *Annual Review of Psychology 43*, 399–441.
57. Bottom, W. P., & Baloff, N. (1994). A diagnostic model for team building with an illustrative application. *Human Resource Development Quarterly 5*, 317–36.
58. Salas, E., Burke, C. S., & Cannon-Bowers, J. A. (2002).
59. Bottom, W. P., & Baloff, N. (1994).
60. Salas, E., Burke, C. S., & Cannon-Bowers, J. A. (2002).
61. Bottom, W. P., & Baloff, N. (1994).
62. Stamps, D. (1997). Training for a new sales game. *Training 34* (7), 46–52.
63. Stamps, D. (1997).
64. Stamps, D. (1997).
65. Connal, D., & Baskin, C. (2002, November). Transforming a sales organization through simulation-based learning: a TELUS Communications case study. *Training Report*, 4–5.
66. Schneider, B., & Bowen, D. E. (1995). *Winning the service game*. Boston, MA: Harvard Business School Press.
67. Anonymous. (1999, May 31). Delta promotes empowerment. *The Globe and Mail*, C5.
68. Schneider, B., & Bowen, D. E. (1995).

69. Schneider, B., & Bowen, D. E. (1995).

70. Schneider, B., & Bowen, D. E. (1995).

71. Schneider, B., & Bowen, D. E. (1995).

72. Schneider, B., & Bowen, D. E. (1995).

73. Peirce, E., Smolinski, C. A., & Rosen, B. (1998). Why sexual harassment complaints fall on deaf ears. *Academy of Management Executives 12*, 41–54.

74. Seppa, N. (1997). Sexual harassment in the military lingers on. *APA Monitor 28* (5), 40–41.

75. Schneider, K. T., Swan, S., & Fitzgerald, L. F. (1997). Job-related and psychological effects of sexual harassment in the workplace: Empirical evidence from two organizations. *Journal of Applied Psychology 82*, 401–15.

76. Murray, B. (1998, July). Workplace harassment hurts everyone on the job. *APA Monitor 29* (7), p. 35.

77. Schneider, K. T., Swan, S., & Fitzgerald, L. F. (1997).

78. Ganzel, R. (1998). What sexual harassment training really prevents. *Training 35* (10), 86–94.

79. Ganzel, R. (1998). Peirce, E., Smolinski, C. A., & Rosen, B. (1998).

80. Ganzel, R. (1998).

81. Peirce, E., Smolinski, C. A., & Rosen, B. (1998).

82. Flynn, G. (1997). Respect is key to stopping harassment. *Workforce Management 76* (2), 56.

83. Tyler, K. (2005, February). Do the right thing: Ethics training programs help employees deal with ethical dilemmas. *HR Magazine, 50* (2), 99–102.

84. Anonymous. (2005, November). Survey says: Ethics training works. *Training, 42* (11), 15.

85. Young, L. (1999, April 19). Employer ethics codes lack supports needed for success. *Canadian HR Reporter, 12* (8), 1,11.

86. Tyler, K. (2005, February).

87. Tyler, K. (2005, February).

88. Greengard, S. (2005, March). Golden values. *Workforce Management. 84* (3), 52–53.

89. Anonymous. (2005, October). Deloitte & Touche USA LLP. *Training & Development, 59* (10), 59.

90. Young, L. (1999, June 14). Ethics training is key. *Canadian HR Reporter, 12* (12), 2.

91. Anonymous. (2005, November).

92. Dolezalek, H. (2003, November). Eye on ethics. *Training, 40* (10), 42–45.

93. Young, L. (1999, April 19); Tyler, K. (2005, February).

94. Mahoney, J. (2005, March 23). Visible majority by 2017. *Globe and Mail*, A1, A7; Crawford, T. (2006, April 1). A better mix. *Toronto Star*, L1, L2.

95. Wentling, R. M., & Palma-Rivas, N. (1998). Current status and future trends of diversity initiatives in the workplace: Diversity experts' perspective. *Human Resource Development Quarterly 9*, 235–53.

96. Koonce, R. (2002, December). Redefining diversity. *Training & Development*, 22–32.

97. Chrobot-Mason, & Quinones, M. A. (2002). Training for a diverse workplace. In K. Kraiger (Ed.), *Creating, implementing, and managing effective training and development: State-of-the-art lessons for practice*, (pp. 117–59). San Francisco. CA: Jossey-Bass; Wentling, R. M., & Palma-Rivas, N. (1998).

98. Noe, R. A., & Ford, J. K. (1992). Emerging issues and new directions for training research. *Research in Personnel and Human Resources Management, 10*, 345–84.

99. Hanover, J. M. B., & Cellar, D. F. (1998). Environmental factors and the effectiveness of workforce diversity training. *Human Resource Development Quarterly 9*, 105–24.

100. Noe, R. A., & Ford, J. K. (1992).

101. Wentling, R. M., & Palma-Rivas, N. (1998).

102. Wentling, R. M., & Palma-Rivas, N. (1998).

103. Rynes, S., & Rosen, B. (1995). A field survey of factors affecting the adoption and perceived success of diversity training. *Personnel Psychology 48*, 247–70.

104. Allerton, H. E. (2001, May). Building bridges in Vancouver. *Training & Development*, 84–97.

105. Henneman, T. (2004, December). Diversity training addresses sexual orientation. *Workforce Management Online, http://www.workforce.com/archive/feature/23/90/44/239046.php?ht= sexual%20orientation*

106. Henneman, T. (2004, December). Acceptance of gays, lesbians is a big part of Kodak's diversity picture. *Workforce Management, 83* (13), 68–70.

107. Koonce, R. (2002, December).

108. Wentling, R. M., & Palma-Rivas, N. (1998).

109. Halcrow, A. (1999). Expats: The squandered resource. *Workforce Management 78* (4), 42–48.

110. Kealey, D. J. (1990). *Cross-cultural effectiveness: A study of Canadian technical advisors overseas.* Hull, QC: Canadian International Development Agency Briefing Centre.

111. Noe, R. A., & Ford, J. K. (1992).

112. Black, J. S., Gregersen, H. B., & Mendenhall, M. E. (1992). *Global assignments.* San Francisco, CA: Jossey-Bass.

113. Kealey, D. J. (1990).

114. Kealey, D. J. (1990).

115. Black, J. S., Gregersen, H. B., & Mendenhall, M. E. (1992).

116. Noe, R. A., & Ford, J. K. (1992).

117. Tung, R. L. (1982). Selection and training procedures of U.S., European, and Japanese multinationals. *California Management Review, 25* (1), 57–71.

118. McEmery, J., & DesHarnais, G. (1990). Culture shock. *Training and Development Journal 44* (4), 43–47.

119. Black, J. S., Gregersen, H. B., & Mendenhall, M. E. (1992).

120. Black, J. S., Gregersen, H. B., & Mendenhall, M. E. (1992).

121. Black, J. S., Gregersen, H. B., & Mendenhall, M. E. (1992).

122. Black, J. S., Gregersen, H. B., & Mendenhall, M. E. (1992).

123. Black, J. S., Gregersen, H. B., & Mendenhall, M. E. (1992).

124. Black, J. S., Gregersen, H. B., & Mendenhall, M. E. (1992).

125. Kealey, D. J. (1990).

126. Black, J. S., Gregersen, H. B., & Mendenhall, M. E. (1992).

Chapter 14

Management Development

Chapter Learning Objectives

After reading this chapter you should be able to:

- define management and management development and explain how it is different from employee training
- describe the main roles, functions, and critical skills of managers
- discuss emotional intelligence and its relevance for management
- describe the models of management skill development
- describe the content of management skills development programs
- discuss the different types of management development programs
- describe outdoor wilderness training programs and their effectiveness for management development
- define job rotation and coaching and discuss the characteristics of great coaches, the five conditions that are necessary to ensure the development of managers, and the challenges of coaching

www.ibm.com/ca

IBM

As an industry leader in training and development, IBM spends more than $1 billion a year on training. IBM is a world leader when it comes to the development of sophisticated training programs. Perhaps, then, it is no surprise that the company recently launched a new two-year company-wide program to transform the role of the manager.

The program is called Role of the Manager@IBM and is the largest management-development initiative in the company's history. It involves 32 000 IBM executives and managers and is designed to transform the role of the manager and to create a new model of 21st-century leadership.

Manager@IBM uses cutting-edge technology to provide managers with a new kind of learning experience that includes a blended program for leadership teams, performance support, and an on-line "e-coach" to guide managers in creating personal management development plans.

The program allows employees to manage their training using three "tracks," thanks to a sophisticated system called Edvisor. In track one, employees can access more than 150 on-line best practice management-support modules. In track two, managers' learning activities are assessed as they prepare for a two-day, face-to-face workshop focused on improving organizational climate and coaching skills. Edvisor helps managers to master specific Web-based program modules that prepare them for the face-to-face learning.

In the third track, an "intelligent agent" analyzes a manager's 360-degree leadership survey feedback and on-line responses. Edvisor then provides leadership advice and assists managers in building a personalized management development plan that includes access to a customized list of management development programs.

More than 22 000 managers have participated in the program and the financial impact of manager action plans has been substantial. More than $280 million in new revenue has been generated resulting in a net gain of $200 million over the $80-million cost of the program. Managers credit the program with enabling them to achieve these results. In addition, survey results indicate that business units with greater participation in Role of the Manager@IBM have greater improvements in employee satisfaction, clarity, and leadership ratings than units with less or no participation.

Another successful program at IBM is called Basic Blue for Managers, which is a blended learning program for new first-line supervisors. The program combines four tiers of training. Three technology-delivered and one week-long classroom learning labs teach first-line managers to become better people managers. This year-long program immerses managers in a combination of on-line self-study, simulations, competency assessments, management coaching, and classroom experiences.

In 2002, *Training* magazine ranked IBM fourth on its list of the Training Top 100, thanks to its Manager@IBM program. In 2003, IBM was ranked second and Basic Blue for Managers was highlighted as a best practice.[1]

The management of our global economy is no simple matter, challenging companies, even smaller ones, to excellence. Evidence indicates that the single characteristic that best distinguishes a successful organization, large or small, from others is the calibre of the management team.[2] As exemplified in the chapter-opening vignette, the development of the skills required of successful managers is a very serious business. This is because, like many companies, IBM understands the impact that managers have on the company's performance. It will be no surprise to learn that *Training* magazine has consistently ranked IBM's training program among the very best in North America (first in 2004–5 and second in 2006.)

This chapter is not placed at the end of the book because the training of managers is unimportant. On the contrary, developing managers is among the most important, complex, and difficult of the challenges that trainers face today. To meet this challenge, management development experts make use of the full slate of principles and techniques described in the earlier chapters.

As you have learned in previous chapters, successful training development involves three key aspects: 1. The identification of training needs, which requires an understanding of the jobs and an identification of the skills required of people who do them (see Chapter 4); 2. The choice of training design and delivery techniques (see Chapters 5-9); and 3. An integration, within the training experience, of elements that contribute not only to learning, but to other psychological forces like motivation and self-efficacy (see Chapter 3). These enhance the odds for successful transfer (see Chapter 10). In this chapter, we describe managers' roles and functions (what managers do) and their competencies (the critical skills they need). We describe the techniques and guiding principles that create the training experience (management training design and delivery) and conclude by describing several types of management development programs and their content. But first, we briefly explain management.

What Is Management?

"**Management** refers to the process of getting things done, efficiently and effectively, through and with other people" (p. 7).[3] The work of managers is to orchestrate the work of others. Although managers and management jobs are all different, they share common aspects that help us grasp their essential natures. Figure 14.1 groups these commonalities by describing what managers

Management

The process of getting things done, efficiently and effectively, through and with other people

FIGURE 14.1

Managerial Roles, Functions, Skills, and Development Approaches

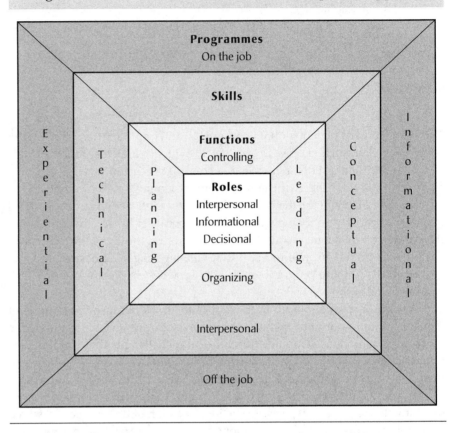

do: their roles (interpersonal, informational, decisional), and the functions these roles serve (controlling, planning, organizing, and leading work organizations). As an example, whereas controlling budgets or organizing a task may have very different meanings for the National Ballet of Canada and Bell Canada managers, accomplishing these tasks requires them to have conceptual, technical, and interpersonal skills as grouped in Figure 14.1.

It is axiomatic to management development that these are learnable skills that can, should be, and are nurtured and developed through training and related experiences. These development experiences (indicated in Figure 14.1) occur on and/or off the job with instructional systems that are informational and experiential.

Management Development versus Employee Training

The topic of management development is separated from employee training for a number of reasons. First, managers are effective when those they manage are effective. That is, managers work mainly through other people. Whereas some management development programs are strictly technical (project planning or budget preparation, for example), most are focused on the development of people and interpersonal skills, a training task of considerable difficulty. Second, and as a result of this different focus and its inherent difficulties, the training design techniques tend to be different (training for managers tends to be experiential and informational). Third, and related to the previous point, the work of management is more influenced by individual managerial preferences and personalities and training must take into account these important individual differences. Fourth, management development is a longitudinal and gradual *process* by which the complex skills and competencies required of managers are built—i.e., developed—over time, with training and with experience. Fifth and most important, incompetent managers can have a catastrophic effect on an entire organization's ability to survive: Management development is different than employee training because it has unique strategic significance.

What Is Management Development?

Management development refers to the "complex processes by which individuals learn to perform effectively in managerial roles" (p. 270).[4] Management jobs are not easy. Managers are responsible for delivering tangible results while tending to unforeseen problems and obstacles of all types: supply problems, machinery breakdowns, personnel issues, etc., all within the current organizational context characterized by change. A diverse and sometimes international work force, frequent technological changes, increased competition, shorter time frames, and a focus on efficiency are all serving to make the job of managing ever more complex. Successful adaptation to this reality requires extensive managerial skills. These skills require strengthening and updating to retain their currency and effectiveness. That is the mission of management development.

Management development
The complex process by which individuals learn to perform effectively in managerial roles

Is Management Development Important?

Management development, a multi-billion-dollar business,[5] is without doubt one of the most important applications of training in organizations. In Canada as well as many other countries, the per capita training expenditures are greater for managers than for any other category of employees: more managers are trained and more is spent on each of them. Corporate expenditures on management education and training are estimated to be $45 billion annually, with approximately $12 billion spent on executive education, and one-fourth spent on university business schools. The average cost of executive education for an organization today is reported to be about $2 million annually.[6] This high level of concern about the development of managers is true in North America as well as in many other areas of the world including the United Kingdom, Lithuania, Spain, and Iran.[7] Why is that? It is because the development of managers is a prudent business investment.

To a very large degree, managers define the organization and it is they who are most responsible for its financial and psychological health. They are responsible for ensuring that the organization functions effectively and efficiently. Organizations are systems composed of people, technologies, procedures, and communications designed to achieve specific valued objectives. It is management's purpose to define these objectives (products and services) and to ensure that they are achieved. In effect, organizations invest more heavily in managers and in their development because theirs is *the* pivotal role in organizations.

Management Development and Leadership

As you will see, the fundamental roles that managers play in organizations are interpersonal, informational, and decisional ones. These three roles are core for the main functions of managers: Controlling, Organizing, and Planning (which makes the convenient acronym, COP). However, the last 20 years have seen a growing recognition of the exercise of leadership as a fundamental function of managers. **Leadership** refers to the individual qualities and behaviours that define and shape the direction of the organization and that inspire others to pursue that direction in the face of obstacles and constraints.

In the past, this "leadership" function was thought to belong more exclusively to the apex of the organizational pyramid: the senior managers.[8] However, in line with current thinking (e.g., Kotter[9] or Whetten and Cameron[4]) we subscribe to the view that the exercise of leadership is a function of *all* management. Hence, the functions of managers are now thought to be Controlling, Organizing, Planning, and Leading (which makes COPL, though some prefer the less literal but more colourful acronym CLOP.)

Adapting to the global economy and its competitive pressures requires ever-increasing levels of resiliency and flexibility in organizations. This flexibility requires that people at all levels of the organization, from the top to the bottom, adapt their job behaviours in response to the changing requirements of their jobs and the contexts in which they are to be performed. As Kotter explains, managers are the motors that propel this process of adaptation to change. From first-line supervisors to CEOs, from production to R&D, managers need to possess the knowledge, skills, attitudes, and behaviours that enable them to foster in the people they manage the attitudes and behaviours that are conducive to the attainment of the individual and organizational goals. The current economic realities compel managers to assume this challenge. They need to lead.

The starting point for a discussion of management development is the identification of training needs. To define these needs, as discussed in Chapter 4, a thorough understanding of the managerial job is required. We therefore begin by reviewing research results that describe what managers do in order to identify the skills they require.

Leadership

The qualities and behaviours that shape the direction of the organization and which inspire others to pursue that direction in the face of obstacles and constraints

The core roles of managers

Interpersonal, informational, and decisional

Core Managerial Roles

Henry Mintzberg analyzed management from the perspective of the manager's day-to-day activities.[11] Derived from the formal authority and status that a manager has, Mintzberg broke these activities into three roles: interpersonal, informational, and decisional. This research is important because it helps define, with greater precision, the skills required of managers and hence the focus of training and development efforts.

Interpersonal Roles

Interpersonal roles refer to the relationship that managers develop with other people because these can provide significant help (or obstacles) to the attainment of group goals. As such, the manager is the organizational person who provides *leadership* (motivates others), and who *liaises* with others both within and outside the unit with the goal of securing information that is of use to the attainment of goals. For example, the training manager who serves on the board of the local community college is better able to gauge the match between the skills taught in the college and those required by his/her organization. The manager also plays a *figurehead* or representational role wherein he or she participates in routine, social, and legal contexts as a representative of the group managed. For example, the Prime Minister, as the manager of Canada, has the duty to meet with his foreign counterparts at annual G8 meetings. Successful achievement of this role requires people skills.

Informational Role

Managers must *monitor* the environment (both internal and external) to accumulate information pertinent to the attainment of organizational goals. He or she reciprocates by assuming the role of *disseminator* of information by informing others about the unit and informing the unit about relevant developments occurring outside the unit. For example, the dean of research in a university might set up systems to provide professors with information about government or private programs that fund research. The manager also acts as a *spokesperson* informing others and "selling" them on the plans, values, or goals of the unit. The manager of an oil company, for example, may be called upon to describe to the community the steps that the organization is taking to curtail greenhouse gas emissions. Hence managers require communication skills.

Decisional Role

Managers must make decisions about people and about goals and the means to attain them. As an initiator of change, the manager is an *entrepreneur* moving the unit in directions that take advantage of opportunities or shifting the activities of the group to reduce threats. For example, to respond to the growing threat from Apple, which had developed a more user-friendly operating system for its computers, Bill Gates moved Microsoft away from the classic DOS systems to the Windows operating environment. The manager *allocates resources,* choosing from competing proposals and projects those that will receive additional funding and personnel and those to be curtailed or discontinued. Downsizing or staff expansions are such resource-allocation decisions. The manager is also called upon to act as a *negotiator,* bargaining with others in the environment to acquire the resources required to meet the planned goals. This negotiation role may involve interactions with the external environment (for example by negotiating with government regulatory agencies or suppliers) or it may be focused internally (for example, securing additional resources for the work group). In addition, the manager is also a *trouble-shooter* reacting to unanticipated and unplanned environmental events that can severely disrupt the unit. For example, when Eastern Canada was hit by a devastating ice storm, Quebec's premier called on the federal government to deploy the armed forces to help. Hence managers require problem-solving skills.

Clearly, managers play a complex role requiring sophisticated skills. Although most managers will have to accomplish each of the roles, the relative emphasis placed on them will depend on the specifics of the hierarchical position, the organizational and social-cultural context, the over-arching organizational strategies, and the technologies and structures in which they operate and exercise their functions. For example, although interpersonal, informational, and decisional skills are all important, the display of interpersonal roles may be particularly significant for the manager of a classical ballet company, while the decisional role may be even more critical for the management of a production department.

Managerial Functions

Functions of management

Controlling, organizing, planning, and leading

The **functions of management** are controlling, organizing, planning, and leading (COPL). That is, managers are responsible for ensuring that things get done. They monitor the work processes and progress towards goal attainment (controlling), they allocate resources and tasks (organizing), establish what should be done and how (planning), and maintain the motivation and zeal of those who do the work (leading). In completing these functions, they play one or more of the interpersonal, informational, or decisional roles and rely on the skills that each implies.

Controlling

Controlling, as its name suggests, refers to the process by which the activities of the organization and its members are monitored to ensure that they contribute positively to the attainment of organization goals and objectives. It involves establishing mechanisms to monitor and resolve performance gaps and address any constraints and problems that hinder the attainment of performance goals.

- For example, the manager of an automobile engine assembly plant is required to monitor quality control indicators to ensure that the engines built meet the quality specifications required, that they start, run smoothly, and function with the fuel efficiency standards specified. Deficiencies from required standards must be identified, diagnosed, and corrected in a timely and efficient manner. In such cases, management would review the quality indicators and institute corrective actions as needed.

Organizing

The accomplishment of most contemporary organizational goals requires the efforts of a diversity of units, each composed of many individuals. Major activities are identified and components of these major tasks assigned to units and individuals. The manager's job is to establish systems that ensure that these efforts are efficiently and effectively coordinated and organized.

- Automobile manufacturing provides a clear example of organizing. One plant may build engines, while another plant builds chassis. Yet another one may place the engines in the chassis. Within each plant (engine, chassis, and final assembly) managers must organize the activities as well. Hence, the engine plant would be organized such that separate units produce the valves, pistons, and fuel injection systems. And each of these sub-systems of the manufacturing process is in turn organized to produce the valves, pistons, and injection systems efficiently and effectively and in such a manner that they all fit together, in a timely manner, to produce the final engine.

Planning

Planning, in the context of management, means defining the direction towards which the efforts of individuals are to be directed. It involves defining objectives and developing goals to be met by the organization and the departments or the units for which the manager is responsible. The scope of the goals and objectives depends on the level of management, and the specifics of the planning tasks depend on the nature of managerial responsibility. As one moves from the lowest to the highest levels of the organization, the objectives and goals become broader and more strategic.

- For example, the highest levels of the automobile industry may choose as a fundamental strategy the production of "high quality" cars and trucks. At lower levels of the organization, meeting this strategic goal require plans that are more local and more specific. Hence mid-level managers may focus their planning efforts on "ensuring that 99 percent of automobile parts meet the established quality standards" while even lower-level managers may plan to "establish a system by which assembly line workers meet once a week to discuss ways of improving the quality of the work that is done" or to ensure "that all employees who provide suggestions for improvements be provided feedback within one week of their making the suggestion."

Leading

Leading is a critical people-oriented function of management. It means influencing the actions of others such that these actions are coordinated to produce the desired outcomes. Managers mainly operate through others. Hence, managers require people skills. Management is responsible for obtaining and keeping employees committed to their goals. This is facilitated when employees believe that the attainment of the goal is important, when they believe that attaining the goals will result in positive outcomes, and when they also believe that their individual efforts make a difference in goal attainment.

A leader, according to Kouzes and Posner, is successful by being a role model (i.e., preaching by example), by inspiring a shared vision, by challenging the status quo, and by encouraging others to do the same (asking why), and by recognizing the contributions of others (through verbal feedback and tangible outcomes).[12]

- In the automobile industry example, building quality cars involves ensuring that people care about quality and view their own work with an emphasis on quality. To inspire all levels, leaders would "sell quality" through their actions and their words. Quality would be one of the important criteria against which all decisions would be weighed.

Although managers are still viewed as those responsible for "getting things done" through the functions of planning, organizing, controlling and leading, increasingly managers must provide support to their employees, assist them in the development of new skills, and act as coaches and facilitators for employee task accomplishment.[13] Leading organizations have formalized these functions by integrating them into the performance management system for managers. To learn more about this, see Training Today 1, "Taking Management Development Seriously: The PricewaterhouseCoopers Story."

Management Skills

In the previous sections, we identified and described the various roles and functions of managers as this process is essential to pinpoint the ensemble of skills and knowledge that are required of managers and that may be developed through training.

Skills

Sets of actions that individuals perform and that lead to certain outcomes

Skills may be defined as sets of actions that individuals perform and that lead to certain outcomes.[14] The literature is replete with descriptions of the types of skills that are needed to accomplish the managerial roles and functions. Two types of approaches have been used to identify the skills required of managers. Some authors rely on their extensive experience with management to infer the skills needed for effective management (or leadership). They then propose mechanisms by which these can be developed.

Others have tended to place a higher emphasis on empirical research to guide their prescriptions. The classic empirical technique for identifying these skills has been to conduct surveys of managers—sometimes within a single firm and sometimes across several firms. Managers rate the importance of many potential skills and statistical analyses are conducted to identify those skills and competencies that distinguish successful managers from their less successful counterparts.

One such study involves observations of 52 successful managers and compares them to less successful ones in three organizations. Successful managers appeared more skillful in a number of ways. They were better than their less successful counterparts in building power and influence, communicating (with insiders as well as outsiders), managing conflict, decision-making, developing others, processing paperwork, planning, and goal-setting.[15]

Taking Management Development Seriously: The PricewaterhouseCoopers Story

PricewaterhouseCoopers (PwC) is one of the largest professional services organizations in the world. PwC takes the development of its people seriously. It has instituted widespread coaching and mentoring programs for managers, but it has gone one step further.

As part of the performance management program, all managers must indicate the steps they have taken to develop their own subordinates. The performance assessment—and the rewards and bonuses paid out to managers based on it—is determined, in part, by the degree to which they have helped their employees achieve higher levels of competencies, both managerial and technical.

Moreover, all partners in the firm are offered a series of workshops delivered by leading professionals to help them gain a deeper understanding of the help that they can provide to their employees and the importance of that function for the organization.

Why would a prestigious organization like PwC attach importance to this policy? Because it is good for their employees and good for business. Such policies help the company retain its valued employees and help them service their clients even better. Developing and growing the competencies of employees also increases their employability, both on client projects with PwC and even if they should leave the organization.

In the end, the value of these practices is that they seamlessly and simultaneously provide benefits both to the organization and to employees. It's a win-win scenario.

Confirmation of these attributes was obtained in a more recent study where, instead of focusing on successful managers, as is usually the case, the authors looked at the problem from the opposite pole. They conducted 166 group interviews (focus groups) with 830 U.S. managers who were identified as *less* successful. These managers tended to be poorer in a number of dimensions that closely mirror those identified by other studies. They tended to display ineffective communication and interpersonal skills, they failed to clarify expectations, they were poorer in delegating and empowering subordinates, they tended to be more distrustful of others, they were less able to organize and encourage teamwork, and they had more trouble motivating others. Furthermore, these less effective managers were poorer at planning, monitoring performance, and providing feedback and they tended to be less effective in identifying and removing obstacles to effective performance that their employees had experienced.[16]

Taking a somewhat different approach, Cameron and Tschirhart asked a large sample of managers working in 150 organizations to identify the most important skills and competencies required of managers. The results showed that the managerial skills fall into four basic clusters.[17] One cluster focuses on human relations skills and includes skills such as providing supportive communication and team building. Another focused on competitiveness and control. A third cluster focused on behaviours that foster individual entrepreneurship and innovativeness, and the fourth focused on order and rationality. Hence, effective managers support and encourage the work of their employees (cluster 1)

TABLE 14.1

The Most Frequently Cited Skills of Effective Managers

Verbal communication (including listening)

Managing time and stress

Managing individual decisions

Recognizing, defining, and solving problems

Motivating and influencing others

Delegating

Setting goals and articulating a vision

Self-awareness

Team building

Managing conflict

Source: Whetten, D. A., & Cameron, K. S. (2002). *Developing management skills* (5th ed.) Upper Saddle River, NJ: Prentice Hall.

while focused on achievement and results (cluster 2). They allow employees to display innovation and creativity (cluster 3), while maintaining control and rationality (cluster 4).

As Cameron and Tschirhart note, the skills required of successful managers are "paradoxical," requiring them to possess a number of skills that may appear contradictory (e.g. cluster 3 versus cluster 4). But Whetten and Cameron[4] showed that successful managers did resolve this paradox: Even as they were controlled, stable and rational, they were still able to be creative and flexible.

As result of these extensive and varied approaches to understanding managerial roles and functions, a number of critical managerial skills have been identified. Table 14.1 presents a summary of the most frequently mentioned skills of effective managers. As you will see, many of these involve "people skills" (communicating, motivating others, delegating, goal-setting, self-awareness, team building, and conflict management). The "people" side of management and its subsequent salience for management development cannot be underestimated. As an example, the Stanford Graduate School of Business produces a large number of briefings videos delivered by corporate and academic stars and intended for the development of managers. They cover a very wide range of topics (such as mergers and acquisitions, preparing financial statements, supply chain strategies, etc.) but the single most frequent topic, about a third of all videos, focuses on dealing with people (such as coaching and providing feedback).

A manager controls, organizes, plans and leads people. In practice, this means that one of the most important aspects of management involves interacting, communicating, and dealing with other people: their peers, subordinates, and superiors, as well as customers and in many cases, members of the general public. You will not be surprised to learn that some managers are better at it than others. Research has shown that those who have superior people skills possess, in addition to other talents, higher levels of a specific type of intelligence called "emotional intelligence," a topic to which we now turn.

Emotional Intelligence

Most human interactions have an emotional component and the success of these interactions often depends on how well emotions are managed. Moreover, because of the heavy responsibilities of the management role and the sheer number of tasks that managers perform, they must often deal with their own emotional issues and pressures. Thus, they have to cope with conflict, performance pressures, and uncertainty. Because much of this involves emotions, managers must develop skills in managing their own emotions and in understanding those of others. The skills that people have in managing emotions—their own and those of others—has been labeled *Emotional Intelligence* (EI).[18] As with coordinating, planning, etc., the training needs of managers now additionally include developing in them greater people skills, and underlying those people skills lie the various aspects of emotional intelligence. It is for this reason that we devote a specific section on this topic. To obtain an appreciation for the prominence of this concept, search "Emotional Intelligence" or "EQ" (Emotional Quotient) on the Internet. You will find thousands of entries!

Emotional intelligence has to do with the ability to manage and cope with emotions—yours and those of others—in your relationships with people. This involves five sets of skills that foster better understanding of oneself and effective interactions with others:

1. *Self-awareness:* Being aware of, and understanding, oneself and one's emotions when interacting with others.
2. *Self-control:* Managing and regulating one's emotions (both positive and negative) that arise from encounters and events.
3. *Motivation or drive:* Channeling emotions and energies in support of one's goals.
4. *Empathy:* "Reading" and recognizing the emotions of others and responding to them appropriately.
5. *Interpersonal skills:* The ability to manage interactions with others in an appropriate and effective manner, through an understanding, integration, and management of emotions—yours and theirs.

Notice that the components of EI (e.g., self-awareness, interpersonal skills, etc.) are listed as skills. That is, they are believed to be controllable and learnable behaviours rather than "fixed" character-like traits. Unlike intellectual intelligence (IQ) which is a relatively stable and enduring characteristic of people's cognitive abilities, EI is believed to be a learnable and changeable factor. In other words, through appropriate management development and training, emotional intelligence can be developed and improved. However, unlike project planning or other "hard skills" associated with management, emotional intelligence involves people-oriented skills that are often labeled as

Emotional intelligence

The ability to manage your own and others' emotions and your relationships with others "soft skills" (see Chapter 13). EI, as with other "soft skills," tends to be developed indirectly, through enhanced skills in dealing with others. As people learn to receive and deliver feedback, to manage stress, or to diffuse conflicts, for example, they also simultaneously enhance their own levels of emotional intelligence.[19] Training in emotional intelligence involves group and individual activities that include role plays, assessments, and practical exercises all intended to enhance self management and empathy.

The fact that emotional intelligence can be developed is extremely important because empirical research has shown that managers with higher levels of emotional intelligence are more effective and successful than managers with lower levels of EI. They are more likely to be promoted and to rise to the highest levels of management in their organizations. Furthermore, emotional intelligence has been found to be much more important than IQ or cognitive ability in predicting a manager's success, and to also predict organizational success. Not surprisingly, research indicates that organizations prefer to hire for management positions people with higher levels of the skills associated with emotional intelligence.[20]

In summary, emotional intelligence involves the ability to manage one's own and others' emotions and relationships with others. Given that managers spend most of their time interacting and communicating with others and that the main functions and roles of management involve people, emotional intelligence is a critical factor in management development and effectiveness. Therefore, in addition to training experiences that are directly focused on its development, those programs that include activities and experiences that encourage self-awareness and self-control, motivation, empathy, and interpersonal skills serve to enhance emotional intelligence.

Clearly, managers require myriad skills. Whereas some fortunate managers excel in all, most managers have strengths and weaknesses, some of which require development. What are the principles that underlie how we are to go about doing that? It is to that end that models of management skill development have been proposed.

Models of Management Skill Development

A model of management skills development is a basic blueprint that identifies the components or steps to be included in the development of programs. Many skill development models exist in the management literature, some specifying a greater number of steps than others (e.g., Whetten and Cameron[4] list five steps while Hunsaker[21] lists 10—see The Trainer's Notebook, "The TIMS (Training in Management Skills) Procedure"). However, most models of management skill development share four basic commonalities. That is, management development programs that have better chances for success will minimally include these four sequenced steps: 1. Initial skills assessment (identifying where people are), 2. Skill acquisition (learning and understanding the basic principles associated with the specific skill of interest), 3. Skill practice (developing procedural learning by integrating the principles into smooth behavioural actions), and 4. Skill application on the job (applying the learned principles in job situations that require the skills).

The TIMS (Training in Management Skills) Procedure

Phillip Hunsaker provides the following 10-step process to management development that he refers to as TIMS or Training in Management Skills.

1. Self-assessment.
2. Learn skill concepts.
3. Check concept learning.
4. Identify behaviours that define the skill.
5. Model the skill (i.e., observe others performing the skill).
6. Practice the skill during training (to build self-efficacy and to contribute to procedural learning).
7. Re-assess skills (to test for progress and to intervene when skill changes are insufficient).
8. Questions to assist in skill application (questioning trainees to ensure that they have a clear understanding of the situations in which the application of the trained skill is warranted and to identify constraints and coping strategies for overcoming these constraints).
9. Exercises to reinforce skill application (as well as self-efficacy and procedural learning).
10. Planning for future development (as a specific preparation for transfer).

The TIMS model (and most other models) helps training developers and management trainers focus their efforts by providing a template of the activities required to increase the odds that managerial skill levels do improve as a result of training. Although the TIMS model is somewhat more detailed than some other models, it reflects the key dimensions common to most management development models: skill-assessment (steps 1 and 7), learning (steps 2 though 5), and practice and preparation for application on the job (steps 6, and 8 through 10).

Source: Hunsaker, P. L. (2001). *Training in management skills.* Upper Saddle River, NJ: Prentice Hall.

TABLE 14.2

The Basic Components of Management Development and Their Expected Impact on Trainees

	MOTIVATION	SELF-EFFICACY	LEARNING	BEHAVIOUR CHANGE (TRANSFER)
initial skills assessment	X			
skill acquisition			X	
skill practice	X	X	X	
skill application on the job	X	X	X	X

Table 14.2 summarizes these four basic components of management development programs and identifies the outcome each is expected to influence.

a. *Skill assessment.* This process identifies the skill level of the manager before development. Initial skill assessment is used to identify the strengths and weaknesses that managers hold relative to the specific skills to be trained and most importantly to help managers become aware of them. Skill assessment is a key component of IBM's

RPC 14.1

Managing@IBM program and it is developed in close symmetry with the learning objectives set for the training program (see Chapter 5). Skill assessment contributes to and builds self-awareness. This is critical because people must recognize a need for development before development can take hold. That is, skill assessment affects and contributes to training motivation. Initial skill assessment also serves to identify the learning and the basic behavioural styles that managers hold. There is general recognition that the purpose of management development is not to change individual personalities or styles, but rather, to help managers translate these personal preferences into practices and behaviours that are appropriate to their work context and that are effective in meeting the goals of the organization.

Initial skill assessment is usually established through self-administered (and often self-scored) standardized validated questionnaires given to training participants at the onset of training. For this reason these questionnaires are relatively short, easily administered, and easily scored under themes that directly reflect the training content. For example, the initial questionnaire for a stress coping program would ask of trainees to describe the degree to which they engage in behaviours that are known to be associated with stress reactions. Typically, trainees retain their answers and after training, answer the questionnaires again, to note changes.

Although initial skill assessment is of importance to all training programs, it is especially critical for management development because "development" is a gradual process where *improvement* in skills is the main objective. Managers will need to practice and rehearse the skill before mastery can be achieved. Keeping managers motivated and confident in the development of the specific skills requires reinforcement. Skill assessment before and after the development experience can be reinforcing as this helps managers perceive the degree of growth in their level of skills mastery. Helping managers perceive improvements helps to build motivation, thus encouraging managers to continue to exert the efforts that lead to mastery. Hence, skill assessment and growth is immediately useful to the trainer (to know how things are going), but it makes an indirect contribution to the motivation of the learner.

b. *Skill learning.* Learning the required principles and behaviours that form the core of the intervention is central and all training programs focus on it. However, as contrasted with most technical training where the trainee is taught specific procedures and steps required to accomplish a task, the managerial role is more diffuse requiring that managers learn how to recognize the need for the skill in a diverse number of circumstances. Hence, management development programs will almost invariably include group discussions where managers help each other discover the opportunities for application that may exist on the job, the obstacles that may inhibit skill use, and the strategies and tactics that may be used to circumvent these obstacles.

In management development, the purpose is to help managers learn managerial principles and processes that can be integrated with their personal styles and applied to the conditions they are likely to meet on the job. Hence, most management development programs will include substantial lectures or presentations that outline the reasons for the training and the principles that will guide their future actions. For example, performance planning and reviews (PP&R) tend to be more constructive when subordinate and managerial anxiety and defensiveness are minimized. To achieve this, most PP&R training programs emphasize the importance for the manager to clearly explain the evaluation process to the subordinate ahead of time. There are many ways of explaining the same thing and no specific manner, or set of words, will be appropriate for all managers and/or with all subordinates. Therefore, the effectively trained manager will have understood the principle (reducing subordinate defensiveness) but will "choose" his or her own specific words and approaches depending on the specifics of the person under review and the specifics of the situation. The ultimate objective of these development programs is to help managers attain procedural learning (see Chapter 3). Attaining that goal generally requires *practice*, the third major component of management development programs.

c. *Skill practice*. As described in Chapter 5, practice is the key to learning how to do most things well. The practice of learned skills serves three fundamental purposes. First and most obvious, practice reinforces learning and more formally, helps shift the learning from the declarative to the procedural learning stage (see Chapter 3). This is essential if the manager is to integrate the learned skill with his or her own style. A second use of practice is to enhance the manager's beliefs in his or her ability to perform the skill. That is, practice contributes to the development of self-efficacy and as you have read in both Chapters 3 and 11, the development of self-efficacy is one of the keys to successful training. Managers who feel more confident in their capacity to learn and display the skill on the job are more likely to learn and transfer that skill. Third, skill practice can take a variety of forms including role plays, simulations, and videotaped behaviour with feedback. These activities are inherently more active, maintaining trainee interest, attention, and motivation on the learning task. However, as training time is invariably limited in the North American context, it is not realistic to expect that the amount of time devoted to practice during training will be sufficient to automatically produce high levels of transfer on the job. As rehearsal and practice on the job is essential, all development models include as a final component "skill application on the job."

d. *Skill application* on the job (transfer), the final step in management development has to do with the transfer process (see Chapter 10). Managers establish, during the training session, specific plans for the application of the learning on the job. Once on the job, however, organizational support in the form of follow-ups, additional coaching, and reinforcement is frequently required to ensure that managers transfer their newly learned skills. The reason for this is that in light of the very numerous tasks that managers perform, usually under pressure, it is very easy and tempting for them to relapse into their traditional, well-honed pre-training behaviours. Specific immediate post-training interventions such as relapse prevention (see Chapter 10) can also be integrated at this point to augment the odds of successful transfer.

In summary, models of management skill development focus on a number of important steps or stages in the development process. This usually begins with self-assessment and then proceeds to skill learning, practice, and application. These steps favour the development of the motivational, self-efficacy, learning, and/or transfer outcomes that lead to successful training.

The Content of Management Development Programs

Based on our earlier discussion, management skills can be clustered around three general categories: conceptual, technical, and interpersonal skills. These three clusters of skills are not completely independent. For example, the mastery of technical skills (planning a project) often requires conceptual skills (such as linear programming), and interpersonal skills (e.g. getting R&D scientists to meet deadlines) often require specific technical skills (understanding the complexities of research). Nevertheless, this categorization provides a useful way to organize management development programs.

In this section, we describe the content of management development programs used to develop some of these skills. More complete descriptions of management development programs may be found in texts specialized in management development (e.g., Whetten and Cameron or Hunsaker) and by consulting the Weblinks identified at the end of the chapter.

Conceptual Skills

To accomplish the planning, organizing, and control functions of management, managers require various conceptual skills. We will limit the discussion to three especially important conceptual skills—problem solving and decision-making, planning, and performance management.

a. *Problem solving and decision-making skills.* Because managers are required to make myriad decisions—small and large—it is essential that they have the skills to do so. Many years ago, James March and Herbert Simon, in one of the most influential studies of managerial decision-making, showed that most people are uncomfortable making decisions, and that they tend to adopt solutions to problems that are not optimal but "adequate." Typically, the first solution that minimally solves the problem is selected.[22]

Contemporary decision-making programs are designed to specifically avoid this tendency. As a result, most programs are organized around four basic steps: 1. Defining the problem, 2. Generating alternative solutions, 3. Evaluating and selecting an alternative solution, and 4. Implementation and follow-up. The actual training programs include introductory lectures where the basic steps required for effective decision-making are explained and defended. Videotapes, role plays, and structured individual exercises are used to reinforce each learning point, and to provide some of the all-important skills practice.

b. *Planning.* Planning is an essential requirement of management. Planning involves first the clarification and specification of the goals the manager wishes to achieve. Next, the manager is taught to scan the environment to ensure that the plans are relevant and have a high probability of being successfully implemented. This second step is referred to as a "SWOT" analysis. That is, the manager is taught how to identify the Strengths and Weaknesses of the unit managed (that is their capabilities and weaknesses) relative to the Opportunities and Threats that exist in the environment. Based on this analysis, the manager is taught to translate these strengths and weaknesses (SW), opportunities (O), and possible threats (T), into specific actions in order to establish the strategies and tactics required for implementation. Finally, managers learn the processes by which the success (or lack thereof) of the plan is evaluated.

c. *Performance management and goal-setting.* Almost all organizations in North America require managers to review, assess, and manage the performance of their units and the people in them. Performance appraisal involves two distinct steps: assessing the performance of people (to provide feedback on past performance and to ensure that rewards and sanctions are applied fairly), and establishing goals and directions for future performance (to encourage improved future performance). Whereas these two steps are usually associated with a yearly formal review session, it is now widely acknowledged that managers need to review the performance of others on an ongoing basis. Motivating employees to improve performance is one of the key skills that successful managers possess. Goal-setting is an integral part of that process. As shown by Edwin Locke and Gary Latham, goals have strong motivational effects and are one of the most important mechanisms for managing one's own performance as well as the performance of others.[23] Goals focus and direct one's efforts and can be self-reinforcing by providing specific feedback information that allows people to evaluate their progress.

However, in order for goals to be motivational, they must be SMART goals. That is, they must be Specific, Measurable, Achievable, Relevant, and specified in Time. Managers need to know how to structure such SMART goals. Moreover, goals are motivating and effective only when there is commitment to goal attainment. Most goal-setting training programs are structured to teach managers how to obtain the employees' commitment to the set goals and to provide feedback relevant to goal attainment.

Goal-setting, which was discussed in Chapter 3, is now an integral part of performance management and many managers are trained in this area in order to enable them to conduct performance appraisals, and to help their employees improve their performance. Many Canadian organizations including PricewaterhouseCoopers, the National Research Council of Canada, and Bell Canada have provided their managers with performance management and assessment training courses that all include goal-setting as one of the key dimensions of the program.

Performance management training programs emphasize, through lectures and discussions, the key advantages of performance reviews and the fundamental difficulties of the process. Such programs include many experiential components such as role plays and simulations.

Technical Skills

Managers of marketing departments know something about marketing, and research directors know something about research. Such knowledge and skills are generally acquired through university programs that may be general (such as a general MBA) or more specialized (such as a university program in Human Resource Management, Marketing, Statistics, or Accounting). Additionally, technical skills can be further developed through targeted training courses and workshops and/or readings. For example controlling budgets requires of managers expertise in computer spreadsheet programs such as Excel and the informational role requires them to have presentation skills, which in turn, often requires them to know how to use presentation programs such as PowerPoint.

As additional examples, university professors tend to build technical skills by reading scientific journals and by attending conferences, and medical doctors and pharmacists in Canada are required to attend a certain number of conferences and workshops that instruct them on new research, treatments, or diagnostic procedures in their areas of practice. Accountants and lawyers are also required to attend periodic specialized information sessions such as when there are changes to auditing standards or tax regulations or when new laws are enacted.

Interpersonal Skills

Interpersonal skills refer to the manager's ability to interact with others in a constructive manner. This includes skills in communication, coaching (see "Coaching" later in the chapter), and in managing conflict and stress. Although we limit our discussion to these skills in this chapter, it is important to note that other skills are also important. For example, there is a growing recognition of the importance for managers to develop "political" skills designed to help them gain power and influence. Moreover, as organizations move towards knowledge-based systems, they require that their members increasingly self-manage their behaviour and show initiative in their own development. Managers need to learn how to function in this new environment by learning how to empower and motivate their employees and to build effective teams.

a. *Communication.* Communication skills are central to most management positions because much of a manager's time involves gathering and disseminating information from the environment to the people in the unit and from the people in the unit to the environment. Often managers must communicate expectations to employees and provide feedback—not all of which is positive—to employees. In communicating effectively, managers are taught to recognize their own *biases and styles* in "hearing" and in "speaking" with others. Hence, managers need to understand their *frame of reference* (knowing "where they are coming from"), how their interpretations of what they hear and communicate are affected by their *values,* and their *trusts* or distrusts of others. These in turn affect *selective listening* (hearing what we want to hear) and *filtering* (telling only that which others want to hear). In addition to alerting managers to these tendencies that obscure communication, most communication training programs teach managers the principles and the practice of effective communication. This involves congruency (ensuring that the message that is sent is in line with their own actions), *clarity* (using language that is appropriate for the listener), and most importantly to ensure comprehension by actively soliciting *feedback* from the listener. Again, in addition to learning the principles of sound communication, trainees are provided with many opportunities to practice these skills during training by analyzing cases and engaging in role plays with other training participants.

b. *Managing conflict.* Managing conflict is an essential skill for managers because they are invariably competing for resources with other managers and because they may be involved in managing the competition and conflict between employees.

    Conflict can be described as being of one of two types—conflict that is *interpersonal* (co-workers who may dislike one another) or *issue-based* (people who may have conflicting views on a problem or its solution).[24] Conflict is not an inherently "bad" thing because issue-based disagreements can often serve to enhance the quality of the final decision.[25] However, when conflict is not properly managed it can quickly create organizational problems.

    There are five ways of managing conflict: *avoidance* (ignoring it), *accommodation* (giving in), *forcing* (getting your way), *compromise* (providing each party with some of the things they want), and *collaboration* (finding a solution together that gives the parties what they both want).

    Collaboration is the ultimate conflict resolution outcome but it is not always possible or appropriate. Which style is appropriate depends on the situation faced by the manager. Forcing, for example, may be appropriate when the resolution requires an unpopular decision and when gaining the commitment of people to that decision is not important. Hence managers are taught to recognize and choose the conflict management response that is appropriate to the circumstances they face. This, above all, requires of managers that they pay attention to the emotional aspects of the conflict. To do so requires that the manager 1. Treats the parties with respect, 2. Listens to the other party and ensures that they know that they have been heard and understood, and 3. Shares his/her needs and feelings.

c. *Managing stress.* Considering the scope, time pressures (managers spend about nine minutes on each problem!), difficulties, responsibilities and ambiguities of managerial life, it is no surprise that managerial jobs tend to be very stressful. A stress reaction is a person's emotional and physical response to a perceived threat. Stress reactions, like pain are useful warning mechanisms that inform people that "something is wrong" and that they should do something about it. However, how a person deals with stress may or may not be particularly functional. Reacting to someone cutting you off on the highway by tearing after them with vengeance on your mind is unlikely to lead to an enjoyable or safe driving experience!

Stress reactions in the context of work are responses to events that may find their source in the work itself and the organization. For example, two well-known work-related stressors are role conflict and role ambiguity. *Role conflict* is associated with having contradictory task demands (for example jobs that require experimentation and innovation in organizations that do not tolerate errors), and *role ambiguity* refers to not knowing what is expected. Stressors that impact work behaviours might also find their source in non-work events (a family or health problem for example). Managers need to recognize stress reactions both in themselves as well as in those they manage because some stress reactions can be quite dysfunctional, damaging one's health and/or work performance.

There are two basic ways to deal with stress. First, one can change the environment by removing or eliminating the stressors. Second, one can learn to cope with and manage stressors more effectively. As individuals are generally better able to learn how to react to stressful situations than they are able to change organizational environments, the second approach is more likely to be successful.

However, most people experience stress and are unaware of it. In learning how to cope with stress, the first and most important step, then, is to recognize the signs of stress: to know when one is in fact experiencing it. As a result, the initial "skills assessment" phase of such training is critical and these programs spend considerable time helping managers become aware of their own reactions to stress. The manager can then learn proactive behavioural and cognitive tactics and strategies (learning how to perceive these situations differently) that will reduce the harmful effects of a stress reaction.

Stress-related training programs rely on the typical informational (reviewing basic principles related to stress and its management) and experiential (principally simulations and role plays) techniques. Usually, these programs offer techniques that can be beneficial to managers' ability to deal with stress not only in the context of work, but also in their non-work lives.

In summary, management development programs are often designed to focus on the development of conceptual, technical, and interpersonal skills. There are of course many different approaches and methods, some "on the job," and others "off the job," for developing these skills, a topic to which we now turn.

Methods of Management Development

🅡🅟🅒 14.2

Whereas virtually all of the on-the-job and off-the-job training methods described in Chapters 6 and 7 can and have been used by some management development programs, management training methods tend to rely on highly informational and highly experiential procedures.

Management training programs are strongly informational and focused on the principles and the applications of the skill or technique being taught. That is they teach principles relevant to specifics in the core roles and functions of management. You may have noticed that in the previous sections describing management training programs (conflict management, decision making, etc.), emotional intelligence, or coaching (see below) we emphasized their principles. Lectures, readings, informative videos, and group discussions structured around these principles and their concrete applications constitute major elements in management training programs. This informational, principles-based approach is of great importance in management development because managers operate in fluid and varied environments and each manager needs to develop his/her own idiosyncratic ways of comfortably applying the principles learned in training. Management development cannot consist of memorizing and applying a set of prescriptions. If, for example, all computer operators can be drilled in exactly the same behaviours for loading a hard drive, all managers cannot be equivalently drilled into using the same words to communicate with all employees effectively. It is only by understanding and integrating the principles taught that different managers can correctly apply them in a manner that is appropriate to themselves and to the work group situation.

Helping managers adapt principles and techniques in conformity with their personal styles, given the context in which they work, requires effort on the part of the learner and that effort requires motivation. Managers who do not believe in the usefulness of a training program are unlikely to exert the efforts required to learn and apply its contents. Focusing on the principles (and their application) contributes motivationally to successful management training: It sells it!

Because of the importance of motivation, management training programs tend to be experiential. **Experiential learning** refers to learning experiences that include skill practice exercises that actively engage and involve the learner: activities likely to be more intrinsically motivating. Hence role plays with feedback, active exercises, and simulations are important components of the programs. Experiential approaches provide, in addition to motivational benefits, two other important ones. First, extensive hands-on practice builds procedural knowledge (see Chapters 3 and 11). That is, direct experience helps managers integrate the newly learned skills. Second, experiential learning is favored because it contributes to managerial self-efficacy which is an important precursor for transfer of training (see Chapter 10). As you will recall from

Experiential learning
Learning experiences that include skill practice exercises that actively engage and involve the learner

The Origins of Outdoor Wilderness Training

During World War II, the allied navies played a major role conveying and protecting ships supplying England. German U-boats opposed these convoys, taking a heavy toll on men and ships. Hundreds of ships were torpedoed, forcing thousands to confront the rigours of survival in rafts and lifeboats. Many successfully escaped their burning ships only to die awaiting a rescue that did not come.

Paradoxically, casualty reports revealed that older, less physically able shipwrecked men had better survival rates than younger, more fit sailors. Discussions held with survivors indicated that younger sailors adopted unsuccessful life strategies such as panic, while the older sailors, those

with greater life experience, remained calmer and hence better able to meet the demands of their extreme situation.

Years after the war ended, this experience spawned "outdoor wilderness training," an experiential team and management development technique. For several days trainees are tasked with arduous and/or hazardous duties that are intentionally stressful.

These stressful situations bring out the best and the worst in ourselves and others allowing us to gain direct experience with what we and others are capable of doing. With its exposure to extreme conditions, outdoor wilderness training is intended to build "life experience" which, in turn, is supposed to contribute to the development of coping skills.

the COMA model (see Chapter 11), motivation, self-efficacy, and procedural knowledge all have important effects on training success and transfer.

Although informational and experiential components are present in most programs, the balance between the two is not always identical. Many short-term programs (such as the Stanford Graduate School of Business DVDs) are essentially informational. Some development programs are more fully experiential providing little if any formal informational components. One such example is Outdoor Wilderness Training. The interesting origins of this popular technique are described in the Training Today 2 feature and its effectiveness as a training strategy is discussed later on in this chapter.

There are three general approaches or techniques to management development: management education programs, management training programs, and on-the-job development.

Management Education Programs

Management education

The acquisition of a broad range of managerial knowledge and general conceptual abilities

The development of managers has typically involved management education. **Management education** refers to the types of activities that are typically conducted by colleges and universities and that develop a broad range of knowledge, principles, and general conceptual abilities relevant to the managerial role.[26] These education programs target the development of the principles and techniques required to effectively control, organize, plan, and lead. Examples and case studies drawn from specific organizations are often used to exemplify the general principles and techniques of management that are presented through lectures and discussions. Three examples of such content areas are "accounting," "organizational behaviour," and "business statistics."

The ever-popular MBA that most business schools offer provides the classic example of a management education program. Executive MBA programs are especially desirable for individuals who are already in managerial roles and want to advance in their organization. These programs provide individuals with a general education in management and are highly informational although they usually include much experiential learning as well. Students not only learn about management concepts and theory, but they are also expected to develop managerial skills. In fact, many MBA programs have managerial skills courses that focus on the kinds of skills listed in Table 14.1. Management education programs make use of a number of experiential methods such as role plays, games, simulations, and behaviour modelling that were described in Chapter 6. The case study method, however, is the most often used method to teach management skills in most MBA programs.

A second, complementary approach to management education has been the development of corporate universities. To learn more, see the Training Today 3 feature, "Are Corporate Universities Useful?"

Management Training Programs

Management training refers to training programs that involve activities and experiences that are designed to develop specific immediately applicable managerial skills (e.g., communication, decision-making) in a particular organizational setting.[27] Many of the specific training programs described in the technical, conceptual, and interpersonal skills development efforts described in this chapter's section on the content of management development programs fall in this category.

Management training programs usually focus on specific topics or particular skills. Some management training programs take place in classrooms and consist of specialized workshops and seminars. Management training programs can also take place outside of the classroom in any number of settings. Outdoor wilderness training is one management development activity that takes place off-the-job.

Outdoor wilderness training programs are typically organized around a series of outdoor tasks that expose individuals to physically and psychologically demanding activities such as rock climbing, white water rafting, or even winter camping experiences, in which the trainees have had little or no prior experience. Though outfitters are careful to provide instructors who are safety conscious, it remains that many of the activities are inherently dangerous. Generally, the successful and safe accomplishment of these tasks requires self-reliance as well as teamwork, strong communication skills, and the development of trust in others. This in turn is expected not only to help enhance the individual skills of trainees—such as leadership skills—but also to improve the individual's ability to function collaboratively with others (teamwork).

A key question, however, is just how effective is wilderness training? Research on Outward Bound Australia trainees indicates that an overwhelming proportion of participants retain highly positive reactions to their training experience. Moreover, the research indicates that such training appears to have effects on a very wide set of variables from leadership ability and mood to social skills and well-being, and that this effect may be very durable and long-lasting. Moreover, these programs appear to have their

Management training
Programs and activities designed to develop specific managerial skills

Outdoor wilderness training
Highly experiential programs designed to help managers develop greater levels of "life experience" by participating in physically and psychologically demanding tasks and activities

Chapter 14: Management Development

Are Corporate Universities Useful?

A corporate university (CU) is a function or department, independent of the human resource department, that offers an integrated set of learning and development experiences that are strategic for that specific organization or industrial sector. The main objective of a CU is to develop individual competencies that are of relevance to the organization. They do not replace training departments. Rather, they operate in parallel to them, developing in managers and employees competencies and attitudes (including attitudes towards learning itself) that will be beneficial to their actual and future performance in the company.

Although they are owned by the companies, corporate universities are sometimes affiliated with universities that provide some of the teaching. The Eaton School of Retailing, developed with Ryerson University in Toronto, is one such partnership. In some cases, CU participation can contribute credits toward formal degrees and diplomas. Other examples of corporate universities include BMO's Institute for Learning (Canada); the Federal Express Leadership Institute (USA); and the Lufthansa School of Business (Europe).

Organizations accept the large investment required by corporate universities because, in part, it is thought that they will contribute to improved individual job performance. However, this remained an untested hypothesis until recently. In 2004, Morin and Renaud conducted an evaluation of a "Canadian financial institution's" corporate university.

Over a two-year period, annual individual job performance data, demographics, and other variables were gathered from more than a thousand employees, some of whom had enrolled in one or more courses provided in the CU (the "experimental" group), while others had not enrolled in any (the "comparison" group). The results showed that CU participation had a very small, though statistically significant, effect on job performance. At first glance, the corporate university's impact on individual job performance appears to be marginal at best.

Whereas advocates of corporate universities may be disappointed that participation in it had such a small impact on overall job performance, they may take solace in that the data also showed a statistically significant interaction between pre-training performance and participation in the CU: those employees who demonstrated the most improvement following participation in the CU were those who had poorer pre-training job performance. This suggests that CU participation may provide its greatest benefit to those organizational members who need it most. The implication of that finding is obvious. Rather than dismissing sub-performing managers and employees, organizations that have CUs may be able to recuperate them through their enhanced job performance.

In addition to providing insight into corporate universities, this study demonstrates the advantage of the pre-post with comparison design over both the post-only and the simple pre-post designs as described in Chapter 11. Had either of these other designs been used, we would have been compelled to conclude that corporate universities have little impact on job performance. However, through the inclusion of "before–after" measurements and the comparison group, it was possible to detect the all-important interaction between CU participation and improvement in job performance. That interaction, more than any other result of the study, may well indicate the true importance and value of corporate universities to organizations.

Source: Morin, L., & Renaud, S. (2004). Participation in corporate university training: Its effect on individual job performance. *Canadian Journal of Administrative Sciences*, 21 (4), 295–306. Reprinted with permission of the authors and the Canadian Journal of Administrative Sciences (CJAS)

largest impact in increasing the participants' self-confidence and their ability to manage time.[28] However, the research also shows that there is considerable variation between programs, some being more successful than others in creating these changes. Beyond some mild indications that shorter programs (one to three days) are less successful than longer ones, we do not know with much clarity what makes one program more successful than another. Hence, whereas it is possible that such programs do lead to improvements in managerial job performance, the research data—being principally based on self reports—remains insufficient to draw a firm conclusion.

Some management training programs are developed in-house by the training group with or without external consultants, while others are purchased from specialized firms (such as Xerox). These training programs are usually of short duration (one-half to three days is typical) and can be delivered by internal staff or by specialized external resources. Moreover, an increasing number of management development programs are being made available through electronic media (see Chapter 8). IPM, for example, offers an integrated package of 12 CD-based training modules that covers key management skills including staffing, performance management, team building, and employee relations (more details are available from www.workplace.ca).

On-the-Job Management Development

On-the-job management development programs are designed to provide individuals with managerial learning experiences on the job. Two of the most common examples are job rotation and coaching.

Job rotation

Recall from Chapter 7 that **job rotation** involves exposing an individual to different areas and experiences throughout the organization. In this way, the individual not only acquires new skills from working on different projects and interacting with people throughout an organization, but also learns about the organization itself. Job rotation as a development technique is particularly useful for the development of managers when the match between the skills the managers possesses and those required in the new job is well thought out: jobs that require the manager's skills and provide opportunity for building others are best. As indicated in the TIMS model, accurate initial skills assessment is especially important when job rotation is contemplated as a development technique for managers.

Coaching

In the last 15 years or so, coaching has grown both as an on-the-job method to develop managers and a function that managers are expected to play with their own subordinates. **Coaching** involves a one-on-one individualized learning experience in which a more experienced and knowledgeable person is formally called upon to help another person develop the insights and techniques pertinent to the accomplishment of their job. The coach interacts with and provides feedback to the manager with the intent of developing his or her insight, skills, attitudes, and motivation.

Coaches may be external or internal to the company depending on budgets, coaching goals and the organizational contexts. For example, the CEO who is struggling with a downsizing decision may well prefer to be

On-the-job management development
Programs designed to provide individuals with managerial learning experiences on the job

Job rotation
Exposing an individual to different areas and experiences throughout the organization

RPC 14.3

Coaching
One-on-one individualized learning experience in which a more experienced and knowledgeable person is formally called upon to help another person develop the insights and techniques pertinent to the accomplishment of their job

coached by an external person. However, the manager who needs to hone her political skills might benefit more from a trusted internal coach. If coaching is to be provided to all employees, on an ongoing basis, relying on internal coaches may be more economically realistic.

Many coaches are specialized in specific sectors such as pharmaceuticals or manufacturing, or in specialized contents such as communication or, as in the following illustration, training.

A marketing manager was promoted to head a different group: the organizational learning group in the Canadian operations of a multinational pharmaceutical organization. Her boss, the vice president of human resources, asked her to develop and present to upper management six weeks hence a training plan for the marketing division. Although experienced in marketing, the new manager lacked direct experience and knowledge of "organizational learning." She therefore signed a six-week contract with an external coach who was an expert in training and development with extensive experience in the pharmaceutical industry. The coach's role was *not* to produce the training plan, but rather to help the manager develop hers. During the weekly two-hour coaching sessions they discussed best practices, what other companies did, the advantages and disadvantages of various options, the obstacles likely to be encountered, and how best to prepare for them, and how to present the plan, including setting up the actual slides for the presentation to her bosses. This coaching episode ended when the manager presented (successfully as it turns out) her training plan.

In this very typical case, the coach was an external consultant hired to help a manager complete one major task within an established six-week deadline. However, many organizations require that managers serve as coaches to subordinate employees and managers on an ongoing basis. In that case the mandate may be much broader (the issues to be coached are not specified in advance) and/or more open-ended (without a specific end date). The coaching system in place in the Canadian branch of PricewaterhouseCoopers (as described earlier in Training Today 1) provides one such example. However, this approach requires that the managers be trained in the science of coaching.

David Peterson lists several characteristics of great coaches of which three stand out: Great coaches are goal-oriented, challengers, and person-focused.[29]

1. *Goal orientation.* Great coaches are great listeners who empathize with the learner and who are honestly interested in helping people achieve their goals.
2. *Challengers.* Great coaches are able to "feel" the mood state of the learner and know when to listen and when to challenge the beliefs and thinking of the learner.
3. *Person-focused.* Great coaches focus their efforts and attention on the learner. They do not try to impose their views on the learner by insisting that there is "one best way" to do things. Rather, they focus on helping the learner use his or her own previous knowledge and experience to develop their own perspective, understanding, and styles in dealing with the problems to be solved.

Managing Performance Through Training and Development

The coach who is goal-oriented, challenging, and person-focused is more likely to develop the manager. This is because these are the skills that will help the person coached to develop insight, motivation, capabilities, real-work practice, and accountability, the five conditions of successfully accomplished coaching. These five form what David Peterson labels the "development pipeline." Coaches are maximally helpful when they structure their efforts to help managers develop:

- *Insight.* Recognizing and understanding their own strengths and weaknesses.
- *Motivation.* Understanding and caring about changing the ways in which they operate.
- *Capabilities.* Identifying resources and best practices for dealing with complex decisions and situations and by exploring alternative ways of dealing with them.
- *Real-world practices.* Identifying opportunities to implement, on a day-to-day basis, the little changes that should be made and to develop the critical perspective needed to assess what works, what does not, and why.
- *Accountability.* Encouraging the manager to demonstrate the new skills and knowledge through commitment to specific actions.

To achieve these objectives, coaches face a number of important challenges. First and foremost, coaches must act to gain the trust of the "coachee." Confidentiality, discretion, and honesty are three of the key behaviours coaches must demonstrate. With this developing trust it becomes easier for the coach to provide feedback that is more likely to prove constructive to the manager. For example, the suggestion that a manager enroll in a specific seminar or read a particular book is more likely to be well received when it is received from a trusted coach.

Applying new skills is difficult and attempts to do so are often subject to obstacles and hurdles that can discourage the use of the new skills. Coaches have a special responsibility to be attentive to these situations and to help managerial persistence. Building self-efficacy, helping managers construe obstacles as "problems" rather than "failures," and providing emotional support are three techniques successful coaches use. Finally, coaches who are in a position to do so sometimes intervene elsewhere in the organization to remove obstacles. That is, successful coaches are sometimes proactive as opposed to strictly passive in their interventions. Compared to external ones, internal coaches are often in a better position to help in this way.

A number of research studies have shown that coaching does help managers become more successful and more effective in accomplishing their tasks.[30] Research has also shown that managers who received coaching experiences as part of their executive education program in a university also reported higher levels of self-confidence and improved skills in developing others. While this evidence speaks highly of coaching, it is important to note that most of the research has relied on self-report measures and/or on the perception of superiors to assess the effectiveness of coaching as a management development technique. Although this is true of most training evaluation of management development programs, the reliance on self-reports as a criterion of success must be viewed with caution. Perceptions may not be accurate substitutes for objective criteria as measures of effectiveness.[31]

Summary

This chapter described the roles, functions, and critical skills of managers and how they are developed. Managers engage in a number of interpersonal, informational, and decisional activities in order to accomplish their organizational goals of controlling, organizing, planning, and leading the work of others. This requires them to master and display conceptual, technical, and interpersonal skills, and to have emotional intelligence. Management development programs are designed to develop these skills. Models of management development involve skill assessment, skill acquisition, skill practice, and skill application. The content of management development programs was described in terms of conceptual, technical, and interpersonal skills. Management development programs involve both informational and experiential learning and include management education, management training, and on-the-job development. Management education programs such as an MBA provide individuals with a general management education. A popular example of a highly experiential management training program is outdoor wilderness training. Examples of on-the-job development include job rotation and coaching.

Key Terms

coaching (page 431)

core roles of managers (page 410)

emotional intelligence (page 417)

experiential learning (page 427)

functions of management (page 412)

job rotation (page 431)

leadership (page 410)

management (page 407)

management development (page 409)

management education (page 428)

management training (page 429)

on-the-job management development (page 431)

outdoor wilderness training (page 429)

skills (page 414)

Weblinks

Bell Canada: www.bell.ca (page 408)

National Research Council of Canada: www.nrc-cnrc.gc.ca (page 424)

Microsoft: www.microsoft.com (page 411)

PricewaterhouseCoopers: www.pwc.com (page 415)

RPC Icons

RPC 14.1 Provides the appropriate assessment tools for determining career development options for employees.

RPC 14.2 Facilitates the implementation of cross-functional development work experiences for employees.

RPC 14.3 Facilitates coaching and post-training support activities to ensure transfer of learning to the workplace.

Discussion Questions

1. What are some of the differences between management development and employee training?

2. Imagine the CEO of a company who has read this chapter and the section on coaching. She decides that coaching is a good idea and sends a memo to all managers telling them to formally take on the role of coach for each of their subordinates. Is this a good idea? How likely is it to improve performance? Had the CEO consulted you prior to announcing her decision, what would you have suggested she do?

3. Compare and contrast management education, management training, and on-the-job development. What are the advantages and disadvantages of each of these approaches for management development? How effective do you think each approach is for teaching the skills listed in Table 14.1?

4. What is emotional intelligence and what does it have to do with management and managerial skills? Can managers be trained to improve their emotional intelligence? If yes, how can this be done?

5. What is outdoor wilderness training and how effective is it for developing managers? What would be your advice to an organization that was considering sending its managers to an outdoor wilderness program?

6. What is the difference between informational learning and experiential learning and when should they be used for management development?

7. Describe the four basic commonalities of models of management skill development.

The Great Training Debate

1. Debate the following: Some people have argued that management development is a waste of time and money because great managers are born, not made. Is it the case that managers cannot be developed?

Using the Internet

1. There are many Internet sources that describe the types of management training programs that exist for different levels of management. Visit

some of these sites via these directories:
http://www.cstd.ca/ctd/search_2005/index.html
www.managementcourses.com/

1. Once you have visited some of these sites, identify the types of programs that are most frequently proposed.
2. How do these "popular" and frequently offered courses relate to the management roles, functions, and skills discussed in the chapter?

2. Coaching is one of the more important one-on-one management development techniques in today's business environment. Go to **http://teragram.ca/coach_preassess_corp.html** and answer the following questions:

1. Suppose you had to implement a coaching program for junior executives and a coaching program for senior managers. Would the content of a coaching training program be the same or different for these two groups?
2. If they did differ, how would they and why?

3. Among the many sources available to find out about wilderness training in Canada are Outward Bound at **www.outwardbound.ca** and the Banff Centre at **www.banffcentre.ca/departments/leadership/**. Prepare a brief report about the kind of programs offered at each site and the skills they focus on.

Exercises

In-Class

1. In an article called "The smart-talk trap," Jeffrey Pfeffer and Robert Sutton (1999) described a phenomenon in organizations that they call the "knowing-doing gap." According to the authors, many managers are knowledgeable and very good at talking but not very good at doing or acting. In other words, talk substitutes for action. An especially dangerous form of talk is "smart talk" where the speaker is particularly good at sounding confident, articulate, and eloquent. Unfortunately, smart talk tends to focus on the negative and is often unnecessarily complicated. It tends to result in inaction or what the authors call the "smart-talk trap." Problems are discussed and plans for action might be formulated, but in the end nothing is done. This can have serious negative consequences for organizations. The authors suggest that one of the main reasons for the knowing-doing gap and the smart-talk trap is that managers have been trained to talk.

   a. What do you think about the knowing-doing gap and the smart-talk trap? Do you think that this is a serious problem in organizations?
   b. The authors argue that one of the reasons for the existence of the knowing-doing gap and the smart-talk trap is the training that

managers receive. Do you agree with this assertion? How can management training result in so much knowing and talking and so little doing?

c. Discuss the knowing-doing gap and the smart-talk trap with somebody you know in a managerial position. Find out what they have to say about the prevalence of it in their organization, why it might or might not be a problem, and what can be done to avoid it.

d. What advice would you give organizations about how to develop managers in order to avoid the knowing-doing gap and the smart-talk trap?

2. This task will help you integrate much of the material in this book. Starting with the TIMS model, construct a table, similar to Table 14.2, in which you indicate for each of the 10 steps of the model the probable impact on trainees for each step.

3. Think of the manager in a current or previous job. Keeping in mind his/her behaviour and performance, how effective do you think he/she was in his/her performance of the core functions and roles of management? What skills do you think he/she needs to improve? What would you recommend your manager do to improve his/her performance and managerial skills?

4. If you were hired in a managerial position and you were told to design your own plan for development, what would you do? Refer to the section on models of management skill development, and for each step in the process develop a plan for your own management development. Be sure to indicate what you will do in each step.

In-the-Field

1. To find out more about management development, contact a human resource professional and ask about management development in his/her organization. To guide your discussion, consider the following issues:

   • Describe the main skills that are the focus of management development programs. What are these skills and why are they the focus of management development?

   • Describe the process of management development. What are the main steps involved in the process?

   • Describe the content of management development programs.

   • What types of management development programs are used and why? Does the organization use experiential learning approaches, and if so, what are they? Does the organization use management education programs, management training programs, job rotation, and/or coaching and how effective are they?

   • How effective is management development for improving managerial and organizational effectiveness?

2. Contact several people who work full-time for an organization. In each case, focus the interview on their perceptions of their own immediate

supervisor/manager/boss. Focus on the skills of managers as described in the chapter. Do they perceive the manager as competent or not and what are the skills they think the manager should most urgently improve? Summarize your results in a report in which you discuss the extent and nature of management skills that subordinates feel should be improved.

Case Incident

Middle Manager Burnout

In a recent article in *Harvard Business Review*, Morison, Erikson, and Dychtwald surveyed more than 7000 mid-career employees between the ages of 35 and 55. The authors report that many middle managers are burned out, dissatisfied, feel that they are in dead-end jobs, and most are no longer energized by their work. Feeling neglected, many are actively searching for new jobs. As a result, many organizations face a stark choice: risk losing some of their best people or continue to work with a host of unhappy managers.

Your consulting advice is requested by the company president. She is asking you to provide suggestions for combating this growing managerial apathy in her organization.

Questions

1. What do you think are some of the causes of this growing problem?
2. In order to improve the situation, what, if anything, should be done with the middle managers, the bosses of the middle managers, and the subordinates of the middle managers, by top management?

Case

Market Research Inc.

Market Research Inc. is a firm that specializes in conducting surveys and interviews with members of the general public in Vancouver. The company has a number of different teams of people that work on many different projects for its many corporate clients. It is usually the case that several projects are conducted at the same time.

The company is composed of three departments: production, technical, and marketing. The marketing group is responsible for selling the company's services to corporate clients. The technical department is mainly composed of research personnel who are responsible for developing and analyzing the results of the surveys, focus groups, and interviewing studies for the clients. The production department is composed of several teams of interviewers. It is that department's job to conduct the data collection. They are responsible for identifying the customers who will be interviewed or surveyed, for enlisting their cooperation, and for interviewing them either personally, by phone or mail, depending on the project.

Market Research Inc. has a wide set of corporate clients who need to better understand customer needs and reactions to company products. This information is crucial to the clients because it helps them better understand how the products and services they sell are perceived by the customers. This information, in turn, can be used by the senior executives to devise strategies to improve products and/or improve the advertising tactics they rely on to promote their products.

Thomas Waterfall (Tom) is the manager of the production department. The department is responsible for ensuring that all of the data collection projects sold by marketing and developed by the technical department are conducted in a professional and timely manner. More specifically, Tom is responsible for ensuring that there is always enough staff on hand to conduct each study (never too many nor too few), for hiring (or letting go) the interviewers, for training them on the specific project requirements, and for ensuring and controlling the quality of the work done by the production department. He must keep himself informed of the activities of the marketing and technical departments to ensure that the production department can meet the demands of these other groups. Finally, the production department is a high-pressure environment where tensions among interviewers and between interviewers and the technical staff can sometimes flare up, threatening the efficient and effective production of the studies. The production manager must often act as an arbiter of disputes and act to soothe people when they get upset, a skill for which Tom is famous.

Mary Milend has been working for the last five years for Market Research Inc. She works in the production department of the company, where she is an interviewer. Her job is to administer the surveys and to conduct focus groups and other interviews with consumers. She has been doing a remarkable job. She conducts her interviews with professionalism and competence, always meets her deadlines, and has never been the object of a complaint, either by consumers or by her co-workers. She has always shown great cooperation, often volunteering to help other interviewers with their tasks when they were submerged. Finally, in the tense atmosphere of conducting the data collection under tight deadlines, she has always maintained extremely good relationships with the technical staff with whom the production department interacts routinely.

Tom, the manager of the production department, has announced that he will be retiring next year. Because of her superb record as an employee and her extensive hands-on knowledge of the production department, the vice president has offered to promote Mary to the job of production manager when Tom retires.

Mary is quite interested in the job, as this would mean a much higher salary, better benefits, vacations, and greater influence in the company. However, as Mary is a very honest person, she told the VP, when he offered her the promotion, that although she was keenly interested in the job, she was not sure that she was the best choice. She explained that she had never acted in a managerial role before and that she felt uncertain that she had the skills to do the job well. Impressed by Mary's honesty, the VP indicated to her that he would be willing to provide her with all of the training she requires to acquire the managerial skills that she will need to perform her new job.

Questions

1. What are the main skills that Mary will need to develop if she accepts the promotion?
2. What are some of the training experiences that might benefit Mary?
3. Should Tom be invited to play a role in Mary's development? If so, what could that role be?
4. How effective do you think each of the following programs would be for Mary's development: management education programs, management training programs (i.e., outdoor wilderness training), and on-the-job development (i.e., job rotation and coaching). What are the advantages and disadvantages of each, and which one(s) do you recommend and why?

References

1. Schettler, J. (2002, March). Training top 100: IBM. *Training, 39* (3), 48–49; Schettler, J. (2003, March). Training top 100: Best practices. *Training, 40* (3), 58–59; Johnson, G., Johnson, H., Dolezalek, H., Galvin, T., & Zemke, R. (2004, March). Top five profile and ranking. *Training, 41* (3), 42–58.
2. McCallum, J. (1993). The manager's job is still to manage. *Business Quarterly, 57* (4), 61–67; Brown, T. L. (1995). Leadership is everyone's business. *Apparel Industry Magazine 56* (9), 14. Tannenbaum, S. I., & Yukl, G. (1992). Training and development in work organizations. *Annual Review of Psychology, 43,* 399–441.
3. Robbins, S P., De Cenzo, D. A. Condie, J. L., & Kondo, L. (2001). *Supervision in Canada today* (3rd ed.). Toronto: Prentice-Hall.
4. Whetten, D. A., & Cameron, K. S. (2002). *Developing management skills* (5th ed.). Upper Saddle River, NJ: Prentice Hall.
5. Baldwin T. T., & Patgett, M. Y. (1994). Management development: A review and commentary. In C. L. Cooper, & I. T. Robertson (Eds.), *Key reviews in managerial psychology.* New York: Wiley.
6. Fulmer, R. M. (1997, Summer). The evolving paradigm of leadership development. *Organizational Dynamics,* 59–72.
7. Marquardt, M. J., Nissley, N., Ozag, R., & Taylor, T. L. (2000). International briefing 6. Training and development in the United States. *International Journal of Training and Development, 4* (2), 138–49; Mabey, C., & Thomson, A. (2000). Management development in the UK: A provider and participant perspective. *International Journal of Training and Development, 4* (4), 272–86; Cornuel, E., & Kletz, P. (2001). An empirical analysis of priority sectors for managers' training. *Journal of Management Development, 20,* 5, 402–13; Agut, S., & Grau, R. (2002). Managerial competency needs and training requests: The case of the Spanish tourist industry. *Human Resource Development Quarterly, 13* (1), 31–51; Analoui, F., & Hosseini, M. H. (2001). Management education and increased managerial effectiveness. The case of business managers in Iran. *Journal of Management Development, 20* (9), 785–94.
8. London, M. (2002). *Leadership development:* Mahwah, NJ: Lawrence Erlbaum Associates; Tichy, N. M., & Cardwell, N. (2002). *The cycle of leadership: How great leaders teach their companies to*

win (3rd ed.). New York: HarperCollins Publishers; Ketz de Vries, M. (2001). *The leadership mystique*. London: Prentice-Hall.

9. Kotter, J. P. (1996) *Leading change*. Boston, MA: Harvard Business School Press.

10. Kouzes, J. M., & Posner, B. Z. (2002). *Leadership challenge* (3rd ed.). San Francisco, CA: Jossey-Bass.

11. Mintzberg, H. (1973). *The nature of managerial work*, New York: Harper and Row; Mintzberg, H. (1975). The manager's job: Folklore and fact. *Harvard Business Review, 53* (4), 49–61.

12. Kouzes, J. M., & Posner, B. Z. (2002).

13. Orth, C. D., Wilkinson, H. E., & Benfari, R. C. (1987, Spring). The manager's role as coach and mentor. *Organizational Dynamics*, 67–74.

14. Whetten, D. A., & Cameron, K. S. (2002).

15. Luthans, F., Rosenkrantz, S. A., & Hennesy, H. W. (1985). What do successful managers really do? An observation study of managerial activities. *Journal of Applied Behavioral Science, 21*, 255–70.

16. Camp, R., Vielhaber, M., & Simonetti, J. L. (2001). *Strategic interviewing: How to hire good people*. San Francisco, CA: Jossey-Bass.

17. Cameron, K. & Tschirhart, M. (1988). Managerial competencies and organizational effectiveness. Working Paper, School of Business Administration, University of Michigan.

18. Goleman, D. (1998). *Working with emotional intelligence*. New York: Bantam.

19. Ryan, A. M., Brutus, S., Greguras, G. J., & Hakel, M. D. (2000). Receptivity to assessment-based feedback for management development. *Journal of Management Development, 19* (4), 252–76.

20. Pfeffer, J. (1998). *The human equation: Building profits by putting people first*. Boston, MA: Harvard Business School Press.

21. Hunsaker, P. L (2001). *Training in management skills*. Upper Saddle River, NJ: Prentice Hall.

22. March, J. G., & Simon, H. A. (1958). *Organizations*. New York: Blackwell.

23. Locke, E. A., & Latham, G. P. (1990). *A theory of goal setting and task performance*. Englewood Cliffs, NJ: Prentice-Hall.

24. Eisenhardt, K. M., Kahwajy, J. L., & Bourgeois, L. J. III (1997, July–August). How management teams can have a good fight. *Harvard Business Review*, 77–85.

25. Haccoun, R. R., & Klimoski, R. J. (1975). Negotiator status and accountability source: A study of negotiator behavior. *Organizational Behavior and Human Performance, 14*, 342–59.

26. Wexley, K. N., & Baldwin, T. T. (1986). Management development. *Journal of Management, 12*, 277–94.

27. Wexley, K. N., & Baldwin, T. T. (1986).

28. Hattie, J., Marsh, H. W., Neill, J. T., & Richards, G. E. (1997). Adventure Education and Outward Bound: Out-of-class experiences that have a lasting effect. *Review of Educational Research, 67*, 43–87.

29. Peterson, D. B. (2002). Management development: Coaching and mentoring programs. In K. Kraiger (Ed.), *Creating, implementing, and managing effective training and development: State-of-the-art lessons for practice*, (pp. 160–91). San Francisco. CA: Jossey-Bass.

30. Burke, M. J., & Day, R. R. (1986) A cumulative study of the effectiveness of managerial training. *Journal of Applied Psychology, 71*, 232–46.

31. Peterson, D. B. (2002).

Chapter 15

Training Trends and Best Practices

Chapter Learning Objectives

After reading this chapter, you should be able to:

- describe how the role of the trainer is changing
- discuss the outsourcing of training and development
- discuss the implications of the aging workforce for training and development
- define just-in-time learning and the implications for the design and delivery of training and development
- discuss the role of ethics in training and development
- discuss the design features for facilitating learning and transfer
- discuss the main reasons why training programs fail and the best practices to make them effective

www.hp.com

www.ibm.com/ca

www.raytheon.com

Hewlett-Packard Co., IBM, and Raytheon Vision Systems

In the 2004 fiscal year, Hewlett-Packard Co. (HP) increased its training budget by $20 million. The following year, it added another $25 million to its training budget, bringing the total to $300 million. Companies like HP recognize that it is more cost-efficient and competitive to develop talent from within rather than compete for talent on the outside.

Another company known for its investment in training and development is IBM. With a training budget of $825 million, IBM maintains one of the world's largest internal training and development programs and employs 1367 training professionals. IBM's commitment to learning goes back generations and the belief that training and development plays a major role in IBM's ability to compete and innovate is embedded in the company's culture. IBM is currently at the forefront of an ongoing transformation in the training industry thanks to its On-Demand Learning, the company's term for its on-line workplace and its approach to training.

On-Demand refers to the company's goal of meeting clients' needs exactly when they occur. This requires the company to develop ways of rapidly training and developing in-house talent. IBM surveys employees to find out what skills and knowledge they need and then catalogues them in a database. This allows employees who have questions and need information to connect with employees who have answers using the Internet and instant messaging. In addition, a series of e-learning packages called the IBM Learning Suite has been developed for various topics an employee might need to receive training or additional education about. The packages can be accessed through the company's intranet on-demand, which means that workers have access to training at the moment they most need it.

The result is a more collaborative learning environment where learning is not just a matter of training courses; it is learning and knowledge-sharing that is embedded in day-to-day work. The on-demand emphasis has helped to drive a cultural and business transformation within IBM.

In 2004, Raytheon Vision Systems, a national defense contractor in California, recognized a looming mass exodus of experienced workers. More than 35 percent of the workforce would be eligible to retire by 2009. In many cases, a person set to retire was the only one in the nation who knew how to do something. The company realized it needed a dynamic solution so they created a training program called

Leave-A-Legacy, which formally pairs employees who have vital knowledge—subject-matter experts—with high-potential subordinate employees. Since it began, the program has successfully encouraged near-retirees to share knowledge on a daily basis, and it has also given them a sense of purpose. In addition, the program is securing the commitment of high-potential employees by giving them higher-level work.

At HP, on-line communities of different professional groups, such as sales and software engineering, have been created to transfer knowledge. They are on-line knowledge repositories for people who do the same kind of work. They post how they do things, solutions, and experience.[1]

Hewlett-Packard Co., IBM, and Raytheon Vision Systems provide examples of some of the trends and best practices of training and development today. Companies today are investing more in training, a clear sign of its importance and relevance in today's marketplace. They are also designing innovative programs and systems that embed learning and information sharing into the work process. They are solving performance problems and implementing systems for knowledge sharing and transfer.

In this final chapter of the text, we review some important trends and best practices in training and development. First, we will discuss how the competencies and role of the trainer are changing. We then discuss the outsourcing of training and development followed by a discussion of the aging workforce and the implications for training and development. We then describe an important trend called just-in-time learning. Next, we discuss some ethical issues associated with training and development. The chapter concludes with a summary of best practices for learning and transfer and an overview of the main reasons why training programs fail and the best practices for making them effective.

The Trainer's Role

As you know from reading this text, a trainer's primary responsibilities revolve around the design, delivery, and evaluation of training and development programs. To get a better idea of what the job of a training manager involves, see Table 15.1.

In recent years, however, the trainer's traditional status as a staff employee of the HR area has begun to change. Trainers have begun to move out of the training department to work with management in solving organizational problems and creating and facilitating learning opportunities. This reflects a movement and evolution of the trainer from a staff employee to a strategic business partner. Thus, while many training professionals still spend most of their time designing and delivering training programs, they are increasingly becoming involved in more strategic functions such as facilitating

TABLE 15.1

Job Description for a Training Manager

Position Title: Training Delivery Manager

Department: Training

Reports to: Director of Training

Supervises: Four Skill Trainers and Two Management Trainers

Position Objective: To manage the training delivery services of the department and implement all scheduled training courses.

Responsibilities:

1. Manages training delivery services within approved budget.

2. Implements all training courses as scheduled.

3. Supervises employees reporting to her/him to ensure they meet performance standards.

4. Creates individual development plans for each employee reporting to him/her.

5. Serves as an active member of the Training Department's management team.

6. Assists the Training Director in developing annual budgets and plans.

7. Works with the Training Development Manager to create new courses and evaluate existing ones.

8. Recommends necessary revisions to existing training courses and possible areas requiring training courses.

Source: McConnell, John H. (2002). How to Identify Your Organization's Training Needs, Copyright 2002 by AM MGMT ASSN/AMACOM (B). This work is protected by copyright and it is being used with the permission of Access Copyright. Any alteration of its content or further copying in any form whatsoever is strictly prohibited.

organizational change, managing organizational knowledge, career planning, and talent management.[2] This trend is expected to continue and trainers who see their primary mission as the design or delivery of training programs are a disappearing breed.[3]

A recent study conducted by the American Society for Training and Development (ASTD) on the areas of expertise and competencies expected of training and development professionals, identified four key roles for training professionals: learning strategist, business partner, project manager, and professional specialist.[4] These four roles are part of the ASTD competency model for learning and performance and the foundation for its professional certification program. Figure 15.1 shows the ASTD competency model. The certification program covers the nine areas of expertise found in the middle tier of the model.

Clearly, being an expert in adult learning is no longer enough to be an effective training manager. When asked about the most important competencies in their jobs, training managers mention things such as long-range planning, building strategic partnerships with line units, understanding business trends, and budgeting. Today's training manager must be a skilled businessperson and have general management skills, which for some companies has become a top priority in selecting training managers.[5]

FIGURE 15.1

ASTD Competency Model

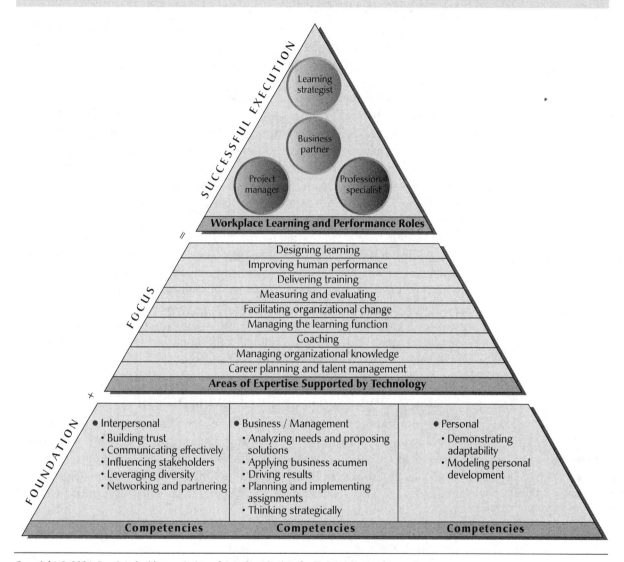

The training and development function is also expected to transform into a learning and performance strategic function. It will focus more on results rather than activities and it will be integrated into the business of the organization at a strategic level and learning will be embedded into the jobs that individuals perform.[6] IBM's on-demand program is a good example of how learning is being embedded into the daily work process. In addition, training functions will become performance consulting centres and training professionals will become performance consultants. As a **performance consultant**, the role of the trainer is not just to provide training and development, but to provide solutions to performance problems. For example, telecommunications company TELUS restructured its learning function into a performance

Performance consultant

Responsible for providing solutions to performance problems

consulting organization. The function works with management to identify performance gaps and training or learning solutions to close them.[7] Finding a solution to the exodus of experienced workers at Raytheon Vision Systems is also a good example of this new role.

Finally, given the increasing importance of life-long learning and the learning organization, the role of the trainer is increasingly shifting from training to learning and the many forms that it might take. Thus, the role of the trainer is to facilitate and create learning opportunities throughout the organization, and to help organizations manage the transition to a learning organization. In fact, we are already seeing changes in the job titles of the most senior person responsible for training in Canadian organizations. Job titles such as "Learning and Development Consultant," "Manager, Learning and Organizational Development," and "Learning and Development Specialist," to name just a few, reflect this new role.[8] All three companies featured at the beginning of the chapter demonstrate how organizations are creating knowledge and learning systems.

In summary, the traditional role of the trainer as a staff person responsible for training and development has been evolving into a much larger role based on the management of learning, knowledge, change, talent, and performance. This involves forming a strategic partnership with management to solve organizational problems and achieve organizational objectives. This will involve a greater focus on learning throughout the organization. It also means that a greater portion of the more traditional training design and delivery functions will be outsourced, the focus of the next section.

Outsourcing Training and Development

While the training and development function is transforming to more of a learning and performance function, it is also outsourcing more of the traditional responsibilities of training and development. **Outsourcing** involves the use of an external supplier to provide training and development programs and services. This follows from the discussion in Chapter 5 on purchasing training programs and services. Outsourcing involves the purchase of training services and products from external suppliers rather than using in-house services.

In the United States, approximately 30 percent of learning budgets were allocated to services provided by external suppliers in 2005 and this is expected to grow to half in the next decade.[9] In addition, a recent survey found that 57 percent of HR and training professionals outsource all or portions of their training and development programs.[10] In Canada, it has been reported that a third (33 percent) of the average total training investment is devoted to external training providers and 25 percent of the survey respondents indicated that their organizations intend to increase payments to outside trainers in the coming year an average of 16 percent.[11]

There are a number of reasons for the outsourcing of training and development. In many cases, outsourcing provides organizations with access to specialists who have a required expertise in a particular training area. In addition, external vendors can provide a greater variety of training programs more

Outsourcing

The use of an external supplier to provide training and development programs and services efficiently and less expensively than in-house training departments.[12] This is especially true for small companies that might not have the in-house expertise or enough people to train to justify the expense of in-house training design and delivery. In addition, the use of external vendors can often result in trainees being trained and back on the job much faster than designing a new training program in-house. A recent survey found that the top reasons for outsourcing included cost savings, time savings, and improvements in compliance and accuracy.[13]

Although the outsourcing of training and development has been found to result in increased performance in the training area, improvements in the design and delivery of training, and training professionals report a high level of overall satisfaction with their training suppliers, outsourcing does have certain risks (e.g., loss of control, vendor does not understand organization's culture, loss of in-house expertise, increased vulnerability) that can result in harmful consequences for an organization.[14] This is why a trusting relationship between the organization and its external vendor is an important factor in successful outsourcing relationships. Furthermore, the positive outcomes associated with outsourcing have been found to be higher when there is frequent vendor-client interaction, when contractual agreements are explicit, when there is greater trust in the vendor, and when the organization's primary motivation for outsourcing is quality improvement.[15] Thus, to increase the likelihood that the outsourcing of training and development will be successful, organizations should take the following actions:[16]

- Establish trusting relationships with suppliers and try to build long-term relationships.
- Make contractual agreements clear and comprehensive and clearly outline each party's responsibilities, explicit performance expectations, and penalties if requirements are not met.
- Work closely with training suppliers, communicate frequently, and always keep abreast of suppliers' actions to retain control of the training program.
- Outsource with discretion—improvements in training occur as a result of systematic and calculated outsourcing that enables effective management of the outsourcing process.
- Outsource for the right reasons—to acquire expertise and enhance the overall design, delivery, and quality of training rather than an emphasis on cost-savings.

To learn about how to determine if training should be outsourced, see The Trainer's Notebook 1, "To Outsource or Not to Outsource."

Aging of the Workforce

The Canadian workforce is getting older as the baby boomers approach their fifties and sixties. This, combined with the fact that there are fewer young people entering the workforce, skill shortages in many areas, the tendency for people to work beyond the traditional retirement age, and the elimination of

To Outsource or Not to Outsource

Outsourcing training and development has become a popular option when it is not cost-effective or timely to develop training programs in-house. But when is it right to outsource training and development? Here is a list of 10 questions to help determine whether to outsource or do it in-house.

1. **What are the capabilities of your training organization? Do you hire it or grow it?** If you have the training staff and they have the competencies or you can grow them, then it is a good idea to keep it in-house.

2. **What's your internal training capacity?** If your training staff do not have the capacity to take on additional training responsibilities and are already maxed out then it is probably better to outsource.

3. **Is the training proprietary?** If the information is critical to the company's competitive strategy and confidentiality is an issue, it is best to keep it in-house.

4. **Does your company value its training organization?** Companies that value their training function and consider it proficient and capable should keep training in-house.

5. **Does the content change rapidly?** If the content changes rapidly (e.g., technology for technical training or compliance for compliance training), it is better to hire training experts in order to keep training up to date.

6. **Are the outsourced trainers viewed as experts? And is that a good or bad thing?** If outside trainers are viewed with cynicism and skepticism rather than as experts, it is better to keep training in-house provided that internal trainers are viewed as credible experts.

7. **Did you do your homework?** You should first research what training is available in-house and what you have before bringing in an external program. Have those who will be involved in the training participate in choosing training if you decide to outsource.

8. **Are you handing over the entire training function?** Outsourcing the entire training function is not the best solution and experts recommend against it, arguing that it is the wrong way to approach outsourcing.

9. **Is there a hidden agenda?** Some managers might have a hidden agenda that involves minimizing the impact of training by outsourcing it and failing to accept responsibility for developing employees. Training can be outsourced but the organization must remain responsible for the training and development of its employees.

10. **Have you considered a combination?** The best solution is usually when an internal consultant works with an external consultant.

mandatory retirement, means that there will be an increasing number of older workers in Canadian organizations. In fact, it is predicted that by the year 2015, 48 percent of Canada's working-age population will be between the ages of 45 and 64 compared to 29 percent in 1991.[17]

There are a number of factors that are associated with the aging process that need to be considered for the purpose of training. In particular, a slowing of basic cognitive processing as well as a decline in the senses is associated with the aging process. On the other hand, long-term memory and quantitative knowledge increase during adulthood. Thus, older workers are most likely to have difficulties when they encounter rapidly changing and unfamiliar job requirements rather than jobs that depend on existing knowledge.[18] Therefore, training programs for older workers must consider these differences.

Computer Training for Older Workers

In recent years, an increasing number of mature adults have been re-entering the workforce in unprecedented numbers. Older workers offer employers advantages such as a strong work ethic, high productivity, a wealth of experience, and low absenteeism and turnover rates. But seniors usually are not regarded as computer-savvy enough to help ease the high-tech labour shortage.

In fact, many employers and trainers assume that older workers can't—or won't—learn to use computers at all. But those who specialize in teaching older learners contend that this impression is dead wrong. Training departments attempting to teach computer applications to older learners often fail to consider their special needs.

For example, an insurance company decided to hire some older workers for its call centre because, it believed, its many elderly customers would relate better to a voice that had some years behind it. So the company recruited and trained a group of mature adults, and then ran them through the same computer training everyone else received. The company's new "old" workers had a high attrition rate during training and substandard performance afterward. The company concluded that hiring seniors was a mistake and that older people couldn't do the job.

But the fault didn't lie with the employees or the material but with the trainers. Trainers often do not think about how to accommodate the needs of an older audience. After adjusting the time allotted for its computer training, the same insurance company tried the experiment again and found that older employees' performance after training was on par with that of younger employees.

Those who specialize in training seniors suggest teaching them in smaller classes of people roughly the same age. A few seniors may find it a challenge to try to keep up with younger trainees, but most will be left behind and won't ask questions if the rest of the class seems to be faster on the uptake. Most experts recommend training seniors in small classes of six to ten. Computer training for older employees can also be improved by slowing it down, using mature trainers from the same peer group as the trainees who can allude to experiences they understand, conducting the training in a learning environment that is comfortable for older learners, and understanding that older learners have some particular problems with computers such as how to use a mouse and line-of-sight problems caused by bifocals. Most importantly, the trainer must adjust his/her instructional style to the needs of an older audience.

For example, providing older workers with extra time for learning, self-pacing, and various job aids are likely to improve their learning. As well, training materials might have to be designed to account for declines in hearing and sight. And as discussed in the Training Today feature on computer training for older workers, trainers must pay special attention to older trainees who might not be comfortable using computers. To learn more about how to respond to the needs of older workers in training, see the Trainer's Notebook 2, "Training Older Workers."

Just-in-Time Learning

Trainers are facing increasing pressure today to deliver training programs at an increasingly rapid pace. Given the rapid pace of change in organizations today, trainers often do not have very much time to design and deliver a

Training Older Workers

The aging process creates special needs for older workers that require accommodation in training. Below are some of the special needs of older workers and how to accommodate them in training to facilitate their learning.

1. **Vision difficulties.**
   - Increase classroom lighting levels.
   - Reduce distracting and uncomfortable glare.
   - Visual aids should have large, easy-to-read print with high-contrast colours and fewer words.
   - Avoid highly reflective table and floor surfaces by closing classroom curtains if necessary.

2. **Hearing difficulties.**
   - Trainers should speak in lower tones.
   - Reduce background noise.
   - Words should be carefully enunciated and amplified.
   - Rooms should have good acoustics.

3. **Memory difficulties.**
   - Use written references, paper-based and on-line guides, summaries, and job aids.
   - Don't use exercises that rely on short-term memory (e.g., oral drills) that discriminate against older learners.
   - Help older trainees combine their strong capacities for integrating new concepts with their large quantities of existing knowledge and established thought processes.

4. **Stress and confidence.**
   - Trainers can reduce stress and increase confidence with a relaxed pace and gentle pressures.

5. **Negative stereotypes.**
   - Older workers should have equal opportunities.
   - Comments, insults, and jokes about being too old to learn are unacceptable.

6. **Participation.**
   - Courses for older adults must be designed for participation and involvement, not just reading and listening.
   - Participants need to take an active role in their learning.

Source: Based on Mingail, H. (2004, September 29). Wise ways for retraining older workers. *The Globe and Mail*, C8. Reprinted with permission from *The Globe and Mail*.

---

training program. Employees increasingly need to obtain new knowledge and skills immediately. This means that trainers must find ways of providing learning opportunities on-demand or what has become known as "just-in-time learning."

Just-in-time (JIT) learning refers to the capability to provide learning and training opportunities when they are needed and where they are needed. To meet this need, trainers will have to find new and innovative ways to design and deliver training. This will further impact the role of the training professional, which will continue to evolve into more of a knowledge structuring and learning facilitation and support role. IBM's On-Demand program is an excellent example of this trend.

Related to JIT learning is the use of technology which, as described in Chapter 8, can be used to deliver training to unlimited numbers of trainees very quickly. Furthermore, as organizations find that they need to provide training more often to increasing numbers of employees, they will continue to look for approaches that are timely and cost effective. A recent trend is something called **rapid e-learning** which refers to developmental software that allows

Just-in-time (JIT) learning

The capability to provide learning and training opportunities when they are needed and where they are needed

Rapid e-learning

Software that allows organizations to develop e-learning more quickly and easily and at a lower price than conventional e-learning development tools

organizations to develop e-learning more quickly and easily and at a lower price then conventional e-learning development tools. The software uses a template approach to develop courses and easy-to-use interfaces that guide trainers through the course development process.[19]

Trainers are also facing demands for shorter training programs. Line managers are becoming increasingly concerned about employees taking too much time off the job for training and are increasingly requesting that courses be condensed. For example, at some companies full-day training courses are being conducted in two hours. This often requires trainers to redesign programs and find creative ways to make up for the reduction in content by assigning more pre-course readings, using more job aids following training, and creating more on-the-job training opportunities.[20]

The Ethics of Training and Development

Ethical dilemmas in our society range from large-scale corporate scandals to day-to-day management situations. Recently, the unethical conduct of senior management at major corporations like Enron and WorldCom has made the headlines. But what do we mean by ethics and what are the ethical dilemmas faced by trainers?

Ethics involves systematic thinking about the moral consequences of one's actions and decisions on various stakeholders. Stakeholders refer to people inside or outside of the organization who might be affected by one's actions and decisions. In organizations, ethics often takes the form of standards of conduct that indicate how one should behave according to an organization's values and principles. For training professionals, ethics involves following a set of standards and principles in the design, delivery, and evaluation of training and development programs.

Training professionals must adhere to a set of ethical principles that guides their behaviour and they must serve as role models of proper ethical conduct to the rest of the organization. These standards can be set by organizations and associations. For example, an association called the Academy of Human Resource Development developed a code of ethics and integrity called the Standards on Ethics and Integrity. It was developed to establish desired standards of behaviour and to bring an increased sense of professionalism to those who do research and practice human resource development.[21] It provides principles and guidance to cover different situations encountered by training professionals such as issues concerning competence and expertise, privacy and confidentiality, and relationships with and responsibilities to others to name just a few. The Canadian Society for Training and Development (CSTD) also has a code of ethics that sets standards of practice and professionalism for its members.

One area of particular concern is the refusal of employees from attending a training program. This not only raises ethical issues, but it can also result in workplace discrimination and human rights complaints. In fact, there have been a number of such cases in recent years in which an employee was denied training and then filed a complaint of discrimination. The Canadian Human

Ethics

Systematic thinking about the moral consequences of one's actions and decisions on various stakeholders

Ethical Guidelines for Trainers

Trainers must conduct themselves according to a set of ethical guidelines and standards as follows:

1. **Voluntary consent:** Trainers should not implicitly coerce unwilling or skeptical participants into self-revealing or physical activities.

2. **Discrimination:** Age, sex, race, or handicaps should not be used as barriers to determine who receives training.

3. **Cost effectiveness:** Training activities should be based on demonstrated utility, should show a demonstrated benefit vis-à-vis costs, and should not be undertaken simply to spend a training budget.

4. **Accurate portrayal:** Claims for the benefits of training need to be accurate; training should be consistent across time and trainers; training materials should be appropriately depicted.

5. **Competency in training:** Teaching methods that do not work, such as talking down to audiences, should be avoided.

6. **Values:** Trainers should believe in the value of what they teach.

Source: Lowman, R. L. (1991). Ethical human resource practice in organizational settings. In D. W. Bray (Ed.), *Working with organizations.* New York: Guilford. Reprinted with permission from The Guildford Press, New York, NY.

Rights Act at the federal level, as well each of the provincial human rights codes, govern human rights issues that can be invoked when an employee is denied training.[22]

In one recent case, a member of the Public Service of Canada was denied entry into its full-time French language training program because testing and evaluation revealed she had a learning disability in auditory processing. Because the employee was denied the training she was not appointed to a bilingual managerial position. The human rights tribunal ruled that the almost exclusive use of auditory discrimination testing to determine her aptitude to learn another language created a discriminatory practice. A number of remedies were ordered, including immediate appointment to the managerial position and a lump-sum payment for lost wages and pension. Access to the training program should not have been denied on the basis of a learning disability as further testing showed that she could learn a second language subject to adaptations to learning methods.[23]

To learn more about the kinds of ethical issues and standards that are important for training and development, see The Trainer's Notebook 3, "Ethical Guidelines for Trainers."

Training and Development Best Practices

Much of what you have read in this text represents best practices for the design and delivery of training programs. However, as a final review and conclusion to the text, we offer you the following two summaries of best practices. The Trainer's Notebook 4 reviews key design factors that facilitate learning and transfer and Table 15.2 provides an overview of the main reasons why training programs fail, along with best practices to make them highly effective, and the relevant chapters in the text.

TABLE 15.2

Main Reasons for Failure and Best Practices

1. **Lack of Alignment with Business Needs**. Training programs often fail because they are not linked to business and organizational needs.

   Best Practices: Effective training programs begin with a needs analysis that links organizational needs and strategies to training programs. Needs must also be translated into clear objectives and evaluation criteria. Training is strategic when it is aligned with business strategy and therefore enables an organization to achieve its strategic goals and objectives.

   Chapter: Chapter 1, "The Training and Development Process" and Chapter 4, "The Needs–Analysis Process."

2. **Failure to Recognize Nontraining Solutions**. Training is often implemented with the intention of improving a performance problem even though it is not always the best solution.

   Best Practices: There are many possible solutions to performance problems that might be more effective and less costly than training and development. It is therefore important to use a performance analysis flowchart like the one presented in Chapter 4 to determine the best solutions to performance problems.

   Chapter: Chapter 4, "The Needs–Analysis Process."

3. **Lack of Objectives to Provide Direction and Focus**. Training programs sometimes fail because they lack clear objectives.

   Best Practices: Training objectives serve a number of purposes for trainers, trainees, and the organization. Training objectives set the stage for training design and indicate the criteria that should be included for training evaluation. Training objectives for most training programs should be set at multiple levels (i.e., reactions, learning, behaviour, results, and ROI).

   Chapter: Chapter 4, "The Needs–Analysis Process" and Chapter 5, "Training Design."

4. **The Solution Is Too Expensive**. Although a training program's ROI is an important measure of effectiveness, a negative ROI does not mean that a training program has failed. There are often many intangible benefits of training programs that add value to an organization.

   Best Practices: Training programs do not have to be expensive to be effective. It is important to estimate the costs and benefits of training programs before making a decision. It is also important to be clear about the main criteria to use when comparing training alternatives and the different criteria for training evaluation.

   Chapter: Chapter 11, "Training Evaluation" and Chapter 12, "The Costs and Benefits of Training."

5. **Regarding Training as an Event**. When training is treated as a separate or isolated event, it is likely to fail.

   Best Practices: Training programs have to be considered as part of a larger process and organizational system that requires ongoing attention and support not only during training, but before and after training.

   Chapter: Chapter 10, "Transfer of Training."

6. **Participants Are Not Held Accountable for Results**. When employees are only expected to attend a training program without any responsibility for what they learn or do after training, they are not likely to show any change in behaviour or improvement in job performance.

   Best Practices: Trainees must be held accountable for what they learn in training and how they will apply it on the job. Managers must also be accountable and responsible for their employees' learning and transfer as well as organizational results.

   Chapter: Chapter 10, "Transfer of Training."

(Continued)

TABLE 15.2 (*Continued*)

7. **Failure to Prepare the Job Environment for Transfer**. Barriers in the job environment can undermine the success of an otherwise effective training program.

   Best Practices: Needs analysis information can be used to identify transfer barriers and remove them before a training program is implemented. Facilitating the transfer of training can involve activities before, during, and after training and include trainers, trainees, and management.

   Chapter: Chapter 10, "Transfer of Training."

8. **Lack of Management Reinforcement and Support**. If management does not support, encourage, and reinforce the use of new knowledge and skills on the job, training programs will not be effective.

   Best Practices: It is extremely important that management be involved with trainees before and after training. Managers need to know how critical their role is and how they can provide support and reinforcement.

   Chapter: Chapter 10, "Transfer of Training."

9. **Failure to Isolate the Effects of Training**. It is especially difficult to be able to demonstrate that changes or effects in employees and the organization are due to a particular training program and not something else. Failure to isolate the effects of training might leave some wondering about the need and value of training and development.

   Best Practices: The traditional way of isolating the effects of training is to conduct an experiment with a training group and a control group. Unfortunately, this type of design is often difficult to implement and is more often the exception than the rule. Therefore, alternative approaches need to be used, such as the internal referencing strategy described in Chapter 11. Other techniques for isolating the effects of training include trainee, supervisor, and management estimates of the impact, as well as estimating the impact of other factors.

   Chapter: Chapter 11, "Training Evaluation."

10. **Lack of Commitment and Involvement from Executives**. Training and development programs are doomed to fail without the commitment and involvement of senior executives. Their commitment is critical for the effectiveness of training and development programs.

    Best Practices: Executives can demonstrate their commitment to the training function by providing resources for programs, and they can become involved by their presence and participation at training sessions.

    Chapter: Chapter 9, "Training Implementation and Delivery" and Chapter 10, "Transfer of Training."

11. **Failure to Provide Feedback and Use Information about Results**. Training programs cannot be improved and are not likely to reach their expectations if the various stakeholders do not receive feedback and information about the results of training. Feedback and information is necessary to make training programs effective for all of the major stakeholders.

    Best Practices: Trainers need to know if their training programs are achieving the objectives; trainees need to know if they have acquired new knowledge and skills; and management needs to know if training has had an impact on business results.

    When training programs are evaluated, it is possible to provide feedback to all of the key stakeholders. Feedback can be used by trainees for learning and performance improvement. Trainers can use feedback to improve the design and delivery of training programs. Management can use feedback to make decisions about future programs and actions needed to solve an organization's problems and improve results.

    Chapter: Chapter 5, "Training Design"; Chapter 9, "Training Implementation and Delivery"; and Chapter 11, "Training Evaluation."

Source: Phillips. J. J., & Phillips, P. P. (2002, September). 11 reasons why training and development fail . . . and what you can do about it. *Training, 39* (9), 78–85. © ROI Institute, www.roiinstitute.net. Used with permission.

The Trainer's Notebook 4

Training Features that Facilitate Learning and Transfer

For training to be effective, trainees must meet four criteria. They must be ready to learn and be motivated, they must learn the content of the training program, and they must transfer the training on the job. The following training design factors have long been recognized as important for enhancing learning and transfer.

1. Trainees understand the objectives of the training program—the purpose and outcomes expected.
2. Training content is meaningful. Examples, exercises, assignments, concepts, and terms used in training are relevant.
3. Trainees are given cues that help them learn and recall training content, such as diagrams, models, key behaviours, and advanced organizers.
4. Trainees have opportunities to practice.
5. Trainees receive feedback on their learning from trainers, observers, video, or the task itself.
6. Trainees have the opportunity to observe and interact with other trainees.
7. The training program is properly coordinated and arranged.

Source: Noe, R. A., & Colquitt, J. A. (2002). Planning for training impact: Principles of training effectiveness. *Creating, implementing, and maintaining effective training and development: State-of-the-art lessons for practice* (pp. 53–79) by Kraiger, K. © 2002 Jossey-Bass Inc. Reprinted with permission of John Wiley & Sons, Inc.

Summary

This chapter began with a review of the changing role of the trainer and the outsourcing of training and development. We noted how the competencies and roles of trainers are changing and shifting towards a greater focus on performance problems and solutions while more traditional training activities are being outsourced. We then discussed how the workforce is aging and the implications of this for training and development. This was followed by a discussion of the increasing demand for just-in-time learning. The importance of ethics in training and development was then discussed, with particular attention to discrimination. The chapter concluded with a brief review of training design features that facilitate learning and transfer and the major reasons why training programs fail as well as the best practices for making them effective.

Conclusion

It should now be clear to you that training and development is an important part of the management of performance in organizations. Training and development plays a critical role in helping organizations meet the challenges of an increasingly complex and competitive environment. Unfortunately, training programs sometimes fail and as a result, restrict an organization's ability to compete and remain competitive. The good news is that the science of training, as described in this text, is full of practical information on how to design, deliver, and evaluate training and development programs. By applying the theories, concepts, and principles described in this text, it is possible to design and deliver effective training and development programs that will benefit individuals, organizations, and society. You now know the science of training; it is up to you to translate training science into practice.

Key Terms

ethics (page 453)

just-in-time (JIT) learning (page 452)

outsourcing (page 448)

performance consultant (page 447)

rapid e-learning (page 452)

Weblinks

Academy of Human Resource Development: www.ahrd.org (page 453)

Canadian Society for Training and Development: www.cstd.ca (page 453)

Discussion Questions

1. What are some of the ethical issues that trainers face, and for training and development?
2. How has the role of the trainer changed over the years and what are the new and emerging roles of trainers?
3. Why do organizations outsource training and development and what are the advantages and disadvantages of outsourcing? Do you think that organizations should outsource training and development?
4. What are the implications of the aging workforce for training and development?
5. What is just-in-time learning and what are the implications for training and development?
6. Why do training programs sometimes fail and how can they be designed to be more effective?

The Great Training Debate

1. Debate the following: Organizations should outsource all of their training and development.

Using the Internet

1. To find out about ethics training in Canada, visit the website of the Ethics Practitioners' Association of Canada (EPAC) at **www.epac-apec.ca/cont-ang/invent-ress-education.htm** where you will find the Inventory of Education and Resources. Find out what kinds of

education resources are available in your province and what kind of training resources are available in Canada. Write a brief report in which you describe the kinds of ethical education programs and training programs available. In addition, click on "Standards" to find out about the Ethical Standards. Review the Code of Ethics and write a brief report in which you summarize the main aspects of the code.

2. To learn about ethical standards of practice for training professionals, visit the website of the Canadian Society for Training and Development (CSTD) at **www.cstd.ca** and click on "About Us" and then "Member Code of Ethics." Review the ethical standards and describe how they apply to the different stages of the training and development process and to training research, practice, and consulting.

3. To find about the American Society for Training & Development's new competency model and certification program, go to **www.astd.org/astd/Competency/Certification+Institute.htm**.

   Answer the following questions:

   1. What is the CPLP?
   2. Click on "Readiness Assessment" and use the chart to determine your readiness; complete the self-assessment using the sample worksheet provided.
   3. Visit the CPLP website to find out about the program requirements. Write a brief report describing what you think about the CPLP.

Exercises

In-Class

1. If an organization wanted to hire a training professional today, what should they look for? Find several job advertisements for a training manager or director in your local newspaper. Bring the advertisements to class and summarize the main competencies and responsibilities of the position. Describe how the job matches the traditional role of a trainer as well as more current roles and expectations described in the chapter.

2. Consider the ethics of the most recent training experience you have had either in a current job or in a previous job. Review the six ethical guidelines listed in The Trainer's Notebook 3, "Ethical Guidelines for Trainers," and determine how well they stand up against your most recent training experience. Based on your analysis, was the trainer and the training program ethical? Be prepared to explain and defend your answer.

3. If you were responsible for training in your organization and management decided that they wanted to outsource most of the company's training and development programs, what would you do? Prepare a brief presentation in which you must present your case to management. What will be your position and what will you present to management in order to defend it?

4. Think about the last time you attended a training program. How accommodating was the program for older workers? What aspects of the program might have facilitated or hindered the learning of older workers? If you were to redesign the program to accommodate older workers, what would you do and why?

5. Think about your knowledge and skills and the extent to which you are prepared for the new competencies and roles expected of training professionals today. Conduct a self-assessment of yourself using the material presented in this chapter with particular attention to the ASTD competency model. What competencies do you have and which ones do you still need to develop? Prepare an action plan that describes some of the things you can do to develop those competencies that you need to develop and improve.

In-the-Field

1. Contact the training manager in an organization to find out how his/her role has changed and how it will change in the future. What was his/her role five years ago? What is his/her role today? What will his/her role be in five years? What skills and experiences do trainers need in order to perform their current and future roles, and how has this changed over the last five to 10 years?

2. Review Table 15.2, "Main Reasons for Failure, and Best Practices," and then contact a manager or director of training in an organization and ask him/her about the success and failure of training and development programs in his/her organization. Make up a question for each of the 11 reasons for failure to find out how the organization deals with them (e.g., Are training programs in your organization based on a needs analysis and linked to business needs?) and if best practices are used in the design and delivery of training and development programs. What recommendations can you provide for the organization to make their training and development programs more effective?

Case Incident

Outsourcing at Nestlé Canada and Hudson's Bay Company

Nestlé Canada has been outsourcing parts of HR services to external providers for years in areas such as payroll, pension administration, and benefits administration. Although the company is using external providers more often for training and development, there are no plans to outsource all of it. If they are planning to develop a course in a particular area, they look for a provider who has experience in that area and then partner with them to develop something specific for the company. For example, the company partnered with an external organizational psychologist to develop a new leadership development program.

Hudson's Bay Company keeps most of its human resources in-house. The company believes it is best served when HR support is delivered by those who most understand the organization—its own employees. In the case of training and development, it is important to have employees who started out working in stores deliver customer service training. They have an understanding of the customer and the way the stores operate.

Questions

1. Comment on the two companies' approaches to outsourcing training and development. What are the advantages and disadvantages of each approach?
2. What advice would you give each company about its current and future outsourcing of training and development?

Source: Cook, T., Household, J., Cormier, B., & Kolida, B. (2003, September 8). HR leaders talk: The constant pressure to add value and control costs combined with the growing desire to play a strategic business role has caused many HR leaders to at least consider outsourcing some part of their operations—if they haven't done so already. *Canadian HR Reporter, 16* (15), p. 13.

Case

Changing Employees' Minds

For many employees, the chance to attend a training course is a wonderful opportunity. SaskTel employees were excited about a six-week training course to prepare them to be part of a team and to learn about process re-engineering to redesign business processes and improve company performance. However, instead of re-engineering training, these employees were part of a social engineering experiment after which half of the 24 participants required psychological counselling or stress leave.

The employees claimed that they were brainwashed. The union claims that this training program was one more reason why SaskTel had its first general province-wide strike in 88 years.

What went wrong? The company included this training as part of a $2-million corporate makeover to make it more competitive. At the outset, the managers believed that they were simply implementing courses that would tap the potential of employees and enable them to become more productive.

SaskTel was not the only company trying to capitalize on the human potential movement, which meant designing ways to tap the values and beliefs of employees to increase performance effectiveness. But the techniques of changing belief systems are not well established, and it is more an art than a science. Other Canadian firms found themselves unknowingly buying training programs from religious cults.

TransAlta paid a consulting company $24 million to train 1500 employees. These employees were subjected to daily sayings that ended with employees saying "amen," and to supervisors conducting daily mood checks so that inappropriate emotions could be monitored and changed.

Public criticisms of employees were encouraged, in an effort to improve performance, but these public humiliations left employees in tears, and some quit the company.

After employees leaked news of this abusive treatment to CBC-TV, the CEO placed ads in newspapers, and sent letters to all workers apologizing for their distress.

The re-engineering program at SaskTel proved more damaging than that at TransAlta. Windows were papered over to prevent people seeing in or out. Employees were discouraged from communicating with each other. There was a lot of jargon (terms such as "blue-skying," "thinking outside the box"), and employees felt that they were trapped in a 1984 Orwellian nightmare. The original program, scheduled to last six weeks, was continually extended. The consultants were highly aggressive, and employees were told to play the game or get out. Fearing for their jobs, the employees played the game, at great personal costs.

Questions

1. Was the training described in the case ethical? Do organizations have a right to provide this kind of training? Do employees have a right to refuse to attend such training programs?

2. The training sessions were designed to change employees' attitudes. Does management have the right to do this? Under what circumstances? What are the ethical issues? Should employees give informed consent? Do these types of training programs violate human rights?

3. What is the role of an organization's training professionals in allowing the kind of training programs described in the case to take place? From an ethical perspective, what is their responsibility?

4. Review The Trainer's Notebook 3, "Ethical Guidelines for Trainers," and conduct an ethical audit of the consultant trainers and the training programs described in the case. Based on your audit, how ethical or unethical were the consultants and their training programs? How ethical were the managers of the organizations who hired the consulting firms to provide the training?

5. If you were a trainer in an organization in which management required employees to attend the kind of training described in the case, what would you do? As a trainer, do you have any ethical responsibility for training that has been approved by management?

Source: Kay, E. (1996, November). Trauma in real life. *The Globe and Mail: Report on Business Magazine*, 82–92.

References

1. Excerpt from: Tyler, K. (2005, April). Training revs up. *HR Magazine, 50* (4), 58–63; Lee, C. (2005, March). IBM: In the top spot for 2005. *Training, 42* (3), 22–24; Weinstein, M. (2006, March). Suite success: On demand delivers for IBM. *Training, 43* (3), 18–21; Speizer, I. (2005, July). IBM builds a new business on its training program. *Workforce Management,* www.workforce.com/archive/feature/24/10/90/241093.php?ht=ibm%20ibm.

2. Vu, U. (2004, July 12). Trainers mature into business partners. *Canadian HR Reporter, 17* (13), 1, 2.

3. Zielinski, D. (2006, January). Wanted: Training manager. *Training, 43* (1), 36–39.

4. Vu, U. (2004, July 12).

5. Zielinski, D. (2006, January).

6. Robinson, D. G., & Robinson, J. C. (2005, Anniversary issue). A heightened focus on learning and performance. *HR Magazine, 50* (13), 65–67.

7. Moralis, M. (2004, November 22). Trainers morph into new role. *Canadian HR Reporter, 17* (20), G2, G10.

8. Harris-Lalonde, S. (2001). Training and development outlook. *The Conference Board of Canada.* Ottawa.

9. Robinson, D. G., & Robinson, J. C. (2005, Anniversary issue).

10. Johnson, G. (2004, August). To outsource or not to outsource . . . that is the question. *Training, 41* (8), 26–29.

11. Parker, R. O., & Cooney, J. (2005). Learning & development outlook 2005. *The Conference Board of Canada.* Ottawa.

12. Kraiger, K. (2003). Perspectives on training and development. In W. C. Borman, D. R. Ilgen, & R. J. Klimoski (Eds.), *Handbook of psychology: Industrial and organizational psychology* (pp. 171–92). Hoboken, NJ: John Wiley & Sons, Inc.

13. Johnson, G. (2004, August).

14. Gainey, T. W., & Klaas, B. S. (2002). Outsourcing the training function: Results from the field. *Human Resource Planning, 25*, 16–22.

15. Gainey, T. W., & Klaas, B. S. (2002).

16. Gainey, T. W., & Klaas, B. S. (2002).

17. Mingail, H. (2004, September 29). Wise ways for retraining older workers. *The Globe and Mail,* C8.

18. Thayer, P. W. (1997). A rapidly changing world: Some implications for training systems in the year 2001 and beyond. In M. A. Quinones & A. Ehrenstein (Eds.), *Training for a rapidly changing workplace.* Washington, DC: American Psychological Association.

19. Boehle, S. (2005, July). Rapid e-learning. *Training, 42* (7), 12–17.

20. Zielinski, D. (2006, January).

21. Hatcher, T., & Aragon, S. R. (2000). A code of ethics and integrity for HRD research and practice. *Human Resource Development Quarterly, 11*, 179–85.

22. Macdonald, N. C. (2004, November 22). Workplace discrimination prohibited—and that includes training. *Canadian HR Reporter, 17* (2), G3, G11.

23. Macdonald, N. C. (2004, November 22).

Index